INSIGHT GUIDES

ITALY

Discovery
CHANNEL

APA PUBLICATIONS
Part of the Langenscheidt Publishing Group

L

INSIGHT GUIDE
Italy

ABOUT THIS BOOK

Editorial
Project Editor
Emily Hatchwell
Editorial Director
Brian Bell

Distribution
UK & Ireland
GeoCenter International Ltd
The Viables Centre, Harrow Way
Basingstoke, Hants RG22 4BJ
Fax: (44) 1256 817988
United States
Langenscheidt Publishers, Inc.
36–36 33rd Street, 4th Floor
Long Island City, NY 11106
Fax: 1 (718) 784 0640
Australia
Universal Publishers
1 Waterloo Road
Macquarie Park, NSW 2113
Fax: (61) 2 9888 9074
New Zealand
Hema Maps New Zealand Ltd (HNZ)
Unit D, 24 Ra ORA Drive
East Tamaki, Auckland
Fax: (64) 9 273 6479
Worldwide
**Apa Publications GmbH & Co.
Verlag KG (Singapore branch)**
38 Joo Koon Road, Singapore 628990
Tel: (65) 6865 1600. Fax: (65) 6861 6438

Printing
Insight Print Services (Pte) Ltd
38 Joo Koon Road, Singapore 628990
Tel: (65) 6865 1600. Fax: (65) 6861 6438

©2006 Apa Publications GmbH & Co.
Verlag KG (Singapore branch)
All Rights Reserved
First Edition 1985
Fourth Edition (updated) 2006

CONTACTING THE EDITORS
We would appreciate it if readers
would alert us to errors or outdated
information by writing to:
**Insight Guides, P.O. Box 7910,
London SE1 1WE, England.
Fax: (44) 20 7403 0290.
insight@apaguide.co.uk**

www.insightguides.com
In North America:
www.insighttravelguides.com

he first Insight Guide pioneered the use of creative full-colour photography in travel guides in 1970. Since then, we have expanded our range to cater for our readers' need not only for reliable information about what to see and what to do in their chosen destination but also for a real understanding of the culture and workings of that destination.

Now, when the internet can supply inexhaustible (but not always reliable) facts, our books carefully marry text and pictures to provide those much more elusive qualities: knowledge and discernment. To achieve this, they rely heavily on the authority and experience of a team of locally based writers and photographers.

How to use this book

Insight Guides has a proven formula of informative and well-written text paired with a fresh photojournalistic approach. The books are carefully structured, both to convey a good understanding of each place and its culture, and to guide readers through its myriad attractions:

◆ The first section, headed by a yellow colour bar, covers Italy's rich **history** and its lively modern **culture** in authoritative **features** written by established experts.

Above: Venice's Piazza San Marco

◆ The main **Places** section, with a blue bar, provides a run-down of all the places worth seeing. Places of major interest are cross-referenced by numbers or letters to specially drawn maps.

◆ The **Travel Tips** section at the back of the book provides recommendations on hotels and restaurants, as well as an Italian phrasebook, with a menu reader. Information may be located quickly by using the index on the back cover flap.

The contributors

This is the Fourth Edition of *Insight Guide: Italy*. To help make a good book even better, managing editor **Emily Hatchwell** enlisted the expertise of Italy specialists, including two Insight regulars: **Lisa Gerard-Sharp** and **Christopher Catling**. **Fred Mawer** wrote a new chapter on Sardinia.

Nicky Swallow helped update the Places chapters and Travel Tips. Editors **Harriet Salisbury, Jeff Evans, Liz Clasen** and **Jane Ladle** brought the new elements together into a coherent whole.

The authors included wine writers **James Ainsworth** and **Margaret Rand**, and **Bruce Johnston**, a *Daily Telegraph* journalist. **Ginger Künzel** wrote on the Italian Alps and the Trentino-Alto Adige region, and **Susie Boulton** contributed to the sections on Venice.

Much of this new edition builds on the work of **Katherine Barrett**, who wrote the chapters on Rome and Famous Travellers. **Clare McHugh** wrote many of the chapters on Italian history and the northern provinces.

It is to **Alberto Rossatti** that the book owes much of its native expertise. Other contributors to the original guide included **Benjamin Swett, Jacob Young, Claudia Angeletti, Kathleen Beckett, Melanie Menagh, Peter Spiro** and **George Prochnik**.

Like all Insight Guides, this book owes a lot to its photographs, many of which are by **John Heseltine, Albano Guatti, Frances Gransden, Phil Wood** and **Bill Wassman**.

Italy specialists **Giovanna Dunmall** and **Adele Evans** contributed to this update with the help of Lisa Gerard-Sharp, who revised the chapters on *Contemporary Italy*, *Making of Modern Italy*, and *The Mafia*. **Sylvia Suddes** proofread this edition.

Map Legend

▬ ▬	International Boundary
▬ ▬ ▬	Region Boundary
⊖	Border Crossing
▬ • ▬	National Park/Reserve
▬ ▬ ▬	Ferry Route
Ⓜ	Metro
✈	Airport
🚌	Bus Station
P	Parking
❶	Tourist Information
✉	Post Office
✝	Church/Ruins
☽	Mosque
✡	Synagogue
	Castle/Ruins
∴	Archaeological Site
∩	Cave
1	Statue/Monument
★	Place of Interest

Places of interest in the **Places** section are cross-referenced to maps by number (e.g. ❶). A symbol at the top of each right-hand page tells you where to find the relevant map.

CONTENTS

Maps

A map of Italy is on the front
inside cover; a map of Rome
is on the back inside cover.

Introduction

History

Features

Portofino
in Liguria,
once a
humble
fishing
village and
now an
exclusive
resort

Travel Tips

Places

THE ETERNAL SEDUCTRESS

Italy, with her unrivalled beauty and baffling contradictions,

continues to seduce and enchant those who are drawn to her

Italy, like the sorceress Circe, tantalisingly beautiful and at the same time treacherous, has attracted kings, scholars, saints, poets and curious travellers for centuries. The spell of the "Eternal Seductress", as men have dubbed her, which once drew people across stormy mountains and seas, now leads them into hardly less turbulent airports and train stations.

Italy has always seemed somewhat removed from the rest of Europe: physically by mountains and sea, spiritually by virtue of the Pope. In the eyes of outsiders, the Italians themselves are characterised by extremes: at one end of the spectrum, the gentle unworldliness of St Francis, and, at the other, the amoral brilliance of Machiavelli; on the one hand, the curiosity of Galileo or the genius of Michelangelo, on the other, the repressive dogmatism of Counter Reformation Jesuits. There have been those who thought the Italians were unworthy of Italy, and others, such as the English novelist E.M. Forster, who considered them "more marvellous than the land".

This book believes that Italy and the Italians are equally worthy of attention. It explores the land and its people, from Calabrian villagers to Milanese sophisticates and delves into their justly famous treasures, from Etruscan statues to Botticelli's radiant *Birth of Venus*. Special features celebrate Italian passions – films, fashion, opera and food – while the history section threads its way through a tumultuous past, from the legendary founding of Rome by Romulus and Remus to the Renaissance, reunification, Mussolini and the Mafia.

In Italy the past is always present: a housing development rises above a crumbling Roman wall; ultra-modern museums display pre-Roman artefacts; old people in tiny mountain villages preserve customs which are centuries old while their grandchildren roar into the future on shiny new Vespas.

This is the country that inspires imagination in the dull, passion in the cold-hearted, rebellion in the conventional. Whether you spend your sojourn in Italy under a brightly coloured beach umbrella on the Riviera, shopping in Milan or diligently examining churches and museums, you cannot be unchanged by Italy. At the very least, you will receive a highly pleasurable lesson in living. Whether you are struck by the beauty of a church facade rising from a perfectly proportioned piazza, the aroma of freshly carved *prosciutto*, or the sight of a stylish passer-by spied over the foam of your cappuccino, there is the same superb sensation: nowhere else on earth does just living seem so extraordinary. ❏

PRECEDING PAGES: St Peter, Rome; welcome to Venice; artistic endeavours at Piazzale Michelangelo, Florence; a quiet afternoon in Scanno in Abruzzo.
LEFT: young visitor to St Mark's Basilica in Venice.

FAMOUS TRAVELLERS

Italy has long been a "paradise of exiles", a haven for visitors in search of classical heritage and humanity, sunlight and passion

As Dr Johnson declared, "A man who has not been to Italy is always conscious of an inferiority", a sentiment still shared by many travellers more than 200 years later. Ever since the Romantic era, Italy has resonated with travellers in search of solace and enlightenment, cultural riches and religious renewal. A reverence for the Classical legacy or the Renaissance has been mingled with affection for the musical culture and an infatuation with art, landscape, Catholicism and cuisine. A clerical creation of E.M. Forster's claims: "I do believe that Italy really purifies and ennobles all who visit her. She is the school as well as the playground of the world."

Above all, Italy has been seen as sublimely civilised, a soothing enchantress who would erase all cares. For past travellers, attitude determined experience: Italy became a picturesque canvas, a place of beauty, longing, moral decay and sexual liberation. In particular, the country represented a holiday haven for repressed northerners drawn to the lotus-eating life of the south. The allure of Italy still draws on this landscape of the senses, a subconscious invitation for projections of aversions and fears as well as desires. Yet whatever their motives, travellers concur on the seductive spell of Italy. On his way to Rome in 1852, the artist Frederick Leighton spoke for many visitors to come: "A faithful lover I return, after six years of longing absence, to the home of my inward heart."

The Grand Tour

The Grand Tourists had great cultural pretensions and treated Italy as a finishing school for the soul. The Victorian itinerary was virtually unchanged since the Romantic era: a brief visit to Venice was followed by autumn in Florence, Rome for Christmas and New Year, then to Naples or Taormina in Sicily until Easter spelt a return to Rome. Gilded youth roamed the summits of Etna and Vesuvius, poked about in

Roman palaces and postured in romantic ruins. Privileged visitors declaimed in Venetian galleries, posed at the Milan opera and gathered in fashionable cafés such as Doney's in Florence and Caffè Greco in Rome. Shelley (1792–1822), the Romantic poet par excellence, had a novelettish affair with an Italian countess and boasted that he had "Florenced and Romed and Galleried and Conversationed".

As for wintering resorts, the Adriatic was ignored in favour of the French or Italian Riviera. Yet while the Côte d'Azur was treated as a sanatorium for the middle and upper classes, Italian cities and resorts were seen as artistic universities and pleasure domes. Historian John Pemble portrays Victorian and Edwardian Italy as appealing to "oversize personalities whose voices, gestures and passions required high ceilings, strong light, and stupendous views". San Remo was a case apart: by the 1880s it was favoured by spinsters, censorious clerics and those who found Monte Carlo too brash.

LEFT: the heroine of Hawthorne's *The Marble Faun* has an assignation in Perugia. **RIGHT:** Percy Bysshe Shelley.

Aesthetes came in search of the picturesque, escaping the frigid capitals of northern Europe and North America. Italy inspired travel memoirs by Goethe and Stendhal, Dickens and Henry James, writers who focused on curious byways rather than the well-trodden highways. In turn, artists such as Poussin and Turner painted the sublime light while the Romantic poets reflected the sunlight of the south in their writings. Virtually no Victorian writer, painter or sculptor of note failed to visit Italy. As for musicians, Liszt, Chopin,

> **AN AMERICAN IN ROME**
>
> In time, American writer Henry James even became fond of "the barbarisms, miseries and uncleannesses of Rome".

Henry James considered the city "the aesthetic antidote to the ugliness of the rest of the world, that is, of Anglo-Saxondom in particular". Yet James, like Marcel Proust, also had an affinity for Venice: "It is a fact that almost everyone interesting, appealing, melancholy, memorable, odd seems to have gravitated to Venice ... the deposed, the defeated, the wounded or even only the bored have seemed to find there something that no other place could give."

Until the 1870s, the British moved as a herd

Tchaikovsky and Wagner were all deeply affected by Italy. Venice inspired Wagner to write *Tristan and Isolde*.

"Infatuated aliens"

This was how Henry James (1843–1916) described his fellow travellers, devoted to Italian art and culture. In literature, Rome, Florence and Venice receive most paeans of praise. This is reflected in Henry James's view of Milan as "perhaps the last of the prose capitals rather than the first of the poetic". By the 1880s, Florence had become the most favoured residential city for foreigners. But each major city had its admirers. John Gibson, the 19th-century sculptor, called Rome "the very university of art", and

in Italy, from Venice to Florence and Rome. The American George Hillard wrote in the 1840s: "No one could visit these cities without being constantly aware of the fastidiousness of English hygiene, the chill of English manners, and the sibilance of English speech." American novelist W.D. Howells declared Venice in October to be "the month of sunsets and the English". As for Rome, stylish Via Condotti was known as "*il ghetto inglese*" while "*inglese*" ("English") became a generic term for all foreigners.

E.M. Forster (1879–1970) saw Italy as liberating "the undeveloped heart" of the English. In *A Room with a View* (1908), his repressed heroine is rescued by voluptuous, pagan Italy. The Welsh poet Dylan Thomas (1914–53) needed no such introduction to Tuscan life. He spent an agreeable time quaffing Chianti and praising the endless pine trees, "the cypresses at the hilltop which tell one all about the length of death, [and] the woods deep as love and full of goats".

In time, what Henry James called "the bark of Chicago" came to be as common as British English in Italy. The Americans tended to be more critical, daring to expose Italy to a burst of realism or mockery. To Mark Twain (1835–1910), "the Arno would be a very plausible river if they would pump some water into it." His compatriot Henry James was equally scathing about the riverside houses: "Anything more battered and befouled, more cracked and disjointed, dirtier, drearier and poorer, it would be impossible to conceive." Yet James, the epitome of the civilised traveller, was the one who best appreciated daily life: "Our picture of Italy is ... of happy processes, accidents, adventures, a generous acceptance of goodly appearances."

A romantic vision

In general, French writers convey a more romantic vision of Italy. In Rome, Emile Zola (1840–1902) succumbed to the melancholy beauty of the Colosseum: "a world where one loses oneself amidst death-like silence and solitude". In Florence, Santa Croce sent Stendhal's head reeling: "I went in constant fear of falling to the ground." This aesthetic sickness, now known as "Stendhal's Syndrome", also affected Maupassant, Proust and Monet. Proust (1871–1922) set part of *A la Recherche du Temps Perdu* in Venice, while George Sand (1804–76) described the city in very sensuous terms: "The bases of the *palazzi*, where oysters used to cling to stagnant moss, are covered in mosses of tender green, and the gondolas glide between two carpets of velvety, beautiful verdure."

The Germans were equally entranced by Italy. In 1788, Goethe (1749–1832) experienced the pleasurable terror of the Roman catacombs. Venice, too, appealed to his poetic nature: "This strange island-city, this heaven-like republic". Thomas Mann (1875–1955) chose ambivalence over waxing lyrical. The protagonist in *Death in Venice* falls under the Venetian spell, but there is an inherent criticism in his praise: "This was

Venice, the fair frailty that fawned and that betrayed, half fairy tale, half snare".

Frederick Faber, a visitor to Pisa in 1843, praised "the voluptuous silent poetry which Italy engenders". To many, the scenery was as aesthetically pleasing as the art. Faced with such a paradise, "nine out of ten English tourists either gush or cant", declared one Victorian visitor. Virginia Woolf (1882–1941) did neither, invoking: "the Arno flowing past with its usual coffee-coloured foam". The Tuscan landscape has inspired some of the loveliest modern poetry. Elizabeth Jennings praises the perfection of the Florentine setting: "Take one bowl,

one valley ... And then set cypresses up/So dark that they seem to contain their repeated shadows/In a straight and upward leap". Charles Tomlinson writes of cypresses "folded in like a dark thought/For which the language is lost".

Italy was unique in offering an equally rich Classical and Christian inheritance. Romantic taste favoured Classical ruins and Renaissance architecture. Then came a Victorian taste for Gothic buildings and medieval madonnas, which prevailed until World War I. Ruskin's writings on Venice and Florence helped to turn the art treasures of Italy into a supremely Christian preserve. By implication, Classical art was seen as spiritually impoverished. Henry James was almost a lone voice in rebelling against the

LEFT: Piranesi's fanciful drawing of Hadrian's Villa.
RIGHT: Mme de Stael, author of *Corinne*, a romance between an Italian poet and a Scottish laird.

prevailing aesthetic: "art is made for us, not we for art". Despite the superiority of Tuscan art, the critic Bernard Berenson (1865–1959) preferred vibrant Venetian art: "The Florentines were too attached to classical ideals of form and composition … too academic, to give embodiment to the throbbing feeling for life and pleasure."

For travellers steeped in Classical lore, the romance of Roman ruins was heightened by nostalgia for lost glory. "Who can visit such a place of beauty and decay", intoned Gladstone, "without feeling that it opens his mind to what he never knew before and cannot hope to recall elsewhere?". The Romantic poet Edgar Allan

Apart from nostalgia, travellers sought escape from the oppressiveness and cold of northern climes. The pessimism of the Protestant mind longed for the perceived sunniness and passion of the Latin disposition. Italy was seen as an incantation, a feminine, luxuriant, sensual country. In a climate of sexual tolerance, the casualties of modern life could seek comfort and acceptance. Italy became a place for elopement, with Robert and Elizabeth Browning fleeing to Pisa in 1846. For moral exiles, this realm of enchantment represented a Faustian pact of temptation and fall. The south, particularly Capri, was known for tolerance towards homo-

Poe marvelled at "the grandeur, gloom and glory" of the Colosseum, then in a parlous state. Sicily and Pompeii provoked a similarly lyrical response: an exquisite sadness and ruminations on the pathos, transience and futility of life.

Sensitive visitors felt a longing for an irrecoverable past, the cultivated melancholy of time travellers who had come too late to a world too old. D.H. Lawrence (1885–1930) lamented the passing of a pagan civilisation: "The Etruscans had a passion for music and an inner carelessness the modern Italians have lost."

LATIN PASSION

Lord Byron (1788–1824) famously declared of Italy: "A woman is virtuous who limits herself to her husband and one lover."

sexuality. In Sorrento, writer Norman Douglas celebrated "elemental and permanent things, casting off outworn weeds of thought" with an illiterate peasant boy.

The perceived moral licence of Italy was an invitation to explore and dare to meet one's destiny. A beguiling story was spun around the poetic yet tragic deaths of Shelley and Keats in Italy. Retreating to sunnier climes was seen as both a promise and a lure, not without torment for the soul. In *Middlemarch*, George Eliot's heroine, Dorothea, has her smothered sensibilities stirred in Rome: on honeymoon there, she compares the sensuous and expansive city with her arid husband. Yet most northern spirits flourished in the noon-day heat. The appeal of expatriate spinsterhood was manifold, with a dizzy round of musical evenings and lively gatherings in Florence and Rome. However, there was little inter-marriage between Italians and foreigners, save for the exchange of a high-sounding southern title for a northern dowry.

Native prejudice

In cultivating the romance of Italy, travellers have had their prejudices. "The country, especially Naples, swarms with pick-pockets", declared one 18th-century guidebook. Yet past travellers generally only knew the natives as servants and rarely commented on the relative poverty of most Italians. Despite his entrée into Italian life, Shelley still ridiculed "countesses [who] smell so of garlic that an ordinary Englishman cannot approach them".

Travellers have always wanted to preserve the mystique, potency and passion of Italy. However, to an Anglo-Tuscan such as Iris Origo (1902–80), "the real gulf lay between the mere tourist and the established Anglo-Florentine". In World War II, she knew old ladies "who preferred the risk of a concentration camp to a return to England". Yet even paradise can become ennervating to exiles such as Alan Moorehead (1910–83): "Presently I began to suffer from that dreadful ennui that must overtake all self-appointed exiles who live in beautiful places in the sun. One lovely day succeeds another ... But as things were, it mattered not in the least to me who won the local elections or whether the hail destroyed the grapes or whether Florence defeated Turin at football."

The decline of paradise has long been a common refrain, with travellers railing against the vulgarity of tourism. "His gondolier, being in league with various lace-makers and glass-blowers, did his best to persuade his fare to pause" – even in Thomas Mann's Venice, the fleecing of tourists was part of the Italian experience. Mary McCarthy, the American critic, wrote: "Contrary to popular belief, there are no back canals where a tourist will not meet himself, with a camera, in the person of the other tourist crossing the little bridge. And no word that can be spoken in this city that is not an echo of something said before." Not that foreign travellers have the last word. Pietro Aretino, the 16th-century writer, indulged in a little *schadenfreude* at the expense of the cultural invaders of his country: "And who would not laugh till he cried at the sight of a boatload of Germans who had just reeled out of a tavern being capsized into the chilly waters of the Canal."

Italy continues to befuddle visitors' senses. When asked what made life worth living,

Harold Acton, the grand old man of letters, replied: "Writing a book, dinner for six, travelling in Italy with someone you love ... I believe Florence has given me all this." Henry James's words will also strike a chord: "One grows irresistibly and tenderly fond of the unanalysable loveableness of Italy ... the whole place keeps playing such everlasting tunes on one's imagination." Nor can the pleasures of serendipity be underestimated as part of the allure. As E.M. Forster realised: "And the traveller who has gone to Italy to study the tactile values of Giotto or the corruption of the Papacy may return remembering nothing but the blue sky and the men and women who live under it." ❏

LEFT: Goethe poses in front of an idealised Italian landscape. RIGHT: Elizabeth Barrett Browning, who together with her husband, Robert, formed the nucleus of an artistic community in Florence.

CARTA
GEOGRAFICA
GENERALE
DELL'
ITALIA

Top border longitude markings: 28 · 29 · 30 · 31 · 32 · 33 · 34 · 35

Left border latitude markings: 45 · 44 · 43 · 42 · 41 · 40 · 39 · 38

I SVIZZERI
Walese

I GRIGIONI

Valtellina
Bergamasco
Lago d'Iseo

VESCOVATO DI TRENTO

Vicentino

DUCATO DI SAVOJA

DUCATO DI MILANO

STATO DELLA REPUBBLICA DI VENEZIA

Brescia
Castiglione

Bergamo
Crema

Verona
Veronese

Padovano

Rovigo

PIEMONTE

MONFERRATO

Lodi
Pavia
Cremona

DUCATO DI MANTOVA
GUASTALLA

Ferrara

Ferrarese

FRONTIERA DI FRANCIA

CONTADO DI NIZZA

DUCATO DI PARMA

DUCATO DI MODENA

Mirandola
Modena
Reggio

Bologna
Bolognese

Romagna

Faenza

REPUBBLICA DI GENOVA

MARE DI GENOVA

REPUBBLICA DI LUCCA

Lucca
Pisa
Pisano
Livorno

GRAN DUCATO DI
Fiorentino

Arezzo

Siena

MONACO

I. di S. Margarita

I. de Gorgona

I. de Capri

TOSCANA

Grosseto

Piombino
Porto Terraio

I. d'Elba
Bastia

Pianosa I.

Porto Longone

MARE DI TOSCANA

S. Fiorenzo

Nebbio
Mariana
Calvi
Aleria

C. Rosso

ISOLA DI
CORSICA

Corsica

Aleria distrutta

Golfo di Ajazzo

Ajazzo
Corbini

Porto Vecchio

I. delle Corsi

Bonifacio

Mare
Tirreno

Scala

Isole della
Maddalena

I. Asinara

C. Artigonese

Lico
Sardi
Terranoua
Tauolaro

Terra Nova

C. Comin

Sassari
Algeri

Oscare
Orose

S. Vito
Iato
Trapani
Mazara

Palermo

Valle di Mazara

C. della Cacca
C. de Bosa

Bosa

ISOLA

Tortoli

C. S. Marco

Dosolo

Orixstagni

E. REGNO DI
SARDEGNA

Toralba
Cagliari

I. di S. Pietro

Villa di Chiesa

S. Michele
M. Santo

I. S. Antioco

Capo Tavolaro

MARE MEDITERRANEO

Decisive Dates

From Origins to the Roman Empire

2000–1200 BC Tribes from Central Europe and Asia, the Villanovans, settle in northern Italy.
circa **900 BC** Etruscans arrive in Italy.
753 BC Legendary date of Rome's founding.
750 BC Greeks start to colonise southern Italy.
509 BC Rome becomes a republic.
390 BC Gauls sack Rome, but are expelled.
343–264 BC Rome gains ascendancy in Italy.
264–146 BC Punic Wars; Rome extends conquests abroad; destruction of Carthage.

58–51 BC Caesar conquers Gaul.
50–49 BC Caesar crosses Rubicon, occupies Rome and is made dictator.
44 BC Caesar assassinated.
27 BC Octavius proclaimed Princeps, as Augustus Caesar; the start of Pax Romana.
AD 96–192 Golden century of peace; empire reaches its greatest extent.
303 Persecution of Christians under Diocletian.
306–337 Constantine makes Christianity the state religion and Constantinople the capital.
393 The empire is divided into eastern and western halves.
5th century Invasions by Visigoths, Huns, Vandals, and Ostrogoths.

410 Sack of Rome by Alaric the Goth.
476 End of Western Roman Empire. Ostrogoth general Odoacer deposes Emperor Romulus Augustus and assumes the title King of Italy.

Medieval Italy

535–553 Justinian brings all Italy within rule of eastern emperor.
568 Lombards overrun much of Italy; peninsula divided into Lombard state ruled from Pavia and Byzantine province centred at Ravenna.
752 The pope asks Frankish king, Pepin the Short, to join fight against the Lombards.
774 Charlemagne, son of Pepin the Short, is made King of the Lombards.
800 Charlemagne is crowned Holy Roman Emperor by Pope Leo III and establishes Carolingian Empire.
827 Saracens capture Sicily.
9th century Carolingian Empire disbands, leaving behind rival Italian states.
951 Saxon King Otto I becomes King of the Lombards; the following year he is crowned Holy Roman Emperor.
11th century Normans colonise Sicily and southern Italy.
1076 Pope Gregory VII and Emperor Henry IV become embroiled in a power struggle that marks the beginning of a 200-year conflict between the papacy and imperial powers.
1155 Guelphs, who take the side of the pope, clash with the Ghibellines, who follow the new emperor, Frederick Barbarossa.
1167 Lombard League of cities formed, to oppose the emperor.
1176 Pope Alexander III and Barbarossa reconciled.
1227–50 The power struggle resumes, and the papacy is, finally, the victor.

Late Middle Ages and Renaissance

1265 Charles of Anjou becomes King of Sicily.
1282 French settlers in Sicily are massacred.
1302 Anjou dynasty established in Naples.
1348 Black Death kills one third of Italians.
1309 Papacy established at Avignon.
1377 Papacy moves back to Rome.
1442 Alfonso V, King of Aragon, is crowned King of the "Two Sicilies" (Naples and Sicily).
1447 Francesco Sforza replaces the Visconti in Milan.
1469–92 Lorenzo de' Medici leads Florence; apogee of Renaissance.
1494 Wars of Italy begin with invasion by French King Charles VIII; Medici driven from Florence.

Centuries of Foreign Despotism

1503–13 Julius II is pope; Rome is now centre of the Renaissance.

1525 Battle of Pavia. Spain captures French king.

1527 Rome sacked by Charles V's imperial troops; Venice is now the centre of artistic activity.

1559 Treaty of Cateau-Cambrésis confirms Spanish control of Italy.

1700–13 War of the Spanish Succession ends Spanish domination; Austria becomes main foreign power on peninsula.

1796 Napoleon invades Italy, brings ideals of French Revolution and founds several republics.

1808 French capture Rome for second time, and exile the pope.

1814 Overthrow of French rule.

Towards Italian Unity

1815 Congress of Vienna; Venice given to Austria, who once again dominates Italy.

1831 Mazzini founds Young Italy movement.

1848 Uprisings across Italy against Austria led by Charles Albert, King of Piedmont.

1852 Cavour is made prime minister of Piedmont.

1854 Piedmont enters the Crimean War.

1859–60 With the help of France, Piedmont annexes most of northern Italy. Garibaldi's "Thousand" conquer Sicily and Naples.

1861 Victor Emmanuel II of Piedmont proclaimed King of Italy.

1866 Venice annexed to Italy.

1870 Italian troops enter Rome; unification completed; Rome becomes capital.

Modern Italy

1882 Triple Alliance agreed between Italy, Germany and Austria.

1896 Italians defeated at Adowa, Ethiopia.

1900 Anarchist assassinates King Umberto I. Victor Emmanuel III is crowned king.

1915 Italy joins Allies in World War I.

1919 Rise of Fascism.

1922 Mussolini's march on Rome.

1935 War against Ethiopia.

1939 Seizure of Albania.

1940 Italy joins Germany in World War II.

1943 Allies land in Sicily. Mussolini deposed, later rescued by Germans to found puppet government in the north. In September, provisional government in the south surrenders.

1944 Liberation of Rome; abdication of King Victor Emmanuel III.

1945 Mussolini killed by partisans.

1946 Italy declared a republic.

1957 Treaty of Rome: Italy joins Common Market as one of six founder members.

1950s–60s Italy's "economic miracle".

1966 Floods in Venice and Florence.

1978 Former premier Aldo Moro is kidnapped and killed. Period of political instability.

1980 Earthquake strikes Campania.

1990 Rise of the secessionist Northern League.

Early 1990s Corruption scandals rock Italy.

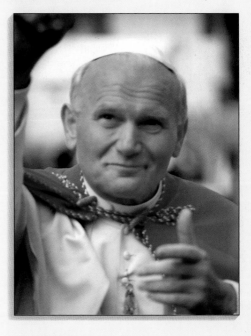

Late 1990s Extensive privatisation as part of the preparation for European Monetary Union.

2000 Millions flock to Rome, where over 700 historic sites are restored for the Holy Year.

2001 Silvio Berlusconi elected Prime Minister. His Forza Italia party governs in coalition with the National Alliance and the Northern League.

2002 The euro becomes the official currency in Italy; first general strike for 20 years.

2004 Genoa is European Cultural Capital.

2005 Pope John Paul II dies and is succeeded by Cardinal Joseph Ratzinger, Benedict XVI.

2006 Berlusconi ousted from power by Romano Prodi and his centre-left coalition, who win the Italian election with the narrowest of margins. ❑

PRECEDING PAGES: 18th-century map of Italy.
LEFT: Francesco Petrarch, Renaissance poet.
RIGHT: the late Pope John Paul II.

BEGINNINGS

*Many primitive tribes settled in Italy, but under the Greeks
and the Etruscans it became the centre of the ancient world*

As schoolchildren have noticed for years, Italy looks like a boot. The long, narrow peninsula sticking out of Europe's underbelly is perpetually poised to kick Sicily westward. This peculiar shape made Italy a natural site for early civilisation. The Alps, which cut across the only land link with the rest of Europe, protected the peninsula from the barbarians who roamed northern Europe, while the Mediterranean, which surrounds the three remaining sides, served as a highway, first to bring civilisation to the peninsula and later to export it.

The land itself contains two separate regions: the northern continental, and the southern peninsular. Together the two parts cover an area of about 250,000 sq. km (97,000 sq. miles). The northern section is a plain, bordered on the north and northwest by the Alps and on the south by the Apennines. Once a vast bay of the Adriatic, this plain was gradually filled with nitrate-rich silt from the Po, the Adige and other rivers, and became the most fertile region in Italy.

Mountainous spine

The Apennine range, the so-called backbone of Italy, dominates the peninsular section of the country. These mountains zig-zag down from the French Alps and the coast of Liguria in the northwest, through northern Tuscany and southeast to the Adriatic coast, and veer west again to the Strait of Messina, between Sicily and the toe of the boot. In the central region of Abruzzo, the peaks of the Gran Sasso d'Italia soar as high as 2,912 metres (9,700 ft).

It is no coincidence that the early inhabitants of Italy flourished in the west, on the lowland plains north and south of Rome. Here there are a few natural harbours and long rivers. The Tiber, Arno, Livi and Volturno are easily navigated by small craft, and their valleys provide easy communication between the coast and the interior. What is more, the plains of Tuscany, Latium and Campania comprise fertile farm-

LEFT: an Etruscan statue of Apollo. **RIGHT:** a Greek temple at Selinunte in Sicily.

land, thanks to a thick layer of ash and weathered lava from the many once-active volcanoes.

Around 200,000 years before the founding of Rome, only cave-dwelling hunter-gatherers lived on the Italian peninsula. However, with the Indo-European migrations (2000–1200 BC), tribes of primitive peoples poured into Italy

from Central Europe and Asia. These tribes lived in round huts clustered in small villages. The Villanovans, as the tribesmen are called, were farmers who could make and use iron tools. They cremated their dead and placed the ashes in tall, clay or bronze urns.

Villanovan culture spread from its original centre around Bologna south to Tuscany and Latium. Nowhere, however, did settlements grow to the size of towns; and Villanovans are not known for any great artistic achievements.

The transformation of Italy from a primitive backwater to the centre of the ancient world was due to the Greeks and the Etruscans. Both sailed across the sea in search of rich new land. They sowed the first seeds of civilisation on the peninsula in the early 8th century BC.

Greek colonists settled in Sicily and on the west coast near modern-day Naples. Most came in search of land to farm, for Greece had insufficient arable land to feed the entire population. Others were political refugees: whenever a Greek king was overthrown, all his followers were forced to flee.

On arriving in Italy, Greek settlers formed independent cities, each loosely linked to their city of origin on the Greek mainland. One of the

MASTERS OF THE VINE

The Greeks were the first to bring both the vine and the olive under cultivation.

soldiers. But after years of inconclusive fighting the Greek leaders gave up the struggle.

The colonists still argued among themselves, and therefore failed to become a dominant political power in Italy. They did, however, become the major cultural and artistic force. Italian natives were eager to trade for Greek luxury goods, the like of which they had never seen. Soon Greek bronze and ceramic ware was dispersed throughout Italy and provided natives with new and sophisticated art patterns to imitate; the architecture and sculpture in the Greek

earliest colonies was at Cumae, by the Bay of Naples. Greeks from Euboea, an island northeast of Athens, settled there in about 770 BC. Other Euboeans founded Rhegion (modern Reggio di Calabria), at the tip of the boot, a few years later. The Corinthian city of Syracuse on Sicily ultimately became the most powerful of the Greek colonies. The colonists farmed the land around their cities, and traded with mainland Greece. They soon prospered and made important contributions to Italian agriculture.

During the 5th century, both Syracuse and Athens tried to establish rival empires out of the Greek colonies in Italy. Numerous battles were fought and many Italian natives were drafted as

cities also served as models. The civilising influence of the Greeks went beyond the visual arts. The natives adapted the Greek alphabet for their own Indo-European tongues and each native group soon had its own letters. By example, the Greeks also taught the Italian natives about modern warfare, lessons that they later used against their Greek teachers. The Italians learnt how to fortify towns with high walls of smooth masonry, and discovered the value of shock troop tactics with armoured spearmen.

But exceptional wealth and knowledge did not enable the Greeks to control Italy, and failure to unify the natives under Greek leadership left great political opportunities wide open.

In about 800 BC, Etruscans settled on the west coast where Tuscany (Etruscany) and Lazio are today. The origins of the Etruscans still puzzle scholars. The Greek historian Herodotus claimed that they came from Asia Minor, driven by revolution and famine at home to seek new lands. However, recent archaeological evidence suggests that Etruscan culture derives from a small group of Phoenicians from Palestine who landed in Italy and imparted to the natives the knowledge they had brought from the East.

Wherever they came from, the Etruscans were a highly civilised people who had a hearty appetite for life. Hundreds of Etruscan tombs but they were grouped in a loose confederation for religious purposes. Representatives of the cities would gather regularly to worship the 12 Etruscan gods, but that was the extent of their political unity. Their fascination with religion far surpassed their desire for political power.

Vital trade routes

Each Etruscan city supported itself by trade. Eager to obtain luxury goods from the Greek colonists, the Etruscans developed overland routes to reach the Greek cities. These cut straight through Latium, the plain south of the Tiber occupied by Italian natives called Latins.

have survived, many with wall paintings depicting dancing, dinner parties and music-making. Other paintings show battle and hunting scenes.

The Etruscans were also extremely skilled craftsmen. Their speciality was metal working. Italy was rich in minerals, and trade in metal goods soon became the basis of an active urban society. Cities sprang up where previously there had been only simple villages. Each of the Etruscan cities (there were 12 in all) was independent,

LEFT: an ancient Greek dives gracefully into the unknown in a fresco from a tomb at Paestum.
ABOVE: the she-wolf suckling Romulus and Remus, the mythical founders of Rome.

One of their trading posts on the route south was a Latin village called Rome, originally only a cluster of mud huts. Under the influence of the Etruscans, the settlement flourished. They drained the swamp that became the Roman Forum and built grand palaces and roads.

For 300 years from the late 8th century BC, Etruscan kings ruled Rome. But, by the 5th century BC, their power was fading. In the north, Gauls overran Etruscan settlements in the Po Valley. Next, Italic tribesmen from Abruzzo threatened the main Etruscan cities. Then, in the south, the Etruscans went to war against the Greeks. The Romans chose this moment to rebel against their Etruscan masters. ❑

ROME RULES THE WORLD

Between its legendary founding by Romulus and its sacking by barbarians,
Rome presided over one of our greatest civilisations

The historians of Ancient Rome wrote their own version of events leading to the overthrow of the Etruscan kings. They drew upon legends about Rome's past and claimed that the city had only temporarily fallen under Etruscan rule. According to legend, Rome was founded by the descendants of gods and heroes.

In his epic, the *Aeneid*, Virgil tells how Aeneas, a hero of Homeric Troy, journeyed west after the sack of Troy to live and rule in Latium. In the 8th century one of his descendants, the Latin princess Rhea Silvia, bore twin sons, Romulus and Remus, fathered by the god Mars. Her uncle, King Amulius, angry because the princess had broken her vow of chastity as a Vestal Virgin, locked her up and abandoned the boys on the river bank to die. They were found there by a she-wolf who raised them. As young men, the brothers led a band of rebel Latin youths to find a new home. As they approached the hills of Rome, a flight of eagles passed overhead – a sign from the gods that this was an auspicious site for their new city.

Rape and revolt

Rome was ruled by Etruscan kings until 509 BC when the son of King Tarquinius Superbus raped a Roman noblewoman, Lucretia. She killed herself in shame and Roman noblemen rose in revolt against the Etruscans.

The leader of the Roman revolt, Lucius Junius Brutus, may have been an actual historical figure. In Roman legend he is the founder of a republic, a vigorous leader, and a puritanical ruler. The historian Tacitus wrote that he was so loyal to Rome that he watched without flinching as his two sons were executed for treason.

In the war against the Etruscans, Rome was also aided by Cincinnatus, a simple Roman farmer who left his plough to help his city. He was so able that he rose quickly to the rank of general. But once the fight was won, he surrendered his position of power and returned to his life as an ordinary citizen.

These stories of Rome's early heroes reveal a lot about the Roman character. For the Romans, *pietas* – dutiful respect to one's gods, city, parents and comrades – was all-important.

Because of this, the heroes of legend were very useful propaganda tools within the empire.

Upon the overthrow of the Etruscans, Rome's leaders founded a republic based on the Greek model, and the Senate, a group of Rome's leading citizens who previously had advisory roles in government, took control of the city.

Roman conquests

During the next 200 years Rome conquered most of the Italian peninsula. But Carthage, a city in North Africa founded by the Phoenicians, controlled the western Mediterranean. If Rome was ever to expand its borders across the Mediterranean, Carthage had to be defeated.

LEFT: the *Augustus of Prima Porta* shows a youthful emperor looking to Rome's future of *Imperium sine fine* (rule without end). **RIGHT:** Hannibal's Carthaginian forces cross the Alps during the Second Punic War.

The initial clash between the two cities, the First Punic War (264 BC), began as a struggle for the Greek city of Messina on Sicily. By the time it was over, in 241 BC, the Romans had driven the Carthaginians out of Sicily completely. The island became Rome's first province. Three years later Rome annexed Sardinia and Corsica, and further military triumphs followed. When Rome conquered Cisalpine Gaul (northern Italy) and extended its borders to the Alps, it alleviated the threat of invasion by the Gauls.

War broke out again in 218 BC when the brilliant Carthaginian general Hannibal embarked on an ambitious plan to attack Rome from the

north via Spain, the Pyrenees and the Alps. Rome eventually counterattacked Carthage, and Hannibal was forced to return and defend his homeland. He was defeated in 202 BC at the battle of Zama, southwest of Carthage.

Final defeat of Carthage

The Third Punic War was almost an afterthought. Carthage, stripped of many of its possessions 50 years earlier, had regained much of its commercial power. When the Carthaginians challenged Rome indirectly, the Romans razed the city of Carthage and ploughed salt into the soil. The Carthaginians were sold into slavery.

The blessings of peace were mixed. Rome

was now more prosperous than ever before, but only the middle class and the rich benefited. For the common people, many of whom had served their city faithfully during the wars, peace meant greater poverty as the menial jobs on which they had depended were now filled by slaves. Independent farmers, who traditionally formed the backbone of the Roman state, sold their land to the owners of great estates, who used slaves to work it. These displaced farmers joined the Roman mob or wandered through Italy seeking work.

The Senate's usual way of dealing with potentially explosive situations was to feed the masses bread and entertain them with circuses. But eventually a patrician, Tiberius Gracchus, challenged the exploitative system. Elected tribune in 133 BC, he campaigned to reintroduce a law limiting the size of the great estates, and proposed redistributing state-owned farming and grazing land among the poor. The Senators, many of them wealthy landowners, blocked Tiberius's plan, and when he persisted and ran for re-election as tribune they engaged assassins to murder him and his supporters.

Gaius the populist

Tiberius's spirit did not die with him. Eleven years later, his brother Gaius was elected tribune. An effective speaker, he was popular with the Roman masses. Once in office, he called for sweeping land reform. Again the Senate struck back viciously. The Roman people were incited to riot, and Gaius was blamed. He was killed or forced to kill himself (the records are not clear), and his followers were imprisoned.

The power of the army commanders now became the determining factor in Roman politics. The general Gaius Marius, son of a farmer, returned to Rome from triumphant campaigns in Africa determined to smash the power of the despised Senate. To the Roman people, Gaius Marius was a god-like figure who had transformed the Roman citizen legions into a professional army. He and his supporters butchered the senatorial leaders and thousands of aristocratic Romans.

This fateful action, taken in the name of liberty, opened the way to dictatorship. The Senate turned to Silla, a rival general and a patrician by birth, who answered Marius's violence with a blood bath of his own. After Marius's death in 86 BC, Silla posted daily lists of people to be executed by his henchmen. He then conducted equally bloody campaigns abroad.

Silla returned to Rome and ruled as absolute dictator. The Senate could put no check on him for it had opened the door for him to take power. The Republic was dead, the victim of three centuries of empire building.

Enter Pompey the Great

For two years the streets of Rome ran with blood. But in 79 BC Silla grew tired of ruling and retired to his estate near Naples. Civil war broke out again. Silla's successor was another general, Gnaeus Pompeius, called Pompey the Great. He

army across the flooded Rubicon river (the border between Cisalpine Gaul and Italy), against the orders of the Senate. With Caesar heading towards the capital, Pompey quickly left for Greece, taking his own small army and most of the Senate with him. Pompey had planned to strike back at Caesar from Greece, having secured an adequate army, but Caesar moved first. He attacked Pompey's allies in Spain, then in Greece, forcing Pompey to flee to Egypt, where he was eventually killed in 48 BC.

Caesar returned to Rome in triumph. The masses believed that his victories proved he was divinely appointed to rule Rome. For the first

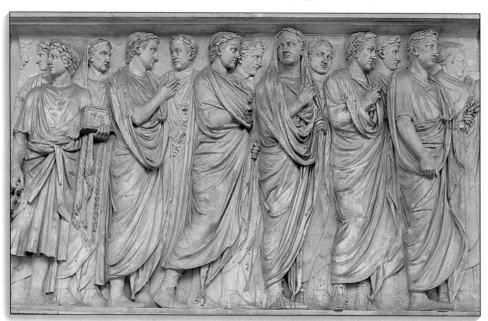

restored many liberties suspended by Silla, but failed to go far enough for the rioting masses.

Pompey's solution was to join forces with two other military men, Crassus and Julius Caesar, and form the Triumvirate, a ruling body of considerable power and influence. This arrangement was successful at first but when Crassus died in 53 BC, the two remaining leaders quarrelled. For several years Pompey and Caesar eyed each other warily. Then, in 49 BC, Caesar, after his successful campaign in Gaul, led his

LEFT: Julius Caesar raised patrician eyebrows when he put his face on a coin. **ABOVE:** Emperor Augustus built the monumental *Ara Pacis* to celebrate peace.

BEWARE THE IDES OF MARCH

An Etruscan soothsayer had warned Caesar to beware of misfortune that would strike no later than 15 March 44 BC. On that day – the Ides of March – Caesar was scheduled to address the Senate. On his way to the Senate chamber he passed the soothsayer. Caesar remarked that the Ides had come safely. The Etruscan replied that the day was not yet over. In the chamber, Caesar was surrounded by conspirators and stabbed 23 times. When he saw that Marcus Junius Brutus, a patrician he had treated like a son, was among his murderers, he murmured "Et tu, Brute?" ("You too, Brute?") and died.

time in decades there were no riots in the capital. But the upper classes were wary of Caesar's autocratic tendencies. While factions within the Senate heaped honours on the new ruler, hoping for favours in return, many patricians watched suspiciously as Caesar had statues of himself raised in public places and his image put on coins. A conspiracy formed against him.

After Caesar's death, Mark Antony, Caesar's co-consul, and Octavian, his grand-nephew, joined forces to pursue and murder the conspirators. Despite their cooperation,

> **CHARACTER BUILDER**
>
> Augustus, first emperor of Rome, outlawed prostitution and drunkenness and strengthened divorce laws.

one", but in fact he was the first emperor of Rome. Unlike his grand-uncle before him, he took care not to offend the republican sentiments of the Romans, and therein lay the key to his success. He allowed the Senate the outward trappings of power and influence, but little of the reality. Uninterested in status symbols or ostentation, he lived and dressed simply. The competence and sensitivity with which Augustus reigned made for an unprecedented period of peace, order and prosperity; and for some 200 years after Augustan

the two were never good friends. Initially they collaborated with an army leader, Lepidus, to form an uneasy Second Triumvirate, but the arrangement faltered when Antony fell in love with the Egyptian queen Cleopatra and rejected his wife, Octavian's sister, to marry her. In revenge, Octavian turned the Senate against Mark Antony, then declared war on his former partner. When defeat was imminent, Antony and Cleopatra committed suicide.

Augustus and the Pax Romana

Octavian's triumphant return to Rome marked the beginning of a new era. He called himself simply "Augustus", meaning "the revered

reform, the Mediterranean world basked in a *Pax Romana*, a Roman peace.

Before Augustus assumed power, the republican institutions had been unable to administer the vast territories Rome now controlled. Military dictatorship had been the result. To meet this challenge Augustus created a personal bureaucracy within his household. In addition to footmen and maids, he also had tax collectors, governors, census takers, and administrators as his "servants". He allowed this personal civil service to grow to a size sufficient to run the empire, but kept it under tight control. At first, many members of the nobility refused to join: they believed that any office in the household, however influential, was too close to personal service. But poor men of talent joined Augustus readily, and throughout his reign the empire ran smoothly.

With peace, art and literature flourished. The poet Virgil, who had lived through the civil wars and military dictatorships, paid tribute to Augustus's achievements in the *Aeneid*; the poet Horace likened the emperor to a helmsman who had steered the ship of state into a safe port. Augustus himself took part in the artistic resurgence and set about rebuilding the capital. He claimed that he had found Rome a city of brick and left it a city of marble.

Augustus reigned for 41 years and set the tone of Roman leadership for the next 150. None of his successors had his ability, but his institutional and personal legacy did much to preserve peace in the flourishing Roman world.

The mad and the bad

The Emperor Tiberius had none of his stepfather's sense of proportion, nor his steadiness. He began his reign with good intentions, but he mismanaged many early problems. He spent the last 11 years of his reign at his villa on Capri, from where he issued a volley of execution orders. The historian Suetonius wrote (in the translation by Robert Graves), "Not a day, however holy, passed without an execution; he even desecrated New Year's Day. Many of his victims were accused and punished with their children – some actually by their children – and the relatives forbidden to go into mourning."

Rome was relieved when Tiberius died, only to find that there was worse to come. Caligula, his successor, ruled ably for three years, then ran wild. His derangement may have been due to illness, or simply the pressures of high office. He insisted that he was a god, formed his own priesthood and erected a temple to himself. He proposed his horse be made consul. Finally a group of his own officers assassinated Caligula, and Rome was rid of its most hated ruler.

The officers took it upon themselves to name the next emperor. Their choice was Claudius, grandson of Augustus, whom they found hiding behind a curtain in the palace after the assassination. Many thought Claudius a fool, for he stuttered and was slightly crippled, but he

proved a good and steady ruler. He oversaw the reform of the civil service, and the expansion of the Roman Empire to include Britain.

Claudius was poisoned by his ambitious wife Agrippina, who pushed Nero, her son by a previous marriage, on to the throne. Like Tiberius before him, Nero started out with good intentions. He was well-educated, an accomplished musician, and showed respect for the advice of others, especially senators. But the violent side of his nature soon became apparent. He poisoned Brittanicus, Claudius's natural son, and tried to do the same to his mother, but she had taken the precaution of building up an immu-

nity to the poison. In the end Nero accused her of plotting against him, and had her executed.

Nero's excesses caused alarm among Rome's citizens. When a fire destroyed the city in AD 64, he was accused of starting it. In fact, he was away from the city at the time and stories of him fiddling while Rome burned are probably untrue.

Nero lost his throne after the Roman commanders in Gaul, Africa and Spain rebelled. When the news reached the capital riots broke out and the Senate condemned him to death as a public enemy. With no hope left, Nero killed himself in AD 68. His suicide threw the empire into greater turmoil. He left no heir and therefore the rebellious commanders fought amongst

---

LEFT: a reconstruction of the Colosseum.
RIGHT: Emperor Nero with his tigress, Phoebe.

themselves for a year until a legion commander, Vespasian Flavius, emerged as emperor.

Vespasian proved a wise emperor, and his rule ushered in a period of peace. There was a short time of troubles when his son, Domitian, became emperor; but, by the time he died, the Senate was powerful enough to appoint its own emperor, Nerva, a respected lawyer from Rome.

Nerva was the first of the "five good emperors" who reigned from AD 96 to 180. He was followed by Trajan, Hadrian, Antoninus Pius and Marcus Aurelius – all educated men, interested in philosophy and devoted to their duties. They were loved by the people of Rome

for administering their vast empire well and successfully defending its borders.

Decline and fall

During the period between the death of Marcus Aurelius and the sack of Rome in the 5th century, it became increasingly difficult to defend the empire from barbarians. Between AD 180 and 285, Rome was threatened in both the east and the west by barbarian tribes. The empire doubled the size of the army. The drain on manpower and resources caused an economic crisis, and the powerful army could place emperors on the throne and remove them at will. Most of these "barracks emperors" served for less than three years and never even lived in the capital. Plague also struck Rome, which weakened the empire and made it more vulnerable to enemy attack. On all sides wars raged. In the east, the revived Persian Empire threatened Syria, Egypt and all of Asia Minor. In the west, Franks invaded France and Spain.

Major political reform was undertaken by Emperor Diocletian in 286. He believed the empire could no longer be ruled by one man, so he divided it into eastern and western regions. He chose Nicomedia in Asia Minor as his capital and appointed a soldier named Maximinus to rule the west from Milan.

Unfortunately this arrangement did not end quarrels about the succession. Constantine marched on Rome in 311 to assert his right to the throne. While on the road, however, he claimed that he had a vision. The sign of the cross appeared in the sky with the words: "By this sign win your victory." As a result, when Constantine defeated his rival, Maxentius, and emerged as the sole emperor, he ruled as a Christian and granted religious freedom to existing Christians.

In 324, he took a step further and confirmed Christianity as the state religion. Not all citizens followed the new faith; some notable families remained true to their pagan beliefs. But Constantine's conversion established Christianity, which had been spreading through the empire since the time of Nero, as the religion of the Roman state and thus of the Western world. Under his auspices, or in the decades which followed his reign, the first Christian churches of Rome were built. These included the earliest constructions of the five patriarchal churches of which the pope himself was the priest: San Pietro (St Peter's), San Giovanni in Laterano, San Paolo fuori le Mura, San Lorenzo fuori le Mura and Santa Maria Maggiore. Together with the catacomb churches of San Sebastiano and Santa Croce in Gerusalemme, along the Via Appia, these soon became centres of pilgrimage.

Despite the conversion to Christianity, the empire continued to decline. In 330, Constantine decided to move the capital east, and make a fresh start in his new city of Constantinople. Back in Italy, the barbarians gradually moved closer. The city of Rome was sacked in 410. ❏

LEFT: one of the "barracks emperors", probably Valerian.

Life in the Empire

I n more than 60 treatises on morality, Plutarch (AD 46–126) laid down what was expected of a Roman gentleman. It was a damnable luxury to strain wine or to use snow to cool drinks. It was "democratic and polite" to be punctual for dinner; "oligarchical and offensive" to be late. Conversation over dinner ought to be philosophical, like debating which came first, the chicken or the egg. Salt fish was scooped up with a single finger, but two could be used if the fish was fresh. There was only one permissible way for a Roman gentleman to scratch himself, and so on.

It would be naive to think that all Romans obeyed Plutarch's strictures. Life was as diverse as in any modern capital, with an elegant high society at one end of the scale, vicious louts at the other, and every permutation in between. The one common factor was probably a passion for bathing. With underground furnaces heating the water, the baths got bigger and bigger. The well-preserved Caracalla baths could disgorge 1,600 glowing Romans per day.

In the early days, relations between patricians and plebeians were codified, as were family matters. Patricians were the source of "tranquillity", mainly by lending an ear to plebeians' problems and dispensing advice. In return, plebeians had to stump up money when the patrician was held to ransom or could not settle his debts. Money made available in such circumstances was not a loan but a plebeian's privilege, for which he was supposed to be grateful. On the other hand, plebeians were not enslaved and could switch allegiance from an unsatisfactory patrician to one more suitable.

Divorce was introduced relatively late. At first, marriage was permanent and wives automatically acquired half the conjugal property. However, husbands exercised the ultimate sanction in that they were legally entitled to murder wives for serious offences, such as poisoning the children or making duplicates of their private keys. Fathers were prevented from selling sons into slavery once the boys had married.

Citizens bombarded bureaucrats with complaints about the quality of life in Rome: disgraceful traffic congestion and refuse collection; preposterous fashions like men experimenting with trousers; escalating inflation; homosexuals getting too big for their boots; the filthy habit of smoking dried cow

RIGHT: a fresco in the Casa dei Vettii in Pompeii.

dung, and so forth. The most castigated men in Rome were unscrupulous property developers who set fire to a building they wanted and then, as the flames went up, offered the uninsured owner a pittance. As soon as the deal was struck, the developer summoned a private fire brigade parked around the corner.

In a spiritual context, the lives of the Romans were wrapped up in astrology and mysticism. The spread of Bacchic rites in republican Rome alarmed the government, which called them "this pestiential evil ... this contagious disease". Senators "were seized by a panic of fear, both for the public safety, lest these secret conspiracies and noctur-

nal gatherings contain some hidden harm or danger, and for themselves individually, lest some relatives be involved in this vice".

The social decadence supposedly behind the downfall of Rome had its own decorum. Petronius Arbiter, author of the *Satyricon*, orchestrated Nero's orgies. He later fell out with Nero and was ordered to take his own life. Petronius invited friends to a farewell banquet where he sat with bandages wrapped around wrists which he discreetly slashed as the evening progressed. The controlled bleeding enabled him to sustain repartee up to the moment his head slumped. It is not known whether he expressed a parting thought on the interesting question of the chicken and the egg. ❑

THE MIDDLE AGES

A period that saw Lombard, Saracen and Norman invasions

and clashes between emperor and pope

For four centuries after the sack of Rome in AD 410, barbarian invaders, including the Goths and the Lombards, battled with local military leaders and the Byzantine emperors for control of Italy. Under these conditions, the culture and prosperity that had characterised ancient times faded. The Roman Empire had unified Italy and made it the centre of the world, but after its demise Italy became a provincial battlefield. Since none of the rival powers could control the whole of Italy, the land was divided, and it remained so until the 19th century.

The Dark Ages began with a series of Visigoth invasions from northern and eastern Europe. The emperors in Constantinople were still in theory the rulers of Italy, but for decades they accepted first the Visigoth and later the Ostrogoth leaders as *de facto* kings. Justinian I, who became emperor in Constantinople in 527, longed to revive the splendour of the empire and sent the brilliant general Belisarius to regain direct control of Italy. But, although he met with initial success – he captured Ravenna from the Goths in 540 – a new group of barbarians soon appeared on Italy's borders: the Lombards.

Invaders from the north

The Lombards were German tribesmen from the Danube Valley. They swiftly conquered most of what is now Lombardy, the Veneto and Tuscany, causing the inhabitants of the northern Italian cities to flee to eastern coastal regions where they were protected by the Byzantines, who still controlled the seas. Many settled around the lagoon of Venice.

Meanwhile, the Lombards altered the system of government. They replaced the centralised Roman political system with local administrative units called "duchies", after the Lombard army generals who were known as *duces*. Within each duchy a *duce* ruled as king. The land was distributed to groups of related Lombard families, each headed by a free warrior, who owed limited feudal allegiance to his king but had a free hand on his own land. This, along with the Byzantines' continuing control of many provinces, meant Italy was effectively divided.

The radical changes that the Lombards brought to Italy's administration did not affect

Kaiser Justinian. (482–565.) Kaiserin Theodora. († 548.)

the Church. Indeed, in Rome the bishopric rose to new prominence because the emperors in Constantinople were too distant to exert any temporal or spiritual authority.

Greatest among the early popes was Gregory I (589–603), a Roman by birth, a scholar by instinct and training, and a great statesman. He persuaded the Lombards to abandon the siege of Rome, and helped achieve peace in Italy. He sent missionaries to northern Europe to spread the word of God and the influence of Rome, and sent the first missionaries to the British Isles.

Gregory's successors reorganised the municipal government of Rome, and effectively became rulers of the city. It was inevitable that

LEFT: the 6th-century Pope Gregory the Great, one of many early popes who was canonised.

RIGHT: Emperor Justinian with his wife, Theodora.

the popes would eventually clash with the emperor in Constantinople. In 726, Emperor Leo decreed that veneration of images of Christ and the saints was forbidden and that all images were to be destroyed. The pope opposed his decree on the grounds that the Church in Rome should have the final say on all spiritual matters, and organised an Italian revolt against the emperor. The Lombards joined the revolt on the side of the popes and used the opportunity to chase the Byzantines out of Italy.

GREGORY THE GREAT

The pope who made peace with the Lombards to save Rome also gave his name to the Gregorian chant, and sent St Augustine to England.

western Europe. To unify his vast territories under Christian auspices, he had Pope Leo crown him Holy Roman Emperor at St Peter's in Rome on Christmas Day 800.

Charlemagne lived only 14 years after his coronation, and none of his successors matched him in ability; authority fell into the hands of Frankish counts, Charlemagne's vassals who had accompanied him south and been granted land of their own. As representatives of the crown, they were required to raise troops, but they used these

After the imperial capital, Ravenna, fell to the Lombard army in 751, the popes, feeling more directly threatened by the powerful Lombards than by an absent emperor, sought a new ally and turned to the Franks for help.

Pepin, king of the Franks, invaded Italy in 754. He reconquered the imperial lands but ceded control to the pope. Twenty years later, Pepin's son, Charlemagne, finished his father's work by defeating and capturing the Lombard king, confirming his father's grant to the papacy, and assuming the crown of the Lombards.

Charlemagne then returned to the north and campaigned against the Saxons, Bavarians and Avars, making himself ruler of a large part of

forces to fight each other for land and power.

This period of feudal anarchy was also marked by invasions. In the south the Saracens invaded Sicily in 827, and for the next 250 years Sicily was an Arab state. Sicily also became a base for raids on the Italian mainland, and Charlemagne's great-grandson, Louis II, who was emperor for 25 years, failed to raise an organised defence against them. The Lombard dukes in the south, whom Charlemagne had not conquered completely, allied themselves with these invaders against the Carolingian emperor. What success Louis had was overshadowed by Pope Leo IV's defence of Rome and the naval victory against the Saracens at Ostia.

The Normans in the south

In the early 11th century, small groups of Normans arrived in southern Italy. Adventurers and skilled soldiers, they would fight for anyone who would pay, Greek, Lombard and Saracen alike. In return they asked for land.

Soon landless men from Normandy arrived to fight, settle and conquer for themselves. The papacy lost no time in allying itself with this powerful group of Christians. In the 1050s, the Norman chief, Robert Guiscard, conquered Calabria in the toe of Italy. Pope Nicholas II "legitimised" Norman rule of the area by calling it a papal fief, then investing Guiscard as its king.

Despite external opposition (from the eastern and western emperors) and occasional domestic rebellions, Roger's son and grandson were able to preserve the regime. Only when William II died in 1189, leaving no heir, did civil war break out and Norman control of southern Italy end.

During the 9th and 10th centuries, the papacy was controlled by Roman nobles. The men they picked for office were often corrupt. After Emperor Otto I arrived in Rome in 962, he insisted that no pope could be elected until the emperor had named a candidate. But, by reforming the papacy, the emperors started a trend that would have far-reaching consequences.

Robert's nephew, Roger, conquered Sicily. He was crowned king in Palermo in 1130 and ruled over the island and his uncle's mainland possessions. He was a tolerant ruler, and his court became a magnet for Jewish, Greek and Arab scholars. Still visible today are the architectural achievements of this sophisticated culture. Brilliant examples of Arab-Norman architecture can be seen in Palermo and at the cathedrals of Monreale and Cefalù.

LEFT: mosaics, such as this one of the Emperor Justinian, are glittering reminders that Ravenna was once the capital of Byzantium.
ABOVE: fresco in Siena's town hall.

In the 11th century, the popes strove to reform the church further by imposing a strict clerical hierarchy. Throughout the Holy Roman Empire, bishops were to be answerable to the pope, and priests to bishops. A single legal and administrative system would bind all members of the clergy together. These reforms immediately angered all lay rulers from the emperor down.

The struggle reached a climax when Emperor Henry IV invested an anti-reform candidate as archbishop of Milan in 1072. As a result, Pope Gregory VII decreed that an investiture by a non-cleric was forbidden and excommunicated Henry. For three days in the cold winter of 1077, the humbled emperor stood in the courtyard of a

Tuscan castle where Gregory was staying, and pleaded for a reconciliation with the pope.

Henry was forgiven. However, he failed to keep his promise to recognise the claims of the papacy, and a new civil war broke out. Gregory's supporters were defeated initially and he was carried off to Salerno and death, but his successors worked to ensure the triumph of Gregory's cause, and the emperors were forced to concede their rights of investiture in 1122.

During the years of the investiture controversy and the ensuing civil wars, the cities of northern and central Italy grew rich and powerful. The emperors were too distracted to admin-

ister them directly. Around the same time, Mediterranean commerce was revived. With new wealth at their disposal, the cities forced the nobles in the countryside to acknowledge their supremacy. The Italian city-states were born. The strong and separate identity of the city-states is one of the leitmotifs of Italian history, influencing the pattern of future political affiliations, fostering separate schools of art, architecture and music, and largely determining regional attitudes today.

The maritime republics of Venice, Genoa and Pisa were foremost among the Italian cities, but inland cities that were situated on rich trade routes also prospered. Milan and Verona lay at the entrance to the Alpine passes, Bologna was the chief city on the Via Emilia, and Florence had sea access via the river Arno and controlled two roads to Rome.

The growing political power of the city-states was an important factor in renewed conflict between emperor and pope during the 13th century. Emperor Frederick II (1197–1250) tried to build a strong, centralised state in Italy. The cities that supported him kept their rights of self-government, but were forced to join an imperial federation. The cities that opposed him, wanting complete political autonomy, found an ally in Pope Gregory IX who secretly had imperial designs of his own. Northern Italy became a battlefield for civil war between the Guelfs, supporters of the pope, and the Ghibellines, allies of the emperor.

By the time Frederick died in 1250, without instituting his reforms, the Guelf cause was won. The alliance of pope and the city-states had ruined imperial plans for a unified Italy.

The age of Dante

The Guelfs beat the Ghibellines decisively, but a feud broke out between two Guelf factions: the Blacks and the Whites. This split was especially severe in Florence where the Blacks defended the nobles' feudal tradition against the Whites, rich magnates who were willing to give merchants a voice in government.

Pope Boniface VIII sided with the Blacks and worked to have all prominent Whites exiled from Florence in 1302. Among the exiles was Dante Alighieri, who went on to write *La Divina Commedia* (*The Divine Comedy*), a literary masterpiece that promoted Tuscan Italian to the status of a national tongue and also reveals much about the politics of the period.

Dante put his faith in the Holy Roman Empire, convinced that it could and should usher in a new period of cultural and political prominence for Italy. When Henry VII became Holy Roman Emperor in 1308, he wanted to revive imperial power in Italy and set up a government that was neither Guelf nor Ghibelline. But the cities refused to support him. Dante's home town, Florence, was the centre of the resistance to imperial plans. ❏

LEFT: an illuminated manuscript made for the Dukes of Milan in the late 14th century. **RIGHT:** Dante Alighieri, as painted by Andrea del Castagno.

THE RENAISSANCE

*Free from foreign interference, the city-states flourished and witnessed
an unprecedented cultural awakening*

The constant fighting in northern Italy subsided in the early 14th century when both the popes and the emperors withdrew from Italian affairs. After Henry VII's demise, the emperors turned their attention to Germany. Meanwhile, the influence of the papacy declined after a quarrel between Pope Boniface and King Philip of France in 1302. The pope insisted that Philip had no right to tax the French clergy; the king's response was to send his troops to capture the pope. French pressure ensured that the next pope was a Frenchman, Clement V, and he moved the papacy from Rome to Avignon, where it stayed until 1377.

The people of Italy were thus free from outside interference during the 14th century and the Italian cities grew stronger, richer and bigger than any in Europe. Against the political background of the supremacy of the city-state, a new culture bloomed and new ideas flourished. Rulers tried new methods of administration. Scholars were allowed to rediscover the pagan past. Wealthy merchants became lavish patrons of the arts. Through their commissions, artists experimented with a new, more realistic style.

Plague and depression

Not even the Black Death – the terrible outbreak of bubonic plague that ravaged Europe in the 14th century – could smother the new cultural awakening. But the plague did cause great human suffering and a prolonged economic depression. During several months of 1347 the death rate was 60 percent in some Italian cities. The merchants' solution to the declining profits of the period was to change the way they did business. Their innovations included marine insurance, credit transfers, double-entry bookkeeping and holding companies – all of which eventually became standard business practice.

To be a good businessman in the early Renaissance required a basic education: read-

LEFT: Titian's portrait of Pope Julius II, a great patron of the arts. **RIGHT:** relief by Ghiberti from the "Gates of Paradise" of the Baptistry of St John in Florence.

ing, writing and arithmetic. But the more complicated business became, the more knowledge was needed, including an understanding of law and diplomacy, and of the ways of the world. Thus the traditional theological studies of the Middle Ages were replaced by the study of ancient authors and of grammar, rhetoric, his-

tory and moral philosophy. This education became known as *studia humanitatis*, or the humanities.

Humanism grew partly out of the need for greater legal expertise in the expanding world of Mediterranean commerce. To learn how to administer their new, complex societies, lawyers looked back at the great tenets of Roman law. As they studied the codes of the ancients, they grew to appreciate the cultural riches of that long-buried civilisation. All aspects of Italian life were re-examined in the light of this new humanism. One way of life was thought to be ideal – that of the all-round man based on classical models. The Renaissance man was a reincarnation of rich, talented Roman philosophers.

Despots and republics

Italians of the 14th century were citizens of particular cities, not members of a national unit. They revered local saints, believed myths that explained the origin and uniqueness of their city, and feuded with other cities. Rulers encouraged artists and writers to glorify their towns.

There were a few experiences and conditions that many cities shared. As the authority of the popes and emperors declined, life in the cities became increasingly violent. Leading families would extend his powers until he controlled the entire city. Then he was in a strong enough position to make his office hereditary. This was how the della Scala family in Verona, the Carrara in Padua, the Gonzaga in Mantua and the Visconti in Milan came to power.

Once established, a despot would centralise all agencies of the government under his supervision. His power would be threatened only if he overstepped what his subjects could tolerate.

Some cities, including Venice, Florence, Siena, Lucca and Pisa, did not succumb to despotism until quite late in their history: the merchants were so powerful that rulers such as

fought each other constantly, and often came into conflict with groups lower on the social ladder that wanted a role in the political life of the city. The remedy to this bloody civil strife was the rule of one strong man. The pattern was repeated over and over again in northern Italy. Traditional republican rule which could not keep order was replaced by a dictatorship. Sometimes a leading faction would bring in an outsider, known as a *podestà*, to end the chaos – for example, the lordship of the d'Este family in Ferrara was established in this way. More often, the future despot was originally a *capitano del popolo* – the head of the local police force and citizens' army. Over time, this captain

the Medici only survived by winning their support. In these cities republicanism flourished briefly, but even so the merchants dominated the organs of the republican government.

During the 14th and 15th centuries, northern and central Italy changed from an area speckled with tiny political units to one dominated by a few large states. Both republics and despots were expansionist in outlook. They would conquer their smaller neighbours and construct out of the lands they gained a new regional state with increased economic resources.

Of the Italian city states, the most successful and the most powerful was Milan. During the 14th century, the authoritarian Visconti family dominated Milan, and led the city to innumerable military and political victories until it was the largest state in northern Italy.

The Visconti regime may have been, in its efficiency, unlike anything Europe had seen for centuries, but for the Milanese people it had great drawbacks. The personal brutality of the Visconti controlled Milan. The regime could not rely on the loyalty of the populace for its survival. When the Visconti line died out in 1447, the Milanese declared a republic, but it was not strong enough to rule over all the restive towns Milan now controlled. When, in 1450, Francesco Sforza, a famous general who had served the Visconti, overthrew the republic and became the new duke, ruling with his wife Bianca Visconti, many Milanese were relieved.

The Republic of Florence

The spectacular transformation of Florence from a small town in the 1100s to the commercial and financial centre it had become by the end of the 14th century was based on the profitable wool trade. The wool guild of Florence, the Arte della Lana, imported wool from northern Europe and dyes from the Middle East. Using the city's secret weaving and colouring techniques, guild members produced a heavy red cloth that was sold all over the Mediterranean area. Wool trade profits had provided the initial capital for the banking industry of Florence. Since the 13th century, Florentine merchants had lent money to their allies, the pope and powerful Guelf nobles. This early experience led to the founding of formal banking houses, and made Florence the financial capital of Europe.

The leading merchant guilds of Florence spent their wealth on art. The city was a showcase of the best of Renaissance sculpture, painting and architecture. In the second half of the 13th century a building boom began with the construction of the Bargello, the Franciscan church of Santa Croce, and the Dominican church of Santa Maria Novella. Arnolfo di Cambio designed the cathedral and the Palazzo Vecchio. The Arte della Lana paid for the construction and decoration of the cathedral. The city hired Giotto to design the Campanile which is named after him, and in 1434 they had Brunelleschi finish the great dome.

The rich men of Florence controlled the city government through the Parte Guelfa. With membership came the right to find and persecute anyone with "Ghibellistic tendencies". Other political non-conformities were also not tolerated. Members of lesser guilds who demanded a greater share of power, or joined with the lower classes to fight the Parte Guelfa,

were annihilated. However, in the early 15th century the violence of class war escalated. The disenfranchised artisans struck back repeatedly. At this point the rich merchants allowed Cosimo de' Medici to rise to the leadership of Florence.

The 15th century was the golden age of the Renaissance. All the economic, political and cultural developments of the previous century had set the stage for a period of unprecedented artistic and intellectual achievement. To live in Italy at this time was to live in a new world of cultural and commercial riches. Italy was truly the centre of the world.

The political history of the century divides into two parts. Until 1454 the five chief states

LEFT: *The Battle of San Romano* by Paolo Uccello, showing the victory of Florence over Siena in 1432.
RIGHT: Cosimo the Elder, the Medici patriarch.

of Italy were busy expanding their borders, or strengthening their hold on territories, which meant fighting many small wars. The soldiers who fought them were mostly *condottieri* (mercenaries). After 1454 came a period of relative peace, when the states pursued their interests through alliances. These years saw the greatest artistic achievement, when Italian states of all sizes became cultural centres.

Italian wars of the Late Middle Ages and Early Renaissance had traditionally been fought by foreign mercenaries, but by the 15th century the mercenaries were more likely to be Italian. Men of all classes and from all parts of Italy joined the ranks of the purely Italian companies to fight northern wars for rival nobles. The *condottieri* looked upon war as a professional, technical skill. In battle, the object was to lose as few men as possible but still be victorious. Soldiers were too valuable to be sacrificed unnecessarily. The countryside, however, suffered heavily as village after village was plundered. The *condottieri* did not hesitate to take what they could even though they were very well paid. They were bound by no patriotic ties, only by a monetary arrangement, so an important captain could always be bought by the enemy.

One of the greatest *condottieri* was Francesco Sforza. Sforza had inherited the command of an army upon his father's death in 1424. He fought first for Milan and then for Venice in the northern wars until Filippo Visconti sought to attach him permanently to Milan by marrying him to his illegitimate daughter, Bianca.

Visconti died in 1447 leaving no heir, and Milan declared itself a republic. Sforza was expected to captain the new republican forces. Instead he went into exile. But when the republican government proved incompetent he turned his forces on the city and starved Milan into surrender. The chief assembly of the republic invited him to be the new duke of the city.

Peace and the Italian League

Sforza, the great soldier, was instrumental in bringing peace to northern Italy. He signed, and encouraged others to sign, the Treaty of Lodi, which led to the Italian League of 1455. This was a defensive league between Milan, Florence and Venice that the King of Naples and the pope also respected. It was set up to prevent any one of the great states from increasing its powers at

the expense of its weaker neighbours, and to present a common national front against attack.

The smaller states of Italy benefited most from the new league. Previously, they had spent vast resources on defence against the larger states. "This most holy League upon which depends the welfare of all Italy", wrote Giovanni Bentivoglio, a citizen of Bologna, in 1460.

During the decades of peace in Italy, Florence experienced its own Golden Age under the rule of the Medici family. The historian Guicciardini described the Florence of Lorenzo de' Medici as follows: "The city was in perfect peace, the leading citizens were united, and their author-

ity was so great that none dared to oppose them. The people were entertained daily with pageants and festivals; the food supply was abundant and all trades flourished. Talented and able men were assisted in their careers by the recognition given to arts and letters. While tranquillity reigned within her walls, externally the city enjoyed high honours and renown."

In part, the success of the Medici was a public relations coup. They allowed the Florentines to believe that the city government was still a great democracy. Only after Lorenzo's death, when Florence was briefly ruled by his arrogant son, did the citizens realise that their state, for all its republican forms, had drifted into the control of one family. They then quickly exiled the Medici and drafted a new constitution. Until then, both Cosimo and Lorenzo de' Medici had dominated Florence while shrewdly never appearing to be more than prominent citizens. They did this partly by manipulating the elections for the *Signoria,* Florence's city council, but the real base of their power lay in their acceptance by the city's leading citizens.

The Medici did more than simply rule and successfully keep the peace. They promoted art

PRINCELY ADVICE

Macchiavelli was inspired by Lorenzo de' Medici when he wrote in *The Prince*: "A ruler must emulate the fox and the lion, for the lion cannot avoid traps and the fox cannot fight wolves."

LEFT: Francesco Sforza married Bianca (**ABOVE**), natural daughter of the last of the Visconti rulers, to become despot of Milan.

and culture in Florentine life. When the famous humanist Niccolò Niccoli died, Cosimo acquired his book collection and attached it to the convent of San Marco, creating the first public library in Florence. Cosimo also had Marsilio Ficino trained to become head of the new Platonic Academy and make Florence a centre of Platonic studies. He supplied Donatello with classical works to inspire his sculpture. Lorenzo de' Medici grew up in the atmosphere his grandfather had created and when he became leader of Florence he also was a great patron of the arts. For his employees he was a peer as well as a patron. His poetry was widely admired.

An end to the peace

When Lorenzo de' Medici died in 1492, the fragile Italian League that had kept Italy at peace and safe from any foreign attacks died with him. Ludovico il Moro, the lord of Milan, immediately quarrelled with the Neapolitan king and proposed to the King of France that he, Charles VIII, conquer Naples and the surrounding states. Ludovico offered finance and safe passage through the north of Italy. Charles readily accepted and so began a truly demoralising chapter of Italian history.

The internal disarray in Italy at the time was so great that the French troops faced no organised resistance. The new leader of Florence, a Dominican friar named Girolamo Savonarola, preached that Charles was sent by God to regenerate the Church and purify spiritual life. Other Italians also welcomed the French. They believed that the invaders would rid Italy of decadence and set up governments with natives in key posts. Only when these ideas proved illusory could Italian patriots recruit an army and challenge the French.

The French and Italians met near the village of Fornovo on 6 July 1495. The Italians, led by General Francesco Gonzaga, looked certain of victory: they outnumbered the French two-to-one, and they could launch a surprise attack against their enemy. But the Italian strategy fell apart. Crucial troops could not cross the river to the French position. General Gonzaga entered the fiercest fighting and did not direct the battle as a whole, and some Italian soldiers left the battle to capture the French king's booty. When the battle ended, four thousand men had died – the majority of them Italian.

"If the Italians had won at Fornovo, they would probably have discovered then the pride of being a united people ... Italy would have emerged as a respectable nation ... a country which adventurous foreigners would think twice before attacking", wrote Luigi Barzini in *The Italians*. Instead, the defeat at Fornovo broke the Italian spirit and led to 30 years of foreign interventions, bloody conflicts, civil wars and revolts. ❏

RENAISSANCE ART

The revolution in art and architecture which began in Florence gave us our
greatest treasures. It also set the stage for Mannerism

Italian art shone brightest during the Renaissance when, as in most disciplines, a revolution took place. The Early Renaissance (1400–1500), the *Quattrocento*, introduced new themes that altered the future of art. Ancient Greece and Rome were rediscovered and with them the importance of man in the here and now. The human body surfaced as a new focal point in painting and sculpture. The discovery of perspective changed architecture.

The Early Renaissance centred on Florence. The city wanted to be seen as "the new Rome" and public works flourished. First was Lorenzo Ghiberti's commission for sculpting the gilded bronze north doors (1403–24) of the Baptistry, won in a competition with Filippo Brunelleschi in 1401. Ghiberti's more famous east doors (1424–52) are so dazzling that Michelangelo called them "the Gates of Paradise".

Classical architecture

It was Filippo Brunelleschi (1377–1466) who championed the new classically inspired architecture. After losing the Baptistry door competition, he went to Rome to study the proportions of ancient buildings. His studies led him to design such masterpieces as the dome of Florence cathedral, the arcade fronting the Innocenti orphanage, the church of San Lorenzo (1421–69), the Pazzi Chapel of Santa Croce (begun 1430–33), and Santo Spirito, all in Florence. You need no yardstick to appreciate the use of mathematical proportions. The overriding impression is of harmony, balance and calm.

If Brunelleschi was the most noted architect, Donatello (1386–1466) excelled in sculpture. His work expresses a new attitude to the human body. The figure of St George, made for the church of Orsanmichele and now in the Museo del Bargello, is not only a realistic depiction of the human form, but also a work of psychological insight. His *Gattamelata* (1445–50) in

LEFT: Michelangelo's *David*, in the Accademia in Florence. **RIGHT:** the anguish of Adam and Eve, from Masaccio's *Expulsion from Paradise*.

Padua was the first equestrian statue cast in bronze since Roman times, and his bronze *David* (1430–32), in the Bargello, was the first free-standing nude statue since antiquity.

The groundwork for the revolution in painting was laid a century earlier by Giotto (1267–1337). His frescoes – in Florence's Santa Croce,

in Padua's Cappella degli Scrovegni, and Assisi's Basilica di San Francesco – depart from the flat Byzantine style and invest the human form with solidity and volume, and the setting with a sense of space and depth. His breakthrough was carried further by the Early Renaissance's most noted painter, Masaccio (1401–28). His Florentine frescoes of *The Holy Trinity with Virgin and St John* in Santa Maria Novella (1425), and *The Life of St Peter* in the Brancacci Chapel of Santa Maria del Carmine (1427), display all the traits characteristic of the Renaissance: the importance of the human form, distinct under its clothing; human emotion; and the use of perspective.

Domenico Veneziano moved to Florence in 1439 and introduced pastel greens and pinks awash in cool light. The palette was picked up by his assistant, Piero della Francesca (1416–92), for his frescoes at San Francesco in Arezzo (1466). These are marvels of pale tone as well as mathematics – heads and limbs are variations of geometric shapes: spheres, cones and cylinders.

The artistic revolution in Florence soon spread to other parts of Italy. Leon Battista Alberti (1404–72), an author of noted treatises on sculpture, painting and architecture, introduced the tracing of classic motifs (columns, arches) on the exteriors of buildings, such as on

Michelangelo, Bramante, Raphael and Titian. Unlike their predecessors, who were thought of as craftsmen, they were considered to be creative geniuses capable of works of superhuman scale, grandeur and effort. Their extravaganzas were made possible by a new source of patronage – the papacy. Having returned to Rome from exile in Avignon, the popes turned the Eternal City into a centre of culture. The art of the High Renaissance is marked by a move beyond rules of mathematical ratios or anatomical geometrics to a new emphasis on emotional impact. The increasing use of oil paints, introduced to the Italians in the late 1400s, began to

the Palazzo Rucellai in Florence (1446–51) and the Malatesta Temple in Rimini (1450).

Giovanni Bellini (1430/1–1516) triumphed in Venice. In his *Madonna and Saints* in San Zaccaria (1505), the grandeur of Masaccio's influence is tempered by Flemish detail.

Detail most delicately expressed is the hallmark of Sandro Botticelli (1444/5–1510). The Uffizi Gallery houses the allegorical *Primavera* (1480) and the lovely *Birth of Venus* (1489).

The High Renaissance

The High Renaissance (1500–1600) was the heyday of some of the most celebrated artists in the entire history of art: Leonardo da Vinci,

replace egg tempera and opened new possibilities for richness of colour and delicacy of light.

Leonardo da Vinci (1452–1519) was born near Florence but left the city to work for the Duke of Milan, primarily as an engineer and only secondarily as a sculptor, architect and painter. In Milan, Leonardo painted the *Last Supper* (1495–98), in Santa Maria delle Grazie. The mural – an unsuccessful experiment in oil tempera, which accounts for its poor condition – is a masterpiece of psychological drama.

Leonardo also exploited new techniques in painting. *Chiaroscuro* (literally, light and dark) – the use of light to bring out and highlight three-dimensional bodies – is vividly seen in the whirl of bodies in the *Adoration of the Magi* (1481–82) in the Uffizi. Another invention was *sfumato*, a fine haze that lends a dreamy quality to paintings, enhancing their poetic potential.

In 1503, Pope Julius II, a great patron of the arts, commissioned the most prominent architect of the day, Donato Bramante (1444–1514), to design the new St Peter's. Bramante had earlier made his mark with the classically inspired gem, *The Tempietto* (1502), in the courtyard of Rome's San Pietro in Montorio. The pope's directive for

CLASSIC REVIVAL

Bramante revived concrete, used by the Ancient Romans and abandoned in favour of brick or cut stone during the Middle Ages.

figures with a dignity, volume and beauty inspired by Hellenistic precedents, yet given new emotional impact. It has been said that Michelangelo sought to liberate the form of the human body from a prison of marble: an allegory for the struggle of the soul, imprisoned in an earthly body, and a condition ripe for themes of triumph and tragedy. The tension imbues his best-known works: *David* (1501–04) in Florence's Accademia; *Moses* (1513–15) in Rome's San Pietro in Vincoli, and the beloved *Pietà* in St Peter's.

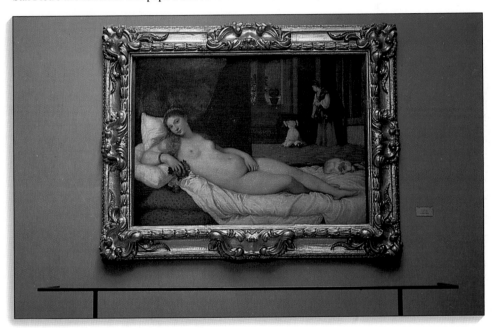

the new project was to create a monument which would surpass any of Ancient Rome. Working with a stock of classic forms (domes, colonnades, pediments) Bramante revolutionised architecture with his revival of another classic technique, concrete, which enables greater flexibility and monumental size.

Bramante died before his design was realised. In 1546, Michelangelo was put in charge of the project, and St Peter's gained its present form.

Michelangelo Buonarroti (1475–1564) first astounded the world with his sculpture: human

LEFT: Botticelli's *Primavera* in the Uffizi in Florence.
ABOVE: Titian's *Venus of Urbino*, also in the Uffizi.

Julius II commissioned Michelangelo to paint the Sistine Chapel ceiling. The result, which was completed in only four years (1508–12), is a triumph of human emotions unleashed by the human condition: man's creation, his fall, and his reconciliation with the Lord.

Michelangelo returned to the Sistine Chapel in 1534 to paint the spectacular *Last Judgement*. In the intervening years he went to Florence to complete the Medici Chapel of San Lorenzo (1524–34) and the Laurentian Library (begun 1524) where the drama of the design outweighs many functional considerations. Michelangelo's architectural genius culminates in his redesign of Rome's Campidoglio (1537–39). This open piazza, flanked by three facades, became the model for modern civic centres.

While Michelangelo was busy on the Sistine Chapel ceiling, a young artist from Urbino was working nearby, decorating a series of rooms in the Vatican Palace. This artist, soon to be known as the foremost painter of the High Renaissance, was Raffaello Sanzio, or Raphael (1483–1520). His masterpiece in this series is the *School of Athens* (1510–11). The dramatic grouping of philosophers around Plato and Aristotle suggests the influence of Michelangelo; the individualised intention of each recalls Leonardo's *Last Supper*.

In Venice, the paintings of Giorgione da Castelfranco (1476/8–1510) have all the charm and delicacy of Bellini's; they also favour poetic mood over subject matter (*The Tempest* [1505] in Venice's Galleria dell'Accademia is a perfect example), prefiguring the Romantic movement.

Also looking ahead to the freer brushwork and shimmering colours of the Impressionists is the Venetian Titian (1488/90–1576). He mastered the technique of oil painting, and left a legacy of richly coloured, joyously spirited religious pictures as well as masterful portraits. ❏

ABOVE: Parmigianino's *Madonna with the Long Neck* in the Uffizi. **RIGHT:** Caravaggio's *Bacchus*.

THE MANNERISTS

The drama of Leonardo, the theatricality of Michelangelo, the poetic moodiness of Giorgione: all set the stage for the Mannerist phase of High Renaissance art, when the serenity and calm classicism that characterised the works of Raphael were abandoned. In Mannerism the human form is paramount, yet it is usually depicted in strained, disturbing poses and violent colours.

Mannerist artists include Angelo Bronzino, Jacopo Pontorno and Rosso Fiorentino, who revelled in the use of bold colours, dramatic poses and heightened emotions. This unnatural look grew out of the work of artists such as Michelangelo, who had begun to exaggerate human features to create tension and drama – in the over-large head and hands of *David*, for example, or the contorted pose of the Virgin in his *Doni Tondo*, in the Uffizi Gallery.

Expression of an "inner vision" at the expense of reality was vital to Mannerism. In Fiorentino's *The Descent from the Cross* (1521) in Volterra's Pinacoteca, the angularly draped figures bathed in an unreal light stir feelings of anxiety and tension. His friend Pontormo (1494–1557) is also known for works of unexpected colour, unnaturally elongated figures and disquieting mood.

Bronzino (1503–72), Pontormo's pupil and adopted son, epitomises Mannerism's achievements in his psychological portraits of Cosimo I, his wife, Eleanor of Toledo, and her son, Giovanni de' Medici (1550), in the Uffizi Gallery.

Parmigianino (1503–40) used distortion merely for effect. In his *Madonna with the Long Neck* (1535), in the Uffizi, the figures are extremely elongated, the setting is fantastical, and the inspiration for the work – Raphael's fluid grace – is exaggerated beyond recognition.

In Venice, Tintoretto (1518–94) combined the bold style, rich colours and glowing light inspired by Titian with a mystical inclination. His attempt to depict religion's great mystery – the transubstantiation of bread into the body of Christ – results in the haunting *Last Supper* (1592–94) in San Giorgio Maggiore, Venice, with its swirling angels created out of vapours.

In architecture, Andrea Palladio (1518–80), like his predecessor Alberti, wrote theoretical studies of ancient architecture. His own designs – including the Villa Rotonda, Vicenza (1567–70) and San Giorgio Maggiore, Venice (1565) – are based on classical concepts, and have influenced architects from Inigo Jones to Thomas Jefferson, and even architects today.

BIRTH OF A NATION

After centuries of foreign domination and a prolonged struggle,
Italy emerged in 1870 as a united independent kingdom

The seeds of Italian patriotism, crushed by the battle of Fornovo in 1495, lay virtually dormant for three centuries. After Fornovo, all the armies of Europe came to Italy and fought among themselves for a share of the spoils. Spain, the most powerful nation in Europe at the time, eventually emerged as the clear master of Italy. The pope crowned King Charles 1 of Spain Holy Roman Emperor in 1530, and Charles and his descendants ruled Italy for more than 150 years. The country was burdened by heavy taxation, and under Spanish influence liberty and native energy and initiative declined. The papacy was no less oppressive; the rules of the Inquisition, the Index and the Jesuit Orders forced many Italians to flee.

Under the Spaniards and later (after the 1713 Treaty of Utrecht) under the equally oppressive Austrians, Italy lost its reputation as a cultural centre. But the 1789 French Revolution inspired many Italians, and the ideals of republicanism spread rapidly. Patriots dreamt of an independent Italian republic modelled on France.

When Napoleon invaded Italy in 1796, the people rose against the Austrians and a series of republics was founded. For three years the whole peninsula was republican and under French rule. But in March 1799, an Austro-Russian army expelled the French from northern Italy and restored many of the local princes. In Naples, the republicans held out for a few months before they, too, had to surrender.

To work against the foreign oppressors and their local sycophants, Italian patriots joined secret societies, such as the Carbonari. In their love of ritual they resembled the Freemasons, but they had a serious goal: to liberate Italy.

The Risorgimento

In 1800 Napoleon won back most of Italy. The kingdom that he founded lasted only briefly but, by proving that the country could be a single

LEFT: Giuseppe Garibaldi, a prominent leader of the Risorgimento. RIGHT: Camillo Benso, Count of Cavour, Italy's first great statesman.

unit, it gave Italian patriots new inspiration. From the Congress of Vienna in 1815, which reinstated Italian political divisions, until Rome was taken in 1870 by the troops of King Victor Emmanuel II of Savoy (who also ruled over Piedmont and Sardinia), the history of Italy was one continuous struggle for reunification.

CAVOUR,
(From a contemporary print in Bianchi's *Cavour*.)

The period is a complex one. Many northern and southern Italians wanted the peninsula to become one nation but there was no agreement as to who would rule or how it should be achieved. Some believed in peaceful evolution. Others, like Giuseppe Mazzini, wanted to revive the Roman republic. Some were for a kingdom of Italy under the House of Savoy.

In 1848, a year of revolt all over Europe, the first Italian war for independence was fought. First, rebellions in Sicily, Tuscany and the Papal States forced local rulers to grant constitutions to their citizens. In Milan, news of Parisian and Viennese uprisings sparked the famous "five days" when the occupying Austrian army was driven from the city. A few days later, Charles Albert of Savoy sent his army to pursue the Austrians, and the revolution began in earnest.

Charles Albert was soon supported by troops from other Italian states; however, the tide turned when the pope refused to declare war on Catholic Austria. The newly confident Austrians drove Charles Albert's army back into Piedmont. He abdicated months later, and the House of Savoy signed a peace treaty.

Garibaldi and Cavour

Venice and the Roman Republic continued the fight. In Rome, Mazzini led a triumvirate that

it was now the only Italian state with a free press, an elected parliament, and a liberal constitution. Piedmont-Savoy was also blessed, from 1852, with a brilliant prime minister, Count Camillo di Cavour, who was devoted to the cause of Italian unity. Cavour went to England and France to raise support for the Italian cause. He contributed Piedmontese troops to the Crimean War, and thus won a seat at the peace conference, where he brought the Italian question to the attention of Europe's most important statesmen. Although Cavour made no tangible gains at this meeting, he won moral support.

Europe was thus not surprised when France

governed the city with a true democratic spirit despite the siege conditions. The commander of the city's armed forces was Giuseppe Garibaldi, a life-long Italian patriot who had honed his fighting skills as a mercenary in the revolutions of South America, where he had fled after being convicted of subversion in Piedmont. Now he and his men faced the combined strength of the Neapolitans, the Austrians and the French. It was French forces that entered the city on 3 July 1849, the day after Garibaldi escaped into the mountains. The following month the Venetians succumbed to an Austrian siege.

The treaty the Austrians had signed with the House of Savoy kept them out of that region, so

and Piedmont went to war with Austria three years later. The French king, Napoleon III, and Cavour had agreed that, after the expected victory, an Italian kingdom would be formed for the Piedmontese king, Victor Emmanuel, and Nice and French Savoy would be returned to France. The people of the Italian dukedoms rushed to proclaim their allegiance to Victor Emmanuel.

Unfortunately, the French soon tired of fighting and decided to make a quick peace with Austria. The Austrians agreed to let Lombardy become part of an Italian Federation (with Austrian troops still in its garrisons), but the Veneto region went back to Austria and the dukes of Modena and Tuscany were reinstated.

In Italy, there was general outrage. Cavour resigned in protest, but first he arranged plebiscites in Tuscany and Modena. Citizens refused to have their dukes back and voted to become part of Piedmont.

Garibaldi and 1,000 red-shirted volunteers sailed for Sicily from Genoa on 5 May 1860. His arrival was a signal for the overthrow of Bourbon rule on the island. Garibaldi quickly declared himself dictator in the name of Victor Emmanuel. After fierce fighting, with the aid of Sicilian rebels Garibaldi entered Palermo

PATRIOT AND DEMOCRAT

Giuseppe Mazzini founded the Young Italy movement and agitated frenetically for unification from 1830–70.

divided over whether to take Rome by force or to negotiate a settlement with the Romans.

Finally, in 1870, after the French were weakened by a defeat in the Sudan, Italian troops fought their way into the city through Porta Pia. The pope barricaded himself in the Vatican. For half a century, no pope emerged to participate in the life of the new Italy.

The new government of all Italy was a parliamentary democracy with the king as executive. The most powerful men in the early days of the Italian state were the loyal

in triumph. Inspired by his success, men from all over Italy now came to help him and, on 7 September, Naples fell to the patriots.

Meanwhile, Victor Emmanuel gathered troops and marched south to link up with Garibaldi and his men. The two groups met at Teano, and the Kingdom of Italy was declared. The new kingdom did not include Rome, however: the pope preached against the patriots, and the French had garrisoned troops there to protect the city. The victorious nationalists were

LEFT: Garibaldi and Victor Emmanuel II of Savoy join forces at Teano.
ABOVE: celebration of Italian unity in Turin.

Piedmontese parliamentarians who were largely responsible for its creation and for designing the administration of the whole peninsula.

However, once the government moved down to Rome, this group began to splinter. The left came to power under a new prime minister, Agostino Depretis. In parliament, Depretis had shown great skill as a legislator and manipulator, but as prime minister he could not organise his party or set forth a coherent national policy. His rivals on the right had done no better, but their opposition made it hard for him to accomplish much. This was the start of the breakdown of the party system in Italy, the effects of which are discernible even today. ❑

THE MAKING OF MODERN ITALY

Wars, Fascism, corruption scandals ... with remarkable resilience,
Italy survived every challenge the 20th century presented to it

As governments so often do during times of rapid change and relative instability at home, Italy began to look abroad for confirmation of its hard-won independence. Relations with France had cooled during the final fight for unification; when France occupied Tunisia, a traditional area of Italian influence, they became positively chilly. Italy's response was to sign the Triple Alliance with Germany and Austro-Hungary, providing for mutual defence in the event of war.

Under the conservative governments of Francesco Crispi (1887–91, 1893–96), Italy also joined the scramble for colonies in North Africa. Crispi successfully colonised Eritrea, but when he tried to subdue Ethiopia (Abyssinia), the Italian army suffered a humiliating defeat at Adwa which led to Crispi's resignation. A later colonising attempt during the Italo-Turkish War (1911–12) ended in victory and the Italian occupation of Libya and the Dodecanese Islands.

North–South divide

At home, the years leading up to World War I were marked by the division that still plagues the country today: relative wealth in the north and extreme poverty in the south. The economy was overwhelmingly agricultural, and the government's protectionist policies left Italy increasingly isolated from other European markets. The industrial boom of the late 1800s, mostly in textiles and refining, was confined to the north. The crushing economic conditions in the south fuelled a wave of emigration. In the last years of the 19th century, nearly half a million people a year set out for the New World.

When World War I began with Austria's attack on Serbia in July 1914, Italy had not been consulted, in breach of the terms of the Triple Alliance. In consequence, on 2 August, Prime Minister Antonio Salandra declared Italy's neutrality. Public opinion began to swing in the direction of the Allies. To help win Italy over,

the Allied governments dangled the possibility of territorial gains: Rome was offered the chance to gain the "unrecovered" provinces of Trieste and Trentino, long held by the Austro-Hungarian Habsburg Empire. In addition, Italy would receive the Alto Adige, plus North African and Turkish enclaves. Finally swayed,

in April 1915 Italy signed the secret Treaty of London and, a month later, broke the Triple Alliance and entered the war on the Allied side.

Seldom had a country been so ill-prepared for war. Italy's army was poorly equipped, and Austrian troops had already dug into defensive positions in Alpine strongholds along the 480-km (300-mile) shared border. For Italy the war was a costly stalemate; of the 5.5 million men mobilised, 39 percent were killed or wounded.

At the post-war conference table, although Prime Minister Vittorio Emanuele Orlando sat with the victors, he was hardly regarded as an equal. Despite his protests, the Treaty of London was ignored. In the end the Treaty of St

LEFT: Benito Mussolini in 1928.
RIGHT: statue of Victor Emmanuel II in Venice.

Germain (10 September 1919) gave Italy Trentino and the Alto Adige (South Tyrol), as well as Trieste. But Fiume, Dalmatia and the other promised territories were negotiated away by the Allies.

Disappointment in the peace talks, combined with the social and economic toll of the war, produced chaotic domestic conditions. Soon there was talk that Italy had won only a "mutilated victory" despite its wartime sacrifice. Inflation soared. Factory workers took to the streets, and peasants clamoured for land reform.

Into this power vacuum marched Benito Mussolini and his Fascist Party. When he

founded the party in 1919, Mussolini played on the worst fears of all Italians. To those who fretted over the "mutilated victory", he was a chest-thumping nationalist. To placate the rich he denounced Bolshevism, although he himself had once been a socialist. To the middle classes he pledged a return to law and order, and a corporate state in which workers and management would pull together for the good of the country.

By mid-1922, Fascism had become a major political force. When workers called for a general strike, Mussolini made his move. On 28 October, 50,000 members of the Fascist militia converged on Rome. Although Mussolini's supporters held only a small minority in parliament,

the sight of thousands of menacing Fascists flooding the streets of the capital was enough to topple the tottering government of Prime Minister Luigi Facta. Refusing to sanction a state of siege, King Victor Emmanuel III instead handed the reins of government to Mussolini.

Once in control, Mussolini quickly pushed through an act assuring the Fascists a permanent majority in the parliament. After questionable elections in 1924, he dropped all pretence of collaborative government. Italy was now a dictatorship. At Christmas of that year, he declared himself head of the government, responsible only to the king. Fascist fronts took over all the rights once held by unions, and management organisations and national corporations were set up to supervise every phase of the economy.

Within two years all parties except the Fascists were banned, and opposition activists were jailed or forced into exile or underground. Anyone Mussolini could not subject by will or law was crushed by force.

Trains that ran on time

Despite its ugly underbelly, on the surface Fascism seemed to work. Weary of inflation, strikes and street disturbances, Italians eagerly embraced their severe new government and its charismatic *Duce*, or leader. This spontaneous response to Fascist rule was reinforced by a strong propaganda campaign. Mussolini promised to restore to Italy the glories of Ancient Rome, and for a time promises were enough.

Soon, however, the government could show results. The economy stabilised, trains ran on time, huge public works projects were launched, and Mussolini even made peace with the Vatican, hammering out the Lateran Treaty (1929), which ended the 50-year rift between Rome and the Catholic Church. He also set out on an imperial campaign, restoring control over Libya, which had been ignored during and after World War I. In October 1935, Italian troops crossed the border of Eritrea and headed for the Ethiopian capital of Addis Ababa. The League of Nations protested, but took no action. Six months later, *Il Duce* announced to an hysterical Piazza Venezia crowd that, finally, Rome had begun to reclaim its empire.

The international outcry over the Ethiopian occupation left Rome isolated. The one government willing to overlook Mussolini's expansionism was in Berlin, where Adolf Hitler's

Nazis had held power since January 1933. Both Germany and Italy had supported General Francesco Franco's nationalist troops in the Spanish Civil War (1936–39), and this cooperation led eventually to the signing of the Pact of Steel between Berlin and Rome in May 1939.

Three months later, Hitler invaded Poland. Within days, Britain and France declared war on Germany. At first the Rome government remained neutral, as it had in 1914, arguing that Berlin's surprise attack on

BLACKSHIRTS

This name was originally given to supporters of Mussolini's Fascist Party, who wore distinctive black shirts in the 1920s; it was later linked with the Nazi SS and with Oswald Mosley's British Union of Fascists.

Eager to pull off his own battlefield coup, in the autumn of 1940 Mussolini set his sights on taking Greece. But the Greeks fought back fiercely. The Italians suffered many casualties, and only Nazi intervention prevented a likely Italian defeat. The war was also going badly for the Axis Powers in North Africa, and eventually even the Nazi General Rommel could not prevent the collapse. Heartened by their desert victories, in 1943 US and British troops captured Sicily.

Poland did not require an automatic military response. In any case, most Italians opposed intervention, and the army was ill-prepared for war. But as Hitler claimed victory after victory – in Denmark, Norway and Belgium, and with France on the verge of collapse – the lure of sharing the spoils of war proved irresistible. On 10 June 1940, Italy entered the war, just before the fall of France. But from the start it was obvious to Mussolini that he was Hitler's inferior in their alliance.

Left: the Palazzo della Civiltà del Lavoro in Rome's EUR district, a prime example of Fascist architecture.
Above: Axis allies – Mussolini and Hitler.

The beginning of the end was in sight. From their base in Sicily, the Allied forces began to bomb the Italian mainland, and Italian public morale sank to a new low. On 25 July 1943, the Grand Council of Fascism voted to strip Il Duce of his powers. Mussolini refused to step down, but the next day, King Victor Emmanuel ordered his arrest. Mussolini was detained in an inaccessible hotel in the Abruzzo mountains. However, in September German air commandos airlifted him to Munich.

Chaos broke out in the final days of the war. To placate the Germans, who would otherwise have occupied the entire country, Prime Minister Marshal Badoglio publicly declared that Italy would fight on. In secret, however, he entered negotiations with the Allies, who by then had fought their way as far north as Naples. Above that line was the hastily organised *Repubblica Sociale Italiana,* headed by the liberated Duce. Better known as the Republic of Salo, based on Lake Garda, this was a puppet regime of Berlin, and Mussolini spent most of his time brooding on the judgement history would pass on him.

As the Allies fought northwards, the Italian Resistance felt safe enough to begin widespread activities. Combined, the forces managed to liberate Rome on 4 June 1944; Florence followed on 12 August. The Germans and Mussolini lasted out the winter behind the so-called "Gothic line" in the Apennines, but by spring 1945 that effort too had collapsed. Mussolini tried to escape into Switzerland disguised as a German soldier, but Italian partisans found him, and the next morning he was shot. His body was hauled into Milan and hung by a rope for the public to see.

Recovery and resiliency

In the immediate postwar period, Italy suffered greatly. At the peace conferences there was no representative from Rome. The Italian colonies, won at such cost, were taken away. Reparations had to be paid to the Soviet Union and Ethiopia.

A MARXIST PARTY WITHOUT MARX

A distinctive feature of Italian politics has been the influence of the Italian Communist Party (PCI). In the postwar years, the party cleaved to the Soviet Union's political line, and Rome's centrist government kept the communists at arm's length.

Under Enrico Berlinguer, PCI secretary 1972–84, the party's orientation changed. It often led the so-called Eurocommunism movement, in favour of more independence from Moscow; it scolded the Soviets for human rights abuses and the Russian invasion of Afghanistan; and on economic issues the PCI grew ever more centrist, prompting some to dub it a "Marxist party without Marx". By 1981 the PCI could count on about a third of the popular vote and it was second only to the Christian Democrats (DC) in size.

Catholicism and communism were the two dominant political cultures of postwar years, with the communist heartland in central Italy. The collapse of communism in Eastern Europe led to the PCI splitting into the mainstream Democratic Party of the Left (DS) and a hardline splinter group. After the upheavals of the 1990s, the DC were dissolved and the DS came to power as part of a left-wing coalition. But now the political scene is awash with new parties, even if many old faces remain.

The political system needed a complete overhaul. In elections in June 1946, voters decided 54 to 46 percent in favour of making the country a republic, thus formally ending the days of the monarchy. The economy was in disarray, but US aid in the form of the Marshall Plan helped to ease the burden from 1948.

After a brief alliance of socialists and communists, the Christian Democrat leader, Alcide de Gasperi, gained control of government, dropping his leftist partners, and for over a decade centrist coalitions ran the country. In the early 1960s, the Christian Democrats, Socialists, Social Democrats and Republicans formed a coalition and ruled, in various combinations, until 1968.

Fuelled by cheap labour, the economy developed rapidly after World War II. During the 1950s there was a steady migration from rural areas to the cities and from south to north. Heavy industry such as chemicals, iron, steel and cars took off. In 1957, Italy became a founding member of the European Community. By the mid-1960s, manufacturing overtook agriculture as the main source of GNP, and observers hailed Italy's "economic miracle".

Terrorism and scandals

A few years later, however, the boom had gone bust, Italy was dubbed the "sick man of Europe", and social ills set in. By far the worst was terrorism. From the late 1970s, kidnappings, knee cappings and murders were a fact of life. The murder, in 1978, of former Christian Democratic prime minister Aldo Moro by the left-wing Brigate Rosse (Red Brigade) spurred new anti-terrorist measures, and eventually 32 Red Brigade members were imprisoned for the deaths of Moro and 16 others. Neo-fascist terrorism also plagued the country, culminating, in 1980, in a bomb blast at Bologna station which killed 84 people. Crime of another sort gripped the nation in May 1981, when Pope John Paul II was shot by Turkish-born Mehmet Ali Agca, but he was not fatally wounded.

Dogged effort helped to cut inflation, and in 1985 Bettino Craxi's government imposed tighter tax-collection laws. Although inflation remained fairly high, and the lira was unsteady,

the economy grew, and Italy briefly overtook France and Britain in the economic league.

Troubles were in store, however. In the 1990s a wave of corruption scandals rocked the state. In 1992, it was alleged that some £67 million (US$100 million) had been shared out among the leaders of the five parties governing Italy in coalition in 1990. Two former premiers were convicted of being chief recipients while veteran prime minister Giulio Andreotti was charged with having links with the Mafia (see page 71), as were other leading figures outside politics, from fashion designers to industrialists. The short-lived first premiership of media

magnate Silvio Berlusconi, in 1994, also stumbled over accusations of corruption.

These scandals unleashed a volley of reforms spearheaded by the first left-wing government in Italy's postwar history. In order to create stronger, more durable governments, the system of proportional representation was changed to a largely first-past-the-post system. Measures were taken to prune the public sector, reform the welfare state, tackle organised crime and meet the requirements of European Monetary Union.

Into the new millennium

In a landslide victory in 2001, Silvio Berlusconi's centre-right government came to power

LEFT: the 6th-century abbey of Montecassino, destroyed by Allied bombs in 1944, but subsequently rebuilt.
RIGHT: 10.25am, the day in 1980 when a terrorist bomb ripped through Bologna train station.

on a tide of populism and nationalism, with a pledge to reform and liberalise the economy. But the country has since sunk into recession and floundered in protectionist measures. Perceived as a free-marketeer, the media mogul was elected to slash red tape, reform labour laws and the tax system. To his fans, he is the embodiment of the self-made man: as owner of an economic empire he is Italy's richest man, estimated to be worth over 15 billion dollars. Grudging admirers see their leader as the nasty medicine to the even nastier complaint. Detractors believe that the premier has failed to resolve the conflict of interest between his public and business roles,

and, as a convicted fraudster, has ties to the tainted insiders of Italian politics and the kickback culture. John Carlin, a commentator on the Italian scene, compares the Milanese mogul with the most megalomaniac of ancient Roman rulers. "The Roman emperors knew that the secret to exercising peaceful rule over the people was to provide them with bread and circus. Well, Berlusconi owns the circus, pretty much all of it – the TV, the football, the magazines, the books. And as a head of government, who also happens to own Italy's biggest supermarket chain, he also controls, in the widest sense of the word, the bread".

CULTURAL BEACONS

Culturally, there is much to celebrate in Italy. Milan now has two state-of-the-art opera houses since the long-awaited reopening of La Scala. At the other end of the country, Palermo's restored opera house, the Teatro Massimo, has become the symbol of the city's cultural resurgence. Even Rome, traditionally ill-served by its concert halls and theatres, has opened its stunning Music Park, giving the capital a cluster of world-class auditoria. The art world has also seen a slew of pristine galleries and successful renovation projects. Thanks to a bequest by the city's patron, the late Gianni Agnelli, Turin now has a magnificent modern art gallery, while

Florence is expanding the Uffizi Gallery. Genoa enjoyed an artistic renaissance as a European Capital of Culture in 2004 and Turin and Piedmont staged a highly successful 2006 Winter Olympics.

More controversially, Berlusconi, wishing to leave his mark, launched several grand projects during his premiership. In Venice, the long-awaited Moses dam, designed to save the city from flooding, has been given the go-ahead. Further south, there is an equally controversial scheme to connect Sicily with the mainland by means of the world's longest suspension bridge, due to be built between 2006–12.

An uncertain future

Italy, traditionally characterised as unstable, is facing an even more unstable future than usual. In 2006, the election of a left-wing coalition under Romano Prodi spelt the end of a turbulent Berlusconi administration in which Italy under-performed in all departments. However, the left's tiny majority gives the administration a weak mandate at a time when the economy is in the doldrums and desperately in need of reform. Romano Prodi, the former EU President, heads a coalition of parties with very different agendas, including Catholics, former Communists and the Greens, so an ideological rollercoaster ride can-

biggest economy in Europe, but industrial output has fallen, and unemployment has risen sharply, especially in the south. Once a vibrant and cre-ative economy, Italy appears yet again to be the "sick man of Europe": uncompetitive, over-reg-ulated, over-reliant on small family businesses, and lacking in investment. The country's experi-ence of the euro has been unpromising, with the currency blamed for price rises, and seen as the cause of the Italian malaise rather than as a symp-tom. Italy is highly exposed to the challenges of globalisation as a disproportionate share of its manufacturing is concentrated in clothing, footwear and white goods where it cannot com-

not be ruled out. Any promised belt-tightening measures will be unwelcome with the far left. Curbing government spending and raising new taxes are hardly popularity-enhancing moves, particularly as the economic forecast is growth at just over 1 percent.

In the meantime, the country faces a spiralling budget deficit and towering national debt, the third highest in the world. Italy remains the fourth

pete with the Asian Tiger economies. In particu-lar, the northern textile firms have been left reeling by the influx of cheap Chinese imports.

The plan is to reach across the divide, and also to inject greater flexibility into the job market without provoking massive protests, as happened in France. It is hoped to liberalise the economy to weaken the straitjacket of guild-like rules that have their origins in the Middle-Ages. Moreover, in a reversal of the previous administration's pol-icy, Prodi is seeking to strengthen relations with the European Union and to weaken links with the United States. In short, Italy finds itself in unchar-tered waters once more – but without a Marco Polo or Christopher Columbus in sight.

LEFT: Italian premier Silvio Berlusconi, Italy's richest man. **ABOVE:** in 2003, after years in exile, the royal family were allowed to return to Italy; the male heirs of the House of Savoy had been banned from entering Italy since 1946.

THE MAFIA

With its tradition of private justice and its code of silence, or omertà, *the Mafia remains Italy's biggest blight*

In Italy, Mafia ghosts often come back to haunt the living. Roberto Calvi, the Italian financier, was found hanging underneath London's Blackfriars Bridge in 1982 but the court case to determine the cause only opened in Rome in 2005. Calvi, known as "God's banker" because of his close ties to the Vatican, was found with his suit stashed with bank notes but weighted down by rocks. Giuseppe "Pippo" Calo, one of the five defendants on trial, is charged with ordering Calvi's killing as punishment for Calvi failing to repay laundered Mafia money. Calo, nicknamed the Mafia's "cashier", was convicted in the 1980s of unrelated Mafia charges.

Calvi created Banco Ambrosiano and turned it into Italy's biggest private bank, but it was on the verge of collapse when he died, and remains Italy's biggest postwar banking scandal. After Calvi's death, the Vatican's bank, which had a stake in Banco Ambrosiano, proffered more than £150m (US$270 million) to creditors, but denied any wrongdoing. Still, whether Mafia murder or suicide, Calvi's death continues to have repercussions in the murky shadows beyond the designer gloss of contemporary Italy.

To many, the notion of the Mafia conjures up images of the *lupara*, or sawn-off shotgun used by the Sicilian underworld; corpses dripping with blood; and onlookers standing by, helpless and resigned. The Mafia may still colour Sicilian life, but local attitudes are changing profoundly, especially among the young. Not that the Mafia is a unified entity confined to Sicily: the all-embracing term may be the "Mafia" but in Sicily it is known as the "Cosa Nostra"; in Naples it mutates into the "Camorra"; and in Calabria becomes the "Ndrangheta".

The revulsion of Sicilians to the 1992 murders of Mafia-fighting judges Giovanni Falcone and Paolo Borsellino helped to weaken the Mafia's grip on public opinion, its greatest weapon, and dented the age-old code of silence, or *omertà*.

Pentiti ("the penitents"), as Mafia turncoats are called, grew from a handful in 1992, when Falcone was killed, to 500 a year later. As a result dozens of dons, including the "boss of all Mafia bosses", Salvatore "Toto" Riina, the Godfather of Corleone, and his deputies, Giovanni Brusca and Leoluca Bagarella, have been jailed.

Women's work

The Mafia, once obsessed with tradition, is changing. In 1995 the Mafia fell into debt, as

income fell (fewer public works and confiscation of Mafia property) and costs rose (mainly legal fees). As the old Mafia guard languishes in jail, their women, once tied to the home, have stepped into the breach, and, unlike their husbands, few have turned informer or state's evidence. In May 2002 women entered the Mafia wars when three were killed in a campaign for control of a valley an hour's drive from Naples. Now that women have entered the wars, the last Mafia taboo has been broken.

To fill the power vacuum, a "criminal mastermind" is thought to be reforming the Mafia, with the help of Cosa Nostra in the US, into a quieter, more secretive and sophisticated entity, based on "old Mafia values". The new generation of gangster is as ruthless on the stock exchange as on the streets of Palermo, and likely to be adept at surfing the Internet – the favoured new medium for laundering money.

Adroitly, the Mafia is also believed to have learned how to exploit the phenomenon of *pentitismo,* infiltrating bogus turncoats, and weaving false evidence, including that of Mafia involvement of institutional figures, together with genuine evidence. The aim is to stall cases, discredit *pentitismo,* and sow uncertainty.

Along with drugs, extortion and property speculation, Mafia activities now include trading arms, nuclear and conventional, between Eastern European and Middle Eastern states. Investment features as much in Moscow as it does in Palermo.

The good old days

Some say the word Mafia first appeared in the 1600s, meaning a witch; others say it derives from Sicilian dialect or the Arabic for "protection", "misery" or "hired assassin". What is certain is that the Mafia as we know it began to take shape in the early 19th century, in the guise of brotherhoods formed to protect Sicilians from corruption, foreign oppression and feudalism. Criminal interests quickly seeped in, corruption became the preferred milieu, and before long the brotherhoods were feeding on the misery from which they pretended to defend their members.

Judges were soon said to be secretly protecting them; nobles to be backing them. The brotherhoods' principal manifestation was as the *gabelotti,* organised minders of the land holdings of an often absent nobility, who distributed jobs and land and policed the countryside.

When Garibaldi set off from Sicily with his red-shirts, he did so thanks to the brotherhoods, which lent the support of some 20,000 men. Turned back by the troops of Turin, they reorganised to oppose the redistribution to private landlords of 200,000 hectares (nearly half a million acres) of Church land in Sicily.

As early as 1838, Mafia brotherhoods infiltrated every walk of Sicilian public life. By 1875 the Mafia had even infiltrated the Bourbon household in Palermo.

Central to the so-called "Southern Question"

was severe economic misery. Between 1872 and World War I, poverty and the defeat of agrarian trade unions forced 1.5 million Sicilians to emigrate. Most went to the Americas. There, many joined brotherhoods based on those back home and the foundations of Cosa Nostra were laid. Elements willing to cash in on illegal activity found a springboard with prohibition. US bootlegging marked the Mafia's graduation from rural bands to a sophisticated urban gangsterism.

In 1925, Mussolini, appalled at the Mafia's new importance as a surrogate state, set out to bring it to its knees. He sent his prefect Cesare Mori to Sicily, with almost unlimited powers.

By 1927, victory was proclaimed for Mori's heavy-handed tactics. Called the "surgical precision of Fascism", they entailed throwing thousands into prison, and laying siege to towns to flush out the Mafia bosses. But Mori was also a threat to powerful agrarian *mafiosi.* Soon Sicily's landed interests struck a deal with the Fascists, and Mori left the island. In return, the agrarian *mafiosi* saw to it that Sicily's more criminal Mafia elements were almost wiped out.

They won a reprieve in 1943, when they were given the job of clearing the way for the Allied invasion. Fearing the effects that war between the US and Italy would have on their interests, Italian and American mobsters such as Lucky Luciano had struck a deal with US authorities in 1940. In return for their help they were to be left alone. Local *mafiosi*, re-armed with weapons taken from Italian forces, and their dons – such as Don Calogero Vizzini (39 murders, six attempted murders) – were installed by the Allies as mayors of key Sicilian towns.

Changing fortunes brought Sicilian and US Mafia elements to cities such as Milan and Naples; Naples, ruled by the less organised local Mafia, the Camorra, became a fiefdom of Cosa Nostra, and was chosen by US gangsters as the site of Italy's first heroin refinery. Sicily's "Americanised" Mafia achieved its quantum leap in the late 1950s with the introduction of drugs. In 1957,

after a crackdown in the US against organised crime, American bosses entrusted their Sicilian counterparts with the importation of heroin, linked to Lucky Luciano, Frank "Three Fingers" Coppola, and his protégé Luciano Liggio, who won his stripes black marketeering during the war.

Clan warfare

Liggio, who died in the mid-1990s, elevated his Corleonese family to the pinnacle of the Cosa Nostra. After he was jailed in 1974 he was eclipsed as head of the Mafia by his lieutenant "Wild Beast" Toto Riina. The tactics of the Corleonesi were simple: the removal of any *mafioso* who coveted power or caused trouble. The Mafia

clan war of the early 1980s left Palermo's streets strewn with blood, the Corleonesi undisputed victors, and Riina linked to some 1,000 murders. Yet not all murders concerned *mafiosi*. In response to the drugs trade which prompted the carnage, a parliamentary anti-Mafia committee had been established. In turn, the Mafia instituted a campaign of terror targeting top officials, the police and politicians. The list of corpses began with Palermo's chief prosecutor Pietro Scaglione in 1971, allegedly murdered by Liggio, Riina and Provenzano. In answer to the 1982 killing, with his wife, of General Carlo Alberto dalla Chiesa, the *carabiniere* who had vanquished terrorism before being sent to Palermo as chief prefect, the government pushed through a law to get at Mafia assets – a law proposed by Pio La Torre, Sicilian regional Communist Party leader, gunned down 100 days before dalla Chiesa.

Dalla Chiesa had begun digging into the island's huge construction industry and is thought to have stumbled on a minefield: the "Third Level" question of who in the country's highest political circles protected, or possibly also issued orders to, the Mafia. The Mafia's chief supergrass, Tommaso Buscetta, claimed that Giulio Andreotti ordered the mob to kill dalla Chiesa and a journalist, because they knew too much. Buscetta's evidence led to "maxi-trials" in the 1980s, where hundreds of *mafiosi* sat in the dock, and launched magistrate Giovanni Falcone's fight against the Mafia.

Failure to use his weight to overturn a guilty verdict concerning the same "maxi-trial" in a supreme court decision in 1992 is believed to have been the reason for Salvo Lima's killing by the Mafia. Lima, a former Palermo mayor and a Euro MP when he died, was the most powerful Christian Democrat in Sicily and the island's representative of the party faction then headed by the wily Andreotti. Lima's murder was the first in a new campaign of terror that saw the assassination of Falcone and his wife in May, victims of a car bomb. Falcone's colleague Paolo Borsellino and five bodyguards were murdered two months later. The terror continued in 1993 with bombs in Milan and Rome which killed bystanders and devastated churches; an explosion at Florence's Uffizi Gallery destroyed minor masterpieces. The assassination of the two Palermo judges and the attempt to destroy the nation's cultural treasures only served to tighten the resolve of Italians and their government against the Mafia.

Recent events seem to bear out public concern over political probity and presumed criminal links. In 2004, Marcello Dell'Utri, one of Berlusconi's close business associates, was sentenced to nine years for complicity with Sicily's Cosa Nostra. For Berlusconi's opponents, that fact alone might explain why his government failed to make much headway in fighting organised crime.

In 2006, the fugitive Mafia Godfather, Bernardo Provenzano, was finally captured after 43 years on the run. "The Phantom of Corleone," also nicknamed "The Tractor" due to his propensity for mowing people down, was caught when a package sent to him by his wife was intercepted. The news caused nationwide celebrations, even if cynics suspected the Sicilian mobster had long been protected in his Corleone power-base. After the arrest of Godfather Toto Riina in 1993, Provenzano led the Mafia underground, consolidating their international financial crime syndicate and abandoning overt violence. However, spectacular plots to murder three major prosecutors emerged in 2005 and were linked to Provenzano, who slipped through the net again, despite the arrest of 46 of the mobster's henchmen. The capture of the Sicilian *capo* may well spark a violent power struggle, with two "super fugitives" in pole position.

Unlike the more centrally controlled Sicilian Mafia, the Neapolitan Camorra, with its 20 rival clans, has always been volatile. Since 2004, well over a hundred people have died in turf wars between gangs eager to control the drugs market. With control of an £11 billion (US$20 billion) a year drugs trade at stake, Naples' poverty-stricken northern suburbs have become a battleground, with protection rackets endemic. Drug-dealers have been executed, while homes and businesses have been torched, leaving children to play truant because their parents are on the run. Since the troubles began, extra police have been drafted in, and made over 1,000 arrests. In 2006, the boss of a Naples' Spanish Quarter crime family was arrested, along with 11 members of his clan, accused of being involved in the drugs trade. Amato Lamberti, a Camorra expert at Naples University, sees no easy solution: "The real problem is the Camorra's roots in Neapolitan society. People hope that with time,

economic development will eliminate the Camorra, but it doesn't work that way."

Many believe that the threat presented by the Sicilian Mafia's rougher cousin, the Calabrian 'Ndrangheta, is just as great. In 2004 it was discovered, during Italy's biggest anti-Mafia operation for a decade, that the drug-running 'Ndrangheta had built a complete underground village below Plati. A year later, the vice-president of Calabria's regional council was brutally gunned down by gangsters.

As for society's relationship with the Mafia, despite a shift in attitudes, criminal practices remain entrenched, from illegal building over

beauty spots to protection rackets. As the Mafia's activities face pressure from aggressive prosecutors and EU regulations, the question that remains is whether the Mafia is being marginalised, or if it only seems so as it slips deeper into the fabric of southern culture. Corleone, the Mafia heartland, considered changing its name to make a fresh start, even opening a "Mafia Museum" and centre dedicated to the study of organised crime. Ironically, it was in a Corleone farmhouse that the Godfather was caught in 2006. *Plus ça change...* Cynical Sicilians also attribute this lethargy to *gattopardismo*, the blight of the south, in which everything appears to change but remains exactly the same. ❑

LEFT: a threatening gesture is made during one of the "maxi-trials". **RIGHT:** former prime minister Giulio Andreotti, allegedly connected to the Mafia.

CONTEMPORARY ITALY

Tradition and rebellion, conformity and individuality, chaos and over-regulation ... Italian life is riddled with paradoxes

According to Sergio Romano, a political journalist on *La Stampa*, "Italy is a constellation of large families, whether ideological, political, professional or criminal – the Church, the business community, the trade unions, the professions, state bureaucracies and the Mafia." He observes that "each family strives for sovereignty", acting as a fierce lobby group and dooming most national reforms to failure.

Curiously, Italian society combines anarchy and cosiness in equal measure, making it both chaotic and stultifying. At the simplest level, Italians create a cosy little world of "their" baker, dressmaker and picture-framer, conveying the social status of a patron rather than of a mere consumer. Personal recommendation is everything. Yet beyond lies the arbitrary world of bureaucracy, in which citizens feel powerless in the face of state indifference. Many commentators conclude that Italy would be a paradise if it could only reinvent the relationship between citizen and state. Yet without political chaos and conflicting social groups, the Italians would cease to be Italians and become Swiss.

The political picture

"It is not impossible to govern Italians, it is pointless." Mussolini's judgement has been borne out by more recent events. In the late 1990s, the country faced secessionist threats, a budgetary crisis, a wave of organised crime and a tide of refugees. Nonetheless, after the corruption scandals of the early 1990s, probity was the basic requirement of the new left-leaning administration. Yet by the new millennium, public opinion had swung back to the right, giving the controversial media magnate Silvio Berlusconi a landslide victory. To make Italy more governable, there have been moves to reduce the power of the fringe parties that frequently hold the country to ransom. Yet the Italian mindset precludes a modern democracy, often seeming to favour an abyss between the state and its citizens. The people

swing between political disaffection and an obsession with politics. Fortunately, however, they also have an innate talent for brinkmanship, coupled with an ability to conjure compromise out of conflict. In 1996 the secessionist Lega Nord (Northern League) marched to the symbolic River Po and in Venice declared indepen-

dence for "the Republic of Padania". In a gesture of rejection of Rome and centralised bureaucracy, protesters waved republican flags and tossed their state television licences into the waters. In response, the Italian president called the country "one and indivisible", while addressing reforms that would allow for greater regional autonomy.

The country has since positioned itself as the new Italy, turning its back on a baroque political structure steeped in *clientelismo* (nepotism). Yet Italy remains deeply old-fashioned, despite its faddism. Italians pride themselves on their free spirit, yet society remains over-regulated while protectionism has preserved many monopolies, including limiting the growth of supermarkets.

LEFT: keeping up with the news. **RIGHT:** anti-global protestors at the G8 summit in Genoa, 2001.

IN GOOD FAITH?

Curiously, the phrase often used to bemoan declining standards is: "There's no religion left any more". Jonathan Keates describes the Italian attitude to religion as "a lackadaisical Catholicism taken out of mothballs at christenings, first communions, weddings and funerals; the religion of photo-opportunity." Increasingly, Italy's practising Catholics prefer to take their cue not from the Pope but from personal conscience or the liberal wing of the Church. Strive as the Church might, civic culture, regional pride and fierce individualism form the real Italian faith today.

Milan is the business capital, a sophisticated modern metropolis dedicated to money-making and pleasure. Most wealth is still created in northern and central regions, such as Lombardy, the Veneto and Emilia-Romagna. However, although the Ferragamo, Berlusconi and Armani fiefdoms are well known abroad, most Italian companies are family-run businesses. Specialised small companies provide more than two-thirds of industrial employment, from textiles in Tuscany to designer sunglasses in the Veneto, and mechanical engineering firms in Emilia. Nonetheless, economic patterns are complex, and high unemployment and low consumer demand mask a thriving black economy and tax evasion.

In the workplace, industrial action is commonplace. The Italian art of conjuring compromise out of conflict in industrial relations is rooted in the social contract, a corporatist pact between government, unions and industry that has historically dominated labour relations, and is only now being gradually eroded.

The impact of the euro, privatisation, and the country's increasing uncompetitiveness are today's major economic issues. Privatisation of the public utilities did not end state interference. Given the traditional monopoly of top jobs in state companies by the political parties, politicians remain reluctant to give up their power. By the same token, the family dynasties who dominate the economy continue to hold sway. With his patrician charm and playboy reputation, the late Gianni Agnelli epitomised the closed, dynastic style of Italian capitalism. After his death in 2003, the Turin football stadium was renamed in his honour, and the family empire survives, even if the fate of Fiat seems to be inextricably linked with General Motors. Despite a rash of mergers, much of the power remains in the same hands: in 2001, the telecommunications industry witnessed the takeover of Olivetti and Telecom Italia by Pirelli and Benetton, the latter responsible for the clothing empire, a Formula One team, all the Italian motorways and service stations.

Under the world's gaze, the country is giving birth to two controversial "grand projects": a bridge over the Straits of Messina, linking Sicily with the mainland, and "Moses", mobile anti-flood barriers guarding Venice's lagoon from the Adriatic. The recession enveloping the country did not prevent the government approving the second stage of Venice's great dam in 2005.

A complex but coherent society

The Italian social system is a rich landscape, not calibrated on class, success or wealth but on more subtle distinctions. In conventional terms, a class system exists but has different connotations. The aristocracy thrives, thanks to its adaptability. Many *marchesi* (marquesses) are entrepreneurs, carving niches in fashion, art, and the wine and food industry. The Strozzi are big in banking, the Tuscan Frescobaldi and Sicilian Tasca are successful wine dynasties, the Pucci and

LEFT: a cheese seller in Marsala.
RIGHT: leather craftsman in his workshop in Rome: skilled artisans are still very much a feature of city life.

Ferragamo fashion empires thrive in Florence.

Although class consciousness and accent are essentially immaterial, the *borghesi* (middle classes) form a recognisable group, as do the *contadini* (encompassing peasants and farmers). Whatever one's profession, honorific titles are important, especially in the south: an engineer is addressed as "*ingegnere*"; *dottore* (doctor) is a mark of respect bestowed on anyone with the right gravitas. Politics rarely impinge on social divisions: a member of the DS, the former Communist Party, may be a Catholic, wear an Armani suit, don a Prada bag, Ferragamo shoes, and have a Filipina maid.

Apart from the north–south divide, the most important distinction is between *statali*, who are government employees or civil servants, and *non-statali*, the rest. Civil servants are seen as utterly cosseted; virtually impossible to fire, they enjoy such privileges as protected pensions. Ranged against the civil servants are the *dipendenti* (company employees), *autonomi* (self-employed), *imprenditori* (entrepreneurs) and, lastly, the *liberi professionisti* (professionals). The company employees claim the moral high ground, charging civil servants with exploiting the system and accusing the self-employed and some professionals of tax evasion.

GUARDIANS OF SO MANY TREASURES

Italians are justifiably proud of their heritage. Italy possesses more UNESCO cultural heritage sites than any other country, matched by an impressive half of the world's artistic wealth.

Clearly, the burden of conservation is great for the authorities. Art fraud is commonplace, a situation compounded by illegal excavations, thefts from churches and the export of priceless artefacts, with penalties ridiculously light. In the 1990s, the state faced a terrorist attack on Florence's Uffizi Gallery, mysterious and devastating fires at Venice's La Fenice opera house and Turin Cathedral, and earthquake damage to San

Francesco in Assisi. Monuments can be closed for years and masterpieces hidden from view. But the proceeds from the state lottery each Wednesday are devoted to cultural investment.

Most collections are publicly owned, and the state offers little support to the private owner. Princess Corsini, who has the last 17th-century Florentine collection remaining in private hands, says such owners are treated as "over-privileged people who have to be kept in line like schoolchildren". As for the sale of art treasures, owners are secretive because selling abroad usually entails breaking Italian regulations.

In truth, this is a strange Italian stalemate in which private sector workers *(non-statali)* justify tax evasion on the grounds that their taxes would only perpetuate the bloated state bureaucracy and southern incompetence.

Popular culture and the arts

Both in the art world and in the broader cultural arena, Italian genius thrives on dissension, diversity and unbridled rivalry. However, music and the performing arts are, arguably, more dynamic than the literary scene: Italy has always been a musical, visual and verbal culture, rather than a literary one. Contemporary fiction is an acquired

taste, with writers often engaged in navel-gazing, esoteric concerns or petty politicking. The classical music scene is not restricted to the great opera houses: Italy boasts some of the best musical festivals in Europe, from the operatic cycles performed in the Roman Arena at Verona to the Puccini Festival at his lakeside home in Tuscany's Torre del Lago. The Macerata opera festival hit the headlines in 1995 when the firing squad in *Tosca* used real bullets and accidentally shot the tenor. But the director of the Rossini Festival at Pesaro, the great composer's birthplace, bemoans Italian conservatism: "The public has no desire for opera to become theatre but only wants it to be about singing and tradition."

Recently, the culture industry has been close to revolt over state plans to slash arts funding, with dire consequences for the country's foremost cultural institutions, from Milan's La Scala opera house to the Venice Film Festival. "In Italy, culture is being undervalued. We have so many great talents that should be nourished, but this won't happen because we won't have the funds", declared the Oscar-winning film-maker Roberto Benigni, responsible for the Holocaust drama, *Life is Beautiful*. The government's response was to stress the need for Italians to take more individual responsibility for their heritage. A shock advertising campaign showed images of mutilated artistic icons, such as Leonardo da Vinci's *Last Supper* with the disciples scratched out. The provocative slogan was: "Without your help, Italy could lose something," which singularly failed to elicit mass donations to save the country's treasures.

Popular culture is dominated by television and by the power of the premier. American-style anti-trust laws do not exist in Italy: telecommunications, publishing and the mass media are aces held in a few family hands. Berlusconi dominates the airwaves by owning the three most popular national television channels and, as head of state, indirectly controls RAI TV's three "public" channels. Mediaset, his media arm, controls channels that draw 60 percent of the audience share to programmes his critics denounce as "trashy TV". With a few exceptions, the output is devoted to political propaganda, poor-quality American imports and platitudinous game shows.

Tobias Jones, author of the polemical *The Dark Heart of Italy*, is acutely aware of the premier's Faustian pact: "When the medium became the message, the mogul became the prime minister." In one sense, having a head of state linked to the lowest form of Italian culture is emblematic of the paradoxical nature of the country. In a society where aesthetics takes precedence over ethics, style triumphs over content, and stylish corruption triumphs over lacklustre probity.

At best, it is partisan broadcasting, but at worst it has been dubbed a "videocracy", in which citizens wake up to a Berlusconi-designed world of vulgar television, political propaganda and venal advertising. In addition, Berlusconi controls 60 percent of television advertising revenue, as well as the national daily, *Il Giornale*, and the Mondadori publishing empire that produces a quarter of all Italian books.

Not that Berlusconi is entirely without a counterweight: De Benedetti, once synonymous with Olivetti, has transmuted into another media magnate and owner of *La Repubblica*, the leading left-wing national daily, and *L'Espresso*, the most influential news weekly, while the Turin-based Agnelli group owns a quarter of all national and provincial newspapers, as well as Fiat and the celebrated Juventus football club.

As any Italian knows, sport and politics are often conflated. Despite a suspended sentence for fraud in 1997, Berlusconi maintains his media empire, high political profile and chairmanship of AC Milan, one of Italy's top football

Spectacle, sociability, conformity

Foremost among the reassuring rituals of modern Italian life is the love of spectacle. During the opera season, La Scala's newly restored marbled and mirrored lobby is awash with Milanese matrons in furs, and rivalled by the Venetians in the faithfully restored Teatro La Fenice. And the Italian love of display cuts across regional and social divides, from the chic Venice carnival to the smallest Sardinian festival. Even so, the recent death of Pope John Paul II entwined several strands of Italian life: the sense of occasion and spectacle, softened by a poignant sense of togetherness.

clubs. Football, like opera, is a national obsession and thrives on classic regional and city rivalries: Milan and Rome have two teams apiece, with Berlusconi's AC Milan a rival to the Agnelli dynasty's Juventus at Turin. Yet, despite AC Milan reaching the Champions League final in 2005, Italian football has been tarnished, at least at team level, by recent allegations of match-fixing. It reflects the cynical ethos in which a premiership player sees the Italian Premier engineer a law under which false accounting is no longer a crime.

Tellingly, there is no Italian term for privacy. The emphasis is on the everyday values of sociability, simplicity and pleasure. The essence of Italian sociability is the *passeggiata*, the evening parade or dating ritual, with pauses for preening, chatting, flirting and gossiping.

Social life is neatly ordered, even underpinned by excessive planning. Commenting on the cloying social packaging of Italian life, novelist and long-term Italian resident Tim Parks says: "Cappuccino until ten, then espresso; *aperitivo* after twelve; your pasta, your meat, your *dolce* in bright packaging; light white wine, strong red wine, *prosecco*; baptism, first communion, marriage, funeral." ❑

LEFT: washing day in Venice. **ABOVE:** supporters of AC Milan, arch rivals of Juventus, the Turin team.

THE UNITED STATES OF ITALY

The diversity of Italian culture spans native Ligurian, Celtic, Etruscan and Roman civilisations and is nurtured by proud regional loyalties

Nationhood is an abstraction to most Italians until it comes to football, cuisine or foreign travel. What counts is *campanilismo* – a love of one's town and its traditions. Until recently, simply by moving from one town to the next, a visitor to Italy could observe marked differences – in clothes, the pronunciation of vowels, even the cooking of pasta. The writer Gore Vidal, who chose Italy as his second home, has complained: "Towns that were once different to the point of hostility are now all unified by TV, Fiat, festivals and soccer matches." Yet deep cultural divisions persist. The Venetian is sardonic and self-contained, the Roman more aggressive, the Florentine aloof. The Piedmontese have a dignified conceit that betrays French influence; the Milanese are renowned for their strong commercial instincts; while Neapolitans are as superstitious as they ever were.

ONE NATION, SO MANY FACES

The Italian look defies simple definition. The Mediterranean type – dark, with olive skin and brown eyes – prevails, but the Latin "Julius Caesar" strain can be found in the mountains around Rome; Arab and Norman features are noticeable among Sicilians; while the farmers of the Veneto, near the border with the former Yugoslavia, have strong Slav traits. The Goths, Lombards and other Germanic conquerors left traces of their physical characteristics in Lombardy and Piedmont. There are Albanian and Greek areas in Calabria and Sicily; and there is a former Austrian province, South Tyrol, within the frontiers of the republic.

▷ **HABSBURG LEGACY**
Germanic influences are clear in bilingual South Tyrol (Alto Adige), part of Austria until 1919.

△ **TRULLI DIFFERENT**
Trulli, strange dome-roofed houses in whitewashed limestone, are found only in Apulia, near Alberobello.

▷ **A WORLD APART**
Venice is still separated from the Italian mainland – both geographically and by its impenetrable dialect.

ARISTOCRATIC ENTREPRENEURS

◁ **WELL MATCHED**
At a traditional wedding in Naples, where ritual has a strong appeal, white doves are released after the ceremony. The southern Italian male still wants to be obeyed, but Neapolitan women often rule the roost.

▽ **OLD VALUES**
In parts of the Sicilian interior, poverty is prevalent and attitudes generally conservative. The role of rural women has hardly changed in a hundred years.

Italians are not naturally snobbish, but a title and an established reputation in the region still count for much. As most Italian firms are family-run, it is no surprise to find aristocrats engaged in enterprise. Building on their traditional bases in banking, textiles and wine, they have infiltrated the state sector, tourism and even the media. Piero Antinori *(above)* is a scion of one of the most reputable Tuscan wine and food dynasties, centred on the family's Florentine palace. In Sicily, Count Tasca d'Almerita, an ardent patriot, flies the Sicilian flag over his ancestral home and runs Regaleali, the family wine estate and cookery school. Near Turin, the Ermenegildo Zegna dynasty controls an exclusive textile and men's fashion concern. As for Tuscan fashion, despite the loss of Marchese Emilio Pucci, the family still runs a fashion empire from the medieval Palazzo Pucci. All over Italy, crumbling *palazzi* are being restored by entrepreneurial contessas with funds from foreign visitors or various paying guests.

▽ **FASHION MECCA**
Window shopping in Milan. The cosmopolitan commercial hub of the north rivals Paris as a fashion centre. A key to its success has been its ability to attract and foster talented designers.

△ **NORTH-EAST FRONTIER**
The spectacular Dolomites on the Austrian border, formed from an ancient coral reef, were the front line of battle during World War I.

▷ **SWISS ROLE**
The Swiss Guard, a corps of 120 men, all Catholic, all Swiss, is charged with protecting the Vatican.

THE ITALIANS

Individualism, a sense of survival and natural ebullience are qualities
almost all Italians share – but there the similarities end

It has been said that Italians do not exist, that those who are thought of as Italian regard themselves as Piedmontese, Tuscan, Venetian, Sicilian, Calabrian, and so on. No one has ever classified the Italians convincingly: to be born in Palermo, Sicily or in Turin, Piedmont is a classification by itself. And sometimes fellow-countrymen can seem like foreigners. In Pietro Germi's film *Il Cammino sella Speranza (The Path of Hope)*, a peasant woman says: "There's bad people in Milan, they eat rice."

According to the writer Ennio Flaiano, being Italian is a profession – except that it doesn't require much studying: one just inherits it. Generations of Italians have learned the art of *arrangiarsi*, of getting along in all kinds of difficult situations. Adjusting to political change and foreign conquest has generated a flexible mentality and a detached attitude towards political institutions and regimes, all of which are considered ephemeral. The forest of rules, statutes, norms, regulations – some many hundreds of years old, others of obscure interpretation – has engendered distrust of the state. The popular saying *fatta la legge, trovato l'inganno* (a law is passed, a way past it is found) is almost a national motto.

North versus south

"Southerners tend to make money in order to rule, northerners to rule in order to make money," declared the writer Luigi Barzini. The conflicting values of north and south reflect different cultures and history. Compared with the industrialised, progressive north, the agrarian, conservative south experienced feudalism, oppression, corruption, poverty and neglect. Known as the *Mezzogiorno,* the region has suffered grandiose white elephants, called "cathedrals in the desert": steelworks sited in remote

places with no proper infrastructure. Cut off from the progress and markets of northern Europe, southerners left for their own survival. Before 1914, more than 5 million emigrated to North America alone. Although emigration is on the wane, the south still suffers from depopulation, perceived backwardness, and a great

gap between rich and poor. Southerners, termed *meridionali*, often encounter prejudice, with northerners resenting "subsidising" the south through taxation. Indeed, some northerners see such aid as pouring their hard-earned money into the pockets of the Camorra in Naples or the Mafia, who are concentrated in western Sicily. The north–south divide, in all its tragicomic aspects, remains at the heart of Italian life.

PRECEDING PAGES: fun and games in the backstreets of Naples. **LEFT:** taking a news break on the piazza; for the residents of Italy's traffic-choked city centres, bicycles are a sensible alternative to the car. **RIGHT:** handicraft in Tuscany.

Politics and individualism

At election time, a higher proportion of people go to the polls in Italy than in most other European countries. Yet the average person in the street expresses a revulsion for politics: *"La politica è una cosa sporca"* ("politics is a dirty thing") is a typical riposte. This is based on a belief that all parties are the same, and that politics work only for politicians – an understandable view in the light of the corruption and political scandals that shook Italy in the 1990s.

The Italians remain sceptical of the state. It is no surprise that they cannot conceive of abstract solutions or trust in ideologies. Even left-wing intellectuals have given up on ideology. And it is widely held that things would be better if everything were left to the common sense of those "who work and produce".

Behind such opinions there is often an unre-

strained individualism that denies social responsibility. Yet hand in hand with such entrepreneurship, there is often a nostalgic yearning for "the strong man", whose power and will is stamped on his face, whose voice captures the needs and desires of the nation. It was a wave of such nostalgia that swept Alessandra Mussolini, grand-daughter of Benito, into parliament in 1992. Similarly, in northern Italy, in the wake of the scandals of the early 1990s, many Christian Democrat supporters were won over by the oratory of Umberto Bossi, leader of the Northern League, a right-wing autonomy movement.

Centuries of authoritarian political and reli-

THE LANGUAGE

The Italian language is the closest to Latin of any of the so-called Romance languages. Modern Italian owes much to writers such as Dante and Manzoni, who assumed as their standard the educated language of Tuscany. Today the best form of speech is said to be *la lingua toscana in bocca romana* (the Tuscan tongue in the Roman mouth).

Italian is considered the most musical language in the world: in the 16th century, the Holy Roman Emperor, Charles V, is said to have spoken Spanish with God, French with men, German with his horse, but Italian with women since it can express many subtleties of thought

and feeling. Italian can be as precise as any other language, yet the style of newspaper editorials, art criticism and political speeches, in particular, is often pompous, pretentious and wilfully obscure.

Until recently, more than 1,500 dialects existed alongside the official Italian language, most of them virtually incomprehensible outside their own village. Many contained a large number of foreign words imported by foreign occupiers. Dialect is still spoken among old people in the countryside, and in some cities, but is fading away among younger generations. The advent of television has done much for linguistic unification.

gious structures, which oppressed the values and needs of individuals have, by forcing people to fall back on cunning and self-reliance, paradoxically produced an over-blown ego. The strong sense that Italians have of their own self-importance is evident in their refusal to queue up at the windows of government offices, or at the bus stop.

Self-regard is reflected in the way the Italians dress. Shoes, ties, beautiful fabrics, and liberty of the imagination all contribute to the "costume". The same

> ## A SENSE OF BELONGING
>
> Italians have an abiding attachment to their home, family and town. According to novelist Tim Parks, "When an Italian leaves a place, it's almost always with the intention of returning victorious and vindicated."

of the Vatican, Italy has the lowest birth rate in Europe. Catholicism has a stronger hold in the south and in the Veneto than in the "red belt" of Emilia-Romagna, Umbria and Tuscany. According to a recent survey, more than 85 percent of Italians claim to be Catholics. However, only about a quarter of them attend Mass regularly. Nonetheless Catholicism still plays an important role in Italian rituals, from first holy communion to the marriage ceremony and Christian burial.

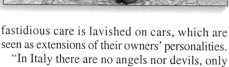

fastidious care is lavished on cars, which are seen as extensions of their owners' personalities.

"In Italy there are no angels nor devils, only average sinners," said Giulio Andreotti, seven-times premier. This tolerant Roman Catholic society is nurtured on the concept of original sin, universal temptation and redemption, so penitence can erase sins, including crimes.

Despite an authoritarian pope, abortion and divorce are legal and artificial contraception is widely accepted. Indeed, much to the chagrin

LEFT: making music through speech in Syracuse.
ABOVE: a monk in an increasingly secular society.
RIGHT: Italian children are cosseted and adored.

Sex and the family

The image of the Italian man as the Latin lover – passionate, impetuously sentimental, and powerful in bed – is a myth. The principal male characteristic is an attachment to his mother which goes far beyond the natural tie to a parent. Its residue is always there, even late in life: the need to feel loved and understood, the wish to receive affection while giving little in return. The classic Italian mother, generous, over-protective and intrusive, reinforces this image. While the family remains the bedrock of traditional Italian society, *mammismo*, the cult of the mother, is its cornerstone. The iconic image of the mother pervades the male approach to courtship and his choice of bride. Once married, however, male infidelity is often quietly condoned, provided that the family is supported and appearances preserved. Yet, within the home, the wife is traditionally the dominant figure.

While women's increasing economic independence is gradually changing the domestic balance, the limitations of Italian feminism are clear. Official forms are not designed for equal partners or female flat-sharers: the imprimatur of the *capo famiglia* (head of the household) is required. Staying together for the sake of appearances, *separati in casa*, is a typically civilised compromise: the couple live under the

same roof but lead separate lives. In terms of morality, a north–south divide prevails, with southern values more traditional and northern mores similar to those of northern Europe.

Yet even here, appearances are more important than reality. A slick young Milanese banker may dress like the proverbial preppy but attaches as much importance to family ties as does the humblest Calabrian peasant. His female counterpart, a Florentine designer, may act like the last of the yuppies but would not dare miss Sunday lunch with her parents. As for sex, discretion counts for much, and provided premarital relationships are not flaunted, family honour is maintained. However, tolerance rarely extends

to relationships openly conducted under the family roof. Since students tend to live at home, and Italian offspring are reluctant to leave the family nest until marriage, romantic assignments can take on the complexity of a Pirandello farce. High rents are a deterrent to leaving home; male offspring may also rely on a doting mother to act as a domestic drudge. But feminism is beginning to seep into family life, and mothers, particularly in northern and central Italy, increasingly expect a career outside the family business.

At least in the urban north, the stereotype of the roly-poly Italian *mamma,* with one eye on the baby and the other on the pasta, is losing its appeal. Indeed, Italy has a declining birthrate, with large families restricted to the south.

In career terms, women in the cities have made great strides in all fields, even politics and the law. Women have always been an important force in education, with the southern upper classes using higher education as a way of escaping strictures against working women. Nonetheless, it is still fair to say that in Italian male eyes, one is a woman first and a person second. To outsiders, Italy may seem a deeply patriarchal society but innate ingenuity and the importance placed upon good relations ensure that compromises are readily reached.

A style of life

How can one judge the national life of the Italians? Many would say that the Italian style of life is a failure because of the persistence of many seemingly insoluble problems. So many things, from the traffic in Rome to the cumbersome paperwork attached to the simplest official action, restrict and frustrate. And Italians seem unable to believe in the possibility of constructive change. For them, life is not about work and progress, but survival and individualism. On the other hand, and perhaps for that reason, Italian life sparkles with a brilliance unmatched anywhere else in Europe. The Italians have perfected a style of life that may be short on efficiency but is long on enjoyment. Simple things, such as eating a meal, taking a walk, watching the world go by, become special in Italy. Life is enjoyed to the fullest, with a flair gained over centuries of practice. ❏

LEFT: Italy's birthrate is declining: the modern *mamma* is more likely to have one or two children than a whole brood. **RIGHT:** true friends in Portofino.

THE ITALIAN LOOK

Supreme visual sense, a feeling for fashion and a creative twist
on classic lines form the essence of the Italian look

Only an Italian fashion editor could be so sweeping: "The Versaces and Armanis are our modern-day Michelangelos, helping dress our dreams. Anything else isn't *moda* – it simply serves to cover us." In other words, from the Renaissance to Romeo Gigli is but a small step, preferably taken in Ferragamo footwear, La Perla lingerie and a Fendi fur coat. In a country where appearances are all, even the Mafia is not immune. According to a recent survey, the successful *mafioso* teams an Armani suit with a Moschino waistcoat and Pollini shoes; while in prison, he insists on Fila and Tacchini sportswear.

Secret conformists

Italians pride themselves on their individuality and exhibitionism. However, dressing appropriately for the season and occasion is more important than dressing to please oneself or one's mood. To be accidentally over-dressed for a visit to a park or pizzeria can be a cardinal sin; equally, a mere "stroll" can be code for parading in one's finery. If in doubt, the look of deluxe anonymity is the safe sartorial badge. Not that designer labels, hip fashion accessories and superior models of cars pass unnnoticed in the social stakes.

Instinctive grace and elegance are insufficient protection against conformity. In such a clannish society, each social group wears its subtle uniform with pride. Off-duty, a young right-winger favours a country gentleman's Barbour jacket and Timberland boots while his left-wing counterpart chooses a checked shirt, jeans, long pullovers and a Loden coat. Italy may be a victim of faddishness but some trends seem more durable than others. Predictably, this nation of consummate conversationalists has 70 percent of the population owning mobile phones.

In a country that worships visual display, conformity is inevitable, yet so too is competitiveness and creativity. This is the joyous paradox of the irrepressible Italian spirit. Style is there-

LEFT and **RIGHT:** high style in Milan, Italy's fashion capital.

fore an emblem of high seriousness, with great attention accorded to the simple purchase of a picture or a place mat. Design is an all-inclusive philosophy involving creative alchemy and a crafts-based aesthetic, brain-storming and problem-solving skills, allied to a talent for interpreting mass culture. The world remains in

awe of Italian taste, inviting native talent to style American furniture, Japanese cameras, German limousines and French family cars. As a result, the inimitable character of *la linea italiana*, Italian style, has a continuing impact on international design.

Milan: fashion mecca

For fashion and design cognoscenti, Milan has a monopoly on "the Italian look". As the design capital, Milan is a well-tailored, cosmopolitan city that knows how to put on a show. During fashion week, the *modelari*, the louche men who chase models, are encased in leather trousers and regulation shades. At a Dolce &

Gabbana party, foreign stars gather by fountains overflowing with rose petals and pick from silver platters piled with pomegranates. Yet this picture of the city at its most hedonistic is only a party snapshot.

Milan's worldwide reputation for fashion has developed not by chance but by design. An innovative industrial culture and sound mass-production techniques set the city on its present successful course, particularly after World War II, when the burgeoning design industry came into its own. The Triennale, the prestigious design institute, and Italian "temple" of design, is now in the 1940s premises that pioneered

mass-production of household objects; it also boasts an exhibition of Italian design, from vintage scooters to early Olivetti computers.

Today, Milan still dominates the fashion and design calendar, from international trade fairs to the spring and summer couture and ready-to-wear collections. The city hosts Salone del Mobile, the furniture trade fair, and fairs dedicated to lighting and home and office design. The fashion and design showrooms are located between the Brera and Piazza San Babila in the *quadrilatero* or "golden triangle". Here, the Japanese buy swathes of Gucci belts or ten Prada bags apiece to offer friends back home.

THE FASHION SCENE

The contribution of fashion to Italy's balance of payments is second only to tourism. Commercially, the industry is more successful than its French counterpart, with the Milan collections considered more wearable and contemporary than those of Paris.

Italian fashion thrives on a long craft tradition, a ready supply of home-grown talent and a contemporary feel, essentially a creative twist on classic lines. Its deep design roots lie in medieval craftsmanship, traditional skills which are prized in haute couture *(alta moda)* as well as in the making of quality fabrics, jewellery, bags and shoes. Native designers also have a highly developed

aesthetic sense dating back to the Renaissance.

Valentino, the Roman couturier renowned for his elegant style, is probably the most highly regarded among Italians. Abroad, however, accolades are accorded to Armani, the master of deconstruction, with his sloping shoulder-lines and minimalist colours, and Versace, his sartorial polar opposite – vulgar, glamorous and sexually explicit – who died in 1997.

Despite the loss of the creative genius, the firm thrives under his sister, Donatella. But in the late 1990s, such pre-eminence was challenged by Prada, Gucci, Dolce & Gabbana and Moschino.

A sense of style and design is in the Italian genes. In 1946, the Italian architect Ernesto Nathan Rogers stated that design should be all-embracing, "from the spoon to the city". Italian designers dutifully filled our world with high-tech telephones and computers; office furniture in fluid shapes; sleek chrome kitchen appliances and twirly pasta quills. Giandomenico Belotti's Spaghetti Chair was literally inspired by pasta.

Italian design encompasses the austere, the provocative, the classically restrained and the kitsch. The roll-call of honour includes the Olivetti typewriter and the Artemide lamp, as well as the Ferrari, a symbol of national pride.

moves with the times: designs can be functional or futuristic, elitist or democratic. Designers confidently switch fields, from interior to industrial or graphic design.

Design diversity

The design field has traditionally cultivated creative cross-fertilisation between the craftsman and architect, designer and artist. Giò Ponti, the 20th century's greatest Modernist, believed that Italy had been created half by God and half by architects. He detested the superfluous and favoured practical, perfect forms such as his Superleggera, the consummate chair, a sculpted

Italy has a reputation for inspired car and motor-bike design, from exclusive Ferraris to basic Vespa scooters *(see pages 94–5)*. In reply, the fashion world fields designers with the aspirations of Renaissance princelings: Armani's fluid lines clash with Versace's camp eroticism, Romeo Gigli's romantic fantasies, and Dolce & Gabbana's Sicilian kitsch.

Aesthetically, Italy is known for its smooth, streamlined objects, from washing machines to motorbikes. Creatively, however, the country

LEFT: the late Gianni Versace at a show in 1991.
ABOVE: a design classic, Piaggio's Vespa was introduced in 1946.

lightweight piece. Ponti designed Milan's Pirelli Tower (1956) as well as creating the espresso machine, founding the magazine *Domus* and establishing the Milan Triennale, Europe's major design exhibition.

The highlights of Italian design history reveal both its readiness to innovate and its essential classicism. In the 1950s, the Modernists abhorred meretricious designs but eclectic designers were eager to experiment. The 1960s avant-garde relished visual disorder and inflatable fantasies. Yet even during the Pop Art period and Swinging Sixties, designers did not abandon their love of craftsmanship or use of high-quality materials, such as leather. The

1970s represented the high point of Italian minimalism, with austere tubular steel chairs. In the 1980s, designers equipped domestic kitchens as if they were for professional chefs. In the 1990s, many designers returned to minimalism, following the "less is more" approach of Mies van der Rohe.

The belief in *bellezza*, beauty for its own sake, means that even high-tech must be aesthetically pleasing. Olivetti is one of many high-profile companies that have always treated their designers as creative artists. The Olivetti typewriter is a design classic, its shape emblazoned over the company headquarters near Turin.

Olivetti launched Italy's first portable typewriter in 1950, with Marcello Nizzoli's Lettera 22. Nizzoli's successors, Ettore Sottsass and Mario Bellini, pioneered ergonomic keyboards and the use of textured plastics and colour.

The Milanese apartment might be a temple of minimalism, decorated with white tubular sofas, stainless-steel shelving, and glass-topped dining tables with an unusual number of legs; however, domesticity *all'italiana* comes in a range of styles. Just as few Postmodernist architects choose to live in their own houses, so few Italian designers practise what they preach. Versace was the high priest of vulgarity yet filled his opulent mansions with antiques. In a grand *salotto* (living room), the clinical effect of Modernist design may be offset by rich Venetian velvets or Florentine brocades. Even in a modern setting, there is a place for family heirlooms, with regional rustic chests or walnut dressers dotted with Venetian vases. Climate, tradition and taste reject carpets in favour of tiles, terracotta or marble flooring dotted with loose rugs. As for superior furniture, the firm of Poltrona Frau make hand-crafted designs out of seasoned beechwood and leather. Their comfortable Art Deco leather armchair, Vanity Fair, has been in production since 1930.

High-tech in the home also has a distinguished pedigree, with cult objects by Aldo Rossi, Ettore Sottsass and Robert Venturi, including coffee pots, chairs and trays in severe metallic designs. Particularly prized are stainless steel kettles by Alessi, or Achille Castiglioni cutlery and his elegant, curiously shaped lamps. The Italians broke the mould of lighting design: "Light does not simply illuminate, it tells a story," says Sottsass. The modern lighting heyday was the 1970s, but certain lamps, from 18th-century Murano chandeliers to Pietro Chiesa's Art Deco funnel lamps, stand the test of time.

Temples of consumerism

Milan may be the design showcase but most cities are citadels of good taste, with smart shops and shiny people committed to sophisticated consumerism. Writer Jonathan Keates refers to the town of Modena as "Middle Italy incarnate, the most unrelentingly consumer-oriented society in Europe". Yet even in poorer southern cities, rampant consumerism is common. If the authentic article is too costly, then dedicated shoppers will settle for a fake: appearances are everything. Naples is the capital of counterfeit culture, where painted marzipan fruit looks finer than real peaches. This is the place for ersatz French cognac or Scotch whisky, Lacoste shirts or Gucci handbags.

Conspicuous consumption is only part of the public picture. An Italian city is a stage for preening and posturing. Whether dressed in Como silks and Armani suits or in the preppy uniform of shades, loafers and designer jeans, Italians make immaculate fashion victims. ❑

LEFT: an exquisite early design from the Murano workshops in Venice. **RIGHT:** Giorgio Armani on the catwalk.

THE LOOK OF THE 20TH CENTURY

Furniture, clothes, cars, typewriters, even kitchen appliances – the influence of Italian design has permeated the way we live and work today

Italian designers bask in their reputation for refinement, innate good taste and eye for colour and line. "Quite simply, we are the best" boasts architect and cultural commentator, Luigi Caccia. "We have more imagination, more culture, and are better mediators between the past and the future. That is why our design is more attractive and more in tune with the times than in other countries." Italian design is nothing if not inclusive. The traditional distinction between architect and industrial designer is blurred, with practitioners dabbling in fields as diverse as factory building and furniture design, office lighting and graphics. In the words of Ettore Sottsass, one of the most influential designers: "Design should be a discussion of life, society, politics, food and the design itself."

MODERNISM TO POP ART

Since the beginning of the 20th century, Milan has led industrial design, reaching its apogee in the 1970s and 1980s. The Italians produced seminal designs for cars and lamps in the 1930s, matched by radios and motorbikes in the 1940s. Milan also pioneered innovative design in the 1950s, with the mass production of household appliances, from cookers and washing machines to kitchen utensils. Italian modernism supplanted the post-war European taste for the safe, hand-crafted homeliness of Scandinavian design. Stylish kettles and coffee percolators became cult objects in the 1960s, followed by quirky Pop Art furniture and the fashion designer chic of subsequent decades, from cool Armani to pared-down Prada. The inimitable character of *la linea italiana*, Italian style, still sets the standard for international design values.

△ **FERRARI FORMULA**
The Ferrari Spider (1993 model) is in a long line of fabulous cars from the most admired Italian manufacturer. Enzo Ferrari (1898–1988), the firm's founder, was also a noted racing-car designer.

▽ **WINDOW SHOPPING**
A highly structured Prada suit adorns Milan's fashion district. Prada is the fashion company that best captures the *Zeitgeist* of the times. Its designs have made it the most copied (faked) label on the city streets.

▷ **WASHED OUT**
Zanussi's rigorous designs, streamlined look and user-friendly features have long made it a European market leader in the field of washing machines, refrigerators and other "white goods".

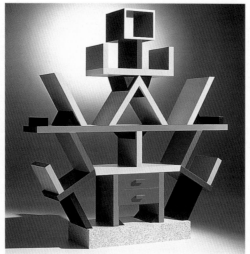

CLASSIC CAR STYLE

△ PLASTIC FANTASTIC
Post-modernist bookcase in laminated plastic, a bold design for the Memphis studio by Sottsass (1981). Memphis was the design event of the 1980s, a playful and much-imitated school inspired by Bob Dylan's song, *Memphis Blues*.

◁ TALKING POINT
Italian design often takes ideas to their extreme, as in these eye-catching New Tone sculptural sofas by Atrium. This is subversive, unconventional, avant-garde living.

Ever since the 1930s, Italian car design has been characterised by stylistic restraint, versatility and timeless elegance. At one end of the scale, the Italians still produce some of the greatest status symbols in the world. In the 1950s, the beautiful Alfa Romeo convertibles spelt playboy raffishness; Ferrari's Spider, the ultimate in glamour, was produced from 1966 to 1992, making it the only sports car to have a longer production run than Germany's Porsche 911.

Yet the Italians have also had great success with Fiat's bland but eminently practical models. Topolino ("the little mouse") was launched to great acclaim in 1939, and continued into the 1950s. Giovanni Agnelli studied North American mass production techniques and from the 1950s the family dynasty had a captive market, with customers eager for the inexpensive Fiat 500. The car industry is based in the north, with Fiat in Turin, Alfa Romeo in Milan and Ferrari in Modena. The huge Fiat Lingotto plant was set up near Turin in the 1920s. Today, the city's fortunes are still inextricably linked to Fiat. The Italians also design for foreign manufacturers, including Mercedes and Rolls Royce.

DESIGN CLASSIC
he Piaggio Vespa ("wasp"), rst produced in 1946, ecame the symbol of eedom for the post- ar generation. The espa Lifestyle bag *bove)*, part of a trend r brand recognition nd product iversification, is an ustere, minimalist fering from the iaggio stable.

ITALIAN CUISINE

*Each region has its own cuisine, from the rich dishes of Emilia-Romagna
to the sparse, intensely flavoured diet of the south*

For Italians, a meal is a celebration of life itself – less of man's art than of nature's wondrously bountiful providence. A deep respect and admiration for ingredients is found throughout the country, although both history and geography have played their part in making the cooking of Italy so strongly regional.

One of the secrets of Italian cuisine, impossible to replicate elsewhere, lies in Italy's soil. After making pulp of Mexico, the Spanish conquistador Hernando Cortés returned to the Old World laden with strange new fruits and vegetables, among them a humble, fleshy yellow sphere smaller than a ping-pong ball which, in 1554, the Italians dubbed the *pomo d'oro* (golden apple). Two hundred years on, thanks to the rich Italian soil, these jaundiced cherries had become huge, lush tomatoes in deep ruby hues; moreover, their relatively demure taste (the contemporary writer Felici had described the original fruit as "more good-looking than good") had been transformed into a piquant yet tantalisingly sweet sensation.

These days, as well as being a key ingredient in many more elaborate Italian dishes, tomatoes are stuffed with beans or rice, offered as an *antipasto* with alternating slices of fresh mozzarella cheese, or simply served lightly dressed in olive oil and topped with sprigs of basil.

A savoury past

Until the Renaissance, the history of Italian cooking largely corresponded with Italy's military fortunes. In the 9th century, the Arabs invaded Italy, introducing Eastern sherbets and sorbets, originally served between courses to refresh the palate. Sicily, where Arab influence was most entrenched, is still noted for its sorbets and sumptuous sweets, including *cassata siciliana*, sweet sponge filled with ricotta cheese or pistachio cream and decorated with almond paste and candied fruit. Two hundred years after the Arabs left mainland Italy, the Italians set off

LEFT: cutting the *parmigiana* in a restaurant in the Italian Lakes. **RIGHT:** olive oil from a small producer.

on their own holy wars. Their return was sweetened by the presentation of sugar-cane which they had discovered in Tripoli. They called it "Indian salt" and for almost a century used it as a condiment for meat and vegetables, not suspecting its natural affinity with dessert.

Some time in the late Middle Ages, pasta

appeared. Nobody knows exactly how it was invented, but the legend of Marco Polo bringing it back from Cathay is firmly refuted by Italians. The Roman gastronome Apicius, writing in the 1st century AD, describes a *timballo* (a sweet or savoury pie made with pasta). Later, in the Middle Ages, Boccaccio recommended the combination of macaroni and cheese.

It was during the Renaissance that cooking became a fine art and evolved along the lines familiar to us today. Bartolomeo Sacchi, a Vatican librarian also known as Platina, composed a highly sophisticated cookbook entitled *De Honesta Voluptate ac Valetudine* (Concerning Honest Pleasures and Wellbeing); within three decades the volume had seen six editions. Florentine merchants spent huge sums on establishing schools for the promotion of culinary knowledge.

Consolidation of the Venetian Spice Route led to fragrant innovations. New pastry cooks invented macaroons, *frangipane* (filled with cream and flavoured with almonds) and *panettone* (a spicy celebration brioche incorporating sultanas). Conquistadors bombarded the Old World with its first potatoes, pimentoes and, of course, tomatoes. When Catherine de' Medici, a keen gourmet, married Henry II of France, she took with her to France her Italian cooks, thus laying the foundations for French cuisine. Until then, France had no cuisine of its own. Even *Larousse Gastronomique* honours Italy as the "mother" cuisine.

Regional flavours

The concept of an Italian national cuisine is highly treacherous. Italy offers the world 23 regional cuisines, a diversity reflecting the country's pre-unification history and the importance of locally available produce (for example, hare, boar, rabbit and chestnuts in Tuscany; pork and truffles in Umbria; buffalo mozzarella, squid and *polpo* – octopus – in Naples). Dis-

SLOW FOOD

The 20th anniversary of the Slow Food movement is to be celebrated in 2006. The founding of this movement in Piedmont was to counter the junk food culture and its manifesto declared: "Let us rediscover the flavours and savours of regional cooking and banish the degrading effects of fast movement." The movement has been so popular that it now has more than 60,000 members spread across five continents.

Carlo Petrini, the founder, explains:"The goal of this movement is the propogation of leisurely, more epicurean eating habits, and a more enlightened and patient approach to life."

tinctive culinary identities evolved as naturally as particular painting styles or costumes. Even more influential than political boundaries were natural variations in soil type, climate and proximity to the sea.

But the single inescapable territorial distinction is that between the north and the south. There are two important culinary differences between the regions. Firstly, northerners eat flat pasta shaped like a ribbon while southerners eat round pasta shaped like a tube. Northern pasta is usually prepared at home with eggs and eaten almost immediately, often *alla Bolognese*, the classic pasta sauce made with lean veal and tomatoes and seasoned with carrot, celery, *prosciutto*, lemon zest and nutmeg. Southern pasta, on the other hand, is manufactured in factories (the first factories opened in the 19th century), does not contain eggs and is purchased dry, a tradition stemming from the days when it was dried in the warm sea breezes around Naples. The classic sauce in the south is *napoletana*, based on pork.

The second difference between north and south concerns the lubrication used for cooking. North of Emilia-Romagna, Italians often line pots and pans with butter when making a meal, whereas south of Bologna it is olive oil which sets the pans sizzling.

Zuppa di pesce, which is more of a stew than a soup, is a stalwart of many menus and usually served in an enormous tureen. Luxury versions include *buridda alla Genovese*, incorporating octopus, squid, mussels, shrimps and clams.

Anchovies and sardines are classic Mediterranean fish. *Pasta con sarde*, a speciality of Palermo, is pasta with a sauce of wild fennel, pine nuts, raisins and fried sardines. A more intricate dish, often found as an *antipasto*, is sardines stuffed with capers, pine nuts, pecorino cheese (often from Sardinia), bread and eggs.

Italy also produces some of the finest meats in the world, which may explain why the Ital-

Situated between the Adriatic and the Tyrrhenian seas, Italy hauls in well over 320 million kilos (700 million pounds) of fish a year. Wonderful fish abound in Emilia-Romagna. Alpine streams make the Adriatic significantly less salty than most oceans, and it is therefore an ideal habitat for *rombo* (turbot), "the pheasant of the sea", and gobies, derived from the Latin *gobius pagenellus* (little pagans). It is said that when St Anthony of Padua went to Rimini in 1221, he preached a sermon for which all the fish, save the gobie, lifted themselves from the water.

ians don't find it necessary to add sauce to their national specialities. Tuscany's Chianina cattle are alabaster in colour and grow to weigh 1,800 kg (4,000 lb). Chianina beef is used to best advantage in *bistecca alla Fiorentina* – a recipe in which the steak is marinated in a little olive oil, wine vinegar and garlic, then rapidly grilled. Baby lamb and kid is popular in hilly regions.

Game birds are also used extensively (Italians are said to eat anything which flies, however small), and warbler, bunting, lark, quail and pheasant are favourites on regional menus. Thrushes and larks are eaten whole, bones as well. *Piccioni* (wild pigeon), served fresh rather than hung, attains new gustatory heights in Italy.

LEFT: the abundant wares of a Naples grocer.
ABOVE: fresh fish for sale on the Adriatic coast.

Look out for *piccioni alle olive*, pigeons wrapped in bacon, roasted and served with green olives.

Of all Italy's provinces, Rome has the most festivals, and Rome's cuisine comes nearest to that associated with feasting. Suckling pigs and suckling lambs are mouth-watering specialities. The justly famous *saltimbocca alla romana* (a thin slice of veal wrapped around a slice of *prosciutto* and a sage leaf, browned in butter and simmered in white wine) lives up to its name – "jump into the mouth". Romans also thrive on *gnocchi* – feathery dumplings incorporating butter, eggs, nutmeg and Parmesan – while their

poor relation, *polenta*, a pudding or cake of yellow maize flour, is popular in Lombardy.

Emilia-Romagna, long celebrated for its gastronomy, has splendid natural resources. Moreover, the entire province has always had one of the world's best road systems, ensuring rapid distribution of ingredients. *Prosciutto* (air-cured ham) is synonymous with Parma, though Tuscany and Umbria also produce a good *prosciutto* rubbed with a garlic and pepper mixture before curing; it is often served with sliced melon or fresh figs. Emilia-Romagna is also the place for sausage. Bologna, the capital of Italian cuisine, lies in the heart of Emilia-Romagna. It is from here that *mortadella*, described by one

connoisseur as "the noblest of pork products", originates. *Mortadella* is made from finely hashed pork, generously spiced and forced into a casing made from suckling pig skin.

Bologna is also the home of *tortellini*, rosebud-shaped pasta filled with spinach and ricotta cheese. "If the first father of the human race was lost for an apple, what would he not have done for a plate of *tortellini*?", goes a local saying. Legends as to *tortellini*'s origins abound. One version gives credit to a young cook of a wealthy Bolognese merchant who modelled the curiously shaped pasta on the navel of his master's wife whom he had seen sleeping naked.

As well as being *polenta* country, Lombardy also boasts the most modern methods of food production in Italy. It produces more rice than any other European region and the famous *risotto alla milanese*, seasoned with saffron, does justice to the native grain, which, as the great cookery writer Elizabeth David pointed out, is ideally suited to slow cooking. Variations on the risotto theme, in which rice is cooked in a broth to absorb its flavour, include *risotto nero*, in which the rice is coloured black by cuttlefish ink.

One way to transform a plain risotto into a dish fit for a king is to shave a little truffle over the top. The truffle, a fragrant mushroom which grows beneath the soil around tree trunks, is prized for its unique flavour and texture. White truffles are found in Piedmont, where they are sniffed out by specially trained dogs; the world's best come from the Astiarca. Black truffles are associated with Umbria.

Bread and pizza

Naples is the place to eat pizza baked over wood in a brick-lined oven – traditionally, *pizza napoletana* (tomatoes, mozzarella, anchovies and oregano), *pizza Margherita* (topped with mozzarella, tomatoes and basil leaves) and *pizza marinara* (topped with tomatoes, garlic, clams, mussels and oregano). A good pizza should be moist and fragrant with a raised rim known as *il cornicione* (large frame).

Bread, eaten without butter, accompanies every meal and is used to mop up juices and olive oil. Every region, even every town, in Italy has its own varieties and the different shapes alone are said to number 1,000. In Tuscany, bread (rough, white and with a floury top) is saltless to counteract the saltiness of the food;

in the south bread comes in large crusty wheels. Favourite speciality breads include *pane alle olive* (a Genoese bread incorporating olives) and *focaccia*, a flat bread drizzled with olive oil and sprinkled with salt, or, in a more elaborate version similar to pizza, topped with olives or onions. Sardinia is noted for its *carta da musica* (music-paper bread), a wafer-thin unleavened bread, which is crunchy and long-lasting. Shepherds traditionally took it with them on long expeditions into the hills with their flocks.

> ### BIG CHEESE
>
> The only authentic Parmesan cheese is Parmigiano-Reggiano, produced around Parma, Reggio nell'Emilia and Modena.

ably similar order. The first course *(il primo)* invariably consists of a pasta or rice dish (especially in the north) or soup. (*Antipasti*, such as toasted bread with olive oil and garlic, seafood salad or grilled vegetables, are generally served only in restaurants or at banquets.) The second course *(il secondo)*, comprising meat or sometimes (especially on Friday) fish, complements or elaborates the theme begun by the first. For example, if the first course was *tortellini* filled with parsley and ricotta, the second would probably be some-

The ritual of the meal

Wherever you are in Italy, the rituals surrounding food and eating remain the same. Devotion to any repast, however humble, is evident in the time Italians spend at the table. In many regions work still stops for a full two hours at midday, and everyone, from the poorest to the richest, is expected to go home and eat. Often the midday meal is the most important event of the day, the time when families swap stories and adventures.

Though their specialities differ greatly, all regions eat their particular dishes in a remark-

LEFT: making pizza in Naples, where it all started.
ABOVE: the best cakes are from Milan, some say.

thing light – such as a sautéed chicken dish with lemon and a little more parsley, echoing the first course. The second course is usually enhanced by at least one, often two or three vegetable dishes, such as *funghi trifolati* (mushrooms sautéed with garlic and parsley), *fave in salsa di limone* (broad beans in lemon sauce) and *cicoria all'aglio* (chicory with garlic sauce).

Afterwards, a light green salad is generally served to cleanse the palate, and to prepare the tastebuds for the grand finale – anything from an exotic pastry *(dolce)* to one of Italy's many cheeses, perhaps served with fruit. Needless to say, each course is washed down with ample quantities of wine.   ❑

WINE IN ITALY

In Italy, wine exists primarily to turn everyday meals
and family get-togethers into hugely pleasurable social occasions

Wine is part of the cultural furniture in Italy. It goes on the table along with salt, pepper and olive oil – and it is made to be drunk with food. This means that the flavours of Italian wine are often both more subtle and more demanding than those of wines from countries where the link is less strong.

Just as there is hardly any such thing as Italian cooking, so the wines of Italy, too, are intensely regional. Vine-growing echoes the north–south divide, largely for climatic reasons. Wines from a delimited region are designated Denominazione di Origine Controllata (DOC). Most DOC wine (which accounts for one in every eight bottles) is produced north of Rome: as one travels south, the grape varieties, and the tastes, become increasingly exotic. Italy grows more grape varieties, and makes more wine (nearly a fifth of the world's total) than any other country. Not all of it is good, but much of it is exciting. Be prepared to take a risk: you will usually be amply rewarded.

Light but quaffable

Soave and Valpolicella illustrate a useful principle. These light white and red wines are produced on a vast industrial scale. The Veneto region – from Venice to Lake Garda, from the Yugoslavian Alps to the flat Po Valley – is the largest producer of DOC wine. Soave, by far the country's biggest-selling dry white DOC, can be as memorable as muzak or waiting-room wallpaper. But for those who are prepared to pay a little more, for Soave Classico made on a small scale by first-rate producers, it can be very good indeed. Any Valpolicella billed as *ripasso* will have more character than straight Valpolicella. Recioto Amarone and Recioto Amabile (made from dried grapes) have extra depth and flavour; the former is dry, the latter sweet and reminiscent of port. Recioto Soave is the white equivalent, a golden, gently honeyed wine.

To the north and east of Venice, Friuli-

LEFT: a variety of fine wines for sale. **RIGHT:** traditional methods in Tuscany.

Venezia Giulia is a source of much crisp, fresh white wine from a long list of grape varieties.

Up above Lake Garda, in the mountain air of Trentino-Alto Adige, the vineyards cling to precipitous slopes under peaks that are snow-covered until well into the spring. The Alto Adige, or South Tyrol, was once part of Austria,

and many growers have distinctly unItalian names. Reds from here can be chewy and plummy, or strawberry-fresh; whites are as crisp as the mountain air, light and ethereal.

Piedmont, Italy's other sub-alpine wine region, is a wonderful place to visit in autumn, when the early morning fog that hangs over the vineyards clears slowly, and the streets of Alba smell of white truffles. The fog, or *nebbia,* gives its name to the main red grape variety, Nebbiolo, which ripens very late; its thick skin enables it to survive the humidity and rot that would threaten thinner-skinned varieties.

The thick skin is also responsible for the wine's deep colour, and for mouth-puckering tannins that make Barolo and Barbaresco such big, powerful, long-lived wines. They are both DOCG, a step up from DOC. These wines are to be taken seriously: wines for long, companiable dinners that stretch well into the night, not wines for an *al fresco* lunch. A glass of sweet, sparkling Asti, aromatic and irresistably quaffable, is more welcome at lunchtime, followed by one of the lighter local reds, such as Nebbiolo d'Alba.

Chianti country

Tuscany challenges Piedmont as producer of the country's most aristocratic wines. Some of the

families in the business today (Antinori and Frescobaldi, for example) have been making wine since before the Renaissance. Chianti is the staple, Italy's best-known red wine, made mostly from the Sangiovese grape. The "blood of Jove" manifests itself in varying forms, from light and fruity to capable of ageing in the bottle. Standards of winemaking in the region have improved so that most Chianti is gratifyingly better than it used to be, even a decade ago.

Brunello di Montalcino and Vino Nobile di Montepulciano, both Sangiovese-based, both expensive, have traditionally represented the heights to which Tuscan reds could aspire. But Super-Tuscans, a loose-knit family of brilliant but quirkily named *vini da tavola* that burgeoned in the 1980s, are now some of Tuscany's greatest stars. Each has its individual style: they sprang from the desire of certain winemakers to produce their dream wine outside the often stultifying law of the time. They have snappy names like Sassicaia or Solaia, and are pricey, but with inimitable richness and complexity.

Dry white wines from Tuscany are less exalted. Galestro is a brave attempt to show that Italy's high-yelding Trebbiano grape can turn into something tasty, especially when blended with Sauvignon Blanc, Chardonnay and others. Vernaccia, from the medieval town of San Gimignano, is made in more traditional style. Tuscany's classiest whites, however, are sweet, made from dried grapes and called Vin Santo.

In Emilia-Romagna, where dishes are gloriously rich and sticky, Lambrusco is the natural partner. Most of it is red, some is dry, and the bubbles vary from a mere prickle to a full-blown sparkle. Much of it, too, is an improvement on the coloured sweet fizz that floods the export market. Look for Lambrusco di Sorbara to get a taste of the real thing.

Further south

Most of the best wines of central and southern Italy are red. Those from the south tend to be cheaper, but don't be fooled: a wine-making revolution has taken place in these sun-baked villages, and wines such as Apulia's Copertino and Umbria's Sagrantino offer tremendous flavours of spices, earth and dried fruit. Montepulciano d'Abruzzo, too, is good, juicy red, with a typically Italian bite.

The whites of the centre and south have their virtues, but character is not always among them.

TOP WINE PRODUCERS

You can always rely on **Allegrini** for serious Valpolicella; **Anselmi** for starry Soave (go for the *cru* and *recioto*); and **Antinori** for quality Chianti, *vino da tavola* Tignanello and stupendous white Castello della Sala. For wonderful Barolo, try **Clerico**, both **Conterno** brothers or **Bruno Giacosa** (also recommended for Barbaresco). **Angelo Gaja** has great Barbaresco at great prices. **Isole e Olena** produce elegant Chianti. **Pieropan's** Recioto di Soave is rich beyond the dreams of avarice (as you'll have to be, too); and **Regaleali** and **Donnafugata** use local grape varieties to produce quality Sicilians with wacky flavours.

HOW TO READ AN ITALIAN WINE LABEL

Denominazione di Origine Controllata (DOC) is a delimited wine region, the equivalent of the French Appellation Contrôlée. Not all DOC wines are very good and some top wines are in fact not DOC; the producer's name is often a surer guide. DOCG (the G standing for *e garantita*) is meant to be a better wine than a straight DOC. Indicazione Geografiche Tipici (IGT) is a classification between DOC and *vino da tavola*, which embraces the two ends of the scale – cheap everyday wine and some high-quality, expensive wines made by producers dissatisfied with DOC restrictions. *Classico* refers to the heartland of a wine region, often producing the best wine. Other words to look for are *abboccato* (semi-sweet); *amabile* (sweet); *secco* (dry); *frizzante* (pétillant); *spumante* (sparkling), which may be made by the *metodo classico* (Champagne method). *Passito* is sweet wine made from semi-dried grapes; *recioto*, a sweet or dry wine made from dried grapes; and *ripasso*, a rich red wine fermented in the barrels previously used for a *recioto*. In Valpolicella, *amarone* is a dry wine of great character made from dried grapes. *Riserva* is wine given extra ageing in the barrel.

All too many are clean, fresh, well made, but bland; often because they are designed for washing down food without drawing attention to themselves.

Exceptions are Orvieto Classico, from Umbria, which can have good nutty fruit, and Frascati, which at its best has an attractive sour-cream tang. But if Frascati did not have Rome on its doorstep it would probably not have achieved the fame it has. Most of it is Trebbiano-based and quaffable, but the better producers use Malvasia.

LEFT: a vineyard and *trulli* house near Alberobello in Apulia. **ABOVE:** decanting an old vintage in Tuscany.

Sweet wines

Sweet, sometimes fortified whites, however, are another matter. The southern half of the country abounds in these, as do the islands, and very good they are too – although calling them whites seems perverse when most age to a rich tawny colour. Look for the names of the Malvasia or Moscato grapes on the label.

In Tuscany, try the Vin Santo ("holy wine") made from grapes which have been hung to dry for months or even years. Traditionally, this was offered to favoured guests as refreshment, along with little sweet almond biscuits, but it can equally well be drunk after dinner – or after lunch if you want to snooze all afternoon. ❏

MUSIC AND OPERA

Italy's contribution to music is unparalleled. And where better to enjoy the art of opera than where it began and flourished?

Italy is rightly known as the home of music, and Milan's image is inextricably bound up with La Scala. When opera houses burn down, as they still tend to do in Italy, people cry in public and the country grieves. Fortunately, the country still has an abundance of major opera houses. However, Italy's contribution to Western music goes beyond operatic rococo interiors and impassioned outpourings of Verdi.

A monk, Guido d'Arezzo, devised the musical scale, while a Venetian printer, Ottavino Petrucci, invented a method of printing music with moveable type. The language of music remains resolutely Italian, including such terms as *soprano, drammatico* and *soprano lirico*. Italy also gave us the piano, the accordion and the fabulous Stradivarius and Guarneri violins and cellos. Cremona has been the capital of violin masters since the 16th century. Indeed, it is not too fanciful to see the curves of violins echoed in the spiral cornices of city palaces.

The food of love

Without the Italian sensibility, the world of music would be without the nobility and intensity of Verdi or the seductive strains of Vivaldi. The lush strings of Albinoni perfectly chime with the public's taste for haunting baroque music, while opera-lovers are rewarded with Rossini's *Il Barbiere di Siviglia*, a comic masterpiece; Bellini's ravishing melodies; or the dramatic flow of Puccini's *Tosca* and *Turandot*. Other musical keynotes are *bel canto*, the traditional Italian art of singing, and Neapolitan love songs, as much part of the passionate city as pizza and Mount Vesuvius. Yet Italian music also embraces Scarlatti sonatas, memorable madrigals, Palestrina's solemn melodies and the purest Gregorian chant – not to mention Mina's soulful pop ballads and Mediterranean rock. Of the old-school balladeers, often witty as well as romantic, Gino Paoli, Francesco de Gregori,

Lucio Dalla and Claudio Baglioni deserve mention. Gianna Nannini is an outspoken firebrand of Sienese feminism and Mediterranean rock, while some of the fusion bands from the south are tinged with North African and Arab notes, a reminder of the Moorish legacy in Sicily and Campania. Eros Ramazzotti, the king of Italian

easy-listening music, has achieved great sales in continental Europe and is designated "the Pavarotti of pop".

Opera was Italy's greatest musical achievement, a rousing art form which came into being in 14th-century Florence and was perfected by Monteverdi. In his opera *Orfeo*, the title role was taken by a *castrato,* a male soprano or contralto with an unbroken voice. *Castrati* were in great demand during the 17th and 18th centuries, thanks to their strong, flexible yet voluptuous voices. Farinelli (1705–82) was the most famous, a soprano whose singing and stage presence caused women to faint from excitement. Italian divas have also graced the stages of the

---

PRECEDING PAGES: a glittering gala at Milan's La Scala.
LEFT: Verdi, great opera composer and Italian patriot.
RIGHT: Claudio Monteverdi, the "father of opera".

great *teatri lirici* (opera houses), including Cecilia Bartoli in the present day, the mezzo-soprano acclaimed for her interpretations of Mozart. Italy, which gave the world Enrico Caruso and Beniamino Gigli, also boasts a clutch of talented tenors, from Luciano Pavarotti to the romantic Roberto d'Alagna, raised in Paris by Sicilian parents.

The world's their stage

Composers such as the modernist, Luciano Berio, also enjoy international renown, experimenting with sound in all its forms, from electronic and rock to folk, jazz and classical. La Scala recently honoured him with a premiere of his opera *Outis*. Gian Carlo Menotti, the founder of the Spoleto Festival, set in a ravishing Roman theatre, is acclaimed for his operas as well as his skills as an impresario. As for conductors, this has been an Italian forte since Toscanini, whose first public performance at the age of 19 was *Aida*, conducted from memory after stepping in at short notice. Riccardo Muti now conducts at Milan's La Scala and runs the Ravenna music festival, close to his home. Muti's respected predecessor, Claudio Abbado, directs productions around the world, as well as in Ferrara. Conductors Daniele Gatti, Riccardo

THE WORLD'S MOST FAMOUS TENOR

Luciano Pavarotti has legendary status, singing with Carreras and Domingo as the "Three Tenors". He is as happy singing Neapolitan love duets as he is crooning with international rock stars, such as Sting, U2 and Tina Turner. The Maestro credits the longevity of his career to his late father who continued singing and recording while in his eighties and was responsible for entering Pavarotti into the Eisteddfod competition, which launched his meteoric rise to fame. More startlingly, Pavarotti attributes his singing technique to his wet-nurse, who breast-fed both him and the accomplished soprano Mirella Freni. He began singing for sweets aged five and his career was launched with the winning of a Welsh choral competition. A connection is often made between the bulkiness of "Big Lucy" and the best cuisine in Italy, boasted by his home region of Emilia-Romagna. Pavarotti remains close to his earthy roots and stages charity concerts in his native Modena. He settled his tax dispute with the authorities, paving the way for a return from tax exile in Monaco. It was suggested that the world's most famous tenor would retire in 2001 after 40 years performing, but he has recently said that he will continue until his 70th birthday in 2005 or, in his own words, "I'll sing while I have the voice."

Chailly and Giuseppe Sinopoli have also found fame abroad, notably at Amsterdam's Concertgebouw, London's Covent Garden and the Dresden opera house.

Conductors working abroad are probably relieved to escape their knowledgeable but critical audiences back home. Italian audiences are hard task-masters, with applause led by the official clapping societies that are present in the major houses. Yet if the opera falls short of perfection, the *loggionisti*, those in the gods, are ready to rain down abuse on fallen divas, with booing and hissing commonplace. Brave visitors who wish to show their appreciation can

lies the key to Italian opera. It is essentially sensual and lush, appealing more to the emotions than the intellect.

The bookends of Italian opera's golden age stand clear: on the one side, the 1815 production of Rossini's classic *opera buffa* (comic opera), *Il Barbiere di Siviglia*; and, on the other, the posthumous 1926 opening of Puccini's last and unfinished opus, *Turandot*. Between the two lies more than a century of operatic triumphs.

During the 19th century, when Giocchino Rossini, Gaetano Donizetti and Vincenzo Bellini dominated the scene, Italian opera

shout *"bravo"* for tenors, *"brava"* for sopranos and *"bravi"* for all. Ultimately, as long as the opera provides a spectacle, of people-watching or, perish the thought, of mellifluous music, then an Italian audience usually goes home happy, whether the fat lady sings or not.

Opera's golden age

Giacomo Puccini once said of himself, "I have more heart than mind". In these characteristics

LEFT: an animated 19th-century audience in San Carlo Opera House in Naples.
ABOVE: composer Vincenzo Bellini.
RIGHT: self-portrait by Gaetano Donizetti.

became infused with vitality, and Europe once again looked towards Italy for operatic innovation. All three composers, born within a decade of one another, shared much in style, and their careers followed similar paths and detours.

Rossini is probably most celebrated for his productions of *Il Barbiere di Siviglia* and *Guillaume Tell*, while Donizetti's masterpieces are *Lucia di Lammermoor* and *La Fille du Régiment*. Bellini is celebrated for his *semi seria* works, *La Sonnambula*, *Norma* and *I Puritani*. These operas are part of standard repertoires constantly performed throughout the world.

The three composers shared a small-town background, and all enjoyed great success at an early age, although Bellini was already 22 years old when he made his operatic debut. Each faced the voracious demands of impresarios and the finicky tastes of leading performers, and they all worked with remarkable speed, producing new works in the space of a few weeks. Not surprisingly, there was a fierce and jealous rivalry between them. Upon hearing that Rossini had composed *Il Barbiere di Siviglia* in 13 days, Donizetti shrugged proudly and concluded, "No wonder – he is so lazy."

They acquired gold and glory all over Europe, but, tragically, all three burnt themselves out. Bellini and Donizetti died young, the latter a

Giorno di Regno (1840), met with lacklustre receptions at La Scala premieres, rave notices for the epic *Nabucco* (1842) marked the beginning of a long and distinguished career. From then on, Verdi saw success after success, highlighted by *Rigoletto* (1851), *Il Trovatore* (1853), *La Traviata* (1853), *La Forza del Destino* (1862), *Don Carlo* (1867), *Aida* (1871) and *Otello* (1887). With premieres in London, Paris, St Petersburg and Cairo, along with those in the theatres of Italy, Verdi was a composer of true international stature.

It was a reputation well deserved. Verdi's sharp, almost brutal dynamism freed Italian

crazed syphilitic, and Rossini's last triumph was achieved before he reached 40. They were followed by the brightest light in Italian opera.

The brightest star

Giuseppe Verdi was born in 1813 (the same year as Richard Wagner) in Le Roncole, a small village 17 km (12 miles) from Parma. His father was a semi-literate peasant, and the family had no history of talent, musical or otherwise, but young Giuseppe made a mark as the local church organist. In 1832, he was denied admission to the prestigious Milan Conservatory. But the young Verdi was persistent, and, although his first two productions, *Oberto* (1839) and *Un*

opera from the lingering vestiges of empty conventions. Verdi also refused to tailor his works to the whims of individual singers, something that no composer had dared do in the past. His independence extended to his personal life. In a very conservative and religious society, he openly lived with his mistress, the soprano Giuseppina Strepponi, for more than a decade before taking her to the altar in 1859.

If Verdi was permitted artistic and personal freedom, he was still constrained by the political realities of his day. Censorship was a constant impediment in an Italy dominated by foreign powers. Verdi was himself an ardent nationalist. His historical works were charged with analogies of the Italians' plight – allusions that were not lost upon native audiences. A dear friend of Count Cavour, Verdi briefly served in the new chamber of deputies after unification. On his death in 1901, Verdi was mourned not only as a composer but also as a patriot.

The best-loved tunes

Although operas of fine quality continue to be composed today, the golden age of Italian opera drew to a close with the career of Giacomo Puccini, who was inspired by Verdi's *Aida* to become an operatic composer. Others contended for the mantle of Verdi, but Puccini had

the advantage of the blessing of the old man himself. "Now there are dynasties, also in art," lamented rival Alfredo Catalani, "and I know that Puccini 'has to be' the successor of Verdi … who, like a good king, often invites the 'crown prince' to dinner!" A dynasty it may have been, but one clearly based on merit. Puccini's success lay as much in his great gift for melody as in his unerring sense of theatre. *La Bohème* (1896), *Tosca* (1900) and *Madama Butterfly* (1904) are today among the best-loved works of opera. ❏

LEFT: curtain call at La Scala.

ABOVE: Giacomo Puccini, composer of *La Bohème*.

ITALY'S OPERA HOUSES

Beyond their gilt and stucco interiors, Italy's glittering opera houses *(teatri lirici)* are mostly neoclassical theatres rebuilt after numerous fires. Historically, the rivalry of noble courts gave birth to countless private opera houses, which gradually opened their doors to the public – the first was in Venice in 1637. The fashion for opera spread, and by the 18th century there were 20 in Venice alone. Most historic opera houses are in Lombardy and Emilia-Romagna, linked to great courts such as Cremona, Parma and Mantua.

Milan's La Scala is the premier opera house. All the great Italian composers have written for La Scala, notably Rossini, Donizetti, Bellini, Puccini and Verdi. It underwent a period of glory with performances of Verdi's patriotic works and spent the early 20th-century under Toscanini's direction. The historic building, a symphony of red, cream and gold, opened in 1778 with a performance of an opera by Antonio Salieri (who is best known today for being an adversary of Mozart). The theatre, which seats 2,000 and has a superb acoustic, celebrated the centenary of Verdi's birth in January 2001. A major restoration programme of the historic venue is currently underway.

San Carlo in Naples enjoys a reputation second only to La Scala. Rebuilt in 1816, it won a name as a "singer's theatre", where vocal gymnastics and artistic rivalry were pre-eminent. While there are major opera houses in Florence and Rome, La Fenice (the Phoenix) in Venice enjoys greater prestige, despite its tragic history. Venice's "Phoenix" lived to rue its name after fires in 1836 and 1996. Australian diva Joan Sutherland mourned the loss of "the most beautiful opera house in the world; singing in La Fenice felt like being inside a diamond". Now, risen from the ashes once more in December 2003, the red and gold rococo confection has been rebuilt exactly as before, although critics complain that it is too bright and brash. On the next rung down in terms of size, but not necessarily in scope, are Parma, Genoa, Bergamo, Modena and Turin.

Opera houses have been buffeted by strikes, budgetary cuts and even arson attacks: La Fenice's last fire, in which it was completely gutted, was a suspected Mafia attack, as was the burning down of Bari opera house. On a more positive note, Palermo's Teatro Massimo reopened recently after 25 years, during which it had opened its doors only once – ironically to allow the filming of *The Godfather*. In response to excessive bureaucracy and a funding crisis, the government has embarked on a privatisation programme, beginning with the magnificent La Scala.

ITALIAN CINEMA

*As windows of the nation's soul, Italian films showed
a vital resurgence, once freed from the fictions of Fascism*

Italian cinema has always flickered between epic spectacles and unabashedly intimate emotions. Before the outbreak of World War I, Italian directors had already filmed *The Romance of a Poor Young Man* and several versions of Bulwer-Lytton's monumental novel *The Last Days of Pompeii*.

When the Alberini-Santoni production company released *La Presa di Roma* in 1905 the Italian feature film was born. The subject is the 1870 rout of the pope by Garibaldi's troops. In its most famous scene, Bersaglieri rallies his forces to breach the wall at Rome's Porta Pia. Because so much of it was shot on location, the film anticipates two dominant currents in Italian film history: realism and historical spectacle.

However, Italian cinema skipped several steps in the development of international cinema. In Britain, the USA and France, early directors associated themselves with vaudeville and music halls and so motion pictures tended to be classed as "low entertainment". By contrast, Italy's first feature film-makers were the most learned and aristocratic in the world, creating what was dubbed "cerebral cinema". At a time when most other countries still saw film as an amusing novelty, Italy was using it to express the meaning of life.

Early extravaganzas

Early in the 20th century, two directors, Enrico Guazzoni and Piero Fosca, revolutionised Italian films. Both directors' historic and melodramatic tastes perfectly complemented Italy's burgeoning nationalism; and both thrived on glorifying the martial exploits of Ancient Rome.

But Guazzoni's significance derives as much from his commercial innovations as from his conceptual ones. *Quo Vadis?* (1913), which established his reputation, ran for two hours and used the world's first gargantuan sets. Guazzoni limited distribution to first-class theatres, and in New York *Quo Vadis?* received the first

personality-spangled premiere. His shrewd marketing enabled future producers to raise unprecedented financial backing. However, *Quo Vadis?* masks any complexity of character with busy sets and costumes; and escapist addiction to costume drama haunts Italian cinema to this day.

Piero Fosca's contribution was more aesthetic and more influential. His grand opus, *Cabiria* (1913), details the adventures of virtuous maidens, strong men, gruesome villains and romantic generals during the wars between Ancient Rome and Carthage. Fosca was one of the first to pan cameras across vast scenes, and introduced live orchestras at screenings. More importantly, *Cabiria* showed it was possible to include subtle characterisation within the epic form.

After the successes of *Quo Vadis?* and *Cabiria*, the world woke up to film's great potential. Industrialists saw many opportunities of making money. Also intrigued was the aristocracy, the source of many of Italy's

LEFT: Marcello Mastroianni, Italy's most sophisticated leading man. **RIGHT:** Maciste, an earlier heart-throb.

film-makers and patrons. (Luchino Visconti, first generation neo-realist, was the heir of an aristocratic Sicilian family; a Roman countess provided Roberto Rossellini with the money to begin filming *Roma, Città Aperta*.)

The support of the nobility is one explanation for the high production standards of early Italian cinema. While directors in France and the United States were still pinning up painted backdrops, Italians hired the nation's finest architects to design and construct full-scale sets. Furnishings in histor-

BIRTH OF AN EPIC

Hollywood drew great inspiration from Italy for its own epics. Fosca's *Cabiria* had a direct influence on D.W. Griffith's 1915 *Birth of a Nation*.

credibility were eligible for up to 60 percent state financing. Particularly patriotic endeavours, such as *Scipione l'Africano*, often received total backing from the government.

The final blow to creative competition was dealt by the new National Body for Importation of Foreign Films. It decided which films could be imported, then insisted they be dubbed into Italian. Unable to compete economically, Italy's better directors went into hibernation.

ical dramas were often borrowed from the personal collections of descendants of the depicted heroes; and if a film included aristocrats, authentic aristocrats were invited to make guest appearances.

This so-called Golden Age of Italian cinema hardly had time to blossom before the Fascists came to power. Mussolini instituted several organisations to regulate the film industry, so convinced was he of the power of the medium. The Direzione Generale per la Cinematografia became an official department of the Ministry of Popular Culture. In addition, the Banco del Lavoro helped provide finance for politically acceptable films. Directors who had ideological

Neo-realism

In 1944, while the Germans were still retreating from Rome, Roberto Rossellini, who had launched his career by filming for Mussolini a patriotic panegyric on dashing navy pilots, made *Roma, Città Aperta*, a film whose unflinching confrontation with truth unnerves audiences to this day. The film follows the lives of several Resistance workers. Every scene, except those set in the Gestapo headquarters, was shot on location. *Roma, Città Aperta* has a rough visceral throb that was revolutionary for the time. Some sequences seem to be documentary footage: the camera jerks and twists and shots break off suddenly.

Despite the unprecedented, relentless immediacy, *Roma, Città Aperta* has a complex symbolic structure. The film elevates drug addicts, priests, German lesbians and Austrian deserters to levels of wider symbolic import without sacrificing their unique personalities. Pina (Anna Magnani), for example, an agonised mother leading a mob of matriarchs to plunder exploitative bakeries in the neighbourhood, is utterly convincing, yet she also symbolises the desperate plight of Italian housewives during the war.

Federico Fellini, who helped Rossellini write the script for *Roma, Città Aperta*, summarised the atmosphere following World War II that pro-

remarkable homogeneity Italy achieved just after World War II, with the widespread conviction that Fascism was wrong. Neo-realist directors spoke from and for an Italy which could confess, if not to chaos, at least to contradictions.

Resurgence

During the 1960s and early 1970s, economic prosperity triggered a resurgence of Italian film, dominated by Federico Fellini, Michelangelo Antonioni and Francesco Rosi – though this was also the period of Luchino Visconti's *The Damned*, Bernardo Bertolucci's *The Conformist* and Paolo Pasolini's *The Decameron*. Rosi was

duced neo-realism: "We discovered our own country … we could look freely around us now, and the reality appeared so extraordinary that we couldn't resist watching it and photographing it with astonished and virgin eyes."

For the next few years, Rossellini, along with Visconti, Vittorio de Sica and Alberto Lattuada, developed a cinema characterised by rapid, seemingly spontaneous juxtaposition. Neo-realism remains the core of what is considered modern in film. The movement arose from the

born in Naples, and southern Italy is a dominant theme in his films. Antonioni's exploration of existential themes and individual crises reached a climax with *Blow Up* (1967). The tireless Fellini, arguably the greatest Italian director, produced a string of classics.

In many ways, Fellini can be viewed as the triumphant culmination of neo-realist philosophy. His characters are torn between the desire to realise their true selves and the urge to conform. His heroes swing wildly between the need to be like no one and the need to be like everyone.

Fellini said that his films were a "marriage of innocence and experience", but they were also about fantasy and loss, tinged with irony, fun

LEFT: Anna Magnani in the neo-realist classic, Rossellini's *Roma, Città Aperta* (Rome, Open City).
ABOVE: Federico Fellini on the set.

ITALY IN THE MOVIES

Rome, Tuscany, Sicily and Venice provide the main backdrops to the cinematic illusion of Italy. Such is the power of the movie myth that Sicilian Mafia murders and Tuscan costume dramas are equally convincing. Fellini, who had a virtual monopoly on Roman sensibility, loved to satirise his fellow-citizens on film: "The Roman is like a grotesque, overgrown child who has the satisfaction of being continually spanked by the Pope." In *La Dolce Vita* (1959) and *Roma* (1972), he held a distorting mirror to Roman reality. Of foreign directors, Peter Greenaway's *Belly of an Architect* (1987) arguably best captures the elusive character of the Eternal City.

Tuscany is a favoured location for foreign films, with the Merchant-Ivory *Room with a View* (1985) both a classic and a cliché, shot in villas in Florence and Fiesole. More quirky are Jane Campion's *Portrait of a Lady* (1996), shot near Lucca, and Tarkovsky's *Nostalgia* (1983), shot in Bagno Vignone, fabulously moody Roman baths south of Siena. Although best-known for *The Last Emperor* (1987), Bertolucci returned to Tuscany to shoot *Stealing Beauty* (1996), a Chiantishire tale, set in a rustic villa and idyllic wine estates. Anthony Minghella's *The English Patient* (1996) and *The Talented Mr Ripley* (1999) were lovingly shot in Tuscany, Rome and Ischia.

Sicily has long drawn directors of the highest calibre, with Rossellini's *Stromboli* (1950) set on a volcanic island, and Visconti's hymn to faded grandeur and Sicilian decadence, *The Leopard* (1968). Coppola's gross yet engrossing *Godfather* trilogy was partly shot in Sicily.

Venice provides an ideal location for moody "art house" films. Stanley Kubrick's film, *Eyes Wide Shut* (2000), features numerous dramatic Venetian scenes, including a masked ball. As for Italian directors, Antonioni's masterpiece, *Identification of a Woman* (1982), shows Venice as a magical yet murky world. In a similar but more ominous vein, *Don't Look Now* (1973) by Nicolas Roeg brings Donald Sutherland and Julie Christie to a eerily deserted Venice shortly after the death of their child. David Lean's *Summertime* (1955) casts Katharine Hepburn as an American abroad who both falls in love and falls into a canal. However, the undisputed Venetian masterpiece is Visconti's *Death in Venice* (1970), based on Thomas Mann's classic novella. Visconti wanted "the light of the *sirocco*, the pale, still pearl light" and, with his artistic decision to use dawn and night shoots, forced his stars into sleeplessness.

and sadness. In *Amarcord* (1975), Fellini's surreal flights of fancy turned Rimini, his home town, into a virtual-reality world. It was sweet revenge on the "inert, provincial, opaque, dull" Adriatic seaside resort he left for Roman chic. In his 1954 masterpiece *La Strada*, he claimed to have based the central character on the lost innocence of his actress wife, Giulietta Masina, who also starred in the film. *La Dolce Vita* (1960) was the first time Fellini worked with his male muse, Marcello Mastroianni, who was chosen for his candour, innocence and "normal face, a face with no personality". The filmic frolicking in Rome's Trevi Fountain turned

Anita Ekberg into an international sex symbol.

In 1967, with *A Fistful of Dollars* and *The Good, the Bad and the Ugly*, Sergio Leone presented world cinema with a new genre: the spaghetti western. These witty and stylised films, which were made on surprisingly low budgets, became the Italian movie industry's most successful exports since Sophia Loren, Gina Lollobrigida and Claudia Cardinale.

Recent trends

In the 1980s the generation of angry young Marxists and Sixties radicals gave way to commercial producers eager to create pale imitations of Hollywood action pictures. Bernardo

Bertolucci is an exception in being free to command Hollywood budgets for international blockbusters or to concentrate on more low-key work. Competition from the highly commercial Italian television networks has had a detrimental effect on feature films, as has the partial demise of Cinecittà, the Roman film studios and former hothouse for young Italian directors. Since privatisation in 1996, the studios have focused on television and advertising, rather than on feature films.

Italy is still suffering from the loss of Fellini in 1993 and of the well-loved actor Marcello Mastroianni in 1996. However, there are some rea-

of a Lady has scenes filmed in the villas of the Lucchesia. In 1997, Roberto Benigni's Oscar winning film La Vita è Bella, in which he acted and was the producer, is set initially around Arezzo and Petrarch. The 1999 version of A Midsummer Night's Dream, starring Michelle Pfeiffer and Rupert Everett, was largely filmed in Montepulciano. Franco Zeffirelli's Tea with Mussolini was filmed in Tuscany, based on Zeffirelli's childhood before and during World War II. Scenes from Ridley Scott's Gladiator (2000) were filmed in Val d'Orcia as well as Rome and, most recently, Under the Tuscan Sun written by Frances Mayes, is centred around Cortona. ❑

sons for hope. Nanni Moretti is a witty maverick attempting to reinvigorate the Roman cinematic scene. He has established a new cinema for less mainstream films in Trastevere. The Son's Room was awarded the Palme d'Or in Cannes in 2001.

Tuscany has always had star quality on the film circuit. As well as Bernardo Bertolucci's Stealing Beauty (1996), in the same year, Anthony Minghella's The English Patient includes scenes set in Pienza and the monastery of Sant'Anna in Camprena. Also, the Portrait

---

LEFT: a young cinema-lover in Cinema Paradiso.
ABOVE: Massimo Troisi, who died during the filming of Il Postino.

"BEAUTY IS IN MY DNA"

All Italian film directors are influenced by their environments to an extraordinary degree. Asked why his films always looked so lush, Bernardo Bertolucci pointed to his upbringing in Parma: "Growing up in such a beautiful city is a kind of dolce condanna, a sweet prison sentence. Look at our local painter, Parmigiano, he was the most decorative of all the Mannerists, the least tortured. I think beauty is in my DNA." Federico Fellini may still be regarded as Italy's greatest director, but Bertolucci remains the more incorrigible romantic, an idealist with considerable power and artistry.

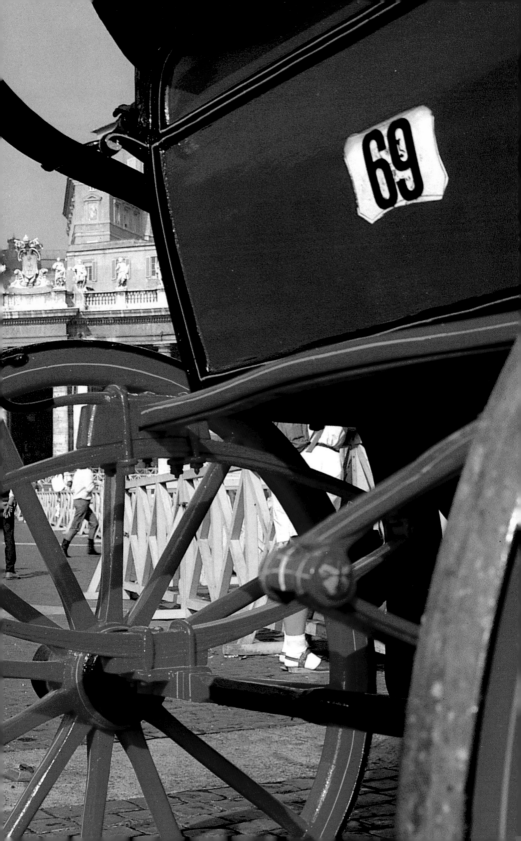

PLACES

*A detailed guide to the entire country, with principal sights
cross-referenced by number to the maps*

Negotiating the tangle of one-way streets in an Italian city takes years of experience. Often a helpful native will point the way, even take you personally to your hotel, restaurant or museum. But if no one materialises, don't panic, simply follow the tourist signs for Centro Storico (historic centre) and Duomo (cathedral), and remember that *senso unico* means "one way". Then find the first *parcheggio* (car park) and abandon your car, for most Italian cities are best explored on foot. If you arrive by train, the station will invariably be in the seedier part of town, so leave it behind for the greener pastures of the Centro Storico.

Modern life has stamped even small villages with a bar and a large population of moped-riding youths. Every town has its Duomo, but how different is the austere Romanesque cathedral of Apulia from the lavish baroque of the one in Turin. Every town has at least one piazza: in the south they are crowded with men smoking and playing cards; in the north, the men are still there, but so are the women and the tourists.

Our favourite places in Italy include many spots less frequented than the tried and true trio of Rome, Florence and Venice. We suggest that, after visiting Rome, you take an excursion east into Abruzzo or Molise, those hitherto remote regions whose architecture, parks, mountains and beaches rank among the most refreshing vacation spots in the country. Or, if you happen to be exploring the Bay of Naples, rent a car and continue down to Italy's heel and toe – Apulia, Basilicata, Calabria – even taking the ferry across to Sicily.

The north has Florence and Venice, of course, but also Milan and Turin, two very modern cities packed with art and history. You could follow the path of generations of travellers who, with Dante and Ariosto in hand, toured the cities of Lombardy, the Veneto, Emilia-Romagna and Tuscany. If you want to catch your breath and relax, retreat into the green hills of Umbria, home of Italy's beloved St Francis of Assisi. ❏

PRECEDING PAGES: Limone, on Lake Garda; St Peter's, Rome; Tricárico, in Basilicata.
LEFT: Castel Tirolo, in the Alto Adige.

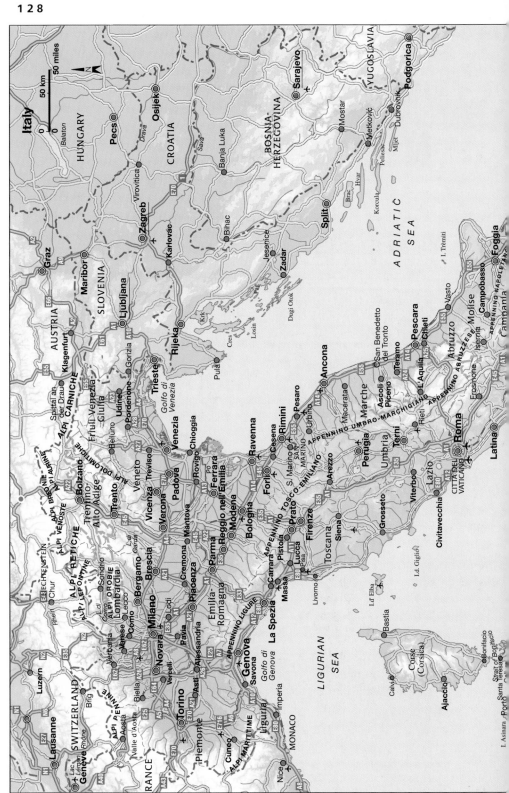

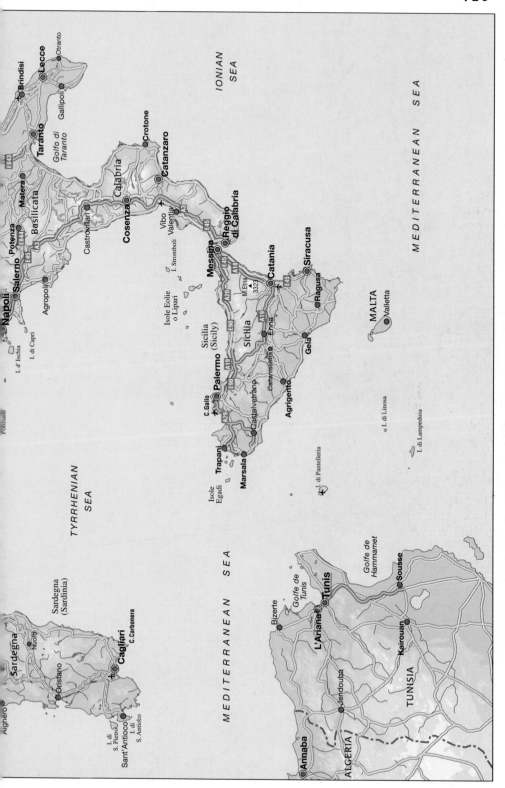

ROME

*Follow in the footsteps of emperors and saints,
discovering the monuments and churches that mark Rome
as the capital of Italy and the ancient world*

Map on
pages
132–3

Lord Byron gave **Rome** (Roma) the epithet "City of the Soul." Poetic hyperbole perhaps, but the description still strikes a chord among visitors to the city. As a result of Jubilee Year (or Holy Year) Rome is now resplendent, the 2,000th anniversary of the birth of Christ having been celebrated in unique style with the refurbishment of over 700 temples, churches, galleries and archaeological sites. Rome can now face the next 2,000 years with an equanimity bordering on smugness.

The Palatine Hill

The best introduction to Rome is not Piazza Venezia, the terrifying roundabout at the centre of the modern city, but the more pastoral **Palatino ❶** (Palatine Hill; daily 8.30am–7.15pm in summer, till 4.30pm in winter; last entry one hour before closing; entrance fee – ticket also valid for the Colosseum), believed by the ancients to be the home of Rome's mythical founder, Romulus. Its claim to be the site of the original settlement is supported by the remains of early Iron Age dwellings in the southwestern corner of the hill. Close by are the remains of the **Tempio di Cibele**, picturesquely planted with an ilex grove. The cult of the Eastern goddess of fertility, also known as Magna Mater, was introduced to Italy during the Second Punic War (218–201BC). Though its mystical rites – involving throngs of frenzied female worshippers, priests committing self-mutilation, and bull sacrifices – were distasteful to old-fashioned Romans, the cult spread widely during the imperial era.

The name Palatine (derived from Pales, goddess of shepherds) is the root of the word palace. In Roman times the Palatine Hill was celebrated for the splendour of its princely dwellings. Earliest, and simplest, of these was the Domus Augustana. A portion of it, known as the **Casa di Livia** (Livia was Augustus's wife), is renowned for its superb wall paintings and floor mosaics.

To the north, alongside the Palazzo di Tiberio (now mostly covered by the Farnese Gardens) runs the **Criptoporticus**, a cool underground passage with a delicately stuccoed vault, built by Nero to connect the palaces of Augustus, Tiberius and Caligula to his own sumptuous Golden House on the Esquiline Hill. To the southeast of this passage extend the remains of the **Domus Flavia**, built at the end of the 1st century AD by the Emperor Domitian. An infamous sadist, who took pleasure in torturing everything from flies to senators, Domitian suffered from an obsessive fear of assassination. According to the ancient historian Suetonius, author of *Lives of the Caesars*, an entertaining if not entirely trustworthy source, the emperor covered the walls of the peristyle (the section with an octagonal maze) with reflective moonstone so that no assassin

LEFT: Piazza della Repubblica. **BELOW:** an umbrella pine shades the ruins of the Palatine Hill.

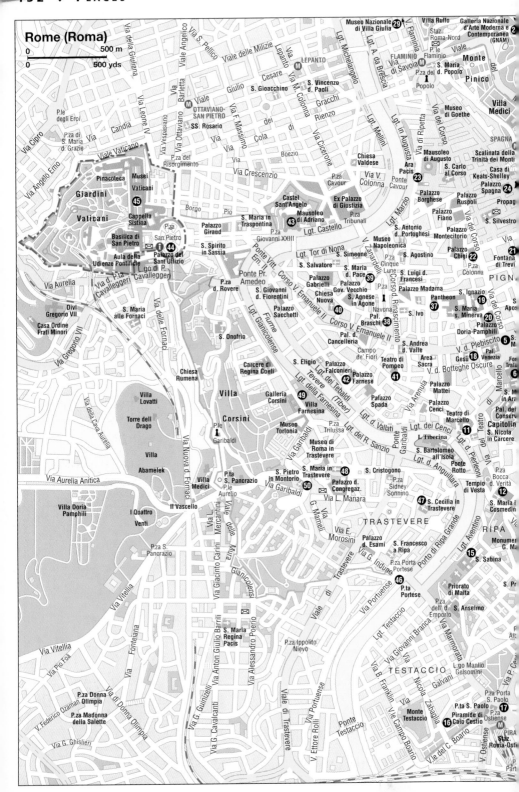

Rome (Roma)

0 ————— 500 m

0 ————— 500 yds

Museo Nazionale di Villa Giulia **29**
Villa Ruffo
Galleria Nazionale d'Arte Moderna e Contemporanea (GNAM) **2**

V. Flaminia
FLAMINIO
Staz. Roma-Nord
P.le Flaminio
Via di Savoia
Monte Pincio
Villa Medici

LEPANTO

Viale delle Milizie
Via Lepanto
Via M. Colonna
P.za del d. Popolo
S. Maria d. Popolo

Via della Giuliana
Via S. Pellico
Viale Angelico
Via Michelangelo
Lgt. A. da Brescia

Cesare
S. Gioacchino
S. Vincenzo d. Paoli
Gracchi
Via F. Massimo
Via Cicerone
Lgt. Mellini
Lgt. in Augusta
Via di Ripetta
Via del Corso
Museo di Goethe

Via Barletta
Giulio
OTTAVIANO-SAN PIETRO
SS. Rosario
dei
Rienzo
Boezio
SPAGNA

Viale
Via Ottaviano
Via Vespasiano
P.za del Risorgimento
Via
Cola
di
Via Crescenzio
P.za Cavour
Via V. Colonna
Ponte Cavour
Ara Pacis **23**
S. Carlo al Corso
Casa di Keats-Shelley
Scalinata della Trinità dei Monti

P.le degli Eroi
Via Leone IV
Candia
Viale Vaticano
Chiesa Valdese
Palazzo Borghese
Palazzo Ruspoli
Palazzo Spagna **24**
Propag

Via Cipro
P.za di S. Maria d. Grazie
Via
Via Angelo Emo
Pinacoteca
Musei Vaticani
Castel Sant'Angelo
Mausoleo di Adriano **43**
Ex Palazzo di Giustizia
P.za Tribunali
Lgt. Marzio
Palazzo Fiano
Palazzo Montecitorio
S. Silvestro

Giardini
Vaticani **45**
Borgo
Pio
S. Maria in Traspontina
Lgt. Castello
Museo Napoleonica
S. Antonio d. Portoghesi
Palazzo Chigi **22**
Fontana di Trevi **21**

Cappella Sistina
Palazzo Giraud
S. Spirito in Sassia
Ponte Vitt. Em. II
Giovanni XXIII
S. Salvatore
S. Simeone
S. Agostino
S. Luigi d. Francesi
Palazzo Madama
S. Agostino
PIGN

Basilica di San Pietro
San Pietro **44**
Aula della Udienze Pontificie
Palazzo del Sant'Ufizio
Lgo di P.
Ponte Pr. Amedeo
P.za d. Rovere
S. Giovanni d. Fiorentini
Palazzo Gabrielli
Chiesa Nuova
S. Maria in Pace **39**
Cinque Lune
Corso Rinascimento
Pantheon **37**
S. Ignazio **19**
Via del Corso

Divi Gregorio VII
S. Maria alle Fornaci
Via d. P.ta Cavalleggeri
Palazzo Gov. Vecchio
S. Agnese in Agone
Navona **40**
S. Ivo
S. Maria s. Minerva **20**
S. Apos

Casa Ordine Frati Minori
Via delle Fornaci
S. Onofrio
Palazzo Sacchetti
Pal. Braschi **38**
Palazzo Doria-Pamphili
V. d. Plebiscito **5**

Chiesa Rumena
Carcere di Regina Coeli
Lgt. Gianicolense
Pal. d. Cancelleria
Campo de' Fiori
S. Andrea d. Valle
Gesù **18**
Pal. Venezia **6**

Villa Lovatti
S. Eligio
Palazzo Falconieri
Palazzo Farnese **42**
Teatro di Pompeo
Area Sacra
V. d. Botteghe Oscure
Marcello

Torre dell' Drago
Villa
Corsini
Galleria Corsini
Villa Farnesina
Lgt. della Farnesina
Lgt. de' Tebaldi
Pafazzo Spada
Palazzo Cenci
Palazzo Mattei
Pal. dei Conserv
Capitolin
S. Nicola in Carcere

Villa Abamelek
P.le Garibaldi
Museo Tortonia
Museo di Roma in Trastevere
P.za Trilussa
Via Garibaldi
L. Tiberina
Lgt. dei Cenci
S. Bartolomeo all'Isola
Teatro di Marcello **11**

Via Aurelia Anitica
Villa Medici
P.ta S. Pancrazio
P.le Aurelio
S. Pietro in Montorio **48**
S. Maria in Trastevere
S. Cristogono
Ponte Rotto
P.za Bocca d. Verità
Tempio di Vesta **12**

Villa Doria Pamphili
I Quattro Venti
Il Vascello
Via Garibaldi
Palazzo d. Congregaz.
Via L. Manara
P.za Sidney Sonnino
S. Cecilia in Trastevere **47**
S. Maria i Cosmedin

P.za S. Pancrazio
Via Mameli
TRASTEVERE
Via E. Morosini
Palazzo d. Esami
S. Francesco a Ripa
Porto di Ripa Grande
RIPA
Monumer G. Ma

Villa Vitella
S. Maria Regina Pacis
Via G. Indune
P.za Porta Portese
S. Sabina **15**

Via Vitellia
S. Maria Regina Pacis
P.za Ippolito Nievo
P.ta Portese **46**
Priorato di Malta
S. Pr

Via Pio Foà
Via di Trastevere
P.za dell d. Emporio
S. Anselmo
S. Alt

P.za Donna Olimpia
P.za Madonna della Salette
Ponte Testaccio
TESTACCIO
L.go Manlio Gelsomini
Via P.

V. Federico Ozanam
Via di Donna Olimpia
Via G. Ghislieri
Monte Testaccio
Piramide di Caio Cestio **16**
P.ta S. Paolo **17**
Staz. Roma-Osti
PIRA
Part

Letters in stone in the Forum.

could creep up on him unobserved. Next to the peristyle lie the remains of a splendid banqueting hall, hailed by contemporaries as "the dining room of Jove."

Following the fortunes of the city as a whole, the imperial palaces fell into disuse during the Middle Ages. Monks made their home among the ruins and the powerful Frangipani family built a fortress here. During the Renaissance, when there was a surge of new building throughout the city, Cardinal Alessandro Farnese bought a large part of the Palatine and in 1625 laid out the world's first botanical gardens on the slope overlooking the Forum. The lush **Orti Farnesiani** are delightful, with their formal landscaping, the sounds of fountains and birds, and good views over Rome.

For lovers of the picturesque, the ruins of the Palatine are hard to beat. Even archaeological excavations cannot deprive this location of its wild charm. It is the last place in Rome where you can find a landscape as it might have been drawn by Piranesi or Claude Lorraine. Roses, moss and poppies growing amid the crumbling bricks and shattered marble give it a romantic rather than an imperial splendour. It is the perfect place in which to wander, sketch or picnic.

The Roman Forum

The Clivus Palatinus leads from the domestic extravagances of the emperors down into the **Foro Romano** ❷ (The Roman Forum; daily 8.30am–1 hr before sunset; free), the civic centre of Ancient Rome. This area, once a swamp used as a burial ground by the original inhabitants of the surrounding hills, was drained by an Etruscan king in the 6th century BC. Until excavations began in the 19th century, the Forum – buried under 8 metres (25 ft) of debris – was known as the "Campo Vaccino" (Cow Field) because smallholders tended their herds among

the ruins. Today it reveals a stupendous array of ruined temples, public buildings, arches and shops.

At the bottom of the Clivus Palatinus, the **Arco di Tito** (Arch of Titus) commemorates that emperor's destruction of Jerusalem and its sacred temple in AD 70. This event marked the beginning of the Diaspora and the shift from the Temple in Jerusalem to local synagogues as the focus of Jewish worship. Until Israel was founded in 1948 and the return to Palestine became possible, pious Jews refused to walk under this arch.

The Via Sacra leads past the three remaining arches of the **Basilica di Costantino**, a source of inspiration for Renaissance architects. Bramante said of his design for St Peter's: "I shall place the Pantheon on top of the Basilica of Constantine." The **Tempio di Antonino e Faustina**, also known as San Lorenzo in Miranda, is a superb example of Rome's architectural layering. Originally a temple erected in AD 141 by the Emperor Antoninus Pius, it was converted into a church in the Middle Ages. During the 17th century a baroque facade was added, as was the case with so many Roman churches.

Across the Via Sacra is the lovely, round **Tempio di Vesta** (Vesta was the goddess of the hearth), where the six vestal virgins took turns tending the sacred fire. The punishment for allowing the fire to die down was a whipping by the priest. Service was for 30 years and chastity was the rule. Few patricians were eager to offer their daughters and the Emperor Augustus had to pick girls by lot. Laxity about vows was common and the Emperor Domitian resorted to the traditional punishment of burying errant virgins alive and stoning their lovers to death. Living in the lovely **Casa delle Vestali** was some compensation for this demanding life. The ruins remain a rose-scented haven.

The Vestals had seats of honour in the circus and theatre, and, in the city, where wheeled vehicles were forbidden, they alone had the right to travel in a carriage.

BELOW: Arch of Titus.

Like modern North Americans, the Ancient Romans were keen litigants. Walk past the three elegant columns of the Temple of Castor and Pollux to the **Basilica Julia** (on the left of the Via Sacra), where trials were held, as many as four at a time. The acoustics were terrible and on one occasion the booming speech of a particularly loud lawyer was applauded by audiences in all four chambers. In cases where an advocate wanted a little extra help, professional applauders, called "supper praisers", could be hired. When not employed, these claqueurs would loiter on the steps of the basilica and play games. Their roughly carved boards can still be seen. The Senate met across the way in the Curia, the best-preserved building in the Forum. Its sombre, solid appearance fits the seriousness of its purpose.

At the western end of the Forum rises the famed **Rostra**, where the orator Cicero declaimed to the Roman masses. After his death, during Octavian's anti-Republican proscriptions, Cicero's hands and head were displayed here. Opposite the Rostra is the single **Colonna di Foca** (Column of Phocas). For centuries the symbol of the Forum, it was described by Byron as the "eloquent and name-less column with the buried base". Unburied and named, it is still, as the Italians say, *suggestivo* (atmospheric). To the right is **Arco di Settimio Severo**.

At the end of the Via Sacra, in the shadow of the Capitoline Hill, rise the eight Ionic columns of the **Tempio di Saturno**. The god's festival, called the Saturnalia, marked the merriest occasion in the Roman calendar, when gifts were exchanged and distinctions between master and slave forgotten. Occurring in the middle of winter, this was the feast that Christians later transformed into Christmas. Behind the temple are, from left to right, the Temple of Vespasian and Titus, and the Temple of the Concordia.

TIP

Taking a picnic into the Forum or Palatine is not officially allowed. But if you are discreet and tidy, there should be no problem.

BELOW: the Victor Emmanuel Monument.

Outside the Forum excavations, across from Pietro da Cortona's Chiesa di Santi Luca e Martina, is the **Carcere Mamertino ❸** (Mamertine Prison; daily 9am–7pm, till 5pm in winter; donation), home of some of Rome's most famous prisoners. According to legend, this dank, gloomy dungeon was where St Peter converted his pagan guards. Miraculously, a fountain sprang up so that he could baptise the new Christians.

The Capitoline Hill

From the **Capitolino ❹** (the Capitoline Hill) the Temple of Jupiter Capitolinus (509 BC) watched over the city. It was also here that modern Italians raised their tribute to Italy's unification. The **Vittoriano** (Victor Emmanuel Monument; daily 9.30am–5.30pm, till 4.30pm in winter; free), completed in 1911 and dedicated to Italy's first king, captures the neoclassical bad taste of the 19th century. The monument is famously despised by locals who call it the "typewriter", "wedding cake" or "false teeth". Beneath the Vittoriano, the **Museo del Risorgimento** (daily 9.30am–6pm; free) contains items relating to the revolution that led to the creation of modern Italy in 1870.

Throughout Rome's history hopes for Italy's future have centred on this hill. In 1300, the poet Petrarch was crowned laureate here; in 1347 Cola di Rienzo roused the Roman populace to support his shortlived attempt to revive the Roman Republic; in the 16th century Michelangelo planned the elegant Campidoglio, thus restoring the Capitoline's status as the architectural focal point of the city.

If you're feeling energetic, climb the 124 steps to the 7th-century **Santa Maria in Aracoeli** (if you happen to be here at Christmas, come for the Midnight Mass). The weak-kneed will probably prefer Michelangelo's regal staircase

Map on pages 132–3

Vercingetorix, leader of the Gauls, was executed in the Mamertine Prison after Julius Caesar defeated his forces in 52 BC.

MAMERTINUM
LA PRIGIONE DEI SS APOSTOLI
PIETRO e PAOLO
IL PIU ANTICO CARCERE DI ROMA
XXV SECOLI DI STORIA

BELOW: the *Dying Gaul* in the Museo Capitolino.

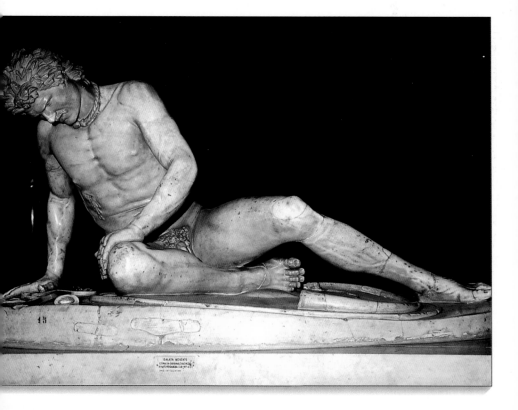

Wine, fish, spices, flowers, shoes, silk – anything could be bought at Trajan's Market.

BELOW: Trajan's Column, celebrating his victories in Romania early in the 2nd century AD.

(known as the **cordonata**), flanked at the top by monumental statues of Castor and Pollux. In the back of the Campidoglio Palazzo Senatorio surmounts the ancient Tabularium, dating from Republican times. On the right of Palazzo Senatorio rises **Palazzo dei Conservatori**; on the left, the **Palazzo Nuovo**. Together they make up the **Capitoline Museums** (Tues–Sun 9am–8pm; entry into the museums is via the Palazzo dei Conservatori; entrance fee), an imposing collection of ancient art and Roman statuary. For an insight into the Ancient Roman character, study the busts of emperors in the Sala degli Imperatori in the Palazzo Nuovo.

Mussolini's legacy

Piazza Venezia ❺, at the foot of the Vittoriano monument, marks the centre of contemporary Rome. You may feel you risk your life by crossing its wide expanse but usually the torrents of traffic will part to allow a pedestrian passage. The Palazzo di Venezia, Rome's first great Renaissance palace (built in 1455), dominates one side. This was Mussolini's headquarters from 1929. Some of his most famous speeches were delivered from the balcony. The light burning in his bedroom at all hours of the night reassured the Italians that the "sleepless one" was busy solving the nation's problems (though according to Luigi Barzini the light was often left on when Mussolini was not there). Now the palace contains the **Museo di Palazzo Venezia** (Tues–Sun 8.30am–7.30pm, last entry one hour before closing; entrance fee) with a collection of paintings, sculptures and tapestries.

"Ten years from now, comrades, no one will recognise Italy", proclaimed *Il Duce* in 1926. One of the most dramatic changes the Fascists wrought on Rome was the Via dei Fori Imperiali. Mussolini cut down old neighbourhoods (reminders of Rome's decadent period) in order to excavate the *fora* and build the road. By such brutal means he hoped to create a symbolic connection between Rome's glorious past and his own regime.

West of the Imperial Fora is **Foro Traiano ❻** (Trajan's Forum), dominated by its famous column. Behind are the splendidly preserved **Mercati di Traiano** (Trajan's Markets; Tues–Sun 9am–7pm, till 6pm in winter; entrance fee), a haunt of Rome's ubiquitous *gatti* (cats). In ancient times the five storeys of the market were abundantly stocked with exotic fare. The top floor contained two fishponds while the other held sea water brought from Ostia. The venue is currently closed for restoration, but Trajan's Forum and the so-called great hemicycle building that forms part of the markets can be seen at a reduced price.

Augustus and Nerva both built their *fora* to accommodate Rome's growing population and passion for litigation. Statues of them stand opposite their *fora*.

Finally, at the end of all this ruined splendour rises the **Colosseo ❼** (Colosseum; daily 9am–1 hr before sunset; entrance fee – ticket also valid for the Palatine), stripped of its picturesque wildflowers and weeds, surrounded by buses and snack stands, encircled by a swirling moat of traffic. This symbol of the Eternal City is less splendid than it was in its marble-clad, imperial days; but after its restoration in 2001, it remains one of the key sights of Rome.

The Colosseum was built in AD 79 when the Emperor Vespasian drained the lake of Nero's **Domus Aurea** ❽ (Golden House; Wed–Mon 9am–7.45pm, closed Tues; advance booking advisable, tel: 06-399 67700 or visit www.pierreci.it). The message was clear: where Nero had been profligate, emptying the coffers of the empire to construct his own pleasure palace, the Flavian prince built a public monument. Also nearby is the **Arco di Costantino** (Arch of Constantine).

Architectural layer cake

From the Colosseum, Via di San Giovanni in Laterano brings you to **San Clemente** ❾, one of Rome's most interesting churches. There are three levels of building. A 12th-century basilica descends to a 4th-century basilica, which in turn leads to a 1st-century Roman apartment building containing, in its courtyard, a Mithraic temple honouring one of the popular cults of imperial Rome.

A little further along, Via di San Giovanni opens up into **Piazza di San Giovanni in Laterano** ❿, containing some of the most important buildings in Christendom. The **Obelisk** is the tallest and oldest in Rome and a suitable marker for the Church of Rome, **San Giovanni in Laterano**, (daily 7am–7pm; free) founded by Constantine the Great. Not surprisingly, such an important church is a hotch-potch of building styles, from the exquisite 4th-century baptistry to the peaceful medieval cloister and the majestic baroque interior. The **Palazzo Laterano** was the home of the popes until the Avignon exile in 1309. The pious may want to ascend the 28 steps of the nearby **Scala Santa** (on their knees of course – daily 6.30am–noon and 4–6.30pm, 3–6pm in winter), said to be the steps Christ walked down after being condemned by Pontius Pilate. Constantine's mother, St Helena, retrieved them from Jerusalem.

Map on pages 132–3

TIP

North of the Colosseum lies the traditional *rione* (neighbourhood) of Monti. In parts, particularly in the hilly, leafy streets between Via Panisperna and Via Cavour, it has retained interesting traces of its medieval past, as well as an intimate village atmosphere.

BELOW: the Colosseum

La Bocca della Verità – the Mouth of Truth.

The ghetto

Rome's old ghetto lies on the western side of the Capitoline Hill, near the ruins of the **Teatro di Marcello** . The city has had a substantial Jewish community since the Republican era, but its isolation dates from the Counter-Reformation and the papacy of Paul IV (1555–59). From then on, the gates to the ghetto were locked from sunset to sunrise, Jewish men had to wear a yellow hat, the women a yellow scarf, and most professions were closed to Jews. "The iron of persecution and insult is every day driven into their souls," wrote one outraged 19th-century American. At that time the Jews were forced several times a year to listen to a tirade from a Dominican friar in the nearby church of Sant'Angelo in Pescheria.

Wandering through the narrow streets or visiting the synagogue on the Tiber, one gets little sense of those years of confinement. A plaque on Via Portico d'Ottavia, however, is a reminder that just over 60 years ago more than 2,000 Roman Jews were deported to a Nazi concentration camp.

The Via del Teatro di Marcello leads south to **Piazza Bocca della Verità**, which yokes together two Roman temples (the Tempio di Portuno and the round Tempio d'Ercole), a baroque fountain and the medieval church of Santa Maria in Cosmedin. In the portico of this church, which uses the Byzantine rites, is the **Bocca della Verit** (daily 9am–6pm, till 5pm in winter), a marble slab resembling a human face and considered to be one of the world's oldest lie detectors. If a perjurer puts his hand in the mouth, so the legend goes, it will be bitten off. In fact, the slab's origin is sadly prosaic: it once covered a drain.

BELOW:
Circus Maximus.

The oldest and largest of the famed Roman circuses, the **Circo Massimo** (Circus Maximus) lies in the valley between the Aventine and the Palatine Hills.

It once seated 250,000 people. In addition to the main event, vendors, fortune tellers and prostitutes plied their trades beneath the arcades.

If the circus has earned the Ancient Romans a bad reputation, their public baths have inspired great praise. In addition to the three pools (hot, warm and cold), the **Terme di Caracalla** ⓴ (Mon 9am–2pm, Tues–Sun 9am–1 hr before sunset; entrance fee) offered exercise rooms, libraries and lecture halls, for the improvement of mind and body. But less salubrious activities also went on here, especially when mixed bathing was permitted. Some took their cleanliness to an extreme: Emperor Commodus is said to have taken eight baths a day. But, for the most part, the baths represent a triumph of the Roman public spirit, demonstrating that cleanliness was not limited to those rich enough to have private facilities; they could accommodate up to 1,600 people. These days they are beautifully lit after dark.

The Aventine and Testaccio

For a contrast to the dusty and barren remnants of the circus and baths, visit the Aventine, one of modern Rome's most desirable residential neighbourhoods. As you climb the Clivo dei Pubblici the smell of roses wafts down from the pretty garden at the top of the hill. Via S. Sabina leads to **Santa Sabina** ⓯, a perfectly preserved basilican church of the 5th century. Inside, shafts of golden sunlight illuminate the immense antique columns of the nave. Outside, in the portico, are some of the oldest wooden doors in existence (5th century).

Bordered by Via Marmorata to the east is **Testaccio**, a genuine Roman working-class district with a real neighbourhood feel and now the "hip and happening" place for nightlife. There is an excellent produce market on Piazza Testaccio and a few trendy boutiques among the old-fashioned grocery stores.

Map on pages 132–3

The 2,000-year old Piramide Cestio

BELOW: Testaccio Market.

South of Testaccio, in the shadow of the Piramide Cestio, lies the **Cimitero Acattolico** ⓰ (Protestant Cemetery; Tues–Sun 9am–4.30pm in summer, 9am–4.30pm in winter; donation), one of the most picturesque spots in Rome. Scores of unfortunate travellers who fell fatally ill on a Grand Tour are buried here. In the old part of the graveyard is Keats's tomb. Its epitaph reads: "Here lies one whose name was writ in water." In accordance with the poet's wishes, the tombstone does not mention Keats by name. The modern part of the cemetery contains Shelley's heart. His body was burned on the shore near Pisa. As his dear friend Lord Byron put it: "All of Shelley was consumed, except his heart, which could not take the flame and is now preserved in spirits of wine."

Outside the **Porta San Paolo** ⓱ is the basilica of **San Paolo fuori le Mura**, one of the major basilicas of Rome. It is believed to house the tomb of St Paul.

Marble, gilt – and flesh and blood

Exuberant, awe-inspiring and outrageous, baroque architecture offers such an over-profusion of detail, painting, gilt and marble that it often overwhelms. But what pleasure there is in discovering a particularly winning putto winking at you from an architrave, in craning to see a fantastic ceiling by Pietro da Cortona or Andrea dal Pozzo, and in seeing saints and biblical figures made flesh and blood by Caravaggio or Bernini.

The baroque style dominates in Rome and the best place to start appreciating it is the **Gesù** ⓲. The church was started in 1568 for the recently approved Jesuit order, champions of the Counter-Reformation. The Council of Trent (1545–63) laid down the rigorous principles for strengthening the Catholic Church against the Protestant heretics. Originally, the Gesù was meant to be austere; its baroque

BELOW: San Paolo fuori le Mura.

ROME AND THE BAROQUE

The baroque (1600–1750) was born in Rome, and nurtured by a papal campaign to make the city one of unparalleled beauty "for the greater glory of God and the Church." One of the first artists to answer the call was Michelangelo Merisi da Caravaggio (1573–1610), whose early secular portraits of sybaritic youths revealed him to be a painfully realistic artist. His later monumental religious painting entitled *The Calling of St Matthew,* in San Luigi dei Francesi, shocked the city by setting a holy act in a contemporary tavern.

The decoration of St Peter's by Gianlorenzo Bernini (1598–1680) was more acceptable to the Romans: a bronze tabernacle with spiralling columns at the main altar; a magnificent throne with angels clustered around a burst of sacred light at the end of the church; and, for the exterior, the classically simple colonnade embracing the piazza (1657).

Bernini's rival was Francesco Borromini (1599–1667), whose eccentric designs were the opposite of Bernini's classics. Many of Borromini's most famous designs hinge on a complex interplay of concave and convex surfaces, which can be seen in the undulating facades of San Carlo alle Quattro Fontane, Sant'Ivo, and Sant'Agnese in Piazza Navona (1653–63).

makeover was performed in the late 17th century. By this time, the Counter-Reformers had discovered art's role as a means of making the intangible more accessible to the faithful. Baroque art also impressed upon the masses the immense power of the Church. Andrea dal Pozzo's altar to St Ignatius in the Gesù is particularly sumptuous. But the supreme example of baroque is the Gesù's ceiling, with Il Baciccia's painting *The Triumph of the Name of Jesus*. White statues cling to the gilt vault, some supporting the central painting which spills out of its frame. Here is the characteristic baroque blend of architecture, painting and sculpture, all working to reinforce the role of a church as a place between this world and the next.

Another Jesuit church, **Sant'Ignazio** ⑲, this time with a ceiling by Andrea del Pozzo, is also an impressive example of baroque. To appreciate its fantastic perspective, stand in the middle of the nave and look heavenwards: the vault seems to disappear as an ecstatic St Ignatius receives from Jesus the light he will disperse to the four corners of the earth. Pozzo also painted a fake dome, since the Jesuit fathers were unable to afford a real one.

Carnival Corso

Via del Corso ("the Corso") stretches from Piazza Venezia to Piazza del Popolo, a distance of almost 1.5 km (1 mile). Lined with elegant palaces and crowded with shoppers, this central artery has always been a good place in which to take the pulse of the city. In ancient times it was the main route north, known as the Via Lata (Wide Way), which gives an idea of how narrow most ancient streets were. Between the 18th and 19th centuries, it was the scene of the Roman Carnival, when aristocrats and riff-raff alike pelted one another with flowers, bon-

Map on pages 132–3

The baroque facade of Il Gesù.

BELOW: Rome is full of stylish boutiques.

Egyptian obelisk in the Piazza del Popolo (12th century BC).

bons and confetti. Masked revellers abandoned all discretion and temporary balconies were attached to palaces to facilitate the ogling of ladies and hurling of missiles. This chaotic setting provided a dramatic background for the climax of Hawthorne's *The Marble Faun* (1860). Alas, Rome has sobered up since it became the nation's capital, and for Carnival you must now head for Venice.

First stop on a tour of the Corso is **Palazzo Doria Pamphili** ⓴ (Fri–Wed 10am–5pm; entrance fee), home of the Galleria Doria Pamphili. The collection is superb (paintings by Titian, Caravaggio and Raphael), but nothing is labelled, so unless you're a connoisseur of 16th- and 17th-century art, use the lively audioguide that comes free with the ticket. The star of the collection is Velázquez's portrait of *Pope Innocent X*. Via delle Muratte, to the right off the Corso, leads to the most grandiose and famous of Rome's baroque fountains: the **Fontana di Trevi** ㉑ (Trevi Fountain) where the voluptuous Anita Ekberg frolicked in Fellini's film *La Dolce Vita* (1960).

But the ancient city rears its head even in the most up-to-date places. **Piazza Colonna** ㉒, about half way down the Corso, is home to the Column of Marcus Aurelius (AD 180–93). Sixtus V (1585–90) crowned this column with a statue of St Paul and Trajan's Column with one of St Peter. (Sixtus was always eager to appropriate Roman triumphal symbols to Christianity: he placed many fallen, forgotten obelisks in front of churches.)

Two particularly impressive relics of the Augustan era, cleaned up and reassembled during the Fascist era, are the **Mausoleo di Augusto** and the **Ara Pacis Augustae** ㉓ (both closed for renovation). The emperor's funeral pyre burned in front of the mausoleum for five days. In the Middle Ages the ill-fated visionary leader, Cola di Rienzo, was cremated there. For centuries the Ara Pacis, built from 13–8 BC to celebrate peace throughout the Empire, was in pieces. Fragments were to be found as far away as the Louvre in Paris and the Uffizi in Florence. Finally, in 1983, the altar was reconstructed with fragments and copies of missing parts.

BELOW:
Trevi Fountain.

The gate of Rome

Everyone – from emperors in triumph to pilgrims on foot – used to enter Rome through the **Porta del Popolo** (Porta Flaminia). On the east rises the lush green of the Pincian hill where, in the Middle Ages, Emperor Nero's ghost was believed to wander. According to legend, a walnut tree infested with crows sprang from Nero's final resting place. In the 11th century, however, Pope Paschal II dreamt that the crows were demons and that the Virgin Mary wanted him to cut down the tree and build her a sanctuary. The existing church of **Santa Maria del Popolo** dates from the late 15th century and contains splendidly decorated chapels of different periods, with works by Pinturicchio, Raphael (the Chigi Chapel) and Caravaggio (the *Conversion of St Paul* and the *Crucifixion of St Peter*).

Take Via del Babuino, on the left of the twin baroque churches, south to **Piazza di Spagna** ㉔. The piazza is shaped like an hour-glass. In the southern section is the Palazzo di Spagna, the seat of the Spanish embassy to the Vatican, which gives the square its name. But it is in the northern part that the famous **Scalinata della**

Trinità dei Monti (Spanish Steps) rises. Neither New York's Times Square nor the Champs-Elysées in Paris provides a better location for watching the world go by. Caricaturists sketch tourists; old women sell roasted chestnuts or coconuts; tired sightseers rinse their hands in Pietro Bernini's fountain; backpackers sunbathe on the steps; hippies play guitars; and shoppers crowd the windows of the elegant shops below. Off this piazza stretch the most fashionable shopping streets in Rome: Via dei Condotti, Via Frattina, Via Borgognona. Underneath the Pincian, the quiet Via Margutta is the place to buy art.

Years ago this area was inhabited by English and American expatriates. John Keats died in the house overlooking the steps, which contains a cluttered collection of memorabilia. The **Keats and Shelley Museum** (Mon–Fri 9am–1pm and 3–6pm, Sat 11am–2pm and 3–6pm – these times do vary, to check tel: 06-678 4235; www.keats-shelley-house.org; entrance fee) is essential viewing for all romantic ghost seekers. Keep an eye out for plaques marking the past residences of famous foreigners. Henry James stayed in Hotel Inghilterra; Shelley in the Via Sistina and Via del Corso; George Eliot in the Via del Babuino; Goethe at 18 Via del Corso, where you can visit the **Goethe Museum** devoted to the writer's travels in Italy (Tues–Sun 10am–6pm; entrance fee). One of the most grandiose plaques marks James Joyce's residences at 50/52 Via Frattina. Joyce, it says, "made of his Dublin, our universe".

The bones and the bees

The street between Trinità dei Monti and Santa Maria Maggiore was cut by Sixtus V, a pope bent on improving Rome and glorifying his own name. The view down the length of the road is dramatic – culminating in the obelisk which

Map on pages 132–3

TIP

Via dei Condotti, which starts at the Spanish Steps, is Rome's most opulent shopping street. Here, and in the surrounding streets, you'll find all the Italian design giants – Armani, Bulgari, Gucci, Prada, Valentino, et al.

BELOW: Spanish Steps.

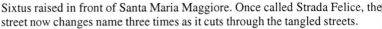

TIP

Rome's glitzy museum of contemporary and modern art (MACRO) just north of Termini station, is being expanded by French architect Odile Decq, and should be ready by winter, 2006. Open Tues–Sun 9am–7pm; entrance fee.

ABOVE and **BELOW:** temples in Villa Borghese park.

Sixtus raised in front of Santa Maria Maggiore. Once called Strada Felice, the street now changes name three times as it cuts through the tangled streets.

The first leg, Via Sistina, leads down to **Piazza Barberini** ㉕, in the centre of which is Bernini's sensual **Fontana del Tritone**. The musclebound sea creature blows fiercely on a conch shell while a geyser of water shoots above him. In the base is the unmistakeable coat of arms of the Barberini family: three bees. The family palace nearby is the work of Carlo Maderno, Bernini and Borromini. Today the Palazzo Barberini houses the **Galleria Nazionale di Arte Antica** (Tues–Sun 8.30am–7.30pm, closed Mon; entrance fee). Don't miss Pietro da Cortona's *The Triumph of Divine Providence*, a baroque celebration of the Barberini Pope Urban VIII – a pope who quarried the ruins of Ancient Rome so extensively that he inspired the witticism: "What the Barbarians didn't do, the Barberini did."

Via Veneto swoops off the Piazza Barberini. Before strolling along its wide streets or retiring to one of its cafés, stop at the **Chiesa dei Cappuccini**, also known as Santa Maria della Concezione (church open daily 7am–noon, 3.30–7pm; free; crypt open Fri–Wed 9am–noon, 3–6pm; donation expected) to see its macabre crypt. According to legend, a group of artistically and ghoulishly inclined friars decided to put the dead brothers' bones (4,000 monks in all) to a cautionary use. Four rooms of rococo sculptures contain a playful filigree of hip bones, a garland of spines and an array of skulls stacked as neatly as oranges and apples on a fruit vendor's stall.

The **Via Veneto** became famous after World War II as the centre of Rome's "Dolce Vita", but today it seems more sleazy than glamorous. Buy a magazine, put on your dark glasses and adjourn to one of the streetside cafés for refreshment, then move on to the Villa Borghese where you can picnic or visit the

Bioparco ㉖ (9.30am–6pm, till 7pm on weekends and holidays, till 5pm in winter; last entry one hour before closing; tel: 06-360 8211), which has very interesting sections on biodiversity and animal reproduction in the new wing. Near the Via Veneto entrance to the park is the **Galleria Borghese** ㉗ (Tues–Sun 8.30am–7pm; visits by reservation only; tel: 06-32810 or book online at www.ticketeria.it), with works by Bernini, Caravaggio, Raphael, Titian, Rubens and Canova among others. If you are interested in Italy's more recent artistic achievements, visit the **Galleria Nazionale d'Arte Moderna e Contemporanea** GNAM; ㉘ (Tues–Sun 8.30am–7.30pm; entrance fee). A wing of the museum opened in 2003 accommodates the collection of paintings, sculptures and prints, largely by Italian artists but including international artists such as Henry Moore, Pollock, Cézanne and Kandinsky, dating from the 1800s to the present.

To the north of the Villa Borghese is another aristocratic palace, built for Julius III. The **Villa Giulia** ㉙ (for opening times refer to the museum) has a beautiful Renaissance garden and, inside, the fascinating **Museo Nazionale Etrusco di Villa Giulia** (Tues–Sun 8.30am–7.30pm; last entry one hour before closing; entrance fee), full of pre-Roman art. The Etruscan terracotta sculptures are particularly interesting. Also well worth seeking out are a touching sarcophagus of a husband and wife and a magnificent statue of Apollo.

Bernini and Borromini

From the intersection of **Via delle Quattro Fontane** (the extension of Via Sistina) and Via XX Settembre you can admire the drama of Roman urban planning: in three directions obelisks scrape the sky. The Via XX Settembre contains a number of splendid baroque churches. First is **San Carlo alle Quattro Fontane ③⓪**, also known as San Carlino. This tiny church, whose interior is the same size as one of the piers under the dome of St Peter's, was designed by Francesco Borromini (1599–1667). The undulating facade is characteristic of this eccentric architect's style. The all-white interior is a fantastic play of ovals. The financially stressed monks who commissioned the church were impressed by Borromini's ability to keep down the costs of the church – by using delicate stucco work rather than marble or gilt – without in any way lessening the beauty of the interior.

Up Via del Quirinale, off the other side of Via delle Quattro Fontane, is another oval gem by Borromini's arch rival, Gianlorenzo Bernini (1598–1680). **Sant' Andrea al Quirinale ③①** offers quite a contrast to its neighbour. Every inch of this church is covered with gilt and marble. Putti ascend the wall as if in a cloud of smoke. Yet the architect's masterful, classical handling of space creates a marvellous sense of simplicity.

For another Bernini masterpiece head in the other direction to **Santa Maria della Vittoria ③②**, in Largo Santa Susanna (off Via XX Settembre) where you'll find his sculpture of the 17th-century Spanish mystic St Teresa of Avila. The artist captures her at the moment when she was being struck by the arrow of divine love.

Across Via XX Settembre, on the north side of Piazza della Repubblica, is **Santa Maria degli Angeli ③③**, a church Michelangelo created from the tepidarium of the **Terme di Diocleziano** (Baths of Diocletian; Tues–Sun 9am–7.45pm;

Map on pages 132–3

Gilded door knob in Santa Maria della Vittoria.

BELOW: the Baths of Diocletian.

Torso of a centurion in the Museo Nazionale Romano.

entrance fee), the largest baths in Rome, built between AD 298 and 306. The *esedra*, the open space surrounded by porticos and seats where the Romans would chat, gave its form to Piazza della Repubblica. The **Fontana delle Naiadi** (Fountain of the Naiads) in the centre of the square, dating from *circa* 1900, caused a scandal when it was unveiled, because of the "obscene" postures of the nymphs. The baths were also once the principal venue of the **Museo Nazionale Romano** ❸ *(see box, page 149)* but this great collection of ancient art was divided up into several sites in a major reorganisation programme carried out in the run-up to the year 2000.

Mary and Moses

Rome has more churches dedicated to the Virgin Mary than to any other saint. The largest and most splendid of these is **Santa Maria Maggiore** ❸ (daily 7am–7pm), one of the four patriarchal churches of Rome. Here the mélange of architectural styles is surprisingly harmonious: early Christianity is represented in the basilican form and in the 5th-century mosaics above the architrave in the nave (binoculars are a must if you want to decipher them). Medieval input includes the campanile (the largest in Rome), the Cosmatesque pavement and the mosaic in the apse. But the overwhelming effect is baroque and as such it is an appropriate resting place for baroque master, Bernini. The coffered ceiling was supposedly gilded with the gold Columbus brought from America.

If your head is spinning with the excess of gilt and marble, head down the Via Cavour to **San Pietro in Vincoli** ❸ (daily 7.30am–noon and 3.30–6pm) where you will find Michelangelo's massive and dignified *Moses*. The statue was to form part of an enormous free-standing tomb for Pope Julius II, but politics and constrained finances curtailed Michelangelo's imagination. Of this one statue Giorgio Vasari, artist and biographer of artists, said: "No modern work will ever approach it in beauty." Moses sits 3 metres (10 ft) high, every inch the powerful lawgiver. The other significant exhibit here is the glass box containing the chains that bound St Peter in his prison cells in Rome and Judaea, hence the name San Pietro in Vincoli (St Peter in Chains).

BELOW: faded grandeur.

Near Santa Maria Maggiore, inside the restored Palazzo Brancaccio, is the most important collection of Oriental art in Italy, the **Museo Nazionale d'Arte Orientale** (Via Merulana 248, Esquiline Hill; Mon, Wed, Fri and Sat 8.30am–1.30pm, Tues, Thur and Sun 8.30am–7.30pm, closed first and third Mon of the month; entrance fee).

The living city

During the Middle Ages, most of Rome's population was crowded either into the region between Via del Corso and the Tiber (Campus Martius to the ancients) or into Trastevere *(see page 159)* across the river. The best time to visit these areas is the early morning, when you will be able to admire the facades of buildings alone, enter churches with only the faithful as companions, and watch the Romans starting their day. Windowless shops give directly onto crooked, narrow streets and workers leave their doors open for light and air. Look in and you will see bakers kneading loaves of *casareccio* bread, furniture restorers rubbing down wood with strong-smelling waxes, and cobblers hammering heels onto worn boots.

Have a *cornetto* (an Italian croissant) and a cappuccino in Piazza della Rotonda and admire the outside of the **Pantheon** ❸ (Mon–Sat 8.30am–7.30pm, Sun 9am–6pm, holidays 9am–1pm; free) – the best preserved of all Ancient Roman buildings. For those who question the greatness of Roman architecture and dismiss it as inferior to Greek, the Pantheon is an eloquent answer. This perfectly proportioned round temple proves how adept the Romans were in shaping interior space. Rebuilt by the Emperor Hadrian, its architectural antecedents are not the Republican round temples – such as the one in the Forum Boarium – but the round chambers used in the baths. Western architecture owes the Romans an enormous debt for their skilful work with vaults and domes. The only light is provided by a large hole set in the centre of the dome – the *oculus* – and this means that the building has been open to the elements for nearly 2,000 years.

Near the Pantheon, in front of **Santa Maria Sopra Minerva** (Mon–Sat 7am–7pm, Sun 8am–7pm), Bernini's much-loved elephant carries the smallest of Rome's obelisks. Inside the church (the only one in the Gothic style in Rome) are a chapel decorated by Fra Filippo Lippi and, to the left of the main altar, Michelangelo's statue of *Christ bearing the Cross*. Other ecclesiastical treasures are just a few blocks away. Caravaggio frescoes adorn both **San Luigi dei Francesi** (*The Calling of St Matthew, St Matthew and the Angel* and *The Martyrdom of St Matthew*) and **Sant'Agostino** (*The Madonna of the Pilgrims*). Borromini's **Sant'Ivo** is tucked into the courtyard of Palazzo Sapienza. Like San Carlino, this church's interior is dazzlingly white. Most startling, however, is its spiralling campanile (bell tower).

Map on pages 132–3

Inside the Pantheon dome.

BELOW: street life around Piazza Navona.

MUSEO NAZIONALE ROMANO

The Museo Nazionale Romano is one of the most important archaeological collections in the world. It is split up into four main sites. The vast **Terme di Diocleziano** (Baths of Diocletian; Via Enrico de Nicola 79 – *see page 147*) was the original home of the museum. The **Aula Ottagona** (Octagonal Hall, Via Romita), an integral part of the baths, still contains some important sculptures. But the bulk of the collection is at the **Palazzo Massimo alle Terme** (Largo di Villa Peretti 1). Highlights include splendid floor mosaics and wall paintings from the villas of wealthy Romans, seen at their best in the delicate frescoes from the Villa of Livia. The **Palazzo Altemps** (Piazza Sant'Apollinari 46) is a 15th-century palace north of Piazza Navona with a beautiful courtyard which houses a fine collection of antique sculptures. The **Crypta Balbi** (Via delle Botteghe Oscure 31) – the remains of the theatre built by Balbus in 13 BC – documents the changing face of Rome through history. All sites open Tues–Sun 9am–7.45pm. A ticket is valid for all the sites of the museums for a period of three days. A €20 ticket (Archeologia Card) is also available and includes the four museum sites, the Colosseum, the Palatine, the Baths of Caracalla, the Tomb of Cecilia Metella and the Villa of the Quintili. Book online at www.pierreci.it or tel: 06-39967700.

Map on pages 132–3

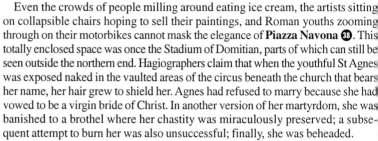

TIP

One of Rome's most photogenic squares is the **Campo dei Fiori**, By day it's the site of a colourful outdoor market (Mon–Sat 8am–1pm). By night it is a favourite meeting place. The hip Vineria wine bar stays open until the small hours.

BELOW: Bernini's fountain, in Piazza Navona. **RIGHT:** the traditional neighbourhood of Monti.

Even the crowds of people milling around eating ice cream, the artists sitting on collapsible chairs hoping to sell their paintings, and Roman youths zooming through on their motorbikes cannot mask the elegance of **Piazza Navona ㊳**. This totally enclosed space was once the Stadium of Domitian, parts of which can still be seen outside the northern end. Hagiographers claim that when the youthful St Agnes was exposed naked in the vaulted areas of the circus beneath the church that bears her name, her hair grew to shield her. Agnes had refused to marry because she had vowed to be a virgin bride of Christ. In another version of her martyrdom, she was banished to a brothel where her chastity was miraculously preserved; a subsequent attempt to burn her was also unsuccessful; finally, she was beheaded.

The church of **Sant'Agnese in Agone** has another curvaceous facade by Borromini. His rival, Bernini, designed the **Fontana dei Quattro Fiumi** in the centre of the piazza. A popular tale claims that the statue of the Nile facing Sant'Agnese is covering its eyes for fear it will collapse. However, the fountain was completed in 1651, before Borromini had even started work on the church.

Stony words

Close by, **Piazza di Pasquino** contains a battered statue that once functioned as the underground newspaper of Rome. The papal censors allowed so little criticism that irrepressible commentators attached their writings to statues in the city. The most famous satirist was Pasquino.

Near the piazza is the elegant church of **Santa Maria della Pace ㊴** (Mon–Fri 10am–12.45pm). Inside there are frescoes by Raphael and a beautiful cloister by Bramante which is often filled with exhibitions of the work of contemporary artists. The front door is often locked, so access is by the Bramante cloister. To the north, Via dei Coronari is lit with torches every night.

At the end of Via dei Cornari, take a left turn and you will soon reach the **Chiesa Nuova ㊵** (daily 8am–noon, 4.30–7pm) dedicated to St Filippo Neri, one of Rome's patron saints, who lies buried here. The apse contains three fine works by Rubens, who lived in Rome from 1606 to 1608. The Oratorio dei Filippini was built between 1637 and 1662 by Borromini as a place of worship for the fraternity of St Philip Neri, who instituted the musical gatherings that later became known as oratorios. The concave architectural elements are typical of Borromini's style.

The last baroque church on this tour is perhaps the most ornate. Puccini chose **Sant'Andrea della Valle ㊶** as a setting for the opening act of *Tosca*. Act II takes place at the nearby **Palazzo Farnese ㊷**, most splendid of Renaissance palaces and suitably intimidating as headquarters for the villainous Scarpia. The palace is now the French Embassy and, alas for the visitor who would like to see Annibale Carracci's frescoes, it is closed to the public. Other grand palaces in the neighbourhood include **Palazzo della Cancelleria** (closed to the public) and the **Galleria Spada** (Tues–Sun 8.30am–7.30pm; entrance fee), which has a handsome gallery.

Act III of *Tosca* takes place on the west bank of the Tiber, in the notorious **Castel Sant'Angelo** prison (Tues–Sun 9am–8pm; entrance fee). Visiting this fortress takes us from Rome into the Vatican City, the world's smallest state *(see page 155)*. ❑

THE COLOSSEUM: BREAD AND CIRCUSES

"While the Colosseum stands, Rome shall stand; when the Colosseum falls, Rome shall fall; when Rome falls, the world shall fall."

The Venerable Bede's 8th-century prophecy has been taken to heart and the Colosseum shored up ever since. The ancient amphi-theatre is the city's most stir-ring sight, a place of stupen-dous size and spatial harmony. The Colosseum was begun by Vespasian, inaugurated by his son Titus in AD 80, and completed by Domitian (AD 81–96). Titus used Jewish captives from Jerusalem as masons. The Colosseum had 80 numbered, arched entrances, allowing over 50,000 spectators to be seated within ten minutes. "Bread and circuses" was how Juvenal, the 2nd-century satirist, mocked the Romans here who sold their souls for free food and entertainment.

FALL AND RUIN

With the fall of the empire, the Colosseum fell into disuse. During the Renaissance, the ruins were plundered to create churches and palaces all over Rome, including Palazzo Farnese, now the French Embassy. Quarrying was only halted by Pope Benedict XIV, in the 18th century, and the site consecrated to Christian martyrs. The Colosseum was still neglected on the German writer Goethe's visit in 1787, with a hermit and beggars "at home in the crumbling vaults". In 1817 Lord Byron was enthralled by this "noble wreck in ruinous perfec-tion", while Edgar Allan Poe, another Romantic poet, celebrated its "grandeur, gloom and glory".

During the Fascist era, Mussolini, attracted to the power that the Colosseum represented, demolished a line of buildings to create a clear view of it from his balcony on Palazzo di Venezia. To celebrate Holy Year (2000), the Colosseum was restored, and it has reopened for festivities and classical drama.

△ **ALL AT SEA**
Renaissance historians believed that, in ancient times, Roman arenas were sometimes flooded to stage mock naval battles, but there is scant evidence to suggest such a display ever took place in the Colosseum.

▽ **GLADIATORIAL COMBAT**
The price of failure: the Gate of Life was reserved for victorious gladiators, with vanquished gladiators doomed to the Gate of Death.

△ **BEHIND THE SCENES**
From the higher tiers stretch views down to the arena and a maze of passages. The arena was encircled by nettir to prevent beasts escaping. The moveable wooden floor was covered in sand, the better to soak up the blood. Below, the subterranean section concealed the anima cages and sophisticated technical apparatus, from winches and mechanical lifts to ramps and trapdoors.

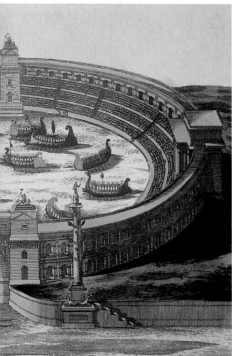

▽ SOCIAL STRATA

Although supremely public, the Colosseum was a stratified affair. The podium, set on the lowest tier, was reserved exclusively for the emperor, senators, magistrates and Vestal Virgins. Above them sat the bourgeoisie, with the lower orders restricted to the top tier, and the populace on wooden seats in the very top rows.

◁ IMPERIAL COINAGE

Bearing the head of Emperor Vespasian, this coin depicts no grape-sucking degenerate but a professional soldier who consolidated Roman rule in Britain and Germany. As the founder of the Flavian dynasty and emperor between AD 69 and 79, he began the stadium. The Colosseum is also known as Anfiteatro Flavio (Amphitheatre of Flavius).

◁ ROMANTIC ROME

This 18th-century view by Giovanni Volpato reflects the nostalgic sensibility of the Romantic era. Visitors on the Grand Tour were beguiled by the ruins bathed in moonlight or haunted by the sense of a lost civilisation. In Byron's words, "Some cypresses beyond the time-worn breach/Appeared to skirt the horizon, yet they stood/Within a bowshot – where the Caesars dwelt".

ENTERTAINMENT FOR THE MASSES

The Roman appetite for bloodshed was legendary, with the barbaric *munera*, or blood sports, introduced as a corrupt version of Greek games. The animals, mostly imported from Africa, included lions, elephants, giraffes, hyenas, hippos, wild horses and zebras. The contests were also a way of eliminating slaves and proscribed sects, Christians and common criminals, political agitators and prisoners of war. Variants included battles involving nets, swords and tridents, mock hunts and freak shows with panthers pulling chariots or cripples pitted against clowns. Seneca, Nero's tutor, came expecting "fun, wit and some relaxation" but was dumbfounded by the butchery and cries of "Kill him! Lash him! Why does he meet the sword so timidly?"

In AD 248, the millennium of the founding of Rome was celebrated by contests involving 2,000 gladiators and the slaying of tame giraffes and hippos as well as big cats. Although convicted criminals were routinely fed to the lions, Christian martyrdom in the arena is less well documented. However, St Ignatius of Antioch, who described himself as "the wheat of Christ", was dutifully devoured by lions in AD 107. Gladiatorial combat was banned in AD 404, while animal fights ended in the following century.

THE VATICAN AND TRASTEVERE

*From the spirituality of St Peter's, with its
extensive museums and magnificent art treasures,
to the earthiness of Rome's medieval quarter*

Map on pages 132–3

T he west bank of the Tiber offers contrasting experiences. Cheek by jowl with the Vatican, with all its papal pomp, is the working-class district of Trastevere, with its tenements, narrow streets, and lively street life.

As you cross the Tiber using Ponte Sant'Angelo, it is not the domed heart of the Vatican you see first, however, but the almost windowless walls of the medieval citadel, the **Castel Sant'Angelo** ❸ (Tues–Sun 9am–7pm; entrance fee). Back in AD 139, this was the site of the mausoleum of the Emperor Hadrian. Later it became a fortress and prison, then a residence to which the popes could flee in times of turbulence. Today it is a museum full of 16th-century furnishings and frescoes. Puccini's heroine, Tosca, plunged to her death from the parapet where visitors now come to admire the views across Rome. Towering over the battlements is a gigantic statue of St Michael, the warlike archangel after whom the castle is named.

Vatican City

From Castel Sant'Angelo, Via della Conciliazione leads to St Peter's, at the heart of Vatican City. If size were the only measure of a nation's power or importance, the Vatican would warrant hardly any attention at all. Yet it serves as an exception to the rule that tiny nations are famous for little more than their postage stamps.

For centuries the Vatican was the unchallenged centre of the Western world. Its symbolic significance, both past and present, and its enduring international role, as both a religious and a diplomatic force, have put this tiny city-state on a par with nations many million times larger. No matter how secular our world has become, divine authority seems still to count and to make the Vatican much more than a geographic oddity, much more than the academic footnote it might otherwise be.

Covering a total area of slightly more than 40 hectares (100 acres), Vatican City is by far the world's smallest independent sovereign entity. What other nation is as small as New York's Central Park? What other nation can lock its gates at midnight, as the Vatican's door-keepers do each night, opening them only at the ring of a bell? What other nation can be crossed at a leisurely pace in well under half an hour?

In Imperial Roman days, the lower part of what is now Vatican City was an unhealthy bog, an area famous among caesars and consuls for its vinegary wine, snakes and diseases. But in the 1st century AD, the dowager empress Agrippina had the Vatican Valley drained and planted with imperial gardens. Under Caligula and Nero, the area was turned over to the circus. Chariot racing and executions – including that of St Peter – were regular events on what later became St Peter's Square.

LEFT: view from St Peter's.
BELOW: Swiss Guards enjoying some time off.

The Lateran Treaty of 1929, concluded between Pope Pius XI and Benito Mussolini, established the present territorial limits of the Vatican. The city is roughly trapezoidal in shape, bounded by medieval walls on all sides except on the corner, where the opening of St Peter's Square marks the border with Rome and the rest of Italy. Of the six openings to the Vatican, only three are for public use: the Piazza, the Arco delle Campane (south of St Peter's Basilica), and the entrance to the Vatican Museums. Pius XI had a special Vatican railway station built in the early 1930s, a facility which no paying passenger has ever used (even popes use it very infrequently). A heliport has been built on a spot where British diplomats whiled away their days during World War II.

Aside from an impressive array of palaces and office buildings, there is also a Vatican prison, a supermarket, and the printing press, which churns out the daily *L'Osservatore Romano* and scripts in a wide range of languages, from Coptic to Ecclesiastical Georgian to Tamil. In short, the Vatican is much more than an oversized museum.

Apart from the area enclosed by the Vatican walls, the Vatican State comprises several other buildings in Rome, plus the Pope's summer residence southeast of the city, Castel Gandolfo.

Piazza San Pietro

Bernini's spectacular, colonnaded **Piazza San Pietro** ⑭ is, according to one's viewpoint, either the welcoming embrace of the Mother Church or her grasping claws. The Via della Conciliazione, constructed in 1937 to commemorate the reconciliation between Mussolini and Pope Pius XI, changed the original impact of the space. Before this thoroughfare provided a monumental approach to St Peter's, the entrance was by way of smaller streets, winding through the old Borgo and arriving, finally, in the enclosed open space, with the biggest church in the world at one end and an enormous Egyptian obelisk in the centre.

BELOW: a public Mass draws thousands to St Peter's Square.

Subjects of the Holy See

To be one of the 800 or so citizens with a Vatican passport is to belong to one of the world's most exclusive clubs – the privilege of citizenship hinges on a direct and continuous relationship with the Holy See. The Pope himself carries passport No. 1 and he rules absolutely over Vatican City.

The word "pope" comes from the Greek *pappas*, meaning "father". Despite two millennia having passed since St Peter first assumed the mantle, the pope's role remains paternal, alternating between concern for humanity and stern warnings against theological or spiritual deviation. John Paul II (1978–2005) asserted his moral authority vigorously. His 1993 encyclical denounced contraception, homosexuality and other infringements of the faith as "intrinsically evil". His successor, Benedict XVI, is cast in the same ethical mould.

The facts and figures

There have been 263 popes. The shortest reign of a pope was that of Stephen II, who died four days after his election in March 752. At the other extreme, the 19th-century's Pius IX, famous for his practical jokes and his love of billiards, headed the Holy See for 32 years. The youngest pope on record, John XI, was just 16 when he took the helm in 931; the oldest, Gregory IX, managed to survive 14 years after his election in 1227 at the age of 86.

While the great majority have been of either Roman or Italian extraction, Spain, Greece, Syria, France and Germany have all been represented, and there has been at least one of African birth (Miltiades, 311–314), and one hailing from England (Hadrian IV, 1154–59). John Paul II was the first Pole to lead the Catholic Church. At least 14 popes abdicated or were deposed from office. Ten popes met violent deaths, including a record three in a row in the 10th century.

The process of electing a new pope is necessarily unique, as the papacy is the world's

only elective monarchy. Members of the Sacred College of Cardinals, a largely titular body of 120 bishops and archbishops, are sealed into the Sistine Chapel soon after the death knell tolls in the Vatican Palace. They cannot leave until a new successor has been chosen. Voting can proceed by acclamation, whereby the cardinals all shout the same name at the same time; by scrutiny, in which four ballots are cast daily until one candidate has captured a two-thirds majority plus one; or, as a last resort, by compromise.

All modern popes have been selected by the second method. Paper ballots are burned after each tally, and onlookers watch the chapel's chimney for dark smoke, which indicates an inconclusive vote, or white plumes, which denote a winner (electors are provided with special chemicals so that there can be no mistake). Finally the cardinal dean announces "Habemus Papam" (We have a pope) to the faithful, and the chosen cardinal appears in one of three robes (sized small, medium and large) kept on hand for the occasion. The coronation takes place on the following day. ❑

RIGHT: part of the substantial gardens behind St Peter's and the Vatican Museums.

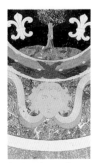

ABOVE: decorative marble in the Vatican Museums.

BELOW: Roman torso in the Vatican's Chiaramonti Museum.

Church, museum, mausoleum; the Basilica di San Pietro, **St Peter's** (daily 7am–7pm, until 6pm in winter; modest dress code; free except for visits to the dome) is all three. No other temple surpasses it in terms of historical significance or architectural splendour. Some may feel the immensity of the interior is more suited to moving commuters through a railway station than to inspiring the intimate act of prayer, but the many architects and patrons of St Peter's intended the building to symbolise worldly power as much as spiritual piety. Just about every important Renaissance and baroque architect from Bramante onwards had a hand in the design of St Peter's. The idea for rebuilding the original 4th-century basilica had been around since the mid-5th century but not until Julius II became pope did a complete reconstruction get underway. Bramante was succeeded by Raphael, Peruzzi, Michelangelo (usually credited with the dome), Giacomo della Porta and Bernini.

The interior is vast – 186 metres (610 ft) long with a capacity for around 60,000 people. On the right, as you walk in, is Michelangelo's *Pietà*, an inspiration to beholders ever since the sculptor finished it in 1500, at the age of 25. At the end of the nave is the bronze statue of *St Peter*, its toe worn away by the kisses of pilgrims.

Over the high altar, which is directly above the tomb of St Peter, rises Bernini's garish bronze baldachin, resembling the canopy of an imperial bed; Pope Urban VIII stripped the bronze from the Pantheon. But Bernini outdid himself in the design for the Cathedra Petri (the Chair of St Peter) in the apse. Four gilt bronze figures of the church fathers hold up the chair. Above, light streams through the golden glass of a window crowned by a dove (symbol of the Holy Ghost). The chair bears a relief of Christ's command to Peter to "feed his sheep". Thus the position of the pope is explained and bolstered by Christ's words and the teachings of the Church fathers, and blessed by the Holy Ghost. Further confirmation of the pope's sacred trust is found in Christ's words inscribed on the dome: "You are Peter and on this rock I will build my Church and I will give you the keys to the kingdom of heaven."

The Vatican Museums

The **Musei Vaticani** ⑮ (Mon–Fri 8.45am–4.45pm, till 1.45pm in winter, Sat and last Sun of the month 8.45am–1.45pm year round; last entry 1hr 30mins before closing; entrance fee except on last Sun of the month) merit a lifetime's study. But for those who have only a few hours, some sights shouldn't be missed. The **Museo Pio-Clementino** contains the pope's collection of antiquities. Be sure to visit the Belvedere Courtyard, home of the celebrated and cerebral *Apollo Belvedere* and the contrasting muscle-bound, sensual *Laocoön*. The Vatican **Pinacoteca** contains superb paintings including Raphael's *Madonna of Foligno* and *Transfiguration*. There are also rooms covered in frescoes: the Stanze di Raffaello comprise three rooms painted by Raphael. Downstairs, colourful frescoes by Pinturicchio decorate the Borgia Apartments.

But the triumph of fresco painting, not only of the Vatican Palace, but of the entire world, is the **Cappella Sistina** (Sistine Chapel). The walls are covered in paintings by Botticelli, Pinturicchio and Ghirlandaio, but the breathtaking star of the show is Michelangelo's ceiling, begun in 1508 and completed by 1512. It is a shallow barrel vault divided into large and small panels tracing the history of the Creation.

No reproduction can ever do justice to the interplay of painting and architecture, to the drama of the whole chapel, alive with colour (considerably brighter since the controversial cleaning of the frescoes finally unveiled to the public in 1994) and human emotion. "All the world hastened to behold this marvel and was overwhelmed, speechless with astonishment", Vasari wrote. The astonishment is no less today than it was in the Renaissance.

Map on pages 132–3

Trastevere

The heart of medieval Trastevere, literally "across the Tiber", is southeast of the Vatican City. Here you can find many reasonably priced restaurants and, at **Porta Portese ㊻**, a popular flea market on Sunday. Traditionally, Trastevere was a working-class neighbourhood with strong communist leanings. Today it is full of trendy restaurants, shops and wine bars.

South of Viale di Trastevere are two churches worth visiting. **Santa Cecilia ㊼** (daily 9.30am–12.30pm and 4–6.30pm; donation) was built on top of the house of a Christian martyr whom the Roman authorities attempted to scald to death in her own *caldarium* (hot bath). When this failed, she was sentenced to decapitation, but three blows failed to sever her head and she lived for a further three days (enough time to consecrate her house as a church). Carlo Maderno's touching statue of the saint curled in a foetal position was inspired by his observations when her tomb was opened in 1599.

ABOVE: stained glass in the Vatican Museums. **BELOW:** instrument restorer in Trastevere.

THE ARTISANS' QUARTER

O ver the centuries, Trastevere's separation from the rest of the city resulted in the development of its own unique customs, traditions and even dialect, and it became home to a proud people who often came to blows with the city dwellers on the other side of the river. In Roman times Trastevere was primarily inhabited by foreign merchants, whose goods arrived in Rome on the Tiber, and was home to a large Jewish colony which later moved to the other bank. The area's largely medieval character was left intact until the second half of the 19th century when, in order to make way for Viale di Trastevere and the Longotevere (riverside boulevards), many historic monuments were torn down and an important part of the area's maze-like network of streets erased.

Despite these changes, and the area's increasing penchant for anything touristy and gentrified (the inhabitants are now more bourgeois than working class), Trastevere retains islands of genuine local atmosphere. Hidden corners remain untouched and provide snap-happy visitors with picturesque photo opportunities of laundry hanging out to dry or old-timers chatting outside their front doors. The winding streets are also the perfect place to seek out an original gift from the area's many artisanal workshops.

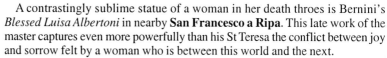

Map on pages 132–3

San Sebastiano is perhaps the most significant of the catacombs in the Appian Way. The Basilica (daily 8am–6pm) contains a large fragment of stone which is said to bear Christ's footprints.

BELOW: Castel Sant'Angelo.
RIGHT: inside St Peter's.

A contrastingly sublime statue of a woman in her death throes is Bernini's *Blessed Luisa Albertoni* in nearby **San Francesco a Ripa**. This late work of the master captures even more powerfully than his St Teresa the conflict between joy and sorrow felt by a woman who is between this world and the next.

In the piazza of the same name, **Santa Maria in Trastevere** ㊽ (daily 7.30am–9pm) is one of the oldest churches in Rome. It has some beautiful Byzantine mosaics illustrating the life of Mary.

After these sobering places of worship, preoccupied with the horrors of this world and the glories of the next, it is a relief to come to the **Villa Farnesina** ㊾ (Mon–Sat 9am–1pm; entrance fee), a jewel of the Renaissance, worldly and pagan. A ceiling fresco by Raphael details the love of Cupid and Psyche. The figures are robust, fleshy, almost Rubenesque. In the next room, Raphael's *Galatea* captures the moment when the nymph, safe from the clutches of the cyclops Polyphemus, looks round. Upstairs, Baldassare Peruzzi, who designed the entire villa, devised a fantastic *trompe l'oeil*. The room seems to open upon a restful village scene. In the bedroom is Sodoma's erotic painting *The Wedding of Alexander and Roxanne*.

To reach another important Renaissance monument, climb the steps up the Gianicolo to the church of **San Pietro in Montorio** ㊿ (daily 8am–noon and 4–6pm; free). In the courtyard is **Bramante's Tempietto** (Tues–Sun 9.30am–12.20pm and 4–6pm, 9.30am–12.30pm and 2–4pm in winter), a circular church that marks what was once mistakenly believed to be the site of St Peter's martyrdom. Climb a little further to the Fontana Paola, an impressive baroque monument that is now a busy car wash. The shady **Passeggiata del Gianicolo** provides panoramic views over the city. The flat dome of the Pantheon, the twin domes of Santa Maria Maggiore and the Victor Emmanuel Monument are all easy to spot from up here.

Into the bowels of the earth

Visitors with more time in Rome should try to see remains from the early Christian era. The secretive beginnings of Christianity are recalled in **Sant'Agnese fuori le Mura** ㊱, about 2 km (1¼ miles) beyond Michelangelo's Porta Pia on the Via Nomentana. Beneath the church run extensive catacombs where the martyred Roman maiden St Agnes was buried.

Also in the complex is the incomparable Santa Costanza, the mausoleum of Constantine's daughter. The ambulatory of this elegant round building is encrusted with some of Rome's most beautiful mosaics.

And for those not averse to tortuous tunnels winding endlessly past burial niches dusty with disintegrated bones, there are countless catacombs outside the walls of Rome. The best way to see them is to spend a day on the picturesque **Via Appia Antica**. You can picnic amid the remains of the Villa of the Quintilii or an unnamed crumbling edifice overrun with wildflowers and lizards. Above ground sits what Byron called the "stern round tower" of the Tomba di Cecilia Metella. Below spread the **Catacombs of St Callisto**, the most famous in Rome (Thur–Tues 8.30am–noon and 2.30–5.30pm, until 5pm in winter; closed Feb; entrance fee) and those of saints Sebastian and Domitilla. ❑

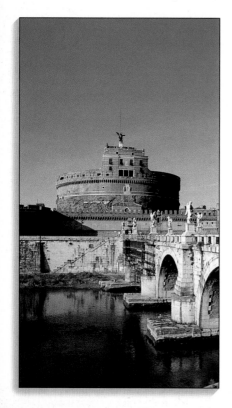

ROME'S ENVIRONS

*Explore ancient towns, villas set among beautiful gardens
and a reconstructed monastery, then visit the Etruscan
tombs to gain a vivid insight into a vanished world*

Map on
page
164

The Fascists boasted that they represented the continuation of Ancient Rome; the official art of the regime appropriated forms of Roman grandeur. Mosaics in the style of Ancient Roman floors pave the avenue and decorate the walls of the **Foro Italico ❶**, the ambitious sports centre created in 1931 northwest of the capital. Bulky square columns support the Palazzo della Civiltà del Lavoro – commonly called the "Square Colosseum" – at EUR (**Esposizione Universale di Roma) ❷**, an area south of Rome intended by Mussolini to showcase imperial Rome and Fascist achievements. Sixty colossal statues of athletes adorn the Stadio Olimpico in the Foro Italico. Stark lines and impressive bulk characterise the church of SS Pietro e Paolo at EUR. The aesthetic of the regime did succeed in creating some striking effects, but mostly the result was phony grandeur. In the city itself, urban planners ruthlessly drove roads through areas of historical importance, tearing down medieval quarters, which they considered an inheritance of dark times, and ripping through the very heart of Rome a triumphal way for the new eagles of the regime.

From this point of view, EUR, an area undeveloped before the Fascist era, is the least offensive of Il Duce's efforts in town planning. In 1938 Mussolini undertook to build, with the designs of Marcello Piacentini, a magnificent Third Rome which would be the natural successor to Imperial Rome and the Rome of the Renaissance. Plans for an exposition in 1942 to commemorate 20 years of Fascism were overtaken by World War II, and the overall design was only partially completed. In the 1950s new buildings were added, government offices and museums moved here and EUR evolved into a residential quarter.

The EUR has a number of interesting museums, including the **Museo Preistorico ed Etnografico L. Pigorini** (Prehistoric and Ethnographic Museum; daily 9am–2pm; entrance fee) and the **Museo della Civiltà Romana** (Tues–Sat 9am–2pm; Sun 9am–1.30pm; entrance fee), devoted to the history of Rome. The latter contains the famous *plastico di Roma*, a reconstruction of the city in the time of Constantine, as well as the new astronomy museum and the city's recently reopened planetarium.

Ancient apartment dwellers

The town of **Ostia Antica ❸** (Tues–Sat 8.30am–7pm in summer, till 5pm in winter; entrance fee) was founded around the end of the 4th century BC as a fortified city to guard the mouth of the Tiber. Later it developed into the commercial port of Rome as well as its naval base. By the time of Constantine, Ostia had turned into a residential town for middle- and lower-class Romans. Ostia's ruins rival those of Pompeii for showing the layout of an ancient Italian city. Houses

LEFT: the Teatro Marittimo, at Hadrian's Villa, near Tivoli.

BELOW: statuary in EUR's Museo della Civiltà Romana.

Sculpture in the Insula dei Dipinti, Ostia Antica.

unearthed in Ostia offer valuable insights into the type of dwellings the same classes presumably had in Rome. Each block contained a four-storey house with numerous rooms, built in brick, reaching a maximum height of 15 metres (49 ft). Each room had a window, covered in mica rather than glass. The *domus*, the typical Pompeiian residence built for the very rich, usually on one floor only, was very rare in Ostia. The Roman theatre, enlarged in the 2nd century by Septimius Severus to hold 2,700 people, houses the summer season of the Teatro di Roma.

The **Lido di Ostia** ➍ is an overcrowded but popular seaside resort. Naturists can drive about 8 km (5 miles) south to the laid-back beaches of Tor Vaianica.

Palestrina

The ancient **Praeneste** ➎ (modern Palestrina) is one of the oldest towns of Latium (Lazio). According to myth, it was founded by Telegonus, son of Ulysses and Circe. The town was flourishing in the 8th century BC but it wasn't until the 4th century that it became a part of Rome. During the civil war between Marius and Sulla, Marius fled to Praeneste, which was besieged by Sulla's troops and eventually destroyed. Sulla wanted to make amends and so ordered the reconstruction of the sanctuary of Fortuna Primigenia, containing an oracle. The temple, which occupied an area of about 32 hectares (79 acres), was one of the grandest of antiquity. It comprised a series of terraces on the slopes of Mount Ginestro connected by ramps. In the Middle Ages a new town rose on its ruins. In 1944 bombs destroyed part of the town bringing the temple to light and prompting excavations. The **Museo Nazionale Archeologico di Palestrina** (daily 9am–8pm; entrance fee) houses many of the local finds including the incomparable Barberini Mosaic.

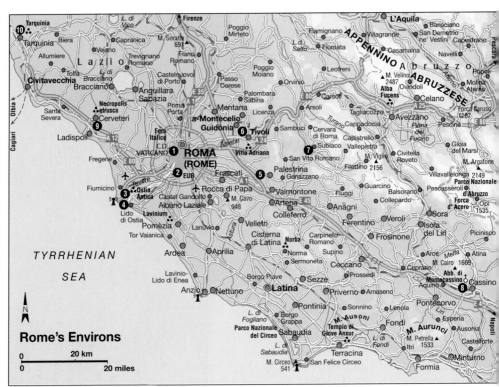

Rome's Environs

Tivoli

At the height of the Roman Empire, the ancient site of **Tibur ❻** (Tivoli), on the lower slopes of the Sabine Hills, was a favourite retreat for poets and Rome's wealthier citizens. The lavish villas scattered around sacred woods and scenic waterfalls attracted such famous visitors as Horace, Catullus, Maecenas, Sallust and the Emperor Trajan. In AD 117 the Emperor Hadrian began building his luxurious retirement home on the gently sloping plain below the foothills on which Tivoli stands. **Villa Adriana** (Hadrian's Villa; daily 9am–1 hr before sunset; entrance fee), which occupies 73 hectares (180 acres), was the largest and richest in the Roman Empire. Hadrian wanted to recreate the monuments and places which had impressed him most during his extensive travelling in the East (the peaceful Canopus, for example, was modelled on a sanctuary of Serapis near Egyptian Alexandria), but Hadrian's overall conception goes beyond mere imitation. The endless succession of terraces, water basins and baths is a joyful reaction against functionality and common sense, but the design doesn't resort to extravagant artifice. Instead, it is a rigorous, geometrical, classical controlling of nature.

See map opposite

The building standing at the heart of the complex, which a romantic archaeologist previously labelled Teatro Marittimo, is a good example of this. It is a circular building with a columned portico and a moated island in the middle. The effect is metaphysical. It suggests escape from reality, retreat into the memory, even the lucid contemplation of death.

ABOVE: stone mask in Ostia's theatre, and **BELOW** mosaic in the ancient baths.

The spirit which pervades Tivoli's **Villa d'Este** (Tues–Sun 9am–1 hr before sunset; www.villadestetivoli.info; entrance fee), the sumptuous residence that Cardinal Ippolito d'Este, son of Lucrezia Borgia, had the skilful architect Pirro Ligorio transform from a Benedictine convent, is very different. The palace is light and has a faded grandeur; with its facade overlooking the park and rooms decorated with frescoes, it is a typical Renaissance mansion. Ippolito, one of the Dukes of Este, was more absorbed by mundane business than spiritual cares. But the real splendour here lies in the symmetrically terraced garden which slopes down the surrounding hillside, covered with luxuriant vegetation, and the unrestrained play of water.

Water here is the prime element. Long, quiet pools, escorted by rows of elegiac cypresses extending into the distance, suggest infinity. Water spouts from obelisks or gurgles from the mouths of mythological creatures and monsters, or gaily springs from the nipples of a sphinx or the multiple-breasted Artemis of Ephesus. In this monument, dedicated to the ephemeral, in this superb triumph of theatricality, are the beginnings of the baroque.

Monastic foundations

Subiaco ❼ already existed when the Emperor Nero began building his villas overlooking one of the three artificial lakes he had created from the waters of the River Aniene. The slaves employed in the construction of the dam and villa founded the town. Five centuries later a rich young man from Norcia, named Benedict, came here in search of a place for meditation and prayer.

The abbey of Montecassino, high on a hill, is easily spotted from the Rome–Naples *autostrada*.

ABOVE: entrance mosaic for Villa d'Este, and **BELOW** the villa's gardens and frescoes.

He stayed for three years, living in a cavern, now known as the Sacro Speco (Holy Grotto). Subiaco, considered the birthplace of Western monasticism, now comprises a series of convents with their numerous cloisters and churches, bell towers, chapels decorated with frescoes and grottoes hewn out of the mountainside, all connected by picturesque stairways.

Around AD 529 Benedict and his faithful monks left Subiaco and moved to **Montecassino ❽** to continue their mystical experience. Here they established one of the most important religious and cultural institutions of the Middle Ages. Five centuries after Benedict's death in AD 547, the abbey he had founded was one of the richest in the world (daily 8.30am–12.30pm and 3.30–6pm, till 5.30pm in winter). The illuminated manuscripts, frescoes and mosaics were so skilfully executed that they became models for others throughout the rest of medieval Europe.

During World War II, Montecassino rose to prominence once more. After US forces entered Naples, Montecassino became the German's front-line (the so-called Gustave Line) designed to defend the environs of Rome. When repeated attacks by the Allies failed to penetrate the powerfully strengthened bulwark, a decision was made to bomb. It resulted in the total destruction of Montecassino. The ancient abbey was swept away. What one sees today is a faithful reconstruction of what existed before the catastrophe.

Cerveteri

Before Rome was the capital of Italy, capital of the popes, or capital of the world, Italy had a highly refined civilisation: that of the Etruscans. Their zest for life and emphasis on physical vitality has fascinated many, including D.H. Lawrence, who saw them as a happy contrast to the puritanical Romans.

The small medieval town of **Cerveteri** ➒, north of Rome on the Via Aurelia, was built on the site of the Etruscan town of Caere. In the 6th and 5th centuries BC, Caere was one of the most populated towns of the Mediterranean. It had strong ties with Hellenic lands, the influence of whose merchants and artists made Caere the centre of a lively and sophisticated cultural life. Its decline began in AD 384, when Pyrgi harbour, its main port, was devastated by a Greek incursion. Eventually the barbaric strength of rising Rome wiped away what had been a refined and joyous civilisation. Nothing remains today of the ancient town of Caere, bar a few walls.

Map on page 164

Caere's necropolis occupies a hill outside the city proper, the **Necropoli della Banditaccia** (Tues–Sun 8.30am–1hr before sunset; entrance fee). From here it could be seen from the ramparts of the city, gay with painted houses and temples. The oldest tombs (8th century BC) have a small circular well carved into the stone where the urns containing the ashes of the dead were placed. (Two modes of burial, cremation and inhumation, continued side by side for centuries.) The first chamber-tombs, also cut into the stone and covered with rocky blocks and mounds *(tumuli)*, appeared as early as the beginning of the 7th century BC. The noble Etruscans were either enclosed in great sarcophagi with their effigies on top, or laid out on stone beds in their chamber tombs.

Excavations of the tombs not already rifled – the Romans were the first collectors of Etruscan antiquities – revealed goods of gold, silver, ivory, bronze and ceramic. The vases show strong Greek influence as well as the excellent quality of the Etruscan craftmanship. Much of this material is now on display in the **Museo Nazionale Archeologico di Cerveteri** (Tues–Sun 8.30am–7.30pm; entrance fee), housed in the Ruspoli Castle, in the Museo di Villa Giulia in Rome, and in the Vatican Museums *(see page 158).*

ABOVE: decorative waterspout at Villa d'Este. **BELOW:** Roman statue on the canal at Tivoli.

Tarquinia

The Etruscan town of **Tarquinia** ➓ stood on a hill northwest of the picturesque medieval town bearing the same name. The town existed as early as the 9th century BC and two centuries later was at its height. In 1924 the **Museo Nazionale Tarquiniense** (Tues–Sun 8.30am–7.30pm; entrance fee) was founded. In it are many Etruscan treasures, including the famous terracotta winged horses (4th century BC).

The **Necropolis of Tarquinia** (Tues–Sun 8.30am–6.30pm, shorter hours in winter, entrance fee), together with that of Caere, is the most important Etruscan necropolis. It stands on a hill south of the original town, occupying an area 5 km (3 miles) long by 1 km (⅔ mile) wide. Some tombs are painted with frescoes that are a precious document of Etruscan lives, costumes and beliefs. Horizontal ribbons of bright colours frame the animated scenes below: the banqueters and musicians in the Tomba dei Leopardi; the hunters in the Tomba del Cacciatore; the erotic scenes in the Tomba dei Tori; the prancing dancers, diving dolphins and soaring birds of the Tomba della Leonessa; the beautiful maiden from the Velcha family in the Tomba di Polifemo o dell'Orco. Ironically, visitors often leave these dusty houses of death feeling shored up by a renewed faith in life and its many joys and mysteries. ❑

THE NORTH

Above all the sense of going down into Italy – the delight of seeing the North melt slowly into the South – of seeing Italy gradually crop up in bits and vaguely latently betray itself – until finally at the little frontier village of Isella, where I spent the night, it lay before me warm and living and palpable ...

—HENRY JAMES (from his *Letters*, Vol. 1, ed. Leon Edel)

For centuries most travellers arrived in Italy from the north. They crossed the mountains from Switzerland or France and often, if physically fit and romantically minded – as was the young Henry James – they made part of the journey on foot. This way Italy came into focus gradually, as they left the cold north behind and made their way south from the lakes to Milan. From there, the cities of the Po Valley beckoned.

If possible, this is still the best way to approach northern Italy. Rather than rush through, with your eyes on the train schedule and your mind checking off each town you have "done", see fewer cities, but see them well. Each one is so rich in history and art that it merits weeks. After all, this is the Italy of Shakespeare – *Romeo and Juliet* (Verona), *The Taming of the Shrew* (Padua) – and of medieval communes and Renaissance princes. The great families – the Visconti in Milan, the Gonzaga in Mantua, the della Scala in Verona – are still remembered for the artistic triumphs, as well as the political scandals, of their courts.

In this section of the book we pass from Byzantine Venice to the great cities of the Veneto – Padua, Verona and Vicenza – magnets for university students since the Middle Ages; and then to Milan, the style and shopping capital of Italy, via the magnificent glaciated landscapes of the Alps and the Italian Lake District.

Northern Italians, although generally more aloof and self-contained than the gregarious southerners, are always pleased to answer questions and make suggestions, always willing to spare a moment to give a stranger a little-known fact or their personal opinion on a historical personage. Quite possibly that native will bear more than a slight resemblance to the figures in the 15th-century frescoes of the local *duomo* – in these regions, the past is always present. ❏

PRECEDING PAGES: brightly painted houses on the Venetian island of Burano.
LEFT: a snow-fed waterfall in the Valle d'Aosta.

VENICE

*... out of the wave her structures rise
As from the stroke of the Enchanter's wand*
—LORD BYRON *Childe Harold's Pilgrimage* (1812)

Map on pages 174–5

When Lord Byron arrived in Venice in 1810, the "Queen of the Adriatic" had been in decline for many years. Though nonetheless enchanted by the beauty of the city, the poet describes her palaces as "crumbling to the shore". The seeds of decline were sown at the turn of the 15th century when the Portuguese stripped Venice of its monopoly of the spice trade. A decade later the League of Cambrai put an end to Venice's hold on crucial cities on the mainland. But even if Venice has been on a downward trend for more than five centuries, it remains one of the most spectacular urban displays in the annals of cultural history. It is not only tourists who are captivated by its charms. For centuries the city has lifted poets, painters and writers to new heights of inspired vision. Proust, James, Waugh and Hemingway are just a handful of the writers who have found her irresistible; few other cities in the world have a more prolific and talented school of painters, from Bellini and Giorgione through Titian and Tintoretto to Tiepolo and Guardi.

Built on over 100 islets, supported by millions of wooden stakes and linked by 400 bridges, Venice is the only city in the world which is built entirely on water. The greatest advantage of this, apart from the obvious aesthetic appeal, is the absence of cars. The biggest disadvantage is the fact that the city is prone to problems of flooding. The sense of precariousness, associated with the city for centuries, inevitably adds to the fascination for the visitor. There is always a feeling that once you turn your back on all this fragile but vibrant glory, the islands, once inhabited by refugees fleeing the hordes of Attila the Hun, will crumble and disappear like a mirage into the sea.

In January 1996 La Fenice, its historic opera house – where Verdi's *La Traviata* and *Rigoletto* were first performed – was razed to the ground. La Fenice finally rose from the ashes once more in December 2003 after the fire which was started by disgruntled electrical contractors. The plush interior, gilt painted ceiling and candelabra lighting have all been re-created. Fittingly, *La Traviata* officially re-opened the tiny theatre in 2004, years behind schedule.

St Mark's Square

The heart of Venice is the vast **Piazza San Marco ❶**. Described by Napoleon as the most elegant drawing room in Europe, this is the great architectural showpiece of Venice. With its café bands and exotic shops under the arcades, it is also the hub of tourist Venice, only in the early evening does it revert to a semblance of solitude. At one end of the piazza, crouching like an enormous, amphibious reptile, the great Basilica di San Marco (St Mark's Basilica) invites visitors to explore its mysterious depths.

LEFT: the ornate Torre dell'Orologio. **BELOW:** St Mark's Square, basilica and campanile.

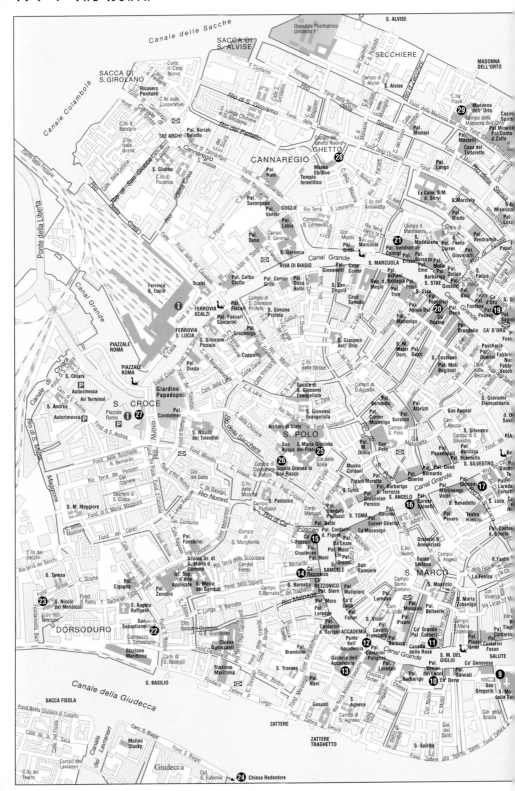

Venice

0   300 m
0   300 yds

BELOW: St Mark's
Basilica.

Basilica di San Marco

The **Basilica di San Marco** ❷ (Mon–Sat 9.30am–5pm, Sun 2–4pm; entrance fee to Sanctuary, Pala d'Oro and Treasury; due to strict security measures all bags now need to be left in the Ateneo San Basso on Piazzetta dei Leoncini – a free left-luggage service) is named after the evangelist St Mark whose remains were recovered (or stolen, depending on your viewpoint) by the Venetians from Alexandria in the 9th century. The then ruler of Venice, Doge Giustiniano Participazio, built a church on this site to house the remains. The original church was destroyed by fire a century later, and was replaced in the late 11th century by the huge ornate edifice we see today.

The sumptuous facade (currently being restored) has five portals decorated with shimmering mosaics. The only original mosaic – in the doorway to the far left – gives a good idea of the appearance of the basilica in the 13th century. Above the main portal are replicas of the famous bronze horses, thought to be Roman or Hellenistic works of the 3rd or 4th century AD and looted by the Venetians from Constantinople in 1204. They were taken to Paris by Napoleon in 1797 and returned in 1815, and are now kept inside the basilica, protected from pigeons and pollution.

The basilica's interior, in the shape of a Greek cross, is thought to have been inspired by the Church of the Apostles in Constantinople. Above the columns of the minor naves, lining the arms of the cross, are the women's galleries or *matronei*, designed in accordance with Greek Orthodox custom, which separates the sexes. The sumptuous atmosphere of the interior is enhanced by the decoration of the walls: marble slabs cover the lower part, while golden mosaics adorn the vaults, arches and domes. Following a complex iconographic plan,

the mosaics cover 4,000 sq. metres (43,000 sq. ft), which is why St Mark's is sometimes called the Basilica d'Oro (Church of Gold). For a brief explanation of the mosaics, join one of the groups that tour the basilica.

Among the many gems housed in the church are the **Pala d'Oro**, a jewel-studded gold and enamel altarpiece dating from the 10th century. The **Treasury** also houses a priceless collection of gold and silver from Byzantium. The **Marciano Museum** (daily 9am–7pm in summer, 9.45am–5pm in winter; entrance fee), reached by steep steps from the entrance narthex, affords fine views of the interior as a whole, while the open-air terrace beyond the museum gives a bird's-eye view of Piazza San Marco. It was here that the doge and other dignitaries gathered to watch celebrations taking place below.

A panoramic view

A striking feature of the square is the soaring **Campanile ❸** (daily July–Aug 9am–9pm, Apr–June & Sept–Oct 9am–7pm, Nov Mar 9am–4pm; entrance fee), a faithful replica of the original tower that collapsed in 1902. Inside, a lift – or, for the energetic, a stairway – climbs 100 metres (330 ft) to the top for a sweeping panorama of the city and lagoon. The piazza's other tower is Coducci's intricate **Torre dell'Orologio ❹** (Clock Tower), designed in 1496 (currently closed for lengthy restoration). Adjoining the piazza and extending to the waterfront is the **Piazzetta San Marco**. On the right as you face the lagoon stands the 16th-century Biblioteca Nazionale Marciana, also known as **Libreria Sansoviniana ❺** (daily 9am–7pm; entrance fee for full tours, tel: 041-520 8788), where classical concerts are occasionally staged. Palladio, Italy's greatest 16th-century architect, considered this structure, with its finely sculpted arcades and detailed

Map on pages 174–5

Mosaic of Christ in St Mark's.

BELOW: Doge's Palace.

Sculptures of Adam and Eve by Antonio Rizzo on the facade of the Palazzo Ducale.

BELOW: the Rio Canonica and Bridge of Sighs.

figures, one of the most beautiful buildings ever constructed. Today it houses the **Archaeological Museum** (daily 9am–7pm; entrance fee), the National Library of St Mark and the Venetian Old Library – with a collection of treasures from the city's golden years.

At the lagoon end of the Piazzetta stand two large 12th-century columns, one crowned with a winged lion, the symbol of Venice, the other with a statue of St Theodore, the original patron saint of the city. Originally a marketplace, the area later became known as a gathering place for politicians waiting to attend meetings. Public executions also used to take place between the two columns.

Across the water lies one of Venice's great landmarks – the majestic **Church of San Giorgio Maggiore ❻** (daily 9am–12.30pm and 2.30–6.30pm; entrance fee for Campanile) on the little islet of the same name. This classical masterpiece by Andrea Palladio has a huge white stone interior with works of art by Tintoretto, and the views from the campanile extend, on a clear day, as far as the Alps.

The Doge's Palace

The **Palazzo Ducale ❼** (Apr–Oct daily 9am–7pm, Nov–Mar daily 9am–5pm; entrance fee) flanks the eastern side of the Piazzetta. This "vast and sumptuous pile", as Byron described it, is the grandest and most conspicuous example of Venetian Gothic in the city. The official residence of the doge and the seat of government during the republic, it stands today as eloquent evidence of the power and pomp of Venice in its heyday.

Inside, the three wings of the palace reveal a seemingly endless series of grandiose rooms and halls. The largest of these is the Sala del Maggior Consiglio (the Great Council Chamber) which could accommodate all 480 (and later 1,700) of the Venetian patricians who sat on the council. The art collection here gives a foretaste of the countless artistic treasures scattered throughout the city, and includes works by the two Venetian giants – Tintoretto and Veronese. Tintoretto's *Paradise* (1588–92) was for many years the largest painting in the world (7 metres x 22 metres/23 ft x 72 ft). In the same room, Veronese's *Apotheosis of Venice* is another compelling masterpiece, though his finest work in the palace is *The Rape of Europa* in the Anticollegio.

Adjoining the palace is the former prison. Once tried and convicted in the palace, prisoners were led across the slender covered bridge to their cell. Since the windowed bridge offered the captive his last glimpse of freedom, it was called **Il Ponte dei Sospiri ❽** (the Bridge of Sighs). However grim its original purpose, it has a romantic air, and is favoured today by young lovers who believe that if they kiss under the bridge (presumably in a gondola) their love will last.

The *Itinerari Segreti* (Secret Itineraries) are fascinating guided tours of lesser-known parts of the doge's palace and prison cells (daily tours in English at 9.45am, 10.45am and 11.35am; for bookings and information tel: 0571-981 064).

A tour of the ducal palace is best rounded off with a coffee break in the piazza. The most famous café here is **Florian**, the once fashionable haunt for high Venetian society. Henry James conjures the atmosphere in *The*

Aspern Papers (1888): "I sat in front of Florian's café, eating ices, listening to music, talking with acquaintances: the traveller will remember how the immense cluster of tables and little chairs stretches like a promontory into the smooth lake of the Piazza."

Map on pages 174–5

The Grand Canal

The **Canal Grande** winds for 3.5 km (2 miles) through the city. This splendid shimmering thoroughfare is flanked by pastel-coloured palaces in a mixture of Byzantine, Gothic, Renaissance and baroque styles, built mostly between the 13th and the 18th centuries.

The best way to see the canal is from a boat. If you are feeling flush, hire a gondola from the San Marco waterfront. Thomas Mann, who commented that the gondolas of Venice were "black as nothing else on earth except a coffin", nonetheless found their seats "the softest, most luxurious, most relaxing in the world". Far cheaper, though less romantic and more noisy, is the No. 1 public waterbus (*vaporetto*) which plies the length of the canal at frequent intervals. Alternatively, try the faster No. 82 service which makes fewer stops.

Starting from San Marco, the entrance of the canal is marked on the left bank by the great baroque church of **Santa Maria della Salute 9**, designed by the 17th-century baroque architect Baldassare Longhena, and erected in thanks for the city's deliverance from the plague of 1630. To the enamoured James, the church was "like a great lady on the threshold of her salon … with her domes and scrolls, her scalloped buttresses and statues forming a pompous crown, and her wide steps disposed on the ground like the train of a robe".

On the same side is the **Palazzo Venier dei Leoni 10** (Wed–Mon 10am–6pm; entrance fee), the famous residence-museum of the late American patroness of the arts, Peggy Guggenheim (1898–1979). This is Venice's leading contemporary art museum with a superb eclectic collection of works representing the major artistic and avant-garde movements of the last century. Paintings by legendary names including Picasso, Braque, Kandinsky and Bacon are all on display alongside a large representation of Surrealist art, which was close to Guggenheim's heart – she was briefly married to Max Ernst, one of the movement's founders. His works, along with those of Dalí, Magritte, Jackson Pollock and de Kooning among many others, are all here. The 18th-century *palazzo* was built for the noble Venier family and was nicknamed the "Nonfinito", because the building remained unfinished, never progressing beyond the first floor. It is a splendidly eccentric setting for the collection, with a lovely garden and courtyard where chained lions were once kept, earning it the sobriquet "dei Leoni".

On the right bank opposite is **Ca'Grande 11**, a three-storey Renaissance residence by Sansovino, now the office of the city magistrate. The first bridge that spans the canal is the wooden **Ponte dell'Accademia 12**, built in 1932 as a temporary structure but retained through popular demand. It is named after the nearby **Gallerie dell'Accademia 13** (Tues–Sun 8.30am–7pm, Mon 8.30am–2pm; entrance fee) housed in the former Scuola della Carità. This contains the world's finest collection

BELOW: Veronese's *Feast in the House of Levi* (Accademia).

BELOW: a journey along the Grand Canal affords vistas unmatched anywhere in the world.

of Venetian paintings, with works by Mantegna, Bellini, Giorgione *(The Tempest)*, Carpaccio, Titian, Tintoretto, Veronese, Tiepolo, Guardi and Canaletto, mostly arranged in chronological order.

Further down the canal on the same side stands the imposing baroque palace of the recently restored **Ca' Rezzonico** ⓮ (Wed–Mon 10am–6pm; entrance fee) housing a museum of 18th-century Venice, dedicated to the swansong years of Venice's Most Serene Republic – La Serenissima. The stately rooms are richly decorated with period paintings, furniture and frescoes. It was here that the poet Robert Browning died in 1889.

Richard Wagner was staying at the second of the two Gothic **Palazzi Giustinian** on the left bank when he composed the second act of *Tristan and Isolde* during 1858–59. Next door, **Ca' Foscari** ⓯ is a 15th-century palace in the Venetian Gothic style, named after the family of the great 15th-century doge who masterminded large Venetian conquests on the Italian mainland.

Beyond the Sant'Angelo landing stage, on the right bank, **Palazzo Corner Spinelli** ⓰ was designed during the early Venetian Renaissance in the Lombardic style by Coducci. Beyond the next side canal, the **Palazzo Grimani** ⓱, now the Court of Appeal, is a late Renaissance masterpiece by Sanmicheli. In front of you, Venice's most famous bridge, **Ponte di Rialto** ⓲, arches over the canal. The former wooden drawbridges built across the canal at this point all collapsed, necessitating the erection of a more weighty stone structure. Antonio da Ponte, one of many eminent contenders for the commission, supervised its construction between 1588 and 1592. The single-span, balustraded bridge has two parallel rows of tightly packed shops selling jewellery, leather, masks, silk and souvenirs.

Ca' d'Oro

The most beautiful Gothic palace in Venice, the **Ca' d'Oro** (Tues–Sun 8.15am–7.15pm, Mon 8.15am–2pm; entrance fee) appears on the right at the first landing stage beyond the bridge. When built in 1420 by the wealthy patrician Marino Contarini, it was covered in gold leaf, hence the name "House of Gold". Inside, the Giorgio Franchetti art gallery comprises a varied collection of paintings, frescoes and sculpture. Further along, on the left bank, the enormous baroque **Ca' Pesaro** ⑳ is another masterpiece by Longhena; this one houses the Galleria d'Arte Moderna and the Museo Orientale (Tues–Sun 10am–6pm; entrance fee). The last building of note before the railway station is **Palazzo Vendramin-Calergi** ㉑, one of the finest Renaissance palaces by Mauro Coducci (1440–1504). Wagner died here in 1883.

The six districts of Venice

The greatest experience the city can offer to the inquisitive visitor is the maze of tiny alleys, the narrow silent canals and the pretty squares and courtyards only minutes away from **San Marco**, the most central of the six districts *(sestieri)* of Venice. Leading north from the Piazza San Marco, starting at the clock tower, is the **Merceria dell'Orologia**. This ancient commercial thoroughfare is still one of Venice's busiest streets, flanked by small shops and boutiques.

Dorsoduro is the most southerly section of historic Venice – an excellent area to stay if you are looking for a quiet *pensione* within easy access of central Venice. To the south, the area is bounded by the **Zattere**, a long, broad and peaceful quayside whose cafés and restaurants afford splendid views across the water to the island of Giudecca. East of the Accademia Galleries, the Dorsoduro is quiet and intimate, characterised by pretty canals, small shops, galleries and chic residences.

Northwest of the Accademia, the area around San Barnaba was traditionally the quarter for impoverished Venetian nobility. Today it is the scene of cafés, artisans and one of the last surviving vegetable barges. Further west, the 16th-century church of **San Sebastiano** ㉒ (Mon–Sat 10am–5pm, entrance fee; Chorus, the association of Venetian churches, issues a special pass allowing access to 13 of the city's most important churches, visit www.chorusvenezia.org; tel: 041-275 04 62) was the parish church of Veronese and provided a Classical canvas for many of his opulent masterpieces, painted between 1555 and 1565.

The area becomes increasingly shabby towards San Nicolò dei Mendicoli, erstwhile home of sailors and fishermen. The charming Romanesque church of **San Nicolò dei Mendicoli** ㉓ was expertly restored by the British Venice in Peril Fund in the 1970s.

The island of **Giudecca**, across the Giudecca Canal, is a quiet working-class area of narrow streets. The main landmark on its waterfront is Andrea Palladio's **Redentore** church ㉔ (Mon–Sat 10am–5pm; Sun 1–5pm), built in gratitude for the city's deliverance from plague in 1576. On the third Sunday in July, the city commemorates this event by building a bridge of boats from the Zattere to the Redentore, where a special Mass is held. That night, a firework display lights up the sky.

Map on pages 174–5

TIP

The signposted routes between St Mark's, the Rialto and Accademia can get very crowded. For respite from the hordes of tourists, just turn off onto any side canal, where you will find equally attractive buildings and a glimpse of genuine Venetian life.

BELOW: Tiepolo's *Abraham visited by the Angels* in San Rocco.

San Polo

The *sestiere* of **San Polo** lies within the large bend of the Grand Canal, northwest of San Marco. The quarter around the **Rialto**, the oldest inhabited part of mainland Venice, became the gathering place of merchants from the East and thence the commercial hub of the city. It is still a bustling area, with shops and market stalls. Fruit and vegetables are laid out under the arcades of the Fabbriche Vecchie while the mock-Gothic stone loggia of the Pescheria marks the site of the morning fish market. Arrive early, as the market begins to close by noon.

The major church of San Polo is the majestic brick Gothic **Santa Maria Gloriosa dei Frari** ㉕ (Mon–Sat 9am–6pm, Sun 1–6pm; entrance fee, or free with Chorus church pass, *see page 181*), usually referred to as the Frari. The interior houses some of Venice's finest masterpieces, including an exquisite *Madonna and Child* by Bellini, Titian's celebrated *Assumption* (crowning the main altar) and his *Madonna di Ca' Pesaro*. Buried in the Frari are the composer Claudio Monteverdi, the sculptor Canova (who lies in a pyramidal tomb he designed as a monument to Titian) and several doges.

Nearby, the **Scuola Grande di San Rocco** ㉖ (daily in summer 9am–5.30pm, restricted hours in winter; entrance fee) is celebrated for its series of religious works by Tintoretto, painted on the walls and ceilings in 1564–87. The scenes from the *Life of Christ* culminate in *The Crucifixion,* of which Henry James wrote: "Surely no single picture in the world contains more human life, there is everything in it including the most exquisite beauty. It is one of the greatest things of art."

Santa Croce ㉗, lying north and west of San Polo, is for the most part a relatively unexplored district. Its core is a maze of covered alleyways lined by peeling facades and criss-crossed by canals barely wide enough for the passage of a barge. Its squares are pleasingly shabby, bustling with local life. The only real concession to tourism is the **Piazzale Roma**, the uninspiring arrival point for those coming by road.

The origins of the Ghetto

Cannaregio is the quietest and most remote district in Venice. Its name derives from *canne* (reeds), for this area was once marshland. The *sestiere* forms the northern arc of the city, stretching from the railway station to the Rio dei Mendicanti in the east. At its heart lies the **Ghetto** ㉘: its name originated from an iron foundry *(getto)* which once stood here. This was Europe's first ghetto, an area for the exclusive but confined occupation of Jews. Built in the early 16th century, it gave its name to isolated Jewish communities throughout the world. It remained a ghetto until Napoleonic times. Though very few Jews live here, the synagogues, tenements and kosher restaurants lend a distinctive Jewish air, and the area's history is well documented in the **Museo Ebraico** (Sun–Fri 10am–7pm, till 6pm Oct–Apr, and earlier closing on Friday – before sunset; closed Sat and Jewish holidays; entrance fee), a small museum in the main square.

The northern part of Cannaregio is the most remote and the area around the lovely Gothic church of the **Madonna dell'Orto** ㉙ (Mon–Sat 10am–5pm, Sun 1–5pm; entrance fee) the most appealing. Tintoretto was born here and lived at No. 3399, near the Campo de'

Venice's scuole *were a cross between professional guilds and charitable societies. Some of them became very wealthy and commissioned fine artists to decorate their headquarters.*

BELOW: Renaissance gateway to the Arsenale, built in 1460 by Antonio Gambello.

Mori. Forming the northern border of Cannaregio, the Fondamente Nuove is the main departure point for ferries to the northern islands. Across the water you can see the walled cemetery on the island of San Michele. Back from the quayside, the baroque church of the **Gesuiti** ⓼ (daily 10am–noon and 4–6pm) has an outrageously extravagant green and white marble interior, and contains Titian's dramatic *Martyrdom of St Lawrence*.

To the east of Cannaregio, it is worth exploring the warren of alleys and canals. With luck, you will stumble upon the church of **Santa Maria dei Miracoli** ⓾ (Mon–Sat 10am–5pm, Sun 1–5pm; entrance fee). Designed in the 1480s by Pietro Lombardo and his workshop, it is one of the loveliest Renaissance churches in the city. Decorated inside and out with marble, it is often likened to a jewel-box.

Castello

The city's western section, **Castello**, varies in character from the busy southern waterfront near San Marco to the humble cheek-by-jowl residences of the north. The area behind Riva degli Schiavoni is worth exploring for its pretty canals, quaysides and elegant faded palaces. Essential viewing for those interested in art is the frieze by Carpaccio in the **Scuola di San Giorgio degli Schiavoni** ⓛ (Tues–Sat 9.30am–12.30pm and 3.30–6.30pm, Sun 9.30am–12.30pm; entrance fee) and Coducci's 16th-century church of **San Zaccaria** ⓝ.

The **Campo Santa Maria Formosa** ⓞ (church: Mon–Sat 10am–5pm, Sun 1–5pm; entrance fee) is a pleasant market square with a fine Renaissance church, which is home to Palma il Vecchio's splendid *St Barbara and Saints* of 1510. The spiritual heart of Castello is the **Campo Santi Giovanni e Paolo** ⓟ, better known in Venetian dialect as San Zanipolo. Standing prominently in this spacious

Map on pages 174–5

Murano Vase.

BELOW: the Casa Bepi on Burano.

Map on
pages
174–5

square is Andrea del Verrocchio's masterly bronze equestrian statue of the fierce mercenary Bartolomeo Colleoni. Presiding over the square is the majestic Gothic church of **Santi Giovanni e Paolo** ㊱ (daily 7.30am–12.30pm and 3.30–7.30pm), where 46 doges are buried. Many of their tomb monuments are magnificent, as is Paolo Veronese's *Adoration of the Shepherds* in the Cappella del Rosario.

Part of eastern Castello is occupied by the **Arsenale** ㊲, the great shipyard of the republic where Venice's galleys were built and refurbished. It is now largely abandoned and inaccessible to the public, but you can see a small part from the No. 52 public waterbus and there is an excellent **Naval Museum** (Mon–Sat 8.45am–1pm; entrance fee) alongside the main entrance gate. To the east of the public gardens is the site of the **Biennale** ㊳, an international exhibition of modern art, film and music (held in odd-numbered years).

Island excursions

There is plenty to see away from the historic centre of Venice. The lagoon was settled from the 5th century and you can still see the remains of the very first Venetian community on the tiny island of Torcello (*see below*). Frequent ferry services link Venice to the main islands.

The island of **San Michele**, just north of Venice, is occupied by the cemetery and the early Renaissance church of San Michele in Isola, designed by Coducci. Napoleon, who forbade burials in the historic centre, established the cemetery. Ezra Pound and Igor Stravinsky were two of the eminent visitors to Venice who are buried here.

Further north, the island of **Murano** is spread over five islets criss-crossed by canals, which make it seem like a mini-Venice. In the late 13th century Murano became the centre of Venice's ancient glass-blowing industry, as factories were moved from the city centre for fear of fire. The **Museo Vetrario** (Thur–Tues 10am–5pm, till 4pm in winter; entrance fee) in the Fondamenta Giustinian has exquisite examples of glasswork.

Venice's justly famous lace industry is based in **Burano**, northeast of Venice. This is a colourful island where canals are lined by brightly painted houses and stalls selling lace and linen. Prices in Burano can be cheaper than elsewhere in Venice, but beware of imitation Venetian lace from factories in the Far East.

Torcello, the most remote of these islands (an hour by ferry), is the least populated and, for many, the most interesting. This rural, marshy island was the site of the original settlement in the Venetian lagoon. Still standing is the magnificent Byzantine cathedral. A large striking mosaic of *The Virgin*, standing above a frieze of apostles, decorates the chancel apse of the church, while the entire western wall is covered by a huge and elaborate mosaic depicting *The Last Judgement*.

To the south of Venice, on a different route, lies the **Lido**, where Thomas Mann's unhappy Aschenbach loitered too long, feasting his tired eyes on the unattainable boy Tadzio, and died of cholera. The Lido is no longer the fashionable resort depicted in *Death in Venice* but in the hot summer months, when the city and its sights can be overwhelming, the sands and sea air provide a welcome break. ❑

Relaxing on the Lido.

BELOW: Burano.
RIGHT: Palladio's San Giorgio Maggiore.

LIFE AS A MASQUERADE

Carnival in Venice is supreme self-indulgence,
a giddy round of masked balls and private parties
suggesting mystery and promising romance

In Venice, Carnival is a 10-day pre-Lenten extravaganza, culminating in the burning of the effigy of Carnival in Piazza San Marco on Shrove Tuesday. As an expression of a topsy-turvy world, Carnival is a time for rebellion without the risk of ridicule. The essence of the "feast of fools" lies in the unfolding Venetian vistas: masked processions heading towards Piazza San Marco past shimmering palaces, with surreal masqueraders tumbling out of every alley. As the revellers flock to Florian's café in Piazza San Marco, the air is sickly sweet with the scent of fritters and the sound of lush baroque music. Carnival capers include costumed balls, firework displays and historical parades, all staged by the carnival societies.

SPIRIT OF RESISTANCE

Carnival is often dismissed as commercialised and chaotic but Venetian traditionalists view it differently. The leader of a venerable carnival company sees the event as saving his city: "Life in Venice is inconvenient and costly. With the Carnival, we give a positive picture and show the pleasure of living here. Carnival is a form of resistance. By resisting the temptation to leave, we are saving the spirit of the city for future generations."

△ SELECT CARDS
A select group of Venetians still appears as *tarocchi*, fortune-telling tarot cards. These famous cards supposedly reached Europe from the East, through Venice. The star of the pack is the Queen of Swords, her costume rich in silver cabalistic signs.

▽ WINDOW DRESSING
Masks originally allowed the nobility to mingle incognito with the common people in *casini* (private clubs), but are now an excuse for all-purpose revelry. This shop window displays fantasy masks, which are creative rather than authentic, and appeal to individual tastes.

▽ THE GREAT LEVELLER
A mask makes everyone equal. Masqueraders are addressed as *"sior maschera"* (masked gentleman) regardless of age, rank or even gender. One way of preserving some individuality is face-painting.

MASTERS OF DISGUISE

Mask-makers had their own guild in medieval times, when a *mascheraio* (mask-maker) helped a secretive society run smoothly. Modern masqueraders must choose between masks in leather *(cuoio)*, china *(ceramica)* or papier-mâché *(cartapesta)*. Papier-mâché and leather masks are the most authentic. Antique masks are rare since neither material readily stands the test of time or the Venetian climate. Authentic mask-makers both reinterpret traditional designs and create new ones. In the case of papier-mâché masks, the pattern is made from a fired clay design, which generates a plaster-of-Paris mould. Layers of papier-mâché paste are used to line the mould and thus create the mask. When dry, the paste gives the mask a shiny surface akin to porcelain. Polish and a white base coat are applied before the eye holes are cut and decorative detail is added. This painting process can be simple or highly artistic. Of the alternatives to papier-mâché, leather masks are hard to fashion; ceramic designs, ideal as hand-held masks or as wall decorations, are often adorned with fine fabrics. Places to browse include Laboratorio Artigiano Maschere (Barbaria delle Tole, Castello 6657, tel: 041-522 3110) and Ca' del Sol (Fondamenta dell'Osmarin, Castello, tel: 041-528 5549). Nearby is Mondonovo – one of Venice's most creative mask-makers (Rio Terra Canal, off Campo Santa Margherita, tel: 041-528 7344).

△ **THE NOBLE LOOK**
Costumes can be historical, traditional or simply surreal. The classic Venetian disguise of the 17th and 18th centuries was known as the *maschera nobile*, the patrician mask. The carnival companies wear noble Renaissance and rococo costumes *(left)* as a matter of course.

▽ **VOLTO FACE**
The patrician *maschera nobile* and witty *commedia dell'arte* masks are among a number of authentic disguises. While this cumbersome ruff is pure fantasy, the white mask looks to the past for inspiration: it is a modern variant on the slightly sinister *volto*, the traditional Venetian mask.

THE VENETO

*Two cities with links to Shakespearean heroines
and a chance to surfeit on the buildings of
Italy's greatest Renaissance architect*

Shakespeare called Italy's second-oldest university city "Fair Padua, nursery of Arts" and described it as a place where Renaissance Englishmen came to "suck the sweets of sweet philosophy". Dante and Galileo both lectured at **Padua ❷** (Padova), and in the mid-17th century a learned woman earned a doctorate here, the first woman in Europe to do so. (Padua's most famous daughter is, without a doubt, Katherina, Shakespeare's tameable shrew.)

But long before the university was established in 1222, Padua was an important Roman town, believed by Virgil to have been founded by the brother of the Trojan King Priam, after the fall of Troy – though, in fact, it had been a settlement of pre-Roman tribesmen. (The Roman historian Livy was born in the nearby hills and was always proud to call himself a Paduan.)

Padua is also a magnet for the faithful. Every June, pilgrims come from all over the world to honour St Anthony of Padua, a 13th-century itinerant preacher whose spell-binding sermons packed church pews throughout Italy. The **Basilica di Sant'Antonio** (daily 7.30am–7pm), built over his remains between 1232 and 1307, celebrates his sanctity handsomely, with works by Donatello (who lived in Padua from 1443–53), Sansovino and Menabuoi. Venice ❶ *(see pages 173–184)* is, of course, very close to Padua, and Venetian influence is evident in

BELOW: Donatello's *Gattamelata.*
BELOW RIGHT: Caffè Pedrocchi.

the church's design. Byzantine domes, an ornate facade and two high, thin bell towers give the exterior an Oriental appearance. The interior also has Byzantine decorative details. The chapel of St Anthony, containing the revered tomb, is a 16th-century design by Biosco.

Padua's piazzas

In **Piazza del Santo**, to one side of the basilica, stands a famous equestrian statue of Erasmo da Narni, called *Gattamelata*, by Donatello. This sculpture of the great Venetian *condottiere* (mercenary) is believed to be the first great bronze cast in Italy during the Renaissance. Also in the piazza is the **Oratorio di San Giorgio** (9am–12.30pm and 2.30–6pm, closes at 5pm in winter; entrance fee), originally a private mausoleum for the prominent Soranzo family. The oratory is decorated with beautiful frescoes by Altichiero and Avanzo. On the corner of the piazza is the entrance to the **Scuola di Sant'Antonio** (daily 9am–12.30pm and 2.30–7pm in summer, till 5pm in winter; entrance fee) which houses paintings by Bellini, Titian and Giorgione, among others.

The Via Belludi leads to another notable square, the **Prato della Valle**, fronted by the **Basilica di Santa Giustina**. A small park at its centre is reached by crossing one of the four stone bridges over a circular moat. In the park, a circle of statues represents famous past citizens of Padua.

The city centres on the crowded **Piazza delle Erbe**, one of its three market squares. Here stands the **Palazzo della Ragione**, called locally **Il Salone** (Tues–Sun 9am–7pm, closes at 6pm in winter; entrance fee), a massive medieval structure. The interior is decorated with fine frescoes and houses a large wooden horse copied from Donatello's bronze masterpiece.

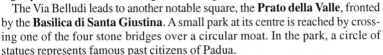

TIP

The upstairs rooms at the Caffè Pedrocchi are used for concerts and other events. The rooms are worth seeing for their extravagant Egyptian, Moorish, Greek and other decor.

BELOW: the Prato della Valle and Basilica di Santa Giustina.

Map on pages 190–1

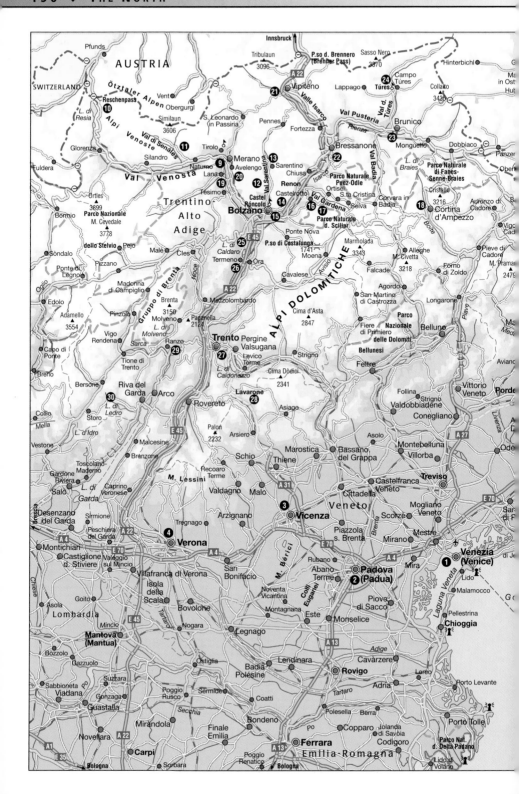

Northeastern Italy

0   20 km
0   20 miles

AUSTRIA

Heiligenblut
er Knopf
nklern
Obervellach
Gmünd
nz
Hochkreuz
2708
Möllbrücke
Spittal an
der Drau
Patergassen
Greifenburg
rdrauburg
Techendorf
Latschur
2236
Radenthein
Kötschach-
Mauthen
Kirchbach
Hermagor
Mösel
Feldkirchen
Gall
Ossiacher
See
rni
voltri
S. Stefan
Villach
Klagenfurt
omeglians
Alpi Carniche
Pontebba
Gentile
76
Paluzza
Podkoren
Gentile
Ampezzo
Chiusaforte
J.di Montasio
2754
Sava
Tolmezzo
amonti
Sopra
Sella Nevea
2571
Triglav
2863
Mrzli
studenec
Friuli-
Venezia
Giulia
Gemona
del Friuli
Zaga
Bohinjska
Bistrica
S. Daniele
d. Friuli
Tarcento
Kobarid
Ljubljana
Spilimbergo
Tolmin
Cividale
del Friuli
Udine
8
SLOVENIA
Codroipo
Cormons
S. Vito
al Tagl
ogruaro
Castions
di Strada
Palmanova
Gorizia
Idrija
Ajdovscina
Cervignano
d. Friuli
Latisana
Aquileia
Monfalcone
7
Sezana
Lignano
Sabbiadoro
Grado
Castello di
Miramare 6
Barcola
Trieste
Caorle
Bibione
Golfo di
Trieste
5
Kozina
Koper
Venezia
Rt Savudrija
Umag
Buje
Buzet
CROATIA
Porec
Baderna
Pazin
ADRIATIC
Vrsar
Zminj
SEA
Rovinj
Labin
Pula

Behind Il Salone is **Caffè Pedrocchi** (closed Mon), famous throughout Italy as a gathering place for intellectuals. During the Risorgimento *(see page 57)*, liberals from the nearby university met here to discuss the founding of the new nation.

From here it is only a short walk through **Piazza dei Signori** to Padua's **Duomo**. Although the cathedral was designed by Michelangelo, many alterations were made to his plans and the result is rather disappointing. The most interesting corner of the church is the frescoed baptistry (daily 9.30am–1pm and 3–7pm in summer, till 6pm in winter; entrance fee).

Miser's Madonna

To the north of the university lies the **Cappella degli Scrovegni** (daily 9am–7pm; by appointment only, tel: 049-201 0020; lines open Mon–Fri 9am–7pm, Sat 9am–1pm; entrance fee includes Eremitani Museum). Enrico Scrovegni commissioned this richly decorated chapel in 1303 to atone for his father's miserliness and usury. It contains a recently restored cycle of frescoes by Giotto depicting the history of Christian redemption. The panels rank among Giotto's masterpieces. The solidity and emotional depth of the figures marked a turning point in Western painting. "In my opinion," wrote Giorgio Vasari in the 17th century, "painters owe to Giotto, the Florentine painter, exactly the same debt they owe to nature, which constantly serves them as a model and whose finest and most beautiful aspects they are always striving to imitate and reproduce."

Thankfully, the chapel escaped the fate of the nearby **Eremitani** church whose apse, covered with precious Mantegna frescoes, was bombed during World War II – Italy's greatest art loss of the war. This bare-walled church stands in poignant contrast to the rich collection of paintings, frescoes, bronzes and mosaics in the **Eremitani Museum** (Feb–Oct Tues–Sun 9am–7pm, Nov–Jan Tues–Sun 9am–6pm; entrance fee includes entrance to Scrovegni Chapel) alongside, which contains outstanding works of art, such as Bellini's *Portrait of a Young Suitor*.

Vicenza

Andrea di Pietro, nicknamed Palladio, and the most prominent architect of the Italian High Renaissance, worked for most of his life (1508–80) in **Vicenza ❸**. Rich and eager to decorate their city with new buildings, the local gentry gave Palladio many opportunities to use his talents. As a result, there is hardly a street in central Vicenza not graced by a Palladian mansion despite the destruction of 14 of Palladio's buildings during World War II.

Palladio's addition of open galleries to Vicenza's Basilica was not just a way of embellishing the market square – the galleries were designed to strengthen the older building, which was suffering from subsidence.

In **Piazza dei Signori**, at the city's heart, stand two of Palladio's masterpieces. The **Basilica**, his first major work, is not a church but a remodelling of a Gothic courthouse (called *basilica* in the Roman sense – a place where justice is administered). Palladio's elegant design features two open galleries, the lower one with Tuscan Doric columns and the upper one with Ionic columns. Facing the Basilica is the **Loggia del Capitaniato**, a later Palladian work commissioned in 1571 to honour the victory over the Turks at Lepanto.

The city's Gothic-style **Duomo** stands just behind the Basilica. It was badly bombed during World War II but has since been completely rebuilt. The interior is unremarkable. A Palladian cupola tops the roof.

North of the Duomo is **Corso Palladio**, the city's main street, lined with many fine villas. Number 163 is the so-called **Casa del Palladio**. With its classic lines and precise geometric proportions, it is a typical example of Palladio's work. Another excellent example of the Palladian style is the **Palazzo Chiericati**, in the Piazza Matteotti, at the end of Corso Palladio. This beautiful building houses the **Museo Civico** (Tues–Sun 10am–7pm in summer, 9am–5pm in winter; entrance fee) and the city's art collection. Tintoretto's *Miracle of St Augustine* and several works by Flemish artists are on permanent display.

BELOW: Palladio's Villa Rotonda, outside Vicenza.

In addition to the fine works in the city museum, the new **Galleria di Palazzo Leoni Montanari** (Contrà di Santa Corona, 25; Fri–Sun 10am–6pm, but variable; tel: 800-57 88 75; entrance fee) has a superb collection of Venetian paintings, including works by Canaletto and Pietro Longhi. On the top floor there is also a notable collection of Russian icons.

Palladio wasn't the only great architect to work here. The younger Scamozzi, who learned much from Palladio, designed the **Palazzo del Comune** on the Corso Palladio; it reflects his strict interpretation of classical architecture.

The finest example of Scamozzi and Palladio's joint work is the **Teatro Olimpico** (Tues–Sun 9am–4.45pm, July–Aug till 7pm; entrance fee), said to have been the first covered theatre in Europe when it was built between 1580 and 1582. Palladio died before its completion and Scamozzi took over. The theatre is a wood and stucco structure with a permanent stage set of a piazza and streets in perfect perspective. The theatre is still in regular use today.

Excursions from Vicenza

Monte Berico, a forested hill visible from all parts of Vicenza, is well worth a visit. Take a bus from the Piazza Duomo, or walk for approximately one hour to reach the **Madonna del Monte**, a 17th-century rebuilding of a chapel that commemorated the site of two apparitions of the Virgin. The final section of the approach is covered by a portico with 150 arches and 17 chapels. Inside, the basilica is spacious and airy, and works of art include a *Pietà* by Montagna. During World War I, the mountains beyond Vicenza were the scene of many great battles. The **Piazzale della Vittoria**, a few yards from the church, is a memorial to all the Italians who died close to here.

Map on pages 190–1

Elegant Verona.

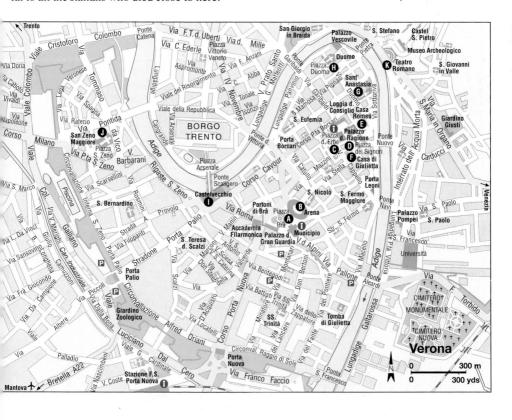

Verona's Giardino Giusti, a superb example of a Renaissance garden, is dotted with statuary.

To the southeast of the town centre is **Villa Capra**, better known as La Rotonda (grounds: mid Mar–early Nov Tues–Thur 10am–noon, 3–6pm; interior: Wed only, same hours; tel: 044-321 793; entrance fee), a famous belvedere built by Palladio in 1551 with a distinctive circle within a cube design. Another fine villa nearby was built in 1688 by Antonio Muttoni. Known as the Villa ai Nani (Villa of the Dwarfs) on account of the statues of comical figures topping the garden wall, it is decorated with the delightful illusionistic frescoes of father and son, Giambattista and Giandomenico Tiepolo.

Verona

Built in the distinctive local pink marble, **Verona** ④ has a rosy hue, as if the sun were constantly setting. What was once a thriving Roman settlement is today one of the most prosperous and elegant cities in Italy.

The **Piazza Brà** ④ is where the Veronese gather day and night to talk, shop and drink together. They sit or stroll in the shadow of the glorious 1st-century Roman **Arena** ⑤ (Sept–June Tues–Sun 9am–6pm, July–Aug Tues–Sun 8am–3.30pm, Mon 1.45–7.30pm; last entry 45 minutes before closure; tel: 045 800 3024; entrance fee), the third-largest structure of its kind in existence. The highest fragment, called the Ala, reveals the Arena's original height. It is often used for city fairs and, in summer, up to 25,000 people at a time fill it to attend performances of popular Italian opera – notably Verdi's *Aida* (if you are fortunate enough to get tickets, take a cushion and do not drink for several hours beforehand – the loos are virtually impossible to reach). *See page 410 for details of booking.*

The Roman Forum was located in what is now **Piazza delle Erbe** ⑥, off the **Via Mazzini**. This large open space has a quirky beauty due to the variety of

Maps on pages 190 & 193

palazzi and towers that line its sides. Among the most impressive is the baroque **Palazzo Maffei**, next to the **Torre del Gardello**, the tallest Gothic structure in the square. The palace with the attractive double-arched windows on the corner of **Via Palladio** is the medieval guild house – the **Casa dei Mercanti**.

The adjoining **Piazza dei Signori** is more formal than its neighbour. The **Palazzo della Ragione**, a massive structure with heavy exterior decoration, stands on the border of the two squares. The interior courtyard has a delicate Gothic stairway. Opposite rises the **Loggia del Consiglio**, considered the finest Renaissance building in the city. Nearby are the tombs of the della Scala family (the Scaligeri), one-time rulers of Verona. The elaborately sculpted monuments stand outside the tiny church of Santa Maria Antica, surrounded by a wrought-iron fence featuring the family's staircase motif (della Scala means "of the stairs").

Verona is, of course, the city of *Romeo and Juliet*. Though the Capulet and Montague families immortalised by Shakespeare did actually exist, the story of the star-crossed lovers was entirely fictional. However, what is now a rather seedy bar on the Via delle Arche Scaligeri was allegedly the **Casa Romeo** . Rather better maintained is **Juliet's House** (Mon 1.30–7.30pm; Tues–Sun 8am–7pm; entrance fee) at No. 23 Via Cappello, near Piazza delle Erbe, a medieval townhouse complete with balcony and recently opened museum. It is also possible to visit Juliet's purported final resting place. The "tomb" (Tues–Sun 9am–6.30pm; entrance fee) is several miles out of the centre on the Lungoadige Capuleti.

If your taste runs to the Gothic, head for **Sant'Anastasia**, which, behind its brick facade, houses a magnificent painting by Pisanello of St George, as well as frescoes by Altichiero and Turone. Verona's **Duomo** (Mon–Sat 10am–5.30pm, Sun 1.30–5.30pm) is nearby. Inside is Titian's *Assumption of the Virgin*.

The **Castelvecchio** (Mon 1.30–7.30pm, Tues–Sun 8am–7.30pm; entrance fee) on the River Adige is a reminder of one of the grimmer chapters in the history of "fair Verona". The castle was first built in 1354 by the hated tyrant Cangrande II Scaliger for protection if a rebellion occurred. But he met his end not at the hands of the mob but through the treachery and ambition of his own brother, who stabbed him. As elsewhere in Italy, this fortress, its closets crammed with skeletons, is now an excellent museum with works by Veronese and Tiepolo.

A saint and a prophet

Every Italian city must have a patron saint, and Verona is no exception. Little is known about St Zeno, a 4th-century holy man, though it seems he was a fisherman. His most famous miracle is depicted by Nicola Pisano on the porch of the **Basilica di San Zeno** (Mon–Sat 8.30am–6pm, Sun 1–6pm; entrance fee). According to the story, the saint was out fishing when he saw a man being dragged into the Adige by crazed oxen. St Zeno made the sign of the cross, exorcised the devils and the man continued safely on his journey. The bronze doors of the church are of splendid workmanship though the artists are unknown. Most people are drawn to Verona because of *Romeo and Juliet* and other Shakespeare plays which are frequently performed in the **Teatro Romano** , an ancient construction of perfect proportion and superb acoustics. ❏

Relief in the Castelvecchio.

BELOW: "Juliet's House".

FRIULI-VENEZIA GIULIA

*The influence of successive invaders has given Italy's
northeastern corner a cosmopolitan feel,
combining flavours of Italy, Austria and Slovenia*

S ince the 2nd century BC – when the Romans took over the northeastern corner
of the Italian peninsula – Friuli-Venezia Giulia has been a victim of foreign
invasions. The Visigoths poured into the area in 403 AD; Attila the Hun earned
his nickname "the Scourge of God" here in 452; and in 489 came Theodoric and
the Ostrogoths. Many of the most gracious modern towns, including **Cividale del
Friuli**, began as barbarian outposts. As a result, Cividale has an outstanding collection of sculpture, jewellery and weapons from this period, displayed in the
Museo Archeologico (daily 9am–7pm in summer, until 1pm on Mon, 8.30am–
1pm in winter; entrance fee), and the **Museo Cristiano** in the cathedral (Mon–Sat
9.30am–noon, 3–6pm, Sun 3–6pm). Subsequent invaders – the Venetians and the
Austrians – left their mark, adding to the cosmopolitan flavour of this region,
which shares a convoluted border with Slovenia. The border runs through the heart
of the bilingual city of **Gorizia**, which has a fascinating castle (Tues–Sun 9.30am–
1pm, 3–7.30pm, till 6pm in winter; entrance fee) and a small war museum.

*While living in
Trieste, James Joyce
finished* Dubliners, *
wrote the final draft
of* Portrait of the
Artist as a Young
Man, *and conceived*
Ulysses.

Trieste

BELOW: the Grand
Canal in Trieste.

Of all Friuli's foreign "invaders", perhaps the best known is James Joyce, who
arrived in **Trieste ❺** in March 1905. He may not be Trieste's favourite son – he

was constantly in debt, often drunk, and given to shouting in the theatre – but the city was to become his home for the following 10 years.

Today the city has an air of faded elegance. Once Venice's rival for trade on the Adriatic, later the maritime gateway for the Austro-Hungarian empire, Trieste is now a port without a hinterland, a city that history left behind. In the Città Nuova, long, straight avenues flank a Grand Canal where tall ships once anchored. Southwest of the canal is the café-filled **Piazza dell'Unità d'Italia** – the largest sea-facing piazza in Italy. At the head of the piazza stands the ornate **Municipio**, of 19th-century Austrian inspiration. At its foot, across the railroad tracks, stretches the long quay with its **Acquario Marino** (Tues–Sun 9am–7pm in summer, 8.30am–1.30pm in winter; entrance fee) exhibiting fish from the Adriatic Sea.

The old city

Behind the Municipio are the narrow, winding streets of the **Città Vecchia**. Stairs by the **Teatro Romano** (closed to visitors) ascend steeply to the 6th-century **Duomo di San Giusto**. Two 5th-century basilicas were here combined into a single four-aisled structure in the 14th century. At the top of the hill here rises a 15th-century Venetian **Castello** with a sweeping view of the city and harbour. The **Museo del Castello di San Giusto** (Tues–Sun 9am–1pm; entrance fee) inside the castle has exhibits of early weapons plus a small art collection. On your way back down, you may want to stop at the **Civico Museo di Storia ed Arte** (Tues, Thur–Sun 9am–1pm, Wed till 7pm; entrance fee), which features relics from the various invaders and inhabitants of Friuli-Venezia Giulia. Also worth a visit is the 12th-century **Basilica of San Silvestro** on the hillside.

Seven km (4 miles) west of Trieste, set in lush green gardens, is the fairytale **Castello di Miramare**, near the seaside town of **Barcola 6**. Built between 1856 and 1860, this mock medieval fortress was the summer home of Archduke Maximilian. A museum (daily 9am–7pm; park open daily 8am–7pm, till 5pm in winter; entrance fee) honours the ill-fated archduke, who later became Emperor of Mexico and died in front of a revolutionary firing squad.

The Romans based their Northern Adriatic fleet at **Aquileia 7**, which now lies several miles inland. Here you can see the ruin of a once-vast harbour, dating from the 1st century AD. Best of all is the **Basilica** (daily, summer 9am–7pm, winter 8.30am–12.30pm, 2.30–5.30pm), begun in AD 313, with its well-preserved floor mosaics.

Udine 8 has an appealing style all its own. Echoes of Venetian rule are everywhere: the 16th-century **Castello** that towers over the city was built as the residence for Udine's Venetian governors and now houses the city's art and archaeology museums. At the foot of the castle hill, lining the monumental Piazza della Libertà, are elegant buildings, Venetian in style, including the graceful **Porticato di San Giovanni**, built in 1523, and the **Loggia del Lionello**, the city hall constructed in the 15th century. This building shows a distinct Venetian influence, with its layered pink and white masonry and windows and arches with pointed tops.

Tiepolo, the greatest Venetian baroque painter, did some of his best work here. The city's **Duomo** has three chapels decorated by him in golds and pinks. ❑

Map on pages 190–1

TIP

The Caffè degli Specchi (the Mirror Café) is one of the most lavish symbols of the belle époque and one of the oldest cafés in Trieste.

BELOW: Piazza della Libertà in Udine, with the 15th-century Palazzo del Comune.

TRENTINO-ALTO ADIGE

The limestone peaks of the Dolomites frame an area of castles, lakes and ancient spas, with its own distinctive mix of Italian and German culture

Map on pages 190–1

This mountainous region, which stretches north to the Italian-Austrian border, first came to the attention of tourists in the English-speaking world in 1837 when John Murray, the London publisher, brought out a handbook for travellers. The book's description of the Dolomites sparked interest particularly among mountaineers who had conquered the Swiss Alps and were looking for new challenges: "They are unlike any other mountains, and are to be seen nowhere else among the Alps. They arrest the attention by the singularity and picturesqueness of their forms, by their sharp peaks or horns, sometimes rising up in pinnacles and obelisks, at others extending in serrated ridges, teethed like the jaw of an alligator."

Today, Trentino-Alto Adige (also known as the South Tyrol, or Südtirol in German) is a popular holiday retreat for hikers, skiers and watersports enthusiasts. It is marked by contrasts, in the landscape as well as in the culture. Here it is possible to hike around a secluded alpine lake in the morning, sample wine in an Italian vineyard at noon, stroll along the palm-lined promenade of a Continental spa in the afternoon and then slip into bed in a medieval castle at the end of the day.

Trentino-Alto Adige actually consists of two different provinces. Trentino, historically a part of Italy except for a period during the 19th and early 20th centuries when it was ruled by Austria, has a definite Italian flair. Alto Adige, on the other hand, was a part of the Austrian Tyrol for six centuries, first becoming an Italian domain in 1919 when the Austro-Hungarian empire was carved up and the European borders were redrawn.

LEFT: the majestic landscape of the Dolomites.
BELOW: Germanic traditions are still flourishing.

Forced assimilation

The Germanic traditions, culture and language have remained, despite post-World War I efforts by Mussolini to stamp them out. The dictator Italianised not only the names of the towns, mountains and rivers but even went so far as to force the South Tyrolean people to adopt Italian family names. Schools were forbidden to teach in German and huge numbers of Italians were sent into the region to run both the government and industries as well as to tip the ethnic balance within the population.

The South Tyroleans, however, insisted on clinging steadfastly to their cultural heritage, turning, in the 1960s, to acts of terrorism in an attempt to gain more autonomy for the province. Today, the atmosphere is once again peaceful as Italians and Germans live side by side, accepting and even appreciating each other's differences. The province is officially bilingual.

The mix of cultures is just one of the factors which makes Trentino-Alto Adige so diverse. The landscape in the east and north is marked by the awe-inspiring peaks of the rocky Dolomites, while the rolling green hills of the south central region are blanketed with

A medieval belfry in Graun.

vineyards and orchards. The castles, of which there are more than 350, vary from crumbling overgrown ruins reminiscent of the one described in *Sleeping Beauty* to those that have been comprehensively restored and now house restaurants, hotels or well-appointed museums documenting the region's history.

Merano

The sleepy spa town of **Merano** ❾ (Meran), with its palm-lined promenades, exclusive shops, fine restaurants and grand old hotels, offers the visitor a taste of old Europe. The largest and most renowned spa in the Alps, Merano has played host to the great and the gracious for well over a century. Those who can afford it come to relax and take the cure in a Mediterranean-like climate. The city owes its famously mild climate to its position in a deep basin, protected to the north by the massive Alpine peaks and opening to the Etsch Valley in the south. Merano flourished between the late 13th and early 15th centuries, when it was the capital of the Tyrol. Thereafter, it passed into relative insignificance until its value as a spa was discovered.

Just a short distance north of Merano is **Castel Tirolo**, one of the only castles in the world to have lent its name to an entire region. During the summer, concerts are performed in the castle. Just down the hill is **Castel Brunnenburg**, where Ezra Pound (1885–1972) spent the last years of his life.

To the west of Merano, the **Venosta** (Vinschgau) Valley extends all the way to the Swiss/Austrian/Italian border. The route leading over the **Reschen Pass** ❿ was first constructed during Roman times as an important link between Augsburg and the Po Valley. Vinschgauer bread, a speciality of the region which is baked in small flat loaves and flavoured with aniseed, is worth sampling.

The **Val di Senales** ⓫ (Schnals Valley), which branches to the north, just past Naturno, passes through the region of the Similaun glacier. It was here that the 5,000-year-old "Similaun Man" was found by hikers in 1991. This frozen corpse (now on view in Bolzano, *see below*), complete with tools, weapons and clothing, has provided valuable new insights into life in the Bronze Age.

In the heart of Alto Adige lies the **Val Sarentina** ⓬ (Sarn Valley), a place where time seems to have stood still. The simple lifestyle of the valley farmers is in marked contrast to the wealth and splendour of Merano. Old farms perch precariously on the mountainsides, rushing brooks carve deep gorges through the mountain walls and the people themselves, celebrating traditional festivals dressed in colourful costumes, all combine to give a feeling of yesteryear. The ancient craft of *federkielstickerei*, or embroidering with peacock quills, is still practised here. The quill is split lengthways with a razor-sharp knife into thin threads used to embroider leather goods such as shoes, braces, handbags and book covers. In **Sarentino** ⓭ (Sarnthein) you can watch the craftsmen at work.

The road leading out of the valley towards the provincial capital of Bolzano winds through numerous tunnels before emerging at **Castel Roncolo** ⓮ (Schloss Runkelstein) (Mar–Nov Tues–Sun 10am–6pm, until 8pm in summer; entrance fee), built on a towering cliff in 1250 and today housing a museum with Gothic frescoes.

Bolzano

Bolzano ⓯ (Bozen) itself provides one of the most vivid examples of the coexistence of Italian and Germanic cultures. The old part of the city, gathered around Piazza Walther and the arcades of the Via dei Portici, is marked by patrician

Map on pages 190–1

Bilingual road sign.

BELOW: fresco in Castel Roncolo.

houses and German Gothic architecture. Adjacent to Piazza Walther is the impressive Gothic **Duomo**, built in the 13th and 14th centuries and reputedly the oldest hall church in Alto Adige. The **Museo Archeologico dell'Alto Adige** (Tues–Sun 10am–6pm, Thur till 8pm; entrance fee) has a fascinating collection including, famously, the mummified body of "Ötzi", the Iceman. Found by chance in the Ötzaler Alps in 1991, the extraordinarily well-preserved remains, including his clothing and copper axe, are estimated to be over 5,000 years old. He is on display in a refrigerated capsule, maintaining the mummy's temperature at -6 °C, and protected behind bullet-proof glass.

On the other side of the Talfer River, in "New Bolzano", the Italian influence is seen in the austere Mussolini-era buildings. As a part of the Italianisation effort after World War I, the city was industrialised and today Bolzano, outside the old town, is an unattractive mass of factories and smoking chimneys.

From Bolzano a cable car takes visitors on a scenic journey up to the **Renón** (Ritten) **Plateau**, a popular resort area. On a clear day, the views of the Dolomite formations are spectacular.

Just east of Bolzano is the **Sciliar** (Schlern) massif, towering like a great stone fortress above the surrounding area. At its base is the **Alpe di Siusi** (Seiser Alm), Europe's largest expanse of mountain pastureland, comprising almost 50 sq. km (20 sq. miles) and offering an abundance of hiking and ski trails.

Following the road from Sciliar to **Castelrotto** ⓰, one emerges in the **Val Gardena** (Grödner Valley) ⓱ with the popular ski resorts of **Ortisei** (St-Ulrich), **Santa Cristina** and **Selva** (Wolkenstein). This valley is also famous for its woodcarvers. From **Wolkenstein**, the Sella Joch Pass winds its way between the jagged peaks of Mount Langkofel and the majestic Sella massif. Travellers

TIP

The Alto Adige produces some good wines. Try the white wines, such as Pinot Grigio or aromatic Gewürztraminer, or the light red wines, which are very good chilled.

BELOW: the Gothic Duomo in Bolzano.
BELOW RIGHT: Lake Carezza.

through this pass enjoy a panoramic view of Mount Marmolada, the region's highest mountain, standing at 3,343 metres (10,965 ft). This route connects with the Great Dolomite Road which leads east to **Cortina d'Ampezzo** ⑱, in the Veneto, the site of the 1956 Winter Olympics and a very chic winter resort, and west over the **Costalunga** (Karer Pass) to Bolzano. The road from Bolzano passes the **Catinaccio** (Rosengarten) massif. During the twilight hours, the rose-coloured rays of the setting sun bathe the cliffs of the Rosengarten (literally "rose garden") in red, which is known as the *enrosadira*.

Lana ⑲, located between Bolzano and Merano, is the centre of the apple-growing region. The parish church in **Niederlana** contains Alto Adige's largest late-Gothic altarpiece, over 14 metres (46 ft) in height. Across the valley is **Avelengo** ⑳ (Hafling), home of the famous Hafling breed of horses.

In central Alto Adige, the **Isarco** (Eisach) **Valley** has, for the past 2,000 years, served as the major route connecting the German north to the Latin south via the Brenner Pass. The former commercial importance of **Vipiteno** ㉑ (Sterzing), the northernmost town on this route, is still evident today in its patrician houses.

Bressanone

Bressanone ㉒ (Brixen), the region's oldest settlement, was a bishopric from 990 until 1964, when the bishop moved to Bolzano. Interesting sights include the prince-bishop's palace and the baroque Duomo, which features impressive marble work and fine ceiling frescoes. A stroll through the Gothic cloisters adjacent to the Duomo is worthwhile. The frescoes here, dating from 1390 to 1509, are among the best examples of Gothic painting in the Alto Adige. The Romanesque chapel of St John at the southern end of the cloisters was built as a baptismal church.

Map on pages 190–1

Decorative sign in Vipiteno.

BELOW: grazing under the Rosengarten massif.

Just north of Bressanone, stretching to the east, is the **Pusteria Valley**. The valley's main town is **Brunico** ㉓ (Bruneck) with its lovely main street lined with houses from the 15th century. West of Brunico, the **Badia Valley** (Gadertal), where the Ladin language is still spoken, branches to the south. From Brunico, the **Túres Valley** leads north to **Campo Túres** (Sand in Taufers), site of **Castle Túres** ㉔. The castle has been restored with many of its original furnishings and is open to the public (for information on guided tours check with the regional tourist office). The Pusteria Valley is the gateway to the Sexten Dolomites where the majestic Three Pinnacles and the Sexten Sundial formations are located. The latter was used by early astronomers as a point of orientation.

Trentino and the Adige Valley

In direct contrast to the rugged mountainous north, the **Adige** (Etsch) **Valley** in south central Alto Adige is marked by a more tranquil landscape. The fertile hills are blanketed with vineyards while orchards stretch across the plains. In addition to the wealth of castles, this region is also the site of numerous aristocratic residences dating from the late 16th and early 17th centuries when it was the fashion among the Tyrolean nobility to build country houses in the Italian Renaissance style. Many of these now serve as luxurious hotels and restaurants. **Lago di Caldaro** ㉕ (Lake Kalterer), nestled between vineyards and a waterfowl preserve, is one of the warmest lakes in the Alps. Further south is **Termeno** ㉖ (Tramin), home of the Gewürztraminer grape.

The capital of the province of Trentino is **Trento** ㉗, site of the Council of Trent which was held intermittently between 1545 and 1563. It was during these sessions, called by the Catholic Church to discuss the rising threat of

The Adige is one of Italy's longest rivers. It rises on the border with Switzerland and Austria, and flows down through Trentino and the city of Verona, before emptying into the Adriatic at Chioggia.

BELOW: in the garden in Castelrotto.
BELOW RIGHT: a baroque church in Tesido, east of Brunico.

Map on
pages
190–1

Lutheranism, that the seeds of the Counter-Reformation were sown. Noteworthy sights include the **Duomo**, built between the 13th and 14th centuries in an austere Romanesque-Gothic style, and the **Castello del Buonconsiglio**, one of Italy's grandest castles and the residence of the prince-bishops who ruled the city for centuries. Today it houses a museum of local art (Tues–Sun 10am–6pm in summer, 9am–noon and 2–5pm in winter; entrance fee).

The region of **Lavarone** ㉘ is located to the southeast of Trento. Here one finds dark green forests, mountain pastures, lakes and caves full of stalactite and stalagmite formations. It was on the shores of the small **Lago di Lavarone** that Sigmund Freud liked to stroll while musing on the relationship between the psyche and human behaviour.

The **Paganella mountains**, considered by many to be the most beautiful in Italy, range to the north of Trento. At the foot of this massif are the lakes of **Terlago**, **Santo** and **Lamar**. Further south is **Lago Toblino**, with a short hiking path leading to **Ranzo** ㉙, a small village with a breathtaking panorama over the valley of the lakes. More ambitious trekkers can follow the *translagorai* route through the wild **Catena dei Lagorai** in the eastern part of the province, passing by numerous serene alpine lakes.

Just west of Lake Garda is **Lago di Ledro** ㉚ where the remains of a Bronze Age stilt village can be seen, as well as a museum (daily 10am–1pm and 2–6pm in summer, reduced hours in winter; entrance fee) with tools, canoes and other relics excavated from the former village. The northern tip of Lake Garda is located within Trentino. Although many towns on the lake have, in the past, been obliged to close their beaches due to pollution, the northern waters remain uncontaminated and off-limits to motorboats, so they are well worth exploring *(see page 225).* ❏

A spring bouquet.

BELOW: exploring Termeno, or Tramin.

MILAN

Map on page 210

For Henry James, Milan's reserved Northern European flavour made it more "the last of the prose capitals than the first of the poetic." But there is poetry in Milan in spite of its modernity

Milan (Milano) is one of the world's fashion capitals, and home to both Leonardo's *Last Supper* and the world's premier opera house, La Scala. Above all, Milan is the centre of business in Italy and it is here and in provincial Lombardy that the demand for federalism – embodied by the right-wing Northern League – is strongest. The prosperous Milanese are courteous but reserved towards visitors and preoccupied with their own lives.

There is no better place to begin a tour of Milan than at its spiritual hub, the **Duomo**  (daily 7am–7pm, crypt; daily 9am–noon and 2.30–6pm), described by Mark Twain as "a poem in marble". This gargantuan Gothic cathedral (the third-largest church in Europe after St Peter's in Rome and Seville's cathedral) was begun in 1386 but not finished until 1813. Decorating the exterior are 135 pinnacles and over 2,245 marble statues from all periods. The "Madonnina", a beautiful 4-metre (13-ft) gilded statue, graces the top of the Duomo's highest pinnacle. The facade is currently under scaffolding while restoration takes place over the next two years.

Inside the Duomo

The English novelist D.H. Lawrence called the Duomo "an imitation hedgehog of a cathedral", because of its pointy intricate exterior. But inside, the church is simple, majestic and vast. Five great aisles stretch from the entrance to the altar. Enormous stone pillars dominate the nave, which is big enough to accommodate some 40,000 worshippers. In the apse, three large and intricate stained-glass windows attributed to Nicolas de Bonaventura shed a soft half-light over the area behind the altar. The central window features the shield of the Visconti, Milan's ruling family during the 13th and 14th centuries. It was Duke Gian Galeazzo Visconti, the most powerful member of the family, who commissioned the Duomo.

A gruesome statue of the flayed St Bartholomew, carrying his skin, stands in the left transept. In the right transept is an imposing 16th-century marble tomb made for Giacomo di Medici by Leone Leoni after the style of Michelangelo. The crypt contains the tomb of the Counter-Reformation saint Charles Borromeo. This 16th-century Archbishop of Milan epitomised the Lombard virtues of energy, efficiency and discipline. Ascetic and rigorously self-denying, he expected no less from his flock. His unbending character led to frequent battles with the lay authorities, especially when he tried to ban dancing, drama and sport.

Outside, a lift goes up to the roof of the Duomo, among the pinnacles and carved rosettes. The view from the top is spectacular: on a clear day it stretches as far as the Alps.

PRECEDING PAGES: high fashion meets high church. **LEFT:** Galleria Vittorio Emanuele. **BELOW:** the roof of the Duomo.

Come down into the recently restored **Piazza del Duomo** ❸ where Milan's many worlds converge. The large equestrian statue standing at one end of the square honours Italy's first king, Victor Emmanuel (after whom major boulevards in cities throughout Italy are named). The piazza is lined on two sides with porticoes, where Milanese of all ages and styles love to gather. To the north is the entrance to the **Galleria Vittorio Emanuele** ❻, Italy's oldest and most elegant shopping mall. Its four-storey arcade is full of boutiques, bookshops, bars and restaurants. But, before you sit down to watch the world go by, be forewarned: the cafés here are pricey.

At the other side of the Galleria is **Piazza della Scala** ❼, site of the famed **La Scala** opera house, which has now been opulently restored. It was built between 1776 and 1778 by Giuseppe Piermarini, and it was here that Verdi's *Otello* and Puccini's *Madama Butterfly* were first performed. The **Museo Teatrale alla Scala** ❺ (Opera House Museum; daily 9am–12.30pm and 1.30–5.30pm; entrance fee) is now housed again at La Scala after its temporary home on Corso Magento. There is a rich collection of memorabilia including original scores by Verdi, Liszt's piano and other objects connected to great musicians and composers. The visit includes a look into the theatre itself from one of the boxes – as long as there are no rehearsals underway.

Follow the Via Verdi from La Scala to the **Pinacoteca di Brera** ❻ (Tues–Sun 8.30am–7.15pm; tel: 02–89421146, www.brera.beniculturalit; entrance fee), home of one of Italy's finest art collections. Paintings of the 15th to the 18th century are especially well represented. Famous works included in the collection are Mantegna's *The Dead Christ* (viewed from the pierced soles of his feet), Caravaggio's *Supper at Emmaus*, and the restored 15th-century *Madonna and Saints* by Piero della Francesca. Raphael's beautiful *Betrothal of the Virgin (Lo Sposalizio)*, a masterpiece of his Umbrian period, was his first painting to show powers of composition and draughtsmanship far in advance of his biggest stylistic influence, Perugino.

A despot's dwelling

Off the Piazza del Duomo is Via Mercanto. From there, Via Dante leads to the **Castello Sforzesco** ❼ (Tues–Sun 9.30am–5.30pm; entrance fee), stronghold and residence of the Sforza family, the despotic rulers of Milan in the 15th century (*forza* means strength in Italian). The greatest of the Sforzas was Francesco, a mercenary general who became the fourth Duke of Milan. To design his stronghold, Francesco employed a local architect, Giovanni da Milano, but the decoration of the principal tower was undertaken by Filarete, a Florentine.

The residential part of the castle, the Corte Ducale, contains a magnificent collection of sculpture, including Michelangelo's last work, the unfinished *Pietà Rondanini*, an almost abstract work charged with emotion. Michelangelo worked on this *pietà* until within a few days of his death in 1564, and it is now especially evocative having been cleaned.

Three blocks west of the castle stands the church of **Santa Maria delle Grazie** ❽, begun in 1466 but expanded in 1492 by Bramante, who also built the exquis-

See map opposite

A bust of Verdi in the Opera House Museum.

BELOW: fortune telling.

Elegant shop on the Via della Spiga.

BELOW: ceiling fresco in the Castello Sforzesco, and **RIGHT:** the castle's Ponticella with a loggia by Bramante.

ite cloister. Next door, the **Cenacolo Vinciano** 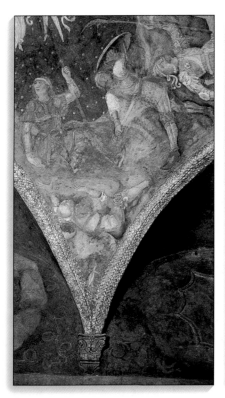 (Tues– Sun 8.15am–7pm, later on Sat; entrance fee), once a refectory for Dominican friars, is home to Leonardo's famous *Last Supper* (1495–7). Since the work was restored in 1999, visitor numbers have been restricted, with visits limited to 15 minutes. To book your time slot, call tel: 02-498 7588 or visit www.cenacolovinciano.it.

Whatever your view of its controversial restoration, the *Last Supper* remains a powerful and moving work. It is far larger than expected –some 9 metres (30 ft) wide and 4.5 metres (15 ft) high. Not all the expressions on the disciples' faces can be discerned, but the careful composition of the work remains completely clear. On either side of Jesus sit two groups of three apostles, linked to each other through their individual gestures and glances. It vividly captures the moment when Jesus announces that one of them is about to betray him. This painting was seminal to the perception of the artist as a creative thinker rather than just an artisan.

From Santa Maria delle Grazie, proceed to the church of **Sant'Ambrogio** 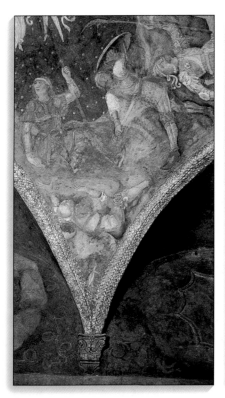 (daily 8am–noon and 2.30–6pm; Via Carducci). This is the finest medieval building in Milan and dedicated to the city's patron saint, St Ambrose. To enter, step down from street level and cross an austere atrium. The church is dark and low, but compelling in its antiquity. Founded between 379 and 386 by St Ambrose, then bishop of Milan – it was he who converted St Augustine – the basilica was enlarged first in the 9th century and again in the 11th. The brick-ribbed square vaults that support the galleries are typical of Lombardic architecture.

Down Via San Vittore from the basilica is the **Museo della Scienza e della Tecnologia Leonardo da Vinci** 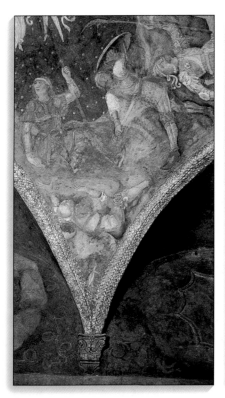 (Tues–Fri 9.30am–5pm, Sat–Sun 9.30am–6pm; entrance fee). Although the large section devoted to applied physics will probably be of interest only to specialists, everyone will enjoy the

huge gallery filled with wooden models of Leonardo da Vinci's most ingenious inventions. Don't miss the reconstruction of his famous flying machine.

Return in the direction of the Duomo to the **Pinacoteca Ambrosiana** , an art gallery founded by Cardinal Federico Borromeo in 1618, along with a major library. The newly restored gallery houses a collection of paintings dating from the 15th to the 17th century (Tues–Sun 10am–5pm; entrance fee). Most notable among the works are Leonardo's *Portrait of a Musician*, Titian's *Adoration of the Magi* and Caravaggio's *Basket of Fruit*.

Fashion avenue

For a break from sightseeing and a glimpse of an important and more contemporary aspect of Milanese life, stroll down **Via Monte Napoleone**, which extends off Corso Vittorio Emanuele between the Duomo and Piazza Santa Babila. This is the most elegant shopping street in Milan. You will find all the star names of Italian fashion here (or on the adjoining Via della Spiga and Via Sant' Andrea) – Armani, Moschino, Valentino, Romeo Gigli, Prada and Versace to name a few – as well as the latest in household design and contemporary art.

If you have time on your visit to Milan, there are two more churches which are worth seeking out. In the Via Torino, near the Piazza del Duomo, stands **San Satiro**, built by Bramante in 1478–80. Inside, the architect cleverly used stucco to create an illusionistic effect, giving the impression that the church is far larger than it actually is. **San Lorenzo Maggiore**, nearby on Corso di Porta Ticinese, attests to Milan's antiquity. The basilica was founded in the 4th century and rebuilt in 1103. Martino Bassi restored it in 1574–88, but its octagonal shape and many beautiful 5th-century mosaics are original. ❏

Map on page 210

TIP

For a gruesome glimpse of the past, venture down into the crypt of Sant'Ambrogio to see the skeletal remains of St Ambrose, Milan's patron saint, along with those of two early Christian martyrs.

BELOW: fresco in Sant'Ambrogio.

CONSPICUOUS CONSUMPTION

Visitors come to Milan as much to shop and dine as to visit the *Last Supper* of Leonardo da Vinci. You will need to book in advance if you plan to eat at a top establishment.

One is the very grand Savini (Galleria Vittorio Emanuele II, tel: 02-7200 3433), where you can try the definitive *risotto alla Milanese*. Just as exclusive is the two Michelin-starred Cracco-Peck, at Via Victor Hugo 4, where you can enjoy a six-course gastronomic menu (tel: 02-876 774). The two Michelin-starred Sadler restaurant in the Navigli district (Via Ettore Troilo 14) is an expensive temple to gastronomy, but for more reasonable prices try the stylish, relatively new offshoot, Sadler Wine and Food restaurant and wine bar, located between the city centre and the exhibition zone (Fiera) at Via Monte Bianco 2/A (tel: 02-481 4677). If your budget doesn't allow for the full gastronomic blow-out, you can always shop for picnic ingredients at Gastronomia Peck, Via Spadari 9 (tel: 02-860842), choosing from the huge and enticing selection of top-quality gourmet cheeses, meats and pastries on display.

Although you need deep pockets to buy designer goods in the Golden Quarter (Quadrilatero d'Oro) – the four streets around Via Monte Napoleone – there are many factory outlets selling seconds or last season's goods.

LOMBARDY

*Beneath is spread like a green sea / The waveless plain
of Lombardy, Bounded by the vaporous air, Islanded by cities fair*
— PERCY BYSSHE SHELLEY

Map on
pages
216–7

From the heights of the central Alps to the low-lying plains of the Po Valley, the province of Lombardy is remarkably diverse. Contrasts abound in this land named after the Lombards, one of the barbarian tribes that invaded Italy in the 6th century. Its cities, renowned for their elegance since Renaissance times, are complemented by dramatic scenery. The Italian Lakes jut into the heart of a steep mountain range, offset by fertile farmlands and fields of gently swaying poplars.

An easy day trip from **Milan ❶**, or a stop-over on a longer journey south, is the **Certosa di Pavia ❷** (Charterhouse of Pavia; May–Sept Tues–Sun 9–11.30am, 2.30–6pm, Oct–Mar till 4.30pm, Apr till 5.30pm). This world-famous church, mausoleum and monastery complex, founded in 1396, is a masterpiece of Lombardic Renaissance architecture, complete with relief sculpture and inlaid marble. The interior of the church is Gothic in plan, but highly embellished with Renaissance and baroque details. Inside stand the tombs of Ludovico Visconti and his child-bride, Beatrice d'Este. Their bodies are not actually buried here, but life-sized effigies on top of the tombs portray them in all their life-time splendour.

Behind the Certosa is a magnificent Great Cloister where Carthusian monks, who had taken vows of silence, once lived in individual dwellings. Each cottage is two-storeys high with two rooms on the ground floor and a bedroom and *loggia* above. Each monk, living in seclusion, took delivery of his food through the small swing portal at the right of his doorway.

Nowadays, Pavia is a country backwater, but between the 6th and 8th centuries it was the capital city of the Lombards. Pavia's fame was augmented in 1361 when the university was founded, and to this day it remains a prestigious centre of learning.

On the Via Diacono, in the old centre of town, is the church of **San Michele**, consecrated in 1155. Here the great medieval Lombard leader, Frederick Barbarossa, was crowned King of Italy. Look for the carefully sculpted scenes of the battle between good and evil above the three doorways. Inside, San Michele is plain and sombre; only the columns are highly decorated.

Eclectic and electric

To reach the **Duomo**, follow the Strada Nuova from San Michele. This cathedral is an eclectic mixture of four centuries of architectural styles. The basic design is Renaissance (Bramante and Leonardo worked on it), but the immense dome, the third-largest in Italy, is a late 19th-century touch, and the facade was added in 1933. The rest of the exterior is unfinished.

If you continue on the Strada Nuova you will arrive at the **Università**, where 17,000 students currently attend classes. One of Pavia's most famous past graduates was Alessandro Volta, the physicist who discovered and

LEFT: the cloister of the Certosa di Pavia, and **BELOW:** sculpture on its facade.

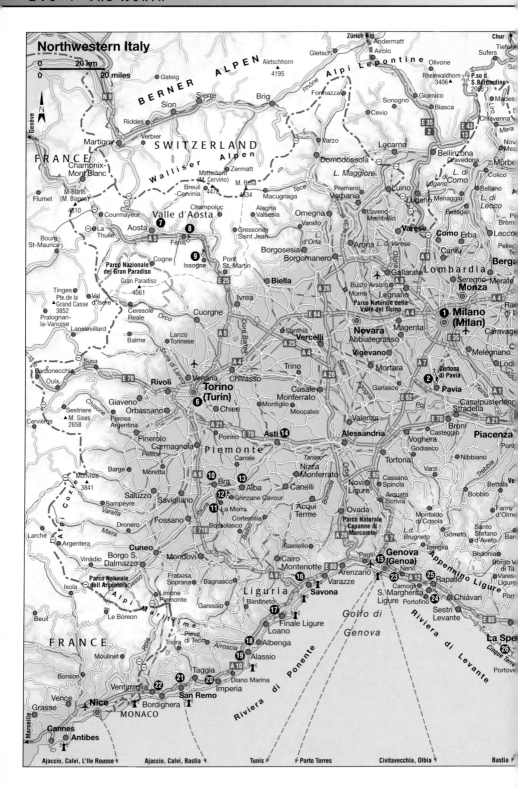

Northwestern Italy

0   20 km
0   20 miles

gave his name to electrical volts. His statue stands in the left-hand court of the university complex.

At the end of the Strada Nuova stands the **Castello Visconteo**, an imposing square fortress built in 1360–65. Today, the castle is the home of the **Museo Civico** (Mar–June and Sept–Nov Tues–Fri 9am–1.30pm, Sat–Sun 10am–7pm; July–Aug and Dec–Feb Tues–Sat 9am–1.30pm, Sun 9am–1pm; entrance fee). Included in the museum's collection are many fine Lombardic Romanesque sculptures and remnants of Roman Pavia including inscriptions, glass and pottery.

Go west from the castle to reach **San Pietro in Ciel d'Oro**, a fine Lombardic Romanesque church, smaller than San Michele, but quite similar. A richly decorated Gothic arch at the high altar is said to contain the relics of St Augustine.

Before leaving Pavia, have a bowl of the town's speciality, the hearty *zuppa alla pavese*, a recipe said to have been concocted by a peasant woman for Francis I of France. The king was about to lose the Battle of Pavia (1525) to the Spanish when he stopped for a bite to eat at a nearby cottage. His hostess wanted her humble minestrone to be fit for a king, so she added toasted bread, cheese and eggs.

Cremona

About two hours' drive from Pavia lies the city of **Cremona** ❸, a pleasant market town on the banks of the Po River and world-famous centre of violin making. The greatest of Cremonese violin makers was Antonio Stradivari (1644–1737) whose secret formula for varnish may account for the beautiful sound of a Stradivarius violin. Some of these glorious instruments are on display in the grandiose 13th-century **Palazzo de Comune** (Tues–Sat 9am–6pm, Sun 10am–6pm; entrance fee) on Corso Vittorio Emanuele and the modern **International School of Violin Making** nearby.

The pink marble **Duomo** was built in the Lombardic Romanesque style. Although consecrated in 1190, it was not completed until much later. Inside the church, 17th-century tapestries on the *Life of Samson* surround some of the heavy columns.

TIP

Try to visit Mantua on a
Thursday, when Piazza
delle Erbe, Piazza
Mantegna and nearby
streets become an
enormous market.

Mantua

Because **Mantua** ❹ (Mantova) lies on a peninsula in the Mincio River, surrounded by a lagoon on three sides, it is known as Piccola Venezia (Little Venice). But history has given the city a more resonant name: "Ducal Mantua", because from 1328–1707 the enlightened but despotic Gonzaga family ruled the town from its sombre fortress. Mantua has a slightly musty medieval atmosphere: the quiet cobbled streets at night could easily be a stage set from a Shakespearean comedy, or a Verdi opera.

During the Renaissance, the Gonzaga court was one of the bright lights of Italian culture, especially under the influence of the Marchioness Isabella d'Este (1474–1539), who modelled her life on *Il Cortegione*, a textbook for courtiers and ladies written by Castiglione. She even gave Castiglione a palace in Mantua. She also hired Raphael, Mantegna and Giulio Romano to decorate the Reggia dei Gonzaga (**Palazzo Ducale**), once the largest palace in Europe. The public can visit a selection of the palace's 450 or so rooms by joining a tour (May–Sept Tues–Sun 8.45am–7.15pm, last entrance 6.30pm; entrance fee). Particularly worth seeing are the nine tapestries in the Appartamento degli Arazzi that were made in Flanders from drawings by Raphael. The Camera degli Sposi (the matrimonial suite) is decorated with frescoes by Mantegna depicting scenes from the lives of the Marquess Ludovico Gonzaga and his wife, Barbara of Brandenburg.

Across town is the **Palazzo Te** (Tues–Sun 9am–6pm, Mon 1–6pm; entrance fee), the supremely elegant Gonzaga summer residence. Designed by Giulio Romano in 1525, this palace is delicate and pleasing. Many rooms are decorated with frescoes of summer scenes and there is a lovely garden. The Giants' Room is the most talked-about in the palace. The illusion of Jupiter hurling thun-

BELOW: outside a
violin workshop in
Cremona.

derbolts at the giants is acted out in paintings of astonishing movement and destruction. Through echoing acoustics, the extraordinary gasps of visitors reverberate in the chamber.

Mantua's **Duomo**, located near the Reggia, has a baroque facade added in 1756. Inside, the cathedral has a Renaissance design and stucco decoration by Giulio Romano. Also worth a visit is the **Basilica di Sant'Andrea** in Piazza Mantegna. The Florentine L.B. Alberti designed most of Sant'Andrea, starting in 1472, but the dome was added in the 18th century. Inside, Sant'Andrea is at once both simple and grand. The frescoes that adorn the walls were designed by Mantegna and executed by his pupils, among them Correggio.

Bergamo

If you want to escape from the hot stillness of "the waveless plain of Lombardy," there is no more restful or picturesque town than **Bergamo** ❺, too often bypassed by tourists racing along the autostrada between Milan and Venice. Bergamo is, in fact, two cities: Bergamo Bassa and Bergamo Alta.

Though pleasant and spacious, the modern **Bergamo Bassa**, where the railway station is situated, is less dramatic than its parent town which rises upon a rough-hewn crag. Beneath its shadow runs Via Pignola, lined with elegant palaces built between the 16th and 18th centuries. But the real treasure of Bergamo Bassa is the **Accademia Carrara** (Tues–Sun 10am–1pm and 2.30–5.30pm; entrance fee). Where else but in Italy can you find, in a small city, a collection of paintings that the grandest metropolis would be proud to have? In this case, it is thanks to the good taste of the 18th-century Count Giacomo Carrara. There is no need to queue to look at paintings by Pisanello, Lotto, Carpaccio, Bellini and Mantegna since the museum is often virtually deserted except for the cordial guards.

If you enjoy mountain climbing, take the creaking funicular to **Bergamo Alta**, a medieval town built in a warm brown stone. The inhabitants keep their ancient town in beautiful condition. The best spot in which to sit and admire it is the central **Piazza Vecchia** – a good place to find the local speciality *polenta con gli uccelli* (polenta with quail). The piazza is flanked by the 17th-century Palazzo Nuovo and the 12th-century Palazzo della Ragione. Beyond the medieval building's arcade is the small Piazza del Duomo packed with ecclesiastical treasures: the Romanesque **Santa Maria Maggiore** and the Renaissance **Colleoni Chapel** (daily 9am–12.30pm and 2–6.30pm, Nov–Feb till 4.30pm), designed by Amadeo who contributed to the Certosa di Pavia, and with an 18th-century ceiling by Tiepolo. The chapel is dedicated to the Bergamesque *condottiere* Bartolomeo Colleoni. The mercenary fought so well for the Venetians that he was rewarded with an estate in his native province, which, at that time, was under Venetian rule. Operatic composer Gaetano Donizetti is buried here. He was born in Bergamo in 1797 to a seamstress mother and pawn-broker father. He died here in 1848, quite insane, having composed 75 operas, of which the best-known today is *Lucia di Lammermoor*. His former home now houses the **Istituto Musicale Donizetti** (Mon–Fri 10am–1pm, Sat–Sun 10am–1pm and 2.30–5pm). ❏

Map on pages 216–7

A window of Bergamo's Santa Maria Maggiore.

BELOW: the Palazzo Ducale in Mantua.

THE LAKES

Although close to the Alps, the Italian Lakes enjoy cool summers and mild winters which make the region ideal for hikers, windsurfers, or anyone who enjoys magnificent landscapes

Map on pages 222–3

The Italian lakes have long been a retreat for romantics. Writers drawn to their shores include Pliny the Younger, Shelley, Stendhal and D.H. Lawrence. "What can one say of Lake Maggiore, of the Borromean Islands, of the Lake Como, except to pity people who do not go mad over them?" wrote Stendhal. Today, they are also a playground for the rich, as well as a popular destination for tourists and honeymooners from all over the world, drawn to their ravishing scenery. But despite the number of visitors, and the lakes' proximity to Milan's international airport (Lake Como, for instance, is a 90-minute drive away), the region has lost none of its allure.

There are five major lakes in the Italian Lake District (from west to east: lakes Maggiore, Lugano, Como, Iseo and Garda), and each has its own character. The lakes were formed during the last Ice Age, which ended around 11,000 years ago, and are the result of glaciers thrusting down from the Alps and gouging out deep valleys wherever softer rock created an easy pathway for the ice. Later, as the ice melted, the lakes were formed in the valley bottoms. All run roughly north to south and all enjoy sheltered microclimates that make them warm and mild in winter (especially on the southern shores which benefit from winter sunshine – the northern shores tend to be overshadowed by Alpine peaks).

LEFT: Bellagio, on Lake Como.
BELOW: statue in the garden of Villa Pallavicino.

Another phenomenon, which makes the lakes – particularly Lake Garda – popular with sailors and windsurfers, is the dependable offshore wind, caused by temperature and air-pressure differences between the warmer water and the cooler surrounding mountains. Sunbathers on the shores of the lake can bask in warm still air, while a stiff wind blows on the lake itself.

Lake Maggiore

The westernmost lake, **Lago Maggiore ❶**, has a special attraction: the **Borromean Islands ❷**, named after their owners, a prominent Milanese family whose members included a cardinal, a bishop and a saint. **Isola Bella**, the most romantic of the three islands, was a desolate rock with just a few cottages until the 16th century when Count Charles Borromeo III decided to civilise the island in honour of his wife, Isabella. With the help of the architect Angelo Crivelli, Charles designed the splendid palace and gardens.

Isola dei Pescatori is, as the name suggests, a fishing village. Another Borromean palace and elaborate botanical gardens decorate **Isola Madre**. All three islands are served by ferries from the main lakeside towns.

The most famous and liveliest settlement on the shores of Lago Maggiore is **Stresa ❸** (put on the literary map by Hemingway's *A Farewell to Arms*) with its many beautiful belle époque villas. Two famous villas adjoin-

Ceiling decoration in Como's cathedral. The building was started in 1396 and only completed in the 18th century.

ing the landing stage are the **Villa Ducale**, residence of the philosopher Antonio Rosmini (1797–1855), and the **Villa Pallavicino** (daily Apr–Oct 9am–6pm; entrance fee) just outside town on the road to Arona, remarkable for its fine gardens. From Stresa, it's a short drive or cable-car ride from Stresa Lido to the summit of **Monte Mottarone**, from where there is a stunning view of the Alps, the lake and the town below.

Baveno ❹, northwest of Stresa, is a small quiet town near the islands and the site of many villas, among them the **Castello Branca** where the British Queen Victoria spent the spring of 1879. The drive south from Stresa to **Arona ❺** along the Lungolago is especially pretty: the road is tree-lined, the views of the lakes and islands spectacular. Arona itself is a rather unremarkable resort town, but it does contain a number of attractive 15th-century buildings.

Lake Lugano

On the map, **Lago di Lugano ❻** (Lake Lugano) looks like a crudely drawn cartoon animal with a very long tail. Much of the lake lies within Swiss territory; only the very eastern tip of the tail is Italian, plus the enclave of Campione d'Italia, a little lakeside town that remains proudly and typically Italian, whilst being entirely surrounded by Swiss territory (and using Swiss currency and postage stamps). Visitors come to Campione for the casino and its nightlife.

Lake Como

Lago di Como ❼ (Lake Como), known locally as "the Lario", is the most dramatic of the lakes. It is almost 50 km (30 miles) long and up to 5 km (3 miles) across; at 410 metres (1,345 ft), it is the deepest inland lake in Europe. At many

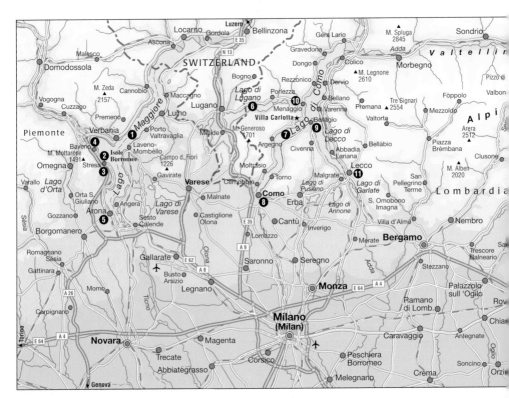

points the shore is a sheer cliff, and the Alps (providing year-round skiing on the glaciers) loom like a wall at the northern end of the lake. **Como** ❽ itself is an historic yet thriving town. Silk weaving, which for many years was confined to homes and small workshops in Como, is now concentrated in several factories.

Como's **Giardini Pubblici** are a pleasant place to relax and look over the lake. In the midst of these gardens stands the Tempio Voltiano (Tues–Sun 10am–noon and 3–6pm, till 4pm in winter; entrance fee), a classic rotunda dedicated to Alessandro Volta, who gave his name to the volt. Many of the instruments he used in his electrical experiments are on display.

It's an easy walk across the town to **Santa Maria Maggiore**, Como's 14th-century marble cathedral. The intricately carved portal is flanked by statues of the two Plinys, who were among the earliest admirers of Lake Como. "Are you given to studying, or do you prefer fishing or hunting, or do you go in for all three?" the younger Pliny asked a friend, and boasted that all three activities were possible at Lake Como.

The 11th-century church of **Sant'Abbondio** (daily 8am–6pm) on the outskirts of Como will transport you back to Como's pre-resort days, when it was a pious and prosperous medieval village. Chances are that you will have this solemn Lombardic church to yourself. The 14th-century frescoes of the *Life of Jesus*, in the apse, make it worth the trip.

Although the distance between the two cities is not great as the crow flies, it can take an hour of driving on narrow, twisting roads to reach **Bellagio** ❾ from Como. Going by public boat from Como's pier is a more pleasant way of getting there. Bellagio sits on the point of land that divides Lago di Como into three parts. From here you can see the entire expanse of the lake and enjoy a spectacular view

Map, see below

The southeastern spur of Lake Como is known as the Lago di Lecco.

BELOW: sculpture by Canova in Villa Carlotta, across the lake from Bellagio.

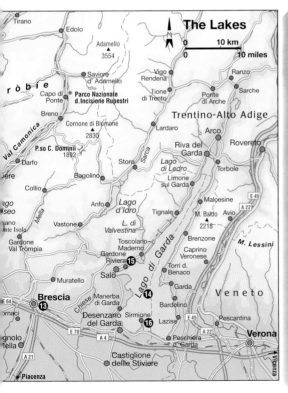

of the Alps. "Sublimity and grace here combine to a degree which is equalled but not surpassed by the most famous site in the world, the Bay of Naples," wrote Stendhal in *The Charterhouse of Parma*. The Frenchman set the opening scenes of his novel in the **Villa Carlotta ⑩** (across the lake from Bellagio) after staying here as a guest. Today the villa (summer daily 9am–6pm; entrance fee), originally built by a Prussian princess for her daughter, and its idyllic gardens provide the perfect setting for a picnic lunch.

Lecco ⑪, a pleasant city at the southeastern end of Lago di Como, is famous as the setting of Alessandro Manzoni's *The Betrothed*, a 19th-century novel which is a classic of Italian literature, and a revealing piece of social history. The author, Italy's greatest 19th-century novelist, was a native of Lecco and a political activist instrumental in bringing about Italy's unification. Visitors can explore his childhood home, the **Villa Manzoni** (Tues–Sun 9.30am–5pm; entrance fee).

Among the more antique attractions of the city is the **Basilica** with its fine frescoes from the 14th century depicting the Annunciation, the Deposition and the Life of San Antonio. The oldest monument in the city is the bridge spanning the Adda River, the **Ponte Azzone Visconti**, built between 1336 and 1338.

Lake Iseo

Lago d'Iseo ⑫ (Lake Iseo) is the fifth-largest of the lakes, measuring 24 km (15 miles) long by 5 km (3 miles) wide. Views of the lake all focus on the large island that sits in the middle: graphically named **Monte Isola** (Mountain Island), this is the largest island of any European lake, and it typifies the rugged mountainous appeal of this lake and its surroundings. Northeast of the lake, the town of **Capo di Ponte** makes a good base for exploring the **Val Camonica**, renowned for

TIP

Lecco is a good base for hikers. It also has good rail connections with Milan and Bergamo.

BELOW: the baroque church of Madonna di Monte Castello, on the west side of Lake Garda.
BELOW RIGHT: the Rocca Scaligera.

its prehistoric rock carvings and designated a Unesco World Heritage Site. Some 158,000 rock carvings have been found, 75 percent of them in the Capo di Ponte area; dating from as far back as 8,000 years ago, they are a record of the hunting and farming activities of the local Camoni tribe. The local tourist office sells guides to the **Parco Nazionale delle Incisioni Rupestri** (National Rock Engravings Park; Tues–Sun 9am–1 hr before sunset in summer, till 4.30pm in winter; entrance fee) with five colour-coded trails, or call 0364-42140 for a guide.

Southeast of the lake is Lombardy's second city, **Brescia ⑬**, which has an exceptional museum – indeed, **Santa Giulia Museo della Citta** (June–Sept Tues–Sun 10am–6pm, Oct–May Tues–Sun 9.30am–1pm and 2.30–5pm; entrance fee) is one of the best historical and archaeological museum complexes in Italy. Santa Giulia showcases Brescia's past in monuments from the Bronze Age to the present day. It incorporates an 8th-century nunnery, the Renaissance church and cloisters of Santa Giulia, the Romanesque oratory of Santa Maria, and the Lombard basilica of San Salvatore. The church alone is a major monument, with Byzantine, Lombard and Roman remains. The Longobard and Carolingian section displays frescoes and gold jewellery, while the Venetian section has Gothic and Renaissance displays, and the Roman section contains mosaics and bronzes discovered during excavations on the site. Also in Brescia, the **Museo delle Armi** in the castle houses Italy's finest collection of antique weapons (June–Sept Tues–Sun 10am–5pm, Oct–May Tues–Sun 9.30am–1pm and 2.30–5pm; entrance fee).

Lake Garda

Lago di Garda ⑭ (Lake Garda) is the cleanest and largest of the Italian lakes. It is especially popular with Northern European tourists, who come to sail, windsurf and water-ski. Its equable climate is responsible for Soave and Valpolicella wines.

On the shores of this lake is a garish remnant of the Fascist era – **Il Vittoriale** – the home of the flamboyant Italian poet and patriot Gabriele d'Annunzio which was given to him by his greatest admirer, Benito Mussolini (daily 9.30am–7pm in summer, 9am–1pm and 2–5pm, closed Wed, in winter; entrance fee). Located in **Gardone Riviera ⑮**, at one time Lake Garda's most fashionable resort, Il Vittoriale is more than a house, it is a shrine to d'Annunzio's dreams of Italian imperialism. Included in the estate is the prow of the warship *Puglia,* built into the hillside. In the auditorium, the plane d'Annunzio flew during World War I is suspended from the ceiling.

From Salò and Gardone Riviera it takes no more than an hour to reach **Sirmione ⑯**, a medieval town built on a spit of land extending into the lake. The **Rocca Scaligera** (Tues–Sun 9am–7pm in summer, till 4.30pm in winter; entrance fee), a fairytale castle, dominates the town's entrance. It was originally the fortress of the Scaligeri family, rulers of Garda in the 13th century, and it is said that they entertained the poet Dante here. An enjoyable hour or two can be spent exploring the local shops, dipping into churches and following the footpath that leads to the tip of the peninsula, with its extensive ruins of a Roman spa, the **Grotte di Catullo** (Tues–Sat 8.30am–7pm, Sun 9am–6pm, till 4.30pm in winter; entrance fee). ❑

Map on pages 222–3

Lily from Gardone Riviera.

BELOW: church in Bardolino, on Garda.

PIEDMONT, VALLE D'AOSTA AND LIGURIA

Maps on pages 216 & 228

If it is not so Italian as Italy it is at least more Italian than anything but Italy – HENRY JAMES

Piedmont (Piemonte) may strike today's visitor, as it did Henry James, as not very Italian. The bordering nations of France and Switzerland have contributed much to the cultural life of this northwestern region. Moreover, the Alpine landscapes of Piedmont, especially in the dramatic Valle d'Aosta, are very different from scenery elsewhere in Italy. But the particular Piedmontese twist on Italian life is not unappealing. It's as if the cool mountain breezes have bestowed a calming effect on the people. No wonder that it was a Piedmontese king, Victor Emmanuel, and his Piedmontese advisor, Count Camillo Cavour, who guided Italy to independence.

Turin ⊙ (Torino), the capital of Piedmont, is a genuinely Italian city, but its proximity and centuries-old ties to France give it a strong Gallic flavour. During the Middle Ages, it was part of a Lombardic duchy, but in the 16th century it became the capital of the French province of Savoy. Following the Risorgimento *(see page 57)*, it was the capital of united Italy from 1861 to 1865.

LEFT: the dome of San Lorenzo in Turin.
BELOW: the city's Royal Garden.

Today, Turin is headquarters for some of Italy's most successful industries, including the Fiat automobile company. But the factories of Turin are a long way from the city's gracious centre, with its wide streets and beautiful squares, gardens and parks where visitors can soak up the sun and sample the spirit of this most modern of Italian cities. Turin hosted a successful 2006 Winter Olympics, endorsing its prestige. Many of the Alpine events were held at the ski resort Sestriere, part of the extensive Franco-Italian Milky Way area.

Historic town centre

The hub of civic life in Turin is the fashionable **Via Roma**, an arcaded shopping street that connects the **Stazione Porta Nuova ⊙** with **Piazza Castello ⊙**, a huge rectangular Renaissance square planned in 1584. In the centre stands **Palazzo Madama**, a 15th-century castle that houses the **Museo Civico di Arte Antica** (Museum of Ancient Art; currently closed for restoration). Included in this museum's collections is a copy of part of the famous *Book of Hours* of the Duc de Berry, illustrated by Jan van Eyck.

Another fine building on the Piazza Castello is the baroque church of **San Lorenzo**, once the royal chapel. The royal residence was the 17th-century **Palazzo Reale ⊙** (Tues–Sun 8.30am–7.30pm; ticket office closes at 6pm, guided tours; entrance fee). From its balcony, Prince Carlo Alberto declared war on Austria in March 1848. Nearby is the **Armeria Reale** (Royal Armoury; Wed and Fri 8.30am–noon, Tues–Thur and Sat–Sun 1.30–7.30pm).

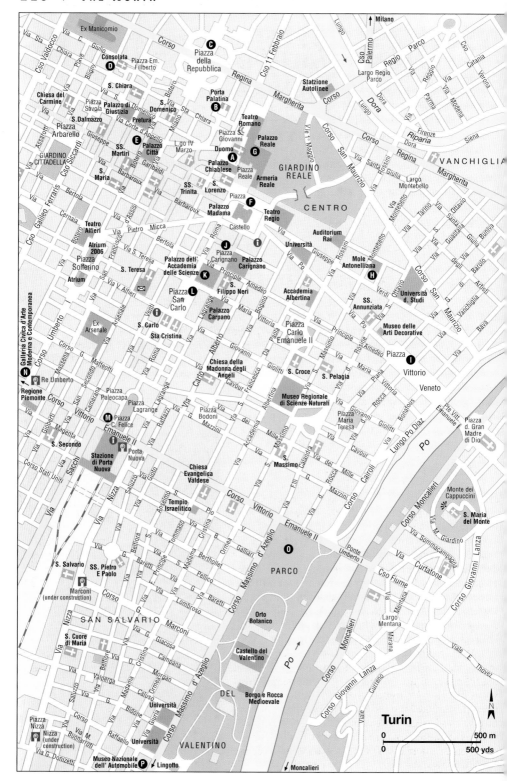

Turin

0   500 m

0   500 yds

Behind the Palazzo Reale, in **Piazza San Giovanni**, are the **Duomo** ❹ (Cattedrale di San Giovanni Battista; Mon–Sat 7am–12.30pm and 3–7pm, Sun 8am–12.30pm and 3–7pm) and **Campanile**. The former is a Renaissance construction designed by the Tuscan, Meo del Caprino; the Campanile is the work of a baroque architect. The Duomo was damaged by fire in 1997, but fortunately the flames did not consume the **Cappella della Sacra Sindone** (Chapel of the Holy Shroud; daily 9am–noon and 3–7pm; entrance fee) – a work of Guarino Guarini. It contains the Turin Shroud, for centuries believed to be the shroud in which Christ was wrapped after the Crucifixion.The cloth is imprinted with the image of a bearded man crowned with thorns. Although carbon dating suggests that the shroud is the work of clever medieval forgers, recent tests imply death by crucifixion. For four centuries the royal House of Savoy owned the shroud, but on his death in 1983, the exiled king, Umberto, left the relic to the Vatican. It will, however, remain in Turin, but only a copy is on view. The real thing is shown every 25 years – every jubilee – the next being 2025.

Vintage car in the Museo Nazionale dell'Automobile.

The Piedmontese capital may seem an unlikely centre for the study of Egyptian art, but it is home to the world's second-largest museum devoted to Ancient Egypt after Cairo: the **Egyptian Museum** (Tues–Sun 8.30am–7.30pm; entrance fee) is housed in the **Palazzo dell'Accademia delle Scienze** ❺, off Via Roma. The collection was assembled by Carlo Emanuele III, and includes the fascinating tomb of the architect Kha. The same *palazzo* also contains a good picture collection on the second floor in the **Galleria Sabauda** (Tues–Sun 8.30am–7.30pm). There are several beautiful Flemish and Dutch works, and many paintings by Piedmontese masters.

BELOW: medieval castle in the Valle d'Aosta.

Turin's enduring city symbol, the Mole Antonelliana now houses the great **Museo Nazionale del Cinema** ❻ (Tues–Sun 10am– 8pm, till 11pm on Sat; entrance fee).The Italian film industry began in Turin in 1904 and the museum traces the history of the cinema from magic lanterns to 21st-century cutting-edge technology. For a stunning view, take the lift to the top of the Mole.

The **GAM** ❼ (Galleria Civica d'Arte Moderna e Contemporanea, Tues–Sun 9am–7pm; entrance fee) has excellent visiting exhibitions and an illustrious permanent collection featuring works by such luminaries as Picasso, Modigliani, Chagall, Renoir and Klee.

It is no surprise that the automobile capital of Italy has a fine museum of cars. It can take hours to explore the **Museo Nazionale dell'Automobile** ❽ (Tues–Sat 10am– 6.30pm, Sun till 8.30pm; entrance fee). Exhibits include the earliest Fiat, the *Itala* that won the world's longest automobile race (between Peking [Beijing] and Paris in 1907) and an elegant Rolls-Royce *Silver Ghost*.

Cross the Po to visit the **Monte dei Cappuccini** ❶, a small hill crowned by a Capuchin convent. From here, take a bus or the rack railway to the **Basilica di Superga** (daily 9am–noon and 3–6pm, till 5pm in winter), a "great votive temple" (Henry James) by Juvarra which houses the tombs of the kings of Sardinia and the princes of Savoy. This basilica sits on a hill commanding a splendid view of the natural amphitheatre of the Alps. The circular church is dominated by the 75-metre (246-ft) dome, flanked by twin 60-metre (196-ft) high bell towers.

Valle d'Aosta

The beautiful Alpine valleys of Piedmont have much to offer. The region is noted for its glaciers, hilltop castles, clear mountain lakes and streams, pine forests and green meadows. The most striking area is the Valle d'Aosta. Here rise Europe's highest mountains: Mont Blanc, Monte Rosa, and the Cervino (Matterhorn). The capital, **Aosta ⓭**, was an important city in Roman times and has many interesting Roman ruins. Roman walls surround the city, and the ruins of the **Roman Theatre** (daily 9am–8pm, till 6.30pm in winter; entrance fee), in the northwest corner of Aosta, include the well-preserved backdrop of the stage. Emperor Augustus nicknamed Aosta the "Rome of the Alps", and it is the Arch of Augustus that guards the main entrance to the city.

The city of Genoa was designated a European City of Culture for 2004. This is the third time an Italian city has been named, after Florence in 1986 and Bologna in 2000.

Dating from Aosta's medieval period are the cathedral and several smaller churches. Among the latter group, the **church of Sant'Orso** (outside the walls on Via Sant'Orso) is the most interesting. The architecture is a strange mix of Gothic and Romanesque. St Orso – he converted the first Christians in the Valle d'Aosta – is buried beneath the altar. Be sure to visit the cloister, which dates back to the 12th century and is known for its unusual carved pillars.

The valley southeast of Aosta contains many fine castles, in particular those at **Fénis ⓮** now magnificently restored (Mar–Sept daily 9am–6.30pm July & Aug till 7.30pm; entrance fee) and **Issogne ⓯** (daily 9.30am–6.30pm in summer, 10am–5pm in winter; entrance fee), which were used as both residences and fortresses. The Lord of Verrès, Giorgio de Challant, commissioned construction of the castle at Issogne in 1497. Today you can stroll through the former seigneurial apartments to see the fine collection of tapestries, jewellery and furniture.

BELOW: Gran Paradiso National Park, south of Aosta.

Southeast of Turin, Piedmont turns into a region of rolling hills and long valleys. In some ways it is reminiscent of Tuscany, and like Tuscany it is an excellent wine-growing area. From Turin head towards Alba along the *autostrada*. If you have time, make a stop at **Bra** ⑩ to see a fine baroque church, **Sant'Andrea**, and an attractive Gothic building called the **Casa Traversa**. The hills surrounding the small town of **La Morra** ⑪, 10 km (6 miles) from Bra, are the source of one of Italy's greatest wines, Barolo. In **Grinzane Cavour** ⑫, between La Morra and Alba, is the Castello Cavour, an imposing 13th-century castle, the feudal home of Count Cavour, which also houses a wine museum (Wed–Mon 10am–12.30pm and 2.30–6.30pm; closed Jan; entrance fee).

Alba ⑬ has long been a favourite with gourmets. It sits at the centre of an area famous for white truffles. These treats are the principal attraction at the city's October fair. Alba also has a fine late 15th-century Gothic cathedral, with a 16th-century inlaid wooden choir.

For more taste treats, proceed to **Asti** ⑭, a city at the centre of a valley that produces Asti Spumante and other famous wines. The Gothic cathedral is a splendid edifice with three ornate portals and circular openings above. The nearby baptistry of San Pietro, dating from the 12th century, is the most interesting of the city's medieval monuments.

The region of Liguria

A narrow strip of coastline sandwiched between sea and mountains, Liguria curves and twists in an east-west arch from the French border to Tuscany. Known as the Italian Riviera, the region is favoured by a year-round mild climate, excellent beaches, and the dramatic Maritime and Ligurian Apennines, which plunge in sheer cliffs or slope gradually to the sea. It is an area of sudden contrasts, not merely between rocky shores and deep green-blue water, but between cosmopolitan resorts and isolated villages, bustling ports and quiet inlets.

Genoa ⑮ (Genova) rises above the sea like a great theatre. Its tiers are elegant *palazzi* and its pit is a noisy, strong-smelling port, the most important in Italy. La Superba, as the city was known in its heyday, rose to prominence between the 11th and 15th centuries, growing rich on trade with the East, and economic and cultural control of Liguria and the island of Corsica. In 2004 it was designated a European City of Culture.

Immediately behind the docks, the lower city begins. Here streets are ancient and narrow with twisting alleys – called *carrugi* – nowadays lined with exotic shops. The afternoon *passeggiata* in Genoa takes place on the elegant **Via Luccoli** Ⓐ, a *carrugio* of slightly wider proportions than most. Strolling along with the prosperous Genoese, you can decide for yourself whether Mark Twain was right to consider the Genoese women the most beautiful in Italy.

Not far from the dock that serves large luxury liners is the **Stazione Principe** Ⓑ, an airy building facing a small square with a striking statue of Christopher Columbus, the most famous Genoese of all time. From the railway station follow the Via Balbi, an avenue lined on both sides with sombre Renaissance palaces. Stop at No. 10, the 17th-century **Palazzo Reale** Ⓒ, famous for

Maps on pages 216 & 232

Door knocker in the Palazzo Ducale.

BELOW: Genoa harbour.

the Galleria degli Specchi (hall of mirrors) and its art collection (Tues–Wed 9am–1.30pm, Thur–Sun 9am–7pm; entrance fee).

In celebration of 2004, Via Garibaldi, "the street of palaces", now links the three most prestigious palazzi – home to the city's most celebrated art museums – to become a museum-street. Palazzo Rosso and Bianco are joined by the Palazzo Grimaldi-Doria Tursi, formerly the town hall and the most important building on the street.

Continue towards the centre on Via Balbi until it becomes the patrician **Via Garibaldi ❶**. This street splits Genoa in two; to your right are the twisting alleys of the old town, and to the left are the newer sections on the hillside. No. 11 Via Garibaldi is one of the most magnificent of Genoese palaces: **Palazzo Bianco ❷**. This 16th-century structure was originally white, but the stone has darkened with time. The facade is baroque, due to major remodelling in the early 18th century. Inside, an art collection features many extraordinary works by Flemish masters.

Across the street is the **Palazzo Rosso ❸** (gallery open Tues–Fri 9am–7pm, Sat–Sun 10am–7pm; entrance fee) featuring a beautiful courtyard. Most of the other Renaissance residences on Via Garibaldi are privately owned and can only be admired from the outside. According to legend, the Romanesque-Gothic **Duomo ❹** (12th–14th century) was founded by St Lawrence in the 3rd century. However, history dates the building to 1118. One of its Gothic portals bears a relief sculpture of the Roman saint's gruesome martyrdom. While being burned alive, St Lawrence said to his tormentors: "One side has been roasted, turn me over and eat it."

The Doria family, who ruled Genoa in the Middle Ages, built their houses and a private church around the **Piazza San Matteo ❺**, lying just behind the cathedral. Each of the buildings on this small, elegant piazza has a black and white facade. Between San Matteo and the port lies the most beguiling part of old Genoa, best explored by day. Also near the cathedral is the 16th-century **Palazzo Ducale ❻**, once the seat of government and now a cultural centre.

BELOW: Palazzo San Giorgio in Genoa.

From here it is a short stroll through labyrinthine alleys to the **Porto Antico**.

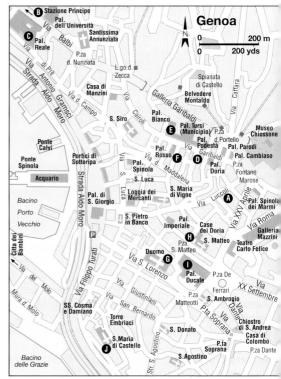

This recently renovated port area maintains its raffish charm, with rough and ready dockside cafés, although the old warehouses and customs buildings have been converted to other uses, such as the new **Museo del Mare e della Navigazione** (Museum of the Sea and Seafaring), which opened in April 2004. It is also the site of Italy's best **Aquarium** (daily 9.30am–7.30pm, Thur and Sat till 10pm, Sun and public holidays till 8.30pm; entrance fee), and the largest in Europe.

To reach another fine Genoese church, go down Via Chiabrera to Piazza Embriaci. Follow the precipitous Salita della Torre degli Embriaci up to **Santa Maria di Castello ⓳** (Mon–Sun 9am–noon and 3.30–6pm, Sun 3.30–6.30pm; entrance fee), an elegant church with a complex of chapels, courtyards and gardens. This was the site of a Roman camp, and several Roman columns have been incorporated into the Romanesque design of the nave. When you're tired of churches and palaces, head down to the bustling waterfront for a plate of *trenette* with *pesto alla genovese* – pasta with a sauce of basil, garlic and cheese.

The Italian Rivieras

Flanking Genoa on either side are two famous and beautiful coasts; each offers ample doses of sand, sun and sea, but they are quite different. The **Riviera di Ponente**, stretching from Genoa to the French border, is the longer of the two, and the one with more popular resorts. The **Riviera di Levante** is characterised by rocky cliffs and promontories and has a large naval port at La Spezia.

Heading towards France from Genoa, you'll pass **Savona ⓰**, a port and industrial centre. With the exception of a small art gallery on Via Quarda Superiore, Savona offers little of interest to the tourist. The town of **Finale Ligure ⓱**, a 30-minute drive further on, is a more inviting place. Visit the **Church of San Biagio**, which has an octagonal Gothic bell tower adjoining.

The most important town on the Riviera di Ponente from an artistic and historic point of view is **Albenga ⓲**. The Romans founded a port on this site in 181 BC, but over the centuries the topography has changed and today the old centre is about a mile from the beach. Surrounding the town is a well-preserved medieval wall and three large 17th-century gates. The cathedral of **San Michele** dates back to the 5th century. Even older are the Roman aqueduct and the ruins of a Roman amphitheatre. In addition to the historic monuments are fine facilities for swimming and boating. The nearby resort of **Alassio ⓳** has long been popular with celebrities. It lies in a pretty bay with a 3-km (2-mile) sandy beach.

Imperia ⓴ was once two separate seaside towns: Oneglia and Porto Maurizio. It was Mussolini's idea to unite the two and name the city after a nearby river. **Corso Matteotti**, a wide boulevard with magnificent views of the coast, links the two town centres. **Oneglia**, in the east, known for its olive oil and pasta production, is the more industrial and modern sector. A large cathedral, **San Maurizio**, towers over the narrow streets of **Porto Maurizio**.

The large resort of **San Remo ㉑** was once a gathering spot for European aristocracy. Its glory days may be well past, but the partially renovated resort offers two enjoyable diversions: walking along the famous palm-lined promenade and gambling at the casino. Near the

Maps on pages 216 & 232

TIP

If you're visiting the resort of Alassio don't miss the Caffè Roma in the centre of town. It has a wall – the Muretto – decorated with tiles bearing the signatures of, among others, Ernest Hemingway, Sophia Loren and Sir Winston Churchill.

BELOW: the harbour at Portofino.

Map on pages 216–7

San Remo's Russian Orthodox church.

BELOW: villa in Santa Margherita. **RIGHT:** relaxing in Borghetto d'Arróscia, inland from Albenga.

tourist office at the city's centre is an authentic Russian Orthodox church, the **Chiesa Russa** (Tues–Sun 9.30am–12.30pm and 3–6.30pm; small entrance fee). Another landmark is the art nouveau **Villa Nobel**, where Alfred Nobel (1833–96), inventor and philanthropist lived.

The gateway to France is nearby at **Ventimiglia ㉒**, a centre of flower cultivation and a pleasant city with an excellent market and a delapidated medieval quarter. The major architectural attraction is the 11th-century **Duomo**. Set on the Cape about 6 km (4 miles) from Ventimiglia in the village of Mortola is the **Giardino Hanbury** (Apr–mid-June daily 10am–5pm, late June–Sept daily 9am–6pm, Oct daily 10am–6pm, Nov–Mar Thur–Tues 10am–4pm; entrance fee), where you will find the colourful flora of five continents.

Riviera di Levante

Among the eastern suburbs of Genoa is **Quarto dei Mille**, famous as the starting point of Garibaldi's valiant 1,000-man expedition that liberated Sicily and led to the unification of Italy. Nearby **Nervi ㉓** is the oldest winter resort on the eastern coast. Here you can take hot sea baths, or follow a 3-km (2-mile) cliff walk.

After the quaint but chic former fishing village of **Camogli**, take the branch off the main road that leads to **Portofino ㉔**. A tiny waterfront village of extraordinary concentrated beauty, it was discovered by wealthy visitors after World War II. Once, only fishing boats docked in the narrow, deep-green inlet, edged on three sides by high cliffs, but it is now a berth for luxury yachts. Part of Portofino's attraction is its size. There are no beaches, and few large shops and restaurants. The pleasures of the port are visual – the reflection of brightly painted houses in the clear water, the ragged edges of stone heights set against the brilliant blue sky. **Rapallo ㉕** is a welcoming family resort, with a large beach and many moderately priced hotels. Other attractions include the 17th-century **Collegiata**, and the 16th-century church of **San Francesco**.

"Paradise on earth" is how Lord Byron described the cluster of five little fishing villages that make up the **Cinque Terre ㉖**. Monterosso al Mare, Vernazza, Corniglia, Manarola and Riomaggiore cling perilously to the steep rocky coast just north of La Spezia. They are indeed a paradise for walkers with a connecting path of 45 km (27 miles), commanding breathtaking views.

From Dante to Shelley, the Gulf of La Spezia has been praised so often by poets that it is also known as the Golfo dei Poeti. On its western point the elongated orange and yellow houses of **Portovenere ㉗** stretch up the precipitous mountain. The resort atmosphere here is friendly and relaxed as locals exchange gossip and tourists stroll alongside the pungent harbour.

Anglophiles and romantics should make a pilgrimage to the grotto from where the virile Lord Byron began his famous swim across the Gulf to visit Shelley in **Casa Magni**. If you take the 20-minute boat ride to **Lerici ㉘** you will appreciate what a powerful swimmer the poet must have been. Shelley had less luck against the waves when his ship sank off the coast. A plaque on Casa Magni commemorates the tragedy: "Sailing on a fragile bark he was landed, by an unforeseen chance, in the silence of the Elysian Fields." ❑

CENTRAL ITALY

Subtle differences in art, cooking, fashion sense and attitude to life – even between neighbouring towns – help to form a destination that appeals both to the heart and the head

To many travellers, Central Italy is the true Italy – that is, the Italy they know from Merchant-Ivory films of E.M. Forster novels, or from the pictures that adorn all the tour brochures. Ironically, the people of this region are reluctant to admit to being Italian at all. They are Tuscan, Florentine, Sienese, Bolognese or Perugian – not a semantic distinction, but a deeply held conviction based on history, culture, and even tribal and genetic differences from the pre-Roman era. And this is an area where history is not the dry stuff of academic books, but a living part of the culture – for anthropologists, Central Italy has long been fertile ground for testing the belief that competition for resources leads people to emphasise their differences. If you want to see this process in action, visit any Umbrian or Tuscan town during its annual festivities – not to mention Siena during Palio, or Florence during Calcio in Costume (Football in Costume) – and feel the intense and elemental atmosphere of inter-parish rivalry.

Such rivalries are reflected in myriad ways that make exploring the region a delight for the sensitive and enquiring traveller. Food is an obvious indicator, whether it be the subtle differences between sheep's-milk cheeses, the more emphatic distinctions between a crisp Orvieto wine and a soft, fruity Chianti, or whether it be the view firmly held by every seafront restaurant along the Tuscan Riviera that theirs is the only authentic fish soup *(cacciucco)*, and that it is far superior to anything the French produce.

Art and architecture is another indicator: labels, such as Florentine, Umbrian School, Lombardic or Pisan Romanesque, at first seem designed to confuse the uninitiated, until continued exposure to some of the world's finest artistic creations leads you to the point where you can distinguish between the light-filled limpidity of the School of Perugino and the crisply delineated and boldly coloured frescoes of Benozzo Gozzoli – unmistakably Florentine even when encountered in the tiny Umbrian hilltown of Montefalco. ❏

PRECEDING PAGES: Siena's Piazza del Campo.
LEFT: a medieval street in Perugia, decorated for a festival.

EMILIA-ROMAGNA

The gastronomic heart of Italy is also noted for its medieval cities and the late-Roman mosaics of Ravenna – all of which are rewarding reasons for visiting this prosperous region

Maps on pages 242 & 246

Emilia-Romagna's winters are cold, wet and foggy, and its summers long and hot. Together with the rich soil of the Po Valley, this climate makes it one of Italy's most prosperous farming regions, famous for its succulent hams and flavoursome Parmesan cheeses.

Emilia-Romagna also has a rich cultural past. The Via Emilia, a road first built by the Romans, cuts through the centre of the region, linking Rimini, Bologna, Modena, Parma and Piacenza – all founded by the Romans as way stations along the road from the Adriatic to the interior. The other major cities of Emilia-Romagna, Ferrara and Ravenna, are off this main thoroughfare. In the Renaissance, Ferrara was home for the d'Este family whose court was a centre of culture and learning. Ravenna was a great international centre from the 4th to the 8th century, originally as the last capital of the Western Empire, then as the seat of the Byzantine emperors.

Bologna ❶, the capital of Emilia-Romagna, is a city of less than half a million people and famous for its university, its cuisine, its traditional left-wing stance and its beautifully preserved historic centre. The old buildings are of a soft orange-red brick and have handsome marble or brick porticoes which shelter shoppers and pedestrians from inclement weather.

The old city evolved around two adjoining squares, **Piazza Maggiore ❹** and **Piazza del Nettuno ❺**. On the south side of the former stands **San Petronio ❻**, the largest church in Bologna. Originally, the Bolognese had hoped to outdo St Peter's in Rome, but church authorities decreed that some funds be set aside for the construction of **Palazzo Archiginnasio ❼** nearby. San Petronio's design is by Antonio di Vincenzo, and although construction began in 1390, the facade is still unfinished. The completed sections are of red and white marble and decorated with reliefs of biblical scenes. The interior is simple but elegant. Most of the bare brick walls remain unadorned. In the fifth chapel on the left is a spectacular 15th-century altarpiece of the *Martyrdom of St Sebastian* by Lorenzo Costa.

Centre of Learning

Behind San Petronio is the **Archiginnasio**, former seat of Europe's most ancient university in whose 17th-century **Sala Anatomica** (Mon–Fri 9am–6.30pm, Sat 9am–1pm) some of the first dissections in Europe were performed.

The Piazza del Nettuno has many attractions. At its centre is the **Fontana di Nettuno ❻**, a 16th-century fountain with bronze sculptures by Giambologna of a muscle-bound Neptune surrounded by cherubs and mermaids. On its west side is the majestic **Palazzo Comunale ❼**, the medieval town hall remodelled in

LEFT: Piazza del Nettuno in Bologna. **BELOW:** delicacies on display in a Bologna deli.

the Renaissance by Fieravante Fieravanti. Part of the palace is now a tourist office. The bronze statue above the gateway is of Pope Gregory XIII, a native of Bologna. To the left is a beautiful terracotta Madonna by Niccolò dell'Arca. Inside are grand public rooms and a fine collection of works by Bolognese artist Giorgio Morandi (1890–1964; Museo Morandi; Tues–Sun 10am–6pm; entrance fee), one of the greatest still-life painters of modern times.

Bologna's leaning towers

Santo Stefano was originally a complex of seven churches; only four remain today. In the court-yard is a fountain in which Pontius Pilate is said to have washed his hands of the fate of Christ.

From Piazza del Nettuno follow the **Via Rizzoli**, a picturesque street lined with cafés, down to **Piazza di Porta Ravegnana ⓖ** at the foot of the **Due Torri**, the "leaning towers" of Bologna. In medieval days, 180 of these towers were built by the city's leading families; now only a dozen remain. Legend has it that the two richest families in Bologna – the Asinelli and the Garisenda – competed to build the tallest and most beautiful tower in the city. However, the Torre Garisenda was built on weak foundations and was never finished. For safety's sake it was short-ened between 1351 and 1360, and is now only 48 metres (157 ft) high and leans more than 3 metres (10 ft) to one side. The **Torre degli Asinelli** (daily 9am–6pm, until 5pm in winter; entrance fee) is still standing at its original height of 97 metres (318 ft), but it too leans more than 1 metre (3 ft) out of the perpendicular. It's a stiff climb to the top up 498 steps, but worth the effort for the wonderful views.

The **Strada Maggiore** leads east from the two towers along the original line of the Via Emilia to the **Basilica di San Bartolomeo ⓗ**. Inside, look for the *Annunciation* by Albani in the fourth chapel of the south aisle, and a beautiful Madonna by Guido Reni in the north transept. Further down the Strada Mag-giore is **Santa Maria dei Servi ⓘ**, a well-preserved Gothic church.

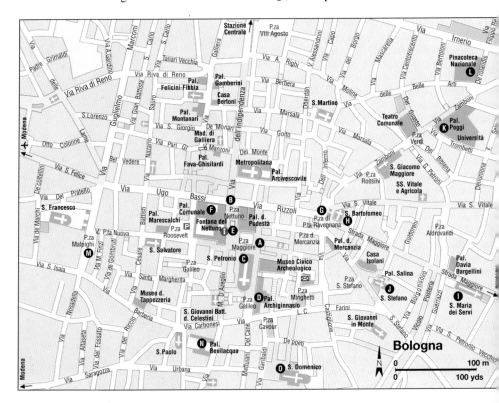

The **Abbazia di Santo Stefano**  (daily 9am–noon and 3.30–6pm) – a complex of churches all dedicated to St Stephen – is located off Via Santo Stefano, just south of the Casa Isolani, a well-restored 13th-century house. Of the several churches, the most interesting is **San Sepolcro**, where San Petronio, patron saint of Bologna, is buried near the striking Romanesque pulpit. To the left is **Santi Vitale e Agricola**, the oldest church of the group, a 5th-century structure containing several Roman capitals and columns. In San Sepolcro is the entrance to the 12th-century **Cortile di Pilato**, "Pilate's courtyard", and beyond this open courtyard is the church of **Santa Trinità**, a dark, 13th-century building.

Bologna's **University**, the oldest in Italy, an institution founded in the 11th century and famous in its early days for reviving the study of Roman law, is located on **Via Zamboni**. Petrarch attended classes here, as did Copernicus. Today, although faculties are spread throughout the city, the official seat is the 16th-century **Palazzo Poggi**.

Past the university, on the left, is the **Pinacoteca Nazionale**, where the National Art Gallery (Tues–Sun 9am–6.30pm; entrance fee) is home to an interesting and varied collection of Italian paintings. The emphasis is on the development of Bolognese and Emilian art from the Middle Ages to the 1700s, including works by Vitale da Bologna (especially the painting of *St George and the Dragon*) and Guido Reni. The stars of the collection are Raphael's great *Ecstasy of St Cecilia* (1515) and Perugino's *Madonna in Glory* (1491).

South and west of the Piazza Maggiore, Bologna has more architectural treasures. Follow the Via Ugo Bassi west to **Piazza Malpighi**. On the west side of this piazza rises **San Francesco**, a church constructed between 1236 and 1263, with a design of French-Gothic inspiration. The larger of San Francesco's two towers and the surrounding decorative terracotta are the work of Antonio di Vincenzo. Though badly damaged in the war, the tower has been skilfully restored.

From San Francesco walk southeast until you reach **Palazzo Bevilacqua**, a 15th-century building in the Tuscan style. Here, the Council of Trent met for two sessions after fleeing an epidemic in Trent. Nearby, **San Domenico** is a church dedicated to the founder of the Dominican order. The tomb of St Dominic stands in a chapel off the south aisle.

Bologna has earned a number of epithets: "La Dotta" (the learned one), "La Turritta" (the turreted one), "La Rossa" (the red one, as much for the rich red of its buildings as for its politics) and finally "La Grassa" (the fat one), for here the rich cooking of Emilia-Romagna is at its best. Specialities are mortadella sausage, tortellini, and tagliatelle, said to have been invented for the marriage feast of Lucrezia Borgia and the Duke of Ferrara. The Bolognese dress their tagliatelle, never spaghetti, with ragù, which in its home town is a rich blend of beef, ham, vegetables, cream and butter.

Modena

Since the Romans conquered **Modena** in the 2nd century BC, the city has thrived. In the past, the sources of Modena's wealth were the rich farmland of the Po plateau that surrounds it, and its position on the Via Emilia. This

Maps on pages 242 & 246

San Domenico contains several statues by Michelangelo.

BELOW: typical arcaded street in Bologna.

TIP

Motoring enthusiasts
will enjoy a visit to the
Galleria Ferrari at 43
Via Dino Ferrari in
Maranello, 20 km
(12 miles) south of
Modena (tel: 0536-
943204). Exhibits tell
the history of the
Ferrari company.

BELOW: stone lion
outside Modena's
Romanesque
Duomo.
BELOW RIGHT: Piazza
Grande in Modena.

famous Roman road still runs through the centre of Modena, but the city has new riches: the car factories where Maserati and Ferrari sports cars are manufactured.

Modena's massive and magnificent Romanesque **Duomo** sits right off the Via Emilia. It dates from the end of the 11th century when Countess Matilda of Tuscany, ruler of Modena, commissioned a cathedral which would be worthy to receive the remains of St Geminiano, patron saint of the city. Matilda engaged Lanfranco, the greatest architect of the time, to mastermind the project.

The partly Gothic, partly Romanesque belltower that stands to one side is the famous **Torre Ghirlandina**. It contains a bucket whose theft from Bologna in 1325 sparked off a war between the two cities. The poet Tassoni immortalised the incident in his celebrated poem *La Secchia Rapita (The Stolen Bucket)*.

Frequently seen strolling around Modena are the smartly dressed students of the **Accademia Militare**, Italy's military academy, housed in a 17th-century palace in the centre of Modena. Another Modenese palace, **Palazzo dei Musei**, contains several galleries including the Galleria Estense (Tues–Sun 8.30am–7.30pm; entrance fee), and the **Biblioteca Estense** (Mon–Sat 9am–1pm; entrance fee), the library of the d'Este family, dukes of Modena as well as Ferrara. On permanent display in the library is a collection of illuminated manuscripts, a 1481 copy of Dante's *Divine Comedy*, and the stunning Borso d'Este Bible which contains 1,200 miniatures.

Parma

There is no better place to become a connoisseur of *parmigiano* (Parmesan), the hard, sharp-flavoured cheese, than in **Parma ❸**, where the cheese is made. It is a medium-sized city that enjoys a cooler, fresher climate than other towns in

the muggy Po Valley. The history of Parma is full of interesting personalities. Napoleon's widow, Marie Louise, was ceded this city after her husband's death. Despite her reputation for immodest behaviour, she did good things for Parma, building roads and bridges and founding orphanages and public institutions. She also founded the Galleria Nazionale (Tues–Sun 8.30am–2pm; entrance fee) in the 16th-century **Palazzo della Pilotta**, a palace which also contains the Teatro Farnese, a Palladian theatre with Italy's first revolving stage.

However, the main aesthetic attraction of Parma is the **Duomo** (daily 9am–12.30pm and 3–7pm) and adjoining Baptistry. Its nave and cupola are decorated with splendid frescoes by Correggio. Contemporaries gushed over them: Titian said that if the dome of the cathedral were turned upside down and filled with gold it would not be as valuable as Correggio's frescoes. Vasari wrote of the *Assumption*: "It seems impossible that a man could have conceived such a work as this is, and more impossible still, that he should have done it with human hands."

The brilliantly restored **Baptistry** (daily 9am–12.30pm and 3.30–6.30pm; entrance fee) is the work of Benedetto Antelami, who built this octagonal building in rich rose pink Verona marble and then sculpted the reliefs that adorn both the interior and the exterior. Inside is a superb cycle of frescoes. Antelami's earliest-known work, the *Deposizione* (Descent from the Cross, 1178), can be seen in the Duomo. This deeply moving sculpture was hewn from a single piece of marble.

In the dome of **San Giovanni Evangelista**, another splendidly sensuous Correggio fresco (*circa* 1520) can be seen. It depicts St John gazing up at heaven where the Apostles are gathered and is matched by frescoes by Parmigiano.

If you are driving northwest on the Via Emilia towards Piacenza, consider making a quick stop in **Fidenza ❹** to see another glorious Romanesque cathe-

Map on pages 246–7

BELOW: Parma hams.

PARMA HAM AND PARMESAN

P arma ham and Parmesan cheese *(parmigiano)* are intricately linked, because it is the whey – the waste-product from Parmesan production – that is used to feed the pigs that produce Parma ham. True Parma ham is branded with the five-pointed crown of the medieval Dukes of Parma, and is produced in the Langhirino hills, south of Parma. Here the raw hind thighs are hung in drying sheds for up to ten months. The air that blows through the sheds is said to impart a sweet flavour to the meat – unlike cheap, mass-produced *prosciutto crudo*, which is injected with brine and artificially dried to speed up the curing process.

Try it as a starter *(antipasto)* in any Parma restaurant, sliced into wafer-thin slivers for eating with bread, melon or figs; and end your meal, perhaps, with slivers of superior *Parmigiano-Reggiano*, the king of Parmesans, which is especially delicious partnered with apples, pears or a good red wine. A lower-quality Parmesan is known as *grana*.

Another speciality of the region is *aceto balsamico* (balsamic vinegar) made from sweet grape juice, boiled slowly and reduced to a syrup, mixed with vinegar, and then aged in wooden casks for many years. It can be used in salads or as a marinade, or even drizzled over fresh berries or ice cream.

dral. Just beyond Fidenza is the turn off for the little town of **Roncole Verdi ❺**, where you can visit the humble cottage in which Giuseppe Verdi (1813–1901) was born in 1813 (Tues–Sun 9.30am–12.30pm and 3–7pm in summer, 9.30am–12.30pm and 2.30–5.30pm in winter; entrance fee).

In the revolutionary year of 1848, when Prince Charles Albert of Savoy called for Italians to assemble under his leadership and form an independent nation, the citizens of **Piacenza ❻** were the first to respond in a plebiscite. This vote of rebellion was a remarkable event in Piacenza's otherwise peaceful history. Situated at the point where the Via Emilia meets the Po, Piacenza has been a lively trading post since 218 BC. Nothing remains of the Roman period, though there are many fine medieval and Renaissance buildings. At the centre of the city is the massive **Palazzo del Comune** (not open to the public), called "Il Gotico". This town hall was built during Piacenza's "Communal Period" (approximately 1200–1400) when the city was an independent and important member of the Lombard League that defeated Emperor Frederick II of Hohenstaufen in his bid to conquer Italy. Il Gotico, begun in 1280, is a remarkably well-preserved building of brick, marble and terracotta. In front of it stand two massive baroque equestrian statues of Piacenza's 16th-century rulers, the Farnese dukes. At the end of the Via Venti Settembre stands Piacenza's Romanesque **Duomo** (daily 7.30am–noon and 3–7pm). Although gloomy on the inside, the cathedral is worth a visit for the frescoes on the columns near the entrance.

Ferrara

A prosperous market town on the banks of the misty Po River, **Ferrara ❼** seems at first glance peaceful and provincial. But the city has a colourful history and

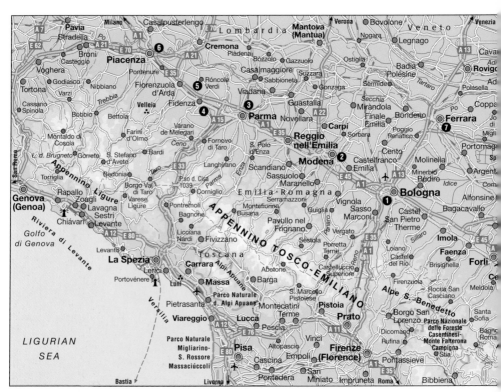

splendid treasures. At the southern end is a well-preserved medieval town, and to the north are long broad avenues lined with Renaissance palaces and carefully groomed gardens. The d'Este family ruled Ferrara from the late 13th century until 1598, a time of prosperity when their court attracted poets, scholars and artists. The Renaissance, the city's golden age, is reflected in all the major monuments.

Dominating Ferrara's skyline is the restored medieval **Castello Estense**, complete with moats, drawbridges and towers (Tues–Sun 9.30am–5pm; entrance fee). Just behind the castle is Ferrara's 12th-century Duomo. Among the noteworthy paintings here and in the adjoining museum (Museo della Cattedrale; Tues–Sun 9.30am–1pm and 3–6pm; donation) are Cosimo Tura's *San Giorgio* and his *Annunciation,* and Jacopo della Quercia's *Madonna della Melagrana* (1408). Across from the Duomo is the **Palazzo del Comune** (not open to the public), a medieval building with a beautiful Renaissance staircase. The piazza in front of this town hall is the hub of life in modern Ferrara, and teeming with bicycles, the number one method of transport in this very flat region of the Po Valley.

Many of the medieval streets south of the cathedral are lined with fortified houses, and, stretching across the **Via delle Volte**, a narrow street near the Po, there are a number of elegant arches. At the beautiful **Palazzo Schifanoia** (Tues–Sun 9am–6pm; entrance fee), one of the d'Este family's summer residences, you can climb the steep stairs to the Salone dei Mesi, a large, high room decorated with colourful frescoes of the months. However, most have deteriorated and their colours dulled. These were executed for the Duke of Borgo d'Este by masters of the Ferrarese school, including Ercole de' Roberti.

Just around the corner is another d'Este palace, the **Palazzo di Ludovico il Moro**, designed by the famous Ferrarese Renaissance architect Biagio Rossetti.

See map below

Ariosto, Petrarch, Tasso, Mantegna and Bellini were just some of the great Italian poets and painters patronised by the d'Este family of Ferrara.

BELOW: the Castello Estense, built in the 14th century.

This houses the Museo Archeologico Nazionale (Via Mellone, Tues–Sun 9am–2pm; entrance fee) which has a fine collection of Etruscan artefacts.

North of the Duomo, Ferrara is a city of broad avenues. Along one of the prettiest streets, Corso Ercole d'Este, is Rossetti's **Palazzo dei Diamanti** (Tues–Sat 9am–2pm, Sun until 1pm; entrance fee), with an art gallery, the Pinacoteca Nazionale, concealed behind a large Renaissance structure with a unique facade. The diamond, emblem of the d'Este family is repeated 12,600 times.

Rimini

Today **Rimini** ❽ is two cities: the old medieval and Renaissance town, and the ultra-modern beach resort a mile distant. In the skyscraper hotels that line Rimini's coast, you are more likely to hear German or English spoken than Italian, but the old centre retains its charm despite the influx of tourists.

The infamous ruler Sigismondo Malatesta has left his mark everywhere in Rimini. It was this anticlerical patron of art who presided over the transformation of a 13th-century Franciscan church into one of the most spectacular Renaissance buildings in Italy. The **Tempio Malatestiano** (Mon–Sat 8am–12.30pm and 3.30–6.30pm, Sun 9am–1pm and 3.30–7pm; free) is considered more a personal tribute to Sigismondo's mistress, Isotta degli Atti (who later became his third wife) than a church. But perhaps that is what Sigismondo intended, since he and Church authorities were never the best of friends. Pope Pius II even went so far as to excommunicate the violent and sensual Sigismondo, and to condemn him publicly to Hell, calling the site "a temple of devil-worshippers".

Sigismondo had better luck with women and artists. He was patron of such great artists as Piero della Francesca and Leon Battista Alberti, among others. It was Alberti who designed the exterior of the Tempio. (He found inspiration in the Roman Arch of Augustus which still stands at the gates of Rimini.) Note the wide classical arches on each side of the entrance. The interior rebuilding was supervised by Matteo de' Pasti, and although the simple, single-nave plan and wooden-trussed roof of the original Franciscan church remain, the side chapels (some added and others only redecorated) are opulent and intricate in design. Immediately on your right as you enter is Sigismondo's tomb. It is decorated with his initials intertwined with Isotta's. Note also the fresco of Sigismondo praying at the feet of St Sigismond, by Piero della Francesca.

To the left of the Tempio is **Piazza Tre Martiri**, which was named in honour of three Italian partisans hanged by the Nazis in this square in 1944. The piazza is also the site of the ancient Roman forum, whose columns now support the porticoes of the two eastern buildings.

Walk out of the piazza along **Corso di Augusto** for four blocks. At the end stands the **Arco di Augusto**, dating from 27 BC. With this archway the Romans marked the junction of the Via Emilia and the Via Flaminia, the primary road north from Rome to the Adriatic Sea.

Ravenna

When the unstoppable barbarians overran Rome in the 5th century AD, **Ravenna** ❾ benefited, gaining the honourable rank of capital of the Western Empire. This

Film director Federico Fellini (1902–93) was born in Rimini. His Oscar-winning film Amarcord *immortalised the area in the 1970s and the Felliniesque atmosphere is still evident in the narrow streets and small houses around the Borgo San Giuliano. The famous "old lady" of Adriatic hotels,* The Grand, *stands in the park named after him.*

BELOW: on the beach in Rimini.

Adriatic port town continued as capital under the Ostrogoths, and the barbarian leaders Odoacer and Teodoric also ruled their vast dominions from here. Later, when the Byzantine emperor Justinian reconquered part of Italy, he too made Ravenna his seat of power, liking it for its imperial tradition under the barbarians and – perhaps more importantly – for its direct sea links to Byzantium.

Under Justinian's rule the Ravenna we know today began to take shape. New buildings arose all over the city, including a handful of churches that are among the wonders of Italian art and architecture. There is no preparation in their simple brick exteriors for the brilliant mosaics within. It is these mosaics that make modern Ravenna, if no longer capital of the Western world, at least a capital of the Western art world.

Start with **San Vitale** (daily 9am–7pm; free), the city's great 6th-century octagonal basilica, famous for the mosaics in its choir and apse. These "monuments of unaging intellect", as the Irish poet W.B. Yeats called them, immediately draw the eye with their marvellous colours and intricate detail. Bright ducks, bulls, lions, dolphins and a phoenix intertwine with flowers and oddly angled corners of buildings to frame Old Testament scenes and portraits of Byzantine rulers with humour and exactitude.

In the dome of the apse a purple-clad and beardless Christ sits on a blue globe flanked by archangels and, at the far sides, St Vitalis and Bishop Ecclesius. Christ hands the saint (Ravenna's patron) a triumphal crown, while the bishop (who founded the church in 521) carries a model of the building as it finally appeared many years after his death. Below stretch imperial scenes of Justinian with his courtiers and Theodora, his beloved wife, with hers.

San Vitale is not the only place to see mosaics in Ravenna. Nearly every

Map on pages 246–7

TIP

Ravenna's medieval Piazza del Popolo is a good place to relax with a cup of coffee after seeing the mosaics.

BELOW: mosaic of the three magi in Sant'Apollinare Nuovo in Ravenna.

Map on pages 246-7

The glorious mosaics depicting an ethereal blue sky sprinkled with gold stars which fill the vaulted ceiling of the Mausoleo di Galla Placidia are said to have inspired Cole Porter to write his timeless song Night and Day.

BELOW: outside the church of San Vitale and **RIGHT:** the apse, with a mosaic of Christ handing a crown to the martyr, Vitale.

church contains a pristine example of the art. Just north, another set may be seen at the **Mausoleo di Galla Placidia** (daily 9am–7pm; free). This interesting lady was born a Roman princess, sister to Emperor Honorius, but after she was captured by the Goths, she married their leader, Athaulf, and ruled with him. He, however, soon died, and she next married a Roman general to whom she bore a son. This son became Emperor Valentinian III. As Valentinian's regent, and a woman with connections in the highest barbarian circles, Galla Placidia played a powerful role in the world of "the decline". The building that houses her tomb has a simple exterior but inside the walls, floors, and ceiling are covered with glorious mosaics, the oldest in Ravenna.

Through the gate that lies between San Vitale and Galla Placidia are two Renaissance cloisters that now house the **Museo Nazionale** (Tues–Sun 8.30am–7pm; entrance fee). The museum includes, as one might expect, many mosaics as well as other relics from Ravenna's past. There's glass from San Vitale and also fabrics from the tomb of St Julian at Rimini.

The baroque Duomo

A pleasant walk along Via Fanni, Via Barbiani and left on to Via d'Azeglio leads to Ravenna's **Duomo** – originally constructed in the 5th century but redone in baroque style in the 1730s. Far more attractive than the cathedral itself is the adjoining **Battistero Neoniano** (daily 9.30am–7pm; free), a 5th-century octagonal baptistry that was once a Roman bath house. The interior combines spectacular Byzantine mosaics with marble inlay from the original.

Across Piazza Caduti from the cathedral complex is **San Francesco**, another 5th-century church almost completely redone in the baroque style. To the left stands the **Tomba di Dante** (daily 9am–7pm in summer, 9am–noon and 2–5pm in winter), not a remarkable building architecturally, but of great historic interest. Dante, the author of *The Divine Comedy*, was exiled from his home in Florence for his political outspokenness and found refuge in Ravenna in 1317. He spent the remaining four years of his life here, putting the finishing touches to his great work.

After Dante's death, the repentant Florentines would dearly have loved to honour their famous son with a splendid tomb, but proud Ravenna refused to give up the poet's remains. The battle over the bones continued for hundreds of years. At one point in 1519, it looked as if Ravenna would lose. The powerful Medici of Florence sent their representatives to Ravenna with a papal injunction demanding the relics. The sarcophagus was duly opened, but the bones were not inside. Someone had been warned of the Florentine scheme and had removed the bones to a secret hiding place. They were not found again until 1865, and now rest within the sarcophagus that is on display. To this day, the city of Florence provides the oil for the lamp which burns on his tomb.

Down the Via di Roma is another church full of mosaics, **Sant'Apollinare Nuovo** (daily 9am– 7pm; free). The scenes are of processions, one of virgins and the other of martyrs who appear to be moving towards the altar between rows of palms. Above, the decorations depict episodes from the *Life of Christ*. ❑

FLORENCE

One of the world's great artistic centres, packed with aesthetic masterpieces, Florence is the essential destination for students of Renaissance art and architecture

Map on pages 254–5

ITALY
Florence
● Rome

Florence (Firenze) is the city that gave birth to the Renaissance and many visitors come here to trace the development of this extraordinary outpouring of artistic talent in the 15th century. A huge number of Renaissance works have remained in the city where they were created; many paintings, statues and whole buildings, such as the Palazzo Pitti, were bequeathed to the people of Florence by Anna Maria Lodovica of the Medici family, whose death in 1743 brought an end to the dynasty that had ruled Florence since 1434.

Her far-sighted bequest ensured that the Medici collections remained intact and were not dispersed all over the globe. Napoleon stole a few choice pieces during his adventures in Italy (including the *Medici Venus*, now in the Louvre), and English collectors bought some splendid paintings very cheaply in the 19th century when the so-called "primitives" were out of fashion. Despite this, you can still see in Florence many of the paintings and frescoes that Vasari, the first art historian, mentions in his entertaining and anecdotal *Lives of the Artists*, first published in 1550. Nearly all works have been superbly restored since the great flood of November 1966, and the bullet-proof glass installed to protect the most important paintings in the Uffizi proved effective when a terrorist bomb exploded in May 1993, reducing some minor masterpieces to shreds.

LEFT: buy a postcard of the city's glories, or **BELOW:** make your own sketch.

Where the Renaissance started

To see where the Renaissance began, it is traditional to begin with Piazza del Duomo. Approaching this massive square, you file through sober streets lined with buildings presenting a stern defensive face. Suddenly the 19th-century face of the **Duomo ❶** (cathedral; open Mon, Tues, Wed, Fri 10am–5pm, Thurs 10am–3.30pm, Sat 10am–4.45pm, Sun 1.30–4.45pm, closed 1st Sat of month; free) is revealed, all festive in its polychrome marble – green from Prato, white from Carrara and red from the Maremma. The design echoes that of the tall **Campanile** (Apr–Sept daily 8.30am–7.30pm, Oct daily 9am–5.30pm, Nov–Mar daily 9am–4.30pm; entrance fee) alongside, designed by Giotto in 1331. You can climb the 414 steps of the belltower for intimate views of the cathedral dome and roofline, or simply enjoy the flamboyant exterior of the cathedral from one of the open-air cafés on the south side of the square.

The little octagonal **Battistero** (Baptistry; Mon–Sat noon–7pm, Sun 8.30am–2pm; entrance fee), to the west of the cathedral, dates to the 6th century, though the interior was redesigned and given its ceiling mosaics of the *Creation* and *Last Judgement* in 1300. The Baptistry has three sets of bronze doors and those to the north have an important place in art history. If it is possible to pin down the start of the Renaissance to a particular event, then it was the competition held in the winter of

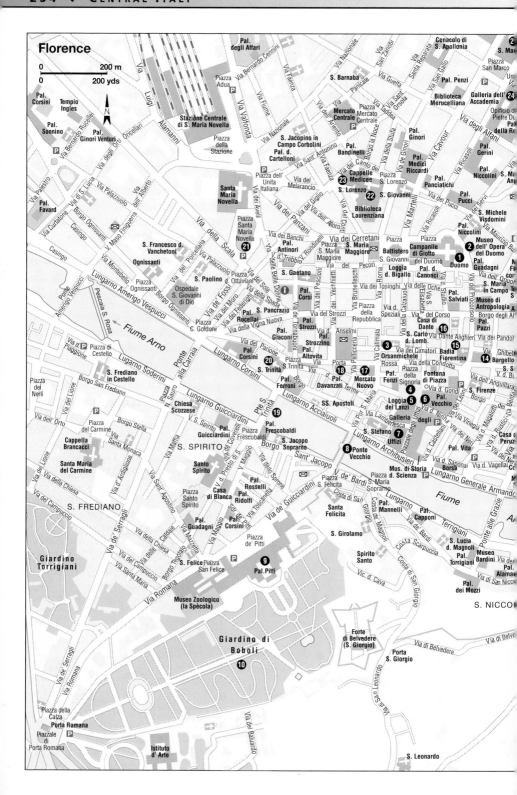

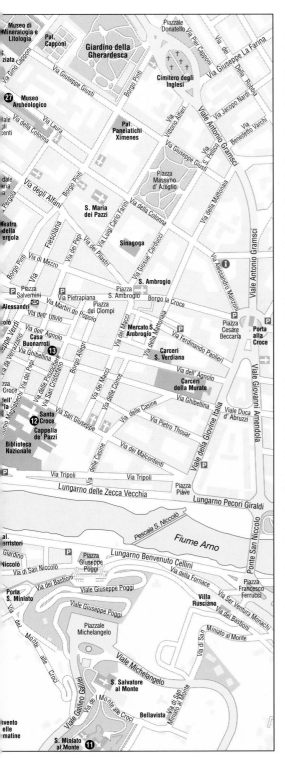

1401 to choose an artist to design these doors. Of the six artists who entered the competition, Ghiberti and Brunelleschi were adjudged joint winners, but Brunelleschi, a fiery-tempered genius, refused to work with Ghiberti and went off in a huff to Rome.

Ghiberti, left with sole responsibility for the doors, did not complete them until 1424, but the resulting work shows many of the key features that define Renaissance art: the realistic depiction of people, fully worked-out perspective, and narrative clarity combined with dramatic tension. Ghiberti was immediately commissioned to design another set of doors, this time for the east portal, and these were unveiled in 1452 when Michelangelo hailed them as fit to serve as the "gates of Paradise"; they are known to this day as the Paradise doors. The third set of doors, to the south, are the work of Andrea Pisano (1330) and tell the story of John the Baptist, patron saint of the city.

Biggest dome in the world

Brunelleschi, meanwhile, spent his time in Rome studying Ancient Roman architecture and he returned to Florence full of confidence that he could accomplish a task that had defeated other architects, namely to complete the cathedral by erecting the vast **dome**. In typically Florentine fashion, the city had decided to build the biggest dome in the world without actually knowing how to achieve it. If you enter the cathedral and climb the 436 steps to the top (Mon–Fri 8.30am–7pm, Sat 8.30am–5.40pm; entrance fee) you can study how the problem was solved – by building a light inner shell of interlocking brick which serves as the support for the outer roof of the dome.

Brunelleschi was hailed as a new Icarus (the mythical hero who similarly defied gravity by inventing flight) and the city passed an ordinance forbidding the construction of any building taller than the dome out of respect for his achievement; to this day, the massive dome rises supreme above the red roofs of the city, rising almost higher than the surrounding hills. Brunelleschi was also buried in the

cathedral – an honour granted to him alone – and his tomb can be seen in the **crypt** (daily 10am–5pm; closed religious hols; entrance fee), among the excavated ruins of Santa Reparata, the city's first (4th-century) cathedral.

Much of the rest of the cathedral is bare. There is an interesting fresco on the north aisle wall, painted by Paolo Uccello in 1436, depicting Sir John Hawkwood, the English mercenary who served as Captain of the Florentine army from 1377 to 1394. Otherwise, to see the cathedral treasures you must visit the **Museo dell'Opera del Duomo ❷** (Mon–Sat 9am–7.30pm, Sun 9am–1.40pm; entrance fee) on the east side of Piazza del Duomo. This restored and expanded museum is full of outstanding sculptures, from Donatello's haggard *Mary Magdalene* carved in wood in the 1460s to the same artist's superb *cantoria* (choir gallery), decorated with angels and cherubs engaged in frenzied music and song. The star exhibit here is Michelangelo's *Pietà*, begun around 1550. Michelangelo intended this for his own tomb, but left it unfinished (a pupil rather clumsily attempted to finish the work). Its magnetic hold over visitors derives from the fact that the tall hooded figure of Nicodemus is Michelangelo's self-portrait.

Lorenzo Ghiberti took themes from the Old Testament for the East Doors (the "gates of Paradise") of the Battistero. This is a detail from the Battle with the Philistines.

BELOW: figure of a saint in an external niche of Orsanmichele.

Showpiece of the guilds

From the cathedral square, **Via dei Calzaiuoli** leads south. This was the principal street of Roman and medieval Florence and, having been restored after World War II bombing, it is lined with good shops. Part way down, on the right, is the church of **Orsanmichele ❸** (a contraction of Orti di San Michele – the Garden of San Michele church, which once stood here). The niches around the exterior walls are filled with Renaissance statues sponsored by the guilds and depicting their respective patron saints. Of these, Donatello's *St George*, made for the Guild of Armourers, is the most important, and for that reason it has been removed to a place of honour in the Bargello museum *(see pages 260–1)* and replaced by a copy.

The same fate befell Michelangelo's *David*, which once stood in the **Piazza della Signoria ❹**, just to the south. The original was moved to the Galleria dell' Accademia *(see page 262)* in 1873 but the copy that now stands in front of the Palazzo Vecchio is faithful to the original. David's companions are the constipated-looking figure of *Hercules* (1534 by Bandinelli), the mythical founder of Florence, and Ammannati's licentious *Neptune Fountain* (1575). Nearby, the **Loggia dei Lanzi ❺** (1382) shelters Cellini's *Perseus* (1554) and Giambologna's *Rape of the Sabine Women* (1583), alongside Ancient Roman statues.

Most of the statues gathered here are symbolic, not least David himself, carved by Michelangelo to represent the aspirations of the Florentine people not long after the citizens had declared themselves independent of all rulers except for God. The fledgling Florentine Republic was threatened by a number of tyrannical Goliaths, including the Pope, the Holy Roman Emperor and the Medici. The combined forces of all three held the city to siege in 1530 and shortly afterwards Cosimo I was crowned Duke of Florence.

This Cosimo was a very different character from his earlier namesake, the humanist, classics scholar and patron of the arts, Cosimo il Vecchio, who ruled the city from 1434 to 1464 without ever holding office. Cosimo I was a no-nonsense military man who set about conquering all those cities in the region not already ruled by Florence. Cosimo I created the Tuscany of today by these means and he set up an efficient administration to rule his dukedom, which remained in place until Tuscany joined the united kingdom of Italy in 1861.

Map on pages 254–5

That administration was based in the **Palazzo Vecchio** ❻ (daily 9am–7pm, until 2pm on Thur; entrance fee), which remains the town hall of Florence, and which was comprehensively redesigned during the reign of Cosimo I. Visiting the ancient town hall, you can see the delicately decorated entrance courtyard with its little fountain – Vasari's copy of the original *Putto and Dolphin* fountain made by Verrocchio in 1470. By contrast, the vast Salone dei Cinquecento (Hall of the Five Hundred) was originally intended as the council chamber of the 500 citizens who governed during the Republic. Cosimo I set his stamp on the chamber by commissioning a series of vast frescoes, painted by Vasari, which glorified his military triumphs. Other rooms of the palace contain mementos of various prominent Florentines, such as portraits of the Medici popes Leo X and Clement VII. A small bust of Machiavelli is located in the little room that he used during his term of office as Chancellor of Florence.

A copy of Michelangelo's David *in Piazza della Signoria.*

The Uffizi

Under Cosimo I, Tuscan bureaucracy grew to the point where new offices were required to house the burgeoning army of lawyers and notaries, the guilds and the judiciary. Thus it was that the **Uffizi** ❼ (Tues–Sun 8.15am–6.50pm, last entry 45 mins before closing; entrance fee) came to be built alongside the Palazzo Vecchio – now a world-famous art gallery but originally intended to

BELOW: the Duomo.

serve a far more utilitarian purpose (the word *uffizi* simply means offices).

Vasari was the architect and he built a well-lit upper storey, using iron reinforcement to create an almost continuous wall of glass running round the long inner courtyard of the Uffizi. It was this glass wall that caused so much damage when a terrorist bomb exploded near the west wing of the Uffizi in May 1993, sending splinters of glass everywhere and destroying a number of paintings in the process. In the 16th century, such lavish use of glass was novel and Cosimo's heirs decided that the airy upper corridor of the Uffizi would make a perfect exhibition space for the family statues, carpets and paintings.

Thus began what has grown to be the greatest collection of Italian art in the world. It is arranged chronologically so that you can trace, almost in textbook fashion, the development of Florentine art from the formal style of the Gothic era (13th and 14th centuries), to the greater realism of the early Renaissance (15th century), and finally to the painterly use of exaggerated colours and the contorted poses designed to show off the artist's skill that is so characteristic of the High Renaissance and Mannerist periods (16th century).

The famous names and familiar works come thick and fast as you explore the collection; essential viewing includes Botticelli's *Primavera* (1480) and the *Birth of Venus* (1485). You should also seek out the portraits of the Medici family that are gathered in the octagonal Tribune, including Bronzino's *Portrait of Bia*, illegitimate daughter of Cosimo I (1542). The corridors of the gallery are lined with ancient Roman and Greek statues, of which the most famous is perhaps the boy removing a thorn from his foot. Look out too for Michelangelo's influential *Holy Family (Doni Tondo*; 1506–8), Raphael's tender *Madonna of the Goldfinch* (1506) and Titian's erotic *Venus of Urbino* (1538).

TIP

Queues for the Uffizi can be achingly long, but tickets can be reserved in advance. Call Firenze Musei, tel: 055-294883, where, for a small fee, you're given a booking number, or log on to www.weekendafirenze.com at least one day in advance (subject to a booking fee). Pre-booked tickets are picked up at a separate entrance.

BELOW: the Ponte Vecchio, built in 1345.

When Vasari planned the Uffizi, he incorporated an aerial corridor (the Corridoio Vasariano) into the design. This consists of a continuous covered walkway linking the Palazzo Vecchio to the Pitti Palace, passing through the Uffizi and along the top of the Ponte Vecchio. The Medici dukes used this corridor to walk between their various palaces without having to mix with their subjects in the streets below. The corridor is currently closed to the general public, though at certain times of year visits can be arranged for small groups (tel: 055-2654321).

En route to the Pitti Palace, the corridor passes over the **Ponte Vecchio ❽**. The bridge was built in 1345 and its workshops were used by butchers and tanners until these noxious trades were banned by ducal ordinance in 1593. Today it has been taken over by jewellers, buskers and streams of tourists shopping for trinkets.

Good shops line the route south of the bridge into the Oltrarno district where you will find the churches of **Santo Spirito**, an architectural masterpiece by Brunelleschi, and **Santa Maria del Carmine** (Wed–Sat and Mon 10am–5pm, Sun 1–5pm; entrance fee), where the Brancacci Chapel contains Masaccio's fresco cycle on the *Life of St Peter*. This is one of the great works of the early Renaissance and the Brancacci Chapel is tiny, with room for only 30 people at a time, so there are likely to be queues at the entrance. Visits are limited to 15 minutes (tel: 055-2382195 to book).

Residence of the Medici Grand Dukes

Space is not a problem at the vast and fortress-like **Palazzo Pitti ❾**. This became the residence of the Medici Grand Dukes in 1550 and, like the Uffizi, it is stuffed with artistic treasures, housed in museums including the Palatine Gallery, the Modern Art Collection, the Argenti (Silver) Museum and the Costume Museum.

The most rewarding of these is the **Palatine Gallery** (Tues–Sun 8.15am–6.50pm, ticket office closes 1 hr earlier; entrance fee), especially the richly decorated rooms with ceiling frescoes by Pietro da Cortona. These illustrate, in allegorical form, the education of a prince under the tutorship of the gods. In Room 1, the prince is torn from the arms of Venus (love) by Minerva (knowledge) and in subsequent rooms learns about science from Apollo, war from Mars and leadership from Jupiter. Finally the prince takes his place alongside Saturn, who, in ancient mythology, presided over the Golden Age.

Among the paintings displayed in these rooms are some wonderful portraits by Titian who even manages to turn the reformed prostitute, Mary Magdalene, into a delectable study of the delights of the female form. More disturbing is Rubens' celebrated masterpiece, the *The Consequences of War* (1638), an allegory of the Thirty Years' War. The artist explained in a letter that the figure in black represents "unfortunate Europe who, for so many years now, has suffered plunder, outrage and misery." Next to her, Venus is trying to restrain the war god, Mars, who is trampling over books, symbolising his disregard for civilisation.

The **Giardino di Boboli ❿** (daily 8.15am–1 hr before sunset; closed 1st and last Mon of month; entrance fee), behind the Palazzo Pitti, was laid out in the 16th century. Here you will find box hedges clipped into formal geometric patterns set against wild groves

So rich is the Uffizi's collection that many of its masterpieces are kept in storage for lack of room to display them. Proposals for expansion have been under discussion for many years, but the powers that be seem incapable of agreeing and, for now at least, plans remain on the table.

Map on pages 254-5

BELOW: San Miniato rises gracefully above Florence.

The Bargello was built in 1255 and became a national museum in 1865.

BELOW: stroking the snout of the bronze boar in the Mercato Nuovo is meant to bring good luck.

of ilex and cypress to create a contrast between artifice and nature. Dotted around the lavishly landscaped gardens are numerous grottoes, statues and fountains.

Jewel on the hill

On one of the hills above Florence sits **San Miniato** ⑪ (daily 8am–7.30pm in summer, 8am–1pm and 2–6pm in winter), a jewel-like Romanesque church. Catch the No. 12 or 13 bus up, and come back down on foot via **Piazzale Michelangelo**, a terrace set high above the city dotted with reproductions of Michelangelo's famous works and with fantastic views across the Arno of the city below.

Prominent in the view, to the east of the city, is the massive Gothic church of **Santa Croce** ⑫, which features in E.M. Forster's novel (and the Merchant-Ivory film) *A Room with a View* (church: Mon–Sat 8am–5.45pm, Sun 3–5.45pm; 8am–1pm for services; free. Cloister, Capella de' Pazzi and museum: Mon–Sat 9.30am–5.30pm, Sun 1–5.30pm; entrance fee). Here you will find frescoes by Giotto and his pupils and the tombs and monuments of famous Florentines, including Michelangelo, Machiavelli and Galileo (born in Pisa but protected by the Medici after his excommunication for holding the heretical view that the earth goes round the sun, rather than the reverse).

Weaving your way back from the church through the alleys of the Santa Croce district you pass the **Casa Buonarroti** ⑬ (Wed–Mon 9.30am–2pm; entrance fee), a house owned by Michelangelo and now containing one of his earliest works, the *Madonna della Scala*, created when he was only 16 years old. Call in at the **Bar Vivoli Gelateria** (Via Isole delle Stinche 7) which serves the best ice cream in Florence. From here it is a short step to the **Bargello** ⑭ (daily 8.15am– 1.50pm, except closed 2nd and 4th Mon and 1st, 3rd and 5th Sun of the month; entrance

fee), once a prison and place of execution but now a museum devoted to sculpture and applied art where you can see works by Donatello, Michelangelo, Cellini and Giambologna. Dante was born in this district and opposite the Bargello you can see the abbey church, the **Badia Fiorentina** ⓰, where the poet watched his beloved Beatrice attending Mass. Round the corner, in Via Dante Alighieri, is the **Casa di Dante** ⓰ (Wed–Mon 10am–5pm in summer, till 4pm in winter; entrance fee), the house in which the poet is supposed to have been born in 1265.

Continuing west, you will reach another important shopping street, Via Roma, which leads south into Via Calimala and the **Mercato Nuovo** ⓱ (Mon–Sat). Despite its name, the "New Market" has been here since 1551 and was known as the Straw Market in the 19th century, on account of its specialism in raffia goods. Today it sells leather and tourist souvenirs. The little bronze boar, **Il Porcellino**, in the south side of the market, has a shiny nose because of the number of visitors who have rubbed it for good luck.

From the north side of the market, Via Porta Rossa will take you to the **Palazzo Davanzati** ⓲, a delightful 14th-century townhouse complete with frescoed walls and contemporary furnishings that present a vivid picture of domestic life in late medieval Florence. The building is undergoing intense restoration work and only certain sections of it are open to the public (Tues–Sat 8.15am–1.50pm). You are now close to the **River Arno** and the bridge called **Ponte Santa Trinità** ⓳, after the adjacent church. The bridge, which features statues of the *Four Seasons*, was blown up by the retreating Nazis in 1944 and dredged up from the river bed to be restored to its original design.

The church of **Santa Trinità** ⓴ (Mon–Sat 8am–noon and 4pm–6pm, Sun 4–6pm) contains frescoes by Ghirlandaio showing the *Life of St Francis* set against

Map on pages 254–5

Relief on a door at Santa Trinità.

BELOW: fresco by Gozzoli in the Palazzo Medici-Riccardi.

Map on pages 254–5

Sculpture in the Accademia.

BELOW: atrium of the Annunziata.
RIGHT: along the Arno embankment.

a background of Florentine buildings. North from here, **Via de' Tornabuoni** is lined with the chic boutiques of high-class couturiers, such as Salvatore Ferragamo and Gucci. At the top of the street, the Palazzo Antinori contains an excellent wine bar and restaurant, but if the prices are too steep you can sample the cheap Chinese restaurants in **Piazza Santa Maria Novella ㉑**, with a view of the Basilica di Santa Maria Novella. The latter features in Boccaccio's *Decameron*, and contains colourful frescoes by Ghirlandaio on the *Life of the Virgin*. In the adjoining **museum** (Mon–Thur and Sat 9.30am–5pm, Fri and Sun 1–5pm; entrance fee) you can see what remains of Paolo Uccello's masterpiece, the *Universal Deluge* fresco, depicting the flood that drowned all but Noah and his entourage, a fresco that was, ironically, badly damaged by the Florentine floods of 1966.

Popular market

Heading back to the heart of Florence, it is easy to get lost in the streets around **San Lorenzo ㉒**, the venue of a crowded street market most days of the week. It is a good place in which to buy almost anything – from picnic food to souvenirs. At the back of San Lorenzo is the entrance to the **Cappelle Medicee ㉓** (Tues–Sun 8.15am–5pm, also 1st, 3rd, 5th Sun and 2nd, 4th Mon of the month; entrance fee), the mausoleum of the Medici family, for which Michelangelo carved two splendid tombs featuring the allegorical figures of *Night* and *Day, Dusk* and *Dawn*. The church itself, entered through the rough, unfinished facade, is an example of Renaissance rationalism in architecture, all cool whites and greys and restrained classical decoration. By contrast, the two huge pulpits carved by Donatello with scenes from the *Life of Christ* are full of impassioned emotion, and Michelangelo's staircase leading to the **Biblioteca Medicea Laurenziana** (Laurentian Library; daily 8.30am–1.30pm; entrance fee), off the cloister, is considerably more exuberant. Just off Piazza di San Lorenzo is the **Palazzo Medici-Riccardi** (opening times vary), the first Medici seat, containing a frescoed chapel, state rooms and a library.

Michelangelo's most famous work, *David*, is in the **Galleria dell'Accademia ㉔** (Tues–Sun 8.15am–6.50pm; entrance fee), two blocks away in Via Ricasoli – be prepared for long queues. Other highlights include Michelangelo's unfinished *Four Slaves*, the plaster cast of Giambologna's *Rape of the Sabines* (on display in the Loggia dei Lanzi) and Fillipino Lippi's striking *Deposition from the Cross*, which was finished by Perugino on the former's death. The collection has been recently expanded to incorporate a display of musical instruments.

The nearby convent of **San Marco ㉕** (church: daily 8.15am–1pm and 4–6pm; museum: Mon–Fri 8.15am–5pm, Sat–Sun 8.15am–7pm; closed 1st, 3rd and 5th Sun and 2nd and 4th Mon of the month; entrance fee), which contains nearly every painting and fresco ever produced by the saintly artist, Fra' Angelico, is equally rewarding.

Return to the city centre via the **Piazza della Santissima Annunziata ㉖**, with its delicate Renaissance colonnade fronting the **Innocenti** orphanage, the work of Brunelleschi, and the **Museo Archeologico Nazionale ㉗** (Mon 2–7pm, Tues and Thur 8.30am–7pm, Wed and Fri–Sun 8.30am–2pm; entrance fee), with its ancient Etruscan and Egyptian treasures. ❑

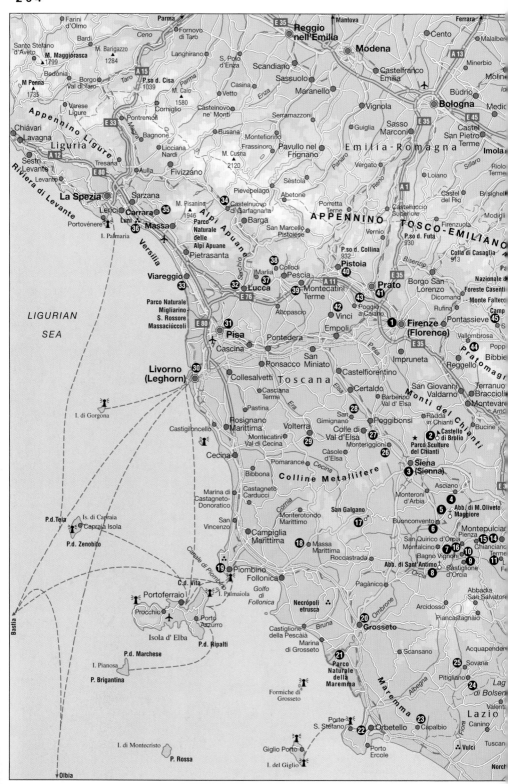

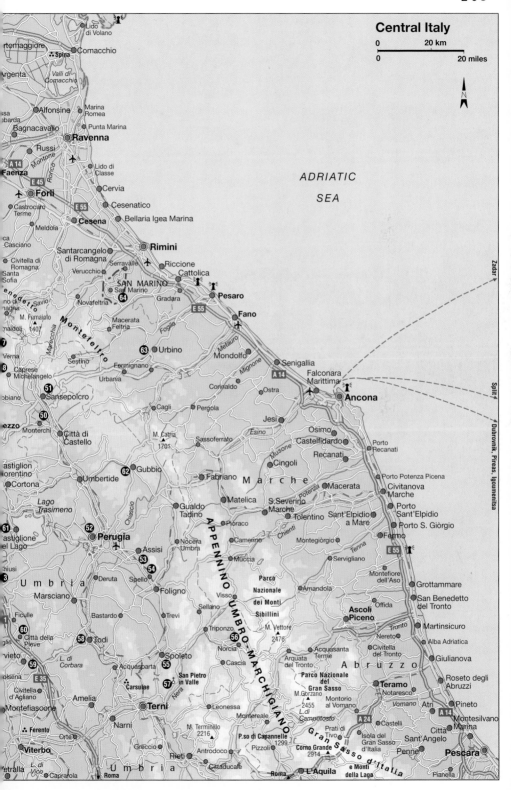

Central Italy

0   20 km

0   20 miles

TUSCANY

Strong architecture, evocative landscapes and soft red wines form an essential part of this region's appeal, and the cities of Siena and Pisa have much to recommend them

Maps on pages 264 & 268

F or those not fascinated by frescoes, the delights of Florence ❶ can quickly fade and the desire to escape the cauldron-like atmosphere of this hot, dry city can prove overwhelming, as it did in the case of the English writer Laurie Lee: "I'd had my fill of Florence, lovely but indigestible city. My eyes were choked with pictures and frescoes … I began to long for the cool uplands, the country air, the dateless wild olive and the uncatalogued cuckoo."

Lee escaped by walking south along the Chiantigiana, the Chianti Way, shown on maps as the N222 road, which takes you to Siena via several pretty towns in the Chianti Classico wine-growing region. If you are driving, the journey will take little more than an hour, unless you are tempted to stop along the route at the scores of *fattorie* (wine estates) offering free tastings and wine sales direct to the public (*vendita diretta*). This is one way to learn about the region's famous red wines; another is to leave the N222 at Castellina in Chianti and drive east, stopping for a walk round the pretty town of Radda in Chianti before rejoining the N429 to the **Badia a Coltibuono** (gardens and cellars open May–Oct Mon–Sat 2.30–6.30pm), a 12th-century abbey set among pines, oaks, chestnuts and vines. Below the abbey are cellars filled with Chianti Classico, the abbey's traditional living. Wine, together with locally produced olive oil and chestnut honey, can be bought on the premises or savoured in the excellent abbey restaurant (tel: 0577-749031; www.coltibuono.com).

South of Gaiole in Chianti, **Castello di Brolio** ❷ (summer daily 9am–noon, 3–7pm; winter Sat–Thur 9am–noon, 3–6pm; entrance fee) is the birthplace of the modern Chianti industry. It was here, in 1870, that Barone Bettino Ricasoli established the formula for making Chianti wines that has been used ever since, requiring a precise blend of white and red grape juice and the addition of dried grapes to the vat to give the wine its softness and fruit-filled flavour.

LEFT: the pageantry of Siena's Palio.
BELOW: a door knocker, typical of the Tuscan nobility's taste for elaborate decoration.

City of narrow medieval lanes

Knowledgeable about the region's wines, you can tackle the traffic headaches that await in **Siena** ❸. Finding space to park may prove difficult, but the medieval core of the city is largely traffic-free, because the alleys that thread between high palaces of rose-pink brick are too narrow for vehicles. All roads in Siena eventually lead to the **Campo** Ⓐ, the huge main central square, which is shaped like an amphitheatre – the Sienese say that it is shaped like the protecting cloak of the Virgin, who, with St Catherine of Siena, is the city's patron saint.

From the comfort of a pavement café on the curved side of the Campo you can note the division of the paved surface into nine segments, commemorating the beneficent rule of the Council of Nine Good Men which governed Siena from the mid-13th century to the early 14th,

A statue by the Duomo shows Remus and the she-wolf. Remus's son is said to have founded Siena.

a period of stability and prosperity when most of the city's main public monuments were built. Twice a year, on 2 July and 16 August, the Sienese recreate their medieval heritage in the Palio, a sumptuous pageant-cum-horserace around the Campo. This is no mere tourist event; the residents of the city's 17 *contrade*, or districts, pack the square as their representative horses and riders career around the Campo, and the rider who wins the race and the Palio, a heraldic banner, becomes an instant local hero. At the square's base is the **Palazzo Pubblico**, with its crenellated facade and waving banners. Erected in the 14th century, it housed the offices of the city government. At its left corner is the slender bell tower, the **Torre del Mangia** (Mar–Oct daily 10am–7pm, July–Aug until 11pm; Nov–Mar 10am–4pm; entrance fee). Climb more than 500 steps for a panorama of the city.

Although bureaucrats still toil in parts of the *palazzo*, as they have for some seven centuries, much of the complex is now devoted to the **Museo Civico B** (daily 10am–7pm in summer, till 5.30pm in winter; entrance fee), which houses some of the city's greatest treasures. Siena's city council once met in the vast **Sala del Mappamondo**, although the huge globe that then graced the walls

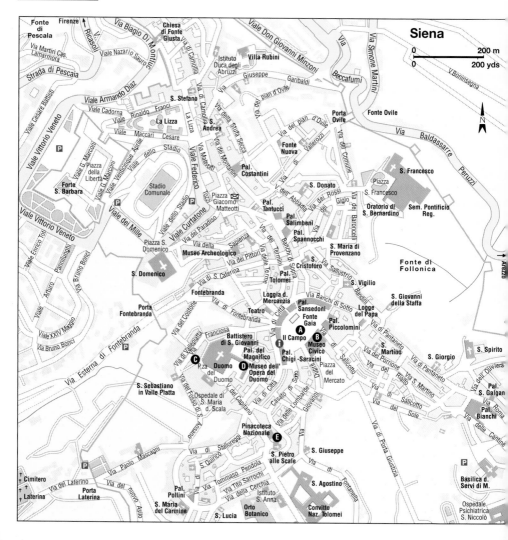

has disappeared. What remains are two frescoes attributed to the medieval master Simone Martini: the majestic mounted figure of Guidoriccio da Fogliano and, opposite, the *Maestà*. The *Maestà* is signed in Simone Martini's own hand, but in recent years doubts have been cast on the authenticity of the Guidoriccio. A smaller fresco recently uncovered below the huge panel may be Simone Martini's original, and the Guidoriccio may have been executed long after the artist's death.

In the Sala della Pace is Ambrogio Lorenzetti's *Allegory of Good and Bad Government*. Intended as a constant reminder to the city fathers of their responsibilities, it depicts the entire sweep of medieval society, from the king and his court down to the peasants working the terraced hillsides outside the city walls.

Exiting again to the Campo, turn left and head up the hill via one of the winding streets to **Piazza del Duomo** ❻. The facade of the vast striped cathedral is a festival of green, pink and white marble, which will help prepare you for the stunning black-and-white geometric patterns of the interior. Take special care to study the 15th- and 16th-century marble inlaid paving of the Duomo, which depicts allegories and scenes from the New Testament (unfortunately, many are covered most of the year to protect them from wear and tear). Off the north aisle is the decorative Libreria Piccolomini, built in 1495 to house the personal papers and books of Pope Pius II. The frescoes by Pinturicchio show scenes from the life of the pope, and in the centre of the room is the famous *Three Graces*, a Roman copy of a sculpture by the Greek artist Praxiteles.

For those with more time, Siena has two other important museums: the **Museo dell'Opera del Duomo** ❼ (Cathedral Museum; daily 9am–7.30pm in summer, 9am–1.30pm in winter; entrance fee), to the right (south) of the cathedral, and the **Pinacoteca Nazionale** ❽ (Picture Gallery; Tues–Sat 8.15am–7.15pm, Sun–Mon 8.30am–1.30pm; entrance fee), in the Palazzo Buonsignori on the Via San Pietro, just south of the Campo. The Cathedral Museum's main attraction is the entire room devoted to the works of Duccio di Buoninsegna, including his moving *Madonna dei Francescani*, the Virgin enthroned.

Rounded hills of the Crete

Siena sits at the geographical centre of Tuscany and whichever way you drive you will be spoilt for choice in terms of attractive historic towns and beautiful countryside. Drive southwest along the N438 to unpromising **Asciano** ❹ and you will pass through the dramatic Crete region, the Tuscany that appears on countless postcards and posters. Here the bare, rounded clay hills have no trees except for the occasional stately avenue of cypresses, winding across the landscape and marking the way to an isolated farm, a simple Romanesque church or a *borgo*, a small defended village.

Asciano's main street, Corso Giacomo Matteotti, is lined with smart shops and classical *palazzi*. At the top end is the simple Romanesque **Collegiata** and the **Museo Archeologico e d'Arte Sacra** (variable opening times; tel: 0577-719510), a revamped museum of Sienese sculpture and archaeological finds from the area. The **Museo Etrusco** (daily 10am–12.30pm and 3–6pm, closed Tues pm), on Corso Matteotti, is a typical small Tuscan museum that celebrates Etruscan inheritance.

Maps on pages 264 & 268

Fresco in Monte Oliveto Maggiore.

BELOW: Siena's Palazzo Pubblico.

Church in the well-preserved town of Buonconvento.

BELOW: antique shop in Montalcino.

A short drive on is the **Abbazia di Monte Oliveto Maggiore ❺** (daily 9.15am–noon and 3.15–5.45pm), a 14th-century Benedictine monastery with an air of aloof dignity, set among groves of cypress trees. The Great Cloister is covered in frescoes on the *Life of St Benedict*, begun by Luca Signorelli in 1495 and completed by Sodoma from 1505. The excellent monastery guidebook gives a detailed description. In one scene Sodoma portrays himself with his pet badgers (one wearing a scarlet collar) looking like a pair of well-trained dogs.

Buonconvento ❻ is worth a brief stop, if only to admire the massive medieval city gates of iron-bound wood, before driving through fertile countryside, scattered with vineyards, to the hilltop town of **Montalcino ❼**, a wine-producing town where every other shop seems to sell the famed Brunello wines. It is also a town of timeless character with several old-fashioned wood-panelled bars where vineyard workers shelter from the midday sun. The streets are narrow and steep and from the airy heights of the walls there are entrancing views. The highest point is the **Fortezza** (Fortress), housing a wine centre or *enoteca* (Tues–Sun 9am–1pm and 2.30–8pm in summer, 9am–1pm and 2–6pm in winter; entrance fee) where regional vintages can be sampled and purchased, and the ramparts explored.

Romanesque abbey church

Further south again is another sight that features on postcards, but which is far more beautiful in the flesh. The ancient abbey church of **Sant'Antimo ❽**, built of creamy travertine and set against tree-clad hills, has inspired numerous poets and painters. The main part of the church was built in 1118 in a style that owes much to the influence of French Romanesque. The simple interior has capitals carved with biblical scenes, and recorded plainsong echoes around the walls as

you explore. The small community of Augustinian monks who tend the church sing the Gregorian chant at Mass every Sunday afternoon throughout the year.

A tortuous mountain route will take you through **Castiglione d'Orcia ❾** and **Rocca d'Orcia**, both with medieval castles built to watch over the valley of the River Orcia, and down to the tiny, fashionable spa town of **Bagno Vignoni ❿**. This has, at its heart, where the main square ought to be, a large stone-lined pool where sulphurous vapours rise above the hot, bubbling waters which well up from volcanic rocks deep under the earth. Some famous bodies have bathed in this pool in times past, including St Catherine of Siena. Bathing is now forbidden but there are several spas and swimming pools nearby.

Just north of Bagno Vignoni, a minor road takes you east along the wide vale of the Orcia river and then up to **Castellúccio** and **La Foce ⓫**, from where there are spectacular views of a cypress-lined, ancient Etruscan road zig-zagging up the hill. The next town is **Chianciano Terme ⓬**, a popular spa resort with chic shops and an historic town centre. More interesting is **Chiusi ⓭**, one of the most powerful cities in the ancient Etruscan League. Chiusi's pride is the **Museo Nazionale Etrusco** (daily 9am–8pm; entrance fee), which has one of the finest collections of its kind in Italy – a thoughtfully arranged display of Etruscan funerary urns, canopic jars, sculptures and Greek-style vases excavated from local tombs. Arrangements can be made at the museum to visit one of the tombs in the vicinity (using the same ticket).

The town's Romanesque church is a delight, built from recycled Roman pillars and capitals and with "mosaics" on the nave walls that were painted by Arturo Viligiardi in 1887. The **Museo della Cattedrale** (daily 9.30am–12.45pm; entrance fee) displays a collection of Roman, Lombardic and medieval sculpture. Included

Map on pages 264–5

People have been taking the therapeutic waters of Tuscany since Roman times. Lorenzo il Magnifico, ruler of Florence, who suffered from arthritis, was one notable spa enthusiast.

BELOW: the timeless Tuscan landscape.

in the ticket price is a fascinating guided visit of an underground network of galleries, dug by the Etruscans and re-used as Christian catacombs in the 3rd–5th centuries. The tour passes a giant Roman cistern and ends under the bell tower, which you can climb for views of Monte Amiata and the Val d'Orcia.

Chiusi stands almost on the border with Umbria, but our Tuscany tour continues north, up the fertile Val di Chiana, where cattle are bred to supply the restaurants of Florence with the raw ingredients of *bistecca alla fiorentina* (steak Florentine), then west to **Montepulciano** ⓮. This splendid hilltop town deserves long and leisurely exploration, with frequent stops to sample the local Vino Nobile wines, either in the city's rock-cut cellars, or in the elegant Caffè Poliziano (27 Via di Voltaia nel Corso).

Some of the best producers of Vino Nobile di Montepulciano are Avignonesi, Le Casalte and Poliziano.

The spacious main square, the **Piazza Grande**, sits at the town's highest point. On one side is the 15th-century **Palazzo Comunale** (Town Hall), a miniature version of the Palazzo Vecchio in Florence. On the other side, Sangallo's intriguing 16th-century **Palazzo Contucci** now houses a hotel and wine cellars (closed 12.30–2.30pm). Between the two is the gloomy **Duomo** (daily 9am– noon and 4–6pm), which contains a masterpiece of the Siena School, the huge *Assumption* triptych (1401) by Taddeo di Bartolo over the high altar.

As the road to Pienza leaves Montepulciano, it is worth diverting right for the church of the **Madonna di San Biagio**, perched on a platform below the walls of the city. This domed church of honey- and cream-coloured stone, a Renaissance gem begun in 1518, is the masterpiece of Antonio da Sangallo.

Model Renaissance city, built for a Pope

BELOW: view along Pienza's town walls.

Pienza ⓯ is a tiny town that would be famous for nothing but its sweet sheep's milk cheeses, had not the future Pope Pius II been born here in 1405. He decided to rebuild the village of his birth as a model Renaissance city, but was swindled by his architect, Bernardo Rossellino, who embezzled most of the funds. Only the papal palace and the cathedral were completed and both are now suffering from serious subsidence – see them before they collapse.

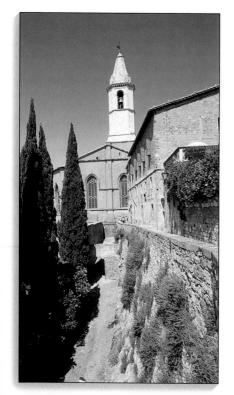

Despite the great cracks and buckled pillars, the cathedral is uplifting, and flooded with light from the great windows that the pope requested – he wanted a *domus vitrea*, a house of glass, to symbolise the enlightenment of the Humanist Age. The **Palazzo Piccolomini** (Tues–Sun 10am–12.30pm and 3–6pm; entrance fee) alongside is filled with the pope's personal possessions and the loggia at the rear was designed to frame views of Monte Amiata, the distant, cone-shaped peak of an extinct volcano.

The last stop after Pienza is **San Quirico d'Orcia** ⓰, with its splendid Collegiata whose Romanesque west portal is carved with dragons and mermaids.

Back in Siena, the N73 will take you southwestwards on a winding and often empty road through the green and sparsely populated foothills of the Colline Metalliferre, the Metal-bearing Hills, so called because they have been a rich source of iron, copper, silver and lead ores since ancient Etruscan times.

Some 20 km (12 miles) out of Siena, be sure to stop off at the ruined Cistercian abbey of **San Galgano** ⓱, with its huge and roofless abbey church, where swallows skim in and out of the glassless Gothic windows and sunlight plays on the richly carved capitals of the nave. On a hill above the church is the beehive-shaped oratory built in 1182 on the site of San Galgano's hermitage. Look out for the sword in the stone, thrust there by the saint when he renounced his military career to become a hermit. An excellent shop alongside sells local herbs, wines, toiletries and books on the history and sights of the region.

Massa Marittima ⑱ is the ancient mining capital of the region, but there are no ugly industrial scars, just two museums devoted to the history of mining in the region (which flourished in the 13th century) and one of Tuscany's finest Romanesque churches, decorated with humorous sculptures illustrating the adventures of St Cerbone, the town's patron saint. Massa Marittima is the gateway to Tuscany's south, a holiday land with many fine and unspoilt beaches and a Mediterranean climate, notably different from that only a short way north.

From **Piombino** ⑲ ferries take visitors to the island of **Elba**, either on day trips to see the villa where Napoleon spent a short period in exile, or for a relaxing week in one of the island's many family-friendly hotels. Further south along the busy coastal road, the Via Aurelia, the city of **Grosseto** ⑳ is worth a stop only if you want to visit the excellent **archaeology museum** (Nov–Feb Tues–Fri 9am– 1pm, Sat–Sun 9.30am–1pm, 4.30–7pm; Mar–Apr Tues–Sun 9.30am– 1pm, 4.30–7pm; May–Oct Tues–Sun 10am–1pm, 5–8pm; free). This has displays and finds that will help you understand the ruins of nearby Etruscan cities such as **Vetulonia** (22 km/13 miles northwest of Grosseto) and **Roselle** (7 km/4 miles north).

Just south of Grosseto is the **Parco Naturale della Maremma** ㉑ (daily; entrance fee), a protected traffic-free nature reserve, rich in wildlife with a long stretch of beautiful unspoilt beaches. The park office in **Alberese** (8 or 8.30am until sunset) issues tickets and supplies information on walking trails.

The symbol of Massa Marittima's "New Town".

BELOW: the harbour of Porto Ercole, on Monte Argentario.

Map on pages 264–5

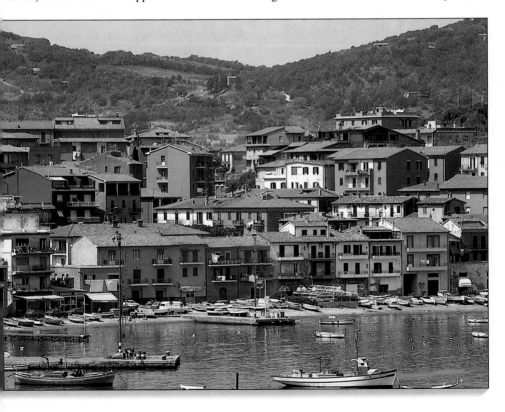

Another wildlife haven is the lagoon north of Orbetello, an important wintering spot for birds. **Orbetello ㉒** was, in the 16th century, a Spanish garrison town, and the baroque architecture reflects this fact. The sea laps right up to the stout city walls and visitors come from afar for the excellent restaurants specialising in fish.

Inland, tiny villages like **Capalbio ㉓** specialise in more robust Tuscan dishes, such as wild boar and even baked porcupine (both are hunted locally). For a totally sybaritic experience, you can swim beneath the stars in the hot falls just south of **Saturnia** before heading into the town for a leisurely meal.

The other villages of this beautiful region, known as the forgotten corner of Tuscany, are situated above dramatic cliffs of soft tufa. These are especially spectacular at **Pitigliano ㉔**, where local people have excavated caves in the rock for storing wine and olive oil, and at **Sovana ㉕**, where the ancient Etruscans excavated tombs in the soft rock below the town. The tiny one-street village has two outstanding proto-Romanesque churches.

Today there are 13 towers in San Gimignano, but historians say there were once 72 in the small, hilltop town.

BELOW: one of the medieval towers of San Gimignano.

West of Siena

More spectacular sights await to the west of Siena. Taking the N2, you will first pass **Monteriggioni ㉖**, a hilltop town built in 1213 to guard the northern borders of Sienese territory, encircled by walls and 14 towers.

Next, drive through the lower, modern town of **Colle di Val d'Elsa ㉗** and, taking the Volterra road, head for the more ancient upper town. Here the main street is lined with 16th-century *palazzi* of unusual refinement and, at one point, the stately procession of buildings is interrupted by a viaduct from which there are splendid views of the surrounding landscape. The shops here are filled with fine glass and crystalware made in the glass factories down in the valley.

Perhaps the most spectacular sight anywhere in Tuscany is the town of **San Gimignano ㉘**, bristling with medieval towers, scarcely changed in appearance since the Middle Ages and richly rewarding – despite the huge number of visitors. (It is best to stay overnight here, in one of the characteristic hotels, to savour the peaceful beauty of the town in the evening and early morning, after the day-trippers have gone.) The main street is lined with shops, many of them selling quality crafts as well as locally produced Vernaccia wines and wild-boar ham.

The tall defensive towers lining the two squares at the highest point of the town were built as status symbols rather than for genuinely defensive purposes. They alone make a visit here worthwhile, but the town also possesses such an embarrassment of artistic riches that few visitors get to see everything. The highlights are the *Wedding Scene* frescoes in the **Museo Civico** (daily Mar–Oct 9.30am–7pm; Nov–Feb 10am–5pm; entrance fee), showing the newly married couple taking a bath together and climbing into bed, plus the frescoes that cover every inch of wall space in the **Collegio**, the collegiate church, depicting the *Last Judgement* and stories from the Old and New Testaments.

Volterra ㉙ is another rewarding place, sited high on a plateau with distant views to the sea. The entrance to the city is dominated by a Medicean castle, now used as a prison, and if you wander through the park that lies beneath its walls you will come to the **Museo Etrusco**

Guarnacci (daily mid-Mar–Oct 9am–7pm, Nov–mid-Mar 9am–2pm; entrance fee) in Via Don Minzoni. This is packed with ancient Etruscan urns excavated from cemeteries uncovered by landslides in the 19th century. The *Married Couple* urn is a masterpiece of realistic portraiture and even more stunning is the bronze statuette known as *L'Ombra della Sera (The Shadow of the Night)*, resembling a Giacometti sculpture but cast in the 5th century BC.

The attractive main square of Volterra has some of the oldest civic buildings in Tuscany, dating from the 13th century, and provides a showroom for the local alabaster carving industry; galleries selling alabaster are located all over the town. The cathedral has a wealth of carvings from an earlier age, including a balletic *Deposition*, sculpted in wood in the 13th century.

As one drives west or north from Volterra, the landscape changes rapidly from hilly terrain to flat marshy coastline. You could be forgiven for missing out **Livorno** ㉚, for, although it has an interesting harbour area and a famous Renaissance statue (the *Four Moors* monument), World War II bombing and modern industry have stripped the city of its character.

Pisa ㉛, by contrast, is a must. All the main attractions lie in the northwestern angle of the city walls, around the well-named **Campo dei Miracoli** (the Field of Miracles). The appearance of the cathedral and baptistry owes much to the influence of Islamic architecture, which Pisan merchants and scholars experienced through their extensive trade contacts with Moorish Spain and North Africa. The gleaming marble surfaces of these buildings are covered in arabesques and other ornamentation, as densely patterned as an Oriental carpet. The **Duomo** (open daily Apr–Sept 10am–8pm; Oct–Feb 9am–5pm, Mar 9am–6pm; entrance fee), built between 1068 and 1118, is one of Italy's major

Map on pages 264–5

Getting the picture by Pisa's baptistry.

BELOW: the Tower, and a statue nearby.

The Casa Museo Puccini (9 Corte San Lorenzo; daily 10am–6pm; entrance fee) is the birthplace of Lucca's famous son, the operatic composer, Giacomo Puccini (1858–1924).

monuments and contains one of its greatest sculptures, the magnificent pulpit by Giovanni Pisano. The **Battistero** (same opening hours as the cathedral), built in the same Pisan Romanesque style as the cathedral, has another fine pulpit, sculpted in 1260 by Giovanni's father, Nicola.

In 2001, after more than a decade under wraps to halt the dramatic tilt, the iconic **Leaning Tower** (Torre Pendente; 8.30am–8.30pm in summer, until 11pm in high season; 9.30am–5pm in winter; www.opapisa.it; entrance fee) reopened to the public. Visits are now limited to 30 people at a time and queues develop quickly, so get there at opening time if you can, or book in advance through the website.

Lucca 𝟛𝟚, a short way north, is a city of many seductive charms, not least the ramparts encircling the city, which were transformed into a tree-lined promenade in the 19th century. The city has more than its fair share of splendid Pisan-Romanesque churches, with ornate facades of green, grey and white marble. The best include **San Michele**, with its tiers of arcading and hunting scenes, **San Frediano**, with its massive Romanesque font, and the splendid **Duomo** (Mon–Fri 9.30am–5.45pm, Sat until 6.45pm, Sun 1–5pm; free). The Duomo contains one of the most famous relics of medieval Europe, the *Volto Santo* (Holy Face), said to have been carved by Nicodemus, who witnessed the Crucifixion – hence it was believed to be a true portrait of Christ (in fact, the highly stylised figure is probably a 13th-century copy of an 11th-century copy of an 8th-century original).

Lucca is the gateway to several regions of Tuscany which all have their own special character. To the west is the Tuscan Riviera, a string of coastal towns known as the **Versilia**. The beaches here are regimented (you pay for access but get facilities such as sun loungers, showers, beach cabins and a bar or restaurant). **Viareggio 𝟛𝟛** is the most interesting for its Liberty-style (art nouveau)

BELOW: decorated columns on the facade of Lucca's Duomo.
BELOW RIGHT: marble quarry in Carrara.

architecture, its plentiful fish restaurants specialising in *cacciucco* (a hearty fish soup) and its atmospheric harbour area.

To the north is the **Garfagnana**, a wild area of high mountains, seemingly covered in snow all year round because the peaks are made of marble. Designated as a huge nature reserve, this is a paradise for walkers. Information on waymarked trails is available from the region's main town, **Castelnuovo di Garfagnana** ❸. On the fringe of the region is the marble town of **Carrara** ❸ with several quarries offering guided tours and workshops. Just outside Carrara is **Luni** ❸, once a Roman town and now a place of well-preserved ruins.

Nearer to Lucca, there are several ornate villas and gardens open to the public, notably the **Villa Pecci-Blunt** (formerly known as the Villa Reale; guided tours of the garden Mar–Nov Tues–Sun on the hour from 10am–noon and 3–6pm; entrance fee), at **Marlia** ❸, whose *teatro verde* (green theatre), surrounded by clipped yew hedges, is the setting for concerts during Lucca's summer music festival. Another splendid villa, with theatrical gardens spilling down the steep hillside, is the **Villa Garzoni** (garden open daily 8.30am–7pm in summer, 9am–noon and 2–4.30pm in winter; entrance fee) at **Collodi** ❸. Collodi was also the pen name of Carlo Lenzini, the author of the *Adventures of Pinocchio* (1881), who spent his childhood here. The Pinocchio theme park in the village (open daily) is a welcome distraction for children and is dotted with sculptures based on episodes from the book.

Montecatini Terme ❸ is the most elegant spa town in Tuscany, with ornate buildings surrounded by flowerbeds and manicured lawns. You can buy day tickets that allow you to sample the waters and admire the marble-lined pools, splashing fountains and art-nouveau tile pictures of water nymphs at the **Terme Tettuccio** (www.termemontecatini.it).

Medieval and modern sculpture

Pistoia ❹ and its neighbour, Prato, are both industrial towns specialising in textiles and metal working, but with attractive historic centres. Pistoia's Piazza del Duomo is graced with the Romanesque **Cattedrale di San Zeno** and Baptistry. The town's churches contain a remarkable number of carved fonts and pulpits from the pre-Renaissance period; they include Giovanni Pisano's pulpit of 1301 in **Sant'Andrea church**, which art historians consider to be his masterpiece, more accomplished even than the pulpit he made for Pisa's cathedral in 1302. In the Palazzo del Tau, you can also see the work of one of Italy's best-known modern sculptors, Marino Marini (1901–66), now the **Museo Marino Marini** (Mon–Sat 10am–6pm; entrance fee), on Corso Silvano Fredi.

Prato ❹ was the birthplace of Francesco di Marco Datini (1330–1410) who died one of the richest men in Europe and left his money to city charities so, as you might expect, the town has several statues of the great man. Another local merchant married a Palestinian woman in 1180 and discovered that her dowry included the Virgin's girdle. The relic is exhibited four times a year from Donatello's external pulpit on the Duomo facade. Inside are superb frescoes by Fra Filippo Lippi and Agnolo Gaddi. Prato's textile heritage can be seen in the excellent **Museo del Tessuto** (Mon–Fir 10am–6pm, Sat

Map on pages 264–5

Terracotta by della Robbia in Pistoia's Ospedale del Ceppo.

BELOW: statue at Collodi.

The chapterhouse of
Prato's church of
San Francesco
contains splendid
frescoes by Niccolò
Gerini.

BELOW: starting life
together in Arezzo's
Piazza Grande.

10am–2pm, Sun 4–7pm; entrance fee). Also worth visiting is the 13th-century **Hohenstaufen castle** (10am–sunset; entrance fee), the only one of its kind in Italy, built for the Holy Roman Emperor Frederick II of Swabia.

City of Leonardo

South of Pistoia is the tiny hilltop village of **Vinci** ㊷, birthplace of Leonardo da Vinci, where the castle has been turned into an entertaining **museum** (daily 9.30am–6pm, until 7pm in summer; entrance fee) dedicated to the great man and his inventions. The displays consist of wooden models of a bicycle, a submarine, a tank, a helicopter, etc., beautifully crafted and based on Leonardo's notebooks.

From Vinci, you can take a winding rural road into Florence, stopping at **Poggio a Caiano** ㊸ (daily 8.15am–sunset, guided tour only; entrance fee), the villa built for Lorenzo de' Medici which became the archetype for many others. Skirting Florence, you can speed south to Arezzo on the A1 *autostrada*, or break the journey by leaving at the Incisa intersection and following signs for **Vallombrosa** ㊹. The reward is not so much the 18th-century monastery as the splendid beech wood that surrounds it; the poet John Milton, visiting in 1638, was so impressed that he wrote a description of Vallombrosa's autumnal leaves in *Paradise Lost*.

More delights await if you go north and take the N70 to **Stia** ㊺. From here, you can visit two sacred sites set high in spectacular woodland, cut by mountain streams and waterfalls. One is the hermitage at **Camaldoli** ㊻ (open only to male visitors), 17 km (10 miles) east of Stia; the other is the monastery at **La Verna** ㊼ further south, best reached by driving east from Bibbiena. It was here that the hands and feet of St Francis were miraculously marked with the stigmata in 1224. The monastery commands panoramic views.

On the way south from here to Arezzo, it is also worth seeking out little **Caprese Michelangelo** ⓭, which has a sculpture park in the grounds of the castle where Michelangelo was born. The views over Alpine countryside explain why Michelangelo attributed his good brains to the mountain air he breathed as a child.

Arezzo ⓮ has a good **archaeological museum** (daily 8.30am–7.30pm; entrance fee) full of Arretine tableware, fashionable for a time during the Roman period. For most visitors, though, the highlight will be Piero della Francesca's painstakingly restored fresco cycle in the church of **San Francesco** (daily 8.30am–noon and 2.30–6.30pm; essential to pre-book a visit, tel: 0575-900404). The frescoes illustrate the *Legend of the True Cross*, a complex story whereby the wood of the Tree of Knowledge, which bore the fruit that Adam and Eve ate, becomes the Cross on which Christ died and then is instrumental in converting Constantine the Great, who made Christianity the religion of the Roman world.

The artist's style, compelling and mysterious, attracts superlatives from art historians and you can easily become hooked on his work, following the Piero della Francesca trail, like the heroine of *A Summer's Lease*, a novel by the English writer John Mortimer. If so, the trail leads from here to **Monterchi** ⓯, 25 km (15 miles) west along the N73, where a former schoolhouse displays his striking *Madonna del Parto*, the Pregnant Madonna. From there, you should continue 12 km (7 miles) north to **Sansepolcro** ⓰, the town where Buitoni pasta is produced. Here the **Museo Civico** (Oct–May daily 9.30am–1pm and 3.30–6.30pm, June–Sept daily 9am–1.30pm and 2.30–7.30pm; entrance fee) has della Francesca's 1463 masterpiece, the *Resurrection*, hailed by Aldous Huxley as "the best picture in the world." To complete the trail, you should visit **Urbino**, in the Marches, to see *The Flagellation of Christ* and other works in the Ducal Palace *(see page 291)*. ❏

Map on pages 264–5

The Casentino region, north of Arezzo, is much loved by walkers. It is also well known for its plentiful wild mushrooms. The Oscar-winning film "La Vita è Bella" (Life is Beautiful) was filmed here and a trail of the film locations covers the main sights.

BELOW: the terracotta roofscape of Arezzo.

ROLLING HILLS, CYPRESS TREES AND TOWERS

The distinctive Tuscan countryside has, for centuries, been a favourite haunt of travellers looking to escape the madding crowds of the cities

As glorious as its historic cities and artistic treasures may be, Tuscany's timeless landscape has long been a draw to visitors. After a hectic, sticky visit to Florence, Siena, Pisa or any of the other major towns, the relative coolness and freshness of a rural ride out is a welcome treat. Small medieval towns, perched on hills to benefit from cooling breezes, overlook a rolling landscape which embraces both controlled agriculture and nature at its wildest. Terraces of vines and silvery groves of olives vie for attention with Tuscany's own peculiar landmark – tall, slender cypresses, often planted in rows as windbreaks. These elegant trees have studded the skyline here for centuries, prompting the writer D.H. Lawrence to accuse them of hiding the secrets of the Etruscans, the early settlers of these parts. He described them as "… the sinuous, flame-tall cypresses/That swayed their length of darkness all around/ Etruscan-dusky, wavering men of old Etruria." These and other images of the Tuscany countryside feature strongly in the background of some of the greatest works of Renaissance art.

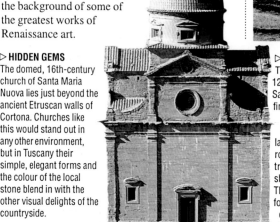

▷ **HIDDEN GEMS**
The domed, 16th-century church of Santa Maria Nuova lies just beyond the ancient Etruscan walls of Cortona. Churches like this would stand out in any other environment, but in Tuscany their simple, elegant forms and the colour of the local stone blend in with the other visual delights of the countryside.

▷ **FLORA AND FAUNA**
The backdrop to the 12th-century church of Sant'Antimo provides a fine example of Tuscan nature at work. Wild flowers (best seen in late spring) fight for room with ancient olive trees and coarse shrubs and grasses. These provide a habitat for moths, lizards and cicadas, whose song is heard in summer.

△ OLIVE GREEN

The silvery leaves of olive groves bring a distinctive colour to a Tuscan hillside. Some wine estates now produce very high-quality (and highly priced) olive oils. Badia a Coltibuono also offers cookery courses in which you can learn how best to appreciate its wines and oils.

▽ CULTIVATION CULTURE

Tuscan farmers use their land for a variety of purposes. Olives, fruit and tobacco are just some of the crops produced alongside cereals like barley and maize. Chianina cattle, native to the region, provide the meat for *bistecca alla fiorentina*, the classic Florentine steak dish.

TOWERS OF POWER AND WEALTH

In the Middle Ages, towers protected the wealthiest families in times of internal and external strife; today, they mark out some of Tuscany's oldest towns, catching the traveller's eye from afar. No better example exists of this distinctive skyscape than San Gimignano *(above)*, which has 13 towers – although at one time it had more than 70.

San Gimignano's many towers date from the 12th and 13th century, and are mostly windowless, possibly to afford further protection; families could retreat into the many rooms inside for months at a time. Defence was not the only purpose of these lofty extensions, however: they were also status symbols. Building a tall, imperious tower was a way of flaunting your wealth and social standing.

Another theory about the the towers concerns the textile trade for which San Gimignano was noted. Towers may have been built to house and protect valuable dyed fabrics, as there was little room to spread them out at ground level.

As many of Tuscany's medieval towns were built on hilltops, a climb to the top of a tower is usually rewarded with magnificent views over the town and the beautiful surrounding countryside.

CHIANTI COUNTRY

...uth of Florence, the hills are ...minated by rows of vines ...wing predominantly ...ngiovese grapes, which are ...ssed to make Chianti wines. ...me vineyards are centred ...und medieval castles; ...ny of these offer tastings ...d sell wine to visitors.

BURNT SIENNA

...e hills around the city of ...na are known for their ...ddish-brown clay, which is ...ed for brick-making and the ...nstruction of most of the ...y's buildings. The ...tinctive pigment in the clay ...s become internationally ...own as burnt sienna.

UMBRIA AND THE MARCHES

Castles cling to ravines and woodland cloaks the
wild mountains in the green heart of Italy,
home to one of Christianity's best-loved saints

Map on
pages
264–5

ITALY
●Rome

Perugia 52 is the sun around which the other towns of Umbria orbit. Like so many of its neighbours, the city suffered considerable damage during the series of violent earthquakes that hit Umbria during the autumn of 1997. Following the earthquakes, many historic churches and buildings were closed as a precautionary measure. Many have since reopened while some remain resolutely closed. Even so, most towns in Umbria are attractive in their own right, and worth visiting even if you cannot get into every church, museum or gallery.

Perugia's **Piazza IV Novembre** is freshened by the 13th-century **Fontana Maggiore**. This splendid fountain is one of the great works of the Pisan sculptors Nicola Pisano and his son, Giovanni. Carved in 1277, it is covered in elegant figures representing sundry subjects: the *Labours of the Months*, Adam and Eve, scenes from Aesop's *Fables*. Such accomplished art, used to decorate a fountain, reveals just how important a reliable water supply was to the survival of any medieval city. Just to the north of the fountain, the steps of the Gothic cathedral are where people and pigeons gather to preen and flirt. Inside, the mystic *Deposition*, painted by Barocci while under the influence of poison fed to him by a rival, inspired the famous painting by Rubens known as the *Antwerp Descent*.

Sweeping down from the piazza is the **Corso Vannucci**. On the right is the 13th- to 15th-century **Palazzo dei Priori** (Town Hall). Up its steps is the **Sala dei Notari**, painted at the end of the 13th century and since restored.

LEFT: Urbino.
BELOW: St Francis, Umbria's best-loved son.

Work of local artists

In the same building is the **Galleria Nazionale dell' Umbria** (daily 8.30am–7.30pm; closed 1st Mon of month; entrance fee) containing works by the most important of the many artists who lived in Umbria, including Francesco da Rimini, Fra Angelico, Piero della Francesca and Pinturicchio. Next door to the gallery is the 15th-century **Collegio del Cambio** (Tues–Sat 9am–1pm and 2.30–5.30pm in summer, 8am–2pm in winter, Sun 9am–1pm all year; entrance fee), distinguished by frescoes of Perugino and his school, and by 17th-century inlaid woodwork.

The rest of the Corso Vannucci is best appreciated at night. Relax in one of the cafés on the street and watch the students watching you. Stop at the end of the Corso in the **Giardini Carducci** to enjoy the second-best view in Perugia: the hills twinkling under the stars.

South of the town is **San Pietro** with its 16th-century choir stalls, carved with a whole medieval bestiary – ducks, crocodiles and elephants included. Closer is the barn-like **San Domenico** with a little-visited tomb that ranks as one of the finest of its age in Italy – that of Pope Benedict XI, who died in Perugia in 1304 having eaten poisoned figs. The adjacent cloister contains Umbria's

Museo Archeologico (Tues–Sun 8.30am–7.30pm, Mon 2.30–7.30pm; entrance fee), with vast quantities of ancient Etruscan pottery and metalwork. West of the city centre is the church of **San Bernardino**, its facade decorated with angels and musicians with diaphanous robes, like the figures in Mucha's art-nouveau posters, except that these date to 1451, not the 1890s.

Assisi and the Vale of Spoleto

There is no place quite like **Assisi ③**. Despite the crowds, despite the damage caused by the 1997 earthquakes, it remains an inspiring and spiritual city. The sight, as you approach Assisi, of the mighty arches supporting the Basilica di San Francesco, rising above the perpetual Umbrian haze, and of Monte Subasio, the great peak towering behind, is sufficient to make the rest of the world seem blissfully far away. The streets are almost too postcard perfect: cascades of flowers fall from wall sconces, alleyway gardens hoard every scrap of sunlight, the smell of roses and wood smoke permeates the air.

The **Basilica di San Francesco** (open daily – Lower Church: 6.30am– 6.50pm in summer, until 6pm in winter; Upper Church: open from 8.30am; closed Sun am for services; audio guides available from tourist office opposite; entrance free) is perfectly situated for sunsets. The facade , designed by a military architect, is like the saint it commemorates, beautiful in its poverty. The main doors lead into the Upper Basilica, decorated with Giotto's famous fresco cycle on the *Life of St Francis*. The frescoes have been restored following the 1997 earthquake: several saints have been reinstated, though the cycle will never look like it used to; the restoration is fragmentary yet faithful. With this cycle, Giotto revived the art of fresco painting in Italy and this is his most accomplished work (though it is now

The artist Pietro Vannucci – "Perugino" – was born near Perugia in c.1450. He found success in Florence and even decorated part of Rome's Sistine Chapel before returning to Perugia and dying near there in 1523.

BELOW: San Bernardino in Perugia.
BELOW RIGHT: Assisi's Basilica di San Francesco, before the 1997 earthquake.

believed that at least three other artists contributed to the cycle, including Pietro Cavallini), admired by all the great artists of the Renaissance for the degree to which it introduced realism into Western art.

The walls of the **Basilica Inferiore** (Lower Basilica) are a jigsaw puzzle of frescoes by many hands, all of them inspired by the example and life of St Francis. They vary between the sweetly cheerful frescoes of Simone Martini, where even the horses seem to smile, to the sternly didactic vault frescoes depicting the monastic virtues of Chastity, Poverty and Obedience. Equally stern is the crypt where St Francis is buried, but the face of the little monk, painted in the transept by Cimabue and said to be a faithful portrait, tells a different story.

Chronologically, a tour of the rest of Assisi begins with the **Roman Forum** beneath the **Piazza del Comune**. The forum's above-ground vestige is the **Tempio di Minerva** (Minerva's Temple), whose interior has been revamped in an unfortunately gaudy manner. In the northeast sector of town, the **Anfiteatro Romano** (Roman Amphitheatre), where live naval battles were staged, has been topped by homes that follow its original oval structure.

The **Rocca Maggiore**, grim and immobile above the town, destroyed and rebuilt, was part of a string of towers guarding Assisi. The **Duomo** (12th-century, dedicated to San Rufino) is best appreciated for the carving of its Romanesque exterior details; its interior was revamped in 1571.

The newly restored **Chiesa Santa Chiara**'s pink and white exterior is supported by buttresses that are decidedly feminine in their generous curves. The chapel houses a 12th-century crucifix said to have spoken to St Francis.

To experience something of the solitude and spirituality that matched the lives of St Francis and St Clare, it is worth visiting a couple of churches on the outskirts

Map on pages 264–5

BELOW: *Francis Casts off His Clothes*, from Giotto's fresco cycle in San Francesco.

of Assisi. **San Damiano**, just 2 km (1 mile) south of the town, is the convent where St Clare spent most of her reclusive life, and it retains the air of a simple religious retreat. More rural still is the favourite hermitage of St Francis, the **Eremo delle Carceri** (daily 6.30am–sunset), a tranquil spot nestling into the tree-covered slope of Monte Subasio, 3 km (2 miles) east of the town.

Unrivalled views of the region can be had from the summit of **Monte Subasio** (1,290m/4,230ft). For centuries the mountain was quarried for its pink stone from which so many of the buildings in the area are made. The road through the Parco Regionale del Monte Subasio begins at the hermitage car park (the barrier is raised at 6am and lowered at 6pm).

Assisi sits on the rim of a dried-up lake bed, called the Vale of Spoleto, which was drained of water in the 16th century. Several other towns of great character line the eastern shore, including **Spello ❺❹**, which has renowned frescoes by Pinturicchio, one of the main artists of the Umbrian school. **Spoleto ❺❺** sits at the southernmost point of the former lake, a city of great cosmopolitan sophistication, renowned for its summer arts jamboree, the Festival dei Due Mondi (of the Two Worlds, meaning Europe and the Americas). The emphasis in this festival is on the avant garde, and the legacy is a number of modern sculptures dotted about the town, plus numerous art galleries selling work of dubious merit.

The town's dominant building, the **Rocca Albornoz** (guided tours only, usually on the hour, see tourist office for times; entrance fee) was built as a papal stronghold, became the home of Lucrezia Borgia, served as a prison where members of the Red Brigade were held and is now a national museum and art gallery. Alongside is the striking **Ponte delle Torri**, spanning the gorge that yawns between the castle and the opposite hill. The Bridge of the Towers, as the

BELOW: Assisi's weeping lion.
BELOW RIGHT: the Eremo delle Carceri on Monte Subasio, outside Assisi.

name translates, was built as an aqueduct in the 13th century and you can walk across the top of the (now dry) water channel.

Spoleto's outstanding treasure is the 12th-century **Duomo** (daily 8.30am–12.30pm, 3.30–7pm in summer, until 5pm in winter). Its medieval porch is surmounted by a rose window. The cathedral floor has an intricate herringbone and spiral Romanesque design. The chapel to the right was decorated by Pinturicchio. The apse is ablaze with Filippo Lippi's final work, the coronation of an exquisite Madonna surrounded by a rainbow and an arc of angels.

On the north side of the stairs leading to the Piazza del Duomo is the 12th-century **Chiesa Sant'Eufemia**; its chaste perfection contrasts with the cathedral's grandeur. Note Sant'Eufemia's massive and ancient stone throne behind the altar.

Visitors to Spoleto with time and a taste for the wild can use the town as a base for exploring the mountainous area to the east of Umbria, where winding narrow roads carry you up to the snowy peaks of the **Monti Sibillini** range, part of the Apennines. You can drive, via Triponzo, to **Norcia** ⑤⑥, the birthplace of St Benedict and a major centre of the truffle and salami industries. From here, roads climb ever higher to the spectacular **Piano Grande**, a vast open plain that is covered in wild flowers and rare Alpine plants in summer. On the return journey you can take in the pleasing 8th-century monastery at **San Pietro in Valle** ⑤⑦ (10.30am–1pm, 2.30–5pm; the monastic complex is now a hotel, but the church is open to the public), with its Lombardic sculpture and 12th-century frescoes.

Hill-top Todi

West of Spoleto is the hill-top town of **Todi** ⑤⑧. Here the lovely view from the **Piazza Garibaldi** is enhanced by the fragrance of a garden beneath. Nearby is

The Edicola, or Tempietto, in Norcia is a curious structure. The 14th-century tower is covered with inscriptions and reliefs of Christian and masonic symbols.

BELOW: the view from Monte Subasio.

the grand **Piazza Vittorio Emanuele** or **Piazza del Popolo**. Facing the **Duomo** is the **Palazzo dei Priori** (13th-century). To the right are the 14th-century **Palazzo del Capitano** and the adjacent 13th-century **Palazzo del Popolo**. The former was built in the Gothic style with a bay of triform windows, the latter in the Lombardic style resting on an impressive network of pillars. The grand staircase leads to a **Museo-Pinacoteca** (city museum and art gallery; Tues–Sun 10.30am–1pm, 2–5 or 6pm) which spans the upper floors of both palaces.

The Duomo itself was begun in the early 12th century. The Gothic campanile, built 100 years later, strays from the fine Romanesque style. The Duomo's rear wall is decorated by a Ferraù da Faenza fresco. To the right is a 16th-century Giannicola di Paolo painting of the Madonna. The interior is softly lit by some of the finest stained glass in the region.

A brisk walk around the hill will bring you to the church of **San Fortunato**. The structure was begun in 1292 and built in stages over a period of 200 years during the architectural revolution. The central portal's sculptures deserve close examination for their tiny, whimsical depictions of humans and beasts. The interior is light and airy; the eggshell whiteness of the stone is enhanced by the deep sable colour of the carved choir and the formidable pillar-mounted lectern.

Through the **Parco della Rocca**, replete with good views, and on down the mountain, the **Tempio di Santa Maria della Consolazione** is perched on a little shelf of green. The 16th-century structure was long thought to be the work of Bramante because of the similarities with St Peter's in Rome, but it is now attributed to one Cola di Capsorala. The altar may seem to some a bit too much, but the space is light and airy, the intricate sunburst of stones on the floor a marvel of geometrics.

BELOW and **BELOW RIGHT:** Santa Maria della Consolazione in Todi.

Vine-growing Orvieto

The hill which supports **Orvieto** ➒ is volcanic in origin, therefore porous, therefore in danger of bringing the city down as it crumbles. The volcanic slopes are covered in the vineyards that produce Orvieto's famously crisp white wines.

After climbing up serpentine curves and through scaffolding-clad streets, you will burst into the unexpected expanse of the **Piazza del Duomo**. With any luck, the late-afternoon sun will be glittering off the mosaics of the 14th-century cathedral's astonishing facade. The cathedral's steps are generally crowded with a mixture of visitors, Orvietans and soldiers garrisoned just down the street. Also on Piazza del Duomo, opposite the cathedral, is the recently renovated **Museo Claudio Faina e Civico** (Tues–Sun 9.30am–6pm in summer, Tues–Sun 10am–5pm in winter; entrance fee). This is home to one of Italy's most important collections of archaeological finds, including Etruscan artefacts and many Greek ceramic works, dating back to the 6th century BC.

The cathedral was begun on 15 November 1290 to house relics of the miracles of Bolsena (1263): principally a chalice cloth onto which blood flowed from the host during a celebration of the Mass. Although the identity of the original architect is a matter of some debate, by its completion the Duomo's construction required the input of legions of architects, sculptors, painters and mosaicists. The facade, designed by Lorenzo Maitani, is bolstered by striped horizontals of basalt and travertine.

Inside the cathedral, the black and white stripes point up the curvilinear arches. The wall of the apse is decorated with scenes from the *Life of the Virgin*. These were begun by Ugolino di Prete Ilario and completed by Pinturicchio and Antonio Viterbo during the late 14th century. On the left-hand side of the altar is the **Cappella del Corporale**, painted by Ugolino and his assistants and depicting the *Miracle of Bolsena*. To the right side of the altar is the **Cappella Nuova**, whose decoration was begun by Fra Angelico in 1447 and completed by Luca Signorelli at the turn of the next century.

Via Duomo and **Corso Cavour** are lined with shops selling Orvietan ceramics whose simple, medieval and Etruscan designs are some of the prettiest in the region. Nearby are elegant restaurants, chic clothiers, and more shops selling wood sculptures. To the right, off Corso Cavour, is the striking 12th-century **Palazzo del Popolo**.

Straight ahead are the **Palazzo Comunale** and the church of **Sant'Andrea** in the **Piazza della Repubblica**. To the left is the **Old** or **Medieval Quarter**, which is easily the most delightful part of the town, with its ancient walls hung with pots of tumbling geraniums, high-walled gardens and the songbirds they attract, and tiny cave-like workrooms of Orvietan artisans.

Lakeside pursuits

The road north from Orvieto will take you to **Città della Pieve** ➏, birthplace of Perugino, father of the Umbrian School of painting, best known for his ability to capture the limpid blues and greens of the Umbrian sky. The town has several of his works, including the *Adoration of the Magi*, which features Lake Trasimeno in the background.

Today that lake is Umbria's summer holiday playground, ringed by campsites offering tennis, swim-

Map on pages 264–5

TIP

Orvieto has lent its name to a white wine of variable quality. Orvieto Classico, though, refers to a special classification and can be very good. Look for wines by Antinori and Bigi. *Secco* wines are dry, while *amabile* are semi-sweet.

BELOW: medieval tower in Orvieto.

ming and trekking on horseback. **Castiglione del Lago ❻** is the lake's capital, and there are splendid views from the ramparts of the 14th-century castle.

North of the lake, the road through Umbertide takes you to the atmospheric town of **Gubbio ❻**, once known as the "city of silence" because of its desolate position in the Umbrian backwoods, but now, thanks to modern roads, a town within easy reach of those who love good food and architecture. Gubbio clings to the side of Monte Ingino, and its major buildings just fit on the narrow terraces that step up the mountainside. At the top of Monte Ingino (it's best to take the funicular railway from the station in Via San Geraloma to the top, then walk back down) rises the **Basilica di Sant'Ubaldo**. The remains of the saint are kept here in a crystal urn above the altar. Legend has it that St Ubaldo intervened in a battle against Perugia, gaining a decisive victory for the badly outnumbered Gubbians. The basilica also displays the three immense candles with which the sturdy men of Gubbio race up the hill in a celebration of the saint's day every 15 May.

Returning to the town, your path should take you to the fine **cathedral** to see the great Gothic ribs of the vault and the 13th-century stained glass. Across a small passage from the cathedral is the **Palazzo Ducale** (Thur–Tues 8.30am–7.30pm; entrance fee), begun in 1476 by Federico da Montefeltro, Duke of Urbino.

The outstanding element of Gubbio's skyline, the belltower of the 14th-century **Palazzo dei Consoli**, is under restoration, but the Museo Civico is open (daily 10am–1pm and 3–7pm in summer, 10am–1pm and 2–5pm in winter; entrance fee). Its Great Hall houses a quixotic collection of medieval paraphernalia, including examples of medieval plumbing. A room on the left of the main hall contains the **Tavole Eugubine**: seven bronze plates upon which a precise hand has translated the ancient Umbrian language into Latin.

BELOW: the Corso dei Ceri festival in Gubbio, which takes place in May.

The Marches

After the stunning hill towns of Umbria, the neighbouring region of the Marches holds very few sights that can compete, with the singular exception of **Urbino** ㊳ with its stronghold of the wise old warrior Duke Federico da Montefeltro. Here he constructed one of the great treasures of 16th-century architecture. Urbino is an eyrie of a town whose golden buildings are set high amid spectacular mountains. Urbino remains one of the few hill towns left in Italy not ringed by the unsavoury intrusions of modernity. The original old city remains almost completely "unimproved", perched at the top of its two peaks.

The **Piazza del Popolo** is a tourist centre by day. By night, groups of university students recline here on the steps or in the cafés, or stand in the street and discuss politics, the latest foreign film, or last night's poetry reading. The facades are old; the faces are generally young. The contrast exemplifies the relaxed symbiosis that exists between Urbino's walls and the lives they enclose.

The duke and his Humanist contemporaries felt man was the centre of the universe – a significant break with Christian philosophy. The courtyard of his **Palazzo Ducale** is paved with a hub, with radiating spokes of marble to symbolise man's central position. The building itself is part palace and part fortress: a graceful, secure nest in the rarefied mountain air for the duke to feather with marvellous works of art. The **Galleria Nazionale delle Marche** (Tues–Sun 8.30am–7pm, Mon 8.30am–2pm; entrance fee), now housed in the palace, has several fine works by Piero della Francesca, including his enigmatic and disturbing *Flagellation of Christ*, and by the town's most famous artist, Raphael. Also remarkable is the *trompe l'oeil* inlay work in the duke's study.

Down the street from the ducal palace is **Casa di Raffaello** (Mon–Sat 9am–1pm and 3–7pm, Sun 10am–1pm in summer, Mon–Sat 10am–1pm in winter; entrance fee) where Raphael spent his first 14 years. In the courtyard is the stone upon which Raphael and his father, Giovanni, also an artist, ground their pigments.

Pocket-sized republic

Urbino stands a little inland from the Adriatic, a sunny coastline marked by hectare after hectare of orchards growing peaches and nectarines for export, and regimented beaches and seaside hotels. You will see something of this if you visit the **Republic of San Marino** ㊴, a self-governing state within Italy that has remained independent for 1,700 years. Stamp collectors will know it as a republic that issues big pictorial postage stamps in a variety of shapes other than square – the philatelic output is on show in its specialist museums.

The republic stands on the peak of Monte Titano, with sweeping views to Rimini and the Adriatic beyond. You can do a complete circuit of the town's historic walls, visiting the several museums that are housed in the bastions, and the diminutive building that serves as the parliament of this pocket-sized republic.

Just west of San Marino is Federico's hill-top fortress of **San Leo**, one of the most impressive sights in Italy, which inspired Dante to use it in the landscapes of his *Divine Comedy*. In the 18th century, the alchemist Cagliostro was imprisoned here. ❑

Map on pages 264–5

Urbino was not on any major trade routes, and had few natural assets, so Federico brought wealth to the town by offering himself and his army as mercenaries.

BELOW: the citadel of San Marino.

ABRUZZO AND MOLISE

*Two huge national parks, Abruzzo and Gran Sasso,
make this a region where the wonders of
nature rule supreme*

**Map on
page 294**

The Apennine Mountains, a geologically unruly region long ignored by most travellers, unravel into three strands as they twist down between Rome and the Adriatic. It is characteristic of this area, formerly known by the single name Abruzzo, that it should have been the birthplace of the priest in Hemingway's *A Farewell to Arms*, who recommended it for winter sport. That has been Abruzzo's traditional image among foreigners and Italians alike.

The image, like all caricatures, leaves out many of the finer points of this old region, but it persists. Visitors flock to the Gran Sasso, the central mountain chain, to climb, ski, birdwatch and hunt, and to Pescara and other beach towns. Yet the region has an indigenous history that may be the oldest in Italy, and its lovely towns, surrounded by snow-capped mountains even in June, contain first-rate monuments. Molise split off from Abruzzo to form an autonomous region in 1963, and has managed to retain its wild spirit more completely than its populous and faster-developing neighbour.

A dip into history

Human habitation of the region goes back more than 13,000 years to so-called Fucino (or Marsicano) Man, whose fragmented bones have been discovered in caves in Ortucchio and Maritza. Evidence of a flourishing indigenous civilisation in the 6th century BC is gathering, hastened by the find of the famous Capestrano Warrior, now at the Museo Archeologico *(see page 297)* in Chieti. Signs of later Roman domination can be seen throughout the region, particularly at the archaeological site of Alba Fucens, near **Avezzano ❶**.

In the Middle Ages and later, the region came under the sway of the various invading kingdoms from the south. The Spanish, for example, were responsible for most of the castles that pepper the region. Earthquakes, particularly the very severe one in 1703, have caused considerable damage, as did the two world wars. Massive migrations of farm workers into the cities after World War II resulted in economic imbalances between the town and the country, but recent efforts to encourage tourism and industry, and the completion of the *autostrade* (motorways), have started to reverse the trend of post-war impoverishment.

Shy animals

Italy's voluptuous landscape is at its most magnificent in the **Parco Nazionale d'Abruzzo ❷**, where over 400 sq. km (154 sq. miles) of high-altitude meadows, beech groves and snow-capped peaks are protected from Abruzzian housing developers. It is still possible to see the shy brown Apennine bear, of which there are between 70 and 100. They feed on berries and insects in the

LEFT: one step at a time, in Scanno.
BELOW: flower-filled corner.

remote upper pastures. The Abruzzo chamois, distinguished by the black-and-white pattern on its throat, also thrives here, as do the Apennine lynx, wolves, otters, song birds, hawks and eagles. About 150 well-marked trails provide access to even the highest sections, most of them within a day's walk of the main road.

Pescasseroli ❸, the administrative headquarters for the park (Tues–Sun 10am–2pm and 3–5.30pm; tel: 0863-91955), was the birthplace of the philosopher Benedetto Croce. Today it is dedicated to physical pursuits such as hiking and skiing, and you can pick up trail maps for the park here or book a guide (Ecotur, tel: 0863-912760). If you are coming at Christmas, Easter or during August, book accommodation in advance. Buses ply daily between Pescasseroli and Avezzano, a more convenient base.

The road and railway skirt the edge of the **Piana del Fucino**, a lake in Roman times but subsequently drained. In what was once the centre of the lake is the important Telespazio communications station, with its forest of satellite dishes. In the surrounding fields bright red poppies burst forth in May.

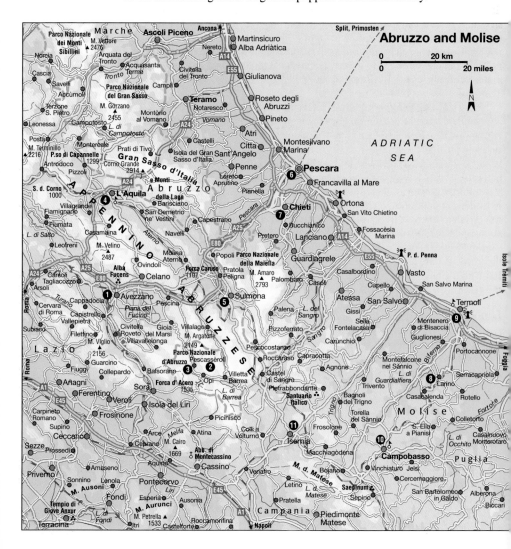

Fountain of 99 spouts

L'Aquila ❹, chief town of Abruzzo, has a turbulent history belied by its fine architecture and the relaxing coolness of its arcaded streets. Founded in 1240 by Frederick II of Hohenstaufen as an outpost against the papacy, the city converted to papal rule shortly after Frederick's death in 1250. Nine years later, Frederick's son, Manfred, reclaimed the city after a siege that destroyed its walls and led to its abandonment for seven years. Charles I of Anjou began rebuilding L'Aquila after defeating Manfred at Benevento in 1266.

According to legend, the city of L'Aquila was formed from 99 palaces, 99 churches, 99 fountains and 99 squares, and in commemoration of this numerical coincidence, the city authorities commissioned a fountain of 99 spouts in 1272. The **Fontane delle Novantanove Cannelle** is one of the highlights of the city. The pleasant courtyard of red and white stone and the sound of water issuing from the 99 masks combine to convey a sense of peace.

L'Aquila's best-known monument is the 13th-century church of **Santa Maria di Collemaggio** (Mon–Sat 8.30am–1pm and 3–8pm, Sun 8.30am–8pm), outside the city wall on the southeast corner of town. It is impossible to miss its red and white facade, whose three rose windows and corresponding doorways subtly combine the Gothic and the Romanesque. The church was begun in 1277 under the guidance of Pietro da Morrone. His lovely Renaissance tomb can be seen to the right of the apse inside. The interior, relieved of baroque flourishes in 1973, has a fine wooden ceiling.

The newly cleaned church of **San Bernardino** (Mon–Sat 7am–noon and 4–6pm, Sun 4–6.30pm) is arguably the finest Renaissance monument in the Abruzzo. The interior, completely rebuilt after the earthquake of 1703, is dominated by its baroque ceiling and organ, both designed by Ferdinando Mosca of nearby Pescocostanzo. In a chapel on the right, the Renaissance tomb of San Bernardino (1488) has a classical precision carried over in its delicate floral frieze. The tomb and the monument to Maria Pereira (1496) in the apse are the work of Silvestro dell'Aquila, a local artist.

On weekday mornings in the **Piazza del Duomo** there is a vibrant open-air market where local cane, wool, lace and copper are sold. The Duomo, completely destroyed by the 1703 earthquake, was rebuilt in the 1900s.

Defensive "ears"

One of the best museums in Abruzzo is L'Aquila's **Museo Nazionale d'Abruzzo** (open Tues–Sat 9am–7pm, Sun 9am–1pm in summer, Tues–Sun 9am–2pm in winter; entrance fee), located in the castle at the north end of town. The *castello* itself, built in 1532 by Piero Luigi Escriba (or Scriba), the architect of Castel Sant'Elmo in Naples, is known for its four protruding "ears" which enabled soldiers to cover every possible angle of approach. The archaeological section on the ground floor has an amusing Medusa's head frieze and the famous remains of a prehistoric mammoth found locally. On the first floor is a collection of medieval religious art, most of it from local churches, while on the second floor are 16th–18th-century works. The modern art on the third floor includes some interesting paintings by local artists.

See map opposite

Pietro da Morrone, a local hermit, was crowned Pope Celestine V at the age of 85. He served only five months in office, claiming that his inexperience with the ways of the world made him unfit to sit on the throne of St Peter.

BELOW: entrance to Santa Maria di Collemaggio.

Unlike the Parco Nazionale, which is of interest for its wildlife and majestic beech groves, the **Gran Sasso d'Italia**, just outside L'Aquila, attracts mountaineers. The Gran Sasso itself, at 2,914 metres (9,560 ft), is the highest peak in the Apennines; the many trails, both for hiking and skiing, that radiate from the nearby Campo Imperatore are known throughout Europe. Trail maps are available from the provincial tourist office in L'Aquila (Piazza SM Paganica; tel: 0862-410808; www.gransassolagapark.it).

Sulmona

One of the most spectacular drives in Abruzzo takes Route 261 from L'Aquila to **Sulmona ❺**, following the valley of the Aterno river past a number of medieval villages, each with its ruined castle and its church. Sulmona, the birthplace of Ovid, is considered by many Abruzzians to be the most beautiful town in the province. The evening *passeggiata* is also worth seeing, when the streets, lined with shops selling *confetti* – sugared almonds that have been made here since the Middle Ages – become packed with people pouring arm-in-arm up the Corso.

The **Palazzo della Santissima Annunziata**, once a combination of hospital, church and storehouse of food donated for the poor, stands at the ancient centre of town. The harmony of its facade is often praised. Each of the three portals has a different size and shape, corresponding to the three windows above. The left portal is Gothic, dating from 1415; the middle one is Renaissance, dating from 1483, and the less interesting right portal from still later. On the first floor is a museum of local archaeology and paintings by local artists (Tues–Sat 10am–1pm, Sun 10am– 1pm and 4–7pm; entrance fee). The church, originally more visibly connected to the *palazzo*, was rebuilt after an earthquake in 1706.

BELOW: L'Aquila's Fountain of 99 Spouts.

Pescara ❻ is the birthplace of the writer Gabriele d'Annunzio (1863–1938) *(see page 225)*, whose home is off Piazza Unione (Mon–Sat 9am–12.30pm, Sun and holidays 9am–1.30pm). But it is the 16 km (10 miles) of wide, sandy beach rather than d'Annunzio that draws so many visitors to this Adriatic coast.

Half an hour outside Pescara is the ancient hilltop town of **Chieti ❼**, famous today for its archaeological museum, but known since antiquity for its views across mainland Abruzzo and the sea. Remains of three Roman temples can be seen off the main Corso Marrucino, just behind the post office. The recently modernised **Museo Archeologico** (daily 9am–7pm; entrance fee), at the far western edge of town in the Villa Comunale, has an extensive coin collection. Particularly interesting is the case containing coins from Alba Fucens: a diagram charts the trenches in which the different coins were found. The museum also contains local anthropological and archaeological finds, including some from the Iron Age, and an interesting collection of Roman statues. The sculpture of the 6th-century BC Capestrano Warrior is the most famous exhibit.

A festival in Molise

If you happen to take the train from Termoli to Campobasso between 25 and 27 May, stop at the medieval village of **Larino ❽**. The Sagra di San Pardo, Larino's annual festival, will be taking place, when ox-carts are paraded through the streets. While there, visit the old cathedral, with its beautiful facade, and climb up the monumental staircase of the Palazzo Reale. Larino is one of the least-known places in Italy, yet one of the most rewarding to visit.

Termoli ❾, on the Adriatic, is a popular beach resort whose old town on the promontory offers fine views in all directions. Well garrisoned behind a small castle built by Frederick II are labyrinthine streets and a fine cathedral. Boats leave from Termoli for the **Isole Trémiti**, a group of offshore islands celebrated for their mysterious grottoes and other marine phenomena.

The town that best illustrates the difference between the old and the new in Molise is **Campobasso ❿**, the region's capital. Presided over by the 15th-century Castello Monforte, from which tumble the steeply stepped streets of the old town, Campobasso's modern quarters spread out to the station below. It is in the new town that two of Campobasso's best-known features can be found: a top-security prison and a training school for the *carabinieri*, the Italian police. Smartly uniformed cadets stroll up the streets in twos and threes or stand talking in the square. Ask them for directions to the old town, in particular to San Giorgio, the 12th-century Romanesque church.

Ninety minutes away by train is **Isernia ⓫**, rich in regional lore and a good starting point for exploring the remote hill towns. In 1979, an ancient settlement was discovered on the outskirts. No human remains were found, but there is evidence that man lived here a million years before the birth of Christ – the oldest traces of humanity discovered in Europe. The discovery of a fireplace indicated that these people used fire. Bones of elephants, rhinoceroses, hippos, bison and bear were also discovered, some now displayed in the excellent archaeological museum, the **Museo Santa Maria delle Monache**, (daily 8.30am–7.30pm; entrance fee). ❑

Map on page 294

The local delicacy in Chieti is torrone di fichi secci, *or nougat with figs.*

BELOW: the hilltop village of Villalago, south of Sulmona.

THE SOUTH

To discover one of Europe's most interesting regions,
venture beyond Naples and Sicily into the Mezzogiorno

When foreign travellers visit Apulia, Basilicata and Calabria, they are usually greeted by stares. The stares are not hostile. Nor are they necessarily suspicious. They're just surprised. So few foreigners – so few northern Italians, even – visit these remote and sunbaked regions that anybody who does is looked upon as a bit of an oddball.

This was the case when the English writer Norman Douglas visited in 1911; it was the case when the anti-Fascist Carlo Levi was banished here in 1935. So few people have come to this area for pleasure or insight that nobody knows of the pleasures and insights to be found. The growing number of travellers who do come follow in the footsteps of the Greeks and Romans to Naples, Pompeii, Cumae and Capri. They flock to Sicily and its temples. But Apulia? Basilicata? Calabria? Italy's heel? Her instep? Her toe?

Then there is northern prejudice. Northerners are industrial, pragmatic, fair-skinned. The southerners are agricultural, superstitious, dark. The northerners are rich. Although there is a wealthy southern upper class, many southerners are poor, and emigrate if they get the chance. Nobody moves south to take their place.

The truth is that southern Italy is one of the most interesting places to visit in Europe. It is a romantic land of castles and churches; vast, wheat-covered plains; and misty mountains where shepherds roam. Apulia is a place for novel architectural forms: the Apulian Romanesque; Leccian baroque; castles by Frederick II – and odd, conical, peasant dwellings known as *trulli*. In Basilicata are the *sassi*, cave-dwellings carved into the side of a ravine, many adorned with frescoes, and La Trinità, an unfinished 11th-century Benedictine monastery covered with Roman inscriptions. In Calabria visitors rediscover the Greeks – in particular, two Greek statues made of bronze, recently dredged up by fishermen off Riace. There are Norman castles, Byzantine churches, rich red wines and landscapes which were first described by Homer.

Naples, the Bay of Naples and Sicily are the richest regions historically, and this is reflected in this guide. Apart from the chapter on Naples, which is best explored on foot, the descriptions are geared towards travelling by car. A car is especially important in the *Mezzogiorno*, where sights are too scattered to justify spending long hours waiting for infrequent trains. ❑

PRECEDING PAGES: the typical Basilicata landscape, unchanged for centuries.
LEFT: an ancient fresco of *Spring* in Naples' Archaeological Museum.

NAPLES

Noisy and crowded, but thrilling, Naples has it all –
fine buildings, world-class museums
and cosmopolitan verve

Map on pages 304–5

Naples (Napoli) has always been the black sheep of Italian cities, the misfit, the outcast, the messy brother that nobody knew quite what to do with. It is burdened by intense poverty, unemployment, bureaucratic inefficiency and organised crime but prompted by a popular mayor, the city has undergone a transformation over the past decade in the renovation of its centre and a less anarchic approach to urban life. However, the irrepressible Neapolitan spirit remains. That Naples is, in fact, one of the most beautiful Italian cities, with a friendly population and a long cultural heritage, evidenced in art, churches, castles and pizza, does not deny its less appealing side. In the end, like all black sheep, troubled Naples is the most interesting member of its family.

Orientation

The city has its own special shape, defined partly by landscape, partly by chance and partly by government edict. The only way to get a feel for the place is to walk its different quarters. To orientate yourself, find **Piazza Garibaldi ❶**. From here, the long **Corso Umberto I** juts down to the southwest to **Piazza Bovio ❷**, where, changing its name to Via Agostino Depretis, it continues on to **Piazza Municipio ❸**. The thoroughfare was forced through the narrow, crowded streets that surround it in 1888, in an effort to improve air circulation following a cholera epidemic. The rather drab **Università ❹** looms halfway down, on the right-hand side.

From Piazza Municipio and the nearby **Piazza Plebiscito ❺** the city fans out to the east, the north and the west. Directly north, up Via Toledo, also known as Via Roma, is the red *palazzo* housing the **Museo Archeologico Nazionale**. East of the museum, in the triangle it forms with the Piazza Plebiscito and the Piazza Garibaldi, lies most of Old Naples, with its medieval streets and churches. North, on a hilltop, stands the art gallery of **Capodimonte**. Further south, on a spur of land out in the bay, rises the egg-shaped Castel dell'Ovo and, along the waterfront, Via Partenope, where the city's most expensive hotels overlook the water. The shoreline then curves away west, passing the delightfully restored **Villa Comunale**, with its famous aquarium, to the marina at **Mergellina**, near Virgil's tomb. From Mergellina views stretch back over the entire city, with Mount Vesuvius looming in the background haze.

The city's roots

The name Naples derives from Neapolis, the New City, founded by settlers from Cumae in the 6th century BC. Nearby stood Paleopolis, the Old City, founded in the 9th century BC, also by Greeks from Cumae. The two cities grew side by side like brother and sister until their violent overthrow by Samnites in 400 BC. Rome wrested

LEFT: Via Tribunali, in the historic quarter.
BELOW: sealing a marriage vow with a toast.

them away after a three-year siege in 326 BC, at which point they began to grow into a single entity called Neapolis. From the beginning, Romans flocked here, drawn by the mild climate, the sparkling bay and the political freedom which retention of the Greek constitution allowed. Virgil wrote the *Aeneid* here; emperors built gardens and bathed.

Eight dynasties

The Dark Ages were indeed dark in Naples – nobody knows quite what happened – and until shortly after the first millennium the city was ruled by dukes loosely allied to Byzantium. Then, in 1139, Roger the Norman took Naples under the wing of his Kingdom of Sicily. The seven dynasties that followed produced most of the architectural landmarks that can be seen today. Their statues, together with one of Roger, peer out from niches in the facade of the Palazzo Reale at the centre of town: Frederick II of Hohenstaufen, who founded the university; Charles I of Anjou, who lived here and left his mark; Alfonso I of Aragon, Charles I of Austria, Charles I of Bourbon, Joachim Murat and Victor Emmanuel II. They line up like wrinkles in the building's broad face, testimonies to the city's past.

Castles and music

When Charles I of Anjou built the **Castel Nuovo ❻** (Museo Civico: Mon–Sat 9am–7pm; entrance fee) in 1282, he could not have known that seven centuries later it would still serve as the political hub of the city. The Municipal Council of Naples meets in the huge **Sala dei Baroni**, where Charles is said to have performed some of his bloodiest executions. The finest architectural element in this imposing fortress is the Triumphal Arch, built from 1454–67 to commemorate Alfonso I's defeat of the French. It is the only Renaissance arch ever to have been built at the entrance to a castle.

A short walk up Via San Carlo brings you to the **Teatro San Carlo ❼** (box office, tel: 081-797 2412), the largest opera house in Italy and one of the finest in the world. It is all red velvet and gold

Naples

0 ——————— 300 m
0 ——————— 300 yds

N

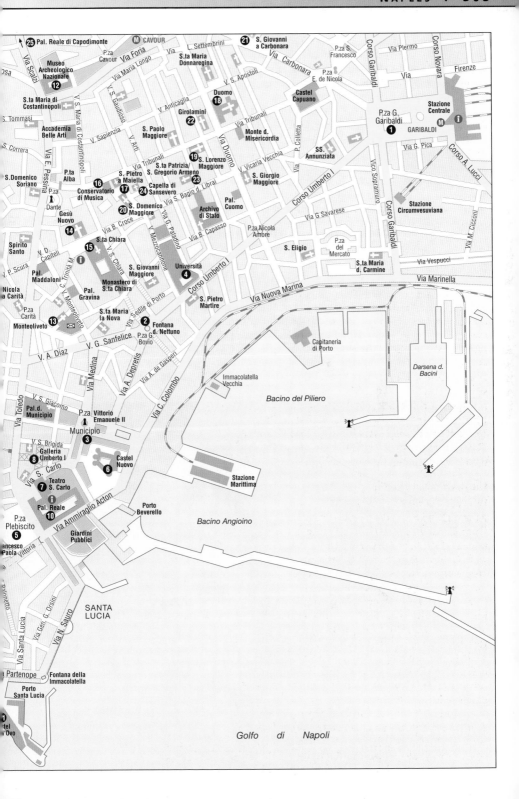

25 Pal. Reale di Capodimonte

Ⓜ CAVOUR

21 S. Giovanni a Carbonara

P.za Cavour
Via Foria
Via Maria Longo
Via Settembrini
L. Settembrini
Via
Via Carbonara
P.za S. Francesco
Corso Novara
Via Plermo
Via Firenze

12 Museo Archeologico Nazionale

S.ta Maria Donnaregina

P.za E. de Nicola

Corso Garibaldi

Via S. Gaudioso
Via S. Apostoli
Via V. S. Apostoli

S.ta Maria di Costantinopoli

18 Duomo

Castel Capuano

1 P.za G. Garibaldi

Stazione Centrale
Ⓜ
ⓘ

Accademia Belle Arti

V. Anticaglia
Girolamini

GARIBALDI

S. Tommasi

22

Via Duomo

Via Tribunali

Via G. Pica

Corso A. Lucci

S. Correra

V. Sapienzia

S. Paolo Maggiore

Monte d. Misericordia

P. Colletta

Via M. Cicconi

Via E. Pessina

Via Arti

Via Tribunali

V. Vicaria Vecchia

SS. Annunziata

Stazione Circumvesuviana

S. Domenico Soriano

P.ta Alba

16

S. Pietro a Maiella

19 S. Lorenzo Maggiore

S. Giorgio Maggiore

Via G. Savarese

Corso Garibaldi

P.za Dante

17

Conservatorio di Musica

24 Capella di Sansevero

S. Gregorio Armeno

23

Pal. Cuomo

Corso Umberto I

Gesù Nuovo

14

20

S. Domenico Maggiore

Archivo di Stato

Via S. Biagio d. Librai

Stazione Marittima

Via B. Croce

Via B. Capasso

P.za Nicola Amore

Spirito Santo

15

S.ta Chiara

V. D. Capitelli

V. P. Scura

Pal. Maddaloni

ⓘ

V.S. Chiara

V. Mezzocannone

S. Eligio

P.za del Mercato

S.ta Maria d. Carmine

Via Vespucci

Nicola a Carità

C. Trinità M.

S. Giovanni Maggiore

Università

4

Corso Umberto I

Via Marinella

P.za Carità

Pal. Gravina

Monastero di S.ta Chiara

Via Nuova Marina

Darsena d. Bacini

13

Monteoliveto

✉

S.ta Maria la Nova

S. Pietro Martire

Capitaneria di Porto

V. G. Sanfelice

Via Sedile di Porto

2 Fontana d. Nettuno

P.za G. Bovio

V. A. Diaz

Immacolatella Vecchia

Bacino del Piliero

V. Medina

V. A. Depretis

Via A. de Gasperi

Via C. Colombo

V.S. Giacomo

Pal. d. Municipio

P.za Vittorio Emanuele II

Via Toledo

Municipio

3

V. S. Brigida

Galleria Umberto I

8

S. Carlo

Teatro S. Carlo

7

Castel Nuovo

6

Stazione Marittima

Pal. Reale

10

P.za Plebiscito

5

ancesco Paola

Via Ammiraglio Acton

Porto Beverello

Bacino Angioino

Giardini Pubblici

Vittoria

SANTA LUCIA

Via Santa Lucia

Via Gen. G. Orsini

Via N. Sauro

Partenope

Fontana della Immacolatella

Porto Santa Lucia

tel 'Ovo

Golfo   di   Napoli

Street vendor.

trim, with six tiers of boxes rising from the stage. Constructed in 1737, under the direction of Charles III of Bourbon, the theatre retains its perfect acoustics, helped by the insertion, after a fire in 1816, of hundreds of clay pitchers between the walls. Even on the sixth tier, you can sit on a red velvet seat in your own private box.

Across the street is the **Galleria Umberto I** ❽, erected in 1887 on a neo-classical design similar to that of its older brother in Milan. Its glass ceiling, 56 metres (184 ft) high, and its mosaic-covered floor were reconstructed after bomb damage in World War II. Pleasant cafés permit a moment's rest.

The wide Piazza Plebiscito around the corner is embraced by the twin arcades of the **Chiesa di San Francesco di Paola** ❾ (1817–32), modelled after the Pantheon in Rome. The square is closed to traffic and is popular with local artists, who often exhibit their work under the arches of the church.

Reminder of turbulent times

The sprawling red facade of the **Palazzo Reale** ❿ (royal apartments: Thur–Tues 9am–8pm; entrance fee) looms across the street with its eight statues illustrating the eight Neapolitan dynasties. At the foot of its monumental marble staircase stand the original bronze doors from the Castel Nuovo. The cannonball lodged in the left door is a reminder of an early siege. Upstairs are a throne room and a small but lavish theatre. Further rooms stretch off in a seemingly endless series of period furniture and Dresden china.

BELOW: the Castel Nuovo, built in 1282.

Another famous castle, the **Castel dell'Ovo** ⓫ (Mon–Sat 9am–6pm, Sun 9am–1pm; free), on the waterfront, is used for hosting exhibitions and cultural events. Its oval shape (hence the name) was commissioned by the Spanish viceroy

Don Pedro de Toledo in 1532, but the original castle was built by William I in 1154, finished by Frederick II and enlarged by the not-to-be-outdone Charles I of Anjou. Pleasant restaurants line the shore, children bellyflop from the causeway, and the speedboats of the Guardia di Finanza (Fraud Squad) lurk just along the quay.

Map on pages 304–5

House of history

The **Museo Archeologico Nazionale di Napoli** ⓬ (Wed–Mon 9am–7.30pm; entrance fee) is one of the great museums of the world, housing the most spectacular finds from Pompeii and Herculaneum and fine examples of Greek sculpture. A trip to the museum will take an entire morning. The highlights include the so-called "Secret Cabinet" (Gabinetto Segreto) which reopened in 2000 after 26 years of unusual Neapolitan prudery (it had been semi-open until 1967). It contains erotic images which lift the lid on the racy ancient world. Graphic sex scenes are depicted on Greek vases, Roman terracottas and Etruscan mirrors.

Relief in the Galleria Umberto I.

The ground floor is devoted to classical sculpture and Egyptian art. In the main entrance hall, a monolithic sarcophagus depicts a famous and important scene: Prometheus creating man out of clay. Another awesome sarcophagus presents a raucous Bacchanalian celebration. Through a doorway to the right, a pair of statues of Harmodius and Aristogeiton, who killed the tyrant Hipparchus, fairly leap out at you as you enter the room. These are actually Roman copies of originals once installed in the Agora in Athens.

In a further room stands a Roman copy of the famous statue of Doryphorus by Polycleitus (440 BC), considered the "canon of perfection" of manly proportions. This statue, found at Pompeii, and others of its period are evidence of the refined tastes of early Greek settlers. The Farnese Collection includes a Hercules and the *Farnese Bull* (the largest piece of antique sculpture ever found) from Rome's Baths of Caracalla.

BELOW: a flying leap off the Castel dell'Ovo.

The rich collection of mosaics on the mezzanine floor at the back of the building come from the floors, walls and courtyards of houses unearthed at Pompeii. The freshness and colour of these works after centuries buried in ash are an amazing tribute to the craftsmanship of their ancient makers.

The Nile scenes in Room LX, from a later period, feature ducks, crocodiles, hippopotami and snakes. These mosaics originally framed the *Battle of Issus*, in Room LXI. In this scene, Alexander the Great is presented in his victorious battle against the Persian emperor Darius in 333 BC. The thicket of spears creates the illusion of an army far larger than that actually shown.

Rooms on the first floor show paintings of Pompeii and a reconstruction of the Villa of the Papyrii in Herculaneum, including an extraordinary collection of marble and bronze sculptures.

Through the large Salone dell'Atlante at the top of the stairs is a series of rooms containing wall paintings from various Campanian cities. Especially startling is the 6th-century BC *Sacrifice of Iphigenia*, the Greek equivalent of the biblical sacrifice of Isaac. The deer borne by Artemis in the top of the picture replaced Iphigenia at the last minute, just as Isaac was replaced by a ram. Far happier is *The Rustic Concert*, in which Pan and nymphs tune up for a Roman celebration.

Wall painting taken from a house in Pompeii depicting Perseus, son of Zeus, and Andromeda, who he rescued from a sea monster.

BELOW: the Battle of Alexander mosaic from the House of the Faun, Pompeii.

Neapolitan churches

The churches of Naples, like the churches of any Italian city, offer glimpses into Italian life. In Italy, a visit to a church, a quick confession, a genuflection in front of an altar are still a daily ritual for many people. Because of this, churches open every day (but close 1–4.30pm), so no opening times are given.

The church of **Monteoliveto** ⓭, about halfway up Via Roma, contains a wealth of Renaissance monuments hidden away in surprising corners. Far in the back of this aisleless basilica, begun in 1411, stands a bizarre group of terracotta figures by the artist Guido Mazzoni. The eight statues, looking almost alive in the dim light that filters into the chapel, represent the *Pietà*, and are said to be portraits of Mazzoni's 15th-century friends. Further back, down a side passage, is the Old Sacristy, containing frescoes by Vasari and wooden stalls, inlaid with biblical scenes. In the very front of the church, to the left of the entrance, another passage leads to the Piccolomini Chapel where a relief of a Nativity scene by the Florentine Antonio Rossellino (1475) is a delight to behold.

Unlike in Rome, which is heavily baroque, no single architectural style dominates Naples. The Gothic, the Renaissance and the baroque are all represented. The late 16th-century church of **Gesù Nuovo** ⓮ at the top of the street called **Trinità Maggiore** presents perhaps the most harmonious example of the Neapolitan baroque. The embossed stone facade originally formed the wall of a Renaissance palace. At noon on Saturdays, when weddings take place here, the massive front doors are thrown open to give a splendid view of fully lit baroque at its best. The interior has a unique design, being almost as wide as it is deep. The coloured marble and bright frescoes seem to spiral up into the dome. Directly above the main portal, just inside the church, stretches a wide fresco by Francesco Soli-

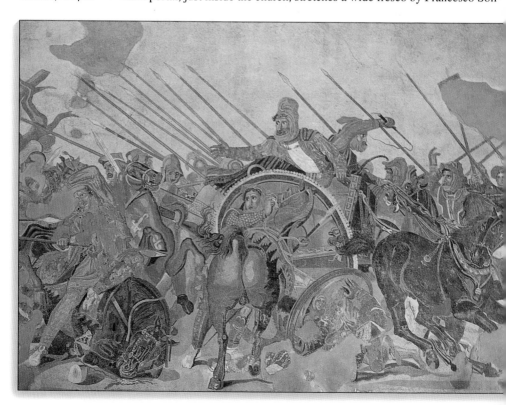

mena (1725) depicting Heliodorus driven from the temple. The ubiquitous Solimena dominated Neapolitan painting in the first half of the 18th century.

Map on pages 304–5

Robert the Wise

A more austere, and older, architectural approach is demonstrated by the Gothic church of **Santa Chiara** ⓫, just across the street. Founded between 1310 and 1328 by Robert the Wise for his queen, Sancia, the huge church – the biggest in Naples – became the favourite place of worship of the Neapolitan nobility. Unfortunately, extensive bomb damage during World War II destroyed many important works of art and 18th-century decorations, but worth seeking out in its vast interior is the Tomb of Robert the Wise (1343) behind the main altar. Through a courtyard to the left of the church is the entrance to its immense and peaceful cloister (built in the 15th century but much altered in the 18th), where majolica-tiled pathways meander through a wild and beautiful garden of roses and fruit trees. The cloister was recently carefully restored and medieval frescoes under the arcades were recovered and the garden replanted with the same species grown here in Bourbon times. Many brightly coloured mosaics discovered in the excavations can also be seen. A museum of sculpture and archaeology is also on site.

The steep **Via Santa Maria di Costantinopoli** leads up to the **Conservatorio di Musica** ⓰, founded in 1537, the oldest musical conservatory in Europe. It has an important library and museum (tel: 081-564 4411), but it is also enjoyable to wander through its courtyard listening to the music of violins, organs, harps and pianos spilling down from upper storeys. Just down the block, the church of **San Pietro a Maiella** ⓱, built between 1313 and 1316, has one of the most famous ceilings in Italy. The Calabrian Mattia Preti began painting it in 1656, at the age of 43, a few months after leaving his native Taverna for the more rigorous artistic challenges of Naples. Five years later he completed his work, establishing himself as one of the most talented painters of his generation. The panels in the nave tell the story of St Celestine V, while the panels in the transept present the life of St Catherine of Alexandria, the virgin martyr who was beheaded for out-arguing pagan scholars.

ABOVE and **BELOW:** majolica tiles in Santa Chiara.

Reliable miracles

The Naples **Duomo** ⓲ is a magnificent Gothic warehouse of relics from every period of the city's history. Kept in a chapel off the right aisle are the head of San Gennaro, the patron saint of the city, and two phials of his blood (chapel open daily 8am–noon). The mysterious powers of the congealed blood are the subject of what Mark Twain called "one of the wretchedest of all the religious impostures in Italy – the miraculous liquefaction of the blood." The miracle has been taking place every year on the first Saturday in May, 19 September and 16 December since the saint's body was brought to Naples from Pozzuoli, the place of his martyrdom, by Bishop Severus in the time of Constantine. It is said that if the blood fails to liquefy a disaster is in store for the city. The last great eruption of Vesuvius in1944 and the earthquake northeast of Naples in 1980 occurred in the years that the blood did not liquefy.

Other notable churches, all in the historical centre of

Display of the sweet lemon liqueur known as Limoncello.

the city, include **San Lorenzo Maggiore ⓭**, where archaeological excavations have revealed the old Decumano (main street) running through its cloister; the Gothic **San Domenico Maggiore ⓴**; the 14th-century **San Giovanni a Carbonara ㉑**; **Girolamini ㉒**; and **Santa Patrizia ㉓** with its **monastery of San Gregorio Armeno**. Via San Gregoria Armeno is famous for its workshops producing *presepi* (Christmas cribs), an important Neapolitan tradition.

The **Cappella di Sansevero ㉔** (Mon and Wed–Sat 10am–6pm, Sun 10am–1.30pm; entrance fee), a small unconsecrated church near the church of San Domenico Maggiore, should not be missed. It contains a moving and remarkably realistic sculpture known as the *Cristo Velato* (Veiled Christ) carved out of a single piece of marble by Giuseppe Sammartino. The chapel was once the workshop of Prince Raimondo, a well-known 18th-century alchemist who was excommunicated by the pope for dabbling in the occult. In the crypt are the gruesome results of some of his experiments.

Museums with a view

BELOW: view from Castel Sant'Elmo.

Two of the greatest museums in Naples stand high on bluffs overlooking the city. The National Gallery of Naples, formerly in the **Museo Nazionale**, has been relocated to the **Palazzo Reale di Capodimonte ㉕** (Tues–Sun 8.30am–7.30pm; entrance fee), the 18th-century palace of King Charles III, set in a shady park directly north of the museum. The gallery contains some of the best paintings in southern Italy. At its heart is the important Farnese collection, which by the late 18th century numbered over 1,700 paintings. Among the high points are Masolino da Panicale's *Foundation of Santa Maria Maggiore in Rome*, in which Christ and Mary ride a cloud as if it were a magic carpet; Bellini's *Transfigu-*

ation; various works of Titian; two startling allegorical paintings by Pieter Breughel the Elder *(The Blind Leading the Blind* and *The Misanthrope)*; and, perhaps the most famous of all, Caravaggio's *Flagellation*. The Salottina di Porcellano is lined throughout with magnificent Capodimonte porcelain tiles which were made in King Charles III's porcelain factory in 1757. These originally adorned the queen's parlour in the royal palace at Portici.

A trip up the Montesanto funicular brings the visitor to the top of the Vomero hill, home of the **Certosa e Museo di San Martino** (Tues–Sun 8.30am–7.30pm; entrance fee), located in the Carthusian monastery of the same name. Like so many buildings in Naples, the Certosa di San Martino was built in the 14th century, but had a complete baroque makeover a few hundred years later, and has recently been beautifully restored. Some of the top painters of the Neapolitan baroque are represented here, including Salvator Rosa, Francesco Solimena and the prolific Luca Giordano. Belvederes give access to the best views in town – the wide sweep of the Bay of Naples.

Good views can also be had from the **Castel Sant'Elmo** (Tues–Sun 8.30am–7.30pm; entrance fee) next door, a 14th-century fortress long used as a prison for political troublemakers. The stately gardens of the **Villa Floridiana** (daily 9am to 1 hr before sunset; free), also on the Vomero, are favoured among young mothers as a place to teach infants to walk. The gardens house the **Museo Nazionale della Ceramica** (Tues–Sun 8.30am–2pm; entrance fee), which contains one of the most extensive collections of porcelain in Italy.

A secret known to sailors in navies around the world is that the Bay of Naples is one of the most beautiful ports in Europe. To appreciate the splendour of the bay, walk through the pleasant and popular **Villa Comunale gardens** to the far-western district of **Mergellina**, from where boats depart to the islands in the bay. The Villa Comunale itself is a mile-long public garden containing a small **aquarium** (Mon–Sat 9am–6pm, Sun 10am–6pm in summer; Mon–Sat 9am–5pm, Sun 9am–2pm in winter; entrance fee) where 200 species of fish cavort in murky tanks.

Birthplace of the pizza

The **Piazza Sannazzaro**, at the heart of the Mergellina district, repays walkers with some of the best pizza in Naples *(see page 406)*. Pizza was originally born in Naples and genuine Neapolitan pizza is unbeatable. Its secret, aside from the fact that it is made with fresh mozzarella – another speciality of the Naples region – lies in the baking. It is cooked quickly, at a high temperature, in a dome-shaped brick oven, over a wood fire. Other local specialities invariably available include octopus *(polpo)*, mussel soup *(zuppa di cozze)*, numerous varieties of fish, various spaghettis made with a fish sauce, such as the Neapolitan catch-all *spaghetti alla pescatora* (fishwife's spaghetti); various kinds of cheese and ham, swordfish, fried mozzarella and spaghetti alla mozzarella.

Naples is a big, brawling city that exists for nobody, ultimately, but itself. It neither actively discourages visitors nor makes any real attempt to draw them in. It just continues on its crowded, noisy, irremediable way, a gypsy caravan of all that is best and worst in Italy. ❑

Map on pages 304–5

TIP

The Campania Artecard costs €13 and is valid for 3 days. During this period it allows you free entry into two museums and half price for another four. Available at participating museums, the main station and tourist information centres (freephone 800-600601; www. campaniartecard.it).

BELOW: Neapolitan personality.

THE CAMPANIA COAST

An endless succession of jewel-like coves
ripples down the Naples coast,
with Pompeii and Herculaneum just inland

Map on
page 314

In Greek times, Naples was a mere stripling overshadowed by its powerful parent **Cumae ❶** (Cuma), 30 km (19 miles) to the west. Founded by Aeolians from Asia Minor around 750 BC, Cumae had become by the 6th century BC the political, religious and cultural beacon of the coast, controlling the Bay of Naples and its islands.

Here Aeneas came to consult the Sybil before his descent into the underworld. The famous **Antro della Sibilla Cumana** (Cave of the Cumaean Sybil; daily 9am–2 hrs before sunset; entrance fee), recently uncovered by archaeologists, consists of a trapezoidal *dromos* (corridor), 44 metres (144 ft) long, punctuated by six airshafts. At the far end is a rectangular chamber cut with niches where the Sybil apparently sat and uttered her prophecies. The eerie echo of footsteps in the corridor recalls Virgil's description of "a cavern perforated a hundred times, having a hundred mouths with rushing voices carrying the responses of the Sybil." From the cave's mouth it is possible to climb up to the acropolis, whose ruined, lizard-haunted temples offer fine views of the coastline and the sea.

The region between Cumae and Naples, known traditionally as the **Campi Flegrei** (Burning Fields), has been a centre of volcanic activity for the whole of recorded history. Unexpected rumblings and gaseous exhalations from below have linked the area to the mythical Greek underworld. The **Lago di Averno**, a once-gloomy lake in the crater of an extinct volcano, is the legendary "dark pool" from which Aeneas began his descent into Hades. No bird was said to be able to fly across this lake and live, due to the poisonous gases. For many years this theory was cruelly tested at the **Grotta del Cane** on the nearby Lago d'Agnano. Dogs were subjected to the carbon dioxide that issued from the floor of the cave until knocked out or killed. "The dog dies in a minute and a half – a chicken instantly", reported Mark Twain. The experiment was repeated nine or ten times a day for the benefit of tourists.

LEFT: the Amalfi coast.
BELOW: the Arco Felice, an ancient brick archway near Cumae.

Volcanic crater

Pozzuoli ❷, a wealthy trading centre in Greek and Roman times but later devastated by wars and malaria, is now famous for its **Solfatara** (daily 8.30am–1 hr before sunset; entrance fee), a volcanic crater releasing jets of sulphurous gases. The Solfatara is thought to have inspired Milton's description of Hell in *Paradise Lost*. Pozzuoli also boasts a magnificent amphitheatre, now newly restored (daily 9am–1 hr before sunset; entrance fee) and used for summer concerts. Pozzuoli was also the birthplace of actress Sophia Loren. On the waterfront, enclosed in a small park, lies a rectangular structure formerly known as the **Serapeo** (Temple of Serapis), but now thought to have been a *macellum* (marketplace). Shellfish encrustation around the bases

TIP

From Naples, the best way to reach Pompeii and Vesuvius is to take the Circumvesuviana railway to either destination. For a convenient route to the top of Vesuvius, take the same train to Ercolano Scavi, then take a bus and walk the final stretch (20 minutes).

of its four Corinthian columns has led to speculation that the ground once sank 5 metres (16 ft) below sea level before rising again to its present height.

Baia ❸ derives its name from Baios, Odysseus's navigator. Here Roman society came to swim. The modern town, with its view across the Gulf of Pozzuoli, contains extensive ruins of Roman palaces enclosed in a picturesque **Parco Archeologico** (Tues–Sun 9am–1 hr before sunset; bookings required, tel: 081-868 8868; entrance fee) on the hillside. At the lowest level of the park is a rectangular *piscina* (bathing pool) from which an arched pathway, hidden in foliage, leads to a domed building believed to have been a bath house. Archaeologists have pinpointed this perfect circular structure as the model for the Pantheon in Rome.

Pompeii and Herculaneum

The two Roman cities of **Pompeii ❹** (Apr–Oct daily 8.30am–7.30pm, Nov–Mar daily 8.30am–5pm, last entry 1 hr before closure; special night openings in summer; tel: 081-8575347; entrance fee; for general information on Pompeii and Herculaneum, tel: 081-8373477) and Herculaneum, buried by the eruption of Mount Vesuvius in AD 79, have solved what the archaeologist Amedeo Maiuri has called "the essential problem in the history of civilisation: the origin and development of the house." Pompeii, originally settled by indigenous Oscans some time before the 8th century BC and later ruled by Etruscans, Greeks and the warlike Samnites, was a commercial centre at the time of its sudden immersion in pumice stone and ash. It was a city of shops, markets and comfortable townhouses, with paved streets, a stadium, two theatres, temples, baths and brothels. Its rediscovery during land reclamation operations in the 16th century, and subsequent years of excavation (sometimes piratical but increasingly

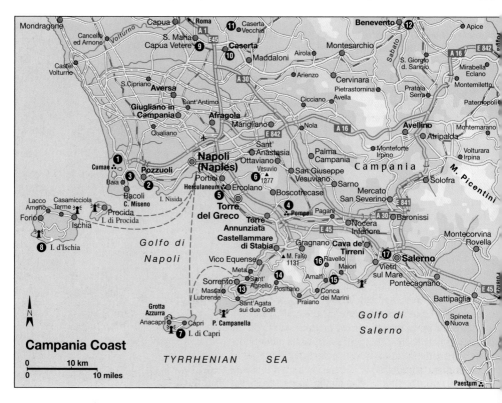

Campania Coast

0   10 km
0   10 miles

TYRRHENIAN   SEA

respectful) have revealed an intimate picture of life in a 1st-century Roman city.

The Pompeiian house is thought to have evolved from the relatively simple design of the Etruscan farmhouse. The structure was built around a central court-yard *(atrium)* whose roof sloped inwards on all four sides to a rectangular open-ing in the centre known as the *compluvium*. Through the *compluvium,* rainwater fell into a corresponding rectangular tank called the *impluvium.* Around the *atrium* itself were the various family quarters, including the bedrooms *(cubic-ula)*, the dining rooms *(triclinia)*, and directly opposite the narrow entranceway *(vestibule)*, the living room *(tablinum)*, the most important room in the house.

As the plan developed, a further peristyle courtyard was added, often con-taining a fountain. Shops were built into the front of the house; sections of the house were blocked off and rented out, with separate entranceways, to strangers (for example, the **Villa di Julia Felix**); another storey was added up top, until the Etruscan prototype had metamorphosed into the comfortable and palatial town-houses typified by the **Casa dei Vettii** and the **Casa del Fauno**.

Wedding whips

A striking feature of the Pompeiian house was the colourful and often highly refined artwork covering its walls. Many of the most beautiful frescoes have been taken to the Museo Archeologico Nazionale in Naples *(see page 307)*, but at the **Villa dei Misteri**, just outside the Porto Ercolano, a series of 10 scenes, apparently depicting the initiation of brides into the Dionysiac mysteries, has been left *in situ*. The meaning of these paintings, which depict, among other things, the whipping of a young bride, is still far from clear, although it is generally agreed that the woman in the final scene is probably a portrait of the mistress of the house, who may have been a Dionysiac priestess.

ABOVE: faun in the Casa del Fauno. **BELOW:** fresco at Villa dei Misteri.

The most remarkable thing about Pompeii is the mass of detail. Carved into the polygonal paving stones of the streets, for instance, are small phalluses pointing to the centre of the city. These are thought by some to have warded off evil spirits, by others to have pointed to the brothel district. And walls and monuments throughout the city are covered with inscriptions of every kind, from lists of upcoming plays to the scribbled accounts of shopkeepers, from election notices to *billets-doux*. "It is a wonder, O Wall," wrote one cynic on the wall of the basilica, "that thou hast not yet crumbled under the weight of so much written nonsense."

Herculaneum ❺ (Ercolano) (Apr–Oct daily 8.30am–7.30pm, Nov–Mar; daily 8.30am–5pm, last admission 90 mins before closure; tel: 081-7390963; entrance fee) was built for the enjoyment of sea breezes and views across the Bay of Naples. Instead of the compact town-houses of Pompeiian businessmen, there are sprawling villas of wealthy patricians. There is a free, spontaneous form of architecture, and the houses, freed of the mud in which they were encased for so long, are generally in a better state of preservation than those of Pompeii.

One of the pleasures of Herculaneum (aside from the fact that it is less crowded with tour groups than Pom-peii) is the carbonised pieces of wooden furniture, door mouldings and screens still inside the houses. Fine fres-coes, such as the *Rape of Europa* in the **Casa Sannitica**,

Transport on Ischia.

adorn the walls, and carpet-like mosaics cover the floors. Particularly striking are the black-and-white mosaics on the floor of the **Casa dell'Atrio a Mosaico**. But the finest building here is the **Casa dei Cervi** (The House of the Deer) which features superb frescoes and statues. After lengthy excavations the **Villa dei Papiri** opened in 2003. Built by Julius Caesar's father-in-law, it is believed to contain the "lost library" of Latin and Greek literary masterpieces. Prior booking is essential for visits. Online reservations and tours for Herculaneum (and Pompeii) can be made through Arethusa call centre, tel: 89111178; www.arethusa.net.

Herculaneum is the best starting point for an afternoon ascent of **Mount Vesuvius ⑥**, which looms directly over the modern city of **Ercolano**. Buses leave regularly from the Ercolano Scavi train station and drop passengers at the roadhead, from where there is a 20-minute climb up a well-beaten track.

Just before the infamous eruption of AD 79, trees and olive groves covered Vesuvius up to its very peak. In the 20th century, a constant plume of smoke billowed from a cone inside the crater until 1944, when, during the volcano's last major eruption to date, the cone was destroyed. Aware that one million people are sitting on a time bomb and that a major eruption is a matter of when and not if, the Italian authorities are offering each family 25,000 euro to move, but the take-up from Neopolitans has been minimal.

Islands of pleasure

Of the three islands just outside the Gulf of Naples, **Capri ⑦**, on the Sorrento side, has traditionally been the most popular. Its mild climate, luxuriant vegetation and seemingly inaccessible coast have drawn visitors for centuries. Emperor Tiberius retired here in AD 27, either to pursue his life-long love of privacy or to indulge in the secret orgies which the historians Tacitus and Suetonius claim characterised the closing years of his reign. While on Capri, writes Suetonius, the emperor "devised little nooks of lechery in the woods and glades … and had boys and girls dressed up as pans and nymphs posted in front of caverns or grottoes; so that the island was now openly and generally called 'Caprineum' because of his goatish antics." The writer Norman Douglas, who also lived on Capri, attributed such legends to the idle exaggerations of resentful peasants.

The modern traveller, arriving by ferry or hydrofoil from Naples or Sorrento, can reach the remains of **Tiberius's Villa** (Villa Jovis; daily 9am–1 hr before sunset; entrance fee) by bus from the town of Capri. The most famous sight on the island, however, is the **Grotta Azzurra** (Blue Grotto), a cave on the water's edge.

From **Anacapri**, on the far side of the island, you can take a chair-lift up **Monte Solaro** (daily 9.30am–sunset in summer, 10.30am–3pm in winter; entrance fee). Its 360-degree view encompasses the southern Apeninnes, Naples, Vesuvius, Sorrento and Ischia. In Anacapri itself, the church of **San Michele** (daily 9.30am–7pm, until 4pm in winter) is worth a visit for its newly restored majolica-tiled pavement depicting the *Story of Eden*.

Ischia ⑧, the largest island off Naples, is famous for its hot mineral springs. The island is of volcanic origin.

Some say the giant Typhoeus, struck by Zeus's thunderbolt, was buried under Ischia, and is the cause of the occasional groanings and shakings that have marked its long history. Compared with Capri, Ischia is larger, wilder and decidedly less manicured than its chic but more touristy neighbour.

The town of **Lacco Ameno**, on the coastal road, is known for its mud baths, which contain the most radioactive waters in Italy. **Sant'Angelo** has some of the best beaches on the island. At **Ischia Ponte**, a causeway crosses to the **Castello Aragonese**, built by Alfonso I of Naples in 1450. The crypt of the ruined cathedral is adorned with frescoes in the style of Giotto. The nearby convent has an interesting cemetery where departed sisters were placed upright in chairs.

Procida, the smallest of the islands in the Bay of Naples, has good beaches and a thriving fishing industry. It is quiet and has not succumbed to mass tourism.

Old Campania

Inland from Naples, at **Santa Maria Capua Vetere 9**, are the remains of the second-largest amphitheatre in Italy after the Colosseum (Tues–Sun 9am–5.30pm). Few tourists are aware of this magnificent crumbling structure, where visitors can actually climb down into the subterranean passages where wild beasts roamed.

Caserta 10 is often called the Versailles of Naples for its lavish **Reggia** (Royal Palace; Tues–Sun 8.30am–7pm; gardens Tues–Sun 8.30am–6pm, till 2.30pm in winter; entrance fee), designed by Luigi Vanvitelli in 1752 for the Bourbon king Charles III. The brick and stone colossus doesn't quite achieve the elegant beauty of Versailles, but it is impressive nonetheless and the vast gardens alone make an excursion worthwhile. **Caserta Vecchia 11**, on a hilltop 10 km (6 miles) northeast, is one of the most beautiful towns in Campania. Founded in the 8th century,

Map on page 314

The royal palace of Caserta took 22 years to complete. The facade is 249 metres (815 ft) long, it has 2,000 windows, and its 1,200 rooms are spread across five floors connected by 34 stairways. Most impressive of all are the 120 hectares (300 acres) of magnificent parkland.

BELOW: view of Sant'Angelo on Ischia, and a neighbouring island.

The freshness and quality of local produce in Campania are superb.

it still looks much as it did then. Its Romanesque cathedral has a wonderful facade with a cow over the central portal. Inside is a monolithic 4th-century baptismal font in which baptism by full immersion was practised. There are some excellent restaurants in the town where you can sample wild boar, the local speciality.

One of the most important cities in Campanian history is **Benevento** ⑫, where the noble king Manfred voluntarily died in battle after the defection of his allies in 1266. The city was named Beneventum upon becoming a Roman colony in 268 BC. In the centre of town, on the route of the ancient **Via Appia** from Rome to Brindisi, stands the **Arch of Trajan**. Of the splendid reliefs depicting scenes from Trajan's life, those on the side facing Rome celebrate the emperor's domestic policies while those on the side facing Brindisi record his foreign policies. The **Museo del Sannio** (Tues–Sun 9am–1pm; entrance fee) is worth visiting not only for its collection of local antiquities but also for the hunting scenes on the column capitals that surround its 12th-century cloister.

Paradise regained

The visitor to **Sorrento** ⑬, whether arriving from the noisy streets of Naples or from the scorched ruins of Pompeii, will find a cool and peaceful town of lemon groves, with a small beach and plentiful cafés. There's not much more to Sorrento, save for a 15th-century **Loggia** with fine column capitals on the Via San Cesareo, and the fact that the poet Tasso was born here in 1544, but that is exactly why the town is such a popular resort among Italians and foreigners alike. It's an excellent starting point for excursions to Capri and the **Amalfi Coast**. This dramatic coast stretches from **Positano** to **Salerno** and has some of the most spectacular scenery in Italy. The **Amalfi Drive** faithfully follows its length, keeping a respectful distance above the waves but doggedly following each frightening twist of the shoreline. Pastel-painted houses cling to the slopes and gardens descend in steps to the sea.

BELOW: Ravello.

Positano ⑭ consists of a semi-circle of houses set back in a cove, with numerous hotels, good swimming and wonderful views. The road then passes through several tunnels before reaching the **Grotta di Smeraldo**, famous for its emerald green light. Through yet more tunnels (watch out for cyclists) lies **Amalfi** ⑮, a major trading centre in Byzantine times and now a major tourist centre. From the main piazza, with its fountain, a flight of steps ascends to the 11th-century bronze door of Amalfi's **Duomo**. In the crypt lies the body of St Andrew the Apostle, delivered from Constantinople in 1208. On either side of the main altar are ambones with fine mosaics.

The loveliest town on the Amalfi coast is **Ravello** ⑯, famous for its architecture, its gardens and admirers. Ravello's **Duomo** is celebrated for its bronze doors by the Apulian Barisano da Trani. Cast in Trani in 1179, the doors were transported to Ravello by ship. Inside, the floor slopes upwards towards God and a fine marble pulpit supported by pillars resting on the backs of six hungry lions. The pulpit was presented to the church in 1272 by Nicola Rufolo and his wife, Sigilgaida, who built the splendid **Villa Rufolo** (daily 9am–8pm; till 6pm in winter; entrance fee) across the street. The villa's lush gardens and Moorish cloister overlook the sea several miles away. The best view, however, is from the more extensive gardens at the **Villa Cimbrone** (daily 9am–8pm, till 6pm in winter; entrance fee), built at the end of the 19th century by a wealthy Englishman, Ernest William Beckett.

Map on
page 314

Salerno and Paestum

It was just south of **Salerno** ⑰ that the Allies began their assault on Italy on 9 September 1943. Recently, there has been a belated restoration of the historic centre and a successful revival of the medieval Fiera Vecchia, a large food and handicrafts fair held in May. The city, strung out along the shore, has a good beach and one of the loveliest cathedrals in southern Italy, which is reached through an atrium incorporating 28 columns from Paestum. Inside, as the removal of 18th-century plaster continues, more medieval frescoes are coming to light.

The English writer George Eliot regarded the **Temple of Neptune** at **Paestum** (daily 9am–1 hr before sunset; entrance fee) as "the finest thing, I verily believe, we have seen in Italy." Her words echo the sentiments of many 19th-century travellers for whom this Greek city was the final stop on the Grand Tour. There are few sights so arresting as Paestum's three well-preserved Doric temples standing empty on the grassy plain that surrounds them. The Temple of Neptune, the most majestic of these, was built in the 5th century BC of a reddish travertine whose warmth, as Eliot wrote, "seems to glow and deepen under one's eyes".

The so-called **basilica** beside the Temple of Neptune dates from the 6th century BC. The third temple, the **Temple of Ceres**, is separated from the other two by the **Roman forum** and **baths**, and a **Greek theatre**. Across the street, in the **museum** (daily 9am–7pm; closed 1st and 3rd Mon of the month; entrance fee) are famous mural paintings from the **Tomb of the Diver** (480 BC). ❏

BELOW: Temple of Neptune at Paestum.

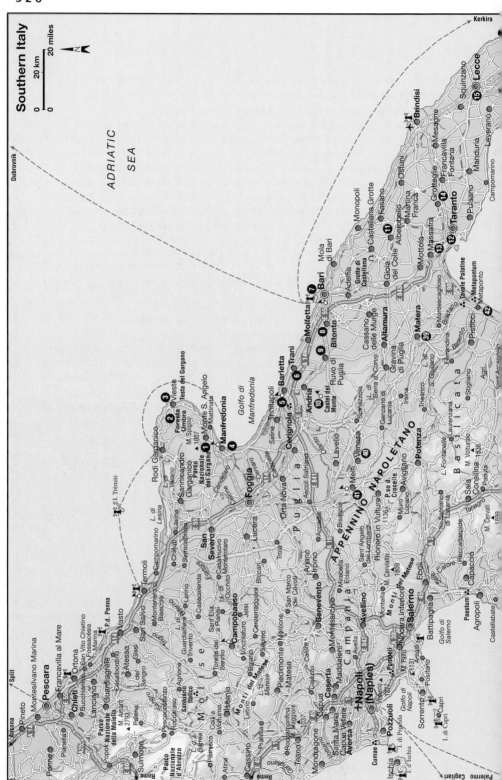

Southern Italy

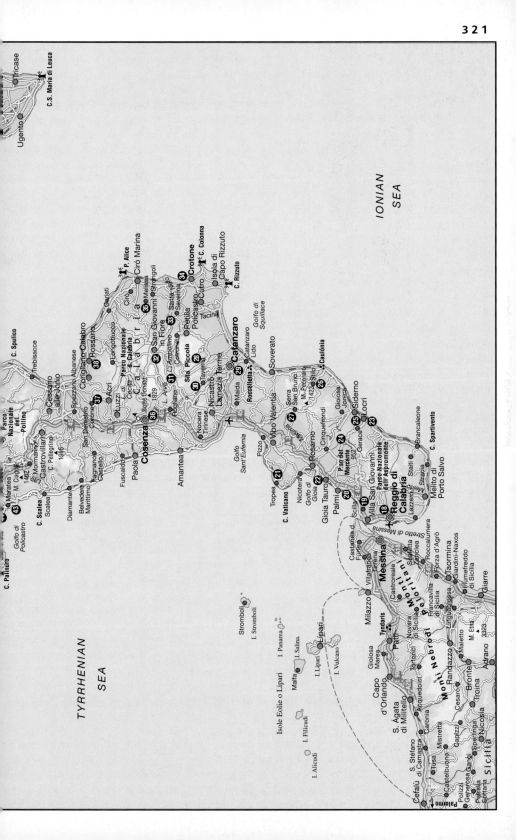

APULIA

Forming the heel and spur of Italy's boot,
Apulia is a region of glorious churches, castles
and sun-bleached beaches

Map on
pages
320–1

Some people visit Apulia (known in Italian as Puglia) for its architecture, some for its landscape, some for its archaeology and some for its food, but all go away haunted by memories of a single man: Frederick II of Hohenstaufen, Holy Roman Emperor, King of Germany and King of Sicily. Known to Dante as "the father of Italian poetry" and to his 13th-century contemporaries as *stupor mundi et immutator mirabilis* – wonder of the world and extraordinary innovator – Frederick built most of the castles that are still the dominant architectural feature of the region.

He also founded many of Apulia's most splendid churches, carrying on the tradition of the Apulian Romanesque begun by his Norman predecessors a century before. An enlightened ruler who waged a bitter and ultimately unsuccessful feud with the popes in Rome, he was also an avid sportsman whose brilliant treatise on falconry still ranks among the most accurate descriptions of the subject. His just laws and tolerance of the Islamic beliefs of the Saracens are legendary. Frederick's death in 1250 and the tragic defeat of his illegitimate son, Manfred, at the Battle of Benevento in 1266 ushered in a period of economic and spiritual decline that is only now being reversed, the former often by illegal means (Puglia has become the preferred gateway for contraband – cigarettes and arms – now flooding into the border-free Europe from former Yugoslavia).

If Frederick II is the dominant figure in Apulia's long and varied history, the Apulian Romanesque is its most important architectural legacy. The style, fusing Byzantine, Saracenic and Italian decorative techniques with the French architectural forms introduced by the Normans, first appeared in the church of San Nicola at Bari in 1087. The plans of most other Apulian churches of the period derived from this elegant cathedral with its short transepts, three semicircular apses corresponding to three naves and three portals, a tall, plain facade, and richly decorated doorways carved with animals, flowers and biblical scenes.

LEFT: Ostuni, a white hill town.
BELOW: rich-flavoured southern tomatoes.

The visiting Archangel

The landscape of northern Apulia is dominated by vast inland plains planted with wheat. The only real mountains are clustered on the Gargano Promontory, a thickly forested peninsula that juts out into the Adriatic to form the "spur" of the boot of Italy. Here, in the medieval town of **Monte Sant'Angelo ❶**, is the **Santuario di San Michele** (Easter–Sept daily 7.30am–7pm, Oct–Easter daily 7.30am–noon and 2.30–5pm; entrance fee), a cave where the Archangel Michael is said to have revealed himself to local bishops in AD 490, 492 and 493. The cave is entered through a pair of bronze doors made in Constantinople in 1076 and decorated with the numer-

TIP

From Vieste you can
catch a ferry to the
Tremiti Islands, 40 km
(25 miles) offshore,
which are sparsely
populated but offer
good beaches and
clear water.

ous deeds of the Archangel; brass rings in the doors were supposed to be knocked loudly to wake the Archangel within. This pleasant town also has a fine municipal museum (currently closed, tel: 0884-561150 for latest information) devoted to the popular arts of the Gargano. Particularly interesting are the presses once used to make wine and olive oil, and a stone flour mill originally turned by mules.

Monte Sant'Angelo is a good place to buy components for a picnic lunch in the **Foresta Umbra ❷**, a parkland in the centre of the peninsula where 100-year-old beech, oak and chestnut trees shade winding trails and pleasant picnic spots. From here, you can drive along the coastline to **Vieste ❸**, a bright town on the tip of the promontory containing a castle built by Frederick II. The road continues west along a serpentine coastline studded with beaches and grottoes, passing en route an impressive 20-metre (66-ft) high rock formation known as *Pizzomuno*, referred to by locals as "the top of the world".

Manfredonia ❹, back on the mainland, is a port and beach resort with a pretty historic centre including a castle, begun by Manfred (son of Frederick II) in 1256 and later enlarged by Manfred's enemy, Charles I of Anjou. Near Manfredonia are the beautiful medieval churches of **Santa Maria di Siponto**, with a 5th-century crypt and an altar made from an early Christian sarcophagus, and **San Leonardo**, with a facade guarded by two stone lions. Siponto, once a thriving medieval port, also has good, if crowded, sandy beaches.

Coastal route

The coastal route to Bari is lined with seaport towns, all carrying on a brisk trade in vegetables, fruit and wine. The oldest, most important and, today, least attractive of these is **Barletta ❺**, where Manfred established his court in 1259. Here,

BELOW: Trani's
Duomo.
BELOW RIGHT: Bari.

at the intersection of the corsos Garibaldi and Vittorio Emanuele, stands the intriguing **Colosso**, a 4th-century Byzantine statue thought to represent the Emperor Valentinian I (364–75). Only the head and torso are original; the rest was recast in the 15th century. Behind rises the **Basilica di San Sepolcro**, with a nice Gothic portal and an octagonal cupola reminiscent of Byzantine designs. Barletta's **Duomo** is a confusing edifice built on a Romanesque plan, with five radiating apses in French Gothic style and a Renaissance main portal. By the sea rises Manfred's 13th-century castle, much expanded in later centuries.

Map on pages 320–1

A far more picturesque town, 13 km (8 miles) south of Barletta, is **Trani ❻**, the centre of the local wine trade and fairly prosperous. Its Romanesque cathedral (daily 8am–noon and 5–8pm in summer, reduced hours in winter), founded in 1097 but not completed until the middle of the 13th century, is perhaps the most beautiful church in Apulia. Beneath its richly carved rose window is a smaller window flanked by pillars resting on the backs of elephants. The wonderful bronze doors are the work of the local artist Barisano da Trani, who is also responsible for the celebrated doors on the cathedral at Ravello. The interior of the church, bright and austere, has the usual three apses and three naves, with triforium arcades above the side-aisles supported, here, by six pairs of columns on either side. Steps descend to the underground church of **Santa Maria della Scala** and the crypt. Even further down is the underground **Ipogeo di San Leucio**, 1.5 metres (5 ft) below sea level, containing two primitive but delightful frescoes.

TIP

When in Bari, be sure to try the local ear-shaped pasta – *orecchiette*. Apulian cuisine is simple but delicious, making use of local tomatoes, wine and oil.

Windy Bari

Ancient **Bari ❼**, founded by the Greeks and developed by the Romans as an important trading centre, was destroyed by William the Bad in 1156 and restored by William the Good in 1169. Today it is the largest and most important commercial centre in Apulia. The city is divided into two distinct parts, the intriguing Città Vecchia, situated at the end of Corso Cavour, with its tight tangle of medieval streets and dazzling white houses, and the Città Nuova, the modern city, with wide grid-like boulevards. The tortuous alleyways of the Moorish-style old city protected the inhabitants from the wind and from invaders.

BELOW: in the old city of Bari.

The church of **San Nicola** was founded in 1087 to contain the relics of St Nicholas, patron saint of Russia, stolen from Myra in Asia Minor by 47 sailors from Bari. Its facade bears many resemblances to the facade of the cathedral at Trani, though it is even plainer. A small round window (oculus) crowns three bifora windows, a monofora window, and a richly carved portal flanked by columns borne by a pair of time-worn bulls.

The interior of the church is best visited in the evening, when sun shoots through the windows of the facade, creating unusual lighting effects on the three great transverse arches (structural additions of 1451). Among the many noteworthy objects in this church are the beautiful column capitals of the choir screen separating the nave from the apse, and the *ciborium* (freestanding canopy) over the high altar, dating from the early 12th century. Behind the *ciborium* is the church's best-known work of art, an 11th-century episcopal throne supported by three grotesque telamones. To the left is a Renaissance altarpiece,

Window of the Castel del Monte.

BELOW: the Duomo (cathedral) in Bitonto.

Madonna and Four Saints, by the Venetian Bartolomeo Vivarini. The crypt contains the precious relics of St Nicholas, said to exude a wonder-working oil and visited by pilgrims for centuries. The Byzantine icon of St Nicholas in the central apse of the crypt was presented to the church by the King of Serbia in 1319.

Bari's **Duomo**, a short walk west of San Nicola, was erected between 1170 and 1178 over the remains of a Byzantine church destroyed by William the Bad during his rampage through the city in 1156. Basilican in plan, the church follows San Nicola in most details of its design, with deep arcades along both flanks and a false wall at the rear that masks the protrusions of the three semi-circular apses. A particularly fine window adorns the rear facade.

Nearby, off the Piazza Federico II di Svevia, is the **Castello** (Tues–Sat 9.30am–1pm and 3.30–7pm, Sun 9.30am–1pm; entrance fee), built in Norman times, refurbished by Frederick II, and considerably enlarged by Isabella of Aragon in the 16th century.

Bari's **Pinacoteca Provinciale** (Mon–Sat 9.30am–1pm and 4–7pm; entrance fee), containing paintings from the 11th century to the present, is in the Città Nuova, along the Lungomare Nazario Sauro. The best painting is undoubtedly Bartolomeo Vivarini's *Annunciation* in Room II. Further rooms contain Giambellino's startling *San Pietro Martire* and a number of works by Neapolitan baroque painters including Antonio Vaccaro and the prolific Luca Giordano. Francesco Netti, the Italian impressionist, a native son of Bari, is also represented and there is a new collection of contemporary art. Bari's small but worthwhile **Museo Archaeologico** (closed for restoration; due to re-open by 2006), in the Piazza Umberto I, has a rich collection of Attic black- and red-figure vases.

Around Bari

An interesting one-day excursion into Apulia's architectural past begins 18 km (11 miles) west of Bari in the olive-oil centre of **Bitonto** ❽, whose famous cathedral, built between 1175 and 1200, represents perhaps the most complete expression of the Apulian Romanesque. The beautiful facade has a rose window and an elegantly carved portal, flanked by the usual lions. The pelican above the doorway is a symbol of Christ – in medieval times, the pelican was thought to peck at its own flesh to feed its young. Bitonto has an attractive historic quarter, and is worth an excursion from Bari.

The town of **Ruvo di Puglia** ❾, 18 km (11 miles) further west, was known as Rubi in Roman times, when it was famous for its ceramics. The 13th-century **Duomo** was widened in the 17th century to provide room for baroque side-chapels and, though restorations have shrunk the interior's width back to its original Romanesque proportions, the wide facade retains its baroque girth, giving the church a somewhat squat appearance. Fortunately, the medieval sculpture on the facade largely remains; the seated figure at the top is thought to represent the ubiquitous Frederick II. Beneath the nearby **Chiesa del Purgatorio** lie some Roman remains. Ruvo's excellent **Museo Archeologico Jatta** (daily 8.30am–1.30pm, and Fri–Sun 2.30–7.30pm; free) is devoted to Rubian ceramics excavated from nearby necropoli and dating from the 5th to the 3rd century BC.

On a hilltop 30 km (19 miles) west of Ruvo stands the **Castel del Monte** (daily 10am–1.30pm and 2.30–7.30pm in summer, 9am–6.30pm in winter; entrance fee), often cited, as is the Colosseum in Rome, as a supreme example of the architectural aims of an age. The eight-sided building has two storeys and eight Gothic towers; curiously enough, the main entrance is adorned with a Roman triumphal arch. Historians differ as to whether Frederick II erected the small fortress as a hunting lodge or as a military outpost, but all agree that he married his daughter, Violanta, to Riccardo, Count of Caserta, here in 1249. In 1266 the implacable Charles I of Anjou imprisoned the hapless sons of Manfred after their father's tragic defeat – and subsequent suicide – at Benevento. The castle served as a refuge for the noble families of Andria, a nearby town, during the plague of 1665, and was later abandoned, becoming a hideout for brigands and political exiles. Restoration began in 1876. The eerie emptiness of the building is reinforced by its isolated position on a hilltop perch that's visible for miles around.

The town of **Alberobello** , 50 km (32 miles) southeast of Bari, is known for its distinctive peasant dwellings known as *trulli*. Nobody knows the exact origins of these conical white-washed houses (the oldest date back to the 12th century), but they did allow for easy home-extension through the addition of another unit, and modern building in the area is often based on the *trulli* shape. Now many of them have been turned into gift shops or are let to foreigners. South of Alberobello, the pleasant hilltop village of **Locorotondo** is another place to find *trulli*. It is also a good centre for local wines.

The **Grotte di Castellana** (daily 8.30am–7pm, guided tours roughly on the hour; entrance fee) is another of the region's great tourist attractions. The 20-km

Map on pages 320–1

TIP

To stay in a *trullo* in Alberobello, contact Trullidea, a company based in the town (tel: 0039-0804 323860; email: info@trullidea.com).

BELOW: *trulli* farm buildings.

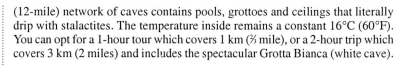

Flamboyant decoration on the facade of Sant'Irene, which also houses one of Lecce's most spectacular baroque altars.

(12-mile) network of caves contains pools, grottoes and ceilings that literally drip with stalactites. The temperature inside remains a constant 16°C (60°F). You can opt for a 1-hour tour which covers 1 km (⅔ mile), or a 2-hour trip which covers 3 km (2 miles) and includes the spectacular Grotta Bianca (white cave).

Spartan Taranto

Taranto ⑫, the ancient Taras founded by Spartan navigators in 706 BC, was in the 4th century BC the largest city in Magna Graecia, boasting a population of 300,000 and a city wall 15 km (9 miles) in circumference. It was, like many towns on this coast, a centre of Pythagorean philosophy and visited by such luminaries as Plato and Aristoxenes (author of the first treatise on music). Today the city, much damaged in World War II, is the home of one of Europe's most important iron works. The old town is effectively an island separated from the modern and industrial quarters by canals.

Taranto's **Museo Nazionale** (closed for restoration, tel: 0994-532112 for latest information), in the modern quarter, is the second most important museum in southern Italy, rivalled only by the Museo Archeologico in Naples for the splendour of its antiquities. The collection includes Greek and Roman sculpture, a series of wonderful Roman floor mosaics and one of the most complete collections of ancient ceramics in Italy. While the museum is being restored, a significant proportion of the collection is temporarily on view at the nearby Palazzo Palanteo (daily 8.30am–7.30pm; entrance fee).

In Taranto's old city is the church of **San Domenico Maggiore**, founded by Frederick II in 1223, rebuilt in 1302 by Giovanni Taurisano, and much altered in baroque times. Nearby, on the Via Cariati, is a lively fish market. Taranto's

Duomo contains fine mosaic floors and antique columns from pagan temples.

For those with the time, a fascinating side trip (21 km/ 13 miles) can be made from Taranto to the nearby town of **Massafra** ⑬, known for its early Christian cave churches hewn into the sides of a deep ravine that snakes through the centre of the town. The Santuario della Madonna della Scala contains a 12th-century *Madonna and Child* fresco. It can be reached via a baroque staircase from the town centre. At the bottom of the ravine is the Farmacia del Mago Gregorio – a maze of caves and tunnels once used by monks as a herb store. Ask in the town about access to these and other cave churches, but avoid visiting in the middle of the day when there will be very few people around.

From Massafra by back roads (37 km/23 miles), or from Taranto by *superstrada* (22 km/14 miles), you can reach **Grottaglie** ⑭, a hilltop town where you can watch Apulian potters make the ceramic pitchers, plates, bowls and cups available in gift shops across the region. The decorative spaghetti plates produced in the town are known throughout Italy.

Baroque Lecce

Lecce ⑮ is known for its profusion of baroque houses and churches. The city owes its appearance to the malleable characteristics of the local sandstone, which is easy to carve when it comes out of the ground but hardens with time. The growth of religious orders, particularly the Franciscans, Jesuits and Theatines, in the 17th and 18th centuries led to intensive building which created an architectural uniformity unique in southern Italy. Churches drip with ornate altars and swirling columns. Outside, shadeless streets meander past curving yellow palaces bright with bursts of bougainvillea.

The heart of Lecce is the cobblestoned **Piazza Sant'Oronzo**. At its centre stands a single Roman column which was stolen from beside its twin in Brindisi. The pair originally marked the southern terminus of the Via Appia from Rome. A bronze statue of St Orontius, patron saint of the city, stands on top of the column. The southern half of the square is dominated by excavations of part of a well-preserved **Roman amphitheatre** (Mon–Fri 10am–1pm, weekends 6–9pm; entrance fee) dating from the 2nd century AD. Discovered in the 1930s, it was re-opened in 2000 as a concert venue, after a six-year restoration. A small museum on the site displays some fine frescoes and mosaics. The unusual Renaissance pavilion used to be the town hall but now houses the tourist information office.

Lecce's harmonious **Piazza del Duomo**, just off the **Corso Vittorio Emanuele**, is framed by the facades of the **Duomo**, the **Palazzo Vescovile** and the **Seminario**, all built or reworked in the 17th century. The Duomo actually has two facades: the lavish one facing the Corso, with its statue of St Orontius, and the more austere (and older) one facing the Palazzo Vescovile. The altars inside the Duomo, carved with flowers, fruit and human figures, are typical of the ornate local style.

Bright basilica

The most complete expression of Leccian baroque is the **Basilica di Santa Croce** (daily 8am–1pm and 4–7.30pm), built in 1549– 1679. Its exuberant facade sports a balcony supported by eight grotesque caryatids. The bright interior has an overall restraint that unifies the different designs of its chapels. A chapel in the left transept contains a series of 12 bas-reliefs showing the life of San Francesco di Paola.

Lecce's modern and informative **Museo Provinciale** (still undergoing lengthy restoration), just outside the old city, is built around a spiral ramp reminiscent of the Guggenheim Museum in New York.

The rewards of travelling in Apulia, as in its neighbours Basilicata and Calabria, include the pleasure of ending the day on a beach. Apulia has the longest coastline in Italy, a fact which has made it peculiarly attractive to foreign invaders, from the ancient worshippers of Zeus to the sun-worshipping visitors of today. Lecce is within easy reach of beaches at **Gallipoli** ⑯ on the Ionian Sea, and **Otranto** ⑰ on the Adriatic. Otranto has the added attraction of a Romanesque cathedral (daily 8am–noon and 3–7pm in summer, 8am–noon and 3–5pm in winter) with an impressive mosaic floor.

In the peace and the wave-song of the pristine Apulian sands, you could lie dreaming for many months, lost in reveries on the passage of so many heroes through these parts, from wily Odysseus to the broadminded, gallant, brooding Frederick II. ❏

Map on pages 320–1

While so much baroque architecture is overblown, "Lecce baroque" is both dazzlingly ornate and exuberant, and at the same time refined. This lovely city is known to many as the "Florence of the South"

BELOW: elaborate figures on the facade of the Basilica di Santa Croce.

CALABRIA AND BASILICATA

Rugged mountains, cave dwellings and ancient
Greek cities combine here with a beautiful
and unspoilt coastline

Map on
pages
320–1

Calabria is closer in spirit than any other region in Italy to the Italy of Byron and Shelley – the land of mouldering ruins that inspired the romantic thoughts of 19th-century travellers. But the region is fast changing. The completion of the *autostrada* from Salerno to Reggio Calabria, governmental support of housing and industry, and vast improvements in the quality of hotels have begun to lure both northern entrepreneurs and foreign tourists to this long-isolated part of Italy. No major city is now without its *Zona Industriale*, no village without its roar of motorcycle engines. But the tourist industry is still in its infancy here. Much of Calabria's heritage lies buried among the roots of the many olive trees.

The landscape of the region is dominated by the backbone of mountains that descends in a series of fantastic foothills to the sea. Only 9 percent of the territory consists of flat land. It was from the sea that Calabria's first invaders, the Greeks, came in the 8th century BC, crossing the Straits of Messina from Sicily.

LEFT: doorway of San Giovanni, in Matera. **BELOW:** one of the Greek bronzes found in the sea in 1972, and now in the museum in Reggio di Calabria.

Spectacular treasure trove

Also from the sea have come the **Bronze Warriors**, Calabria's most celebrated reminder of those early settlers. Discovered by fishermen off Riace in 1972, these two colossal Greek statues, thought to have been lost overboard from a ship sailing between Calabria and Greece 2,000 years ago, are the star attractions in the **Museo Nazionale della Magna Graecia** in **Reggio di Calabria** ⓲ (daily 9am–7.30pm, also late-night openings in summer, closed 1st and 3rd Mon of the month; entrance fee).

The coastline just north of Reggio was first described by Homer in Book XII of the *Odyssey*, the earliest navigational guide to the Tyrrhenian Sea. Here lurked the infamous monster Scylla, whose "six heads like nightmares of ferocity, with triple serried rows of fangs and deep gullets of black death" did away with six of Odysseus's best men. Today the Rock of Scilla provides the foundation for a youth hostel. Modern **Scilla** ⓳ has an excellent view across the Straits of Messina.

Further north, **Palmi** ⓴ is worth visiting for its **ethnographic museum** (Mon–Fri 8am–2pm and 3–6pm, entrance fee), which has an extensive collection of ceramic masks designed to ward off the evil eye, and collections of agricultural and maritime life, music and art, religion and magic. The museum is housed in a modern complex just outside the town.

Tropea ㉑, suspended from a cliff over one of the many fine beaches that line the shore, is perhaps the most picturesque town on the coast. The old town has a beautiful Norman **cathedral** containing, behind the high altar, the *Madonna di Romania*, a portrait that is said to have been painted by St Luke.

Highway ss111 is the loneliest road in Calabria. It

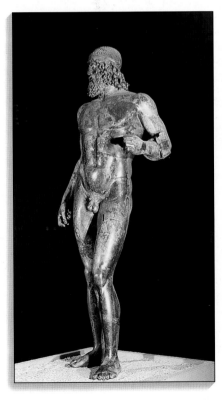

twists across the central mountain chain following what is believed to be an ancient trade route connecting **Gioia Tauro** ㉒ on the Tyrrhenian with **Locri** ㉓ on the Ionian Sea. Fierce brigands once ruled the woods through which it passes. From the **Passo del Mercante** ㉔, the road's highest and loneliest point, both seas are visible. From here the road descends to the beautiful town of **Gerace** ㉕, situated on the hump of a nearly inaccessible crag. It is best to visit Gerace in the evening, and on foot, to appreciate the romantic sunset views from the grassy ruins of its castle. It is said that in the 10th century the city's inhabitants survived an Arab siege by subsisting on ricotta cheese made from mothers' milk.

In still earlier times, a miracle-working saint, San Antonio del Castello, conjured up a spring of pure water in a cave in the cliff that surrounds the castle. The imprint of the saint's knees, they say, can be seen in the floor of the cave.

Gerace is a city of many layers, justifying the phrase, "If you know Gerace, you know Calabria." Its cathedral is the largest in Calabria. It was begun in 1045 on top of an older church – now in the crypt. Both cathedral and crypt contain columns from the Greek settlement at Locri. Some parts of this 7th-century BC town, including walls and temples, can still be seen.

The famous **Cattolica** at **Stilo** ㉖, one of the best-preserved Byzantine churches in existence, is a reminder that in medieval times Calabria's rugged interior was a vibrant religious centre. The tiny 9th-century church, built on a square floor plan with five cylindrical cupolas, clings to the flank of Monte Consolino, just above Stilo, like a miniature castle overlooking its town. Its bright interior is adorned with fragments of frescoes. The four columns supporting the vault are from a pre-Christian temple, but were placed upside-down to symbolise the church's victory over paganism.

Another important religious centre further inland is the Carthusian monastery at **Serra San Bruno** ㉗, where you can visit the Museo della Certosa (Tues–Sun 9am–1pm and 3–8pm in summer; 9.30am–1pm and 3.30–6pm in winter; entrance fee).

In this peaceful sanctuary, reconstructed around the ruins of an abbey destroyed by earthquake in 1783, 16 bearded, white-robed monks live according to the vows of silence, solitude and poverty prescribed by Bruno of Cologne in the 11th century. The monks eat no meat, but make an excellent cheese, which is sold in the town.

Where shepherds wander

Of Calabria's four great mountain clusters – the Aspromonte, the Sila Piccola, the Sila Grande and the Sila Greca – the **Sila Piccola** ㉘, in the middle, has most to offer. Among its dense pine groves and cool meadows shepherd boys still wander with their flocks. The climate up here is refreshing after the dry heat of the coast. The twisty road up from **Catanzaro** ㉙ climbs first to **Taverna** ㉚, a serene town whose name suggests that it was once a way-station. In 1613, the baroque painter Mattia Preti was born here. He left Calabria at the age of 43 to become one of the most influential painters in Naples. The church of **San Domenico**, just off the main square, contains the best of Preti's local work; paintings of his may also be seen in the churches of **Santa Barbara** and **San Martino**.

"Calabria! – No sooner is the word uttered than a new world arises before the mind's eye – torrents, fastness, all the prodigality of mountain scenery – caves, brigands and pointed hats... costumes and character – horrors and magnificence without end."

– EDWARD LEAR

BELOW: the 10th-century Cattolica at Stilo.

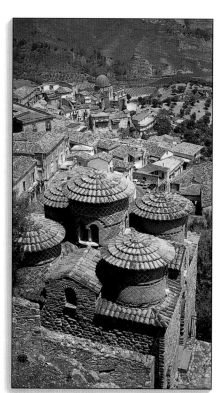

A few "tourist villages" have been developed in the vast pine-covered area of the inner Sila as skiing or fishing centres but they have not altered its sense of isolation. The roads are empty and winding and barred when the snow gets too deep in winter. Even the **Lago Ampollino** ㉛, a man-made lake created in the early 20th century to encourage tourism and produce electricity, lacks the crowds found at even the most remote Italian holiday spots. Here, nature still rules.

San Giovanni in Fiore ㉜, the biggest town in the Sila, is noted for the black and purple costumes of its women. More compelling is the lovely hilltop town of **Santa Severina** ㉝, famed for its medieval scholastic tradition. Attached to the cathedral is an 8th–9th-century Byzantine baptistry built originally as a *martyrium* (a shrine for the sacred relics of honoured members of the local Christian community) when it stood alone. At the entrance to the town, the Byzantine church of **San Filomena** has a cylindrical dome of Armenian inspiration, and three tiny apses that seem to anticipate Romanesque designs. The long central Piazza Vittorio Emanuele leads to the 10th-century castle which is now a school.

The coastal town of **Crotone** ㉞ was founded by Greeks in 710 BC. Here the mystical mathematician Pythagoras came up with his theorem on right-angled triangles and taught the doctrine of *metempsychosis*, in which the soul is conceived as a free agent which, as John Donne later imagined, can as easily attach itself to an elephant as to a mouse before briefly inhabiting the head of a man. Other than these scholarly associations, the modern town on its crowded promontory has little to offer the tourist apart from an interesting **archaeological museum** (daily 9am–7.30pm, closed 1st and last Mon in the month; entrance fee) and an excellent wine from the nearby village of **Melissa** ㉟.

Northern Calabria and Basilicata

The old town of **Cosenza** ㊱ stands on a hilltop surrounded by the flat and sprawling modern city that has grown around it. In the heart of the *centro storico* stands a beautiful Gothic cathedral, consecrated in the presence of Frederick II in 1222. In the **Tesoro dell'Archivescovado** behind the cathedral is a Byzantine reliquary cross that Frederick II donated to the church at the time of its consecration. The partially ruined **Castello** (daily 8am–8pm; free) at the top of the old town has excellent views.

When the travel writer Norman Douglas visited the Albanian village of **San Demetrio Corone** ㊲ in 1911, he was told by the amazed inhabitants that he was the first Englishman ever to have set foot in the town. Although tourists are no longer a rarity in these parts, be prepared for the curious stares of barbers, policemen, shopkeepers and women in bright Albanian dresses. The Albanians first fled to Calabria in 1448 to escape persecution by the Arabs. Today they form the largest ethnic minority in the region. They have their own language, literature and dress, and their own Greek Orthodox bishop. As isolated as San Demetrio is in the backhills of the Sila Greca, this was once one of the most important centres of learning in Calabria, the site of the famous Albanian College where the revolutionary poet Girolamo de Rada taught for many years. Inside the college, the little church of Sant'Adriano contains a Norman font and a wonderful mosaic pavement.

The inimitable Norman Douglas, during his lengthy sojourn in the "flesh-pots of Crotone", speculated that the cows he encountered wandering along the beach might very well be "descendants of the sacred cattle of Hera".

BELOW: mending nets in a fishing village.

Map on pages 320–1

The Tavole Palatine at Metaponto was built in the late 6th century BC. A nearby museum displays vases, coins and jewellery found at the site.

On the Ionian coast, overlooking the sea, stands lonely **Rossano** ❸❽, the most important city of the south between the 8th and 11th centuries. It is home of the famous **Codex Purpureus**, a rare 6th-century Greek manuscript adorned with 16 colourful miniatures drawn from the Gospels and the Old Testament. This extraordinary book can be seen in the **Museo Diocesano** (Tues–Sun 9.30am–12.30pm and 4–7pm; tel: 0983-525263; entrance fee) beside the cathedral. At the top of the greystone town, the five-domed Byzantine church of **San Marco** offers breathtaking view across the valley. Below the old town lies the bustling resort of Rossano Scalo.

Land of poverty and history

Basilicata is the poorest and most underdeveloped region in southern Italy, yet it is a land of considerable historical and sociological interest with a remarkably varied landscape. Its beaches on both the Tyrrhenian and Ionian coasts are among the finest in the south.

Matera ❸❾, the second-largest city after Potenza, presents perhaps the most unsettling example of the clash between the ancient and modern in southern Italy. Until quite recently, people in Matera literally lived in caves. Their rock-cut dwellings, called *sassi* by local inhabitants, date back to Byzantine times when they were built as churches. In later years, many of the churches were converted into homes where humans and livestock crowded together in unsanitary dankness, watched over by Byzantine frescoes painted on the rock. The *sassi* area – now a Unesco World Heritage Site – has recently been developed as a tourist attraction. You can pick up maps and itineraries from the **tourist office** (9 Via de Vitti de Marco; tel: 0835-331983) or book a guide through the

BELOW: Matera.

Cooperativa Amici del Turista (tel: 0835-330301; www.materaturistica.it).

The church of **Santa Lucia**, in the main part of town, contains the two most famous frescoes in Matera, the *Madonna del Latte* and *San Michele Arcangelo e San Gregorio*, both dating from the second half of the 13th century. Nearby, the Apulian Romanesque **Duomo** has a striking rose window.

Venosa ⓴, in northern Basilicata, was the birthplace of Horace, the 1st-century BC Roman poet and satirist. Here lie the remains of **La Trinità**, a Benedictine abbey begun in the 11th century and never completed. The structure, built of stones from an earlier Roman temple on the site, is a topless treasure trove of inscriptions, portals, sarcophagi and frescoes romantically situated in a grassy park, surrounded by olive trees and close to some Roman remains. **Melfi** ㊶, just to the west, has a fine Norman castle containing the **Museo Nazionale del Melfese** (Tues–Sun 9am–8pm, Mon 2–8pm; free) with interesting archaeological finds. It was here that Frederick II promulgated his *Constitutiones Augustales*, the just code of laws for which his regime is still remembered by local inhabitants.

Of the many beautiful coastal towns in Basilicata, **Metaponto** ㊷, on the Ionian sea, is best known, mainly on account of its **Tavole Palatine**, a Doric temple dating from the 6th century BC, with 15 standing columns. The Greek city of Metapontum was founded in the 7th century BC and the excavation site is open to the public.

Over on the Tyrrhenian coast **Maratea** ㊸ rivals Ravello in Campania for its atmospheric streets and breathtaking views over the sea. Maratea in fact comprises several coastal villages dotted along the spectacular, jagged coastline: Porto di Maratea, Fiumicello, Castrocucco and **Acquafredda** ㊹, which has a charming hotel, the Villa Cheta Elite, just above the beach. ❑

Map on pages 320–1

Built into a hillside across the valley from Matera is the church of the Madonna delle Tre Porte, with an exquisite fresco of the Virgin.

BELOW: the Norman castle at Melfi.

SICILY

*The island of Sicily, set in the middle of the Mediterranean
and once the centre of the known world, has the finest array of
Classical and Moorish sites in Italy*

Map on
page
340

Nature and history have made Sicily a land of considerable and striking contrasts. The greatest island in the Mediterranean Sea, Sicily was for centuries the centre of the known world. Its peculiar geographic position – smack in the middle of the Mediterranean – made the island vulnerable to attacks by foreigners, but at the same time a meeting-place of Mediterranean civilisations, a bridge between East and West. Witness the Greek colonisation (8th–3rd century BC), the Arab invasions (9th–10th century) and the Norman domination (11th–12th century). These were Sicily's great epochs, when commercial towns were founded and developed along the coast.

Invaders generally confined themselves to the coast because of the difficult, mountainous terrain inland. Sicily's volcanic features, represented by Mount Etna and the Aeolian Islands, testify to relatively recent geological origins. The island still suffers violent earthquakes occasionally, and intermittent lava flows have made the plain below immensely fertile *(see Italy's Volcanoes on page 348)*.

The reasons for the island's relative state of underdevelopment are rooted in its feudal past. Land in the interior is still organised along semi-feudal lines while industry suffers from mismanagement and Mafia involvement.

PRECEDING PAGES:
the hill-top town of
Calascibetta, in the
centre of the island.
LEFT: Arab-Norman
cloisters at
Monreale.
BELOW: under
the almond trees,
near Etna.

The Ionian coastline

A ferry plies between Villa San Giovanni in Calabria and **Messina ❶** in half an hour. Travellers arriving at Messina are invariably surprised to find themselves in a modern grid-like city with low-rise buildings and wide avenues; the surprise turns to astonishment when they see the wonderful scenery which is offered by the **Peloritani Mountains** that cradle the city.

Although founded in the Classical Age by Greek settlers and developed mostly between the 15th and 17th centuries, Messina has little to show for its ancient origins. On a fateful morning in 1908, terrifying earthquake jolts, followed by a violent seaquake, shook the city and razed it to the ground. Despite this disaster, several fine churches survived, including the **Duomo** and the nearby Orion fountain, by a pupil of Michelangelo, Giovanni Montorsoli. At midday, the astronomical clock of the Duomo's campanile puts on a spectacular show with mythological and religious figures and sound effects such as a cock crowing and a lion's roar.

In the shadow of Etna

After 45 km (28 miles), the road from Messina winds up to a town that is the essence of Sicily. "It is the greatest work of art and nature!" exclaimed Goethe in *Italian Journey*. **Taormina ❷** knows no greys. Its beauty is made up of light, colour and sea. Lying on a short terrace of the coast against a mountain, it slopes down a

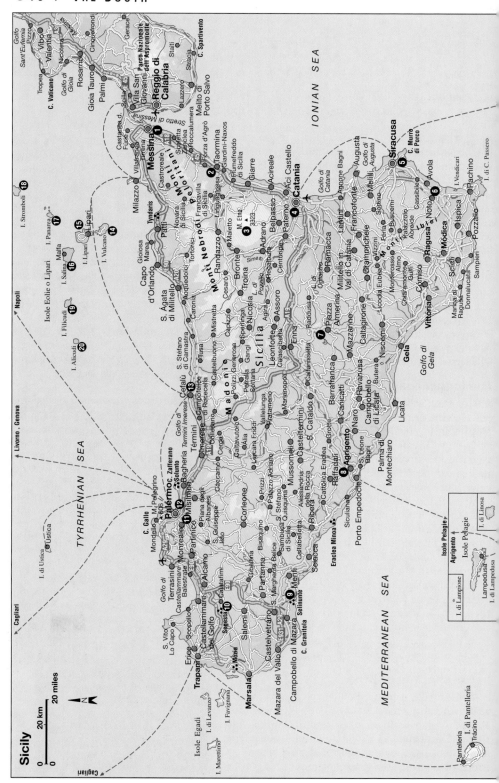

cliff "as if", wrote Guy de Maupassant, "it had rolled down there from the peak." Its shoulders are embraced by the looming Mount Etna.

Climb the hill to the **Greek Theatre** (daily 9am–7pm in summer, till 4pm in winter; entrance fee; also open for summer concerts, opera and drama July–Sept, tickets and information from the tourist office, tel: 0942-23243; www.taormina-arte.com), Taormina's most famous monument, celebrated by many writers for its magnificent position. Built in the 3rd century BC, but completely remodelled by the Romans in the 2nd century AD, it illustrates the Greeks' knack of choosing settings where nature enhances art. The jagged coastline of Taormina is dramatic: outcrops of rocks are intercut by narrow creeks, ravines and inlets.

In town, **Corso Umberto**, which cuts through the old centre, is the place for shopping and people-watching. The bars here are usually packed with an international crowd, but the atmosphere somehow remains that of a village. You can see this village in its churches or in the grand *palazzi* with their mullioned windows, marble tracery, scrolls and billowing balconies. The village atmosphere, however, does not disguise the fact that Taormina is a resort for the well-heeled.

Sicily's smokestack

The landscape south of Taormina is dominated by **Mount Etna ❸**, the majestic volcano (3,323 metres/10,959 ft) with its snow-capped peak. It is one of only a few volcanoes in the world which are active. Its surface is punctuated by about 200 cones, smaller craters, accumulated layers of lava, gashes and valleys. Etna's history is a series of more or less ruinous eruptions, from the one in 396 BC, which halted the Carthaginians, to one in 1981, which destroyed part of the cableway. Even a smaller eruption in 1992 required help from the US marines to staunch the lava flow. The volcano has been in eruptive mode again since 1999 – the last major eruption was in October 2002. What happens next, of course, is as unpredictable as ever. To discuss options of getting close to Mount Etna, usually by the northern route via Linguaglossa, contact Etna Natural Touring (Via Marconi 98, Linguaglossa; tel: 095 643613). For general advice on current conditions and hiking routes visit the Etna Regional Park in Nicolosi (Via Etnea; tel: 095 821111), or visit the information centres in Catania or Taormina.

In the fertile plain stretching from the southern foot of Mount Etna rises the city of **Catania ❹**. It was an important Greek and Roman colony and suffered from the various powers that succeeded in dominating the island. Destroyed twice by violent earthquakes (in 1169 and 1693), the city was covered in 1669 by lava which even advanced into the sea for about 700 metres (2,300 ft).

Catania is the economic centre of the richest area of Sicily: its continuing development is based mainly on citrus fruits, vineyards and market gardening, but commercial and high-tech enterprises also flourish.

Catania has a modern feel, with an urban plan characterised by wide streets designed in the 18th century baroque style. Its main axis is the elegant, austere **Via Etnea**, where people gather for the *passeggiata* and window shopping. But Catania's baroque soul is better tasted in the smaller **Via Crociferi** in which churches and monastic buildings open like wings of a

See map opposite

Traditional puppets of Crusader Knights.

BELOW: grapevine on Etna.

Sicilian bread comes in a variety of shapes.

theatre. The street is covered by a baroque arch leading to **San Benedetto**, a vast yet unfinished Benedictine monastery.

Another landmark in the history of the baroque style is the church of **San Nicolò**, which is reached by following Via Gesuiti. And any visit would be incomplete without seeing **Castello Ursino** (Tues–Sun 9am–noon and 4–7.30pm), erected by Emperor Frederick II (1239–50) and since sympathetically restored. The Swabian castle contains an art museum. You can then rest in the landscaped gardens of **Villa Bellini**.

Town of tyrants

From the wide plain of Catania head for **Syracuse ❺** (Siracusa) through landscapes of classical beauty, counterpointed by archaeological remains. Built in 734 BC by a group of Corinthian farmers who settled on the small isle of **Ortigia**, Syracuse developed so rapidly that in a short time it was establishing new colonies along the Sicilian coast. In 485 BC, when it had developed into a prosperous town, it was conquered by the tyrant Gelon. Syracuse then enjoyed its greatest political, economic and artistic magnificence, becoming one of the most important centres of the Mediterranean. It defeated the Carthaginians, Etruscans and even Athenians and eventually it ruled over almost the whole of Sicily. After a short dalliance with democracy, Syracuse flourished under despotism. Dionysius, the city's most enlightened tyrant, presided over Syracuse's golden age.

Great monuments and public works testify to the epoch's glory and wealth. After many years of decay, Syracuse is benefiting from restoration work. Much of Ortigia is under scaffolding, but this much-needed work has brought a new confidence to the city. At the ancient but still lively heart of town, you can admire

BELOW: nuns visiting the archaeological park at Syracuse.

the grandiose **Tempio di Atena** (5th century BC), which later became the **Duomo**.

Leave Ortigia across the **Ponte Nuovo** and head north to **Neapolis** (daily 9am to 2 hrs before sunset; entrance fee), the sprawling archaeological park with the **Teatro Greco**, one of the greatest theatres in the Greek world (spanning 138 metres/ 452 ft in diameter and with a capacity of 15,000 seats). Here, in summer, a series of high-quality classical performances is held; if you buy a ticket, you may end up in the very spot where Plato or Archimedes sat for their night on the town. Call the tourist office for details (tel: 0931-464255).

Nearby lie the **Latomie**, which are ancient honeycombed quarries. Later, these were used as prisons for Athenians sentenced to hard labour. In the **Latomia del Paradiso** there is a man-made cave known as Dionysius's Ear, which has an amazing echo. A whisper is amplified by the walls, a phenomenon that permitted the tyrant Dionysius to eavesdrop on prisoners. If you relish ancient legends, stop at the lively bars by the **Aretusa Fountain** back in Ortigia. According to local lore, the beautiful nymph jumped into the sea in order to escape from the river god Alfeo and was transformed into this spring.

An interesting destination close to Syracuse is the small town of **Noto ⑥**. It stands on a ridge of the **Iblei Mountains**, furrowed by a long and straight road which widens out into wonderful scenes of inclined squares. Here Spanish baroque architecture triumphs in churches, palaces, monasteries and squares, all in a golden-coloured stone. Noto's most interesting vantage point is Piazza Municipio, a baroque square that encompasses a riot of pilasters, adorned windows, loggias, terraces and belltowers. Another highlight is **Palazzo Villadorata**: a facade incorporating Ionic columns and baroque balconies awash with lions, cherubs, medusae and monsters.

Map on page 340

The original town of Noto was destroyed by an earthquake in 1693. A Spanish-Sicilian noble, Giuseppe Lanza, was put in charge of the rebuilding, and he decided to start the town afresh, 16 km (10 miles) further south.

BELOW: mosaics from the Villa Romana del Casale in Piazza Armerina.

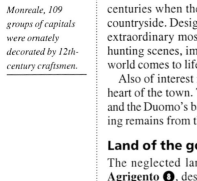

At the cloisters in Monreale, 109 groups of capitals were ornately decorated by 12th-century craftsmen.

BELOW: the Tempio della Concordia at Agrigento.

Sicily's harsh and imposing heart

From the coast, an excursion leads through the bare interior, with its reddish sulphur mines, vivid vegetation and little villages clustered on hills. One hill-top town is **Piazza Armerina ❼**, famous for the **Villa Romana del Casale** (daily 8am–6.30pm; entrance fee), an imperial mansion or grand hunting lodge outside the town. This is a complex construction, built between the 3rd and 4th centuries when the great noble families of the Roman Empire relaxed in the countryside. Designated a Unesco World Heritage Site, the villa has a series of extraordinary mosaics, the work of African and Sicilian artists, representing hunting scenes, imaginary creatures, and natural landscapes; an entire ancient world comes to life before your eyes. This is Sicily's greatest Roman wonder.

Also of interest is the baroque **Duomo**, crowning a terraced hill back in the heart of the town. Theatrical staircases also accentuate the spacious belvedere and the Duomo's baroque facade. A Catalan-Gothic campanile with blind arcading remains from the original church and sets the tone for the lavish interior.

Land of the gods

The neglected landscapes of the mining area lead to the solar beauty of **Agrigento ❽**, described by the Greek poet Pindar as "the most beautiful city of mortals." The symbol of the city is a group of magnificent temples occupying a valley. The origins of Agrigento (Akragas to the Greeks) date from 581 BC. The 5th century marked the apogee of the town, and it was then that the main temples were erected. The town was later conquered by the Carthaginians and the Romans. Its importance diminished under the successive Byzantine and Arab dominations, but grew again with the arrival of the Normans. The classical city, **Valle dei Templi** (Valley of the Temples; main zone daily 8.30am–1 hr before sunset; entrance fee) comprises magnificent temples and tombs. The finest are: Tempio di Giove (Olympian Zeus), the largest Doric temple ever known; Tempio di Giunone (Juno/Hera), which commands a view of the valley; and Tempio della Concordia, one of the best-preserved temples in the world despite the present need for some scaffolding. Opposite the Temple of Olympian Zeus is the newlyrestored Kolymbetra Mediterranean garden.

The splendid temples of **Selinunte ❾** (daily 9am–7pm, till 4pm in winter; entrance fee) can be seen from afar, on a promontory between a river and a plain in the middle of a gulf with no name. Selinunte looks like a puzzle made of stone pieces: divided columns, chipped capitals, and white and grey cubes are all heaped together, as if a giant hand had mixed the pieces to make the reassembling of the original image more difficult. However, the stones speak volumes, revealing libraries, warehouses, courthouses, temples – all testifying to a prosperous ancient town in the middle of fertile lands. Amid the stones grows *selinon*, the wild parsley which gave its name to the powerful Greek colony.

Selinunte was destroyed in its attempt to expand at the expense of Segesta: in 409 BC, 16,000 citizens of Selinunte were slain by their Carthaginian rivals. To complete the plunge into the past, go to the rival **Segesta ❿** (daily 9am–7pm in summer, till 4pm in winter; entrance fee). In spite of the frequent devastations of wars between the Greeks and the Carthaginians, an imposing Doric **temple** has survived. It stands on the side of an arid and wind-beaten hill and is propped up by 36 columns. Further up is the **theatre** (Teatro), constructed in the 3rd century AD over the top of Mount Barbaro and from which stretches a splendid view over the **Gulf of Castellammare**; during July and August there are open-air performances.

Map on page 340

The Conca d'Oro

Enclosed by a chain of mountains, the Conca d'Oro, an evergreen valley that widens as it approaches the sea, is still irrigated and cultivated according to old custom. The valley is dominated by **Monreale** ⓫, which was founded in the 11th century around the famous Benedictine abbey bearing the same name.

Next to the monastery is the **cathedral** (daily 8am–6pm; chapel and terraces closed noon–3pm), a masterpiece of 12th-century Norman architecture. The church owes its fame to the mosaics, made by Byzantine and Venetian artists and craftsmen. The mosaics illustrate biblical scenes, from the Creation to the

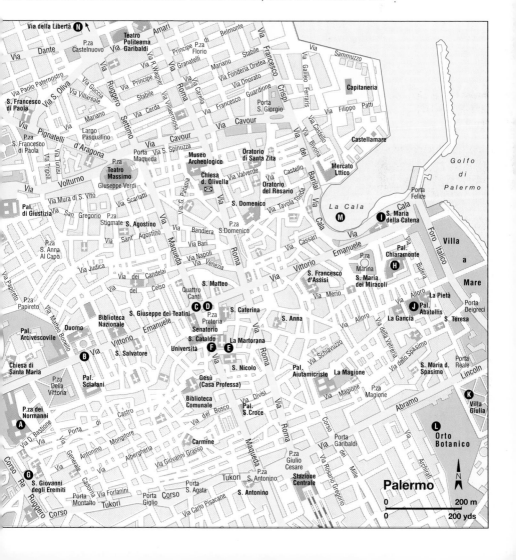

Apostles, in a golden splendour which fades away into grey, giving a tone of "sad brightness" summed up by the gesture and glance of the huge Pantocrator (Almighty). To pass from the cathedral to the cloister is to move from the East to the West. Here, the beauty lies in the 109 groups of capitals whose sculptures show an unusual freedom in execution, typical of the Romanesque style.

After admiring the view of the Conca d'Oro from the church's terraces (180 steps), proceed to **Palermo** ⓬, chief town and port of Sicily, at the bottom of a wide bay enclosed to the south by Capo Zafferano and to the north by Mount Pellegrino, which Goethe described as "the most beautiful promontory in the world."

Discovering Palermo

The puppet theatre in Sicily goes back centuries, re-telling the story of the battles between Charlemagne's knights (the Paladins) and the Saracen invaders.

The best place to start an itinerary is from the **Palazzo dei Normanni** Ⓐ, the splendid Norman palace and seat of the Sicilian parliament (also known as the Palazzo Reale). Inside are the **Cappella Palatina** (Mon–Fri 9–11.45am and 3–4.45pm, Sat 9am–noon, Sun 9–10am and noon–1pm; free) and the **Sala di Re Ruggero** (guided tours available; enquire at Cappella Palatina), featuring glittering chambers enlivened with mosaics of Eastern influence. From there, follow the city's oldest thoroughfare, the **Via Vittorio Emanuele** Ⓑ. This street leads down to the **Quattro Canti** Ⓒ, a busy crossroads in the centre of the old town, cut by **Via Maqueda**, the other axis of Palermo. Here the baroque dominates in four monuments decorated with fountains and statues. Another beautiful 16th-century fountain stands in nearby **Piazza Pretoria** Ⓓ. Once nicknamed the Piazza Vergogna (Square of Shame), due to its saucy nudes cavorting in its fountain, the Piazza Pretoria celebrated the 500th anniversary of this sculptural masterpiece by unveiling the restored fountain in 2004. In Piazza Magione, the

BELOW: in the gardens of Villa Giulia.

Cistercian church, **La Magione**, has been restored. Near to the Vucciria market, the **Oratorio di Santa Zita** is due to re-open after restoration in December 2004, while the nearby **Oratorio del Rosario di San Domenico** is scheduled to re-open in 2005.

A few more steps lead to the Norman age, when Palermo was defined by the geographer Idrisi as the "town which turns the head of those who look at it." Here are two churches: the **Martorana** Ⓔ, decorated with Byzantine mosaics, and **San Cataldo** Ⓕ, which preserves three red Moorish domes. The nuns of the church of Martorana are famous for inventing *pasta reale,* the popular marzipan fruit-shaped sweets.

Between Via Maqueda and the Palazzo dei Normanni extends the **Albergheria Quarter**. In spite of the desolation, it is still possible to discover old Palermo near the lively **Ballarò market** in the quarter's centre. Isolated by an oasis of green is the small church of **San Giovanni degli Eremiti** Ⓖ (daily 9am–6.30pm, closed Sun afternoon), a masterpiece of medieval architecture. Its five Moorish domes recall the 500 mosques that once dotted the town, as described by the traveller Ibn Hawqal in the 10th century. The dilapidated southeastern quarter of the old town, called the **Kalsa**, is at the heart of an urban regeneration programme. A witness to its turbulent history is the splendid 14th-century **Palazzo Chiaramonte** Ⓗ (not open to the public), a Catalan-Gothic fortress which became the headquarters of the Inquisition in the 17th century. Nearby in the ancient harbour, the church of **Santa Maria della Catena ❶** is a synthesis of Gothic and Renaissance art. Via Alloro, the hub of the quarter, contains Sicily's most important art gallery in the imposing **Palazzo Abatellis ❿**. The **Galleria Regionale della Sicilia** (daily 9am–2pm, until 1pm on Sun; Tues–Thur also 2.30–7.30pm; entrance fee) has a collection of medieval paintings.

Stroll in the park of **Villa Giulia ⓚ**, a typical Italian garden, planted in 1777 with rigorous symmetry. Close by is the **Orto Botanico ⓛ** (Mon–Fri 9am–6pm, Sat–Sun 8.30am–1.30pm; entrance fee), among whose exotic plants and rare trees Goethe loved to rest. You can then continue along the **Foro Italico**, an esplanade leading to the **Cala ⓜ**, the old port. Although it no longer functions as a port, the Cala remains a picturesque shelter for gaily coloured fishing boats. Today's city centre is in **Via Ruggero Settimo** and the first part of the bland **Viale della Libertà ⓝ**. Here are the most elegant shops, several bookstores and cinemas. Palermo's picturesque side is still visible in the food market of the **Vucciria** and in the **Castello di Zisa** in the suburbs (Mon–Fri 9am–6.30pm, Sat–Sun 9am–1pm; entrance fee), built in 1160 by William I, which recalls the time when Palermo was virtually the centre of the known world.

Along the Tyrrhenian coast

Along the intense blue Tyrrhenian Sea the road is bordered by flowers and luxuriant citrus and olive groves. The winding road offers glimpses of **Cefalù ⓭**. A panoramic view of the town, possible only from the sea, is extraordinary: a little town clinging to a promontory at the foot of an enormous rock and, to the west, a beautiful sandy beach crowded with bathers and flanked by hotels. Cefalù's fame lies in its medieval charm and great Norman cathedral.

Aeolian Islands (Isole Eolie)

The Sicilian experience should end with a taste of adventure. The best place for this is an archipelago of seven little isles emerging in the **Golfo di Patti** off the north coast of Sicily: the **Aeolian Islands**, a name alluding to Aeolus who, in Greek mythology, is the god of the winds. **Vulcano ⓮**, the first stop for the ferry, offers yellow sulphurous baths and volcanic craters. **Lípari ⓯**, the largest and most populated island, is the most complex geologically and the richest historically. Its pumice beach has the only white sand in the whole archipelago. **Salina ⓰**, the highest and the greenest, is topped by two symmetrical volcanos.

The smallest and most exclusive island is **Panarea ⓱**. With its little white houses framed by luxuriant vegetation, it is a refuge for rich tourists and luxury yachts. **Stromboli ⓲**, the "black giant", has just two villages separated by burning lava flows. Like Etna, it is constantly active and rumblings can be heard at between 5- and 25-minute intervals.

The visitor to **Filicudi ⓳** and **Alicudi ⓴** has to forget modern comforts, for there is no running water on these islands. Despite such inconvenience, they are a paradise not only for divers and marine-life enthusiasts but also for people who love peace and solitude. ❑

Maps on pages 340 & 345

In April 2006, after more than 40 years eluding the Italian police, Italy's most wanted man, mafia "boss of bosses", Bernardo Provenzano, was arrested near his home town of Corleone.

BELOW: a freshly caught swordfish in Lípari.

THE LIVING EARTH: ITALY'S VOLCANOES

Bubbling, seething and angry, or silent, solemn and threatening, Italy's volcanoes dictate the way of life of those in their shadow

The area from the island of Sicily north to Campania on the Italian mainland is notoriously unstable geologically. Here, the earth's crust continues to suffer earthquakes, changes in land levels and volcanic activity. From Vesuvius brooding over the Bay of Naples to imperious, seething Etna on Sicily, Italian volcanoes have shaped the way of life for local people for centuries. The destruction and devastation that has followed major eruptions has on the one hand caused trepidation and exodus but, on the other, has offered long-term compensation in the legacy of fertile soil enriched with volcanic extract.

SPREADING THE WORD

The fame of Italy's volcanoes owes much to its classical writers. Virgil and Pliny the Younger both described the might of volcanic activity in the region. Pliny, in particular, left us a detailed account of the eruption of Vesuvius in AD 79 which saw the death of his uncle, Pliny the Elder, and destroyed the towns of Herculaneum and Pompeii. In turn, Vesuvian mud and ash has preserved for us a unique picture of life in Roman times *(see page 314).*

▽ VOLCANIC ISLES

Stromboli, one of the volcanic Aeolian (or Lípari) Islands northeast of Sicily, was believed by the ancient Greeks to be the home of Aeolus, the god of wind. The waters around these islands are enriched with minerals and are known for their curative properties, making them popular with bathers.

△ THE TOURIST TRAIL

Volcano tourism really began in the 19th century when Vesuvius, then Etna *(above)* became part of the traveller's itinerary. Sedan chairs or donkey-power was used to convey lazy visitors to the top, and wily, business-minded local guides led the way.

▷ FIRE PREVENTION

Vesuvius, although officially "active", has not shown any major activity since 1944. Etna, however, remains a constant threat. In 2001 lava flows reached the nearby town of Nicolosi and in 2002 the volcano was awakened again by earthquakes.

▷ MUD, GLORIOUS MUD

The seas around the Aeolian Islands can be radioactive and in places are warmed by underwater jets of steam. Sulphurous mud pools are sought out for the treatment of rheumatism. The island of Lípari also has the notable hot springs of San Calogero, where the water temperature rises to over 60°C (140°F).

◁ KEEP YOUR DISTANCE
Etna is Europe's largest active volcano and Italy's highest mountain outside the Alps. Though it is prone to eruption, and the area around the main crater is now out of bounds, it is possible to climb – providing common sense and local advice are heeded. Wear warm clothing and strong shoes.

△ ROCKY RAVINE
Etna's Valle del Bovo (Valley of the Ox) is a bleak, rocky chasm, 5 km (3 miles) wide, on the mountain's eastern face. It was created by a volcanic explosion and pot holes still puff out plumes of smoke. Geologists marvel at the clear stratification of rock forms in the valley walls.

RIVERS OF FIRE
vesome rivers of fire like s lava flow on Etna reveal raw power of volcanoes d the wonder they have uced over the centuries. In *Spéronare*, Alexandre mas described Etna's mmense crater, roaring, full flames and smoke; heaven ove one's head, hell neath one's feet."

THE MIGHT AND POWER OF GODS

The power of Italy's active volcanoes is a phenomenon which defied explanation in ancient times. The Romans attributed the fiery convulsions to Vulcan, the god of fire and metal-working, whom they believed lived deep beneath the island of Vulcano in the Aeolian Islands. In addition, the poet Virgil told of the giant Enceladus who, he declared, was interred below Mount Etna, his groanings and rumblings accounting for the earth-shaking, violent eruptions.

Early Christians, too, saw divine activity in volcanic outbursts. In the year 253, the mere production of the veil covering the tomb of the recently martyred St Agatha was said to have staunched the lava flow from Etna that threatened to envelop Catania and its people. Even in relatively modern times, the citizens of Naples have been quick to turn to their patron saint, Januarius, for help whenever Vesuvius has begun to belch smoke.

However, some observers over the centuries have been more pragmatic about the causes of volcanic activity. One anonymous Roman poet suggested that the phenomenon was wind induced: "It is the winds which arouse all these forces of havoc: the rocks which they have massed thickly together they whirl in eddying storm ..."

ITALY
●Rome

SARDINIA

*Seven thousand prehistoric stone towers, countless
beaches and more sheep than people make Sardinia the
perfect place to get away from it all*

BELOW: Cala di
Volpe, a luxury hotel
in the form of a
medieval castle.

ardinia has little in common with the rest of Italy. The Mediterranean's
second-largest island offers a restricted diet of art and architecture; rather,
its appeal lies in its beaches and rugged landscape. Much of its 1,600-km
(1,000-mile) coastline is given over to duney sands and romantic coves nestling
in pine and juniper woods. Much of its interior, where sheep outnumber humans,
is wild and mountainous, and covered in a knotty carpet of herby, shrubby *macchia*. Even the island's cuisine is different from the mainland's. Here, robust,
country fare comes in the form of *pecorino* cheese made from ewes' milk, roast
lamb and suckling pig, *seadas* or cheese pastries served with honey, and *carta
da musica* – crisp, wafer-thin bread said to resemble sheets of music.

Most holidaymakers come for stay-put beach holidays. Many base themselves
in the purpose-built, ritzy resorts that has put the island on the tourist map, but
there are more down-to-earth alternatives. The large distances involved and the
paucity of sights make Sardinia less than ideal for a touring holiday. There are,
however, some unique attractions, notably the intriguing remnants of the prehistoric, nuraghic civilisation: an astonishing 7,000 stone towers, or *nuraghi*,
which from a distance look like giant dung heaps, litter the countryside.

Lying within Gallura, the sparsely inhabited northeastern region of Sardinia where pinky, granite rocks tower like castles over swathes of *macchia* and juniper, cork and oak woods, is the **Costa Smeralda ❶**, or Emerald Coast. In the early 1960s, the Aga Khan and associates bought up this impossibly picturesque little piece of coastline – a mere 10 km (6 miles) end to end by road – and turned it into a hedonistic bolthole, now the flagship of the island's tourism. Development is rigorously controlled. Virtually every hotel and apartment complex comes in regulation "Mediterranean" style, with pantiled roofs, and pink and russet walls, distressed to give the appearance of age.

Even if you can't afford to partake in the jet-set lifestyle, it makes great spectator sport. Head for **Porto Cervo**, the only resort where Armani and Versace boutiques compete for attention with extravagant yachts, and **Cala di Volpe**, half Moorish castle, half rustic homestead and the most stylish of the hotels. Many of the gorgeous coves are inaccessible, but you can wander through groves to those on the Cappriccioli peninsula. Impressive **Cala Liscia Ruja**, just south, is the area's biggest beach. The resort of **Baia Sardinia**, just north of the Costa Smeralda proper, is equally contrived, but far less pretentious and more affordable.

Much of the rest of the Galluran coastline is being spoilt by the onset of ranks of apartments and self-catering villages. This is true of scruffy **Palau**, the departure point for ferries to **La Maddalena ❷**, part of the Maddalena archipelago. The island is a NATO military zone but there is public access to good beaches, and it is connected to **Caprera ❸**, where you can visit the house in which Garibaldi spent his last years. Back on the mainland, **Santa Teresa di Gallura ❹** is a study in pink, and there are a couple of great sandy beaches at nearby **Capo Testa**, fringed by bizarre rocks the size of houses.

Alghero

Northwestern Sardinia is a more benign, softer region than the northeast, with sandy strands cupped in pine woods. But its big draw is **Alghero ❺**, the only resort on the island which has genuine character and history: in the 14th century, the port was occupied by Catalans, and street names are still written in that language.

Its old centre, half surrounded by medieval walls, could hardly be more entrancing: cobbled lanes are lined with high-sided, shuttered buildings dripping in peeling stucco and washing. The best beach in the vicinity is **Spiaggia di Maria Pia**, and there is a popular boat trip across the bay to the **Grotta di Nettuno ❻**, a cave system at the foot of a towering, tilted cliff with memorable rock formations. Untouristy **Sassari ❼**, a 45-minute drive inland, is Sardinia's second city, which has enjoyably earthy backstreets between the overblown, neo-Gothic **Piazza d'Italia** and the baroque-fronted cathedral; and a large **archaeology museum** (Tues–Sun 9am–8pm; entrance fee), which, after Cagliari's, is the best place to immerse yourself in the nuraghic culture.

Sardinia's dramatic interior – with imposing tablelands, pine woods, massive walls and granite amphi-theatres – is the historic, cultural and geographic heart of the island. Here, safely sheltered from foreign invaders, a population of shepherds developed a fierce and isolated society.

Map on page 352

TIP

Alghero is arguably the best place on the island for fresh seafood. Stop at the market in Via Sassari for lobster, sea urchins and squid, or try the local restaurants.

BELOW: oleanders and *macchia* in the Monti del Gennargentu, south of Nuoro.

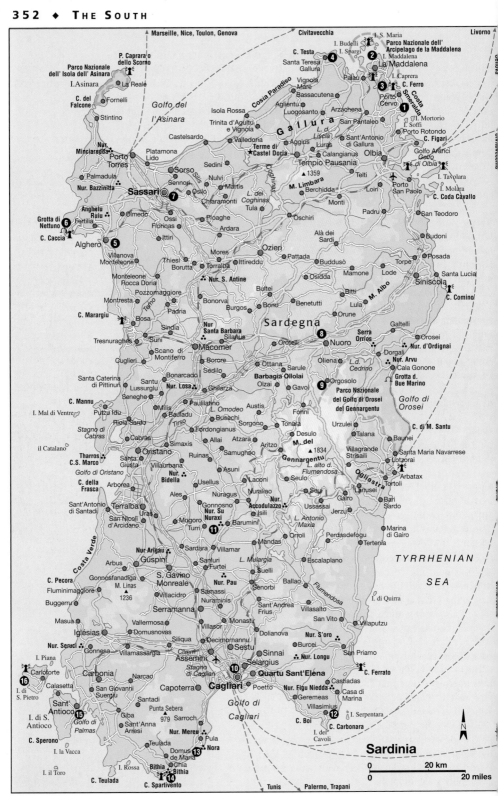

Sardinia

There are no urban centres of interest – **Nuoro ❽**, the area's capital, is only worth visiting for its folklife museum, the **Museo della Vita e delle Tradizioni Sarde** (Tues–Sat 9am–8pm in summer, 9am–1pm and 3–7pm in winter; entrance fee). Immediately south is the most accessible part of the region, where vineyards and olive groves are intensively cultivated across the hillsides. Many visitors end up at the **Hotel Su Gologone** near Oliena, which lays on superb Sardinian cooking and guided expeditions into the mountains. Just down the road lies unwelcoming but fascinating **Orgosolo ❾**, once the Barbagia's "bandit capital", where politicised, anti-capitalist murals cover much of the wallspace along its high street. The long lonely drive south on the SS125, which clings unnervingly to mountainsides from Dorgali to Arbatax and beyond, is the island's most exhilarating.

The south

Cagliari ❿, the island's hectic capital, is rewarding if you ignore the traffic-ridden port and climb up into **Castello**, the medieval centre where steep, gloomily atmospheric streets lie within 13th-century walls and towers. The cathedral, a hotchpotch of styles, and a Roman amphitheatre are outshone by the **Museo Archeologico Nazionale** (Tues–Sun 9am–8pm; entrance fee), famous for exquisite bronze statuettes and votive boats from the nuraghic culture.

An hour's drive north, skirting the fertile **Campidano** plain, brings you to the island's most impressive *nuraghe*, **Su Nuraxi ⓫** (open daily 9am–8pm; entrance fee) at Barumini. Dating from the 13th–16th century BC, the colossal fortification is made up of beautifully formed beehive-shaped rooms; the maze of low stone walls at its base was once a dependent village.

The coastal road east from Cagliari leads to enormous tranches of the finest sand in the island's isolated southeastern corner. However, **Villasimius ⓬** and the **Costa Rei**, the unfancy resorts that have grown up around them, are rather characterless, comprising mainly campsites and self-catering complexes.

The gentle, pine-clad coastline southwest from Cagliari, scattered with holiday homes and a few smart hotels, is more interesting. Punic and Roman **Nora ⓭** (open daily 9am–7pm; entrance fee) is Sardinia's most extensive classical site, with clearly defined houses and mosaics and a temple and small theatre. Equally rewarding is the waterside location, on a little peninsula next to a long curve of sand. Many of the finds from Nora are housed in the **Museo Archeologico** (daily 9am–8pm, till midnight in Aug; entrance fee) in nearby **Pula**. A few miles south lies the **Forte Village**, a luxurious, beautifully landscaped and family-orientated complex where the service runs to flower petals being placed in bedroom lavatory bowls. It sits next to a good beach, but the area's best is at **Chia ⓮**, backed by hillock-high dunes. The drive beyond along the **Costa del Sud** passes craggy headlands and azure waters in deep inlets on its way to **Sant'Antíoco ⓯**. Linked to the mainland by an ancient causeway, the island's eponymous town has Christian catacombs under its main church.

Ferries run to **San Pietro ⓰**, known for the bloody *mattanza* in early summer, when schools of tuna are slaughtered en masse. ❑

See map opposite

Traditional folk costume can often be seen at festivals.

BELOW: the sandy beach at Nora. **OVERLEAF:** door of San Zeno, Verona.

INSIGHT GUIDES
Travel Tips

In this ever changing world,
Singapore Girl, you're a great way to fly.

SINGAPORE
AIRLINES

A STAR ALLIANCE MEMBER

singaporeair.c

BANGKOK · TOKYO · AMSTERDAM · AUCKLAND · NEW DELHI · LOS ANGELES · OVER 55 MAJOR CI

CONTENTS

Getting Acquainted

The Place

Area 301,164 sq. km/ 116,280 sq. miles
Capital Rome
Highest Mountain Mont Blanc (4,760 metres/15,617 ft)
Principal rivers Po, Tiber, Arno and Volturno
Population approx. 58 million
Language Italian
Religion Roman Catholic
Time Zone Central European Time (GMT plus 1 hour, EST plus 6 hours: add one hour in summer)
Currency The euro (€)
Weights & Measures Metric
Electricity 220 volts – you will need an adaptor to operate British three-pin appliances and a transformer to use 100–120 volt appliances
International Dialling Code +39

Climate

There are three main kinds of climate affecting Italy:
● In the mountainous areas (Alps and Apennines), winters are typically long and cold, and summers are short and cool. Even for summer visits, you are advised to bring sweaters and light boots.
● In the Pianura Padana region (around Milan), the climate is characterised by foggy winters and hot, humid summers.
● In the rest of Italy, winters are fairly mild, and hot, dry summers are tempered by sea-breezes (more along the Tyrrhenian coastline than the Adriatic). Summers can be torrid in the south and on the islands.

Geography

The Alps form a natural boundary between Italy and Austria, France and Switzerland. Further south, running at a right-angle to the Alps and heading right down the country, are the Apennines. Between the two is the fertile Po valley, where most of the country's cereals are grown. Below the Alps are the Italian Lakes, notably Maggiore, Lugano and Como. The landscape is not without drama: there are four active volcanoes including Etna, near Catania on Sicily, and Vesuvius, on the Gulf of Naples. The islands of Sicily and Sardinia both feature largely mountainous terrain.

Government

Italy is a republic headed by a president who is elected by Parliament for a term of seven years. Parliament is composed of two houses: the Senate (with 315 members) and the Chamber of Deputies (comprising 630 members). The president nominates the prime minister and, on the prime minister's recommendations, the Cabinet.

After a period of constitutional corruption in the early 1990s, Italy reduced its dependence on proportional representation and moved towards a "first-past-the-post" system, more in line with the British or French electoral systems. Under the new system, the country elected its first left-wing government, a loose centre-left coalition (known as l'Ulivo), in 1996, which remained in place until recently. The government was headed by Romano Prodi, who then moved to Brussels; his successor was the former Communist, Massimo d'Alema. Following the collapse of this loose left-wing coalition, a technocratic administration run by Massimo d'Amato was put in place until the general elections in May 2001. They resulted in a clear swing to the right and the election of the "House of Freedom" coalition led by Silvio Berlusconi (a party which includes Umberto Bossi's Separatist

Population

About 58 million people live in this democratic republic. Parliament and government are based in Rome, the capital and largest city (pop. around 3 million). The second-largest city is Milan (pop. just over 1.5 million), the third largest is Naples (pop. 1 million) and the fourth largest is Turin (pop. about 1 million).

Northern League). The individual regions tend to have strong political affiliations, with the north influenced by a Federalist agenda, the centre and certain major cities historically left-wing, and the south in a transitional phase, though traditionally more right-wing. However, even Italy is breaking the mould of traditional political affiliations, particularly at a local level. Bologna has returned to its traditional left-wing roots and is governed by former trade union leader, Sergio Cofferati. Likewise, despite a right-wing government, both the region of Lazio and the city of Rome are in left-wing hands. Since 2001, Rome has been run by Walter Veltroni who served in Romano Prodi's left-wing government.

In the south, several remarkable city mayors enjoy considerable local support, particularly in the cities of Catania, Naples and Palermo. These mayors are well attuned to the local mood, responding to the public's insistence on probity. The re-awakening of civic duty is matched by a new political commitment to take care of the city heritage.

In 2004 Romano Prodi returned to Italian frontline politics as the national leader of the left, and in the 2006 elections dethroned Berlusconi as Italian prime minister by the narrowest of margins.

Economy

As a general rule, traditional industry (cars, electrical goods, the manufacture of white goods, chemicals, sulphur, mercury, iron and steel) is concentrated in northern Italy, while agriculture is based mostly in the south. However, each region makes its own mark using its own local skills. Turin is synonymous with Fiat and car-making, while the Veneto is home to the clothing manufacturer Benetton and to Italy's sunglasses industry. Milan is the centre of the Italian design industry and rivals Paris as the fashion capital of Europe. (Italy is Europe's foremost producer of designer clothes and silk garments.)

The country also has a long tradition of craftsmanship, witnessed by the prestige of Murano glass from Venice, Como silk from the lakeside region near Milan, Tuscan leatherware and marbled paper, Sicilian ceramics and Piedmontese textiles. Carrara marble, from a mountainous patch of Tuscany, is famous throughout the world.

As for agriculture, each region has its specialities, whether Parma ham and Parmesan from Emilia or olive oil from Liguria and Tuscany – note that Italy is the main producer of olive oil in the world. Wine-making is a major industry across the country: the north produces crisp Friuli wines and full-bodied Trentino reds as well as the Piedmontese heavyweights of Bardolino and Barolo. The Veneto, Emilia, Tuscany and Sicily have fine wine-making traditions, to name but a few sound wine-producing regions. In recent years, good wine-makers in the south have greatly improved the overall quality of Italian wine.

No simple solution has yet been found to the struggling economy of the south and its huge levels of unemployment, institutionalised corruption and inefficiency, but none of these flaws is genetic. Recently, economic inroads have been made, with beacons in the form of Catania, which is developing a high-profile, high-tech industry and operating an intelligent approach to tourism by promoting active holidays around the currently very active Mt Etna.

Planning the Trip

What to Wear

Although the Italians are known for their sense of style, this does not mean that one should always dress formally in Italy. However, when sightseeing, both men and women are advised to cover their shoulders and avoid wearing shorts (or short skirts in the case of women), as some churches bar visitors who are deemed unsuitably dressed. Unless you are visiting mountain areas, the moderate climate makes heavy clothing unnecessary in summer. A light jacket should be adequate for summer evenings. In winter (November–March), the climate can be cold and wet throughout Italy.

Visas & Passports

EU citizens do not need a visa or a passport to enter Italy: an identification card valid for foreign travel is sufficient.

Visitors from the following countries need a passport but are exempt from needing a visa providing they do not stay for more than three months: Australia, Austria, Barbados, Canada, Iceland, Jamaica, Japan, Kenya, South Korea, Kuwait, Malaysia, Maldives, Malta, Mexico, Monaco, New Zealand, Nigeria, Norway, Paraguay, Poland (for a stay up to 30 days), Singapore, Switzerland, Trinidad and Tobago, United States, Uruguay and Venezuela (up to 60 days). Other nationalities should contact their nearest Italian consulate for information on entry regulations.

You are supposed to register with the police within three days of arriving in Italy. In fact, this procedure will be taken care of by

Customs

Used personal effects may be imported and exported into Italy without formality. Importing narcotics, weapons and pirated materials is forbidden. Alcoholic drinks, tobacco and perfume may be imported in limited quantities, depending on your nationality.

Goods on which duty has already been paid in another EU country may be freely imported, provided the amount falls within what might be reasonably described as "for personal use", for example for a wedding or family party.

However, the recommended allowances for each person over 18 years of age are still given. They are as follows:
• 10 litres spirits or strong liqueurs over 22 percent vol.
• 20 litres fortified wine
• 90 litres wine (of which no more than 60 litres may be sparkling)
• 200 cigars
• 400 cigarillos
• 3,200 cigarettes
• 110 litres beer
• 3 kilos tobacco

If you are any in doubt about what you can bring back, check with your local customs office. In the **UK**, contact HM Revenue & Customs, Dorset House, Stamford Street, London SE1 9NG (tel: 0845 010 9000) or log onto www.hmrc.gov.uk

For **US** citizens, the duty-free allowance is: 200 cigarettes, 50 cigars or 3 lb tobacco; 1 US quart of alcoholic beverages and duty-free gifts worth up to $100.

your hotel, whatever the level of accommodation. If you are not staying in a hotel, theoretically you should contact the local police station, but virtually no one does.

Foreign Consulates

The following consulates and embassies are all based in Rome but employees there can put you in

Animal Quarantine

Pets must be vaccinated against rabies and you should obtain an officially stamped document stating that your animal is healthy no more than one month before you arrive in Italy.

touch with other consulates (eg, in Milan or Venice), should one of those be more convenient. Generally, appointments are necessary, so always ring before visiting. (Remember to dial the Rome code, even if calling from within Rome.)
Australia: tel: 06-852721 (emergencies, toll-free: 880877780)
Canada: tel: 06-445981 (24-hour emergency service)
France: tel: 06-68806437
Germany: tel: 06-492131
Great Britain: tel: 06-42202600
Ireland: tel: 06-6979121
New Zealand: tel: 06-4417171
United States: tel: 06-46741

Money Matters

The currency in Italy is the euro (€), which is available in 500, 200, 100, 50, 20, 10 and 5 euro notes, and 2 euro, 1 euro, 50 cent, 20 cent, 10 cent, 5 cent, 2 cent and 1 cent coins. There are 100 cents to one euro.

Italy is a society that prefers cash to credit cards, except for large purchases, or, for instance, hotel bills. In the case of modest restaurants and smaller shops, it is usual to pay in cash. Check beforehand if there is any doubt. Most shopkeepers and restaurateurs will not change money, so it is best to change a limited amount at the airport when you arrive, especially if it is the weekend, when banks are closed. Try to avoid changing money in hotels, where the commission tends to be higher than in banks.

Travellers' cheques are still recommended in Italy, as they can be replaced if stolen or lost. Note, however, that commission will be charged for changing them.

Banks are generally open 8.30am–1.30pm and for one hour in the afternoon (usually between 3pm and 4pm). Unfortunately, most banks are notoriously inefficient, and currency conversion can easily turn into a tedious saga, so use cashpoints where possible. You can also change money at airports and main railway stations. You will find current exchange rates are published in the press and posted in banks. Rates fluctuate greatly.

Cash Machines & Credit Cards

Given the long queues for money changing in Italy, it is simplest to get cash from cashpoint machines, which are widely available. Most Switch cards work in Italian machines, with your normal PIN number, as do credit cards, though you may sometimes have to look for particular "Bancomats" (cashpoint machines) that take your card.

In cities, many restaurants, hotels, shops and stores will take major credit cards (Visa, American Express, MasterCard and Carte Blanche), but in rural areas, especially, you may be able to pay only in cash.

Public Holidays

- **January** New Year's Day (1)
- **March/April** Good Friday, Easter Monday
- **April** Liberation Day (25)
- **May** Labour Day (1)
- **August** Assumption of the Blessed Virgin Mary (15)
- **November** All Saints' Day (1)
- **December** Immaculate Conception of the Blessed Virgin Mary (8), Christmas Day (25), St Stephen's Day (26)

In addition to these national holidays, almost all cities have a holiday to celebrate their own patron saint, for example St Mark, 25 April (Venice); St John the Baptist, 24 June (Turin, Genoa and Florence); Sts Peter & Paul, 29 June (Rome); St Rosalia, 15 July (Palermo); St Gennaro, 19 September (Naples); St Petronius, 4 October (Bologna); St Ambrose, 7 December (Milan).

Getting There

BY AIR

Low-cost airlines now operate from many of Italy's smaller provincial airports, thus opening up Italian routes to greater competition. In addition to the national airline, Alitalia, many major scheduled airlines fly direct to Italy, as well as charter flights, which tend to offer lower fares, and often fly to more convenient provincial airports. (Alitalia, for instance, only fly directly to Rome or Milan; to reach other Italian destinations, you have to catch a connecting flight.) However, transfers into the nearest town may be less easily available than at the smaller airports, so it might be worth considering hiring a car, especially if arriving late in the evening.

The country has two airports designed for intercontinental flights: Roma Leonardo da Vinci (Fiumicino) and Milano Malpensa 2000.

ROME

Leonardo da Vinci/Fiumicino

Rome's main airport is 35.5 km (22½ miles) southwest of central Rome, and is Europe's fourth-busiest airport. Rome is a good gateway to other destinations, including Naples, the south and even parts of Tuscany. (fast, reliable trains connect the city with Chiusi-Chianciano, for instance.) The airport is served by most major carriers, from Alitalia to British Airways and British Midland.

There is a direct **train service** that runs every 30 minutes (daily from 6am to midnight) between Fiumicino Airport and Termini station. Tickets (around €9.50) are sold at the airport and all counters at the station, as well as from vending machines, and many newsagents. The train journey takes 30 minutes. Another slower local train (around €5) runs roughly every 15 minutes to the stations of Trastevere, Tiburtina and Ostiense, from which taxis, metro and bus services are also available; the journey to Trastevere takes about 20 minutes.

Catching a yellow or white **taxi** with a meter (unofficial taxis can charge extortionate fares and may even be dangerous) from the air-port can be a good alternative to public transport; but do negotiate a fare beforehand. Surcharges are made for luggage and for travel at night and on Sunday, and there is also a special airport supplement. Typical fares are in the region of €45, even more at night.

Roma Ciampino

The low-cost airlines Easyjet and Ryanair are just two of many carriers who fly to Ciampino. At the arrivals hall you can buy a one-way or return ticket for an efficient and private **bus shuttle service** to Via Marsala, near Stazione Termini (for more information see www.terravision.it; tickets can also be bought in advance on line). Alternatively, an

airport bus (COTRAL) goes roughly every 30 minutes from the airport to Anagnina metro station at the end of Linea A. From there, it's 30 minutes to Stazione Termini and the centre of town (trains leave every 5 minutes until 9pm when the metro is replaced by an efficient bus service, see Metro page 367). Bear in mind that buses stop running at 11pm, so late arrivals will need a taxi. **Taxis** are far more convenient and typically cost around €36–40. If you're travelling by **car**, take the GRA ring road, coming off at exit 23 for Rome.

NORTHERN ITALY

Bergamo
Bergamo Airport is small, but convenient for exploring the Lakes, including Lake Iseo and Lake Como, as well as Milan, Mantua and the rest of Lombardy. Among other airlines, Gandals flies here from London City Airport.

Brescia
Brescia airport is very convenient for Lake Garda, Lake Iseo, Verona, the Dolomites and Trentino-Alto Adige and is served by charter flights, including Ryanair (from London-Stansted).

Genoa
Genoa Airport (Genova) is convenient for exploring Genoa and the Ligurian coast. This small airport is served by Ryanair, which runs from London-Stansted and by British Airways from Gatwick.

Milan
Milano Malpensa 2000 Airport.
Milan's intercontinental airport is served by major carriers, from Alitalia to Lufthansa, British Airways, British Midland, Easyjet, BMIBaby and Flybe. The airport is 46 km (28½ miles) from the centre of Milan, which is rather inconvenient.

The **Malpensa Express** runs from the airport's Terminal One to the centre of Milan (Cadorna station, which is on the metro; note that this is different from Stazione Centrale, Milan's main railway station). The

service takes about 50 minutes and operates from 5.30am to 1.30am.

Alternatively, an **Air Pullman** shuttle bus ferries passengers between the airport and the Air Pullman office outside Stazione Centrale. You can buy a ticket (around €8) up to a few minutes before departure from the Air Pullman office. The journey takes approximately 50 minutes and shuttles run every 30 minutes.

For **drivers**, a new link road to central Milan is under construction but in the meantime, follow signs to the A8 Autostrada (motorway) that runs to Milan. A **taxi** to the centre will take about 45 minutes and cost around €80; it's sensible to try and negotiate a price beforehand.

Milano Linate, Milan's other airport, is around 8 km (5 miles) from the centre. International flights are being phased out from Linate, but some carriers continue to use this airport rather than Malpensa, including Easyjet from the UK. The ATM bus 73 runs regularly (5.30am–midnight) in front of the airport (Piazzale del Aeroporto) to its terminus on Piazza San Babila at the corner of Corso Europa. There's also the STAM shuttle to Milan's Stazione Centrale, running about every 30 minutes.

Turin
Turin Airport is small but very handy for exploring the Piedmontese hinterland and the vineyards of Barolo and Bardolino, as well as the Gran Paradiso National Park and even the Valle d'Aosta. The airport is served by British Airways, as well as Ryanair.

Venice
Venice's **Marco Polo Airport** is at Tessera on the mainland 9 km (5.5 miles) north of Venice. The airport is served by major carriers, from Alitalia to British Airways and Easyjet to Volare. To reach Venice there is a **public bus** to Piazzale Roma (30 minutes), a private **land taxi** (20–25 minutes) or the hourly **Alilaguna waterbus**, which crosses the lagoon to Piazza San Marco via the Lido and takes about 75 minutes, depending

on your stop. The waterbus (*vaporetto*) is quicker between 11.30am and 3.30pm and it costs €10; for further details, tel: 041-5416555. The luxury option is to take a private **water-taxi** identifiable by their black-on-yellow numbers; these cost about €85 and carry up to four people with luggage.

Venice/Treviso

Treviso Airport is an alternative for travellers to Venice or the Lakes. Charter flights are available from London-Stansted, and a reliable coach service runs to Venice. When some low-cost airlines (eg Ryanair) refer to "Venice airport", they actually mean Treviso airport.

Verona

Verona Airport is probably the most convenient for the Lakes or the Veneto region. Charter flights arrive from cities including London, Paris and Frankfurt, and British Airways also flies here. Again, there is often confusion about which airport is correct for Verona. Ryanair's "Verona airport" is actually Brescia airport.

CENTRAL ITALY

Ancona

Ancona Airport is small but convenient for exploring the Marche region, as well as parts of Tuscany, Emilia and Umbria. Ryanair flies here from London-Stansted.

Bologna

Bologna Marconi Airport is handily placed for exploring Emilia Romagna, or even travelling on to Florence and Tuscany. The airport is served by Alitalia and British Airways. A **shuttle-bus** service called Aerobus goes to the city centre and takes 20 minutes; a **taxi** takes 15 minutes but it will cost around three times as much as the bus.

Bologna's second airport at **Forlì**, 60km (38 miles) south of the city, is served by Ryanair. Forlì is convenient for exploring the southern "Romagna" part of the region and the Adriatic beaches.

Florence

Peretola-Florence, is 4 km (2 miles) northwest of the city centre. Some international flights land here, but these tend to be more expensive than flights to Pisa *(see below)*. From the UK, Meridiana flies regularly to Florence.

Parma

Parma Airport is small but a handy alternative to Bologna for exploring Emilia Romagna. Ryanair has introduced a new service.

Pescara

Pescara Airport is served by Ryanair and is a good option for exploring the lesser known central regions of Abruzzo and Molise.

Pisa

Galileo Galilei Airport is the more usual airport for international visitors to Florence, although Bologna provides an acceptable alternative *(see above)*. Pisa airport is served by charter and scheduled airlines, including Ryanair, Mytravelite, BMIBaby and British Airways. **Trains** to Florence (hourly; journey time: about one hour) leave from just outside the airport.

Rimini

Rimini Airport is small but handy for exploring the Adriatic Coast and the rest of Emilia Romagna. Mytravelite flies from Birmingham and Volare from Luton.

SOUTHERN ITALY

Bari and Brindisi

Both city airports are handy for exploring Italy's heel – the regions of Puglia and Basilicata. Alitalia, British Airways and Ryanair all operate services to Bari, and Brindisi is served by Ryanair.

Calabria

Calabria's Lamezia Airport may be in the middle of nowhere, but it's convenient for the north coast of Sicily, since you can catch the ferry at the port of Villa San Giovanni (every half hour until 10pm, then

hourly throughout the night) to Messina. Cheap carriers, such as Ryanair, offer incredible savings on standard fares.

Naples

Naples Airport is served by major carriers from Alitalia to British Airways and Easyjet. The airport **bus** stops outside the terminal every hour and takes just 20 minutes to reach Piazza Municipio in Naples. A **taxi** takes the same time and costs about €20 – make sure that the meter has been turned on before the journey begins. For **drivers**, the Autostrada A2 exits into the Naples bypass *(tangenziale)*, which is also a toll road.

Sardinia

Cagliari-Elmas is the main airport on Sardinia, but there are also airports at **Olbia** (the airport for the famous Costa Smeralda) and **Alghero**. Ryanair flies to Alghero from London-Stansted. Meridiana flies to Sardinia (Olbia) via Florence, while Alitalia also runs regular flights.

Sicily

Palermo's Punta Raisi Airport is 32 km (20 miles) west of Palermo. The airport is served by major carriers and charters, from Alitalia to Meridiana and Air Sicilia. Scheduled flights involve a change at Milan or Rome, but many charter flights are direct and save time. The airport is small but convenient for Palermo and Sicily's north and west coasts.

Fontanarossa Airport, Sicily's other main base, is 7 km (4 miles) southwest of Catania and is served by such carriers as Alitalia, Air Malta and British Airways, as well as a large number of charters. This airport too is small but it's handy for Sicily's east and south coasts, from Taormina to Siracusa.

BY CAR

When calculating the cost of travelling to Italy by car, allow for the price of motorway tolls as well as accommodation en route and petrol. A number of new motorways have

Car Trains

The following rail services will transport cars to Italy:
- Paris–Milan
- Boulogne–Lille–Milan
- Schaerbeek (Brussels)–Milan
- Hertogenbosch (Holland)–Domodossola–Genoa–Milan
- Hertogenbosch–Chiasso–Milan
- Düsseldorf–Cologne–Milan–Genoa
- Hamburg–Hanover–Verona
- Munich–Rimini
- Düsseldorf–Cologne–Bolzano
- Vienna–Venice
- Boulogne–Bologna
- Boulogne–Rome
- Boulogne–Alessandria
- Boulogne–Livorno

been built in recent years, including one on the north coast of Sicily and others around Milan. The most heavily tolled motorway is the one along the Ligurian coast.

The usual route from France is via the Mont Blanc Tunnel (between Chamonix and Courmayeur) or from Switzerland through the Gran San Bernardo Tunnel (between Bourg St Pierre and Aosta). Some of the many Alpine passes are seasonal, so it is best to check with the tourist board or a motoring organisation before setting off.

To take your car into Italy, you will need a valid driving licence (with an Italian translation if it's not the standard EU licence), the vehicle registration document (which must be in the driver's name or be supported by the owner's written permission for the driver to use the vehicle) and Green Card insurance. You must carry a warning triangle in case of breakdown. Most petrol stations accept credit cards, as do toll booths, but cash is always most welcome, especially in the south.

BY COACH

The cost of travelling to Italy from Great Britain by scheduled coach is not much cheaper than travelling by air. National Express Eurolines runs coaches from London Victoria, via Paris and Mont Blanc, to Aosta, Turin, Genoa, Milan, Venice, Bologna, Florence and Rome.
To book from London, contact: National Express Eurolines, Victoria Coach Station, Buckingham Palace Road, London SW1; tel: 0870-514 3219; www.eurolines.com

BY RAIL

Rail travel is slow and not particularly cheap (except Inter-Rail, which provides a month's unlimited rail travel in Europe for anyone under 26 at a very reasonable price), but it can be a very attractive way to travel, especially if you are planning to stop off en route. The journey from the UK is quicker now that the Eurostar service exists. From Great Britain the usual route when travelling to Rome, for example, is via Paris, where you change trains (from Gare du Nord to Gare de Lyon). Arriving in Rome's Termini station is a pleasure after its impressive restoration, and the station has both left-luggage lockers and a left-luggage office.

ES (Eurostar), IC (Inter City) and EN (Euronight) trains are top-of-the-range trains running between the main Italian and European cities. A special supplement is charged and seat reservation is obligatory.

For train information, call the same number from anywhere in Italy: 147-888 088. The Italian rail system is operated by Trenitalia. (www.trentialia.it).

The Rail Pass, Family Card and Kilometric Card (which allows one or more people to travel a specified number of kilometres at a special rate) can be purchased at any major train station in Italy. The fastest trains operate on the networks between the major cities while the regional trains are fairly slow:

Be aware that once you have purchased your ticket you must stamp it before entering the train in one of the special machines that can be found on station concourses and platforms. Failure to do so will result in a fine.

Practical Tips

Business Hours

Shops are open 9am–12.30pm and 3.30pm or 4pm–7.30 or 8pm. In areas serving tourists, hours are generally longer than these, for instance in Taormina, Venice and popular towns in Tuscany, many shops remain open on Sunday, while elsewhere almost everything is closed on that day. Shops often also close on Monday (sometimes in the morning only) and some shut on Saturday.

Tipping

It is customary to tip various people for their services, especially in restaurants and hotels, although Italians don't always adhere to this practice. Most restaurants continue to impose an outdated cover and bread charge (coperto and pane) of around €5, although it has "officially" been eliminated in most cities. Often, in addition, a 10 percent service charge is added to the bill. If the menu says that service is included, a small extra tip is discretionary. If service is not included, it is usual to leave 12 to 15 percent of the bill.

Media

The Italian press is concentrated in Milan and Rome. The biggest papers are La Repubblica and Il Corriere della Sera, which publish regional editions. Il Mattino is the main newspaper for Naples, while Il Giornale della Sicilia and La Sicilia are widely read in Sicily. However, Il Corriere dello Sport, the pink sports paper, is probably the one you will notice most.

It is worth buying the local newspaper for entertainment listings and bus and ferry timetables. Most major cities publish weekly listings magazines: *Roma C'e*, which has a section in English at the back, is a guide to everything going on in Rome and is available from newsstands every Thursday. *La Repubblica* also publishes *Trovaroma*, a what's-on section, every Thursday and *Enjoy Rome* is a similar publication. Listings magazines for Milan include the monthly *Milano Mese*.

Television stations include RAI (the national network with three channels, which is due to be privatised), the Vatican network, plus various privately owned national channels, and over 450 local commercial stations. Many European channels and the US channel CNN are available by cable.

Postal Services

Some post offices open from 8am–1.30pm only, but many towns have a main post office that is open throughout the day. The post office can provide such services as *raccomandata* (registered post), *espresso* (express post) and telegrams. Stamps can also be bought at tobacconists *(tabacchi)*.

You can receive mail addressed to *Posta Restante*, from the *Fermo Posta* window of the main post office in every town, picking it up personally with identification. However, Internet cafés are now a more popular way for travellers to keep in touch.

Telephones

Public telephones are widespread, particularly in major cities – Rome even introduced a new-style telephone box for Holy (Jubilee) Year 2000. Most accept phonecards *(carte telefoniche* or *schede telefoniche)*, available from tobacconists or post offices; few telephones accept coins. From post offices and some bars you can call *scatti* (ring first, pay later).

You can also make calls using a British BT chargecard or one of the

Area Codes

When dialling numbers either inside or outside your area in Italy, dialling must always be preceded by the area code, including the zero. Area codes of some of the main cities are:

Bologna	051	**Palermo**	091
Florence	055	**Pisa**	050
Genoa	010	**Rome**	06
Milan	02	**Turin**	011
Naples	081	**Venice**	041

To call abroad from Italy, dial 00, followed by:
Australia.............................61
Canada 1
Ireland..............................353
New Zealand.........................64
UK 44
USA 1
Then dial the number, omitting the initial "0" if there is one.

cards issued by AT&T, Sprint, NCI and other North American long-distance telephone companies. This allows more flexibility by charging the calls to your home address.

The cheapest time for long-distance calls is between 10pm and 8am Monday to Saturday, and all day Sunday.

For directory enquiries dial 12. For international enquiries, call 176 and to make a reverse-charge (collect) call, dial 170.

Italy has an extremely high ownership of mobile phones and in the major cities, such as Rome, Milan, Venice and Florence, it is possible to hire one.

Security & Crime

Throughout Italy, Jubilee Year (2000) sparked an increased police presence and therefore brought greater security for visitors than in the 1990s. Rome, in particular, has benefited from increased police presence. As for the north, Venice is generally the safest city in Italy. Milan now has a heavy police presence at Stazione Centrale, the main train station and traditionally one of the most crime-prone areas in the city.

Semi-official vigilante groups of Guardian Angels also act discreetly in dodgy areas of the city. Crime campaigns, increased civic pride, and the greater number of bars and restaurants in southern cities have also helped reduce crime.

Although violent crime is rare, many offences in the north have recently tended to be gang- or drug-related, with an increase in crimes committed by or on immigrants or refugees. With rising numbers of people entering Italy, the harassment of foreigners (essentially from former Yugoslavia, Eastern Europe, Albania or Africa) is unfortunately on the increase in a country that is traditionally unused to dealing with incomers. Terrorism resurfaced in the form of bomb blasts in Milan, Florence and Rome in the early 1990s, but the situation is relatively calm at the moment.

The main problem for tourists is petty crime – pick-pocketing, bag-snatching and theft from cars; it is wise to have insurance coverage against this and to take basic, sensible precautions against theft. Always lock your car and never leave luggage, cameras or other valuables inside. This applies particularly in major cities, and in the south. If walking, especially at night, in the tiny alleys of historic city centres of, for example, Bari, Genoa or Palermo, try to blend in and avoid wearing flashy jewellery that may attract attention.

If you are the victim of a crime (or suffer a loss) and wish to claim against your insurance, it is essential to make a report at the nearest police station and get documentation to support your claim. If you need a policeman, dial **113** (**112** for the *Carabinieri*, a national police force).

Useful & Emergency Numbers

General Emergency Assistance and police: 113 (24-hour service)
Caribinieri **(Police):** 112
Fire Brigade: 115
Medical assistance, ambulance: 118
Breakdown service: 803116

Route information; motorway tolls; weather forecasts: 1518
Train information: 892021
International operator assistance: 170

Health

To receive free treatment in cases of illness, accident or childbirth, EU citizens (and citizens of countries with other ties to Italy, such as Brazil, Monaco and the former Yugoslavia), should obtain form E111 before leaving home. However, this will not entitle you to repatriation in the event of serious illness. Citizens of non-EU countries must pay for medical assistance and medicine. Health insurance is recommended, and you should keep receipts for medical expenses if you want to claim. Most hospitals have a 24-hour emergency department (*Pronto Soccorso*) but a stay in an Italian hospital can be a grim experience, particularly in the south.

For minor complaints, seek out a *farmacia* (signs have a red cross in a white circle). Normal opening hours are 9am–1pm and 4–7.30 or 8pm, but outside these hours the address of the nearest *farmacia* on duty is posted in the window.

Women Travelling Alone

The difficulties encountered by women travelling in Italy are often overstated, but women – especially young blondes – usually have to put up with much male attention. Though often annoying, it is rarely dangerous, but take particular care in Genoa, Bari, Naples, Palermo and Catania. Ignoring whistles and questions is the best way to get rid of unwanted attention, and the less you look like a tourist, the fewer problems you will get.

Tourist Information

REGIONS & PROVINCES

Administratively, most of Italy is divided into regions *(regioni)* such as Tuscany and Sicily, then into provinces *(provincie)*. Certain regions, such as Sardinia and Sicily, are autonomous.

Every major town has an **Azienda Provinciale per il Turismo (APT)**, possibly with subsidiary IAT offices. As well as helpful information, main APT offices should offer a free city map, a hotel list and information about museums. The tourist offices in the main cities are listed below.

As another source of information, major cities have a **Touring Club Italiano** (TCI) office, which provides free information about points of interest. Telephone numbers are listed in the local telephone book. The club also produces some good maps and food and wine guides.

ITALIAN STATE TOURIST BOARD

The Italian State Tourist Board, known as ENIT (Ente Nazionale per il Turismo), provides general tourist information. ENIT's headquarters are in Via Marghera 2/6 Rome (tel: 06-4971222).

In the UK, ENIT, 1 Princes Street, London W1R 8AY; tel: 020-7408 1254; fax: 020-7493 6695, www.enit.it.

In the US, ENIT, Suite 1565, 630 Fifth Avenue, New York, NY 10111; tel: 212-245 4822/212-245 5633; fax: 212-586 9249, www.italiantourism.com. There are also offices in Chicago, Los Angeles and Canada.

KEY ITALIAN TOURIST OFFICES

Arezzo: APT Arezzo, Piazza della Repubblica 28; tel: 0575-377678; fax: 0575-20839; www.apt.arezzo.it
Assisi: APT Assisi, Piazza del Comune 12; tel: 075-812450; www.bellaumbria.net/assisi.
Bergamo: APT del Bergamasco, Viale V Emanuele 20; tel: 035-213185/210204; fax: 035-230184; www.apt.bergamo.it

Bologna: APT Bologna, Via De' Castagnoli 3; tel: 051-218756/7; www.provincia.bologna.it
APT Bologna, Piazza Maggiore 1e, Palazzo del Podestà, Bologna; tel: 051-246541; fax: 051-6393171; www.comune.bologna.it
Bolzano (Bozen): APT Bolzano, Piazza Walther 8, Alto Adige; tel: 0471-307000; fax: 0471-980128; www.sudtirol.com/bolzano.
Capri: APT Capri, Piazza Umberto I; tel: 081-8370686; www.capri.it.
Catania: AAPIT Provincia di Catania and Acireale, Via Cimarosa 10–12; tel: 095-7306211/7306222; fax: 095-7306233; www.apt.catania.it
Genoa: Aeroporto C. Colombo; tel: 010-6015247; Stazione Principe, Piazza Acqua Verde; tel: 010-2462633; www.apt. genova.it.
Ferry Terminal; tel: 010-2463686.
Elba: APT Elba; Calata Italia 26, Portoferraio; tel: 0565-914671; fax: 0565-914672; www.aptelba.it.

The Lakes

Lake Como (Lago di Como):
IAT **Bellagio:** Piazza Mazzini, Bellagio, Lombardy; tel: 031-950204.
IAT **Como:** Piazza Cavour 17, Como; tel: 031-269712.
APT del Comasco (Como area): tel: 031-3300111; fax: 031-261152; lakecomo@tin.it; www.lakecomo.org.
Main APT Lake Garda: Via Roma 8 Gardone Riviera, tel: 0365-290411; fax: 0365-290025; www.lagodigarda.it
Lake Garda (Lago di Garda):
APT Desenzano, Via Porto Vechia 34, Desenzano; tel: 030-914 1510.
APT Riva del Garda: Giardini di Porta Orientale 8, Riva, Trentino; tel: 0464-554444.
APT Sirmione, Viale Marconi 8, Sirmione, Lombardy; tel: 030-916114.
Navigation on Lake Garda: tel: 030-9149511; freephone number: 800-551 801.
Lake Iseo (Lago d'Iseo):
APT Iseo, Lungolago Marconi 2, Iseo, Lombardy; tel: 030-980209.
Navigation on Lake Iseo: tel: 035-971483; freephone: 800-551 801.

Lake Maggiore (Lago Maggiore):
Navigation on Lake Maggiore:
tel: 0322-2332000; freephone
number: 800-551 801
Stresa: Piazza Marconi 16 (near the
Navigazione Lago Maggiore ticket
office) tel: 0323-30150; fax: 0323-
31308
Verbania: Corso Zanitello 6/8; tel:
0323-503249; fax: 0323-556669;
www.lagomaggiore.it

Milan

APT Milano, Via Marconi 1 (by the
Duomo); tel: 02-725243; fax: 02-
72524301
IAT Milano, Via Marconi 1 (by the
Duomo): tel: switchboard: 02-
72524300; fax: 02-72524350);
IAT Stazione Centrale
(tourist office in Milan's central
railway station): 02-72524360/
72524301.
www.milanoinfotourist.com

Naples

APT, Palazzo Reale, Piazza
Plebiscito tel: 081-2525711;
fax: 081-418619
www.inaples.it
EPT Napoli, Piazza Del Gesù Nuovo;
tel: 081-5523328;

email: ept@netgroup.it; open
Mon–Sat 9am–8pm; Sunday
9am–3pm.
Stazione Centrale (Naples' main
train station): tel: 081-20 6666.
Orvieto: APT Orvieto, Piazza Duomo
24, Orvieto; tel: 07633-41772; fax:
07633-44433; info@iat.orvieto.tr.it.
Padua: Padua APT, Riviera dei
Mugnai 8; tel: 049-8767911;
fax: 049-650794;
www.padovanet.it
Palermo: Palermo APT, Piazza
Castelnuovo 35;
tel: 091-586122/583847;
fax: 091-586338; www.aapit.pa.it.
Perugia: APT Perugia, Palazzo Dei
Priori, Piazza IV Novembre 3;
tel: 07557-36458.
Pisa APT: Via Pietro Nenni 24;
tel: 050-929777; fax: 050-929764
www.pisa.turismo.toscana.it
Rimini APT: Piazzale F. Fellini 3;
tel: 0541-56902; fax: 0541-56598
www.riminiturismo.it
San Gimignano: Piazza Duomo 1;
tel: 0577-940008; fax: 0577-
940903; www.sangimignano.com
Siena: APT Siena, Piazza del Campo
56; tel: 0577-280551;
fax: 0577-270676; open Mon–Sat
8.30am–1pm, 3–7pm;

closed Saturday afternoon;
aptsiena@turismo.toscana.it;
www.terresiena.it
Siena Hotels Promotion: Piazza
San Domenico; reservation on tel:
0577-288084; fax: 0577-280290;
hotel information, email:
info@hotelsiena.com.
Sorrento: APT Sorrento, Via Luigi
De Maio 35, Sorrento; tel: 081-
8074033; fax: 081-8773397;
www.sorrentotourism.it
Taormina: APT Taormina, Piazza S.
Caterina, Sicily, tel: 0942-23243;
fax: 0942-24941;
www.gate2taormina.com
Trentino: Via Romagnosi 11,
Trento; tel: 0461-839000;
fax: 0461-260245;
www.trentino.to (information in
English)
Trento: APT Trento, Via Manci 2,
Trento; tel: 0461-983880;
fax: 0461-984508.
Turin APT: Piazza Castelli 161;
Torino; tel: 011-535181/535901;
fax: 011-530070;
www.turismotorino.org
Urbino APT: Piazza Rinascimento 1
– 61029 Urbino; tel: 0722-2613;
fax: 0722-2441;
www.comune.urbino.ps.it/turismo

Top Three Tourist Destinations

Rome

APT Rome (main office): Via
Parigi 5; tel: 06-488991;
open Mon–Sat 9am–7pm. There is
also a multi-lingual **tourist call
centre** (tel: 06-82059127) that
operates daily 9am–7.30pm.
Stazione Termini (opposite
platform 4): tel: 06-48906300;
open daily 8am–9pm.
Fiumicino airport (International
Arrivals, Terminal B) open daily
8.15am–7pm.
There are several other tourist info
points around town, all open daily
9.30am–7.30pm.
Piazza dei Cinquecento (opposite
Termini station); **Piazza Pia** (in front
of Castel Sant Angelo); **Piazza del
Tempio della Pace** (on Via dei Fori
Imperiali); **Piazza Sonnino** (in
Trastevere); **Piazza delle Cinque
Lune** (near Piazza Navona).

Florence

APT Florence: Via Manzoni 16; tel:
055-23320; fax: 055-2346286;
apt@firenze.turismo.toscana.it;
info@firenze.turismo.toscana.it;
www.firenze.turismo.toscana.it.
**APT Firenze & Provincia
(Florence & Province):**
Via Cavour 1 (just north of
the Duomo); open weekdays
8.15am–7.15pm; tel: 055-
290832; fax: 055-2760383;
infoturismo@provincia.fi.it.
APT Airport (Vespucci
Peretola): 055-315874.
APT Fiesole (in the hills above
Florence): Via Portigiana 35; tel:
055-598720; fax: 055-598822.
Firenze Comune (Florence Council,
tourism section): tel: 800-055055;
fax: 055-2381226; open weekdays
8.30am–5.30pm, weekends
8.30am–1.45pm. www.comune.fi.it.

Venice

Head office: APT Venice, Castello
4421; tel: 041-529 8711;
fax: 041-523 0399;
www.provincia.venezia.it.
Santa Lucia train station:
tel: 041-5298727; open 8am–7pm
(little literature available but the
staff are helpful).
Lido di Venezia (on the island of
the Lido): Gran Viale S.M.
Elisabetta 6/A; tel: 041-529 8720;
only open from the beginning of
May to the end of October.
Marco Polo Airport: 041-541
5887; open daily 9.30am–7pm.
San Marco, 71F Piazza San Marco;
tel: 041-529 8711; open
9.30am–5pm or later in summer,
until 4.30pm winter.
**Hoteliers freephone number for
bookings in Venice,** tel: 800-843
006 (calls from within Italy only).

Verona: Verona APT, Via degli Alpini 9; tel: 045-8068680; fax: 045-8003638; info@tourism.verona.it www.tourism.verona.it; **Arena di Verona** (for booking opera tickets in the Verona Arena): Piazza Brà 28, Verona; tel: 045-8051811; fax: 045-8005151; Ticket Office, Via Dietro Anfiteatro 6/b, Verona.
Vicenza APT: Piazza Matteotto 5 – Vicenza; tel: 0444-320854; Piazza Duomo 5; tel: 0444-544122; www.ascom.vi.it/aptvicenza

Useful Websites

ROME

Official site of the Rome municipality: www.comune.roma.it
Information on the Vatican museums: www.vatican.va
Cultural information and special events: www.whatsoninrome.com
English-speaking guided tours and walks: www.enjoyrome.com
Museum and cultural listings and news on Rome and Italy (plus classifieds): www.wantedinrome.com

THE NORTH

Venice
Venice water transport (ACTV Venezia): www.actv.it
Clear site in English and Italian.
The City of Venice: www.comune.venezia.it/museicivici
Official site of Comune di Venezia.
La Fenice opera house: www.teatrolafenice.it
Saving Venice (Salviamo Venezia): www.savevenice.org
Venice Carnival (Carnevale di Venezia): www.carnivalofvenice.com
Museums in the Veneto (Musei del Veneto): www2.regione.veneto.it/cultura

Veneto
Padua (Padova) APT : www.turismopadova.it
Arena di Verona: www.arena.it
Verona tourist office (APT Verona): www.verona-apt.net

Consorzio di Verona: www.veronatuttintorno.it
Consortium promoting Verona's churches, hotels and restaurants.
Verona general information: www.turismoverona.it

Milan
La Scala: www.teatroallascala.org
Milan general information: www.milanoinfotourist.com

The Lakes
Lake Garda: www.lagodigarda.it
Trentino: www.trentino.to
Information on the Trentino area of Lake Garda
Turin general information: www.turismotorino.org

CENTRAL ITALY

Emilia Romagna
APT site: www.emiliaromagnaturismo.it

Pisa
Pisa general information: www.pisa.turismo.toscana.it

Florence
The Uffizi Gallery: info@uffizi.firenze.it
E-mail address for booking a precise time-slot in which to visit the gallery.
Agriturismo in Tuscany: www.agriturismo.regione.toscana.it
Official site giving information on rural farm stays in this popular area
Tuscany: general information: www.turismo.toscana.it

Umbria
Umbria general information: www.umbria2000.it
www.umbriaonline.com
Umbria jazz festival: www.umbriajazz.com
Perugia city: www.comune.perugia.it
Perugia province: www.bellaumbria.net/perugia

General Sites

The following is just a selection of the many general sites on Italy that are available on the web :
Database on all Italian cities: www.thecity.it
Culture, tourism and practical information.
Database on all Italian museums: www.museionline.com/ita
Best routes in Italy: www.virgilio.it/mappa
Plan your journey from one Italian destination to another.
Piazze d'Italia: www.mediasoft.it/piazze
Visit different squares in Italy, including virtual tours.

Abruzzo
Abruzzo national park headquarters: www.parcoabruzzo.it
Abruzzo general information: www.terradabruzzo.com

THE SOUTH, SICILY & SARDINIA

Naples
Naples hotels: www.napleshotels.na-it
For details of cumulative card for several museums:
www.napoliartecard.com

Campania
Guide to the island of Capri: www.caprinet.it
On-line magazine on the Campania coast: www.giracostiera.com

Puglia (Apulia) & Calabria
The city of Bari, capital of Puglia: www.barionline.cjb.net
General information.
Calabria's official site: www.it/eng/Regioni/calabria
General Caabrian site: www.madeincalabria.com

Getting Around

Travelling within Italy

Local newspapers offer reasonably trustworthy information on bus, train and ferry timetables, including up-to-date telephone numbers of bus and ferry companies. If you are planning to travel much by train, it's worth buying an *Orario Generale* (General Timetable), an infallible yet inexpensive, source of information. Booking (including train tickets) through a travel agency often proves easier than doing it yourself.

The latest transport novelty in a few Italian city centres is the "Motobeep", an egg-shaped capsule on wheels that is a cross between a covered scooter and a tiny car. (The passenger sits in an covered seat behind the driver, who acts like a tour guide.) Motobeeps are proving popular in Palermo and Rome and are due to be introduced in Naples.

By Air

The major cities – Rome, Milan, Florence, Venice, Naples – and other tourist centres are connected by flights, most provided by Alitalia. Smaller Italian airlines include AirOne, Air Sicilia (for Sicily) and Alisarda (for Sardinia). Flying in Italy is expensive compared to the train but it can be useful for long distances. Discounts are often available if you are prepared to travel on certain days, but these must be booked in Italy. For information, contact your nearest travel agent or Alitalia office. Children under two (accompanied by an adult) get a 90 percent discount, and those between two and 12 get 50 percent off; young travellers of 12–21 years get a 25 percent discount.

By Rail

In general, the cheapest, fastest and most convenient way to travel in Italy is by train. For long distances or major lines, the fast *InterCity (IC), EuroCity (EC)* and *Eurostar (ES)* services (reservations recommended) are well worth the extra cost for comfort and time. The *Pendolino* is the fastest and most comfortable train, and requires a "supplement" *(supplemento)* and a reservation. It is also worth reserving a seat for long journeys as trains tend to be crowded, especially in peak season. Most travel agencies make reservations, along with the stations.

Local trains are called *Regionale, Diretto, Interregionale* and, rather inappropriately, *Espresso* – much slower than you might expect.

Trains are generally cheaper and more convenient than buses – at least on main routes such as Milan–Bologna–Florence–Rome. However, in the south, especially in Sicily, buses are the better option, because many southern trains suffer from a lack of investment, and maintenance, comfort and reliability all suffer. Exceptions to this rule are the fascinating Circumetnea service around Etna and the Naples Circumvesuvio, which is the best way of seeing Pompeii, Herculaneum and other Classical sites.

Significant reductions and special offers are available for groups and young travellers; make enquiries on arrival in Italy.

Train Information

- Train information is available from staff at *Uffici Informazioni* at most major stations.
- For train information anywhere in Italy, tel: **892 021** or **199 166 177** (in Italian). From the UK call Rail Europe on **08705-848848; www.raileurope.co.uk**
- You can also check routes on the official railway website: **www.trenitalia.com**

Train Tickets

Tickets are valid for two months. Passengers must stamp tickets in the station before boarding and if, for some reason, that is not possible, you must find the conductor before he finds you.

By Bus

Each province in Italy has its own inter-city bus company and each company has its own lines. This can lead to some confusion since, particularly in Sicily, the rival firms do not provide information about one another and connections are not always co-ordinated. However, in some areas, such as the south, and if you are going in to the mountains, buses are the best method of travel. The journey from Siena to Florence is also is faster by bus than by train. Some of the main bus companies operating long-distance travel from the principal cities are listed below.

Rome

COTRAL (toll-free information: 800-150008, www.cotralspa.it) covers the region of Lazio efficiently. Buses leave from different metro stations around town.

Milan

Autostradale, Piazzale Castello 1, tel: 02-801161. Services across Lombardy and the Lakes, and to Venice and Turin. The firm uses the fastest motorway routes and also organises guided tours, which can be booked through tourist offices.

Trentino

Atesina, tel: 0461-821000, is a bus company based in Trento; it runs services throughout the province of Trentino and further afield, including abroad.

Alto Adige

SAD, Via Conciapelli 60, Bolzano, tel: 0471-450111, www.sad.it. This company operates services in the province of Bolzano and further afield, including the entire Alto Adige (South Tyrol) Dolomites area.

Florence

Lazzi, Via Mercadante 2, tel: 055-215154, www.lazzi.it. This firm runs services to Tuscany and all over Italy. **Sita**, Viale dei Cadorna 105 (tel: 055-278611). Sita operate services to most of Italy.

Ferries & Hydrofoils

There are daily car-ferry connections between Reggio di Calabria and Sicily, Villa San Giovanni and Sicily, Naples and Sicily; between Civitavecchia and Sardinia, Livorno and Sardinia; and between Naples and the islands of Capri and Ischia. Regular boat services link Genoa, Sardinia, Naples and Sicily and connect the mainland with Italy's many smaller islands. Ferries and hydrofoils also operate between towns and sites on the northern lakes of Como, Garda and Maggiore. For information on timetables and fares, consult a travel agency or the regional tourist office.

In the UK, **SMS Holidays**, 40 Kenway Rd, London SW5 ORA. tel: 020-7244 8422, can make ferry bookings for passengers.

Ferry information can be found online at the following websites:
www.traghetti.com
www.fun.informare.it
www.viamare.com

Inner-city Travel

ROME

Most visitors have to rely on public transport, taxis and their feet to access the centre of Rome, as only residents' cars are allowed there. There is a large underground car park at the foot of the Gianicolo, with space for 800 cars and 200 coaches, so you can park there and take public transport or a taxi into the centre. There are plenty of taxi ranks, or you can call for one on 06-3570, 06-4994 or 06-5551.

The Roman metro covers a limited area but it is efficient. There are also night buses and tourist bus routes. Other options include hiring a Vespa or rollerblades (the latter from Villa Borghese).

Roman Travel

Public transport information: freephone 800-431784.
Train enquiries, tel: 892021.

Buses

Tiburtina station is the main terminus for buses coming or going to places outside Rome and the surrounding Lazio region. To reach the centre from Tiburtina, take metro line B towards Stazione Termini, the main train station.

ATAC/COTRAL bus information is available from the kiosk in Piazza dei Cinquecento in front of Stazione Termini or from tourist offices or tourist information kiosks. Free route maps are available at some of the principal metro stations, such as Ottaviano. Buses run from 5.30am to midnight, after which time there is a night service. Tickets, once validated, are good for 75 minutes on all ATAC (orange, red or green) buses and for one journey on the metro or on some urban railways, excluding Roma-Lido di Ostia, the beach route.

Bus and metro tickets must be validated with a time stamp from the machines at the entrance to the metro and at the rear of buses. Ticket machines are located in every metro station but tickets can also be bought from most tobacconists (marked with a large T outside) or newsagents. A standard single-use ticket (biglietto a tempo) is valid for a journey of up to 75 minutes. A one-day ticket (the Metrebus, also known as a biglietto integrato giornaliero) allows you to use all modes of transport excluding the airport bus and the so-called "tourist bus" (line 110); it expires at midnight on the day purchased. Three-day (biglietto turistico integrato), weekly and monthly passes are also available.

Of the public buses, number 64 is especially useful since it connects Stazione Termini with Piazza Venezia and the Vatican. As for tourism, the 110 open (an open-top double-decker bus) covers all the main sites, including the

Colosseum, Piazza Navona and St Peter's, in a two-hour tour that leaves every 20 minutes from Piazza dei Cinquecento in front of Stazione Termini daily between 8.40am and 8.20pm. Tickets allow you to get on and off all day and can be bought from the kiosk in Piazza dei Cinquecento, or on board if you get on at another stop.

To minimise pollution, the city has several "electric buses" which can cope with the narrow alleys of the historic centre. Line 119, for instance, connects Piazza Venezia with Piazza del Popolo passing via the Trevi fountain and Piazza di Spagna, while the 116 passes through or close to Piazza Navona, Campo de Fiori and St Peter's.

Metro

The metro system (Metropolitana) has two lines, A and B, which meet at Stazione Termini, the city's main train station, and runs between 5.30am and 11.30pm (until 12.30am on Saturdays). Until 2008 Line A will close down early at 9pm for major engineering and renovation

Taxis

In Italy, cabs are found at taxi ranks or may be booked by phone. Hailing them in the street is less common. When you telephone, you will be given the call letters of the taxi and approximately how long it will take to arrive. Fares are clocked up on meters but do check that the driver has switched the meter on when you set off. There is a fixed starting charge, then a charge per kilometre (and a standing charge for traffic jams). If asked, taxi drivers are obliged to show the current list of additional charges, which should also be posted on the back of the seat. Extra charges are added for journeys at night (10pm–7am), on Sundays and holidays, for luggage, and trips outside town.

The general rule for tipping is to round off the fare to the nearest few euros or so.

work. Between 9–11.30pm (12.30pm on Saturdays) the service is replaced by two above ground buses, MA1 and MA2 that follow more or less the same route as the metro.

Metro tickets can be bought from machines at stations, or from tobacconists and some bars. They must be validated in the metro station before starting your journey. If a ticket inspector catches you without a ticket you will be given a hefty on-the-spot fine.

MILAN

Milan's **bus** and **tram** service (ATM) is fast and efficient. Standard tickets must be purchased in advance at tobacconists (tabacchi) or news kiosks and are valid for 75 minutes of travel.

The **Metropolitana Milanese** (MM), which has recently been extended, is the best subway in Italy. MM has four lines including the blue Passante Ferroviario (in addition to red MM1, green MM2 and yellow MM3), which serve almost all the city and the hinterland. Tickets are sold at machines in stations and in most tobacconists (tabacchi) and news kiosks; they must be validated at the start of travel. Once metro tickets are stamped, they can be used for other forms of transport within the specified time period. Although basic tickets allow 75 minutes of travel, they cannot be used twice on the metro. However, there is also a flat-fare day ticket, valid on all forms of transport and for multiple journeys. You can also buy 24-hour tourist tickets, 2-day tickets, carnets (books of 10 tickets) and weekly passes.

For **taxis**, which are all white, go to one of the many ranks (eg, at San Babila or Stazione Centrale) or call 02-8383, 02-6767 or 02-8585.

Milanese Travel

Public transport (ATM): freephone 800-016857.
Train information: 1478-88088
Malpensa Express rail service: 02-27763 (see page 359).

FLORENCE

The main **bus** company is ATAF and their office at Piazza Stazione should have a free bus map of the city. Tickets are sold at bars, tobacconists (tabacchi) and news kiosks with the ATAF sticker and are dispensed by machines near bus stops. They are valid for 60 or 120 minutes of travel, and you can change buses during that time. You can also buy 24-hour and multiple tickets.

Cars are discouraged from the city centre, with strict traffic and parking regulations, but large car parks are provided on the edge of town (eg, Piazza Independenza), linked by public transport. The city has a complex traffic system known as ZTL (Zona a Traffico Limitato). In certain zones, only pedestrians are allowed, while in others, residents may drive, deliver or even park at some times of day. Really, the simplest and most reliable way of getting around is on foot.

Florentine Travel

• **Train information:** 1478-88088
• **Florentine public transport:** freephone 800-424500
• To learn more about Florentine transport, call the Florence tourist office (see page 364) or check the traffic situation on: **www.comune.firenze.it**

VENICE

The city is small enough to be covered on foot but a good map is essential for exploring the maze of small streets and squares. Pick one up from one of the tourist offices. Note that Venice's tourist offices do not supply public transport maps.

The main form of public transport in Venice is the **vaporetto** (water bus). Routes and times are subject to change, and information is available at the ACTV water-transport offices on Piazzale Roma, tel: 041-5287886, or consult their website, www.actv.it. The cost of maintaining Venice and the difficulties of protecting this unique environment

prompted increases in the cost of water transport, particularly a high fare for tourists travelling the Grand Canal. A single fare is €3.50 (plus €3.50 for each piece of luggage). 24-hour tickets are €10.50, and a 3-day travelcard costs €22.

The most scenic, but slowest line remains the No. 1 Accelerato, which takes you down the Grand Canal. Line 82 provides a faster service on the same route, taking 25 minutes and making only six stops; it goes west as far as Tronchetto (the car-park island) and east to San Zaccaria (and the Lido in summer). The 52 provides an enjoyable circular ride around the periphery of Venice and takes in Murano.

Buy a ticket before boarding, or you will be surcharged. Day (24-hour) and three-day passes are available. Children under 1-metre (just over 3-ft) tall travel free, but there are surcharges for excess luggage – a suitcase costs as much as an adult.

Water-taxis take up to four people and, like regular taxis, display meters. You can find water-taxi "ranks" at main points in the city. The system of charges for water transport is complex; pick up a free copy of A Guest in Venice from any major hotel or look out for Meeting in Venice, a similar publication.

The flat rate for hiring a **gondola** during the day is around €60 for 50 minutes and about €30 for each 25 minutes thereafter, and after 8pm it's €80, though it is advisable to haggle. A singing gondolier costs extra. A maximum of six people are accepted and gondolas booked as a group convoy may be cheaper. A recommended route is Bridge of Sighs–Santa Maria Formosa–Rialto Bridge–Grand Canal.

Very much cheaper are traghetto gondolas, which cross the Grand Canal where there are no bridges.

NAPLES

In general, Neapolitan transport has improved dramatically in terms of

Neapolitan Travel

- **Train enquiries,** tel: 892 021.
- **Taxis:** take one from an official rank or call: 081-5560202/081-5564444 (Napoli taxis).
- A flat-fare **ticket** is available covering city buses and metro.

efficiency, reliability and safety. Napoli Centrale, the main railway station, is now tightly controlled by the police and therefore safer than stations in many cities.

Buses run to most places in the city and they are the only public transport along the waterfront. However, they are generally very crowded during rush hours. Owing to congested traffic, **taxis** are not much faster than buses, although they are much more expensive.

Naples' main **metro** line, the Metropolitana FS, covers most of the city and suburbs. It connects Piazza Garibaldi with Piazza Cavour, Monte Santo, Mergellina, Campi Flegrei and Bagnoli.

Two good **local railways** for tourists include Circumvesuviana, which goes from Piazza Garibaldi to Pompeii, Herculaneum and Sorrento, and the Circumflegri, which leaves from Piazza Montesanto for Cuma.

Private Transport

Italian motorways *(autostrade)* are generally fast and uncrowded, except in summer and on key holidays, such as Easter. Nearly all *autostrade* charge tolls, which can be paid for by cash or by major credit cards including Visa, MasterCard, American Express and Diners Club. A convenient method of payment is by ViaCard, a pre-paid card that will take off the amount for each toll that you go through. It can be bought from various outlets including the main motorway service stations and some tobacconists. Entering the automatic toll meter lanes if you haven't already pre-registered may well incur you a fine.

Note that it is compulsory to wear seatbelts at all times. Infants up to nine months must travel in a baby seat, and children up to four years must sit in the back seat of the car.

It is obligatory to use headlights on motor vehicles during the day as well as at night.

Hitchhiking is forbidden on motorways and is not advised for solo women, especially in the south.

When travelling into the mountains in winter, check road conditions with the nearest tourist information centre, or ring the Italian Automobile Association (ACI) on 803-116. When there is ice and snow on the roads, you will need to put chains on your wheels.

PARKING

Pay attention to street signs advising "no parking" because Italian police are strict and will remove vehicles found in these areas. You'll need plenty of cash to reclaim your car. Try to park in a garage for the night: it will be fairly expensive but much safer. Ideally, leave your car in your hotel car park, a designated car park (of which there are few) or an official car park. Never leave valuables inside and do not leave any objects visible to passers-by.

In the south, especially in Naples, Palermo and Catania, where it is hard to find parking, it is best to leave your car with official car-parking attendants – although there are also few of these. Many locals leave their car (often with the keys) with unofficial attendants but this is not recommended.

Car Rentals

Hiring a car is expensive in Italy, as is petrol. Car rental firms, such as Avis, Hertz and Europcar, are represented in most cities and all airports, though local firms often offer better rates – look in *Yellow Pages* under *Autonoleggio*. Collision damage waiver and

breakdown recovery are usually included in the price but check this; additional insurance cover is usually available at fixed rates. Ensure that the fee includes the 19 percent VAT (IVA).

The renter must be over 21 and must be in possession of a valid driver's licence (an EU licence, an international driving licence or a national driving licence with Italian translation). A deposit equal to the cost of hiring the vehicle is usually required, or a credit-card imprint.

Speed limits

Urban areas:
50 km/h (30 mph)
Roads outside urban areas:
90 km/h (55 mph)
Dual carriageways outside urban areas:
110 km/h (70 mph)
Motorways *(autostrade)*:
130 km/h (80 mph);
for cars less than 1100cc:
110 km/h (70 mph)

Where to Stay

Italy has a wonderful variety of accommodation in all categories, from grand villas to small family-run hotels, as well as the *Agriturismo* sector *(see below)*. In major cities, there are even bed and breakfasts.

Agriturismo

Tuscany and Umbria are probably the two areas where *agriturismo* (rural or farm-stay holidays) is most developed. In Tuscany, most of the best places are around Florence, Siena and San Gimignano. In the Chianti area properties are prized for their proximity to wine estates, while many of those in Lucca are in exquisite patrician villas. Lesser-known areas such as the Mugello (north of Florence), wild Lunigiana, Massa Marttima and the Lucca hinterland can also be promising places to stay.

Most regional tourist offices (and a number of those in cities and provinces) should be able to supply lists of *agriturismo* properties. The term can mean different things in different areas, so check carefully what is on offer when you book. The *agriturismo* website for the whole of Italy is www.agriturismoinitalia.com.

Tuscany: Ask for the *Agriturismo in Toscana* brochure from: Regione Toscana Giunta Regionale, Dip. Dello Sviluppo Economico, Via di Novoli 26, 50127 Firenze (Florence), Italy. Also check www.agriturismo.regione.toscana.it.

Villa Holidays

Private villas with their own pool usually cost a premium in Italy, and such properties tend to be booked up very quickly. Some so-called "villas" are actually apartment complexes, so always ask exactly what you're getting.

Tuscany tends to be the most expensive region but Umbria is catching up in terms of price and quality; there are also a number of magnificent Palladian villas in the Veneto, but the weather can be disappointing compared with areas further south. In the south, except for some chic sites in Sardinia, Capri and the Amalfi coast, prices tend to be lower than elsewhere, but quality is also more variable.

Since many properties are in the heart of the countryside, expect your car to take a bit of a battering along unpaved tracks.

Selected UK operators who offer villa holidays: Another Italy, tel: 01635-863030; Bridgewater Villas, tel: 0161-787 8587; Cottages to Castles, tel: 01622-775217, www.cottagestocastles.com, covers both villas and small complexes; The Individual Travellers – Vacanze in Italia; tel: 08700-780186, www.indiv-travelers.com.

International Chapters, tel: 020-7722 0722, features top-of-the-range properties; Italtourism, tel: 020-8879 0345, has a range of properties across Italy, including some in Tuscany. CV Travel Italian World, tel: 0870-603 9018, www.cvtravel.net.

The following specialise in villa holidays in **Tuscany:** Invitation to Tuscany, tel: 020-7603 7111; Italian Life, tel: 08704-448811, www.italianlife.co.uk; Traditional Tuscany, tel: 01877-382999; Tuscany Now, tel: 020-7272 5469; and Travellers Way, tel: 01527-578100.

Useful Websites

General
Agriturist (Farmhouses):
www.agriturist.it
B & Bs
www.caffelletto.it (upmarket)
www.bbitalia.it (general)
Hotels in Italy:
www.giroscopio.com/ (then insert the name of the city)
Dreamclick:
www.dreamclick.com
Romantic or exclusive hotels and courses, including sailing, ballooning, art, gladiator skills.
Citalia: www.citalia.co.uk
Artscape: www.artscape.uk.com
Painting holidays.
Arblaster and Clarke Wine Tours:
www.arblasterandclarke.com
Elegant resorts:
www.elegantresorts.co.uk
Tours and hotels include the Amalfi and Campania coasts.
Exclusive Italy:
www.exclusiveitaly.co.uk
Italian Cookery holidays
www.italian-cookery-weeks.co.uk
www.flavoursholidays.com
www.italiansecrets.co.uk
Liaisons Abroad:
www.liaisonsabroad.com
Musical and cultural holidays.

The Magic Travel Group:
www.magicgroup.co.uk
Wide range of general holidays.
Last-minute holidays in Italy:
www.vib.it

Rome
Database of hotels:
www.venere.com
www.expedia.it
www.hotelreservation.it
www.gotoroma.com

Naples
Hotels: www.napleshotels.na-it
www.itwg.com/naples

Skiing
Aosta (Valle d'Aosta):
www.aosta.shop.com
Bormio:
www.provincia.so.it/aptvaltellina
Cortina d'Ampezzo (Veneto):
www.sunrise.it/dolomiti
Courmayeur:
www.courmayeur.net
Dolomites:
www.sunrise.it/dolomiti
Madonna di Campiglio (Trentino): www.aptcampiglio.it
San Martino di Castrozza (Trentino): www.sanmartino.com

Apartment Holidays

Venetian Apartments, tel: 020-8878 1130, www.venice-rentals.com, are market leaders for Venice but they also have apartments in Rome, Verona and Florence.

Italtourism, tel/fax: 020-8879 0345, email: ptafi@italtourism. freeserve.co.uk, offers over 1,000 self-catering apartments across Italy; most of their rural properties have pools.

International Chapters, tel: 020-7722 0722, and Carefree Italy, tel: 01293-552 277, offer apartment and other self-catering holidays in locations throughout Italy.

Bed and Breakfasts

Rome is the city where the Bed and Breakfast system has taken off, particularly for budget travellers. Although the quality of accommodation is extremely variable, places are generally clean, simple and welcoming. A list of authorised B&Bs is available from any Rome tourist office or information point; alternatively, consult the Rome B&B association website at www.b-brm.it or call tel: 06-55302248. It offers over a hundred bed and breakfasts and apartments in the centre of Rome. Bookings can be made online.

Choosing a Hotel

All the main international chains are represented in Italy, with Jolly and Hilton being two of the most prominent groups. There are also many independent hotels with style and atmosphere in different areas. Be sure to call or write beforehand to verify facilities and reserve. Smaller hotels are not necessarily cheaper than large ones – some of the more exclusive small hotels match the grand hotels in style and expense; however, even inexpensive hotels usually offer basic comforts and good service.

UK Tour Operators

Abercrombie & Kent, tel: 0845-0700 610; www.abercrombiekent. co.uk. ATG Oxford, tel: 01865-315678; www.atg-oxford.co.uk. **Andante Travels**, tel: 01722-713800; www.andantetravels.co.uk. **Citalia**, tel: 0870-9097555; www.citalia.co.uk. Simply Sardinia, tel: 020-8541 2213; www. simplytravel.co.uk. **Exclusive Italy**, tel: 020-8256 0231; www.exclusiveworldwide.com. **Italian Connection**, tel: 01424-728900; www.italian-connection.co.uk. **Italian Expressions**, tel: 020-7435 2525; www.expressionsholidays.co.uk. **Magic of Italy**, tel: 0800-9803378; www.magictravelgroup.co.uk. **Italiatour**, tel: 0870-7333000; www.italiatour.co.uk. **Long Travel Southern Italy**, tel: 01694-722193; www.long-travel.co.uk

Hotel Listings

The following listings include a selection of reputable city hotels, villa hotels, converted castles, rural inns and apartments. Your travel agent or the tourist offices in Italy should be able to give more details on these and many other hotels.

ROME

Rome has an impressive range of accommodation, particularly at the top end of the scale. However, the large demand means that, like in Venice, prices are relatively high, and it is worth booking in advance if you wish to stay in a good hotel. The alternative is to book with a reputable tour operator, who ought to have a fixed allocation in some of the best hotels. You could also consider staying in Tivoli or in the Colli Romani hills around the city.

Grand Hotels

Aldrovandi Palace Hotel
Via Ulisse Aldrovandi 15
Tel: 06-3223993
Fax: 06-3221435
www.aldrovandi.com

Price Categories

Price categories are based on a double room without breakfast:
€ = under €80
€€ = €80–160
€€€ = €160–280
€€€€ = more than €280

This imposing 18th-century palace overlooking the Villa Borghese gardens is in the prestigious Parioli district. A former college, it is now one of Rome's leading hotels and its suites are among the most expensive in the city. Décor is sumptuous rather than stylish – a mood that is reflected in both the facilities and service. The hotel's many amenities include a business centre, several restaurants, private parking, a fitness centre, gardens, and, exceptionally for Rome, an outdoor swimming pool. €€€€
Capo d'Africa
Via Capo d'Africa 54
Tel: 06-772801
Fax: 06-77280801
www.hotelcapodafrica.com
One of a recent slew of boutique hotels in Rome. The dramatic, palm-tree lined entrance bodes well and the 64 rooms are cosy yet refreshingly contemporary – one suite has its own private terrace. Views are delightful and the Colosseum only a five-minute walk away. Any worries that you won't be in the thick of things will vanish once you realise how well connected you are. €€€–€€€€
Cavalieri Hilton
Via Cadlolo 101
Tel: 06-35091
Fax: 06-3509 2241
www.cavalierihilton.it
This resort-style hotel with superb views has great sports facilities, including a two swimming pools, fitness centre, jogging track and tennis courts. It has two renowned restaurants – La Pergola and Giardino dell'Uliveto – an efficient congress centre, an executive floor and several shops. €€€€
Celio
Via Santissimi Quattro 35/C
Tel: 06-70495333

Fax: 06-7096377
www.hotelcelio.com
This boutique hotel is just a stone's throw from both the Colosseum and the Forum. It occupies a charming *palazzo* that has been completely and sensitively restored, including its fine mosaics. The atmosphere is elegant and the bedrooms achieve a particularly high standard of comfort. €€€
De Russie
Via del Babuino 9
Tel: 06-328881

Fax: 06-32888888
www.hotelderussie.it
A favoured 19th-century haunt of the Russian imperial family, dignitaries and luminaries, this hotel was later frequented by Picasso and Jean Cocteau. Set among terraced, shady gardens, and beautifully restored, it's a verdant, tranquil oasis in the heart of town. Designed in an elegant minimalist style, it offers the ultimate in luxury blended with up-to-the-minute technology. A fully

equipped health spa and a superb restaurant – Le Jardin du Russie – make it very popular with celebrities. €€€€
D'Inghilterra
Via Bocca di Leone 14
Tel: 06-699811
Fax: 06-69922243
www.royaldemeure.com
Old-fashioned it may be, but this hotel, in the main shopping area close to Trinita dei Monti, is arguably the most atmospheric of the grand hotels. Bedrooms are

Hotel Groups

The following is a selection of the most noteworthy hotel groups.

Abitare La Storia: Operating under the banner of "Living History", this is an association of independently run hotels, each of which occupies an historic *palazzo* or villa, often with lovely grounds. You can book directly or through a central reservation system in Rome, tel: 06-4464399, fax: 06-445 2845, www.logis.it. General enquiries, tel: 0322 772156; www.arbitarelastoria.com

Bonaparte Hotel Group: This is a Milan-based group of independent hotels. Essentially good, reliable 4-star hotels with a personal touch, they are suitable for business or leisure. One, the Century Tower, has only spacious suites, but prices still compare to a 4-star hotel. To book from within Italy, call the freephone number: 167-249901 for Century Tower and several others in Milan; or 167-877446 for the Bonaparte, Scandinavia, and four others in Milan, Brescia and Bergamo. From outside Italy, either call the hotels directly or contact head office in Milan on: 02-725521; fax: 02-8692278.

Charming Hotels: This group of luxurious, independent hotels is characterised by its impeccable taste in atmospheric locations, antiques and excellent traditional cuisine. There are Charming Hotels in Como, Siena and Venice, among other places. You can book through

head office in Rome: Via Pinciana 25, tel: 06-8411940, fax: 06-8521 0210; in the UK through Liaisons Abroad, tel: 020-7376 4020, fax: 020-7376 4442, or in the USA through European Connection, Roslyn Heights, New York, tel: 310-541 0028, fax: 310-541 1359, toll-free 800-541 5412. Call, toll-free, outside Italy from Australia, Belgium, France, UK, Spain, Switzerland and US 800-24276464; in Italy call 840-707575; www.thecharminglife.com

Jolly Hotels: formed in 1949, this is now the largest Italian hotel group; tel: 00800-0005 6559 (toll-free); www.jollyhotels.it

Leading Hotels of the World/ Leading Small Hotels of the World: Consortium of upmarket properties. From the UK, tel: 00800-2888 8882; www.lhw.com

Logis d'Italia: Similar to the French group, Logis de France, this group has hotels all over Italy and these are listed in the *Logis d'Italia* guide. The group's principles are founded on value for money, size and hospitality (many are small and family run). Book through a central reservations system in Milan, tel: 02-48519285, fax: 02-48519265, or directly with hotels.

Sina Hotels: This small hotel group, founded by an Italian aristocrat, runs stylish and luxurious hotels in Milan, Parma, Viareggio, Florence, Perugia and Rome. They have a certain

elegance and formality in common. You can book directly or through Sina Hotels in Rome: Piazza Barberini 23, tel: 06-4870222, fax: 06-4874778. For central reservations, tel: 800-273226; www.sinahotels.com

Starhotels: This Italian group specialises in hotels in the heart of cities, such as the four-star Savoia Excelsior in Trieste. For reservations from the UK, tel: 00800-8602 0000; from the USA, tel: 800-816 6001; in Italy, tel: 800-860200; www.starhotels.it

Starwood Hotels and Resorts: Upmarket properties located throughout Italy and the world. For reservations from the UK, tel: 0800-353 535; www.starwood.com

Turin Hotels: This group began in Turin and manages traditional, classic hotels in the regions of Piedmont and Liguria. The hotels are characterised by high Piedmontese standards of service, classical or Neo-classical buildings and excellent cuisine. They are all 4-star and can be booked through Turin Hotels International, Turin, tel: 011-5151911, fax: 011-5617191, www.thi.it.

Travelling Around Italy Hotels: This chain has just 14 elegant hotels, which are closely linked to their surrounding areas and cater for lovers of good food and wine. The group is based at Via della Purificazione 4, Rome, tel: 06-4872001; fax: 06-485994; www.travellingarounditaly.com

mostly spacious and elegant, with marble bathrooms. In the public areas, frescoes, antiques, chandeliers and antiquarian prints add to the elegant atmosphere. Lizst, Ernest Hemingway, Anatole France and Alec Guinness all stayed here. The roof garden is one of the loveliest in the city and the restaurant has been newly renovated. €€€€

Forum
Via Tor dei Conti 25
Tel: 06-6792446
Fax: 06-6786479
www.hotelforumrome.com
This is a lovely hotel close to the Colosseum with a view of the ancient city, including the Forum, from its roof garden. 79 rooms. €€€–€€€€

Grand Hotel Parco dei Principi
Via G. Frescobaldi 5
Tel: 06-854421
Fax: 06-8845104
www.parcodeiprincipi.com
Beautifully located in a park on the edge of the gardens of the Villa Borghese, this luxurious, modern hotel prides itself on exquisite attention to detail. Excellent facilities include a swimming pool, well-appointed rooms, 20 panoramic suites and three restaurants. €€€€

Hassler-Villa Medici
Piazza Trinità dei Monti 6
Tel: 06-699340
Fax: 00-6789991
www.hotelhasslerroma.com
Located at the top of the Spanish Steps, this hotel is one of the best in Rome. It provides excellent food and service and even has free bicycles available for exploring the city. Run by the same family since circa 1900, it was recently redesigned by the owner's wife. The bedrooms are luxurious, and some have four-poster beds. The roof-garden restaurant has fine views over the city. €€€€

Lord Byron
Via Giuseppe de Notaris 5
Tel: 06-3220404
Fax: 06-3220405
www.lordbyronhotel.com
Situated close to the Villa Borghese in the exclusive Parioli district, this distinguished hotel has the elegant,

Price Categories

Price categories are based on a double room without breakfast:
€ = under €80
€€ = €80–160
€€€ = €160–280
€€€€ = more than €280

ambience of a private club, sustained by old-fashioned décor and individually designed rooms with Irish linen sheets, French beds and good Roman service. There's a piano bar and the renowned Sapori del Lord Byron restaurant. €€€€

St Regis Grand
Via Vittorio Emanuele, Orlando 3
Tel: 06-47091
Fax: 06-4747307
www.starwoodhotels.com
Between the railway station and the Via Veneto area, this exclusive and dignified hotel occupies a patrician palace, graced with Oriental rugs, chandeliers and antiques. It has recently been beautifully restored, but retains its original style. Facilities include tea-rooms, a bar and gourmet restaurant. Personal butler service available. €€€€

Westin Excelsior
Via Vittorio Veneto 125
Tel: 06-47081
Fax: 06-4826205
www.starwoodhotels.com
This grand hotel has been a meeting place for celebrities and society figures since the 1950s. The hotel claims that this was the location of the Ingrid Bergman–Roberto Rossellini affair, and where the last Shah of Iran courted his future wife. Regardless of whether either claim is true, to many, this hotel is quite simply synonymous with Roman dolce vita, even if some of this indefinable quality has otherwise moved on from the Via Vittorio Veneto. €€€€

Small Hotels

The Beehive
Via Marghera 8
Tel: 06-44704553
www.the-beehive.com
A chic but incredibly cheap option

near Termini station run by an American couple with a dorm room, apartments and private rooms decorated in a colourful and contemporary style. It has a welcoming garden, its own café for guests and knowledgeable staff. €

Columbia
Via del Viminale 15
Tel: 06-4883509
Fax: 06-4740209
www.hotelcolumbia.com
This charming hotel is centrally located near to the Via Nazionale. Rooms are large and elegantly furnished. There is also a roof terrace where you can enjoy breakfast. €€€

Dei Consoli
Via Varrone 2/d
Tel: 06-68892972
Fax: 06-68212274
www.hoteldeiconsoli.com
Occupying a 19th-century building that has been well restored in the Empire style, this new hotel overlooks St Peter's. The cupola is visible from the spectacular rooftop terrace and from many of the 28 bedrooms. There is a direct internet connection in each room. €€–€€€

Gregoriana
Via Gregoriana 18
Tel: 06-6794269
Fax: 06-6784258
Close to the Spanish Steps, in a central location, this former 17th-century monastery is now a three-star hotel with a quiet, cosy atmosphere. Especially admirable is the art deco interior, with room letters designed by the celebrated 1930s' fashion illustrator Erté. Although there is no restaurant, the hotel does have a pleasant terrace where breakfast is served. €€

La Residenza 'A'
Via Vittorio Veneto 183
Tel: 06-486700
Fax: 06-42012435
www.hotelviaveneto.com
On the first floor of a palazzo in the swanky but dull Via Veneto, this features modern rooms with art on the walls. Computers with free internet in every room. €€€

Margutta
Via Laurina 34
Tel: 06-3223674

Fax: 06-3200395
Near Piazza del Popolo, this little hotel occupies an 18th-century *palazzo*. Rooms are simple and there is no restaurant, but atmosphere and value are compensation enough. €€

Santa Maria
Vicolo del Piede 2
Tel: 06-5894626
Fax: 06-5894815
www.htlsantamaria.com
This hotel takes its name from the nearby church of Santa Maria in Trastevere. A former 17th-century cloister, this jewel of a small hotel has been sympathetically renovated and offers high standards of comfort. There is an attractive courtyard garden which is an oasis of calm, yet close to all the main sights of Trastevere. Excellent service. €€€

MILAN

Always book a Milan hotel well in advance because, except in July and August, rooms tend to be scarce. During the main trade fairs it can be almost impossible to find a room, leaving no alternative but to stay outside the city. If no rooms are available, consider saying on Lake Como, which is only 30–40 minutes from the centre of Milan and can be easily reached by train.

Grand Hotels
Excelsior Gallia
Piazza Duca d'Aosta 9
Tel: 02-67851
Fax: 02-66713239
www.excelsiorgallia.it
Located beside Stazione Centrale, this luxurious historic hotel is now part of the Forte-Meridien group,

but still feels like a real Milanese institution. Public rooms are gracious and appealing, and the bedrooms vary greatly in style and size; most feature wonderful original art deco marble bathrooms. The hotel has a beauty parlour and an excellent restaurant. €€€€

Four Seasons
Via Gesù 8
Tel: 02-77088
Fax: 02-77085000
www.fourseasons.com
This is one of Milan's most exclusive hotel, with the highest staff-to-client ratio in the world, assuring attentive, but unobtrusive service. The setting is delightful, with the former monastic cells converted into supremely luxurious bedrooms. Many choose the hotel for its proximity to the prestigious Quadrilatero shopping district. Book well in advance. €€€€

Hermitage
Via Messina 10
Tel: 02-318170
Fax: 02-33107399
www.monrifhotels.it
Elegant and characterful hotel with 119 rooms (and eight suites). A lovely garden and veranda, plus stylish décor and attentive service have made this hotel very popular with celebrities. €€€–€€€€

Principe di Savoia
Piazza della Repubblica 17
Tel: 02-62301
Fax: 02-6595838
www.luxurycollection.com
Set on the same square as the Duca di Milano, this hotel revels in old-fashioned luxury, with self-consciously grand interior. More than 400 rooms include the most splendid presidential suite in the city, favoured by celebrities, super-models and heads of state. The suite's private pool is an over-the-top fantasy inspired by Pompeiian baths. Apart from such glitzy touches, this is essentially a classic luxury hotel, offering superb service and excellent facilities. Reception rooms are elegant, and the rooftop fitness centre includes a sauna and swimming pool, with glorious views over the city. €€€€

Distinctive Milanese Hotels

Park Hyatt, Via Tommaso Grossi 1, tel: 02-88211234; www.milan.park.hyatt. Cool understatement has been combined with opulence in Milan's newest designer hotel. Beautiful bedrooms with travertine-clad walls, Venetian stucco and lovely touches such as hand-blown Venetian-glass light sconces. Very "designer" bar in graphite, and a spa. The location is ideal: just a stone's throw from La Scala, the Duomo and a Prada shop. €€€€

UNA Hotel Century, Via Fabio Filzi 25b, tel: 02-67504, fax: 02-66980602; www.una.century@unahotels.it. Despite occupying a tower, this hotel located close to Stazione Centrale has a friendly atmosphere and offers both the luxury of space and a sense of privacy. Bedrooms here are probably the largest in their price range in Milan – all 150 rooms are cleverly designed suites that can easily be transformed into a separate bedroom and office space. Other amenities include a small fitness centre and a good restaurant which serves Milanese and classic Italian cuisine. €€€€

The Century Tower is part of a small group of very different hotels, so you might opt for the boutique **Hotel Bonaparte**, Via Cusani 13, tel: 02-85601, fax: 02-8693601, a discreetly upmarket affair near the Castello Sforzesco and the financial district. €€€

For those wishing to be close to the Fiera, Milan's Trade Fair, try the **Radisson SAS**, Via Fauche 15, tel: 02-336 391, fax: 02-33104510, www.radissonsas.com. A stylish modern hotel with rooms overlooking peaceful gardens. €€€

Hotel Ariston, Largo Carrobbio 2, tel: 02-72000556, fax: 02-72000914. Set in a rather noisy, traffic-filled area, this ecologically minded hotel is an experiment in healthy living. This hotel is an asthma-sufferer's dream: rooms come equipped with atomisers and ionisers. Recycled paper and biodegradable products are used and the restaurant uses organic products. The 48-roomed hotel takes itself rather seriously: décor is minimalist but the lozenge-shaped desks add a note of fun to the austere proceedings. €€€

Price Categories

Price categories are based on a double room without breakfast:
€ = under €80
€€ = €80–160
€€€ = €160–280
€€€€ = more than €280

The Westin Palace
Piazza della Repubblica 20
Tel: 02-63361
Fax: 02-63366337
www.westin.com
The third main hotel on the Piazza della Repubblica, the Palace, like the Principe di Savoia, offers wonderful fitness facilities, notably its indoor golf range. Guests have access to the Principe di Savoia's rooftop pool and fitness club. The renovated bedrooms, some with steam rooms, are comfortable, and the restaurant has a sound reputation. €€€€

Small, Old-fashioned Inns
Antica Locanda dei Mercanti
Via San Tomaso 6
Tel: 02-8054080
Fax: 02-8054090
www.locanda.it
This delightfully intimate hotel has only 14 rooms and is cosy as an inn, despite its setting in the heart of the financial district. The hotel has no sign (and no TV), and guests are woken in the morning by an old-fashioned bell before being served breakfast in bed. There are well-stocked bookshelves and the bedrooms have fine views. €€€
Antica Locanda Solferino
Via Castelfidardo 2
Tel: 02-6570129
Fax: 02-6571361
Old-fashioned furniture and a gracious atmosphere create a pleasant ambience in this 11-bedroom hotel in the elegant Brera quarter. In tune with the low-key mood, breakfast is served in your room. Book well in advance. €€€

Small, Friendly Hotels
Antica Locanda Leonardo
Corso Magenta 78
Tel: 02-48014197

Fax: 02-48019012
www.leoloc.com
Small, family-run hotel with 20 rooms offering a warm welcome. Enviable location very close to the church of Santa Maria delle Grazie and Leonardo's Cenacolo. €€€
Aspromonte
Piazza Aspromonte 12/14
Tel: 022-361119
Fax: 022-367621
www.venere.it/milano/aspromonte
Small and gracious with very attentive service from the young proprietors. In summer breakfast is served in the garden. €€
Hotel Vittoria
Via Pietro Calvi 32
Tel: 02-5456520
Fax: 02-55190246
This pleasant, family-run three-star hotel, with friendly, helpful staff, is about ten minutes' walk from the cathedral. Refurbishment has given all 18 bedrooms air-conditioning and noise insulation, although some are a little small (typical for Milan). No-smoking rooms and suites are available. The cosy breakfast room overlooks a nice garden where breakfast is served in fine weather. The hotel does not have a restaurant but there's a bar, which is open 24 hours a day. Car park (supervised) nearby. €€€

Standard Business Hotels
Executive Hotel
Viale Luigi Sturzo 45
Tel: 02-62942807
Fax: 02-62942713
Freephone from Italy: 800-014207
This hotel, with 414 rooms, offers good service and has a recommended restaurant.
€€€–€€€€
Jolly Hotel President
Largo Augusto 10
Tel: 02-77461
Fax: 02-783449
A good, large chain hotel. There are three other Jolly hotels in Milan.
€€€–€€€€
Michelangelo
Via Scarlatti 33
Tel: 02-67551
Fax: 02-6694232
Close to the Central Station, this is one of Milan's best-run business

hotels, and, despite its anonymous setting in a tower, it maintains a personal touch. €€€–€€€€
Milano Hilton
Via L. Galvani 12
Tel: 02-69831
Fax: 02-66710810
The Milano Hilton is a large recently renovated hotel, decorated in a modern, if rather characterless, style. It is located in the city's new commercial centre, near Stazione Centrale. €€€€

LOMBARDY & THE LAKES

Many of the best hotels in Lombardy, Piedmonte and the Veneto occupy lakeside sites, with glorious views. For further details on some of the following and on the area in general, visit: www.inlombardia.it

Bergamo
Excelsior San Marco
Piazza della Repubblica 6
Tel: 035-366111
Fax: 035-366159
This modern hotel offers slick service, good facilities and a roof garden. €€€

Bellagio
Du Lac
Piazza Mazzini 32
Tel: 031-950320
Fax: 031-951624
www.bellagiohoteldulac.com
Very centrally located, overlooking the embarkation point for boats.

Piedmont

Piedmont (Piemonte) has considerable appeal, especially for wine-lovers, who are attracted to the many specialist wine tours on offer in the region, and nature-lovers, wanting to visit its national park. Albi is popular as a chic destination, and in winter the ski resorts of Sestriere, Sansicario and Sauze-d'Oulx and the whole Milky Way are pulling in a growing number of visitors and will feature in the Winter Olympics in 2006.

Pleasant roof garden and dining room with excellent, panoramic views. Good value. €€–€€€

Grand Hotel Villa Serbelloni
Via Roma 1 Lago di Como
Tel: 031-950216
Fax: 031-951529
www.villaserbelloni.it
This fabulous patrician villa has been converted into one of the finest hotels in northern Italy. The views, grounds, facilities (including two swimming pools, tennis courts and full health spa) and service are all impeccable. The villa has a gorgeous location, and the terrace restaurant overlooks the palm-filled grounds and the lake. €€€€

Tremezzo
Grand Hotel Tremezzo
Via Regina 8, Lago di Como
Tel: 0344-42491
Fax: 0344-40201
www.grandhoteltremezzo.com
Set on the western bank of Lake Como, this art nouveau-style villa-hotel has fine views over the lake on one side and an Alpine panorama on the other. The Grand, popular as a congress centre, has three restaurants, one of which produces gourmet feasts. Enjoy the new floating swimming pool in the lake waters. €€€–€€€€

Lake Como

Lake Como has long been a tourist favourite. The resort of Como has a handful of good hotels on the lakeside and, of the other resorts around the lake, Bellagio, although tiny and touristy, is the most lovely.

Como
Barchetta Excelsior
Piazza Cavour 1
Tel: 031-3221
Fax: 031-302622
www.hotelbarchetta.com
This rather anonymous modern hotel is redeemed by its location in the heart of Como and by the spacious, balconied bedrooms overlooking the lake. €€€–€€€€

Sirmione
Grand Hotel Terme
Viale Marconi 7
Tel: 030-916261
Fax: 030-916568
www.termedisimione.com
This is an elegant, well-modernised hotel overlooking the lake. Good sports facilities include a pool, sauna and fitness centre. €€€€

Lake Iseo
L'Albereta
Via Vittorio Emanuele 11,
Erbusco, Provincia di Brescia
Tel: 030-7760550
Fax: 030-7760573
www.albereta.it
Although this fully modernised 19th-century villa is a good hotel in its own right (with 57 rooms), most Italians associate it with gastronomic feasting, as its restaurant is run by one of Italy's best-known chef, Gualtiero Marchesi. The "hotel" is actually a compact rural estate, consisting of a couple of farmhouses and a tower-house. €€€

TURIN

Turin is trying to broaden its appeal, even though most of the hotels still cater largely to a business clientele. The Turin Shroud display has helped give the city more appeal, and the fact that low-cost airlines now fly here has made this an accessible city break from the UK and France. In 2006 Turin hosts the Winter Olympics.

Jolly Hotel Ambasciatori
Corso Vittorio Emanuele II 104
Tel: 011-5752
Fax: 011-544978
Freephone tel: 167017703
www.jollyhotels.it
This typical Jolly hotel is favoured by a business clientele. It is large, modern and efficient and offers a good location and service. €€€

Turin Palace Hotel
Via Sacchi 8
Tel: 011-5625511
Fax: 011-5612187
www.thi.it
This, the flagship of the Turin Hotel Group, is a classic, elegant hotel,

designed in grand Piedmontese style, and handy for Porta Nuova station. The public rooms house large paintings and period furniture. The staff are highly professional and the cuisine is good. €€€

Villa Sassi
Strada Traforo del Pino 47
Tel: 011-8980556
Fax: 011-8980095
www.villasassi.com
This hotel is housed in a splendid 18th-century villa surrounded by lovely parkland. There are only 16 bedrooms, some of which have private terraces overlooking the park. You can expect excellent service and every comfort in an exclusive ambience. Rooms on the first floor are more romantic than the ones on the modern floor above. Dinner is served in the elegant, frescoed dining room. €€€

VALLE D'AOSTA

The Valle d'Aosta is best known for its ski stations in Breuil-Cervinia and Courmayeur, so hotels are busy in winter. Recently, the area has been promoted as a summer destination, with outdoor holidays linked to the Gran Paradiso National Park.

Aosta
Classhotel Aosta
Corso Ivrea 146
Tel: 0165-41845
Fax: 0165-236660
www.classhotel.com
At the old gates of the city, this hotel is popular with tourists and business clients. The recently refurbished rooms offer a good standard of comfort. €€–€€€

Europe
Piazza Narbonne 8
Tel: 0165-236363
Fax: 0165-40566
Set in the historic centre, this is a traditional hotel, noted for its tranquillity and elegance. €€–€€€

Cogne
Hotel Miramonti
Viale Cavagnet 31
Tel: 0165-74030
Fax: 0165-749378

This friendly and welcoming family-run hotel is an ideal base for exploring Gran Paradiso National Park. It's furnished with antiques and antiquarian books, with a blazing fire in winter. The hotel's Coeur de Bois restaurant has a cosy, panelled interior and is noted for its local specialities and mouth-watering desserts. Swimming pool and fitness centre. €€–€€€

LIGURIA & THE ITALIAN RIVIERA

Genoa has a shortage of individual and historic hotels in the city centre. However, this is more than compensated for by the huge range of stylish accommodation on the Ligurian coast. Remember, though, that a number of the hotels, especially standard beach hotels, close in winter. For more information, visit: www.apt.genova.it.

Genoa
Bristol Palace
Via XX Settembre 35
Tel: 010-592541
Fax: 010-561756
www.hotelbristolpalace.com
Traditionally Genoa's grandest hotel, the Bristol Palace is on the city's most elegant shopping street, close to Old Genoa. The modest entrance belies its history and though rooms vary greatly in quality, some have appealing features, such as old marble bathrooms. The bright and stylish dining-room is decorated in Louis XVI style. €€€–€€€€
Jolly Plaza
Via Martin Piaggio 11
Tel: 010-83161
Fax: 010-8391850
Freephone: 167017703
This small but distinguished *palazzo* has been transformed into a four-star hotel. Bedrooms vary in style but all of them are well-equipped and many have Jacuzzis. The restaurant is in the adjoining Villeta di Negro. €€€
Locanda di Palazzo Cicala
Piazza San Lorenzo 16
Tel: 010-2518824
Fax: 010-2467414

Price Categories

Price categories are based on a double room without breakfast:
€ = under €80
€€ = €80–160
€€€ = €160–280
€€€€ = more than €280

www.thecharminghotels.com
The first floor of this historic *palazzo* has been renovated and transformed into a charming city hideaway. Large, airy rooms with high arched ceilings embellished with stucco combine a nostalgic atmosphere with modern convenience. The pleasant lounge overlooks Piazza San Lorenzo and the cathedral. €€€

Alassio
Beau Rivage
Via Roma 82
Tel/fax: 0182-640585
This late-19th century villa has an old-fashioned charm. Some rooms feature frescoed ceilings; others have terraces. Guests have use of a private beach nearby. €€–€€€

Bordighera
Grand Hotel del Mare
Via Portico della Punta 34
Tel: 0184-262201
Fax: 0184-262394
www.grandhoteldelmare.it
This exclusive hotel overlooks the sea and is popular for its peace, comfort and beautiful rooms. Health centre and thalassotherapy. €€€–€€€€
Grand Hotel Parigi
Lungomare Argentina 16/18
Tel: 0184-261405
Fax: 0184-260421;
www.hotelparigi.com
Centrally located with panoramic views over the beach and sea, this elegant hotel is very comfortable. The rooms are spacious and there is also a fitness centre. €€€

Camogli
Cenobio dei Dogi
Via Cuneo 34
Tel: 0185-7241
Fax: 0185-772796
www.cenobio.it

Overlooking the sea and surrounded by a lovely park, this hotel is known for its beautiful rooms, restaurant, salt-water pool, solarium and private beach. Also has a summer nightclub. €€€–€€€€

Portofino
Eden
Vico Dritto 20
Tel: 0185-269091
Fax: 0185-269047
www.hoteledenportofino.com
This three-star hotel, set in a 1920s' Ligurian villa, is a lovely family-run alternative to the Splendido *(below)*. There are only 12 rooms but the ambience is delightful, as are the tropical gardens. The Ristorante da Ferruccio is praiseworthy. €€–€€€
Splendido
Viale Barratta 16
Tel: 0185-267801
Fax: 0185-267806
Freephone: 167877293;
www.splendido.net
This is without doubt one of the finest hotels on the Ligurian Riviera, and in all of Italy. In an exclusive little port that draws celebrities, it's a peaceful oasis with a splendid view of the Portofino promontory. Every comfort is provided, plus fine dining, health and beauty centre, and a private speedboat. Open end Mar–mid-November. €€€€

Rapallo
Excelsior Palace Hotel
Via San Michele di Pagana 8
Tel: 0185-230666
Fax: 0185-230214
www.excelsior@thi.it
This elegant hotel is beautifully appointed, overlooking the Gulf of Tigullio and Portofino. It combines a rich history with every modern, stylish amenity, including swimming pools and a health spa. €€€€
Hotel Europa
Via Milite Ignoto 2
Tel: 0185-669521
Fax: 0185-669847
Part of the Turin Hotels group, this art-nouveau hotel was restored to its former glory a few years ago. It now houses a fine restaurant, as well as a fitness centre. €€

Santa Margherita Ligure
Imperiale Palace
Via Pagana 19
Tel: 0185-288991
Fax: 0185-284223
www.hotelimperiale.it
This grand hotel in a tropical garden is located in the neighbouring, but less chic, resort to Portofino. The appeal lies in the old-fashioned décor, antique furnishings, spacious rooms and excellent service. Private beach. €€€–€€€€

San Remo
Royal
Corso Imperatrice 80
Tel: 0184-5391
Fax: 0184-661445
www.royalhotelsanremo.com
This luxurious hotel is surrounded by terraced gardens with palm trees and an illuminated fountain. This is the choice of high-rollers at the casino and Italian stars during the annual February San Remo Song Contest (when hotels are usually full). Large rooms overlook sea or hills and facilities include a fitness centre, pool, tennis courts and Fiori di Murano restaurant. €€€€

Sestri Levante
Grand Hotel dei Castelli
Via alla Penisola 26
Tel: 0185-487220/485780
Fax: 0185-44767
The Grand, in a pleasant setting in front of San Niccolò church, is surrounded by a large park. It features a converted tower and retains some original features, including stone fireplaces. There's a lift down to the private beach. Good service. €€€

Ventimiglia
La Riserva di Castel d'Appio
Castel d'Appio 71
Tel: 0184-229533
Fax: 0184-229712
www.lariserva.it
Set 5 km (3 miles) outside the town of Ventimiglia, this is a small place with a wonderful view of the Riviera dei Fiori and the Costa Azzurra. Service is courteous and homely. €€–€€€

VENICE

Since there is almost no off-season in Venice, only a small blip in late January, many hotels are full all year round. Unfortunately, this means that many hoteliers try less hard than they might to keep guests happy. In addition, the unique location and environmental circumstances mean that hotel prices can be up to 30 percent higher than on the mainland. The basic rules here are: book early, check what view your room has and ask what the price differential is between "good" rooms and "bad" rooms (the same hotel can offer expensive large rooms overlooking the canal and pokey back rooms with little natural light.)

If you would rather someone else found accommodation for you, contact the efficient official Association of Venetian Hoteliers, even for last-minute bookings, tel: 041-522 2264, fax: 041-522 1242. Or, in Italy, call them on the freephone number: 800-843006 or visit www.veniceinfo.it (email: info@veniceinfo.it). Alternatively, contact the tourist office on: 041-529 8711, fax: 041-529 8734. The switchboard will connect you to the relevant information office in the city. For accommodation complaints, while in Italy call the freephone number 800-355 920, which puts you in touch with the tourist board.

Top Hotels
Many of these are magnificent but with a few notable exceptions they tend to rest on their laurels.
Cipriani
Isola della Giudecca 10
Tel: 041-520 7744
Fax: 041-520 3930
www.hotelcipriani.it

Booking Advice

When booking a hotel, act like a Venetian. Don't just request its official address, which can be singularly unhelpful in actually finding the hotel. Instead, ask which is the nearest square, church and ferry stop.

A small oasis on the tip of the Giudecca, the Cipriani is the most glamorous of Venetian hotels and the destination for travellers on the famed Orient Express. Lavish bedrooms are furnished with Fortuny fabrics, and amenities include one of the only private swimming pools in Venice. There are gardens, tennis courts, a yacht harbour, piano bar and a water-launch service, which whisks guests in a couple of minutes to San Marco. On the down side, service here, although professional, can verge on the indifferent and quality of individual rooms is variable. €€€€
Danieli
Riva degli Schiavoni 4196, Castello
Tel: 041-522 6480
Fax: 041-520 0208
www.danieli@luxurycollection.com
In a dominant position on the bustling waterfront, just a stone's throw from St Mark's Square, this prestigious hotel is rich in memories of eminent guests: George Sand, Alfred de Musset, Dickens, Balzac and Wagner. The splendid covered Gothic foyer, built around a courtyard, is an attraction in itself, and the rooms in the old part of the hotel are very plush, with parquet floors and gilded bedsteads. Avoid the hotel's modern extension, which is devoid of charm. The roof garden restaurant, La Terrazza, has a splendid view over the lagoon, but the cuisine is less impressive. Unless you are a celebrity, a regular or a big tipper, service can be supercilious to the point of arrogance. €€€€
Gritti Palace
Campo Santa Maria del Giglio 2467, San Marco
Tel: 041-794 611
Fax: 041-520 0942
www.grittipalace@
luxurycollection.com
The 15th-century Gritti, decorated with Murano-glass chandeliers and 16th-century damask furnishings, is the most legendary Venetian hotel and has a price tag to match. Doge Andrea Gritti lived here and it retains the air of a private *palazzo*.

Renowned for its formal luxury, fabulous setting on the Grand Canal and discreet, attentive service, it has hosted Ernest Hemingway, Winston Churchill and Greta Garbo. Distinguished cuisine can be enjoyed on the canalside terrace. €€€€

Londra Palace
Riva degli Schiavoni 4171, Castello
Tel: 041-520 0533
Fax: 041-522 5032
www.hotelondra.it
This elegant hotel on the scenic Riva degli Schiavoni, overlooking the lagoon, has been recently (and radically) restored to its neoclassical splendour. Tchaikovsky composed his *Fourth Symphony* here in 1877. The hotel has a romantic bar and the excellent Do Leoni restaurant, serving authentic Venetian and classic Italian cuisine. The staff are welcoming and far less supercilious than in many other Venetian top hotels. Rooms differ greatly, so it is worth paying extra for one overlooking the waterside. €€€€

Westin Europa & Regina Hotel
Corte Barozzi 2159, San Marco
Tel: 041-2400001
Fax: 041-5231533
www.europaregina@westin.com
Five minutes from San Marco, facing the baroque church of Santa Maria della Salute, this luxury hotel occupies an 18th-century palace that has been recently renovated; the stucco-work and tapestries are now shown to great effect. The spacious bedrooms and suites are all decorated in traditional Venetian style. The restaurant spills onto a romantic terrace, and the service is first-class. The pastel-coloured rooms overlooking the Grand Canal are in great demand. €€€€

Superior Hotels
In terms of comfort and degree of luxury, but alas also in price, there is sometimes little to choose between these hotels and the "top hotels", but there can be big price differentials between "star", "superior" and "standard" rooms.

Hotel Giorgione
Calle Larga dei Proverbi 4587, Cannaregio

Price Categories
Price categories are based on a double room without breakfast:
€ = under €80
€€ = €80–160
€€€ = €160–280
€€€€ = more than €280

Tel: 041-522 5810
Fax: 041-523 9092
www.hotelgiorgione.com
Situated near the Ca d'Oro, quite close to San Marco and the Rialto Bridge, this hotel dates back to the 13th century, with 15th- and 19th-century additions. The recently refurbished interior is a tribute to Venetian style, with lots of chandeliers and Murano glass. Superior rooms are considerably bigger than standard ones, and are worth the slightly higher price. The restaurant, Osteria Giorgione, is good. €€€–€€€€

Luna Baglioni
Calle Larga dell'Ascensione 1243, San Marco
Tel: 041-528 9840
Fax: 041-528 7160
Freephone: 1678-21057
www.baglioni hotels.com
The Luna is the oldest hotel in Venice, dating back to 1118, when it was founded as a Knights Templar lodge for pilgrims travelling to Jerusalem. Countless restorations and refurbishments mean that the hotel does not really look its age, and the décor is currently in traditional Venetian style: a riot of Murano glass, inlaid marble, swagged curtains and frescoes. There is an 18th-century ballroom with original ceiling frescoes.The hotel has an impressive restaurant and the grandest breakfast room in Venice. €€€€

Metropole
Riva degli Schiavoni 4149, Castello
Tel: 041-520 5044
Fax: 041-522 3679
This popular patrician residence is decorated in fine 19th-century style and is dotted with well-chosen antiques. There are excellent views over courtyards and the lagoon and the hotel is noted for its attentive

service. The hotel is a little tricky to find, so request directions or, better still, take a private gondola to the hotel jetty. €€€€

Monaco & Grand Canal
Calle Vallaresso 1332, San Marco
Tel: 041-520 0211
Fax: 041-520 0501
This reputable hotel faces Santa Maria della Salute church, where the Grand Canal flows into the lagoon. During Venice's notorious high tides and flooding, guests have to walk on raised boards through the reception to reach their rooms – a rather surreal experience. The hotel is intimate and comfortable, although the rooms are a little on the small side and sometimes noisy. The best rooms are on the ground floor overlooking the Grand Canal. Service is good. €€€€

Saturnia & International
Calle Larga XXII Marzo 2398, San Marco
Tel: 041-520 8377
Fax: 041-520 7131/5858
www.hotelsaturnia.it
This distinctive hotel is housed in an historic 13th-century palace close to a busy shopping street by Piazza San Marco. The hotel has a medieval air, which, depending on taste, comes across either as romantic or somewhat austere. Bedrooms are intimate and comfortable. €€€€

Pensione & Small Hotels
Accademia Villa Marevege
Fondamenta Bollani 1058, Dorsoduro
Tel: 041-523 7846
Fax: 041-523 9152
Set in the Dorsoduro district at the Grand Canal end of Rio San Trovaso within easy walking distance of the Accademia gallery, this remodelled Gothic palace maintains its charm, with delightful gardens front and back. The building was remodelled in the 17th century and was once the Russian consulate. Reserve months in advance. €€€

Bucintoro
Riva San Biagio 2135, Castello
Tel: 041-522 3240
Fax: 041-522 2424
This is a simply furnished, family-run two-star hotel on the waterfront,

with splendid views over the Basin of San Marco and the island of San Giorgio Maggiore – there are stunning views from each of the 28 bedrooms, especially those on the top floor. The side rooms have a sweeping vista over the Riva degli Schiavoni. €€–€€€

Flora
Calle dei Bergamaschi 2283/a (off Larga XXII Marzo), San Marco
Tel: 041-520 5844
Fax: 041-522 8217
www.hotelflora.it
This friendly three-star hotel is set in a quiet alley off a prestigious shopping street, just five minutes'

Venetian Apartments

Given the high cost of Venetian hotels (and the poor quality offered by many of them), apartments, particularly for a family or small group, can represent not just a more attractive option, but also excellent value for money. Note, however, that it is extremely difficult to book an apartment from within Venice itself, since most of the owners are linked to specific foreign agents or tour operators.

The London-based **Venetian Apartments**, tel: 020-8878 1130, fax: 020-8878 0982, www.venice-rentals.com, are market leaders for Venice and they have a wide selection of individualistic apartments on offer. Try to book well in advance to secure a good choice. Apartments must be booked for at least a week. €€–€€€

Palazzetto Pisani, Canale Grande, tel: 041-523 2550 Set close to the Accademia Bridge on the Grand Canal, this patrician palace is owned by a descendant of Alvise Pisano, who was elected Doge of Venice in 1735. There is a choice of two apartments, one small and the other larger, which has delightful views over the Grand Canal, and a vast drawing room. €€–€€€€

walk from Piazza San Marco. As for the interior, the art nouveau-style touches, such as the staircase, are particularly appealing. Bedrooms vary enormously. Some of the best bedrooms are numbers 45, 46 and 47. The secluded garden, complete with a Venetian well-head, has recently been remodelled. The courtyard provides a lovely breakfast setting. €€–€€€

La Fenice et des Artistes
Campiello della Fenice 1936, San Marco
Tel: 041-523 2333
Fax: 041-520 3721
www.fenicehotels.it
This highly individual hotel is set within a stone's throw of La Fenice, and has traditionally been popular with actors, musicians and artists. €€–€€€

San Cassiano Ca' Favretto
Calle della Rosa, Santa Croce 2232
Tel: 041-524 1768
Fax: 041-721 033
www.sancassiano.it
One of the few hotels actually on the Grand Canal, the three-star San Cassiano is a converted 14th-century *palazzo*. About half the rooms have canalside views looking across to the Ca' d'Oro, one of the city's loveliest Gothic palaces, but, as everywhere in Venice, these rooms vary dramatically in size and quality. Given that the stairs are steep and there is no lift, less agile visitors are advised to stick to rooms on the ground floor. The hotel has its own jetty, so you can arrive in style in a gondola. €€–€€€

Hotels on the Lido

Des Bains
Lungomare Marconi 17
Tel: 041-526 5921
Fax: 041-526 0113
This prestigious, well-established four-star hotel is remembered for its role in Thomas Mann's *Death in Venice* and still finds favour with stars who flock to the September Venice Film Festival. This hotel is among the grandest on the Lido and is across the road from its private

beach. Facilities are similar to those at the Excelsior *(below)* but this one is more atmospheric and characterful. €€€–€€€€

Westin Excelsior Hotel
Lungomare Marconi 41
Tel: 041-526 0201
Fax: 041-526 7276
Situated on the Lido, a short ferry-ride from San Marco, this is a huge five-star beach hotel – the grandest hotel on the Lido – with a facade that is reminiscent of a Moorish castle. Attractions include numerous sports facilities and a free launch service into Venice. Although the hotel is impressive, the fact that it is located on the Lido rather than in historic Venice makes it somewhat lacking in romance. On the other hand, the beach location makes it a popular choice for visitors with young families. €€€€

THE VENETO

Verona and Vicenza have long been sought-after destinations for visitors, particularly with the continuing success of the operatic season in Verona. At the top end of the market, the Veneto has a good selection of Palladian villas, which make a good alternative to hotels. The Veneto is home to Italy's most prestigious winter ski resort, Cortina d'Ampezzo, and accommodation here should be booked well in advance for the winter season. For details of Cortina d'Ampezzo accommodation, contact: Cortina Turismo, Corso Italia 83, Cortina d'Ampezzo, Veneto 32043, tel: 0436-866252, fax: 0436-867448, www.cortina. dolimiti.org. A useful website for checking hotels in the Dolomites area is: www.sunrise.it/cortina

Asolo

Asolo, with its picturesque historic centre, is a popular destination for foreign visitors and it makes a handy base for exploring Verona, Vicenza, Treviso and even Venice.

Lake Garda

Lake Garda borders several regions, so see also entries in the Trentino-Alto Adige and Veneto sections *(pages 380 and 382–3)*. Although less exclusive and intimate than Lake Como, Garda has its own appeal and is excellent for watersports. Sirmione is one of the loveliest resorts, followed by Gardone Riviera and Riva del Garda.

Hotel Villa Cipriani
Via Canova 298
Tel: 0423-523411
Fax: 0423-952095
This luxurious ochre-washed Palladian villa was once the home of Robert Browning. Set in the low Veneto hills, the romantic Cipriani has a welcoming, lived-in feel. The pastel-coloured bedrooms overlook manicured grounds. Local facilities include golf, tennis courts and horse-riding. €€€€

Bassano del Grappa
This old-fashioned town is popular with foreigners in search of peace, quiet and *grappa*.
Bonotto Hotel Belvedere
Piazzale Giardino 14
Tel: 0424-529845
Fax: 0424-529849
Some rooms in the centrally based Belvedere are nicely old-fashioned, while others are more modern, and consequently have less character. The hotel also has a noted restaurant, Il Ristorante di Buon Ricordo. €€–€€€

Lake Garda
Hotel Gardesana
Torri del Benaco
Piazza Calderini 20
Tel: 045-722 5411
Fax: 045-722 5771
www.hotel-gardesana.com
This delightful medieval harbour-master's house, which overlooks Lake Garda, has been converted into a welcoming, well-furnished three-star hotel. Bedrooms on the third floor are the quietest and they have lovely views over the lake. €€€

Padua (Padova)
If Venice is fully booked or too pricey, consider making Padua your base. This historic city, famed for its ancient university and Giotto's frescoes, has much to offer, and while it lacks the obvious romance of Venice, it has culture aplenty. And Padua is infinitely preferable to the garish resorts nearby (such as Lido di Jesolo), or so-called "mainland Venice", the grim commercial and industrial area around Mestre
Majestic Toscanelli
Via dell'Arco 2
Tel: 049-663244
Fax: 049-8760025
This small, cosy four-star hotel lies in the heart of the old quarter, close to Piazza delle Erbe, an area that is gradually being renovated. Although the hotel is neither majestic nor Tuscan, despite its name, it is well run. Some of the bedrooms are lovely, if rather small. There is no restaurant, but the hotel is handy for exploring haunts in historic Padua, including the good local *osterie* and boutiques. €–€€

Verona
One of Italy's most romantic destinations, Verona is ideal for a city break, particularly since several low-cost airlines now run flights here or to nearby airports such as Brescia, Bergamo and Treviso. Beds can be hard to find during the annual wine trade fair, Vinitaly, or when operatic performances are being staged at the Roman Arena, so check these dates with the Verona tourist office.
Due Torri Baglioni
Piazza Sant'Anastasia 4
Tel: 045-595044
Freephone in Italy: 167821057
Fax: 045-8004130
www.baglionihotels.com
This grand classical *palazzo* , a

Price Categories

Price categories are based on a double room without breakfast:
€ = under €80
€€ = €80–160
€€€ = €160–280
€€€€ = more than €280

Veronese institution, has been refurbished and converted into a luxury hotel. It has an excellent, if rather formal, restaurant with a fine wine list. There are eight suites as well as luxurious bedrooms. €€€€
Giulietta e Romeo
Vicolo Tre Marchetti 3
Tel: 045-8003554
Fax: 045-8010862
Set in the historic centre, close to the celebrated Roman Arena, this is a popular, good-value hotel. The comfortable rooms are decorated in good taste and have spacious bathrooms, but there is no restaurant. Parking is in a nearby alley. €€
Victoria
Via Adua 6
Tel: 045-590566
Fax: 045-590155
Set in the heart of the old quarter of Verona, this historic 12th-century *palazzo* has been creatively yet sensitively converted. The bedrooms are superbly inviting and the reception rooms feature original Roman and medieval decoration. The owner is friendly and the staff are generally helpful. €€–€€€

Vicenza
Giardini
Via Giuriolo 10
Tel/fax: 0444-326458
E-mail: info@hotelgiardini.com
This recently renovated *albergo* is modern, comfortable and offers good value for money. €€–€€€
Villa Michelangelo
Via Sacco 35
Arcugnano, near Vicenza
Tel: 0444-550300
Fax: 0444-550490
Set in Arcugnano, 7 km (4½ miles) south of Vicenza, this handsome 18th-century villa surveys the vine-clad slopes from its eyrie on a hill. Now converted into a stylish four-star hotel, it has a well-regarded restaurant. €€–€€€

TRENTINO

Trentino is best known for its ski stations in the Dolomites, so the hotels in the ski resorts here tend to do excellent business during winter. The jewel in the crown is Madonna di Campiglio, Italy's most prestigious ski resort after Cortina d'Ampezzo. Prices are relatively high but you can also choose to stay in furnished apartments, which are less expensive than hotels. Lake Garda is the other area in Trentino that is in great demand throughout the year.

Cavalese
Hotel La Stua
Via Baldieroni 2
Tel: 0462-340 235
Fax: 0462-231120
This rustic-style hotel is set in the heart of the Alpine resort of Cavalese, which is popular both for winter skiing and summer rambling. La Stua is named after the traditional large mountain stove that is on display here. Pleasant wood-panelled rooms are cosy, individualistic and well equipped. The hotel has a steam room, sauna and hay baths, a popular therapeutic treatment here that involves lying under a huge pile of clean hay and sweating your cares away. The restaurant serves filling local specialities. €–€€

Cognola (near Trento)
Villa Madruzzo
Via Ponte Alto 26
Tel: 0461-986220
Fax: 0461-986361
This grand hill-top villa is set in lovely grounds and is generally more appealing than most of the hotels in Trento, the provincial capital, 3 km (1½ miles) away. The villa's elegant interior is matched by pleasing service and good traditional cuisine, with dishes featuring mushrooms a local speciality. It's a good base for exploring Trento and the Dolomites, and non-residents can eat at the restaurant. €–€€

Levico Terme
Imperial Grand Hotel Terme
Via Silva Domini 1
Tel: 0461-706104
Fax: 0461-706350
Freephone number: 167265211

This grand, sensitively restored Hapsburg villa is a lasting reminder of what this area must have been like under Austrian domination. The atmosphere here is formal rather than welcoming but the impressive facilities include a health and fitness centre, indoor and outdoor pools, and tennis courts. There is also a convention centre. €€–€€€

Madonna di Campiglio
Diana
Via Cima Tosa 32
Tel: 0465-441011
Fax: 0465-441049
www.hoteldiana.net
This Alpine chalet is in the heart of the province's most stylish ski resort, and its wood-finished interior has a gentrified rustic air and is extremely popular during the skiing season. Bedrooms are in quiet good taste. Facilities include a sauna, steam room and solarium. Here, as in many other ski resorts, you will be encouraged to take half-board at peak periods. €€–€€€

Trento
Hotel Accademia
Vicolo Colico 4–6
Tel: 0461-233600
Fax: 0461-230174
Set in a medieval building in the historic heart of Trento, this family-run hotel has great character. The charm lies in such details as wooden shutters, geranium-filled window boxes, vaulted ceilings and gentrified rustic bedrooms, which have been fully modernised. The panelled suite on the top floor is popular with celebrities. The restaurant serves good local dishes and there is also an *enoteca*, for snacks and sampling the local wines. Good service. €€€
Hotel del Buonconsiglio
Via Romagnosi 16/18
Tel: 0461-272888
Fax: 0461-272889
This pleasant modern hotel is well equipped, comfortable and set close to the historic centre. In true Italian style, it believes in providing a lot of marble for its money, but the overall effect is a touch soulless. €€

Riva del Garda
Hotel du Lac et du Parc
Viale Rovereto 44
Tel: 0464-551500
Fax: 0464-555200
This part-old, part-modern hotel enjoys a lakeside location in Trentino's most popular lake resort, on a section of Lake Garda where motor boats are banned. As well as the hotel, there are holiday chalets in the spacious grounds and facilities include many restaurants, a piano bar, tennis courts, a sailing and wind-surfing school and a fitness centre. The hotel is also geared to conferences and congresses. €€€–€€€€

ALTO ADIGE (SOUTH TYROL)

The overriding atmosphere here is more Germanic than Italian, as befits this bilingual province. The accommodation ranges from quaint flower-bedecked Tyrolean chalets to family-run inns and grand castles.

Merano
Castel Rundegg
Via Scena 2
Merano, Provincia di Bolzano
Tel: 0473-234100
Fax: 0473-237200
This fairytale Tyrolean castle is promoted as a health and beauty farm, with a range of treatments. The castle is in fact a fortified manor house, dating from the 12th century and set in landscaped grounds close to Merano. Some rooms have Gothic vaulting, beams and panelling. It's atmospheric, but the style may seem a little too contrived for some tastes. The upmarket restaurant can cope with special diets as well as classic Mediterranean cuisine. Facilities include an indoor pool, gym, fitness centre and a sauna. There is also a golf course nearby. €€€–€€€€
Villa Tivoli
Via Verdi 72
Tel: 0473-446282
Fax: 0473-446849
www.villativoli.it
Peacefully located within its own

gardens, this small Liberty-style hotel is an oasis of tranquillity, and deservedly attracts high acclaim. In summer, meals are served alfresco on a terrace with panoramic views. €€–€€€

FRIULI-VENEZIA GIULIA

Trieste
Grand Hotel Duchi d'Aosta
Piazza Unità d'Italia 2
Tel: 040-760 0011
Fax: 040-366092
This luxurious hotel, set in a handy position in the old part of town, is old-fashioned and dignified. Big, well-furnished rooms are matched by efficient service. €€€–€€€€
Jolly
Corso Cavour 7
Tel: 040-760 0055
Fax: 040-362 699
www.jollyhotels.it
This modern hotel is typical of the Jolly style, so good service and comfort abound. The downside is the anonymous décor, in keeping with the chain's desire to also attract a business clientele. €€€

EMILIA-ROMAGNA

Emilia Romagna has a great range of accommodation, with particularly fine hotels set in Bologna, Ferrara and Modena.

Bologna
Dei Commercianti
Via dei Pignattari 11
Tel: 051-233 052
Fax: 051-224733
www.cnc.it/bdegna
This historic hotel was formerly Bologna's city hall and it retains several original features. All the bedrooms are different – some have private terraces and lovely views to the church of San Petronius – but a few of the singles are cramped. There is no restaurant. €€€–€€€€
Grand Hotel Baglioni
Via dell' Independenza 8
Tel: 051-225445
Fax: 051-234840
Freephone: 167821057

www.ghb.bologna@baglionihotels.com
This sophisticated hotel in the heart of Bologna is ideal for shopping and all the main sites. Bedrooms are comfortable, staff are courteous and the restaurant is good. Baglioni is generally a reliable hotel chain at the upper end of the market and more appealing than the anonymous international chain hotels. €€€€
Hotel Elite
Via Aurelio Saffi 36
Tel: 051-6459011
Fax: 051-6492426
This comfortable modern hotel is convenient for the airport. Some rooms have kitchenettes, designed for long-stay visitors. The hotel also has one of the best restaurants in Bologna. €€–€€€
Jolly de la Gare
Piazza XX Settembre 2
Tel: 051-281611
Fax: 051-249764
This large, comfortable four-star hotel is set close to the station and the Alitalia air terminal. €€€€
Orologio
Via IV Novembre 10
Tel: 051-231253
Fax: 051-260552
www.orologio.hotel-bologna.net
In the heart of the historic centre, this newly refurbished former palazzo offers every comfort and excellent service. There are 29 very stylish rooms and five suites. €€€
Royal Carlton
Via Montebello 8
Tel: 051-249361
Fax: 051-249724
This large hotel is very comfortable and handily located close to the centre of Bologna. Recently renovated. There are a number of well-equipped suites so the professional ambience and convenient location makes this a

Price Categories

Price categories are based on a double room without breakfast:
€ = under €80
€€ = €80–160
€€€ = €160–280
€€€€ = more than €280

popular choice for executives and tourists alike. €€€€

Ferrara
Duchessa Isabella
Via Palestro 70
Tel: 0532-202121
Fax: 0532-202638
This small, frescoed 15th-century palazzo is the finest hotel in Ferrara, which, given the choice of lovely Gothic residences here, is quite a compliment. Authentic features include inlaid ceilings and the reception rooms are studded with antiques. Facilities on offer include bicycles, an extremely popular form of transport in flat Ferrara. In summer, breakfast is served in the hotel's lovely garden. Considerate, helpful staff. €€€–€€€€
Hotel Ripagrande
Via Ripagrande 21
Tel: 0532-765250
Fax: 0532-764377
www.ripagrandehotel.it
This Renaissance palace, with a grand entrance hall, air of refinement and good cuisine (served in the courtyard in summer), is set in the heart of historic Ferrara, close to the intriguing former Jewish ghetto. The only jarring note is the huge difference in size and quality between the bedrooms: a single can mean a box room unless you make it very clear that this is not acceptable. €€€

Parma
Grand Hotel Baglioni
Via dell' Indipendenza 8
Tel: 0512-25445
Fax: 0512-34840
Freephone: 167821057
www.baglionihotels.com
This is a sophisticated modern hotel, well placed for the historic centre. The building has an ugly exterior, but the advantages come in the form of spacious bedrooms, an impressive, if coolly clinical, marble interior, and a good restaurant. Best suited to business visitors. €€€–€€€€
Villa Ducale
Via del Popolo 35/a
Tel: 0521-272727
Fax: 0521-780756
This charming, welcoming villa is

set in appealing and award-winning grounds. Attentive service. €€€

Ravenna
Bisanzio
Via Salara 30
Tel: 0544-217111
Fax: 0544-32539
This modern, comfortable hotel is located close to such notable Byzantine monuments as San Vitale and the Mausoleum of Gallia Placidia. Also on offer are marble-clad interiors, spacious bedrooms, good breakfasts and a pleasant garden. €€–€€€

FLORENCE

Florence has lots of delightful accommodation but there is often a severe shortage and prices are relatively high. You need to book well in advance if you want to have any chance of staying in a good hotel, or book with a reputable tour operator, who will probably have a fixed allocation of rooms. Instead of staying in the city centre, which can be very hot in summer, you could head for the cool hills above the city, in such engaging villages as Fiesole.

Grand Hotels
Brunelleschi
Piazza Santa Elisabetta 3
Tel: 055-27370
Fax: 055-219653
www.hotelbrunelleschi.it
Close to the Duomo, this luxurious place was once a medieval prison. It is the most atmospheric city-centre hotel in Florence, with a beautifully restored church, Byzantine tower and private museum incorporated into the building. Another unique feature are the remains of Roman baths that were discovered here and are now on general view. The bedrooms and suites overlook the cupola that surmounts the Duomo. The Santa Elisabetta restaurant specialises in Tuscan dishes. €€€–€€€€
Grand Hotel Villa Medici
Via Il Prato 42
Tel: 055-277171
Fax: 055-2381336

Price Categories

Price categories are based on a double room without breakfast:
€ = under €80
€€ = €80–160
€€€ = €160–280
€€€€ = more than €280

With its huge bedrooms, roof-garden restaurant and swimming pool, this 18th-century villa-hotel offers everything you could desire, including a good location near the railway station. €€€€
Helvetia & Bristol
Via dei Pescioni 2
Tel: 055-26651
Fax: 055-288353
www.charminghotels.it
This is among the best luxury small hotels in the city, with many famous names on its guest list. Elegant and extremely comfortable rooms and suites (45 rooms, 13 suites). There is a good restaurant and a delightful winter garden. €€€€
Hotel de la Ville
Piazza Antinori 1
Tel: 055-2381805
Fax: 055-2381809
This is a quiet and elegant hotel, now completely restored, located in the centre next to Via de' Torna-buoni. The atmosphere is elegant but understated, and the service is discreet but correct. Bar, sitting room and terrace. €€€–€€€€
Lungarno
Borgo San Jacopo 14
Tel: 055-27261
Fax: 055-268437
This stylish hotel overlooks the Arno between Ponte Vecchio and Ponte Santa Trinità. A medieval tower is incorporated into the otherwise modern structure of the hotel but, somehow, this seems to work. The Lungarno, unusually for Florence, houses a fine collection of modern art. Room number 891 is especially recommended – it is lavishly furnished with antiques, and has a terrace overlooking the river. €€€€
Savoy
Piazza della Repubblica 7
Tel: 055-27351
Fax: 055-2735888

Set on one of the city's grandest squares, the Savoy is a Florentine institution and now beautifully restored. It is still undoubtedly an Italian classic in style and service, with many rooms decorated in the Venetian style. €€€€
Westin Excelsior
Piazza Ognissanti 3
Tel: 055-264201
Fax: 055-210278
Set in the historic heart of the city, this luxurious hotel unfortunately rests rather on its laurels. It does, however, occupy an ancient palace overlooking the Arno and features 16th-century frescoes, marble floors, antique tapestries and period furniture. The terrace restaurant has river views. Service tends to be under par but the location is wonderful. €€€€

Small Hotels
Annalena
Via Romana 34
Tel: 055-229600
Fax: 055-222403
www.hotelannalena.it
Located across the Ponte Vecchio, opposite the rear entrance to the Boboli Gardens, this little hotel offers a lovely Florentine experience at a reasonable price. The frescoed entrance leads to tasteful antique-furnished bedrooms. €€€
Beacci Tornabuoni
Via Tornabuoni 3
Tel: 055-212645
Fax: 055-283594
www.bthotel.it
This small and atmospheric hotel occupies the top floors of a Renaissance *palazzo* on the most elegant shopping street in Florence. Roof-garden restaurant; half-board compulsory. €€€
Regency
Piazza Massimo d'Azeglio 3
Tel: 055-245247
Fax: 055-2346735
www.regency-hotel.com
This small 19th-century villa is perfect for those in search of tranquillity. The hotel has a lovely garden, beautiful furniture, a gourmet restaurant, impressive service, a central position and a price to match. €€€€

Florentine Hills

The hills around the city are always an attractive proposition, especially in the hot summer months. Fiesole, 8 km (5 miles) outside the city, makes a good summer base.

Grand Hotel Villa Cora
Viale Machiavelli 18
Tel: 055-2298451
Fax: 055-229086
www.villacora.it
Although this luxurious villa-hotel is located in the Florentine hills, it is still convenient for the city centre. Built by Baron Oppenheim in Neo-classical style, Cora once hosted Eugenia di Montijo, the widow of Napoleon III, and the rich Baroness Von Meck, a patron of both Tchaikovsky and Debussy. Has a huge park and a pool. €€€€

Pensione Bencistà
Via Benedetto da Maiano 4,
Fiesole
Tel/fax: 055-59163
Situated outside the city, between Fiesole and San Domenico, this small 15th-century villa is decorated with low-key rustic good taste and attracts a loyal clientele for its peaceful grounds, pleasant summer terrace and the typically Tuscan cuisine. Half-board only. Closed December and January. €€

Villa Le Rondini
Via Bolognese Vecchia 224
Trespiano
Tel: 055-400081
Fax: 055-268212
www.villalerondini.it
Set in the hills 4 km (2½ miles) from Florence, this period villa has been modernised out of all recognition yet remains a characteristic villa in lovely grounds. Reception rooms are airy, bedrooms are comfortable, and the restaurant is excellent, serving produce from the owners' family farm. What really sets this hotel apart from most of the city-centre hotels is the sense of space and the great views over the city. Facilities include a heliport, tennis court and a delightful pool set in olive groves. There is a regular shuttle service to the centre of Florence.
€€€–€€€€

TUSCANY

As a region with centuries of tourism behind it, Tuscany has the best range of accommodation in Italy. However, the popularity of vine-clad Chiantishire and the delightful medieval hill-top towns makes bargains scarce. In summer, the appeal of the Siena–Florence–San Gimignano golden triangle still makes finding the right place tricky, at least at an affordable price.

Abetone

Abetone is one of the best-equipped ski resorts in the Apennine range. The pistes are well kept and easily accessible from the town centre. The resort is equally appealing in summer when the heat of the Tuscan cities drives residents to the mountains or the sea. Abetone is a lovely base for summer walking holidays, with clearly marked trails suitable for people of all ages and levels of fitness.

Hotel Bellavista
Via Brennero 383
Tel: 0573-60028
Fax: 0573-60245
The Bellavista is the best hotel in Abetone, in a great central location with lovely views. Once a hunting lodge owned by the noble Florentine Strozzi family, it was later converted into a welcoming Alpine-style four-star hotel, which gets very busy in the ski season. The interior is in a rustic, cosy style and is framed by balconies and a large terrace for summer dining. The situation, layout and security aspects of the rooms make the modern part especially suitable for young children or more elderly guests. Cuisine, including a creative breakfast, is tasty and filling. The owner and her family do their utmost to satisfy individual requirements. €€

Arezzo

Arezzo is a prosperous city thanks to the gold jewellery trade and other local enterprises. The recent restoration of Piero della Francesca's masterpieces in San Francesco has also helped make Arezzo a firm fixture on the tourist trail. The countryside around Arezzo is worth exploring, particularly the rugged Casentino.

Castello di Gargonza
Monte San Savino 52048
Tel: 0575-847021
Fax: 0575-847054
www.gargonza.it
This meticulously restored medieval hamlet lies in the Tuscan hills between Arezzo and Siena. Visitors stay in modernised 13th-century apartments and cottages. The excellent restaurant serves Tuscan dishes. There is a swimming pool in the grounds and horse-riding in the hills nearby. The hotel is part of the excellent Abitare La Storia group of independent hotels. €€–€€€

Val di Colle
Località Bagnoro, Scopeto
Tel/fax: 0575-365167
Set in a tranquil position, this beautifully restored 14th-century house is 4 km (2½ miles) from the centre of Arezzo. There are elegant bedrooms with a rustic theme. Antique furniture co-exists harmoniously with modern art. €€

Lucca

Hotel Villa Rinascimento
Santa Maria del Guidice,
Tel: 0583-378292
Fax: 0583-370238.
This beautifully restored Renaissance villa lies on the road to Pisa and is 9 km (5 miles) from Lucca. The interior is simple yet lovely and the grounds include a pool and olive groves. Open March to October. €€–€€€

Villa La Principessa
Via Nuova per Pisa 1616, Massa Pisana, 4.5 km (3 miles) from Lucca.
Tel: 0583-370037
Fax: 0583-379136
This peaceful rambling patrician villa is decorated in stately 18th-century Parisian style. Bedrooms are dotted with antiques, while public rooms, including the two drawing rooms, are hung with works of art. €€€–€€€€

Pietrasanta

Pietrasanta makes a good base for exploring the Tuscan coast all the way to Viareggio and Forte dei Marmi. You can also make forays from here into the hinterland to visit such historic towns as Lucca.

Albergo Pietrasanta
Palazzo Barsanti Bonetti
Via Garibaldi 35
Tel: 0584-793726
Fax: 0584-793728
Pietrasanta is at the forefront of Italian sculpture, thanks to its famed marble quarries – Michelangelo. Henry Moore and Pomodoro were regular visitors. The village is home to sculptors of international renown and this relatively new hotel in a 17th-century *palazzo* has great appeal to visiting artists, with hand-decorated ceilings and doors, works of art and elaborate period furniture. It has the feel of a stylish private home, and breakfast is served in the winter garden. €€€

Radda in Chianti
Villa Miranda
Radda, Siena province
Tel: 0577-738021
Fax: 0577-738668
This appealing Chiantishire villa, which has been run by the same family since the 1840s, is ideally placed for trips into the vineyards. Bedrooms have beamed ceilings and brass bedsteads. €€

San Gimignano
Villa San Paolo
Strada per Certaldo, (Casini)
Tel: 0577-955100
Fax: 0577-9551113
This delightful classical villa is set on a hillside 4 km (2½ miles) from San Gimignano, and its terraced grounds include a pool and tennis courts. The bedrooms are very cosy and the service is friendly. €€€

Sinalunga
Locanda dell'Amorosa
Tel: 0577-677211
Fax: 0577-632001
www.amorosa.it
Sinalunga is certainly not the most attractive of Tuscan towns but it matters little to guests at the Locanda, who find an oasis of calm beyond the town. This lovely medieval complex has long been

famed for its gastronomic excellence, but the romance of the building means that the 14 bedrooms and six suites are as sought after as tables in the restaurant. The Locanda is a typical member of Abitare La Storia, a traditional Italian association of independent historic hotels. Swimming pool; wine bar. €€€€

Siena
Visitors choosing Siena as a base need to decide between an historic city hotel or a rural retreat in Siena province. Bear in mind that, in summer, city accommodation may be scarce, particularly during the Palio race in July and August.

Borgo Monastero
Castelnuovo Berardenga
Tel: 02-90960931
Fax: 02-90969365
Set in the heart of Siena province, this *borgo medeovale*, or fortified village, is one of many such Italian sites that has succumbed to large-scale *agriturismo*. Its restoration has been meticulous, and from the outside, no-one would guess that the Borgo is no longer a classic Tuscan village. It is divided into 64 self-catering apartments, all with access to the excellent facilities, including pools, tennis courts and mountain bikes. The landscape is typically Tuscan, with olive groves, vineyards and woods. Open all year. €€–€€€

Certosa di Maggiano
Strada di Certosa 82
Tel: 0577-288180

One option is to book with a reputable tour operator, who will probably have a fixed allocation in some of the best hotels. The alternative is to book a villa holiday or stay in an *agriturismo* property. However, although it has been an *agriturismo*-seller's market until now, the greed of certain Tuscan property owners means that there has been an explosion of self-catering properties in this sector, with great differences in quality.

Fax: 0577-288189
This unique 14th-century Carthusian monastery is the oldest such building in Tuscany. Now converted into a five-star hotel, it is adorned with antiques and offers a prestigious restaurant, library and lovely cloisters. €€€€

Garden
Via Custoza 2
Tel: 0577-47056
Fax: 0577-46050
This 18th-century patrician villa is now a comfortable hotel with formal Italian gardens and an indoor swimming pool. The hosts are welcoming and the restaurant has panoramic views. €€€

Palazzo Ravizza
Piano dei Mantellini 34
Tel: 0577-280462
Fax: 0577-221597
www.palazzoravizza.it
This atmospheric family-run villa is five minutes' walk from the historic centre of Siena. Although it is far from being one of the most expensive city hotels, it remains one of the most appealing and arguably the most typically Sienese. The *palazzo* retains its original 17th- and 18th-century frescoes and furnishings and some of the bedrooms are huge and decorated in imposing Empire style. The breakfast room overlooks the garden and there is a good restaurant. Half-board encouraged in summer. €€€

Villa Scacciapensieri
Via Scacciapensieri 10
Tel: 0577-41441
Fax: 0572-70854
This delightful villa is set on a hill 3.5 km (2 miles) from Siena and has sweeping views down to the centre of town. The villa is surrounded by landscaped classical gardens and it also has a pool. The bedrooms are relatively simple. €€€

Grosseto
Fattoria San Lorenzo
Via Aurelia Antica
Grosseto province
Tel: 0564-28423
This traditional farmhouse lies 9 km (5½ miles) from the sea, off the Principina-Castiglione della Pescaia road from Grosseto. Dating from the

late 17th-century, it is at the heart of a working agricultural estate that produces vegetables, fruit and sunflowers (which guests can buy). Maremma is noted for its magnificent white cattle, which feature in an annual rodeo nearby. A number of cottages and outbuildings have been converted into *agriturismo* self-catering apartments, but don't expect real privacy because it can house up to 100 people. There is a pool, a lake for fishing and a restaurant, plus opportunities for horse-riding and country walks. €€

Porto Ercole
Il Pellicano
Località Lo Sbarcatello
4.5 km (3 miles) southwest of Porto Ercole
Tel: 0564-858111
Fax: 0564-833418
www.pellicanohotel.com
This luxurious modern hotel and villa complex, located in the region's chicest port, is composed of independent villas and cottages, all set among the pine and olive groves by the beach. Guests have the privacy of villa-living but all the services and facilities of a top hotel. Facilities include a private beach, heated pool and fitness centre. The cuisine is inspired by Mediterranean fare. €€€€

UMBRIA & THE MARCHES

In some respects, Umbria is the new Tuscany, at least to many discerning travellers. The quality and range of accommodation is excellent, with the region particularly good at supplying individualistic accommodation, whether in historic frescoed city *palazzi* or on grand estates. The earthquake in the late 1990s damaged certain areas in Umbria, including Assisi, Spello and Norcia, but large subsidies have helped to deal with the renovation and rebuilding work, at least on major monuments. The Marche, with the notable exception of Urbino, is far less developed, although this may well change in the near future.

Assisi
Subasio
Via Frate Elia 2
Tel: 075-812206
Fax: 075-816691
The columns of this hotel link to the church of San Francesco, and the terraces command a wonderful view of the town and countryside. Many famous people have stayed here, including the Belgian royal family, and actors Charlie Chaplin, James Stewart, Marlene Dietrich and Gabriele d'Anunzio. Good rooms and service. €€–€€€
Umbra
Vicolo degli Archi 6
Piazza del Comune
Tel: 075-812240
Fax: 075-813653
Bordering the Piazza del Comune, the Umbra is set in an atmospheric spot and is also the most central hotel in Assisi. Though small, the 25 rooms are comfortable, if low-key. The restaurant is very good, with alfresco service on the terrace in summer. €€

Campello sul Clitunno
Vecchio Molino
Via del Tempio
Pissignano 34
Tel: 0743-521122
Fax: 0743-275097
This former mill – a rough-hewn stone, creeper-clad structure – retains many medieval features, and is one of the most romantic hotels in Umbria. €€–€€€

Gubbio
Park Hotel ai Cappuccini
Via Tifernate
Tel: 075-9234
Fax 075-9220323
Set at the foot of the Gubbio hills, this austere 17th-century convent is now a striking hotel blessed with

every modern comfort. The restoration has retained the basic spirit of the place, and the original terracotta floors and marble-faced arches remain, as does the old well in the centre of the cloisters. However, the hotel also has a heated pool, gym, tennis courts, solarium and Jacuzzi, as well as a very good collection of modern art. The restaurant serves delicious Umbrian dishes, which are matched by a good wine list. €€€

Perugia
Brufani Palace
Piazza Italia 12
Tel: 075-5732541
Fax: 075-5720210
This luxurious, recently remodelled 19th-century hotel is furnished with antiques, but the slightly precious décor makes it look rather affected. The terrace of the restaurant, where truffles are a speciality, has lovely views over the valley. €€€–€€€€
La Rosetta
Piazza Italia 19
Tel/fax: 075-5720841
La Rosetta is a good hotel with a new and an old wing. Eat in the courtyard under pergolas and palms in the summer. Fine service and a menu featuring Umbrian specialities. €€
Le Tre Vaselle
Torgiano Perugia, via Garibaldi 48
Tel: 075-9880447
Fax: 075-9880214
A little way from Perugia (15 km/ 9 miles), this is a wonderful small hotel and health centre in a 17th-century villa owned by Giorgio Lungarotti, one of Italy's most famous wine collectors. Great cooking in Le Melograne restaurant, and a pleasant ambience. €€€

Spello
Hotel Palazzo Bocci
Via Cavour 17
Tel: 0742-301021
Fax: 0742-301464
This lovely early 14th-century palace has some wonderfully quirky corners and many tiny decorative niches. The public rooms feature vaulted, frescoed ceilings and

hidden architectural details. *Il Mulino* restaurant, facing the hotel, is noted for its Umbrian and classic Italian cuisine. €€–€€€

Urbino
Bonconte
Via delle Mura 28
Tel: 0722-2463
Freephone: 176867148
Fax: 0722-4782
www.viphotels.it
This delightful villa-hotel is set within the famous walled town, near the Ducal palace. The interior is comfortable and elegant and the restaurant is well reputed. €€–€€€

ABRUZZO & MOLISE

Although gradually improving, these regions are still woefully behind most others in Italy in their range and quality of accommodation. However, the same does not apply to Abruzzese cuisine, which is popular across Italy.

L'Aquila
Hotel Duomo
Via Dragonetti 6
Tel: 0862-410893
Very centrally located within a few steps of the Piazza del Duomo, this hotel is charming and offers a warm welcome. It is also extremely reasonably priced. €–€€

Pescara
Esplanade
Piazza 1 Maggio 46
Tel: 085-292141
Fax: 085-4217540
This is an old-style elegant hotel with a modernised interior with spacious rooms. The Esplanade overlooks the beach, so it affords good views. €€–€€€

Price Categories

Price categories are based on a double room without breakfast:
€ = under €80
€€ = €80–160
€€€ = €160–280
€€€€ = more than €280

NAPLES

Thanks to the partial regeneration of the city centre, the successful clean-up of several problem areas and the opening of new routes to the city by low-cost airline carriers, Naples is once again becoming an appealing destination.

Excelsior
Via Partenope 48
Tel: 081-7640111
Fax: 081-7649743
This luxurious hotel is set on the seafront, just across the street from the Castel dell'Ovo. It has a wonderful view of the Gulf of Naples and the terrace is lovely. €€€€

Grand Hotel Parker's
Corso Vittorio Emanuele 135
Tel: 081-7612474
Fax: 081-663527
This chic and well-known hotel – the first choice for many visitors to Naples – is located in a 19th-century *palazzo*. There are stunning views over the Gulf of Naples. The décor is refined yet casual and the service is excellent. €€€€

Grand Hotel Santa Lucia
Via Partneope 46
Tel: 081-7640666
Fax: 081-7648580
www.santalucia.it
From this classically grand hotel there are wonderful views over the Bay of Naples and the Castel dell'Ovo. Very stylish, elegant rooms (88 rooms and 8 suites), and courteous service. €€€€

Grande Hotel Vesuvio
Via Partenope 45
Tel: 081-7640044
Fax: 081-7644483
This luxurious 19th-century hotel overlooks the marina and the Gulf of Naples. Many of the bedrooms are very grand, with marble bathrooms. The style is supposedly *belle époque* but there are lapses in taste, as well as some less attractive modern additions. The staff are attentive and professional. €€€€

Miramare
Via Nazario Sauro 24
Tel: 081-7647589
Fax: 081-7640775
www.hotelmiramare.com
This art nouveau hotel, which

Booking in Naples

If you need to find a room, even at short notice, contact the Naples tourist office, tel: 081-5512701, or the Neapolitan Hoteliers Association, tel: 081-5520205, fax 5529660, www.napleshotels.na.it.

overlooks the old port, has such elaborate touches as an amber-lacquer panel in the lobby. The hotel is run by an enthusiastic owner (and his exuberant dog), so hospitality and helpful advice make up for the small bedrooms. The highlight is breakfast on the roof terrace, with views over Vesuvius. There is no restaurant here but guests are entitled to a 10 percent discount at several local places. Ask for a room with sea views. €€€–€€€€

Paradiso
Via Catullo 11
Tel: 081-2475111
Fax: 081-7613449
www.bestwestern.it
This elegant Best Western hotel is located in a quiet area in the hills of Posillipo, the slightly anonymous residential district above the historic city. Good views of the sea and the port. €€€

Royal
Via Partenope 38
Tel: 081-7644800
Fax: 081-7645707
www.hotelroyal.it
An elegant hotel in a prime site on the seafront, with good service. Each of the guest rooms has a balcony. It's popular with business travellers and has a large conference hall. €€€–€€€€

Splendid
Via Manzoni 96
Tel: 081-7141955
Fax: 081-7146431
www.hotelsplendid.it
Overlooking the bay, this hotel is set in the peaceful, panoramic, residential quarter of Posilippo. Many rooms have private terraces and it is especially convenient for the funicular down to the Lungomare. €€–€€€

CAMPANIA COAST & ISLANDS

Capri, Ischia and the Amalfi Coast are the main poles of attraction in Campania, with tiny Positano and the chic island of Capri taking most of the laurels (and the euros). Ischia is increasingly sought after, particularly for the water cures and mud-bathing in the island's radioactive pools. Sorrento has long been popular with package tourists and it still has great appeal, not least for the number of hotels that are luxurious or welcoming in a typically southern way. It is also well located for exploring the Amalfi coast, Pompeii and Capri. Bear in mind that some coastal hotels are closed between January and April, and in summer, guests are often expected to take half-board.

Amalfi
Hotel Cappuccini Convento
Via Annunziatella 46
Tel: 089-871877
Fax: 089-871886
The monastic cells of this former monastery have been converted into comfortable rooms featuring period furniture. There is a pleasant garden, an Arab-Norman cloister and panoramic views. Good value for money. €€–€€€

Capri
Grand Hotel Quisisana
Via Camerelle 2
Tel: 081-837 0788
Fax: 081-837 6080
This is Capri's grandest hotel, a dowager that began life as a sanatorium in 1845 but was converted into a quaint *pensione* 20 years later. Now, it is a luxury hotel with elegantly furnished rooms and a *bijou* pool. From the outdoor terrace, known as the island's open-air drawing room, guests can watch the world go by on Capri's quaint Piazzetta. Closed November to April. €€€€
Punta Tragara
Via Tragara 57
Tel: 081-8370844
Fax: 081-8377790

The Punta Tragara is comfortable and quiet, with a beautiful view of the Faraglioni. There is a three-night minimum stay in July and August. €€€€
Villa Brunella
Via Tragara 24
Tel: 081-8370122
Fax: 081-8370430;
www.villabrunella.it
Small, quiet hotel with a lovely flower-filled terrace, comfortable family atmosphere and classically elegant rooms. The restaurant has panoramas over the sea and the surrounding landscape. Swimming pool. €€€

Ischia
Grand Hotel Punta Molino Terme
Lungomare C. Colombo 23, Ischia Porto
Tel: 081-991544
Fax: 081-991562
Located near the tourist port and a small pine wood, this hotel specialises in curative bathing in the hotel's radioactive pool. The hotel service is good, but since you are paying for the privilege of indulging in water cures, it is worth booking elsewhere on the island if therapy of this type is not to your taste. €€€–€€€€
Regina Isabella
Piazza Restituta 1, Lacco Ameno
Tel: 081-994322
Fax: 081-900190
Here, guests can sample the curative baths that are typical of the area and indulge in various restorative cures from mud baths to thermal baths. A minimum three-night stay is expected in July and August. €€€€

Positano
Le Sireneuse
Via Colombo 30
Tel: 089-875066
Fax: 089-811798
In an 18th-century patrician villa, this luxurious hotel has long been a mecca for celebrities. Highlights are too numerous to list, but include wonderful views from the terrace and most bedrooms and delicious Campanian cuisine in the atmospheric restaurant. There's a

fitness centre, private boats, a cooking school and one of Italy's finest swimming pools. €€€€
Palazzo Murat
Via dei Mulini 23
Tel: 089-875177
Fax: 089-811419
Set close to the cathedral in this chic spot on the Amalfi coast, the hotel occupies a charming 18th-century *palazzo*. Some of the rooms are designed in rustic style and the overall effect is pleasing rather than twee. Recitals, concerts and exhibitions are sometimes held here. Compared with Le Sireneuse *(see above)*, this is good value. €€€–€€€€

Prices on the Coast

Much of the Campania coast is a popular destination at all times of year, so restaurant prices tend to be higher here than elsewhere in the region. Prices on the Capri and the Amalfi coasts are especially elevated.

Sorrento
Grand Hotel Ambasciatori
Via Califano 18
Tel: 081-8782025
Fax: 081-8071021
The Ambasciatori is a quiet Sorrento retreat, with a swimming pool and a large garden. €€€
Grand Hotel Excelsior Vittoria
Piazza Tasso 34
Tel: 081-807 1044
Fax: 081-8771206
Freephone in Italy: 800 90053
This is a well-established, elegant hotel, affording views across the Gulf of Naples and the Bay of Sorrento. Built in 1834, the gracious building is set among lemon and olive groves. Most bedrooms have a balcony overlooking the sea or the grounds and a private lift connects the hotel with the Bay of Sorrento. The renowned restaurant specialises in Neapolitan and Campanian cuisine. There are also two self-catering apartments in the grounds. €€€€

APULIA (PUGLIA)

Although Apulia has largely been overlooked by package holidays until now, green tourism looks set to be the future for the region. Hotels are often of a poor standard outside Bari, but regional accommodation includes the delightful trulli (see below) in Alberobello, and agriturismo, villa holidays and specialist holidays are also beginning to open up here. The experience of staying in a masseria pugliese, a fortified manor house, is something quite unique to Apulia.

Alberobello
This village is famed for its trulli, quaint conical houses that are available in various sizes (with one or two cones), depending on your needs.
Dei Trulli
Via Cadore 32
Tel: 080-4323555
Fax: 080-4323560
www.hoteldeitrulli.it
Furnishings here are simple to the point of austerity but somehow that is all part of the fun. However, if the novelty of living in a cone does wear off, the pleasant grounds with swimming pool at Dei Trulli may compensate. Half-board is available here in summer. €€–€€€

Savelletri
Masseria San Domenico
Località Petolcchia (65 km/40 miles from Bari; 54 km/33 miles from Brindisi)
Tel: 080-4827990/4827769
Fax: 080-4827978
www.imasseria.com
Lovely old masseria, whose origins date back to the 5th century, in secluded gardens with a large pool. Very peaceful location with gracious bedrooms, attentive service and very pleasant outdoor terrace. There is also a thalassotherapy centre and golf club. €€€€

Cisternino/Ostuni
Il Frantoio
(5 km/3 miles from Ostuni)
Tel/fax: 0831-330276
arbales@tin.it

This 16th-century wine estate is set in the Itria Valley, not far from the medieval town of Ostuni; it is an example of a masseria pugliese, a fortified manor house designed to house both the landowners and the workers' families. Here, organic oil produced in an ancient underground mill is sold in the farm's cave shop. This agriturismo offers superb Apulian country cooking and a great way of getting to know the people and customs of rural Italy. €€–€€€

Lecce
President
Via Salandra 6
Tel: 0832-456111
Fax: 0832-456632
This recommended hotel offers good service among rather uninspiring competitors. Located in the centre of town. €€–€€€

BASILICATA & CALABRIA

Although slowly improving, Basilicata and Calabria are still far behind most other Italian regions in their range and quality of accommodation.

Cosenza
Grand Hotel San Michele
Località Bosco 8/9
55 km (34 miles) from Cosenza, 16 km (10 miles) northwest of Cetrano
Tel: 0982-91012
Fax: 0982-91430
This hotel is in a magnificent setting, with a sheer drop down to the sea. It offers lots of comforts, including tennis courts, a swimming pool and a lift to the beach. €€€

Reggio di Calabria
Grand Hotel Excelsior
Via Vittorio Veneto 66
Tel: 0965-812211
Fax: 0965-893084
www.excelsior@reggiocalabria
hotels.it
This first-rate hotel which faces the Museo Nazionale offers some of the best facilities in the region, as well as comfortable rooms and good service. It serves both the business and leisure markets. €€€

SICILY

Accommodation in Sicily has improved greatly in recent years. Taormina remains the prime resort on the island, but other centres, from Cefalù to Agrigento and Erice, are gaining in popularity.

Agrigento
Villa Athena
Via Passeggiata Archeologica 33
Tel: 0922-596288
Fax: 0922-402180
This is a stylish 18th-century villa located very close to the Temples (building permission would never be granted today!) and consequently has a very fine view of the Temple of Concord. The rooms are modern and comfortable and the restaurant and service are both good. €€€

Cefalù
Cefalù is the rival resort to Taormina but, despite a wonderful Norman cathedral, it does not have the prestige, nor the facilities or luxury hotels, of that established east-coast holiday spot, Nevertheless, it can make quite a good base for exploring Palermo and the north coast of Sicily. Note that, unlike in Taormina, hotels here close between October and March.
Baia del Capitano
Località Mazzaforno (5 km/3 miles east of Cefalù).
Tel: 0921-420003
Fax: 0921-420163
This is a comfortable recently renovated Mediterranean-style modern hotel in an olive grove 5 km (3 miles) west of the town. There's a pool and tennis courts at the hotel and a beach nearby. €€–€€€
Kalura
Via Cavallaro 13
Località Caldura
Tel: 0921-421354
Fax: 0921-423122
www.kalura.it
Lying 2 km (just over a mile) out of town, this hotel has spacious rooms, all with a terrace. The grounds are attractive and there is a pool, as well as access to a private beach. Good for families, with an emphasis on sports facilities. €€–€€€

Erice

This lovely old village makes a far better base than Trapani for exploring the west of the island. The sea is some distance away but Erice is restful and atmospheric.

Baglio Santa Croce
Tel/fax: 0923-891111
www.bagliosantacroce.it
Set just outside the village of Erice on the flanks of Mt Erice, this 17th-century former farmhouse with beamed ceilings and brick floors is the loveliest place to stay in this area. It has a swimming pool and great views towards Trapani. €€

Elimo
Via V. Emanuele 73
Tel: 0923-869377
Fax: 0923-869252
www.charmerelax.com
This is a welcoming, cosy boutique hotel, converted in good taste and set in the middle of Erice. Formerly a 17th-century *palazzo*. Panoramic views. €€–€€€

Moderno
Via V. Emanuele 63
Tel: 0923-869300
Fax: 0923-869139
This is a pleasant if unremarkable hotel in the heart of the village. It's fairly old fashioned and decorated in simple yet good taste. Acclaimed restaurant. €€

Palermo

Excelsior Palace
Via Marchese Ugo 3
Tel: 091-6256176
Fax: 091-342139
Set off the chic and central Viale della Libertà, the Excelsior offers old-world charm, comfort and excellent cuisine, although it is now looking rather faded. It overlooks a pleasant park and is well located for a visit to the beach at Mondello. Note that there is a considerable difference between the size and quality of individual rooms. €€€€

Grand Hotel et des Palmes
Via Roma 398
Tel: 091-6028111
Fax: 091-331545
This old-fashioned, slightly dilapidated but centrally located historic hotel has art nouveau-style public rooms and a chequered history that includes a Mafia convention on the premises. It is also where Wagner composed his *Parsifal*. Rooms variable in quality and size. €€€

Grand Hotel Villa Igiea
Via Salita Belmonte 43
Tel: 091-6312111
Fax: 091-547654
Located near the Lido di Mondello, under Monte Pellegrino 3 km (2 miles) north of the city, this is Sicily's most prestigious hotel. The palace was built for the Florio dynasty and has lush gardens, sea views and a grand dining room. The villa, designed by the architect Basile, is meant to look like a Norman palace from the outside, although the interior is richly decorated with stucco-work and art nouveau furnishings. €€€€

Principe de Villafranca
Via G. Turrisi Colonna 4
Tel: 091-6118523
Fax: 091-588705
www.principedivillafranca.com
This charming boutique hotel is very popular. Spacious rooms have vaulted ceilings and there is a pleasing blend of contemporary and antique furnishings and furniture. Very good bar and restaurant. €€€

Siracusa

Grand Hotel Villa Politi
Via Maria Politi Laudien 2
Tel: 0931-412121
Fax: 0931-36061
This elegant, restored hotel has a cosseted atmosphere. The setting, in landscaped grounds overlooking the archaeological zone, is slightly inconvenient for those without a car, but the delightful secluded atmosphere makes up for it. Good service. €€€

Price Categories

Price categories are based on a double room without breakfast:
€ = under €80
€€ = €80–160
€€€ = €160–280
€€€€ = more than €280

Hotel Roma
Via Roma 66
Tel: 0931-465626
Fax: 0931-465535
www.hotelroma.sr.it
This very attractive small hotel is set in the heart of the lovely island of Ortygia. Recently totally renovated, it still retains its *palazzo* elegance and style and has plenty of period features. The restaurant, Vittorini, is very good, as is the service from the friendly staff. €€€

Taormina

This is Sicily's most prestigious resort, so accommodation is sometimes difficult to find here. Bear in mind that a number of Taormina hotels try to insist on guests taking half-board, especially in high season.

Grand Hotels

Grande Albergo Capo Taormina
Via Nazionale 105
Tel: 0942-572111
Fax: 0942-625467
Set just below the village, with stunning views of the bay, this large modern hotel is carefully landscaped into the rocks. Rooms are spacious and calming, with lovely views. Other big attractions include the grounds and the pool overlooking the rocky private beach. Of the hotel's two main restaurants, the best one, the fish restaurant *Il Pirata*, is romantically set on the beach. Ask for a room with a view overlooking Etna or Isola Bella. A shuttle service links the hotel with the village, which is 3 km (2 miles) away up a steep hill. €€€€

Grand Hotel Timeo & Villa Flora
Via Teatro Greco 59
Tel: 0942-23801
Fax: 0942-628501
This exclusive place is one of Taormina's top hotels, with spectacular views over the Greek Theatre, the coast and Mt Etna. It has an elegant, old-world atmosphere, impressive public rooms and sleek service. €€€€

San Domenico Palace
Piazza San Domenico 5
Tel: 0942-613111
Fax: 0942-625506

This is one of the best hotels in Sicily, as the former US president George Bush (senior), a past guest, would be the first to admit. The 15th-century monastery here has been converted into a glorious luxury hotel and has an elegant swimming pool. San Domenico is famous for its location, its floral park and the vast, high-ceilinged rooms with extraordinary views over Mt Etna and the sea. €€€€

Villa Hotels
Villa Ducale
Via Leonardo da Vinci 60
Tel: 0942 28153
Fax: 0942- 28710
This small villa with only 13 rooms has a delightful atmosphere. The cosy mood is enhanced by a small library and period furniture. There is also a romantic terrace for breakfast and views of Etna from certain rooms. Bedrooms, decorated with Sicilian ceramics, feature wrought-iron beds. €€€
Villa Fiorita
Via Pirandello 39
Tel: 0942-24122
Fax: 0942-625967
This atmospheric villa has lovely gardens and grand reception rooms adorned with coffered ceilings. The bedrooms are decorated in good taste and some have balconies or even terraces. Breakfast can be taken on the terrace or in an attractive dining room. There is also a pleasant pool. €€€
Villa Sant'Andrea,
Via Nazionale 137 (in Mazzaro, 5 km/3 miles east of Taormina)
Tel: 0942-23125
Fax: 0942-24838
This elegant, recently renovated old-fashioned villa, dotted with antiques, is surrounded by exotic gardens, and the gorgeous setting includes a breakfast terrace overlooking the sea with stunning views. €€€€

Where to Eat

What to Eat

Italian **breakfast** *(colazione)* is usually a light affair, consisting of a *cappuccino* and *brioche* (pastry), biscuits or crispbreads, or simply a *caffè* (black, strong *espresso*).

Lunch *(pranzo)* is traditionally the main meal of the day but this is gradually changing as Italy comes more into line with Northern Europe. Although, by preference, lunch would be the centrepiece of an Italian day, this is certainly no longer the case in the north of Italy, in the industrialised cities, or for dedicated workaholics across the country. A traditional lunch is increasingly the preserve of the south or the leisured classes. However, when Italians have the time to indulge in such lunches, then an ideal one might run as follows: after an *antipasto* (hors d'oeuvre), there follows a *primo* (pasta, rice or soup) and a *secondo* (meat or fish with a vegetable (known as a *contorno*) or just a salad. To follow, comes cheese or fruit. Italians usually drink an *espresso* after lunch and sometimes a liqueur, such as *grappa*, *amaro* or *sambuca*. Traditionally, **dinner** *(cena)* is similar to lunch, but lighter. However, in cities, as well as in the north and the centre of the country, as it becomes more normal to eat less at lunchtime, dinner is becoming the major meal of the day.

Every region in Italy has its own typical dishes: Piedmont specialises in pheasant, hare, truffles and *zabaglione* (a hot dessert made with whipped egg yolks, sugar and Marsala wine). Lombardy is known for *risotto alla Milanese* (saffron and onions), minestrone, veal and

panettone (a sweet, Christmas bread made with sultanas and candied fruits). Trentino-Alto Adige is the place for dumplings and thick, hearty soups to keep out the cold; Umbria is best for roast pork and black truffles, and Tuscany is good for wild boar, chestnuts, steak and game. Naples is the home of Mozzarella cheese and pizza and is good for seafood, and Sicily is the place to enjoy delectable sweets.

Italy still claims the best ice-cream in the world, as well as the Sicilian speciality *granita* (crushed ice with fruit juice or coffee).

Restaurant Listings

It is difficult to generalise about prices since much depends on the choice of dishes and menu selection – even noted chefs may offer a less expensive, but restricted menu in conjunction with the main menu. The price ranges should therefore only be taken as guides to value.

ROME

Agata e Romeo
Via Carlo Alberto 45
Tel: 06-4466115
www.agataromeo.it
This little temple to gastronomy has been the proud bearer of a Michelin star for over eight years. Traditional and creative forms of Roman and southern Italian cuisine are seamlessly blended and the wine list is among the best in Rome. Vegetarians are well catered for. Reservations essential. Closed weekends and from August 13–September 11. €€€€
Agustarello
Via Giovanni Branca 100
Tel: 06-5746585
Traditional, long-established *trattoria* specialising in real *cucina romana* or offal. The sons of the late owner reverently use every part of the animal and create delicious offerings such as *coda alla vaccinara* (oxtail with tomatoes, pinenuts, raisins and bitter chocolate) and *trippa alla romana* (tripe). Popular with the locals, so reservations are

recommended. Closed Sunday and August holidays. €€

Alberto Ciarla
Piazza San Cosimato 40
Tel: 06-5818668
Set on Trastevere's friendliest square, this fish restaurant is one of the best in Rome. The elegance, discretion and beautifully served food make a clear contrast to the friendly chaos of the market outside. Reserve. Closed Sunday and lunchtimes. €€€€

Bio Restaurant
Via Otranto 53
Tel: 06-45434943
As its name suggests this place is organic. You will eat well in these calming, earth-toned surroundings. €€

Cantina Cantarini
Piazza Sallustio 12
Tel: 06-485528
Informal, bustling taverna serving simple but very good dishes. From Thursday to Saturday evening only fish features on the menu. At other times the menu is meat-based Roman and *marchigiana* (from the Marche region). Closed middle two weeks in August. €€

Checchino dal 1887
Via Monte Testaccio 30
Tel: 06-5743816
The place for an authentic old-time family atmosphere, plus Roman cuisine of the offal variety – hardly surprising since this area, Testaccio, was the home of the slaughterhouse and Roman meat-processing industry. Not one for vegetarians. Closed Sunday, Monday, Christmas and August. Reserve.€€€–€€€€

Cul de Sac
Piazza Pasquino 73
Tel: 06-68801094
One of the best-stocked wine bars in Rome. Middle Eastern influenced snacks, hearty soups and salads are

Price Guide

The price of a three-course meal for one (not including wine):
€ = under €25
€€ = €25–45
€€€ = €45–70
€€€€ = €70 or more

on the menu. It gets packed so be prepared to queue as bookings are not taken. €–€€

Da Benito e Gilberto
Via del Falco 19
Tel: 06-6867769
Tucked away in the Borgo area between St Peter's and the Castel Sant'Angelo, this intimate, family-run restaurant is a great favourite both with locals and celebrities. Its speciality is superb fresh seafood and there is no menu, but you are guaranteed a gourmet feast. Reservations essential. Closed Sunday and Monday and lunchtime. €€€

Ditirambo
Piazza della Cancelleria 74
Tel: 06-6871626
Numerous vegetarian options such as ricotta flan with raw artichokes and pomegranate vinaigrette. Extensive wine list. €€

Il Convivio
Vicolo dei Soldati 31
Tel: 06-6869432
Run by three brothers, Il Convivio is one of the city's foremost temples to food and innovation. Equal emphasis is placed on vegetable, fish and meat options but they are always combined with the unexpected. Lunch and dinner Tuesday–Saturday, dinner only Monday. €€€€

Il Gonfalone
Via del Gonfalone 7
Tel: 06-68801269
Recently renovated, this smallish space is a quiet gourmet experience. Lovely outdoor seating on a quiet cobble-stoned street. The bread is home-made and the cuisine is a nouvelle take on Mediterranean. €€

Il Pagliaccio
Via dei Banchi Vecchi 129
Tel: 06-68809595
This smart restaurant has a limited but creative menu with an emphasis on beautiful presentation and quality ingredients. €€

Il Simposio
Piazza Cavour 16
Tel: 06-3211131
This Liberty-style restaurant adjoins the Bacchanalian paradise of the Costantini *enoteca* (wine bar). The

cellars hold over 4,000 bottles of wine to accompany the delicious, creative cuisine featuring seasonal specialities. There is a good selection of cheeses and snacks. Closed Sunday and August. Reservation recommended. €€€–€€€€

La Pergola
Via Cadlolo 101
Tel: 06-35092152
This sophisticated, rooftop restaurant with two Michelin stars belongs to the Cavalieri Hilton Hotel. The views are spectacular, the interior sumptuous and the menu a gastronome's dream. The place for a special celebration. Reservations essential. Closed Sunday and Monday, a period in January and August. Evenings only. €€€€

Myosotis
Vicolo della Vaccarella 3/5
Tel: 06-6865554
Warm and welcoming family-owned restaurant, close to the Piazza Navona. Fresh seafood, fresh pasta and excellent meats reflect the owners' commitment to using only the best raw materials. Excellent wine cellar. Closed Sunday, Monday lunch and August holidays. €€

Obikà
Via dei Prefetti 26 (corner of Piazza Firenze)
Tel 06-6832630
Rome's only Mozarella bar, but they serve plenty of main courses too. Minimal but welcoming setting. Cheap lunch menus available. €€

Piperno
Via Monte de' Cenci 9
Tel: 06-68806629
Traditional yet discreetly upmarket *trattoria* on a little piazza in the heart of the Ghetto district. The menu features classic Roman dishes such as *animelle con i carciofi* (lamb entrails with artichokes) and *saltimbocca* (veal cutlets with sage). Closed Sunday evening, Monday, part of August and Christmas. €€€–€€€€

Roscioli
Via dei Giubbonari 21
Tel: 06-6875287
This deli-cum-restaurant has had rave reviews for its authentic produce and inventive food

combinations. Try their signature dish, tonarelli with grouper fish, pistachios and fennel seeds. €€
Sora Lella
Via di Ponte Quattro Capi 16
Tel: 06-6861601
This authentic Roman *trattoria* is in a *palazzo* situated on the magical Isola Tiberina, right next to Trastevere. Here you will find ªtraditional food as well as home-made pasta. Closed Sunday and August. Reserve. €€€
Taverna Angelica
Piazza Amerigo Capponi 6
Tel: 06-6874514
This is a warm and welcoming establishment, ideal for a romantic, candlelit dinner. It is set in the labyrinth of lanes in front of St Peter's, known as the Borgo area. A constantly changing menu reflects the seasons with a strong emphasis on seafood. Also ideal for after-theatre suppers as the kitchen closes around midnight. Monday–Saturday dinner only. Lunch and dinner Sunday.
€€€–€€€€
Trimani Wine Bar
Via Cernaia 37b
Tel: 06-4469630
This very popular *enoteca* is the place to enjoy a glass or two chosen from an extensive selection of wines. Tasty snacks include *torte salate* (savoury tarts). There's also a fine daily specials menu. Closed Sunday and during August holidays. €€

ROME'S ENVIRONS

When the Roman heat gets too much to bear, escape to the sea at Ostia, or consider a trip to the Colli Romani, the Alban Hills to the southeast of the city. Tivoli, with its lovely water gardens, makes for a good excursion in summer – you can dine out on the way back to Rome. Frascati, of wine fame, is one of the best-known towns just outside Rome, but there are many others that are equally good. Frascati is the place to eat *porchetta* (pork from a suckling pig), followed by a leisurely walk. Nemi has a strawberry festival, where the red fruit is served in white wine. Castel Gandolfo is the place to try *guanciale*

(similar to bacon), smoked with olive, oak and laurel wood and flavoured with red pepper. Quite a few places in this area offer special tasting menus *(degustazione)* at reasonable prices.

Civitavecchia
L'Angoletto
Via P. Guglielmotti 2
Tel: 0766-32825
Serves good, traditional seafood, soups and home-made pasta. Warm welcome and attractive setting near the promenade. Closed Monday and Christmas. €€

Frascati
Cacciani
Via A. Diaz 13
Tel: 06-9420378
Located in the centre of Frascati with panoramic views over the hills from the terrace. Local dishes and fish are the specialities and, of course, Frascati wine. Closed Monday, two weeks in January and two weeks in August. €€€

Nemi
La Taverna
Via Nemorese 13
Tel: 06-9368135
This inn is rustic and charming with a nice fireplace. Traditional cooking is on offer. Closed Wednesday and January. Best to reserve. €€

Ostia Antica
Allo Sbarco di Enea
Vicolo dei Romagnoli 675
Tel: 06-5650253
Set in a Roman seaside port, this restaurant is perennially popular. Closed Monday and February. €€€

Palestrina
Stella
Piazza della Liberazione 3
Tel: 06-9538172
Modern ambience combined with regional cuisine in this long-established three-star hotel. €€

Tarquinia
Arcadia
Via Mazzini 6
Tel: 0766-855501
The young owners offer a warm welcome in this very pleasant,

central restaurant. Fish is the speciality. Closed Monday (except July–August) and January. €€–€€€

Tivoli
Adriano
Via di Villa Adriana 222
Tel: 0774-535122
Close to the entrance of the Villa Adriana (Hadrian's Villa), this elegant restaurant features good, local specialities. Closed Sunday evening in winter. Reserve. €€€
Vesta
Piazza della Mole 19
Tel: 06774-335638
A new restaurant which offers a contemporary take on Italian cuisine. Lots of fish and various home-made interpretations of the beloved *tiramisù* dessert. Closed Wednesday and lunchtime (except Sunday when it is open for lunch and dinner). €€–€€€

MILAN

Milan is home to some of the best restaurants in Italy, many of which are institutions, such as Boeucc or Savini *(see below)*, as famed for their formality and stuffiness as for their cuisine. Milanese food is fine, if you like risotto and escalopes, but most gastronomic menus also offer classic Italian dishes. There is also a huge range of foreign cuisine on offer here, plus culinary examples from every Italian region.

Restaurants in the centre of the city (within easy walking distance of the Duomo), vary greatly, ranging from gourmet temples to *pizzerie* and fast-food joints. If you want a lively, more bohemian atmosphere, try Milan's canal quarter, the Navigli. The Brera is the place for fashionable dining. Since Milan is essentially a business city, some top restaurants close during high summer.

Al Mercante
Piazza di Mercanti 17
Tel: 02-8052198
This friendly restaurant is in a great central location on the lovely Piazza di Mercanti. Specialises in local cuisine and a rich selection of antipasti. In summer, the ancient *loggia* makes a very pleasant place to eat. Closed Sunday, August and 1–7 January. Best to reserve. €€€

Armani/Nobu
Via Pisoni 1
Tel: 02-62312645
Minimalist ambience and innovative cuisine in the Emporio Armani. There is a sushi bar and a restaurant which offers fusion food combining the flavours of Japan with South America and the West. Reserve. Closed Sunday, Monday lunch, August and Christmas. €€€–€€€€

Bice
Via Borgospesso 12
Tel: 02-76002572
This is a Milanese institution of the best kind: a reliable top-class restaurant serving unpretentious yet exquisite food with friendly, attentive service. Classic Italian dishes, with some Tuscan specialities. During the seasonal fashion shows or when there is a big event in town, Bice tends to be full. Book in any case, since it is among the trustiest of celebrity restaurants in Milan. Closed Monday, Tuesday lunch and August. €€€€

Bistrot Duomo
Via San Raffaele 2, 7th floor,
La Rinascente, Piazza del Duomo
Tel: 02-877120
This airy and modern restaurant is on the top floor of La Rinascente, Milan's most upmarket department store. Recommended as much for its setting overlooking the Duomo as for the cooking. Milanese specialities predominate but classic Italian cuisine is also on offer. Closed all day Sunday, Monday lunch and 3 weeks in August. €€€

Boeucc
Piazza Belgioioso 2
Tel: 02-76020224

This temple of old-school gastronomy, set in an old palace, is a Milanese institution. The atmosphere is formal but more characterful than that of its rival, Savini. Classic Italian cuisine is leavened with Milanese dishes and there is a cool portico for summer dining. Smart dress is expected and reservations are necessary. Closed Saturday and Sunday lunch, August, and Christmas/New Year. €€€–€€€€

Cracco-Peck
Via Victor Hugo 4
Tel: 02-876774
This Michelin two-starred bastion of gourmet cuisine is now under the guidance of top chef, Carlo Cracco, a disciple of the fabled Alain Ducasse. Expensive and outstanding. Closed Sunday and Saturday lunch, Christmas/New Year; lunchtime mid-June–August. Reservations essential. €€€€

Il Luogo di Aimo e Nadia
Via Montecuccoli 6
Tel: 02-416886
Acclaimed as one of the top places to eat in Italy, with one Michelin star. Some Tuscan influence characterises the deceptively simple but superbly executed dishes. Closed Saturday lunch, Sunday, August and Christmas. Reservations are essential. €€€€

Il Teatro
Hotel Four Seasons, Via Gesù
Tel: 02-77088
Superlatives abound in descriptions of Milan's Four Seasons Hotel and its two restaurants – especially Il Teatro, where the exclusive and creative cuisine is hard to fault. Reservations essential. Closed lunchtime, Sunday and August. €€€€

Joia
Via Panfilo Castaldi 18
Tel: 02-29522124
Very popular, gourmet restaurant specialising in creative vegetarian and fish dishes. The Swiss owner/chef, Pietro Leeman, now holds a Michelin star. Reflecting his time in the Far East, many of his dishes have exotic touches. Reservations essential. Closed Saturday lunch, Sunday and August holidays. €€€€

La Fabbrica
Alzaia Naviglio Grande 70
Tel: 02-8358297
This lively pizzeria in the heart of the Navigli canal district is set in a former factory and attracts a young crowd. Open daily. €–€€

Le Langhe
Corso Como 6
Tel: 02-6554279
This is an exclusive Piedmontese restaurant offering such typical dishes as *tartuffo bianco* (white truffle) and *carpaccio*. Excellent Piedmontese wines including Barolo and Barbaresco. Closed Sunday and August. €€€

Sadler
Via Conchetta
corner of Via Ettore Troilo 14
Tel: 02-5810 4451
Creative cuisine in a modern and prestigious setting. Currently holds two Michelin stars. Professional service. Specialities include fish and white truffles (in season). Closed lunchtimes, Sunday and periods in January and August. Must book. €€€€

Sadler Wine and Food
Via Monte Bianco 2/a,
Tel: 02-481 4677
Elegant, but informal, this is a smaller version of Sadler on Via Conchetta, with continuous opening

Eating Options

With such a variety of restaurants on offer, how should you choose where to eat? Even the names are confusing – what is the difference, for example, between a *ristorante* and an *osteria*? Although *osteria* means an inn, it can refer to a chic restaurant decorated in a gentrified rustic style. The number of courses may seem confusing too: if you don't want a multi-course meal, you could have a snack at a bar, *tavole calde* or *rosticcerie* (grill), or forego the *antipasto* and take a *primo* and a *secondo* instead.

Pasta Dishes

Common Pasta Shapes

cannelloni (large stuffed tubes of pasta); *farfalle* (bow- or butterfly-shaped pasta); *tagliatelle* (flat noodles, similar to *fettuccine*); *tortellini* and *ravioli* (different types of stuffed pasta packets); *penne* (quill-shaped tubes, smaller than *rigatoni*).

Typical Pasta Sauces

pomodoro (tomato); *pesto* (with basil and pine nuts); *matriciana* (bacon and tomato); *arrabbiata* (spicy tomato); *panna* (cream); *ragù* (meat sauce); *aglio e olio* (garlic and olive oil); *burro e salvia* (butter and sage).

from midday–11pm. Innovative cuisine based on classical favourites. Closed Sunday and periods in January and August. €€–€€€

Savini

Galleria Vittorio Emanuele 11

Tel: 02-72003433

Formal décor, an ultra-professional approach and classic Italian cuisine can be expected from a restaurant that has been perfecting its formula since 1867. However, the effect is somewhat marred by supercilious service and a cool atmosphere. Closed Sunday, August and first week of January. Reservations and smart dress required. €€€€

Torre di Pisa

Via Fiori Chiari 21

Tel: 02-874877

Set in the liveliest street in the elegant Brera district, this is an intimate and appealing *trattoria* with gourmet cuisine inspired by seasonal produce. Arrive early to allow time for a drink in one of the Brera's numerous bars – try the Orient Express (Via Fiori Chiari 8), which recreates the atmosphere of the legendary train. Closed Saturday lunchtime and Sunday. €€€

LOMBARDY & THE LAKES

Also see the entries under *Where to Stay, page 375,* as a number of the best hotels in the Lakes have equally good restaurants. Villa-hotels, in particular, often provide lovely lakeside settings, and the cuisine makes use of fish from the lakes, as well as some more traditional Lombard specialities.

Bergamo

Da Vittorio

Viale Papa Giovanni XXIII 221

tel: 035-213266

One of Italy's top restaurants, the young chefs are very enthusiastic and creative using the finest, seasonal ingredients. This is matched by attentive service. Vittorio's many acclaims include two Michelin stars. Closed Wednesday and August. Reservations essential. €€€€

Lio Pellegrini

Via San Tomaso 47

Tel: 035-247813

Set in an atmospheric former sacristy, this restaurant serves Tuscan specialities alfresco in the garden in summer. Must book. Closed Monday and Tuesday lunch. €€€–€€€€

Taverna Colleoni dell'Angelo

Piazza Vecchia 7, Città Alta

Tel: 035-232596

Lombard specialities are served in a 14th-century palace linked to the famous *condottiere* (mercenary) Colleoni. This elegant restaurant has been in business since 1740. Excellent service. Closed Monday. €€€

Trattoria del Teatro

Piazza Mascheroni 3, Città Alta

Tel: 035-238862

This old-fashioned restaurant has 19th-century furniture as a backdrop to simple but delicious, traditional food where specialities include polenta. Closed Monday. €€–€€€

Cremona

Martinelli

Via degli Oscasali 3

Tel: 0372-30350

This is an elegant restaurant located in an 8th-century *palazzo* specialising in local, traditional cuisine and fish dishes. Closed Sunday, Wednesday and August. €€€

Mantua (Mantova)

Il Cigno Trattoria dei Martini

Piazza Carlo d'Arco 1

Tel: 0376-327101

Set on a wonderful piazza, Cigno offers delicious regional cooking and excellent service. Closed Monday, Tuesday and August. Reserve. €€€

Pavia

Il Cigno

Via Massacra 2

Tel: 0382-301093

Well-presented creative and modern cuisine is served in this small, atmospheric and intimate restaurant. The historic town of Pavia is 35 km (22 miles) from Milan. Closed Monday, August and beginning of January. Reserve. €€€

LAKE GARDA

Gardone Riviera

Villa Fiordaliso

Corso Zanardelli 150

Tel: 0365-20158

Set in a splendidly converted villa with links to Mussolini, this excellent restaurant (one Michelin star) is one of the best in the region, perhaps even in the country. During the Fascistic, and ultimately doomed, Republic of Salo, Mussolini entertained his mistress, Claretta Petacci here. Set in lovely grounds, the villa is a luxurious place, dotted with antiques and tastefully restored in the art-nouveau style. Expect creative cuisine, with the emphasis on fish, seafood and pasta. Closed Monday and Tuesday lunch and 20 November–10 February. €€€€

Sirmione

Vecchia Lugana

Piazzale Vecchia Lugana 1

Tel: 030-9196023

Price Guide

The price of a three-course meal for one (not including wine):

€ = under €25

€€ = €25–45

€€€ = €45–70

€€€€ = €70 or more

Set in an ancient palace close to the Sirmione peninsula, this *trattoria* on the lake shore was a favourite of the operatic diva Maria Callas and numerous Italian literary figures. Fish features heavily. One Michelin star. Closed Monday and Tuesday, 7 January–15 February; in November open only Friday evening, Saturday and Sunday. €€€–€€€€

PIEDMONT

Piedmontese cuisine is considered one of the best in Italy and worthy of a gastronomic pilgrimage in itself. The keynotes are elegant French flourishes and filling country food. Dishes include truffle-scented risotto, creamy, buttery risotto, game, and Alpine cheeses. Typical dishes can be tasted in Turin's grandest hotels and restaurants.

Turin
Del Cambio
Piazza Carignano 2
Tel: 011-543760
This formal establishment, which opened in 1757, is one of the most impressive-looking restaurants in Italy, decorated with grand 19th-century furniture. The equally formal staff serve classic Italian cuisine with an excellent selection of Piedmontese wines. It is strange to think that Casanova, the great libertine, appreciated this symbol of restraint. Closed Sunday and August. Reserve. €€€€
Hosteria La Vallée
Via A. Provana 3/b
Tel: 011-8121788
Great care is given to using the finest, seasonal ingredients in this highly acclaimed restaurant. Splendid service and excellent location near to the historic Piazza Cavour. Closed lunchtime, Sunday and August. Reservation essential. €€€–€€€€
La Capannina
Via Donati 1
Tel: 011-545405
Although this restaurant is set in a fine *palazzo*, the ambience remains rustic. The food is strictly cooked in the Piedmontese style – the *fritto*

Piedmontese Wine
The region has a monopoly on many of Italy's best wines, including Barolo and Barbaresco, which are produced on the western shore of Lake Maggiore. The success of the wine business has brought quiet prosperity to the villages of Asti and Alba, places traditionally connected with truffles and other gastronomic treats.

misto (mixed fried fish) is superb. Closed Sunday, August and 1–7 January. Reserve. €€
Spada Reale
Via Principe Amedeo 53
Tel: 011-8171363
This modern *trattoria* and restaurant is especially popular with young professionals, not only for its eclectic mix of Tuscan and Piedmontese cuisine but for its lack of stuffiness. Wine and beer are both available. Closed Saturday lunch, Sunday and August. Reserve. €€–€€€
Tre Galline
Via Bellezia 37
Tel: 011-4366553
Tre Galline is a typical old-fashioned *piola,* and has recently been refurbished. As well as the Piedmontese specialities, there are lighter salads, pastas, soups and cheeses. Closed Sunday, lunchtime and August. Reserve. €€
Villa Sassi-Toula
Strada Traforo del Pino 47
Tel: 011-8980556
This 18th-century former cardinal's villa converted into a chic small hotel has an equally exclusive restaurant. Superb, subtle cuisine, including *carpaccio* and asparagus *frittata*, with sea bass to follow. Closed Sunday and August. Reservations necessary. €€€€

VALLE D'AOSTA

Fontina, arguably the best cow's milk available, comes from the Valle d'Aosta, a region that is also noted for its fondues, salami, terrines and cured meats. *Larda*, a rasher of

pure fat, is traditionally served here with a plate of cold cuts.

Aosta
Le Foyer
Corso Ivrea 146
Tel: 0165-32136/41845
Located just outside Aosta, this renowned hotel belongs to Classhotel Aosta. The restaurant offers "tastes of Aosta" – especially good cheeses. Closed Monday evening and all day Tuesday. €€–€€€
Vecchio Ristoro
Via Tourneuve 4
Tel: 0165-33238
This former watermill is now home to one of the best restaurants in the area. It has one Michelin star for its excellent seasonal cuisine which features fish and specialities such as *bollito misto* (beef broth). Good, attentive service and very pleasant atmosphere. Must book. Closed Sunday and Monday lunch, June and 1–7 November. €€€€

Breuil-Cervinia
Les Neiges d'Antan
Località Cret Perrères 10
Tel: 0166-948775
Situated on a mountain around 4.5 km (2 miles) southwest of Breuil-Cervinia, this quiet inn comes into its own during the skiing season, when it is much in demand. Typical Valdostana cuisine predominates, from soufflés to trout. The *fonduta* (fondue) is particularly tasty. Excellent wine list. Seasonal opening: 6 December–1 May and July–15 September. Reserve. €€€

Gignod
Locanda La Clusaz
Località La Clusaz, Statale Gran San Bernardo (St Bernard motorway)
Tel: 0165-56075

Local Tipples
In the chilly Alpine region of Valle d'Aosta, the locals might recommend a warming *caffe valdostano nella grolla*, coffee laced with wine and *grappa*, which is set alight.

Reservations

It is always advisable to reserve at more upmarket restaurants but if one catches your eye, then call in – it might be a quiet day.

Located 9 km (6 miles) north of Aosta, this delightful inn (with 14 rooms) offers specialities including grain soups, polenta and dishes made with chestnuts or bacon. Closed 10 May–15 June and 3 November–3 December; at lunchtime except Saturday, holidays and August. €€€

LIGURIAN RIVIERA

Ligurians have the longest lifespan in Italy, thus prompting hordes of researchers to investigate the merits of the local diet. Certainly, the cuisine is one of the healthiest in Italy and it has the greatest appeal to vegetarians of all Italian regional diets. Oddly, the Ligurians do not eat nearly as much fish as one would expect of a coastal region. Typical dishes include basil-scented *pesto* sauce, the region's signature dish, often served with *trennette*, ribbon-shaped pasta. Other specialities include olive oil, second in prestige only to Tuscan oil, salt-cod stew, excellent artichokes, salad leaves, and a range of vegetables.

Genoa

In the past, Genoa has had a reputation as an unsafe city, and the locals may try to dissuade you from exploring the restaurants of the historic centre at night. To avoid the centre, however, would mean missing out on much of what is best about the city: the rough-and-ready atmosphere of the tiny *trattorie* hidden in the back streets. If you feel remotely nervous, you could take the precaution of checking out a few places for lunch and then returning to one nearby in the evening. If you dress down a little, walk confidently, and know roughly where you are going, then you should be as safe as you would be

anywhere else. At heart, Genoa is a city for culinary surprises: don't be afraid to peer into a few places before deciding, on impulse, on a place that suits your mood. Most such tucked-away eating places are fairly cheap and yet they often have far more atmosphere than the grander restaurants in the rather soulless modern quarter.

Antica Osteria del Bai

Via Quarto 12, Quarto dei Mille
Tel: 010-387478
This illustrious restaurant set inside a fortress overlooking the sea is where Garibaldi dined in 1860 – not, however, its only claim to fame. On offer are Genoese dishes, although much richer than is generally typical of the local cuisine, and seafood also plays a greater role, whether in pasta sauces or as elaborate Adriatic fish dishes. Closed Monday. Must book. €€€€

Gran Gotto

Viale Brigata Bisagno 69r
Tel: 010-564344
Set near Stazione Brignole, this is a classic and elegant spot dedicated to regional cooking and seafood. Try the seafood pasta, the hot seafood *antipasto* or the *trenette al pesto*, Genoa's signature dish. Closed Saturday lunch and all day Sunday. Reserve. €€€€

La Bitta nella Pergola

Via Casaregis 52r
Tel: 010-588543
This acclaimed, elegant restaurant specialises in fresh seafood and offers regional cooking in a comfortable maritime atmosphere. One of Genoa's best restaurants, it has one Michelin star. Closed Sunday evening, Monday, and August; also Sunday lunchtime in July. Must book. €€€€

Le Cantine Squarciafico

Piazza Invrea 3 Rosso
Tel: 010-2470823
Lying between the old town and the port, the restored wine cellars of a lovely 16th-century *palazzo* make this an atmospheric wine bar and restaurant. Wines from every region of Italy are on offer, accompanied by, predominantly, Ligurian dishes. Closed Sunday and lunch in summer. €€

Pansön dal 1790

Piazza delle Erbe 5
Tel: 010-2468903
This lovely restaurant is situated in a safe but slightly dilapidated square close to Via XX Settembre. The restaurant is very popular with the locals, especially with families. Many Genoese dishes are on offer, including *pansoti al sugo di noci* (pasta with walnuts) and *pesto alla genovese* (pasta with basil sauce). Closed Sunday dinner and 2 weeks in August. €€€

Zeffirino

Via XX Settembre 20
Tel: 010-591990
Set in the centre of the city, off the smart shopping district, Zeffirino is a prestigious restaurant and was once popular with Frank Sinatra. It is famous for the legendary *pesto alla genovese*. However, veal, lobster and fresh fish are cooked fairly inventively. The chef is renowned for giving away his cooking secrets, so ask, if you're interested in the recipe. Reserve. €€€–€€€€

Lerici

La Calata

Via Mazzini 7
Tel: 0187-967143
This restaurant in the port is known for its seafood prepared with top-quality fresh ingredients. In summer you can dine on the terrace with fabulous views over the Gulf. Closed Tuesday and December. €€€

Portofino

This is a chic destination, so expect even the simplest restaurant to charge above-average prices. *(See Where to Stay page 377 for details on dining in hotels here.)*

Da u'Batti

Vico Nuovo 17
Tel: 0185-269379
An intimate restaurant with a very pleasant veranda. A bounty of good seafood is on offer. Closed Monday and December–mid-January. €€€

Il Pitosforo

Molo Umberto 19
Tel: 0185-269020
Numerous VIPs and the international yachting fraternity meet here to

compare boats and bank balances. Ligurian specialities are available, as well as international cooking. Closed Sunday and 1 January–28 February. Reserve. €€€€

San Remo

This destination is especially popular during the February San Remo Song Contest and in summer.

Il Bagatto
Via Matteotti 145
Tel: 0184-531925
The emphasis here is on Ligurian dishes, both meat and fish-based. Lovely setting in the old *palazzo* Borea d'Olmo. Extensive, well-chosen wine list. Closed Sunday and 30 June–30 July. Reservations advised. €€€

Paolo e Barbara
Via Roma 47
Tel: 0184-531653
Elegant, small Michelin-starred restaurant right in the heart of town. Reservations essential. Closed Wednesday and Thursday; 19–30 December; 23–29 January; 22 June–7 July. €€€€

Vernazza

Gambero Rosso
Piazza Marconi 7
Tel: 0187-812265
Vernazza is the most popular of the scenic Cinque Terre coastal villages, and Gambero Rosso, a small *osteria* set by the port noted for its seafood, tends to be full at lunchtime. It is, however, strangely peaceful and quiet in the evening. Closed Monday (except August) and mid-December–February. €€€

VENICE

The following restaurants are listed according to the area *(sestriere)* in

Price Guide

The price of a three-course meal for one (not including wine):
€ = under €25
€€ = €25–45
€€€ = €45–70
€€€€ = €70 or more

which they are located. However, the official geography of Venice is fairly complex and the best way of working out where a restaurant is located is often to just call up beforehand and ask which main church or square is nearest.

An unpleasant snag of Venetian life is that most foodstuffs are imported and restaurants are consequently not only at least 10 to 15 percent dearer than on the mainland but tend to be of lower quality. In the grandest eateries, you are often also paying for the service, the atmosphere and the fabulous views from their terrace rather than for top-class cuisine. However, on the plus side, many Venetian restaurants are famed for the stunning views they offer.

Castello

L'Aciugheta
Campo San Filoppo e Giacomo
Tel: 041-522 4292
Excellent, good value *bacaro* but also has a proper menu featuring a variety of dishes from Adriatic fish to truffles and oysters. Popular with Venetians and also for its fine Friuli wines. Closed Monday. €–€€

Al Covo
Campiello della Pescaria 3968
Tel: 041-5223812
Set close to the Arsenale ferry stop, this enthusiastically run restaurant serves fish fresh from the lagoon, wild duck (when in season) and wonderful home-made desserts; it also has a great wine list. Lunch is less expensive than dinner. Closed Wednesday and Thursday. €€€€

Dorsoduro

Ai Gondolieri
Fondamente de l'Ospedaleto 366
Tel: 041-5286396
Close to the Guggenheim museum, this popular restaurant serves up exceptional risottos. Must book. Closed Tuesday. €€€€

Antico Pignolo
Calle dei Specchieri 451, San Marco
Tel: 041-522 8123
Classical Venetian ambience in this highly regarded restaurant. Venetian and traditional specialities include fresh fish. Exceptional wine list and

attentive service in four spacious dining salons where well-spaced tables ensure your privacy. €€€€

(Antica Trattoria) La Furatola
Calle Lunga San Barnaba 2870, Dorsoduro 30123
Tel: 041-5208594
This unpretentious place is where local foodies go for fish dishes. Closed Monday lunchtime and Thursday, January and August. €€€

Cantinone Gia Schiavi
Fondamente Nani, Dorsoduro 992
Tel: 041-5230034
On Rio di San Trovaso, this canal-side wine bar is extremely popular with locals. Do as the Venetians do and enjoy *cichetti*, typical bar snacks, with a glass of wine. It is especially atmospheric at the cocktail hour, from 7–8pm. Closed at 9.30pm and Sunday dinner. €–€€€

Taverna San Trovaso
Fondamenta Priuli 1016
Tel: 041-5203703
This cheap and cheerful inn serves decent Italian food in a lovely spot by the canal, near to the gondola repair yard. Closed Monday. €€

San Marco

Al Graspo de Ua
Calle dei Bombaseri 5094/a
Tel: 041-5200150
Located close to the Rialto Bridge, this well established fish restaurant is centuries-old and an absolute delight for those seeking local colour and traditional Venetian fare, leavened by classic Italian dishes. Closed Monday and a period in January. €€€–€€€€

Al Volto
Calle Cavalli
San Marco 4081
Tel: 041-5228945
This is Venice's oldest *enoteca* (wine bar) where you can choose between tastings from several thousand different wines. Extremely popular. Open: 10am–2.30pm, 5–10.30pm. Closed Sunday. €

Antico Martini
Campo San Fantin 1983
Tel: 041-5224121
Set close to the site of the Fenice opera house, this place serves Venetian and international cuisine.

Price Guide

The price of a three-course meal for one (not including wine):
€ = under €25
€€ = €25–45
€€€ = €45–70
€€€€ = €70 or more

It was popular with such celebrities as Igor Stravinsky and Laurence Olivier. Serves Venetian and international cuisine. Closed Tuesday and Wednesday lunch. Reservations recommended. €€€

Caffè Quadri
Procuratie Vecchie
Piazza San Marco 120
Tel: 041-5222105
Situated in the most prestigious area of Venice, this fine restaurant is awash with Murano glass and sumptuous furnishings. It is also renowned for its innovative and classical Italian cuisine and features traditional Venetian dishes. Prices are predictably high, but acceptable by Venetian standards. Reservations essential. Closed Monday from November to March. €€€€

Canova
Luna Hotel Baglioni
Calle Larga dell'Ascensione 1243
Tel: 041-5289840
Exquisite dishes served in the very gracious surroundings of the Canova restaurant of the Baglioni Hotel. An extensive menu includes Venetian specialities as well as international cuisine, all prepared with freshest, seasonal ingredients. Excellent service and very extensive wine menu. Must book.
€€€€

Harry's Bar
Calle Vallaresso, San Marco 1323
Tel: 041-5285777
For many people, Harry's Bar is a symbol of gastronomic Venice. Although prices are high, standards are also impressive and if you can't afford a full meal here, you could consider coming for a cocktail instead. This bar and restaurant, which was once a favourite haunt of the writer Hemingway, is now patronised mainly by very wealthy Venetians, expatriates, and

American tourists. Expect good home-made pastas at exorbitant prices, with a small discount for paying in cash and further discounts for favoured guests. Reserve.
€€€€

San Polo

Da Pinto
Campo delle Beccarie, San Polo 367
Tel: 041-5224599
This is a rough-and-ready *bacaro (see below)* set in the market area in the middle of the Rialto district. It's a good place to begin a wine crawl and great for authentic Venetian snacks and a chat over some wine. This is also a good place to sample the snacks known as *cicchetti* – the seafood variety are particularly tasty. Open 7.30am–2.30pm and 6–8.30pm. Closed Monday. €

Osteria Da Fiore
Calle del Scaleter 2202/a
Tel: 041-721308
This is a small but chic gastronomic restaurant near Campo San Polo; many have come to consider it the city's best. It has one Michelin star and its good food, wine and elegant ambience attract Venetian celebrities. Must book. Closed Sunday and Monday.
€€€€

"Bacari"

Venice's **San Polo** district is home to a number of cheap and cheerful *bacari* (singular: *bacaro*), wine bars that also serve simple but good snacks. Most close early (usually by 9.30pm) and they normally keep rather odd hours, so telephone first to check opening times if possible. Most *bacari* are hidden away in the warren of alleys around the Rialto district. **Recommended places** are: Da Pinto; Da Mori (Calle de' Do Mori); and Do Spade (Calle de' Do Spade). The addresses are usually meaningless: to reach your destination, you're best advised to go to the Rialto Bridge and then ask a friendly native for directions from there.

Trattoria alla Madonna
Calle della Madonna, San Polo 594
Tel: 041-5223824
This is a popular fish and seafood restaurant near the Rialto. The place is large and, owing to its good-value food (by Venetian standards), always crowded, but there's still a good atmosphere. Service, however, can be a little brusque. Closed Wednesday and a period in August. Reservations advised. €€€–€€€€

Cannaregio

Vini da Gigio
Fondamenta San Felice 3628/a
Tel: 041-528 5140
This cosy, atmospheric inn has a canalside setting and good food, featuring both meat and fish. Closed Monday, and periods in January and August. Reserve. €€

Santa Croce

Antica Bessetta
Salizada de Cà' Zusto 1395
Tel: 041-721687
This authentic family-run *trattoria*, one of the city's oldest, is set somewhat off the beaten track, near San Giacomo dell'Orio. It serves regional cuisine and is fairly good value despite recent price rises. Closed Tuesday and Wednesday lunch. €€€–€€€€

THE VENETO

The Veneto has a distinguished culinary tradition. At Christmas, Verona produces *pandoro*, a distant cousin to *panettone* and just as delicious. Seafood is also on the menu, with specialities from the Adriatic including squid, mussels, mackerel, brill, bass and mullet. The region is also the biggest producer of poultry in Italy, so chicken is generally good here; salami is also recommended. Local pasta includes *bigoli*, wholewheat spaghetti, often served with *salsa*, a classic sauce made with anchovies and garlic. As for wine, you can follow wine trails to explore the vineyards that produce Soave, sparkling Prosecco and full-bodied Bardolino and Merlot.

The Island of Burano

Trattoria Da Romano
Piazza Galuppi 221
Tel: 041-730030
Set on the colourful island of
Burano, this is a popular, artistic
trattoria, overlooking the sea.
Many people have professed to
being charmed by the artistic
ambience, casual welcome and
straightforward cuisine. Catch
motonave No. 12 back to central
Venice. Closed Tuesday and in
December. €€

Padua (Padova)
Dotto di Campagna
Via Randaccio 4, Località Torre
(Ponte di Brenta)
Tel: 049-625469
This rustic restaurant is set 6 km
(3¾ miles) north-east of town but it's
worth the trip, as this is the place for
authentic Veneto cuisine. Try the
gnocchi, roast meats, *pasta e fagioli*
(pasta and beans) and *baccalà* (salt
cod). Closed Sunday evening,
Monday and August. Reserve.
€€–€€€

Verona
Expect above-average prices in
this chic, perenially popular city.
Many restaurants here are great,
matching unusual cuisine with
atmospheric settings and lovely
Veneto wines such as Bardolino.
Bottega Del Vino
Via Scudo di Francia 3
Tel: 045-8004535
Set in the historic heart of town,
just off Piazza delle Erbe, this
traditional Veronese inn *(osteria)*
was a haunt of the Futurist painters
such as Boccioni. It is still
frequented by an intellectual and
artistic set, as well as by those who
simply appreciate Veronese and
classic Italian cooking, notably
stuffed pasta. Closed Tuesday
except July and August. €€€
Locanda di Castelvecchio
Corso Castelvecchio 21/A
Tel: 045-8030097
This elegant restaurant on a beautiful corner of the old town still has
the ambience of an old *osteria*.

Friendly service, exquisite Veronic
cuisine. Closed: Tuesday and
Wednesday lunch. €€
12 Apostoli
Vicolo Corticella San Marco 3
Tel: 045-596999.
Just off Piazza delle Erbe, this
atmospheric family-run restaurant
is one of the best places to eat in
Italy. It is located in an ancient
frescoed palace. The restaurant
produces Veronese and classic
Italian cuisine, including rabbit
tagliatelle and squid risotto.
Closed Sunday evening, Monday
and mid-June–5 July. Reserve.
€€€–€€€€
Il Desco
Via Dietro San Sebastiano 7
Tel: 045-595358
Located in a lovely old *palazzo*, this
is a very elegant, highly acclaimed
restaurant (two Michelin stars), one
of Italy's best. Elia Rizzo's superb
cooking combines rare and
expensive ingredients with the more
traditional. Closed Sunday, Monday
and festivals. Must book. €€€€

Vicenza
Antico Ristorante Agli Schioppi
Contrà del Castello 26
Tel: 0444-543701
In the historic heart of the city this
rustic yet elegant restaurant housed
in a *palazzo* specialises in traditional
cuisine from the Veneto. Outside
dining in the summer. Closed
Saturday evening, Sunday, 1–6
January and 20 July–15 August.
€€–€€€

TRENTINO–ALTO ADIGE

The regions of Trentino and Alto
Adige offer mountain food with an
Italian or Austrian twist. Wholesome
dishes prevail, from hearty pork and
beef sausages to polenta and
pulse-filled soups. By Lake Garda
and Trentino's lakes and mountain
streams, fish dishes include Alpine
trout poached in white wine.
In Alto Adige, Austrian influences
are strong, with foods including
smoked meats, sauerkraut, red-
cabbage goulash, dumplings,
gnocchi and apple strudel all

popular. Many of these dishes are
also typical of Trentino. Check
Where to Stay, pages 382–3, for
entries on such excellent castle-
restaurants as Castel Rundegg.

Bolzano (Bozen)
Laurin
Parkhotel Laurin, Via Laurin 4
Tel: 0471-311000
Liberty-style, very pleasant
restaurant. The Mediterranean
cooking of chef Luca Verdolini is
highly innovative. Very good wine
list and an especially attractive bar.
Closed Sunday lunch. €€–€€€

Pinzolo
Mezzosoldo
Spiazzo Rendena, Near Pinzolo,
Trentino
Tel: 0465-801067
This cosy inn is located in the
mountainous Val Rendena area
south of Pinzolo, within acceptable
driving distance of the ski resort of
Madonna di Campiglio. (You can
always stay in the inn overnight, if
you can't face the drive back.) The
reason for making the journey is
simple: great home-cooking. The
Lorenzi family pick the ingredients,
including herbs and mushrooms,
themselves. Meals begin with home-
made breads and ten (light) starters,
including *radicchio dell'orso*, an
edible root only exposed by
avalanches. Other courses include
pheasant, alpine vegetables and
pine-kernel-covered ice-cream. Open
daily but closed during periods in
May and October. €€–€€€

Trento
Chiesa
Parco San Marco 64
Tel: 0461-238766
Set on one floor of a 17th-century
cloistered palace, this elegant
restaurant serves very refined food.
Closed Sunday. €€–€€€
Lo Scrigno del Duomo
Piazza del Duomo 29
Tel: 0461-220030
Elegant, minimalist restaurant set in
a former 17th-century *palazzo*. The
restaurant (which holds a Michelin
star) is noted for its regional
cuisine, while the *enoteca* (wine bar)

downstairs has a good selection of snacks and a very wide choice of wines. Booking advised. Closed Monday. €€€–€€€€

FRIULI-VENEZIA GIULIA

The cuisine of Friuli-Venezia Giulia, like the region, is often described as "not really Italian", which is hardly surprising given that the frontiers touch both the former Yugoslavia and Austria. Expect a lot of goulash, boiled pork and Viennese sausages, as well as rice and polenta. As a general rule, the cuisine of the hinterland is more frugal, while Venetian culinary influences prevail on the coast, with seafood generally good in Trieste. As for Friuli wines, the Italians have long recognised them as being among the great regional wines but the rest of the world has been slower to catch on.

Trieste
Antica Trattoria Suban
Via Comici 2
Tel: 040-54368
Run by the same family for generations, this restaurant is probably the most traditional of Trieste's eating places. Friendly and simple in style, it serves good regional cuisine. Summer bower. Closed Monday lunch, all day Tuesday and periods in January and August. Reserve. €€€

Udine
Alla Vedova
Via Tavagnacco 9
Tel: 0432-470291
This is a very old Friulian restaurant, with outdoor tables in summer. Good traditional cooking. Closed Sunday evening and Monday. Reserve. €€

EMILIA-ROMAGNA

Although it is the gastronomic capital of Italy, Bologna also has its fair share of traditional taverns serving simple hearty cuisine. The city is famous for pasta of every

description, although perhaps most famously for spaghetti bolognese, and for velvety sauces, salami and cold meats. Food is good across the region and each major town has its own specialities, from Parmesan and Parma ham in Parma to *aceto balsamico*, Italy's best vinegar, in Modena. Emilian wines include Trebbiano, Cabernet Sauvignon and Lambrusco.

Bologna
Buca San Petronio
Via de'Musei 4
Tel: 051-224589
Excellent-value restaurant set in a *palazzo* in the historical centre. Traditional, regional cooking and freshly made pasta. Outdoor dining in summer. Closed Wednesday evening (except during holidays/festivals) and August. €–€€
Caffè Commercianti
Strada Maggiore 23/c
Tel: 051-266539
Well-known watering hole for the litterati and intelligentsia of Bologna, including luminaries such as Umberto Eco. Also reputedly serves the best martini in town. €–€€
Cantina Bentivoglio
Via Mascarella 4b
Tel: 051-265416
Set in the cellars of a *palazzo*, this restaurant attracts a young crowd. Emilian specialities are eaten to the accompaniment of live music. Closed Monday. €€
Da Bertino e Figlio
Via delle Lame 55
Tel: 051-522230
This is a lively Emilian *trattoria*, with good cooking, notably the gnocchi. Closed Sunday and Monday evening on alternate months, Saturday evening in July and 5 August–4 September. €€
La Pernice e La Gallina
Via dell'Abbadia 4
Tel: 051-269922
Highly acclaimed restaurant in the historical centre of Bologna. Traditional and innovative cuisine are skilfully blended to produce gourmet delights. Closed Sunday and Monday lunchtime, and for a period in August.
€€€–€€€€

Price Guide

The price of a three-course meal for one (not including wine):
€ = under €25
€€ = €25–45
€€€ = €45–70
€€€€ = €70 or more

Le Stanze
Via di Borgo San Pietro 1
Tel: 051-228767
Housed in a former chapel from the Bentivoglio dynasty, this 16th-century spot is the place where the smart set go to be seen. Closed Saturday lunch. €€
Pappagallo
Piazza della Mercanzia 3c
Tel: 051-231200
Very popular restaurant not only for its location, near the two towers, but also for its Bolognese specialities. Good fish dishes. Closed Sunday, and a period in August, and Saturday in June and July.
€€€–€€€€
Trattoria Battibecco
Via Battibecco 4
Tel: 051-223298
This elegant one-star Michelin restaurant with excellent service is the place to sample the rich flavours of Bolognese cuisine. Must book. Closed Saturday lunch, Sunday and holidays. €€€€

Ferrara
La Romantica
Via Ripagrande 36
Tel: 0532-765975
Set in a romantic spot in the heart of the medieval quarter, this well-established restaurant serves classic Italian cuisine with a few Jewish *Ferrarese* dishes. Closed Sunday evening, Wednesday, and periods in July and August.
€€–€€€

Modena
Oreste
Piazza Roma 31
Tel: 059-243324
This traditional restaurant has a pleasant, rather "retro" atmosphere. The specialities are meat and home-made pasta.

Closed Sunday evening and Wednesday; 26 December–6 January and period in July. €€

Fini
Rua Frati Minori 54
Tel: 059-223314
This is a classic smart yet homely Michelin-starred restaurant, offering traditional regional cuisine. Try the *bolliti* (boiled meat) and cured meats for which Fini is renowned. A broad range of Emilian and international dishes is also available. Closed Monday, Christmas/New Year and two weeks in August. Reserve. €€€€

Parma
The home of Parma ham and Parmesan cheese is a centre of gastronomic excellence. It is pretty difficult to eat out badly in town, but prices often reflect this.

Ravenna
Antica Trattoria Al Gallo 1909
Via Maggiore 87
Tel: 0544-213775
This elegant Liberty-style restaurant has been run by the same family for almost a century. Al Gallo serves good regional food, which changes according to the seasons. Typical dishes include courgette flowers, rabbit and olives, fried mushrooms, and several good vegetarian options. Closed Sunday evening, Monday, Tuesday, 20 December–10 January and Easter. €€–€€€

San Marino
Righi-La Taverna
Piazza della Libertà 10
Tel: 0549-991196
Good rustic food in the pocket-sized Republic of San Marino. Closed Wednesday in winter, and 1–14 January. €€–€€€

FLORENCE

Florence has a reputation for its proliferation of rather nasty fast-food joints and fake "tourist menu" places. Certainly, many restaurants are only too ready to produce indifferent food to indiscriminating tourists they will never see again. However, many restaurants are as good as any you will find in Italy, even if their prices are high. That said, the city still has a selection of simple inns where you can eat well on a reasonable budget. In the Florentine hills, there are some stunning gastronomic restaurants set in gorgeous palaces or villas.

Alle Murate
Via Ghibellina 52r
Tel: 055-240618
Intimate restaurant which is very fashionable, especially with young Florentines. The atmosphere is relaxed and the excellent cuisine covers creative Tuscan as well as international dishes. Closed Monday, lunchtime and 7–28 December. Must book. €€€€

Cibrèo-Cibreino
Via del Verrocchio 8r (restaurant)
Via dei Macci 122r *(trattoria)*
Tel: 055-2341100
Cibrèo is a universally respected Tuscan restaurant that operates a double-pricing system. Those who are unfamiliar with the system book in the expensive restaurant, where they can expect delicious food. Those in the know eat virtually the same things in the adjoining, more modest-looking *trattoria* for a fraction of the price. Best to reserve. Closed Sunday, Monday, 31 December–6 January and 26 July–6 September. €€ *(trattoria)*; €€€–€€€€ (restaurant)

Del Fagioli
Corso Tintori 47r
Tel: 055-244285
Traditional Florentine cuisine is on offer in this typical, family-run *trattoria*. Fresh fish is served on Fridays. Good value. Reservations advised. Closed Saturday, Sunday and August. €€

Enoteca Pinchiorri
Via Ghibellina 87
Tel: 055-242777
With three Michelin stars, this is one of the city's, and Italy's, most prestigious restaurants, set on the ground floor of a 17th-century palace, with a delightful courtyard for dining in the open air. The culinary highlights include a superb, updated version of *nouvelle* French and Tuscan cuisine, with dinner treated as a work of art; there is also an impressive wine collection (almost 60,000 bottles). Closed Sunday and Monday, Tuesday and Wednesday lunchtimes, December–January and August. Reserve. €€€€

La Baraonda
Via Ghibellina 67r
Tel: 055-2341171
Located in the historic Santa Croce quarter, this very pleasant *trattoria* is rustic and atmospheric. Tuscan cuisine and good fish dishes are on offer, as well as excellent hand-made pasta. Closed Monday, lunchtimes and 9–31 August. Reserve. €€€

La Loggia
Piazzale Michelangelo 1
Tel: 055-2342832
Set outside the historic centre, part way up the hill on a grand square, where a copy of Michelangelo's *David* reigns supreme, La Loggia restaurant has a bewitching view down over the bowl of Florence. Serves international and Italian delicacies. Good service. Closed Monday. €€€–€€€€

Omero
Via Pian de' Giullari 11r, Località Arcetri (5 km/3 miles from Florence)
Tel: 055-220053
Set on a hill above the panoramic square of Piazzale Michelangelo, this is a gentrified rustic *trattoria* with outside tables in summer. The splendid view is matched by the Tuscan cuisine, prepared with excellent ingredients. Tasty dishes include ravioli stuffed with ricotta and herbs, grilled meats, steaks and pigeon. Closed Tuesday and August. Reserve. €€€

TUSCANY

Tuscan cooking is essentially *cucina povera*, peasant food, albeit delicious enough to make you want to cast off any pretence at urban sophistication. This being the case, it is wise to eat the food in its natural habitat, in unpretentious yet atmospheric country-style inns.

Address tips

If there is an "r" in a restaurant's address after the street number, this identifies the property as commercial premises.

Arezzo
Antica Osteria l'Agania
Via Mazzini 10
Tel: 0575-295381
Very pleasant, family-style restaurant specialising in good, simple local cuisine. Excellent value. Closed Monday except June to September. €–€€

Colle di Val d'Elsa
Ristorante Il Cardinale
Relais della Rovere, Via Piemonte 10
Tel: 0577-924696
Fax: 0577-924489
www.chiantiturismo.it
The Relais della Rovere began life in the 11th-century as an abbey but it was promoted to a cardinal's residence during the 15th century. The gentrified rustic restaurant, Il Cardinale, occupies the ancient wine cellars of the estate. The menu, which is essentially Tuscan, is matched by excellent regional wines. The charm of the setting may well tempt you to stay the night. Closed 15 January–February. €€–€€€

Cortona
Il Falconiere
Località San Martino a Bocena (4 km/2½ miles north of Cortona)
Tel: 0575-612679
In a lovely setting in the hills, this elegant Relais hotel makes you feel as though time stands still. Good, imaginative cuisine includes both fish and meat dishes and service is excellent (one Michelin star). There is a lovely panoramic terrace. Must book. Closed Monday and Tuesday lunchtime (except from March to October). €€€–€€€€

Gaiole in Chianti
Badia di Coltibuono
Tel/fax: 0577-749031
www.chiantinet.it/ristbadia
Situated in Chianti country, outside the wine-producing village of Gaiole, this estate was founded by Vallombrosan monks *circa* 1000. The rustic-style restaurant makes good use of local produce. From May to October, guests can visit the wine cellars, gardens and cloisters. It's slightly twee, so it might not be to everybody's taste. Closed Monday (except May to October); 10 January–10 March. €€–€€€

Lucca
Da Giulio
Via delle Conce 47
Tel: 0583-55948
Good plain food, such as minestrone and bean soups. Closed Sunday (except third Sunday in the month), Monday and August €
La Buca di Sant'Antonio
Via della Cervia 1/5
Tel: 0583-55881
This traditional *osteria* (inn) is arguably the best in town for reliable rustic cooking. Closed Sunday evening, Monday, 12–19 January and 11–19 July. €€

Montalcino
Taverna Il Grappola Blu
Via Scale di Moglio (off Via Mazzini)
Tel: 0577-847150
This intimate, well-run inn is the best in the quaint medieval village of Montalcino, 40 km (25 miles) south of Siena. The atmosphere is rustic but the cuisine is above average, and service is friendly but correct. Typical dishes include filling soups, rabbit dishes and pasta with *funghi porcini* (ceps). The Taverna has an excellent wine list – wines produced by Fabio Pellegrini of La Cerbaia estate are particularly recommended. Closed Friday. €€€

Pisa
Sergio
Lungarno Pacinotti 1
Tel: 050-580580
This famous restaurant offers elegant décor in a medieval setting and sound regional food. Closed Sunday, January and August. €€€

San Gimignano
Dorandò
Vicolo dell'Oro 2
Tel: 0577-941862
This is a friendly and stylish restaurant specialising in Tuscan recipes with ancient origins. Notes on the recipes are provided. Closed Monday (except from Easter to October) and 10 January–28 February. Booking advised. €€€

Siena
Guido
Vicolo del Pettinaio 7
Tel: 0577-280042
Set in a 15th-century building, this is an elegant restaurant in the gentrified-rustic style that Tuscans have perfected. Good service and traditional regional cooking including Etruscan-style *pici* (Tuscan spaghetti) and Florentine steak. Closed Wednesday and January. €€–€€€
Tullio Ai Tre Cristi
Vicolo Provenzano 1/7
Tel: 0577-280608
Managed for 40 years by the same family, this *trattoria's* specialities include pasta and soups. Try the *pici*, a variant on home-made Tuscan spaghetti. Lovely frescoed walls. Closed Tuesday. €€

Sinalunga
Locanda dell'Amorosa
Tel: 0577-677211
Fax: 0577-632001
www.amorosa.it
This fine restaurant is part of an enchanting medieval hotel complex long famed for its gastronomic excellence. Closed early January–early March. €€€€
Locanda La Bandita
Via Bandita 72, Località La Bandita (north of Sinalunga)
Tel: 0577-623447
The family-run La Bandita is set in an 18th-century farmhouse in the countryside near Bettolle, a village east of Sinalunga. (On the Florence–Rome motorway, take the Val di Chiana exit, and La Bandita is 1 km (¾ mile) from there, sign-posted along country lanes.) Highlights include homemade pasta, subtle *antipasti* and unusual Tuscan-inspired desserts. The restaurant is called Walter Redaelli. Closed Tuesday and February. Reserve. €€–€€€

UMBRIA & THE MARCHES

What Umbria does best on the food front is unpretentious home cooking. Specialities include pork, cured meats, *carpaccio* of *funghi porcini* and nourishing soups. Umbria is also black-truffle *(tartufo nero)* country, with the prized tuber added to anything, from scrambled eggs upwards. Since black truffles are less prestigious than the white Piedmontese truffles, the Umbrians feel they can use them more liberally. The cuisine of the Marches celebrates all manner of seafood and fish soups, plus salami, lasagne with truffles, and roast meats.

Perugia
Il Falchetto
Via Bartolo 20
Tel: 075-5731775
Il Falchetto serves authentic, unpretentious local food using the best ingredients. Closed Monday and period between January and February. €–€€

Ancona
Passetto
Piazza IV Novembre 1
Tel: 071-33214
This is an elegant spot, serving traditional seafood cuisine. Sea views from the terrace. Closed Sunday evening, Monday and period in August. Reserve. €€€

Assisi
San Francesco
Via S. Francesco 52
Tel: 075-812329
This is the place for Umbrian dishes served in front of a fine fireplace, with views over the basilica. Umbrian dishes include *carpaccio* of *funghi porcini*, lentil-based dishes, wild herbs and lamb, ricotta cheese from Norcia and wines from Montefalco. Closed Wednesday and 1–15 July. €€–€€€

Foligno
Villa Roncalli
Via Roma 25
Tel: 0742-391091
Local specialities feature strongly on the menu in this lovely old

Patrician villa, which is a restaurant with rooms. Dine alfresco in the summer with splendid panoramic views. Reservations advised. Closed Monday and 5–30 August. €€–€€€

Orvieto
I Sette Consoli
Piazza Sant'Angelo 1a
Tel: 0763-343911
Refined, excellent interpretations of local cuisine are on offer here. Dishes include *crostini* with ricotta cheese, stuffed rabbit, *baccalà* (salt cod) marinated in apple vinegar, and bean soup with fennel. Closed Wednesday and Sunday evening November– March. Reservations essential. €€–€€€
La Grotta
Via Lucca Signorelli 5
Tel: 0763-341348
Set just off the Piazza Del Duomo, this restaurant is particularly recommended for its roast meats. Closed Tuesday. €–€€

Spello
Il Molino
Piazza Matteotti 6/7
Tel: 0742-651305
The restaurant is housed in a converted 14th-century mill. Typical dishes include lamb and *funghi porcini*, with meats often roasted on the spit in front of diners. Closed Tuesday and 7–22 January. €€

Spoleto
Il Tartufo
Piazza Garibaldi 24
Tel: 0743-40236
The recently renovated Il Tartufo serves traditional cuisine in a quiet, dignified setting. The dining room has a 4th-century Roman floor. Typical dishes include *baccalà* and asparagus, rich soups, pork dishes and pear soufflé. Truffles are the main ingredient. Call in advance. Closed Sunday evening, Monday, 10 February–10 March and July. Must book. €€–€€€

Todi
Umbria
Via San Bonaventura 13
Tel: 075-8942737

This restaurant is set in a 14th-century building, with a delightful terrace overlooking the hills. Good local food. Closed Tuesday and Christmas to 9 January. €€–€€€

ABRUZZO & MOLISE

Abruzzo has far greater culinary riches than the rather deprived Molise region. Mutton, lamb and kid represent the most important meats here, with lamb generally roasted or grilled. Adriatic fish is also in abundance, as is salami from the mountains and garden produce from the hinterland. Peppers, potatoes, figs and grapes are also specialities. Molise produces good pasta, prepared with simple chilli or tomato sauce.

Campobasso
Vecchia Trattoria da Tonino
Corso Vittorio Emanuele 8
Tel: 0874-4152000
This lovely old *trattoria* in the heart of Campobasso has a welcoming, family atmosphere. It has also been awarded a Michelin star for the quality of its modern, creative cuisine, which makes reservations essential. Closed Sunday and Monday from September to June and Saturday and Sunday in July and August; also 20–30 July. €€–€€€

Chieti
Venturini
Via Cesare de Lollis 10
Tel: 0871-330663
This restaurant, set in a former convent, has a traditional atmosphere and a nice terrace. Specialities include roast game and fish dishes. Closed Tuesday and part of July. €€–€€€

Price Guide

The price of a three-course meal for one (not including wine):
€ = under €25
€€ = €25–45
€€€ = €45–70
€€€€ = €70 or more

L'Aquila
La Grotta di Aligi
Viale Rendina 2
Tel: 0862-65260
This well-established restaurant is very popular with celebrities as well as locals. It features exceptionally good local cuisine, stylish décor and attentive service. Closed Sunday. €€–€€€

Tre Marie
Via Tre Marie 3
Tel: 0862-413191
This old-fashioned restaurant has a homely atmosphere and offers good traditional local cuisine. Closed Sunday evening, Monday (excluding August) and 24–31 December. Reservations recommended. €€

Teramo
Duomo
Via Stazio 9
Tel: 0861-241774
This modern restaurant, close to the Duomo, serves traditional local food. Closed Monday, Sunday evening and 7–27 January. Reserve. €€

NAPLES

Naples is the original home of the pizza – you should not leave without sampling this at least once during a visit. Don't be deterred by the pizza chains back home – these are far superior. The simple, inexpensive *pizzerie* are often the best, so don't turn your nose up at a place simply because of its scruffy exterior. The pizza crust tends to be thin and crispy here, with a tastier yet more limited filling than many people are used to abroad. Apart from pizza places, the city offers a wide range of restaurants and, given Naples' location, seafood figures heavily on any menu, as do *mozzarella di bufalo*, tomato sauce and pasta.

Caruso
Grand Hotel Vesuvio, Via Partenope 45
Tel: 081-76400044
Dedicated to the great tenor, Caruso, who was a guest of the hotel, this is a very stylish and elegant restaurant. Specialities include both Neapolitan and national Italian cuisine. The views across the Bay of Naples and the Castel dell'Ovo are breathtaking. Must book. Closed Monday and 5–25 August. €€€€

Ciro a Santa Brigida
Via Santa Brigida 73
Tel: 081-5524072
In the old heart of Naples, this well-established restaurant has the reputation of being among the best places in town to sample the authentic Neopolitan pizza. The full menu also offers good meat and fish dishes. Closed Sunday (excluding December) and 7–25 August. €–€€

Da Michele
Via Cesare Sersale 1–5
Tel: 081-553 9204
This popular *pizzeria* off Corso Umberto serves classic pizza margherita and tasty fishy pizza marinara. Open late. Closed Sunday and August. €

Di Matteo
Via Tribunali 94
Tel: 081-455262
This is the place for authentic rustic wood-fired pizzas. Closed Sunday and August. No credit cards. €

Don Salvatore
Strada Mergellina 4a
Tel: 081-681817
This lively modern restaurant/pizzeria is very popular – both for its food and location. Specialities include the buffet of *antipasti* and delicious fresh fish. A large bay window opens onto the seafront and port giving excellent views. Closed Wednesday. €€–€€€

Giuseppone a Mare
Via Ferdinando Russo 13
Tel: 081-5756002
Set at Posillipo, right on the seafront, so expect great seafood. Closed Sunday evening, Monday, 18 August–4 September and 24–25 December. €€€

La Cantina di Triunfo
Riviera di Chiaia 64
Tel: 081-668101
Traditional Neapolitan dishes are served and the menu varies according to the days of the week and what ingredients are in season. A brief menu is based on finds at the market on that day. Closed lunchtimes, Sunday, public holidays and August. €€–€€€

La Cantinella
Via Cuma 42
Tel: 081-7648684
Set on the seafront, this is an elegant yet modish seafood restaurant, with a telephone on every table (so you can close that business deal while eating your sea bass). Closed Sunday from June to September, part of August and 24–25 December. Must book. €€€€

La Chiacchierata
Piazzetta Matilde Serao 37
Tel: 081-411465
This tiny family-run *trattoria* is one of the best places to eat in the historic centre. Neapolitan specialities feature, such as tender *polpette* (octopus) and hearty soups of flageolet bean, broccoli and leek. Closed evenings (except Friday), August, and Saturday and Sunday from June to September. Must book. €€€

La Fazenda
Via Marechiaro 58/a
Tel: 081-5757420
La Fazenda overlooks the Gulf of Naples and Capri and serves fine Mediterranean food. In summer, you can dine outside. Closed Sunday evening, Monday lunch and 15 August–1 September. €€€

Sbrescia Antonio
Rampe Sant'Antonio a Posillipo 109
Tel: 081-669140
Set on a steep street, this restaurant offers a fresh seafood menu and a beautiful view of the Gulf. Closed Monday and part of August. Reserve. €€€

CAMPANIA COAST & ISLANDS

Thanks to the rich volcanic soil, the fruit, vegetables and herbs grown in Campania are among the best in the country. Also expect good seafood from sea bass to squid and swordfish.

Amalfi
Da Gemma
Salita Fra' Gerardo Sasso 9
Tel: 0898-71345

Next to the Duomo, this stylish *trattoria* offers good, traditional cooking, especially seafood. If you have space, try the curious dessert from Salerno. Tables on the street in summer. Closed Wednesday and January. Reservations recommended. €€€

Capri

Given the number of foreigners pouring onto the island in summer, some of the cuisine is neutral "international style" to appeal to what some restaurateurs think their cruise-liner day-trippers will be expecting. However, if you scratch the surface, you will find true Campanian cuisine flourishing on this island. Value for money is probably not as good in Capri as elsewhere in Italy, but the fabulous views and ample opportunities for people-watching go a long way towards compensating for the price you have to pay.

Canzone del Mare
Via Marina Piccola 93
Tel: 081-8370104
Founded by the singer Gracie Fields, who settled here at the height of her popularity, the atmosphere is reminiscent of the 1950s and the restaurant's customers read like a celebrities' *Who's Who*. The location remains as stunning as ever, set beside a swimming pool surrounded by gardens with views of the Faraglioni; and the food is good. Open Easter–October for lunch only, plus evenings in August. €€€€

La Capannina
Via de Botteghe 12/14
Tel: 081-8370732
This chic restaurant serves classic, traditional seafood, as well as regional and international cuisine. Closed Wednesday (except June–September) and 10 November–10 March. Reservations recommended. €€€–€€€€

La Pigna
Via do Palazzo 30
Tel: 081-8370280
This elegant restaurant is the perfect place for a romantic dinner, especially on the terrace, with its

view over the Gulf of Napes. The ambience brings together international and local influences, and the Neapolitan cuisine is served with flair. Closed Monday and February. €€–€€€

Le Grottelle
Via Arco Naturale 13
Tel: 081-8375719
There is a unique view of the Arco Naturale, which overlooks the Gulf of Salerno, in this rustic-style restaurant and pizzeria housed in a natural grotto. Dishes include home-reared rabbit and barbecued fish. Closed Thursday, except during summer, and late October–mid-March. €€€–€€€€

Ischia

Da "Peppina" di Renato
Via Montecorvo 42, Località Forio
Tel: 081-998312
Furnished with old barrels, this enticing *trattoria* offers local cuisine, such as *pasta mischiata* (pasta with beans, lentils or chickpeas) and home-made *crostate* (tarts) and cakes. Closed lunchtime and Wednesday, except June–September, and November–March. Must book. €€–€€€

Il Melograno
Via Giovanni Mazzella 110
Tel: 081-998450
Located in Forio on the west side of the island, Il Melograno is noted as much for its gastronomy (one Michelin star) as its picturesque setting among olive groves. Creative fish cuisine is the speciality of the house. Must book. Closed 7 January–15 March, Monday October–January, Tuesday and Wednesday lunch November–January. €€€€

Paestum

Nettuno
Via Principi di Piemonte 2, Zona Archeologica
Tel: 0828-811028.
This place offers good views of the temples and some fine Italian classic cooking. Closed 12–26 November and evenings, except Friday and Saturday during July and August. Reservations recommended. €€–€€€

Positano

Chez Black
Via del Brigantino 19/21
Tel: 089-875036
A popular restaurant and pizzeria overlooking the beach at Spiaggia Grande. Fish is the speciality, and the mixed seafood grill is justly famous. For a less expensive option try perhaps *spaghetti alla Black*, cooked in squid ink. Excellent selection of wines. Closed 7 January–7 February. €€€

La Buca di Bacco
Via Rampa Teglia 4
Tel: 089-875699
In a beautiful location overlooking the sea, this hotel has a large veranda where the renowned restaurant serves good, regional food. Closed November to March. €€€–€€€€

Price Guide

The price of a three-course meal for one (not including wine):
€ = under €25
€€ = €25–45
€€€ = €45–70
€€€€ = €70 or more

Salerno

Al Cenacolo
Piazza Alfano 1, 4/6
Tel: 089-238818
Good fish and pasta, and tasty desserts. This is probably Salerno's best restaurant. Closed Sunday evening, Monday, part of August and 24 December–2 January. €€€

Sorrento

Don Alfonso 1890
Corso Sant'Agata 11, Sant'Agata sui due Golfi (9 km/5½ miles from Sorrento)
Tel: 081-8780026
This is a shrine to gastroromy and widely considered to be the best in the whole of southern Italy. The two Michelin-starred restaurant features fresh, seasonal dishes, exquisitely executed and served in gracious surroundings. Reservations essential. Closed Monday and Tuesday lunch from June to

September, Monday and Tuesday in alternate months. €€€€

La Fenice
Via degli Aranci 11
Tel: 081-8781652
This recently renovated restaurant/ pizzeria has a pleasing décor and a nice welcoming atmosphere. Seafood and delicious *antipasti* are the specialities here, on a menu that has something for all budgets. Closed Monday, except during August. €€–€€€

APULIA (PUGLIA)

The heel of the boot of Italy has a rich agricultural heritage, with a healthy cuisine based on pasta, lamb, seafood and vegetables. The most common form of pasta here is *orecchiette* ("little ears"), served with a variety of delicious sauces. Herbs also play a major role in this region's cooking, and olives, olive oil, almonds, aubergines, figs and watermelons are significant ingredients in many dishes.

Bari
Ai Due Ghiottoni
Via Putignani 11
Tel: 080-5232240
This is a smart restaurant specialising in Puglian dishes with great food and a superb wine list. Closed Sunday. €€–€€€
Murat
Via Lombardi 13
Tel: 080-5216551
The elegant Murat restaurant of the renowned Palace Hotel offers an interesting choice of regional dishes, a good selection of cheeses and moderately priced set menus are Another draw is the panoramic view. Closed August. €€€

Barletta
Il Brigantino
Litoranea di Levante
Tel: 0883-533345
Il Brigantino is a large, elegant restaurant offering traditional cuisine, especially fish, efficient service and sea views from the terrace. Closed January. €€€

Brindisi
La Lanterna
Via Tarantini 14
Tel: 0831-564026
Set between the Colonno and the cathedral, La Lanterna is housed in a 15th-century *palazzo* and specialises in inventive twists on regional cuisine, with lots of new recipes. Closed Saturday lunch, Sunday and August. €€

Foggia
In Fiera – Cicolella
Viale Fortore, corner of Via Bari
Tel: 0881-632166
This elegant restaurant/pizzeria belongs to the Hotel Cicolella and specialises in Puglian and Mediterranean dishes. This is a good place to try the local delicacy, *orecchiette* (ear-shaped) pasta. Closed Monday and Tuesday and 7–24 November. €€–€€€

Lecce
Picton
Via Idomeneo 14
Tel: 0832-332383
In a baroque *palazzo*, this elegant restaurant specialises in local cuisine with an emphasis on inventive, light, seasonal dishes. Closed Monday and periods in June and November. €€–€€€

Manfredonia
Coppola Rossa
Via dei Celestini 13
Tel: 0884-582522
Coppola Rossa is a friendly *trattoria* offering good local fish and home-made desserts. Closed Sunday evening, Monday, Christmas–10 January. €–€€

Taranto
Ponte Vecchio
Piazza Fontana 61
Tel: 0994-706374
Stylish seafood and fish restaurant where lobster and clams are specialities. Lovely terrace for alfresco dining. Closed Tuesday. €€

Trani
Il Melograno
Via Bovio 189
Tel: 0883-486966

A welcoming, family-run restaurant in the centre of town. Fish is the speciality but local seasonal dishes and fresh ingredients also feature. Closed Wednesday and January. €€–€€€
Palazzo Giardino Broquier
Via Beltrani 17
Tel: 0883-506842
In the heart of the city, this acclaimed restaurant has stylish surroundings in a former *palazzo* matching its excellent food. Summer dining in the very pretty garden. Closed Tuesday and 10–26 November. Must book. €€–€€€

Price Guide

The price of a three-course meal for one (not including wine):
€ = under €25
€€ = €25–45
€€€ = €45–70
€€€€ = €70 or more

BASILICATA & CALABRIA

The food in Basilicata is a vegetarian's delight, with baked aubergines, pepper stew, and salads of bitter wild onions all popular. By comparison, the food in Calabria is richer, with plenty of home-made pasta, focaccia and spicy dishes featuring swordfish, anchovies, tuna and cuttlefish.

Cosenza
L'Arco Vecchio
Piazza Archi di Ciaccio 21
Tel: 0984-72564
This renowned, pleasing restaurant in the historic centre of town specialises in Calabrian cuisine. In summer dine alfresco. Closed Sunday and 10–18 August. Must book. €–€€

Matera
Casino del Diavolo-da Francolino
Via La Martella Ovest (1.5 km/ 1 mile out of town)
On the outskirts of Matera, this restaurant is scenically set amid olive groves. The typical local dishes have made it very popular and the long buffet of *antipasti* is a

special delight. In summer meals are served in the garden. Closed Monday. €€

Reggio di Calabria
Baylik
Vico Leone 3
Tel: 0965-48624
Lying close to the port, this restaurant offers the freshest fish. It's possible to dine till midnight on the catch of the day and the swordfish accompanied with pumpkin flowers is highly recommended. Closed Thursday and part of August. €€

SICILY

Sicilian food is rich in all areas, and the island's historic influences are perpetuated in its food. The Arab legacy has given Sicilians a sweet and spicy cuisine, and Spanish rule brought a more cultivated and refined style of cooking. Typical dishes include *pasta con le sarde* (pasta with sardines), *pasta alla norma* (with aubergines), fish couscous, stuffed aubergines, deep-fried rice balls and chickpea fritters.

The surrounding Mediterranean provides lobsters, tuna, swordfish and octopus, while the volcanic soil is particularly suitable for growing oranges, lemons and grapes, along with a great range of vegetables.

Palermo
Charleston le Terrazze
Viale Regina Elena, Mondello (11 km/7 miles from Palermo)
Tel: 091-450171
Located on the pier at Palermo's fashionable seaside resort, Mondello, this stylish restaurant attracts a chic clientele in summer. The menu features fish and seafood dishes served in the attractive Liberty-style dining room. Closed Wednesday (except May–October) and 10 January–10 February. €€€–€€€€
Santandrea
Piazza Sant'Andrea 4
Tel: 091-334999

Sicilian Wine

Sicily now produces some excellent wines, with any of the bottles produced by Corvo, Donnafugata or Regaleali especially recommended.

The Santandrea is located just behind the colourful Vucciria market, this well-regarded restaurant treats customers to the freshest market produce, skilfully and imaginatively presented. Specialities include fresh sardines with spaghetti and rich chocolate tart. Closed Tuesday, Wednesday lunch, January and Sunday and Monday in July and August. €€–€€€

Catania
La Siciliana
Viale Marco Polo 52/a
Tel: 095-376400
This is a classic, elegant restaurant, with a long family tradition of cooks. Specialities include *pasta all norma* and rice with cuttlefish. Closed Sunday evening and Monday. Reserve. €€€
Osteria I Tre Bicchieri
Via San Giuseppe al Duomo 31
Tel: 095-312294
This elegant restaurant is among the best in Sicily. One area is reserved for the *enoteca* (wine bar), while the vaulted dining room serves very creative, excellent Mediterranean dishes. Fish and seafood feature strongly, but carnivores are also well catered for. Extensive wine list. Closed lunchtimes and August. €€€–€€€€

Siracusa
Archimede
Via Gemellaro 8
Tel: 0931-69701
Arguably the most authentic *trattoria* and pizzeria in the lovely quarter of Ortygia. The tasty fish dishes are rivalled by mouth-watering, mostly vegetarian, *antipasti* and typical Sicilian pasta dishes. Good service. Closed Sunday. Book. €€

Taormina
Al Duomo
Vico Ebrei 11
Tel: 0942-625656
Stylish restaurant which offers some of the best dining in Taormina with excellent service. Try the Sicilian specialities menu. Must book. Closed Monday, January and November. €€€
La Giara
Vico la Floresta 1
Tel: 0942-23360
This restaurant/piano bar is among the most fashionable places in town owing to its good food, excellent service and fabulous views. Closed lunchtime and Monday (except July to September) and February, March, November (except Friday and Saturday); Reserve. €€€–€€€€

Sardinia

Sardinian cooking is different from classic southern fare. The terrain is less forgiving than in much of the south, resulting in a distinctive cuisine. Specialities include suckling pig roasted on a spit, or lamb, kid and various forms of offal. The star seafood is lobster, whether grilled or served in a salad. Sardinians make pasta, including huge ravioli filled with chard, but they are better known for their bread, which ranges from wafer-thin "music paper" to heavy loaves. Other specialities are pecorino cheese and a variant on couscous. Compared with the quality and range of Sicilian wines, Sardinian wines will never be great – they're fine but are designed to be drunk young.

Palau
Da Franco
Via Capo d'Orso 1
Tel: 0789-709558
This is a good place for a business meeting, with refined service and a terrace overlooking the little port. Seafood dominates the menu. Closed Monday (except June–September) and 23 December –10 January. €€€€

Culture

Italy has such a long recorded history that the biggest problem facing the traveller on the culture front is how to choose between the nation's countless attractions. All main centres, most provincial cities and many small towns have fine museums. Theatres, galleries and concert halls also offer something for every interest.

Regeneration & Restoration

The Jubilee effect: The wraps have finally come off many of the country's monuments after years of restoration. The whole country, but especially the capital, has felt the winds of change, largely thanks to the impetus given by Holy Year (2000), and the pope's insistence that the event be commemorated by restoration of the city's churches.

However, the influence and political commitment of Rome's former mayor, Francesco Rutelli, a dedicated environmentalist, has also been considerable. Under his administration, attempts have been made to pedestrianise historic areas, such as Piazza del Popolo and a route linking the Fontana di Trevi and the Pantheon.

Parts of the south are also improving greatly in terms of regeneration, renovation and even cultural life, but much depends on the political will of the local administration. As soon as a major city in the south has a good (i.e. uncorrupt and entrepreneurial) administration, investment in culture swiftly follows. This has been the case in Catania, Palermo (formally opened to the public on 23 December 2002) and Naples, for example.

Opera & Concerts

Classical music and opera lovers will feel very much at home in Italy. Opera, for instance, is not at all a minority taste here, as it is in so many other countries, and magnificent concerts can be enjoyed all year round.

Rome

The city's most important music venue is the **Auditorium Parco della Musica** (www.auditoriumroma.com). Designed by Genoan architect Renzo Piano, it features its own set of Roman ruins, three indoor halls and an outdoor amphitheatre, and hosts concerts that range from the classical to electronica.

Opera, ballets and concerts are also held at the **Teatro dell'Opera**, Via Firenze 72, (which relocates to the Baths of Carcalla in high summer) www.operaroma.it. Concerts are also held in various churches, smaller auditoriums and outdoor venues during the summer long festival called *Estate Romana*.

Florence

The most important musical event in Florence is the international music and arts festival, **Maggio Musicale Fiorentino**, which takes place in May and June at the Teatro Comunale, the principal opera house and concert hall.

Open-air concerts are held in the **Boboli Gardens** and in the cloisters of the **Badia Fiesolana** on July and August evenings. Another younger, but important, summer festival is **Estate Fiesolana**, which runs from June until August. This event fills the ancient Roman theatre in Fiesole and several churches in Florence with opera, concerts, theatre, ballet and films.

Milan

Milan's hallowed Teatro alla Scala has undergone a complete renovation. The programme is available at the La Scala website, where you can also buy tickets (www.teatroallascala.org). Reservations open two months before the date of the

performances. Most sell out on the first day. Any tickets unsold one month before the performance are available at the La Scala box office, located in the Duomo metro station opposite the ATM point (which provides information on the public transport service in Milan). The ticket office is open noon–6pm daily. For information call 02-7200 3744 between 9am and 6pm. Expect to be on hold for some time.

Turin

In Turin, classical music is at its peak from late August until the end of September, when **Settembre Musica** takes over the city. This is an international music festival and features the cream of national and international performers.

Venice

Venice's renowned **La Fenice** opera house (www.teatrolafenice.it) was razed to the ground by a mysterious fire in 1996. It rose from the ashes and officially re-opened in November 2004 with a celebratory performance of Verdi's *La Traviata*.

Verona

Verona's annual open-air opera season runs from June to August. Performances are held at the **Fondazione Arena di Verona** at Piazza Brà 28. For bookings tel: 094-8005151, fax: 045-8011566 or book online at www.arena.it. The marvellous open-air acoustics make it a memorable occasion. Classics like *Madame Butterfly*, and Verdi's *Aida* are performed.

Naples

Naples is blessed with the largest opera house in Italy – **San Carlo** – a place with fine acoustics that draws performers and audiences throughout the year. The San Carlo Opera House's season runs from January to mid-July. Tel: 081-7972331. In the **Teatro delle Palme** (Via Vetriera 12, tel: 081-418134), a classical music season runs from January to April. Pick up a free copy of *Qui Napoli* from the tourist office to find out what's on when in the city.

Palermo

Here, opera is also performed in a grandiose setting. Bari's opera house may have been burnt down in a suspicious fire but Palermo's **Teatro Massimo** (Piazza Giuseppe Verdi; guided tours Monday–Friday 9am–1pm, tel: 091-605 3515, www.teatromassimo.it) opera house has been finely restored after languishing in a state of abandonment for over 20 years. Ask the tourist office for a copy of its *Agenda* magazine, an up-to-date listing of events throughout the city (in English and Italian) or visit www.palermotourism.com.

If your Italian is fluent enough for you to enjoy a play in the vernacular, make enquiries at the relevant city's tourist office *(see page 363–5)* or check listings sections of local newspapers for information on performances.

In **Rome**, the principal theatres are: **Teatro Sistina**, Via Sistina 129; www.ilsistina.com; tel: 06-4200711, **Teatro Valle**; Via del Teatro Valle 21; www.teatrovalle.it; tel: 06-68803794, and **Teatro Argentina**; Largo Argentina 52, www.teatrodiroma.net; tel: 06-684000345.

In **Milan**, you can go to the **Piccolo Teatro**, Via Rovello 2, and its offshoot, **Teatro Studio**, Via Rivoli 6, as well as the new **Nuovo Piccolo Teatro** next door (booking number for all three theatres: 02-77333222; or visit www.piccoloteatro.org).

In **Florence**, you can take in an Italian production at **Teatro Comunale**, Corso Italia 12, tel: 16-27791 or 055-2779236, at **Teatro della Pergola**, Via della Pergola 12/32, tel: 055-2479652, or at **Teatro Verdi**, Via Ghibellina 101, tel: 055-213220 or 055-2396242.

In **Naples**, there are two notable theatres: the **Mercadante Piazza Municipio**, tel: 081-5524214, a small but beautiful theatre rebuilt in the 1940s, and the **Bellini**, Via Conte di Ruvo, tel: 081-5491266.

Nightlife

In recent years, **Milan and Florence** have been the main centres of hip Italian nightlife: Milan for its rock and discos and Florence for its clubs. In the south, **Naples** and **Catania** have the liveliest nightlife. In Naples, which is famed for its stylish clubs, nightlife is concentrated in the newly revitalised historic centre and the Pozzuoli area by the port as well as Posillipo and Mergellina.

In **Palermo**, nightlife was, until recently, fairly non-existent, concentrated only around the chic summer resort of Mondello. Now, however, although Mondello is still thriving, the historic centre of Palermo is coming to life again. Small bars and cafes remain open at night and such exciting ventures as Lo Spasimo cultural centre – a former monastic complex where concerts, exhibitions and other events draw visitors of all ages – are helping to regenerate the area.

In **Rome**, jazz and blues have long been fashionable but now a taste for the Latin beat has emerged, with Brazilian dance music popular, as well as techno and house music. Roman nightlife has been rejuvenated with the success of the Jubilee Year and the growing popularity of the Testaccio area. The traditional heart of Roman nightlife, Trastevere, remains lively, although mainly for bars and restaurants.

Venice, by contrast, is less of a city for nightlife. Although there are piano bars, the casino and the odd folk club, most people prefer sitting in cafés and walking through the beautiful, labyrinthine streets here. Those desperate to go clubbing tend to drive at breakneck speed to the **Lido di Jesolo** coastal resort, a world away from sleepy Venice in atmosphere.

In **Turin,** the best nightlife from a visitor's point of view lies in the seductive 19th-century cafés. The most famous are **Baratti E Milano** in Piazza Castello and **Caffè Torino** on Piazza San Carlo.

Below is a list of the current hotspots. Trust advice on the ground as the scene is always changing.

To find out what's on in Rome, check in *La Repubblica* and *Il Corriere della Sera* newspapers or the weekly *Roma C'e*, a useful listings booklet that comes out every Wednesday and has a section in English. Also *Wanted in Rome*, a fortnightly magazine in English.

NIGHTSPOTS

Campo de' Fiori

On summer nights, this lovely, rambling square and its lsurrounding medieval streets become a lively and popular rendezvous point. An all-time classic on the square is the **Vineria**, but any other bar will do just as well to indulge in some memorable people-watching.

Piazza Navona

This elegant Renaissance square becomes a good place for a night-time amble. Try the legendary *tartufo* ice from **Tre Scalini** at no.30.

The Pantheon

Just east of Piazza Navona is the Pantheon district, which is extremely lively and beautifully illuminated at night. Apart from the sheer romance of this locality, the fine *gelaterie* (ice-cream parlours) especially the **Cremeria Monteforte**, are another great draw.

Trastevere

Situated on the other side of the Tiber, Trastevere is an intimate and atmospheric part of town, though it is becoming quite touristy. Even so, its alleyways and tiny squares are lined with family-run inns and restaurants, and convivial bars.

Testaccio

This district, and above all its leafy and winding thoroughfare, Via di Monte Testaccio, is dotted with nightclubs and bars.

MUSIC CLUBS, CABARET & CINEMA

Alien
V. Velletri (13–19)
Tel: 06-841 2212
One of Rome's biggest clubs. Amazing lighting and special effects.

Black Out Rock Club
Via Saturnia 18
Tel: 06-70496791
The place for indie, punk and rock music, with some performances by British and US bands.

Caffè Latino
Via de Monte Testaccio 96
Tel: 06-57288556
Live Latin American music on most nights feeds the current Roman craze. Later, DJs play funk, acid jazz and Latin American sounds and, on some nights, there are film screenings and cabaret.

Il Bagaglino al Salone Margherita
Via due Macelli 75
Cabaret in Italian that's only worth visiting if your Italian is up to it.

Jackie O'
Via Boncompagni 11
Tel: 06-42885457
Very glamorous club with restaurant and piano bar – be prepared to queue. It pays to don your finest gear and emulate the Romans' style of *la bella figura*.

L'Alibi
Via di Monte Testaccio 40/47
Tel: 06-5743448
A social and cultural centre with various activities on offer such as gay discos on Tuesdays. Other nights are open to all and themed; Rome's oldest gay venue.

Nuovo Sacher
Largo Ascianghi 1
Tel: 06-5818116
Trendy cinema, founded by director Nanni Moretti as a venue for art-house films shown in "V.O." (original version) on Monday and Tuesday; it also acts as an open-air cinema in summer. Bookshop; friendly bar.

Milan

Given the eclectic nature of Milanese nightlife, it is tricky to categorise places – sometimes the same place peforms several functions. Nightlife, of the hot, youthful variety, is centred on the Navigli district, the canal quarter. You should just be able to turn up in the evening and see what is on offer. However, if you like to plan ahead, check what's on in the *ViviMilano* insert in Wednesday's *Corriere della Sera* or visit www.hellomilano.it. More refined nightlife, especially in the form of bars and low-key clubs, takes place in the Brera area. Outside these areas, Milan can be oddly quiet at night. If there are no taxis at the ranks, call: 02-8383, 02-6767, 02-8585 or 02-5251.

Alcatraz
Via Valtellina 25
Tel: 02-69016352
One of the trendy mega clubs with two dance floors, three bars, two performance areas and a pub.

Bar Daila Café
Via San Vicenzo 15
Tel: 02-581 12288
This friendly jazz café has live music on Thursday and Friday evenings. (Happy hour is between 6 and 8pm; open until 2am but closed Sunday.)

Bar Giamaica/Jamaica
Via Brera 32
Tel: 02-876723

Roman Bars & Cafés

Many Romans prefer going on café-crawls to hitting the latest club. Many of the following open until late and the clientele varies according to the time of day.

Antico Caffè della Pace
Via della Pace 3/7
Classic ivy-swathed café that also serves good *aperitivi* and *digestivi*.

Bar Navona,
Piazza Navona 67
Familiar Roman spot on one of Rome's loveliest squares.

Bar San Calisto
Piazza San Calisto 4
Gritty and rough-hewn, but no

This bar in the Brera has no special gimmicks and doesn't look anything special, but it is a piece of Milanese history – a traditional meeting place for artists, intellectuals and celebs. Despite its fame, it's a calm place for drinking cocktails or sampling Italian regional dishes. Open in the day.

Beau Geste
Piazza Velasca 4
Tel: 02-8900692
Part-club, part-disco, this nightspot plays music to suit most tastes.

Blue Note
Via Borsieri 37
Tel: 02-69016888
This is Europe's only franchisee of the legendary New York jazz club, featuring some of the biggest names around. Restaurant, bar and Sunday brunch (increasingly popular in Milan). Open daily.

Blueshouse
Via Sant'Uguzzone 26
Live music on most nights with tribute bands honouring legendary names such as Led Zeppelin and the Rolling Stones. At other times bands play blues, rock and even folk.

Café Cavalieri
Corso Genova 26
Tel: 02-8323557
This is a great place for an *aperitivo* from 6–9pm, accompanied by plates of cured ham and seafood. There is always a warm welcome from the owner. Open daily 7am–2am.

less classic. It serves cheap coffee, beer, alcohol and ice cream.

L'Oasi della Birra,
Piazza Testaccio 41
The place for beer and *grappa* in the fun Testaccio district.

Rosati
Piazza del Popolo 4/5
A historic bar that affords great views over the elegant Piazza del Popolo.

Tazza D'Oro
Via degli Orfani 84
Bustling bar and coffee roastery that sells the city's best coffee. No seating.

Café Teatro Nobel
Via Asciano Sforza 81
Tel: 02-89511746
Shows, jazz and cabaret in the lively
Navigli canal quarter. Take the
metro to Porta Genova, then walk.
Capolinea
Via Lodovico Il Moro 119, Navigli
Tel: 02-89122024
Big-name bebop bands meet in this
jazz club in the canal quarter, where
you can dine on Milanese and
Tuscan specialities. Closed Monday.
El Brellin
Vicolo dei Lavandai,
Via Alzaia Naviglio Grande 14
Tel: 02-58101351
This sophisticated Navigli piano bar
and restaurant is set in a quaint,
converted wash-house. Only
Milanese dishes are served. Open
Monday–Saturday 12.30–2.30pm
and 7pm–2am, Sunday noon–3pm.
Grand Café Fashion
Via Vetere, Porta Ticinese,
The bar on the first floor attracts all
those of the *bella figura*.
Hollywood
Corso Como 15
Tel: 02-6559 8996
One of the top nightspots in Milan.
The crowd is high energy. Be
prepared to queue. Open
Tuesday–Sunday 11pm–4am.
Especially popular with the *glitterati*
on Sundays. R&B night on Tuesday.
La Salumeria della Musica
Via Pasinetti 2
Tel: 02-56807350
Cabaret and live music in this
former factory, now transformed into
a buzzing club. Just like a real
salumeria, hams and sausages
dangle over the bar. Closed Sunday.
Le Scimmie
Via Asciano Sforza 49
Tel: 02-89402874
An established, reputable jazz and
blues club in the Navigli area. You
can also dine on Italian or French
cuisine. Closed Tuesday.
Pasticceria Ricci
Piazza della Repubblica 27
Pastries are served during the day,
but at night it's a gay club and one
of the trendiest bars in Milan.
Radetsky
Corso Garibaldi 105
Tel: 02-6572645

A chic minimalist bar playing to the
thirty-something crowd. Open daily.
Shocking Club
Via Bastioni di Porta Nuova 12
Tel: 02-86454630
This smart club is favoured by
models and showbiz types. Friday
night is "shocking" night. Open
10.30pm–4am. Closed on Monday.

Florence

CLASSIC CAFES

Caffè Gilli
Piazza della Repubblica 39r
Tel: 055-213896
This historic café, an institution on
the piazza, is also an excellent
patisserie. Stand at the bar where
prices are far lower than at tables.
Caffè Rivoire
Piazza della Signoria 5r
Still one of the best places to be
seen in Florence. Closed Monday.
Caffè Strozzi
Piazza Strozzi
This is a low-key meeting-place,
popular for evening *aperitivi*.
Vivoli
Via Isola delle Stinche 7r
Vivoli is universally acknowledged
as the city's best ice-cream parlour,
so expect queues in summer.
Closed Monday.

FASHIONABLE BARS

Most trendy bars lie in the more
bohemian Oltrarno, on the far side
of the river, Florence's answer to
the Parisian Left Bank. At night,
lively quarters include the vaguely
alternative Santo Spirito area and
the bohemian-chic Santa Croce.
However, good Florentine bars and
clubs are dotted throughout the city,
and even in the Tuscan countryside.
Dolce Vita
Piazza del Carmine 5
Tel: 055-280018
This glamorous spot is the place to
go for cocktails, live music and
general hanging out. Open daily
5.30pm–11.30am.
Rose's
Via del Parione 26r
Tel: 055-287090

This was Florence's first sushi bar.
Good for cocktails and long drinks.
Salamanca
Via Ghibellina 80r
Tel: 055-2345452
Spanish restaurant and bar, open
till 2am. Live music, including
flamenco every Monday and Latin
singer-songwriters on Thursday.

CLUBS

Given the number of special events
in Florentine clubs, it pays to check
times carefully; places only start to
fill up very late, after young
Florentines have had their fill of
hanging out in *pizzerie* and *gelaterie*.
Escopazzo Garden
Lungarno Colombo, Bellariva
Tel: 0556-76912
This eclectic Latin club has regular
themed nights, from Cuban to
Caribbean music. After midnight
however, you are more likely to be
dancing to mainstream sounds.
Maramao
Via de Macci 79r
Tel: 055-244341
Sample the famous *dolce vita* in this
club, currently one of the hippest in
town. Closed Monday and May–
September. Open 11pm–3am.
Meccanò
Parco della Cascine
Viale degli Olmi 1
Tel: 055-331371
Set in the Cascine park, Meccanò is
the best-known Florentine club and
appeals to a wide age group. It is
home to La Piccionaia restaurant,
where dinner is accompanied by a
floor show. The club is the place to
spot visiting VIPs and Florentine
poseurs. Even the armchairs are
fashioned by the French designer
Philippe Starck. Open 11pm–4am
Tuesday–Saturday in summer,
Thursday–Saturday in winter.
Space Electronic
Via Palazzuolo 37
Tel: 055-293082
This established club is an old
favourite with the younger crowd.
Universale
Via Pisana 77r
Tel: 055-221122
This former cinema has been trans-

formed into a huge venue, where you can eat, drink, dance, and watch shows and concerts. A very versatile club. Open 8.30pm–3am. Closed Monday, Tuesday and June–September.

Naples

Neapolitan nightlife is concentrated in the chaotic but characteristic historic centre, the area stretching towards the sea, and the Pozzuoli district by the port. The Borgo Marinaro area, which used to be patronised by pensioners, is now popular with all ages, although the bars and *trattorie* are just the same as they were 30 years ago.

CLASSIC CAFES, WINE BARS & LIVE MUSIC

The top chic places change all the time, so pick up a copy of the latest *Qui Napoli* listings magazine in both English and Italian. There is a selection of venues on the official Naples website www.inaples.it. If you speak Italian visit www.napolinapoli.com. As well as classic cafés, such as the legendary Gambrinus, Naples has a decent range of bars, including several atmospheric wine bars. Note that most places here close on Monday.

A Ret' A' Palm
Piazza Santa Maria La Nova
Called "Behind the Palms" in Neapolitan dialect, this wine bar and inn *(osteria)* is set in a *palazzo* run by the Austrian-Neapolitan Alan Wurtzburger. This unpretentious place has an excellent wine list and good bar snacks at very reasonable prices. The music includes live performances every Wednesday by the musician-owner himself.

Caffè Gambrinus
Via Chiaia 1–2, Piazza Plebiscito
Tel: 081-414133/417582
This is the city's most famous bar, an elegant place adorned with gilt-and-plaster reliefs. The terrace is a good spot for watching the world go by, sipping *aperitivi* or downing a sweet coffee. Open from early morning until about 10 or 11pm.

Chez Moi
Via di Parco Margherita 20
Tel: 081-407526
Located in the upmarket Chiaia area, this well-established music bar caters for all ages, depending on the night (call ahead first).

Chiatamon
Via Chiatamone
This is an informal and fashionable bar overlooking the seafront of Via Caracciolo. Music and dancing is courtesy of DJs on most weekends.

Murat Live Club
Via Bellini 8
Tel: 081-5445919
The emphasis here is on live music and especially jazz, including modern and contemporary. The action usually starts around 10pm. Located in the San Carlo Arena district.

Otto Jazz Club
Piazzetta Cariata 23
Tel: 081-5524373
Has jazz sessions from 10.30pm. Entrance fee includes first drink.

Sannakura Club
Via Santa Chiara 10
Tel: 339-2849423
This club specialises in rap and hip-hop sounds.

Slovenly R 'n' R Bar
Vico San Geronimo 24 (next to Via Benedetto Croce)
Tel: 335-6115857
Live rock with an international flavour in an underground cellar.

Velvet Club
Via Cisterna dell'Olio 11
This club buzzes from 11pm till 6am. Different sounds range from pop to techno, hip-hop, rock and more.

Vinarium
Via Cappella Vecchia 7
Tel: 081-7644114
This centrally located, classic wine bar is particularly popular with trendy professionals over the age of 30. The ambience is smart/casual, with a relaxing feel in spite of the relatively formal surroundings. A quick stroll away, Via Carlo Poerio is bursting with bars, pubs and wine bars.

Vineria
Via Palladino 8
This atmospheric wine bar was once a student haunt, but now attracts a wider cross-section. The atmosphere is defined as

"intellectual yet homely", a mood enhanced by low lighting and wood and marble fixtures and fittings. Closed Monday.

Virgilio Sports Club
Via Tito Lucresio Caro 6
Tel: 081-5755262
The name is a bit misleading, even if there is a sports club here too, since this is now a music bar for twenty- and thirty-somethings. However, in true Neapolitan style, different sets of people have their favourite nights, with Thursday a typical night for *per bene* (well-bred) over 30s. There are sea views from the terrace.

Clubs in Naples

The following are among the most stylish or fashionable places for dancing in Naples, but the city is not known for cutting-edge clubs and avant-garde music. Most places tend to play a similar mix of classics from the 1970s and '80s to rap, house or the current chart hits, and are closed on Monday.

Chez Moi
Via del Parco Margherita 20
Tel: 081-407526
Similar in approach to **My Way**, another trendy club in the Chiaia area, with different nights (unofficially) for different crowds.

Kiss-Kiss
Via Sgambati 47
Tel: 081-5466566
Located in the Vomero district, this large club has a restaurant and attracts a student clientele.

La Mela
Via dei Mille 40b, Chiaia
Tel: 081-413881/410270
This is a smart, trendy place. However, allegations of Mafia involvement mean that there are occasional shootings, after which the place is closed for a while. Whatever its associations, many locals miss it when it's gone.

Dug Out
Mergellina
Tel: 081-662183
This club is hewn out of soft tufa rock, a cavern in a courtyard, echoing its name. Check what the night's theme is prior to going.

Festivals

The year is packed with special events, some linked to festivals of the Catholic church, others to the changing seasons, especially the harvest, and to local produce. There are also historical re-enactments connected to jousting or costumed cavalcades. Locals often consider their home festival the best, no matter how tiny; however, as far as outsiders are concerned, the festive set-pieces in Tuscany, Venice and Sicily probably provide the biggest spectacle. These are some of the highlights of the festival calendar.

Carnevale. This period of festivities preceding Lent (February and March) is celebrated in unrivalled style in Venice. Apart from Venice, there are other excellent carnivals in Viareggio on the Tuscan coast, and in Acireale and Sciacca in Sicily.

Easter involves major celebrations in Italy, especially in Sicily. The most dramatic and passion-filled festivals are the Mysteries *(I Misteri)* at Trapani, the Easter Devils at Prizzi and the Albanian festivities outside Palermo.

The **Scoppio del Carro**, or Explosion of the Carriage, takes place in Florence on Easter Sunday. A mechanical dove swoops through the cathedral and ignites a golden carriage filled with fireworks. The event symbolises the Resurrection. This is an event the Florentines themselves follow with great enthusiasm so the centre of the city is always packed.

The **Festival dei Due Mondi di Spoleto**, in late June–early July, at Spoleto, in Umbria, offers theatre, concerts, ballet and exhibitions. Although the future of the festival has been under threat for many years, last-minute administrative solutions have always been found.

Biennale. This is a major exhibition of international modern art, held in Venice every June–October in odd-numbered years. The sites are not just in the Biennale pavilions and gardens, but also in unusual and striking buildings dotted throughout the city, including the old Arsenale.

Gioco del Calcio (also known as Calcio in Costume) is another Florentine event, held on 19, 24 and 28 June. This is a type of football played by men wearing 16th-century costumes.

The **Palio** horse race is held on 2 July and 16 August in Siena's Piazza del Campo. The bareback riders, who take part in a two-hour procession before the race, wear 15th-century costumes. This is the highlight of Siena's festive calendar, so book accommodation well in advance. You may find it difficult to see in the crowds, but the atmosphere is usually wonderful.

The **Festa del Redentore** is held in Venice, on the night of the third Saturday of July. A bridge of boats is built across the Giudecca Canal to the Redentore, the church that was built in gratitude for deliverance from the Plague in 1567. People row out to picnic on the water to watch the wonderful firework displays launched from Giudecca island.

The **International Film Festival** is held at the Lido in Venice at the end of August each year. Recently, the new administration decided to focus less on Hollywood blockbusters and more on art-house and European films. However, since the Venetians like a celebrity-driven event, the changes have been minor.

The **Festa di Noiantri** is a Roman tradition, celebrated in the last half of July. This street festival, involving music, fireworks and food, is centred on Trastevere, one of the oldest quarters of Rome.

In Tuscany, the city of Arezzo hosts the **Giostra del Saracino** on the last Sunday in August and the first Sunday in September. This medieval jousting match echoes the events of the Crusades.

Outdoor Activities

National & Regional Parks

Italy has some stunningly beautiful national parks *(see below)*. The regions of Abruzzo, Piedmont, Trentino and Alto Adige are just a few of the many areas that should be able to supply information on parks in their territory *(see pages 363–5)*. A useful website for all parks is www.parks.it

The Dolomites
The Dolomites has some of the most spectacular natural landscape in italy, and can be explored on skis or along marked hiking trails. For information contact the Trentino information service in London (tel/fax: 020-8879 1405), who will be able to supply brochures on parks, refuges, hiking, lakes, activities and accommodation. You can also check the English-language Trentino website: www.trentino.to.

Etna, Catania, Sicily
An intriguing and well-organised park, centred on the active volcano of Mt Etna. Many excursions explore this strange area, which encompasses fertile areas from ancient eruptions and the volcanic moonscapes of the most recent lava flows. Contact the Catania tourist office (AAPIT Provincia di Catania & Acireale, Largo Paisiello 51, Catania, Italy 95100; tel: 095-7306211, fax: 095-316407) for free maps, brochures and descriptions of trips to the top or around the base, or contact Gruppo Guide Alpine Etna Sud, Via Etnea 49, Nicolosi, tel: 095-7914755. Access is currently restricted due to continued volcanic

activity. Visit the Mt Etna Regional Park website: www.parcoetna.it.

Parco Nazionale del Gran Paradiso

Home of the last steinbocks in Italy, this Alpine park is the oldest in the country and covers 720 sq. km (278 sq. miles). Spreading over parts of Valle d'Aosta and Piedmont, it has refuges and trekking facilities. For details contact the tourist boards of **Piedmont**, Via Magenta 12, 10128 Torino, tel: 011-43211, fax: 011-4322440, www.regione.piemonte.it, and **Valle d'Aosta**, at Piazza Chanoux 3, 11100 Aosta, tel: 0165-236627, fax: 0165-34657, www.regione.vda.it/turismo or www.aostavalley.com/regione/index.

Parco Naturale dello Sciliar

This park is in the Alto Adige (South Tyrol) region and overlooks the vast plateaux of the Swiss Alps, with jagged rock faces, steep peaks and impressive ledges. Wildlife include chamois, marmots, and golden eagles. The park was established by the authorities of Bolzano (Bozen) – call the tourist office there on 0471-307001 or visit www.bolzano-bozen.it.

Parco Nazionale dello Stelvio

Italy's biggest park, at 1,350 sq. km (520 sq. miles), is situated close to Switzerland and is rich in forests and animal life. The mountains are beautiful and there are plenty of hotels nearby. For information tel: 0342-910100/901654 or visit www.stelviopark.it. (Open all year.)

Parco Nazionale dell'Abruzzo

This park extends from the southern section of the Abruzzan Apennines and includes limestone and a Dolomitic landscape. King of the beasts here is the brown bear – some of the last of the species in Italy live in remote splendour in one of the highest sections of the Apennines. Other wildlife includes the Apennine wolf, the white-backed woodpecker and the Orsini's viper, which is less poisonous than the majority of other Italian vipers. Tel:

Hiking in the Alps

If you want to go hiking in the mountains, pick up a map of the network of walking paths, with more than 80 overnight areas with shelters. Paths are marked with numerous red signs and distinctive small flags. Every stage calls for 5 to 7 hours of hiking time at an average of around 1,000 metres (3,300 ft) in altitude.

At the overnight rest areas (known as *rifugi*, or refuges) there are shelters with double-decker bunks, essential services and a kitchen. While many are in idyllic but fairly isolated spots, others are situated near hamlets or resorts, where it is possible to buy food, phone home, rest for a day, visit rural museums, chat with the local inhabitants and, last but not least, eat a good meal at an inn.

An itinerary can last a month, a week or a day. A lot of regions provide lists of recommended guides, members of the reputable Italian CAI association. From the Maritime Alps in the west to Lake Maggiore, on a route stretching for 650 km (400 miles) that spans five provinces, the hiker crosses many splendid parks, such as the Gran Paradiso, the Orsiera-Rocciavrè, the Alta Val Pesio and the Argentera. All national park areas are open to the public between July and September.

0863-910715 or visit www.parcoabruzzo.it for information.

Parco Nazionale della Maremma

This wonderful Tuscan park is a mixture of meadows, pine forests, sandy shores and swampland along the Tuscan coast. Wildlife includes wild boar, porcupines, peregrine falcons and the pond tortoise. There are countless trails and opportunities to go riding. However, you will need to check itineraries and facilities before you arrive with the Grosseto tourist office in Tuscany.

Sport

Spectator Sports

FOOTBALL (SOCCER)

The national sport in Italy is football. Almost every city and village has a team and the most important national championship is the "Serie A" (First Division), the winner of which is eligible to play in a kind of European championship, the "Champions' League", against other top European teams.

The "Serie A" championship runs from September to May, and each of the 16 teams has to play the other teams twice. Traditionally, the most successful Italian team is Juventus FC from Turin, followed by Internazionale ("Inter") from Milan, but in recent years, other teams have had significant victories, including sides from Verona, Parma, Florence and Rome.

From September until late May, Rome's two teams, Roma and Lazio, play nearly every Sunday at the Stadio Olimpico. The cheapest tickets are about €20 and can be purchased at the Stadium's box office or one of the many Roma or Lazio stores around the city. (To get to the stadium take Metro Line A to Flaminio, then Tram 225 to Piazza Mancini and follow the crowds. Or take Metro Line A to Ottaviano and then bus 32 up to the stadium.)

If you want to see a game, check the newspaper listings, but it is generally difficult to get tickets for an important match. Prices vary according to the importance of the team, the game, and the location of the seat you want. Unlike some European countries, matches here tend to be safe, family affairs.

Milan matches: You can book a football visit to Milan with certain

UK tour operators, including Liaisons Abroad. You can also do a tour of Milan's San Siro football stadium (for details contact the Milan tourist office, *see page 364).* Contact the club for tickets to matches: AC Milan administrative office, Via Turati 3; tel: 02-62281. Curiously, you can also buy tickets at any branch of the Cariplo bank.

OTHER SPORTS

Almost every other sport is enjoyed in Italy, including basketball, golf, water polo, horse racing, rugby union, rowing and sailing. In addition, you can ski in the Alps, Dolomites and the Apennines.

May is an important month for sport in Italy. The *Giro d'Italia* cycle race is a major event on the cycling circuit, but it has recently been damaged by drug allegations. Also in May, there is the Italian Open tennis tournament, held at the Foro Italico in Rome. Equestrian sports followers also enjoy their major competition of the year in May, which takes place in Rome's Villa Borghese gardens.

BUYING TICKETS

For tickets for any sporting event, consult the local tourist office or, alternatively, buy the pink *Gazzetta dello Sport* newspaper, which should give you the lowdown on what's on when and how to book.

Motor-Racing

In Italy citizens typically support Ferrari and, consequently, the German champion, Michael Schumacher, who currently races for them. There is always a large crowd at the circuits in Imola (where the San Marino Grand Prix is held) and Monza (Italian Grand Prix). Although the car industry is centred on Turin, motor racing is based in the regions of Lombardy and Emilia-Romagna.

Shopping

Shopping is an Italian passion, not just because the natives are natural consumers, in love with the latest designs, but also because it's often viewed here as an art, involving the search for the beautifully crafted object, the right coffee cups, or the right garment in the right shade and fabric. Italians are expert at marketing their designer labels around the world, so much so that Milan now rivals Paris as Europe's fashion capital. In addition, since most Italians also attach great importance to finding the right foodstuffs, you are likely to find good quality just about everywhere, even in the simplest street market.

Shopping Areas

ROME

The best shopping district is around the bottom of the Spanish Steps, the heart of Rome's design world, with the elegant **Via Condotti** lined with the most exclusive fashion boutiques (Gucci, Ferragamo, Prada, Armani and Bulgari). Other fashionable streets run parallel to Via Condotti, such as **Via Borgognona** (with the shops of Dolce & Gabbana and Hogan); **Via delle Carrozze** or **Via Frattina** (for ceramics, lingerie and costume jewellery); **Via Vittoria** (where the boutique of Laura Biagiotti can be found) and **Via della Croce**. Make sure you check out the new Fendi megastore in **Largo Goldoni** off Via Condotti. Most of these streets are closed to traffic.

For antiques, go window-shopping along **Via del Babuino** (do not miss the Giorgio Armani boutique there), along **Via Margutta** (the place for even more antiques) or **Via dei Coronari** (even more antiques in the streets leading to Piazza Navona).

Another fine shopping section is along the Via del Corso between Piazza del Popolo and Largo Chigi, where **Via del Tritone** begins.

Less expensive and more popular shopping streets include **Via Nazionale**, near the railway station, which is good for everyday clothes shops; this is also where Fiorucci (sportswear and shoes) has his main outlet, and **Via Cola di Rienzo**, a busy shopping thoroughfare in the Prati district.

"The other face of fashion" is represented by the open markets, such as the one in Via Sannio, which sells new and second-hand clothes, and, of course, the famous one at Porta Portese, open only on Sunday, from sunrise–1.30pm, where you can find almost everything. "Armani-style" second-hand clothes can be found in Via delle Carrozze.

MILAN

Milan is home to the major fashion houses and is a consumer paradise during the twice-yearly showing of the new collections. This city, more than Rome, is Italy's principal centre for international fashion.

For those with expensive tastes, the most chic shopping streets are: Via Montenapoleone, Via della Spiga and Via Sant' Andrea, an area known as the "Quadrilatero" or "Golden Triangle" within walking distance of the Duomo and La Scala. These elegant streets are home to such fashion icons as Krizia, Giò Moretti, Trussardi, Kenzo, Sanlorenzo, Giorgio Armani and Ferragamo, as well as Versace, Gucci, Ermenegildo Zegna, Comme des Garçons, Valentino, Dolce e Gabbana, Hermès, Chanel, Moschino, Prada, Ferre and Fendi.

The **Brera district** is also a smart and discreet shopping location, with a good selection of clothing and antiques. Pick up a shopping guide from the Milan tourist office.

FLORENCE

The whole centre of Florence could be considered a huge marketplace, crowded as it is with tourists and well-dressed locals. Handicrafts are fast disappearing, leaving the place to smart clothing shops. The most fashionable streets are still **Via dei Calzaiuoli**, **Via Roma**, and **Via de' Tornabuoni**, home to the famous Ferragamo fashion house – visit its shoe museum in Palazzo Spini-Feroni – as well as **Via della Vigna Nuova** and **Via degli Strozzi** for the likes of Neuber, Principe and Diavolo Rosa.

Ponte Vecchio is famous the world over for gold and silver jewellery and antique shops, but prices can be extortionate. To buy gold or jewellery, you will probably get a better price and range in Arezzo, or in Verona, in the Veneto.

The area near the church of **Santa Croce** is full of top-quality leather goods, while for other handicrafts check out the city's two open markets, sprawling **San Lorenzo** and covered **Mercato Nuovo**, near Piazza della Signoria.

The **Oltrarno area**, over the Ponte Vecchio bridge, is home to what remains of Florence's renowned craft industries, from picture restorers to makers of marbled paper. Request a list from Florence tourist office *(see page 364)*.

Just 27 km (17 miles) away, at **The Mall**, you can snap up designer labels at up to 80 percent off the original price. The Mall is at Via Europa 8, Leccio Reggello; tel: 55-865 7775; www.outlet-firenze.com. Call for details of shuttlebus pick-ups from hotels in Florence or take the train to Rignano sull'Arno and taxi to Leccio.

VENICE

The most exclusive shopping area in Venice is the **Via XXII Marzo** and the streets around **St Mark's Square**. Try the Rialto Bridge and San Polo for local shopping. A market is held on the **Lido** on Tuesday morning.

Bargains in this city include shoes, clothes, gifts and fur coats. However,

Size Chart

Women's dresses:

Italian	UK	US
38	8	6
40	10	8
42	12	10
44	14	12

Men's shirts:

Italian	UK	US
36	14	14
38	15	15
41	16	16
43	17	17

Women's shoes:

Italian	UK	US
37	4	6
38	5	7½
39	6	8½
40	7	9

Men's shoes:

Italian	UK	US
40	6½	7½
41	7	8
42	8	8½
43	9	9½

few tourists leave without a supply of at least one Venetian craft, such as hand-blown Murano glassware, or colourful carnival masks.

NAPLES

Naples is the capital of Italian fakes, so look out for cheap copies of designer goods on the streets or in markets. However, the city also has its own designer shops and crafts, such as Christmas cribs and their accompanying tiny figurines (a local art form) and Capodimonte porcelain.

The best shopping area is around **Piazza Amedeo** to **Piazza Trieste e Trento**. Via dei Mille and **Via Filangieri** are home to numerous famous-name designer shops. Mariella, one of Italy's most famous and expensive men's wear outlets, is located nearby, in **Via Riviera di Chiaia**. A less expensive street is the **Via Roma**, quite near to the San Carlo Opera House.

Language

Basic Communication

Yes/No *Sì/No*
Thank you *Grazie*
Many thanks *Grazie mille/tante grazie/molte grazie*
You're welcome *Prego*
Alright/Okay/That's fine *Va bene*
Please *Per favore/Per cortesia*
Excuse me (to get attention) *Scusi* (singular), *Scusate* (plural)
Excuse me (to get through a crowd) *Permesso*
Excuse me (to attract attention, e.g. of a waiter) *Senta!*
Excuse me (sorry) *Mi scusi* (singular), *Scusatemi* (plural)
Wait a minute! (informal) *Aspetta!* (formal) *Aspetti!*
Could you help me? (formal) *Potrebbe aiutarmi?*
Certainly *Ma certo*
Can I help you? (formal) *Posso aiutarLa?*
Can you show me...? (formal) *Può indicarmi...?*
Can you help me? (formal) *Può aiutarmi, per cortesia?*
I'm sorry *Mi dispiace*
I don't know *Non lo so*
I don't understand *Non capisco*
Do you speak English/French/ German? *Parla inglese/francese/ tedesco?*
Could you speak more slowly, please? *Può parlare più lentamente, per favore?*
Could you repeat that please? (formal) *Può ripetere, per piacere?*
slowly/quietly *piano*
here/there *qui/là*
What? *Cosa?*
When/why/where? *Quando/perchè/dove?*
Where is the lavatory? *Dov'è il bagno?*

Greetings

Hello (Good day) *Buon giorno*
Hello/Hi/Goodbye (familiar) *Ciao*
Good afternoon/evening *Buona sera*
Goodnight *Buona notte*
Goodbye *Arrivederci*
Pleased to meet you (formal)
Piacere di conoscerLa
I am English/American/Canadian
Sono inglese/americano/canadese
Irish/Scottish/Welsh
irlandese/scozzese/gallese
Do you speak English? *Parla
inglese?*
I'm here on holiday *Sono qui
in vacanza*
How are you (formal/informal)?
Come sta/come stai?
Fine thanks *Bene, grazie*
See you later *A più tardi*
See you soon *A presto*
Take care (formal) *Stia bene,*
(informal) *Stammi bene*

Telephone calls

the area code *il prefisso telefonico*
**I'd like to make a reverse charges
call** *Vorrei fare una telefonata a
carico del destinatario*
May I use your telephone, please?
Posso usare il telefono?
Hello (on the telephone) *Pronto*
My name's *Mi chiamo/Sono*
Could I speak to...? *Posso parlare
con...?*
Sorry, he/she isn't in *Mi dispiace,
è fuori*
Can he call you back? *Può
richiamarLa?*

I'll try again later *Riproverò più tardi*
Can I leave a message? *Posso
lasciare un messaggio?*
Please tell him I called *Gli dica, per
favore, che ho telefonato*
Hold on *Un attimo, per favore*
Can you speak up please? (formal)
Può parlare più forte, per favore?

In the Hotel

Do you have any vacant rooms?
Avete camere libere?
I have a reservation *Ho fatto una
prenotazione*
I'd like... *Vorrei...*
a single/double room (with double
bed) *una camera singola/doppia
(con letto matrimoniale)*
a room with twin beds *una camera
a due letti*
a room with a bath/shower *una
camera con bagno/doccia*
for one night *per una notte*
for two nights *per due notti*
**Could you show me another room
please?** *Potrebbe mostrarmi
un'altra camera?*
How much is it? *Quanto costa?*
on the first floor *al primo piano*
Is breakfast included? *È compresa
la prima colazione?*
Is everything included? *È tutto
compreso?*
half/full board *mezza
pensione/pensione completa*
It's expensive *È caro*
**Do you have a room with a
balcony/view of the sea?**
*C'è una camera con balcone/con
vista sul mare?*

Can I see the room? *Posso vedere
la camera?*
What time does the hotel close?
A che ora chiude l'albergo?
I'll take it *La prendo*
big/small *grande/piccola*
What time is breakfast? *A che ora
è la prima colazione?*
Please give me a call at... *Mi può
chiamare alle...*
Come in! *Avanti!*
Can I have the bill, please? *Posso
avere il conto, per favore.*
dining room *la sala da pranzo*
key *la chiave*
lift *l'ascensore*
towel *l'asciugamano*

Eating Out

Bar snacks and drinks
I'd like... *Vorrei...*
coffee *un caffè* (espresso: small,
strong and black)
un cappuccino (with hot, frothy milk)
un caffè latte (milky coffee)
un caffè lungo (weak)
uno corretto (laced with alcohol –
usually brandy or grappa)
tea *un tè*
lemon tea *un tè al limone*
herbal tea *una tisana*
hot chocolate *una cioccolata calda*
orange/lemon juice (bottled) *un
succo d'arancia/di limone*
fresh orange/lemon juice *una
spremuta di arancia/di limone*
orangeade *un'aranciata*
water (mineral) *acqua* (minerale)
fizzy/still mineral water *acqua
minerale gasata/naturale*
a glass of mineral water *un
bicchiere di minerale*
with/without ice *con/senza ghiaccio*
red/white wine *vino rosso/bianco*
beer (draught) *una birra (alla
spina)*
milk *latte*
a (half) litre *un (mezzo) litro*
bottle *una bottiglia*
ice cream *un gelato*
sandwich *un tramezzino*
Anything else? *Desidera
qualcos'altro?*
Cheers *Salute*

In a Restaurant
I'd like to book a table *Vorrei
riservare un tavolo*

Pronunciation & Grammar Tips

Italian speakers claim that
pronunciation is easy: you
pronounce it as it is written. This
is roughly true but there are a few
rules to bear in mind: *c* before *e*
or *i* is pronounced "ch", e.g. *ciao,
mi dispiace, la coincidenza. Ch*
before *i* or *e* is pronounced as "k",
e.g. *la chiesa*. Likewise, *sci* or *sce*
are pronounced as in "sheep" or
"shed" respectively. *Gn* in Italian
is rather like the sound in "onion",
while *gl* is softened to resemble
the sound in "bullion".

Nouns are either masculine (*il*,
plural *i*) or feminine (*la*, plural *le*).
Plurals of nouns are most often
formed by changing an *o* to an *i*
and an *a* to an *e*, e.g. *il panino, i
panini; la chiesa, le chiese*.

Words are stressed on the
penultimate syllable unless an
accent indicates otherwise.

Italian has formal and informal
words for "You". In the singular, *Tu*
is informal while *Lei* is more polite.
It is best to use the formal form
unless invited to do otherwise.

Have you got a table for... *Avete un tavolo per ...*
I have a reservation *Ho fatto una prenotazione*
lunch/supper *il pranzo/la cena*
I'm a vegetarian *Sono vegetariano/a*
Is there a vegetarian dish? *C'è un piatto vegetariano?*
May we have the menu? *Ci dà il menu, per favore?*
wine list *la lista dei vini*
What would you like? *Che cosa prende?*
What would you recommend? *Che cosa ci raccomanda?*
What would you like to drink? *Che cosa desidera da bere?*
a carafe of red/white wine *una caraffa di vino rosso/bianco*
fixed-price menu *il menu a prezzo fisso*
the dish of the day *il piatto del giorno*
VAT (sales tax) *IVA*
cover charge *il coperto/pane e coperto*
That's enough; no more, thanks *Basta (così)*
The bill, please *Il conto per favore*
Is service included? *Il servizio è incluso?*
Where is the toilet? *Dovè il bagno?*
I've enjoyed the meal *Mi è piaciuto molto*

Antipasti (Hors d'Oeuvres)
caponata **mixed aubergine, olives and tomatoes**
insalata caprese **tomato and mozzarella salad**

Emergencies

Help! *Aiuto!*
Stop! *Fermate!*
I've had an accident *Ho avuto un incidente*
Call a doctor *Per favore, chiami un medico*
Call an ambulance/the police/ the fire brigade *Chiami un'ambulanza/la Polizia/ i Carabinieri/i pompieri*
Where is the nearest hospital? *Dov'è l'ospedale più vicino?*
I would like to report a theft *Voglio denunciare un furto*

insalata di mare **seafood salad**
insalata mista/verde **mixed/ green salad**
melanzane alla parmigiana **fried or baked aubergine** (with parmesan cheese and tomato)
mortadella/salame **salami**
pancetta **bacon**
peperonata **vegetable stew** (made with peppers, onions, tomatoes and sometimes aubergines)

Primi (first courses)
Typical first courses include soup, risotto, gnocchi or numerous varieties of pasta in a wide range of sauces. Risotto and gnocchi are more common in the north than in central Italy.
il brodetto **fish soup**
il brodo **consommé**
gli gnocchi **potato dumplings**
la minestra **soup**
pasta e fagioli **pasta and bean soup**
il prosciutto (cotto/crudo) **ham**
tartufi **truffles**
la zuppa **soup**

Secondi (Main Courses)
Main courses are typically fish-, seafood- or meat-based, with accompaniments *(contorni)* that vary greatly from region to region across Italy.

La Carne (Meat)
arrosto **roast meat**
ai ferri **grilled**
al forno **baked**
al girarrosto **spit-roasted**
alla griglia **grilled**
stufato **braised, stewed**
ben cotto **well-done** (steak, etc.)
al puntino **medium** (steak, etc.)
al sangue **rare** (steak, etc.)
l'agnello **lamb**
la bistecca **steak**
il capriolo/cervo **venison**
il cinghiale **wild boar**
il coniglio **rabbit**
il controfiletto **sirloin steak**
le cotolette **cutlets**
il fagiano **pheasant**
il fegato **liver**
il filetto **fillet**
il maiale **pork**
il manzo **beef**
l'ossobuco **shin of veal**
il pollo **chicken**

1	*Uno*	**16**	*Sedici*
2	*Due*	**17**	*Diciassette*
3	*Tre*	**18**	*Diciotto*
4	*Quattro*	**19**	*Diciannove*
5	*Cinque*	**20**	*Venti*
6	*Sei*	**30**	*Trenta*
7	*Sette*	**40**	*Quaranta*
8	*Otto*	**50**	*Cinquanta*
9	*Nove*	**60**	*Sessanta*
10	*Dieci*	**70**	*Settanta*
11	*Undici*	**80**	*Ottanta*
12	*Dodici*	**90**	*Novanta*
13	*Tredici*	**100**	*Cento*
14	*Quattordici*	**200**	*Duecento*
15	*Quindici*	**1,000**	*Mille*

le polpette **meatballs**
la salsiccia **sausage**
saltimbocca (alla romana) **veal escalopes with ham**
le scaloppine **escalopes**
lo stufato **stew**
il sugo **sauce**
il tacchino **turkey**
la trippa **tripe**
il vitello **veal**

Frutti di Mare (Seafood)
surgelati" **frozen**
alla griglia **grilled**
fritto **fried**
ripieno **stuffed**
al vapore **steamed**
le acciughe **anchovies**
l'aragosta **lobster**
il baccalà **dried salted cod**
il branzino **sea bass**
i calamari **squid**
i calamaretti **baby squid**
i crostacei **shellfish**
le cozze **mussels**
il fritto misto **mixed fried fish**
i gamberi **prawns**
i gamberetti **shrimps**
il granchio **crab**
il merluzzo **cod**
le ostriche **oysters**
il pesce **fish**
il pesce spada **swordfish**
il polipo **octopus**
il risotto di mare **seafood risotto**
le sarde **sardines**
la sogliola **sole**
la trota **trout**
il tonno **tuna**
le vongole **clams**

I Legumi/La Verdura (Vegetables)

gli asparagi **asparagus**
le carote **carrots**
la cipolla **onion**
i funghi **mushrooms**
i fagioli **beans**
i fagiolini **French (green) beans**
il finocchio **fennel**
l'insalata mista **mixed salad**
l'insalata verde **green salad**
la melanzana **aubergine**
le patate **potatoes**
le patatine fritte **chips/French fries**
i peperoni **peppers**
i pomodori **tomatoes**
il radicchio **red, bitter lettuce**
la rughetta **rocket**
i ravanelli **radishes**
gli spinaci **spinach**
la verdura **green vegetables**
gli zucchini **courgettes**

I Dolci (Desserts)

al carrello **(desserts) from the trolley**
un semifreddo **semi-frozen dessert (many types)**
la cassata **Sicilian ice-cream with candied peel**
le frittelle **fritters**
un gelato (di lampone/limone) **(raspberry/lemon) ice cream**
una granita **water ice**
una macedonia di frutta **fruit salad**
il tartufo (nero) **(chocolate) ice cream dessert**
il tiramisù **cold, creamy cheese and coffee dessert**
la torta **cake/tart**
lo zabaglione **sweet dessert made with eggs and Marsala wine**
la zuppa inglese **trifle**

La Frutta (Fruit)

le albicocche **apricots**
le arance **oranges**
le banane **bananas**
il cocomero **watermelon**
le ciliegie **cherries**
i fichi **figs**
le fragole **strawberries**
i lamponi **raspberries**
la mela **apple**
il melone **melon**
la pesca **peach**
la pera **pear**
il pompelmo **grapefruit**
l'uva **grapes**

Basic Foods

l'aceto **vinegar**
l'aglio **garlic**
il burro **butter**
il formaggio **cheese**
la frittata **omelette**
i grissini **bread sticks**
l'olio **oil**
la marmellata **jam**
il pane **bread**
il pane integrale **wholemeal bread**
il parmigiano **parmesan cheese**
il pepe **pepper**
il riso **rice**
il sale **salt**
la senape **mustard**
le uova **eggs**
lo zucchero **sugar**

Sightseeing

Si può visitare...? **Can one visit...?**
Suonare il campanello **ring the bell**
aperto/a **open**
chiuso/a **closed**
chiuso per la festa/ferie/restauro **closed for the festival/holidays/restoration**
Is it possible to see the church? È possibile visitare la chiesa?
We have come a long way just to see ... Siamo venuti da lontano proprio per visitare ...

At the Shops

What time do you open/close? A che ora apre/chiude?
Closed for the holidays Chiuso per ferie
Pull/push Tirare/spingere
Entrance/exit Entrata/uscita
Can I help you? Posso aiutarLa?

Tourist Signs

abbazia (Badia) **abbey**
basilica **church**
belvedere **viewpoint**
castello **castle**
centro storico **historic centre**
chiesa **church**
duomo/Cattedrale **cathedral**
fiume **river**
giardino **garden**
lago **lake**
monastero **monastery**

What would you like? Che cosa desidera?
I'm just looking Stò soltanto guardando
How much does it cost? Quant'è, per favore?
How much is this? Quanto viene?
Do you take credit cards? Accettate carte di credito?
I'd like... Vorrei...
this one/that one questo/quello
Have you got ...? Avete ...?
We haven't got (any) ... Non (ne) abbiamo...
Can I try it on? Posso provare?
the size (for clothes) la taglia
What size do you take? Qual'é la sua taglia?
the size (for shoes) il numero
Is there/do you have ...? C'è ...?
Yes, of course Sì, certo
That's too expensive È troppo caro
cheap economico
It's too small/big È troppo piccolo/grande
I (don't) **like it** (Non) mi piace
I'll take/leave it Lo prendo/lascio
Anything else? Altro?
Give me some of those Mi dia alcuni di quelli lì
a (half) kilo un (mezzo) chilo
100/200 grams un etto/due etti
more/less più/meno
with/without con/senza
a little un pochino
That's enough/No more Basta così

Types of Shops

antique dealer l'antiquario
bakery/cake shop la panetteria/pasticceria
bank la banca
bookshop la libreria
boutique il negozio di moda

monumenti **monuments**
museo **museum**
parco **park**
pinacoteca **art gallery**
ponte **bridge**
ruderi **ruins**
scavi **archaeological site**
spiaggia **beach**
tempio **temple**
torre **tower**
ufficio turistico **tourist office**

bureau de change *il cambio*
butcher's *la macelleria*
chemist's *la farmacia*
delicatessen *la salumeria*
department store *il grande magazzino*
dry cleaner's *la tintoria*
fishmonger's *la pescheria*
food shop *l'alimentari*
florist *il fioraio*
grocer's *l'alimentari*
greengrocer's *il fruttivendolo*
hairdresser's *il parrucchiere*
ice-cream parlour *la gelateria*
jeweller's *il gioielliere*
post office *l'ufficio postale*
shoe shop *il negozio di scarpe*
supermarket *il supermercato*
tobacconist *il tabaccaio*

Travelling

Transport
airport *l'aeroporto*
arrivals/departures *arrivi/partenze*
boat *la barca*
bus *l'autobus/il pullman*
bus station *l'autostazione*
car *la macchina*
ferry *il traghetto*
ferry terminal *la stazione marittima*
first/second class *la prima/seconda classe*
flight *il volo*
left-luggage office *il deposito bagagli*
motorway *l'autostrada*
no smoking *vietato fumare*
platform *il binario*
railway station *la stazione (ferroviaria)*
return/single ticket *un biglietto di andata e ritorno/di andata sola*
sleeping car *la carrozza letti/il vagone letto*
smokers/non-smokers *fumatori/non-fumatori*
stop *la fermata*
taxi *il taxi*
ticket office *la biglietteria*
train *il treno*

At the Airport
Where's the office of British Airways/Alitalia? *Dov'è l'ufficio della British Airways/dell'Alitalia?*
I'd like to book a flight to Venice *Vorrei prenotare un volo per Venezia*
When is the next flight to ...? *Quando parte il prossimo aereo per?*

My suitcase has got lost *La mia valigia è andata persa*
The flight has been delayed *Il volo è rimandato*
The flight has been cancelled *Il volo è stato cancellato*

At the Station
Can you help me please? *Mi può aiutare, per favore?*
Where can I buy tickets? *Dove posso fare i biglietti?*
at the ticket office/at the counter *alla biglietteria/allo sportello*
When does the train leave/arrive? *A che ora parte/arriva il treno?*
Can I book a seat? *Posso prenotare un posto?*
Are there any seats available? *Ci sono ancora posti liberi?*
Is this seat free/taken? *É libero/occupato questo posto?*
You'll have to pay a supplement *Deve pagare un supplemento*
Do I have to change? *Devo cambiare?*
You need to change in Rome *Bisogna cambiare a Roma*
Which platform does the train leave from? *Da quale binario parte il treno?*
The train leaves from platform one *Il treno parte dal binario uno*
When is the next train/bus for Naples? *Quando parte il prossimo treno/pullman per Napoli?*
When does the bus leave for Siena? *Quando parte l'autobus per Siena?*
How long will it take to get there? *Quanto tempo ci vuole per arrivare?*

Days & Dates

morning/afternoon/evening *la mattina, il pomeriggio, la sera*
yesterday/today/tomorrow *ieri/oggi/domani*
the day after tomorrow *dopodomani*
now/early/late *adesso/presto/ritardo*
Monday *lunedì*
Tuesday *martedì*
Wednesday *mercoledì*
Thursday *giovedì*
Friday *venerdì*
Saturday *sabato*
Sunday *domenica*

Next stop please *La prossima fermata per favore*
Is this the right stop? *È la fermata giusta?*
The train is late *Il treno è in ritardo*
Can you tell me where to get off? *Mi può dire dove devo scendere?*

Directions
right/left *a destra/a sinistra*
first left/second right *la prima a sinistra/la seconda a destra*
Turn to the right/left *Gira a destra/sinistra*
Go straight on *Va sempre diritto*
Go straight on until the traffic lights *Va sempre diritto fino al semaforo*
Is it far/nearby? *È lontano/vicino?*
It's 10 minutes by car *Dieci minuti con la macchina*
opposite/next to *di fronte/accanto a*
up/down *su/giù*
traffic lights *il semaforo*
junction *l'incrocio, il bivio*
Where is ...? *Dov'è ...?*
Where are ...? *Dove sono ...?*
Where is the nearest bank/petrol station/bus stop/hotel/garage? *Dov'è la banca/il benzinaio/la fermata di autobus/l'albergo/l'officina più vicino/a?*
How do I get there? *Come si può andare/faccio per arrivare a ...?)*
How long does it take to get to ...? *Quanto tempo ci vuole per andare a ...?*

On the Road

Where can I rent a car? *Dove posso noleggiare una macchina?*
Is comprehensive insurance included? *È completamente assicurata?*
Is it insured for another driver? *È assicurata per un altro guidatore?*
driving licence *la patente (di guida)*
petrol *la benzina*
petrol station/garage *la stazione di servizio*
oil *l'olio*
Fill it up *Faccia il pieno*
lead free/unleaded/diesel *senza piombo/benzina verde/diesel*
My car won't start *La mia macchina non s'accende*
My car has broken down *La mia macchina è guasta*

Health

Is there a chemist's nearby?
C'è una farmacia qui vicino?
Which chemist is open at night?
Quale farmacia fa il turno di notte?
I don't feel well *Non mi sento bene*
I feel ill *Sto male/Mi sento male*
Where does it hurt? *Dov'è Le fa male?*
It hurts here *Ho dolore qui*
I suffer from ... *Soffro di ...*
I have a headache *Ho mal di testa*
I have a sore throat *Ho mal di gola*
I have a stomach ache *Ho mal di pancia*
antiseptic cream *la crema antisettica*
sunburn *scottatura da sole*
sunburn cream *la crema antisolare*
sticking plaster *il cerotto*
tissues *i fazzoletti di carta*
insect repellent *l'insettifugo*
mosquitoes *le zanzare*

Road Signs

alt **stop**
autostrada **motorway**
avanti **go/walk**
casello **toll gate**
dare la precedenza **give way**
deviazione **diversion**
divieto di sosta/sosta vietata **no parking**
divieto di passaggio/senso
vietato **no entry**
entrata **entrance**
galleria **tunnel**
incrocio **crossroads**
limite di velocità **speed limit**
parcheggio **parking**
pedaggio **toll road**
pericolo **danger**
rallentare **slow down**
rimozione forzata **parked cars will be towed away**
semaforo **traffic lights**
senso unico **one-way street**
sentiero **footpath**
solo uscita **no entry**
strada interrotta **road blocked**
strada chiusa **foad closed**
strada senza uscita/Vicolo cieco **dead end**
tangenziale **ring road/bypass**
uscita **exit**
vietato il sorpasso **no overtaking**
vietato il transito **no thoroughfare**

Further Reading

General

Across the River and into the Trees, by Ernest Hemingway.
A Room with a View, by E.M. Forster.
The Architecture of the Italian Renaissance, by Peter Murray.
The Aspern Papers, by Henry James.
Autobiography, by Benvenuto Cellini.
Christ Stopped at Eboli, by Carlo Levi.
Le Città Invisibili, by Italo Calvino. Translated as *Invisible Cities*.
The Civilization of the Renaissance in Italy, by Jacob Burckhardt.
D.H. Lawrence and Italy, by D.H. Lawrence.
The Doge, by A. Palazzeschi.
Etruscan Places, by D.H. Lawrence.
Florence, a Traveller's Companion, by Harold Acton and Edward Chaney.
The Gallery, by John Horne Burns.
Graziella, by Alphonse de Lamartine
Il Fuoco, by Gabriele d'Annunzio. Translated as *The Flame of Life*.
Italian Hours, by Henry James.
Italian Journey, by J.W. von Goethe.
The Italian Painters of the Renaissance, by Bernard Berenson.
The Italians, by Luigi Barzini.
The Italian World, by John Julius Norwich.
The Last Medici, by Harold Acton.
Lives of the Artists, Vols 1 & 2, by Giorgio Vasari.
Love and War in the Apennines, by Eric Newby.
The Love of Italy, by Jonathan Keates.
The Mafia, by Clare Sterling.
The Mediterranean Passion, by John Pemble.
The Merchant of Prato, by Iris Origo.
Memoirs, by Giacomo Casanova. Translated into many languages.
Naples '44, by Norman Lewis.
Pictures from Italy, by Charles Dickens.
Renaissance Venice, edited by J.R. Hale.
The Rise and Fall of the House of Medici, by Christopher Hibbert.
Rome, Naples and Florence, by Stendhal (published 1817).

Siren Island, Summer Islands, South Wind and *Old Calabria*, by Norman Douglas.
Slow Food, The Case for Taste, by Carlo Petrini.
The Stones of Florence and Venice Observed, by Mary McCarthy.
The Stones of Venice (1851–3), by John Ruskin.
The Story of San Michele, by Axel Munthe.
Those Who Walk Away, by Patricia Highsmith.
Thus Spake Bellavista, by Luciano de Crescenzo.
Der Tod in Venedig, by Thomas Mann. Translated as *Death in Venice*.
A Tramp Abroad, by Mark Twain.
A Venetian Bestiary, by Jan Morris.
Venetian Life, by William Dean Howells. 1866.
Venetian Red, by P.M. Passinetti.
Venice, by Jan Morris.
Venice: A Thousand Years of Culture and Civilisation, by Peter Lauritzen.
Venice and its Lagoon, by Giulio Lorenzetti.
Venice for Pleasure, by J.G. Links.
Venice: The Greatness and the Fall, by Mark Twain.
Venice: The Rise to Empire, by John Julius Norwich.
The Wings of the Dove, by Henry James.
The Dark Heart of Italy, by Tobias Jones.

Other Insight Guides

Other *Insight Guides* to Italian destinations include: Northern Italy, Southern Italy, Rome, Venice, Florence, Umbria, Tuscany, Sicily, Sardinia and South Tyrol.

Insight Pocket Guides, including a pull-out map, feature tailor-made itineraries and are ideal for short breaks. Guides in the Italian series include: Venice, Rome, Milan, Florence, Sicily, Sardinia and Tuscany.

Insight Compact Guides are handy, information-packed books, which are ideal for on-the-spot reference. There are *Compact Guides* to: Florence, Milan, Rome, Tuscany, Venice, the Italian Riviera and the Italian Lakes.

ART & PHOTO CREDITS

AKG 31, 54, 62, 109, 261
American Nunismatic Society 32
Anne Hamann Picture Agency 102
APA Photo Agency 120/121, 343, 354
Axiom/Jim Holmes 141, 163
Gaetano Barone 33, 40, 44, 47, 55, 251, 259, 283, 325, 331
BBC Hulton Picture Library 60
Marcello Bertinetti 176, 177
Bilderberg 285
Bridgeman Art Library 92
Crollolanza/Rex Features 67
Steve Day 203
Jerry Dennis/Apa 208, 209
Bernard & Catherine Desjeux 156
Edizioni Storti Venezia 181
Annabel Elston 85L, 96, 220, 221, 222T, 223
Ente Provincial Per Il Turismo 26, 30
Gil Galvin and George Taylor 83, 97, 184, 257T, 268T, 269T, 258, 269, 270, 271, 272, 274, 275L&R, 276, 278, 278T
Glyn Genin 27, 72, 76, 84, 86, 173, 176, 178, 272T, 277T, 336/7, 341, 341T, 342, 342T, 344, 344T, 346, 346T, 347
Patrizia Giancotti 6/7
Giovanni Giansanti/Sygma/Corbis 65
Frances Gransden spine, all back cover pictures, 29, 45, 131, 134T, 135, 137T, 138T, 140T, 141T, 142, 143T, 143R, 144T, 146, 146T, 147T, 147, 148T, 150T, 157, 158, 158T, 159T, 160, 162, 164T, 165, 165T, 166T&L, 167T, 167, 253, 256T, 261T, 262T, 262, 263
Albano Guatti 8/9, 10/11, 14, 78/9, 80/81, 122/3, 206/7, 236/7
Hans Höfer 48, 49, 53
John Heseltine 12/13, 104, 124/5, 168/9, 183, 188L, 196, 197, 218, 219, 226, 238, 240, 245, 284L, 286L, 287, 292, 294T, 296, 298/99, 322, 324R, 326, 326T, 327, 328T, 328, 329, 330, 332, 333, 334, 334T, 335
Image Bank 155
Italian Cultural Institute 34, 300
Michael Jenner 50, 87, 211
Lyle Lawson 154, 338, 339
Alain Le Garsmeur 24
Lelli & Massotti/La Scala Archives 106/7, 112
Magnum 68
Marka/Kay Reese & Associates 20, 22/3, 25

Mary Evans Picture Library 35, 39
Fred Mawer 350, 353
Metropolitan Opera Archives 111L&R, 113
Nial McInerney 88, 93
Ros Miller front flap top, back flap bottom, 178T, 179L, 182, 183T, 184, 184T, 208, 209, 211T, 212L, R&T, 213, 214, 215, 219T
Robert Mort 105, 267
Museo Teatrale Alla Scala 108
Museum of Modern Art/Film Still Archives 114, 115, 116, 117
Peter Namuth title, 16, 18, 19, 38, 56, 57, 58, 59, 110
National Portrait Library 17, 21
Mike Newton 103, 277, 293
Gisela Nicolaus 290
Popperfoto 71
Susan Pierres 28, 37
Mark Read front flap bottom, back flap top, 91, 231T, 232, 233, 234, 234T, 235
Nicholas Reese 180, 284R, 288R, 319
Robert Harding Picture Library 249, 297, 324L, 351, 353T
Alessandra Santarelli 75, 89, 130, 136, 139, 141, 143L/R, 148, 150, 151, 159
Sipa Press/Rex Features 73, 93
Scala Palazzo Pubblica/Siena 41
Scala Uffizi/Florence 46, 52
Spectrum 189, 195, 227
Sporting Pics/Rex Features 77
Swett, Benjamin 36, 295
Thomas Schöllhammer 161, 257
George Taylor 193T, 194T, 195T, 224L&R, 225, 225T, 260T
Paul Thompson/Eye Ubiquitous 149
Topham Picturepoint 63, 64, 66, 69, 73, 74, 90, 118, 119
Turismo de Roma 137
Venezia Accademia 179
J. Viesti 143L, 144, 273
Bill Wassman 2T, 3, 4T, 70, 82, 85R, 99, 101, 126, 134, 138, 140, 144,

145, 147, 149, 170, 172, 185, 188R, 192, 198, 199, 200, 200T, 201T, 201, 202L&R, 203T, 204L&R, 205T, 205, 229, 229T, 230, 241, 242T, 243, 244 L&R, 245T, 247, 248, 248T, 250, 252, 256, 260, 266, 279, 282, 286R, 288L, 291
Gerd Weiss 289
Phil Wood 98, 100, 302, 303, 306, 306T, 307T, 307, 308, 308T, 309, 309T, 310, 310T, 311, 312, 313, 314T, 315T, 315, 316T, 316, 317, 318T, 318, 323

Picture Spreads

TL = top left; TCL = top centre left; TC = top centre; TCR = top centre right; TR = top right, CR = centre right; BCR = below centre right; BC = below centre; BR = below right; CL = centre left; C = centre.
Pages 94/5: TL National Motor Museum; TC Aldo Ballo; C Atrium Ltd; BL Zanussi; BCL Bill Wassman; BCR Vespa
Pages 76/7: TL Phil Wood; TCL Phil Wood; TCR APA/Glyn Genin; TR CEPHAS/Mick Rock; CL John Heseltine; BL Bill Wassman; BCL Ros Miller; BC Bill Wassman; BCR Bill Wassman; BR ACE/Peter Adams
Pages 152/3: TL Blaine Harrington; TC AKG; TR AKG; R Blaine Harrington; CL Scala; CR Blaine Harrington; C AKG/Erich Lessing; BL AKG/Erich Lessing; BR AKG
Pages 186/7: TL John Heseltine; TC John Heseltine; TR John Heseltine; C Blaine Harrington; BL Blaine Harrington; BC Bill Wassman; BR John Heseltine
Pages 280/1: TL John Heseltine; TCL G. Galvin & G.Taylor; TCR Blaine Harrington; TR G. Galvin & G.Taylor; C Axiom/Chris Coe; BL G. Galvin & G.Taylor; BC: Axiom/Chris Coe; BR G. Galvin & G.Taylor
Pages 348/9: TL Glyn Genin; TCL Glyn Genin; TCR Agencia Contrasto/ Katz; TR Mary Evans Picture Library; CL Agencia Contrasto/Katz; CR Glyn Genin; BL Apa/Glyn Genin; BC Glyn Genin; BR Agencia Contrasto/Katz
Map Production ERA Maptec Ltd

Cartographic Editor **Zoë Goodwin**
Design Consultant **Klaus Geisler**
Picture Research
Hilary Genin, Monica Allende

Index

Note: page numbers in italics refer to illustrations

INSIGHT GUIDES

The classic series that puts you in the picture

Alaska
Amazon Wildlife
American Southwest
Amsterdam
Argentina
Arizona & Grand Canyon
Asia's Best Hotels & Resorts
Asia, East
Asia, Southeast
Australia
Austria
Bahamas
Bali & Lombok
Baltic States
Bangkok
Barbados
Barcelona
Beijing
Belgium
Belize
Berlin
Bermuda
Boston
Brazil
Brittany
Bruges, Ghent & Antwerp
Brussels
Buenos Aires
Burgundy
Burma (Myanmar)
Cairo
California
California, Southern
Canada
Cape Town
Caribbean
Caribbean Cruises
Channel Islands
Chicago
Chile
China
Colorado
Continental Europe
Corsica
Costa Rica
Crete
Croatia
Cuba
Cyprus
Czech & Slovak Republic
Delhi, Jaipur & Agra
Denmark

Dominican Rep. & Haiti
Dublin
East African Wildlife
Eastern Europe
Ecuador
Edinburgh
Egypt
England
Finland
Florence
Florida
France
France, Southwest
French Riviera
Gambia & Senegal
Germany
Glasgow
Gran Canaria
Great Britain
Great Gardens of Britain
 & Ireland
Great Railway Journeys
 of Europe
Great River Cruises:
 Europe & the Nile
Greece
Greek Islands
Guatemala, Belize
 & Yucatán
Hawaii
Hong Kong
Hungary
Iceland
India
India, South
Indonesia
Ireland
Israel
Istanbul
Italy
Italy, Northern
Italy, Southern
Jamaica
Japan
Jerusalem
Jordan
Kenya
Korea
Laos & Cambodia
Las Vegas
Lisbon
London

Los Angeles
Madeira
Madrid
Malaysia
Mallorca & Ibiza
Malta
Mauritius Réunion
 & Seychelles
Mediterranean Cruises
Melbourne
Mexico
Miami
Montreal
Morocco
Moscow
Namibia
Nepal
Netherlands
New England
New Mexico
New Orleans
New York City
New York State
New Zealand
Nile
Normandy
North American &
 Alaskan Cruises
Norway
Oman & The UAE
Oxford
Pacific Northwest
Pakistan
Paris
Peru
Philadelphia
Philippines
Poland
Portugal
Prague
Provence
Puerto Rico
Rajasthan
Rio de Janeiro
Rome

Russia
St Petersburg
San Francisco
Sardinia
Scandinavia
Scotland
Seattle
Shanghai
Sicily
Singapore
South Africa
South America
Spain
Spain, Northern
Spain, Southern
Sri Lanka
Sweden
Switzerland
Sydney
Syria & Lebanon
Taipei
Taiwan
Tanzania & Zanzibar
Tenerife
Texas
Thailand
Tokyo
Toronto
Trinidad & Tobago
Tunisia
Turkey
Tuscany
Umbria
USA: The New South
USA: On The Road
USA: Western States
US National Parks: West
Utah
Venezuela
Venice
Vienna
Vietnam
Wales
Walt Disney World/Orlando
Washington, DC

INSIGHT GUIDES

The world's largest collection of
visual travel guides & maps

TRULY ADVENTUROUS

TRULY ASIA

In the heart of Asia lies a land of many cultures, wonders and attractions. Especially for the adventure seeker to whom fear is not a factor. There are hundreds of thrills to experience. Mount Kinabalu. Mulu Caves. Taman Negara. These are just a few places where you'll always find that rewarding adrenaline rush. Where is this land, so challenging and exhilarating? It can only be Malaysia, Truly Asia.

Malaysia
Truly Asia